BATM

CHRONICLES

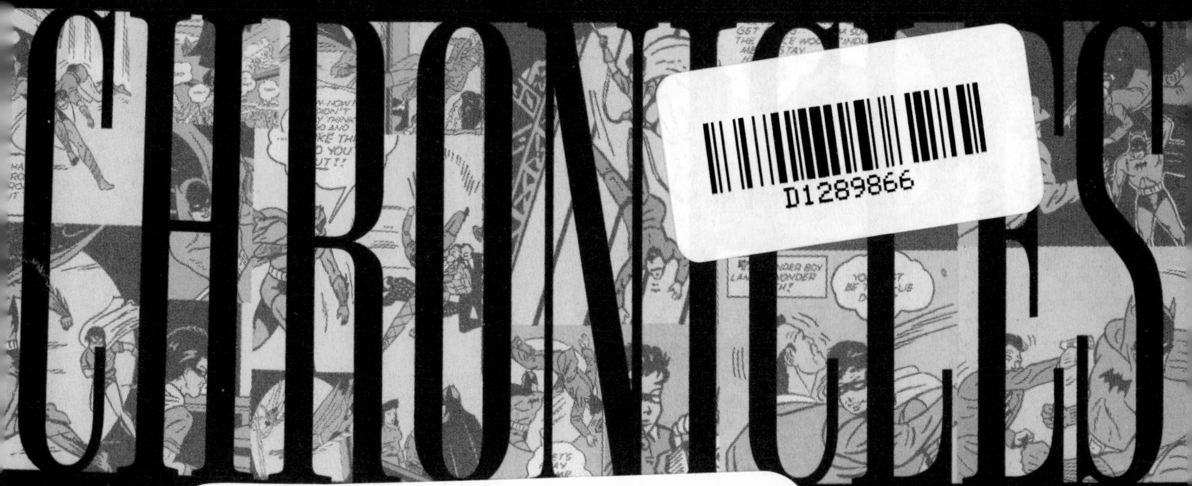

THE BATMAN CHRONICLES VOLUME 2. Published by DC Comics. Cover and compilation copyright ©2006 DC Comics.
Originally published in single magazine form in BATMAN 2-3, DETECTIVE COMICS 39-45, NEW YORK WORLD'S FAIR 1940.
Copyright 1940 DC Comics. All Rights Reserved. Batman and all related characters, the distinctive likenesses thereof and related
elements are trademarks of DC Comics. The stories, characters and incidents featured in this publication are entirely fictional.
DC Comics does not read or accept unsolicited submissions of ideas, stories or artwork.

DC Comics, 1700 Broadway, New York, NY 10019

A Warner Bros. Entertainment Company
Printed in Canada. First Printing.
ISBN: 1-4012-0790-1.
ISBN 13: 978-1-4012-0790-8.

Cover art by Bob Kane.

BATMAN CHRONICLES

VOLUME TWO

BATMAN CREATED BY BOB KANE

* These stories were originally untitled and are titled here for reader convenience.

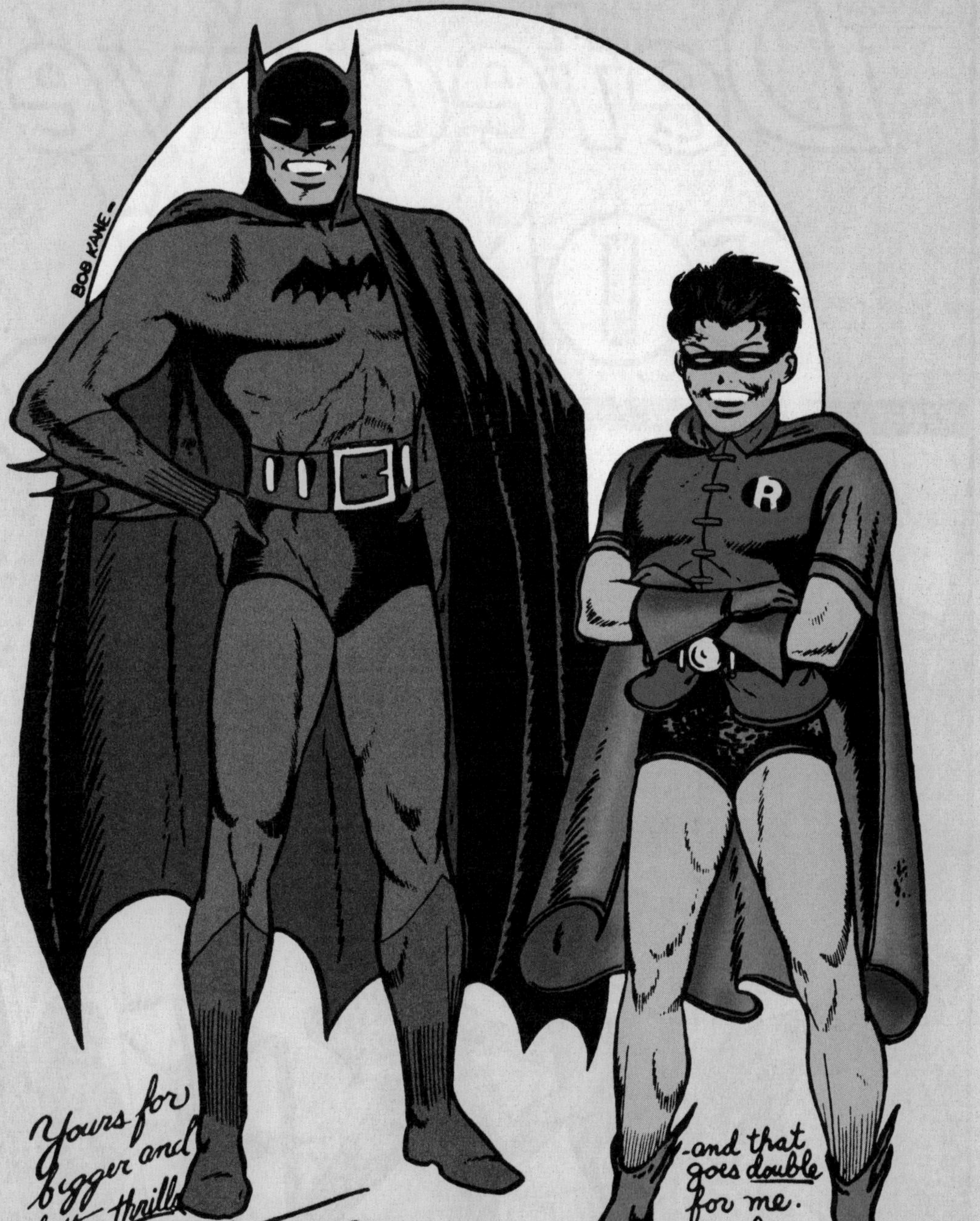
BOB KANE-
Yours for bigger and better thrills
Batman
-and that goes double for me.
Robin

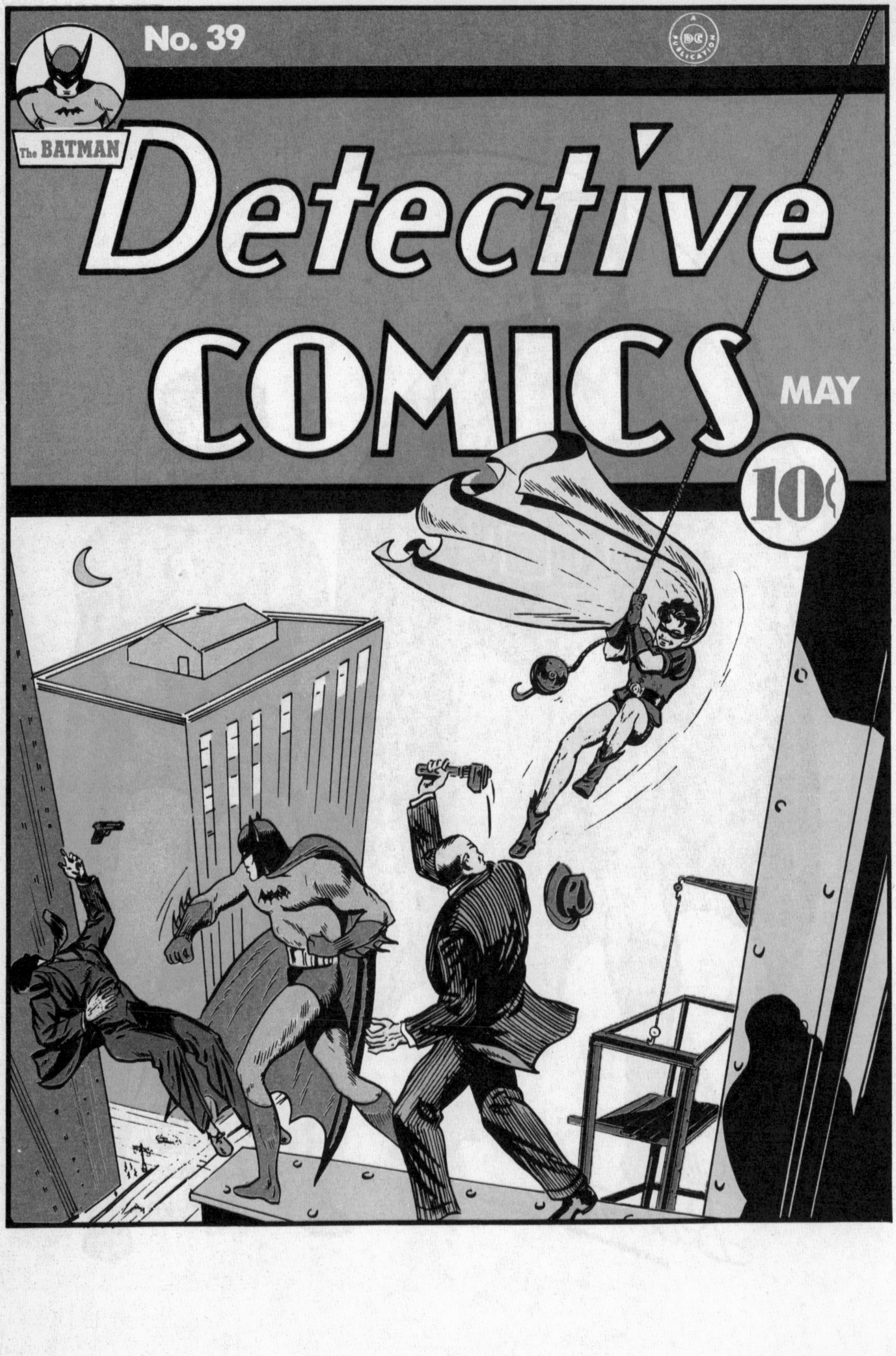
No. 39
The BATMAN
Detective
COMICS
MAY
10¢

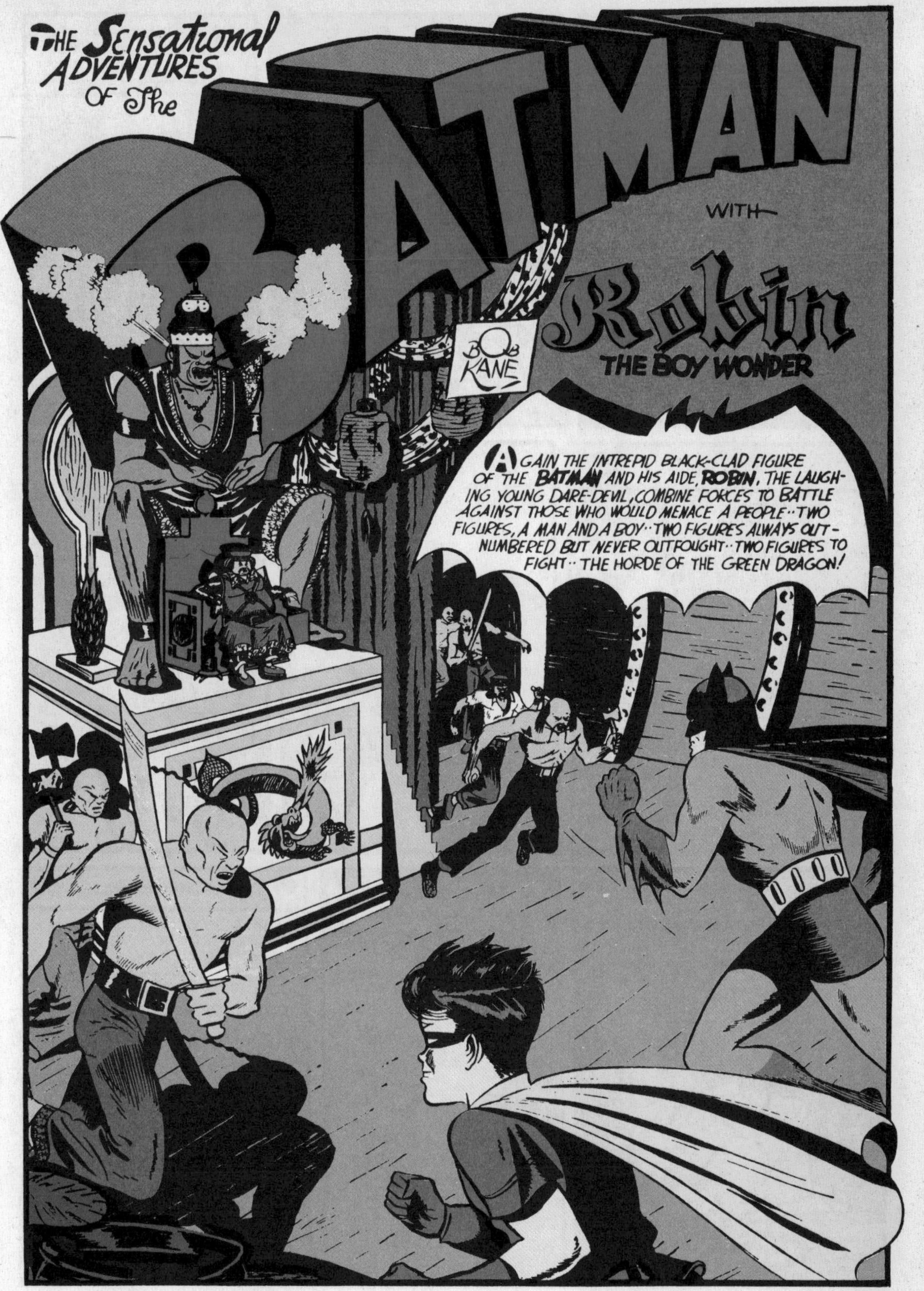
THE Sensational ADVENTURES OF The
BATMAN
WITH
Robin
THE BOY WONDER
BOB KANE
AGAIN THE INTREPID BLACK-CLAD FIGURE OF THE BATMAN AND HIS AIDE, ROBIN, THE LAUGHING YOUNG DARE-DEVIL, COMBINE FORCES TO BATTLE AGAINST THOSE WHO WOULD MENACE A PEOPLE·· TWO FIGURES, A MAN AND A BOY·· TWO FIGURES ALWAYS OUT-NUMBERED BUT NEVER OUTFOUGHT·· TWO FIGURES TO FIGHT·· THE HORDE OF THE GREEN DRAGON!

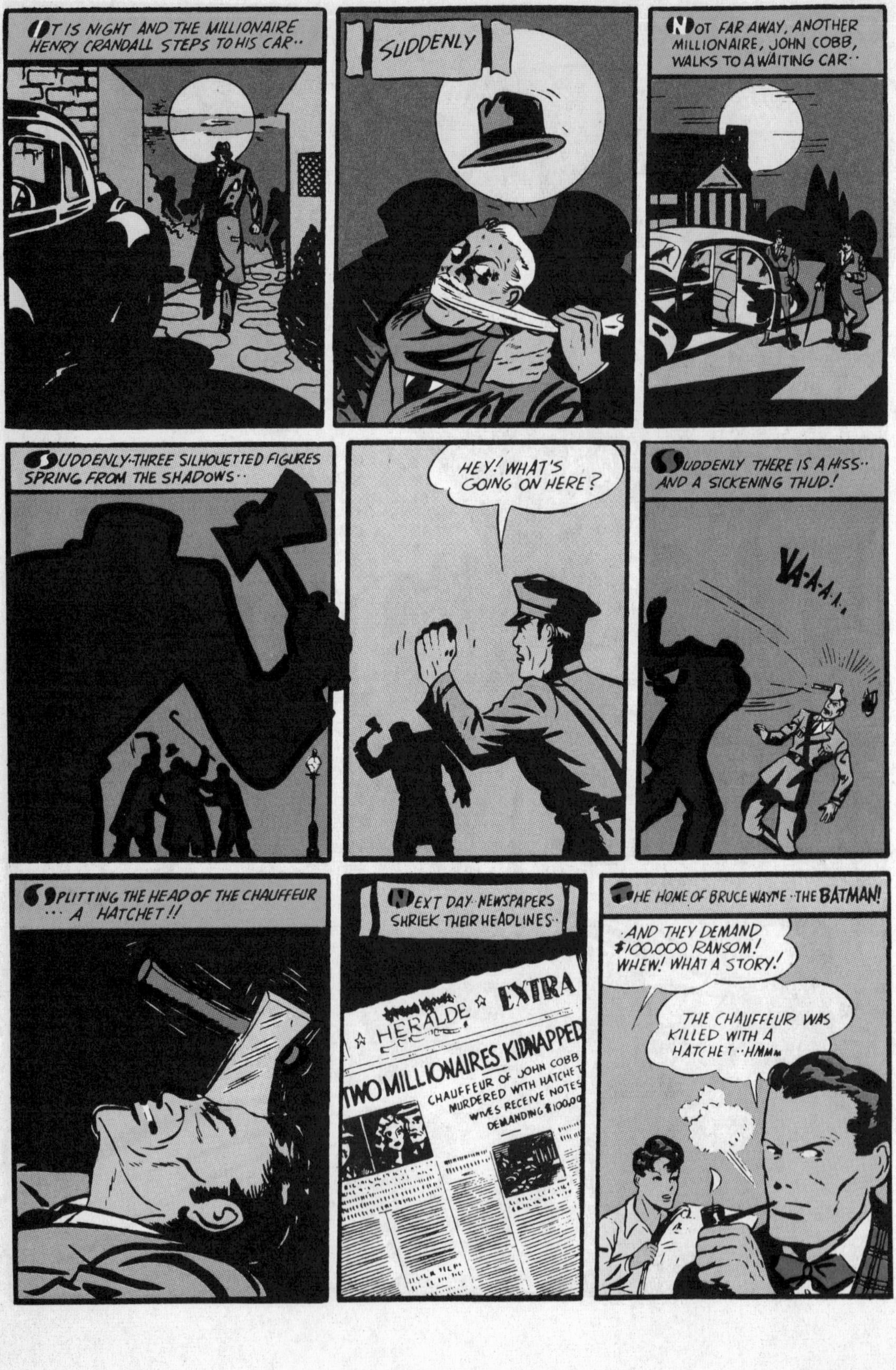
IT IS NIGHT AND THE MILLIONAIRE HENRY CRANDALL STEPS TO HIS CAR..
SUDDENLY
NOT FAR AWAY, ANOTHER MILLIONAIRE, JOHN COBB, WALKS TO A WAITING CAR..
SUDDENLY-THREE SILHOUETTED FIGURES SPRING FROM THE SHADOWS..
HEY! WHAT'S GOING ON HERE?
SUDDENLY THERE IS A HISS.. AND A SICKENING THUD!
SPLITTING THE HEAD OF THE CHAUFFEUR ... A HATCHET!!
NEXT DAY NEWSPAPERS SHRIEK THEIR HEADLINES..
EXTRA
TWO MILLIONAIRES KIDNAPPED
CHAUFFEUR OF JOHN COBB MURDERED WITH HATCHET WIVES RECEIVE NOTES DEMANDING $100,00
THE HOME OF BRUCE WAYNE..THE BATMAN!
AND THEY DEMAND $100,000 RANSOM! WHEW! WHAT A STORY!
THE CHAUFFEUR WAS KILLED WITH A HATCHET..HMMM

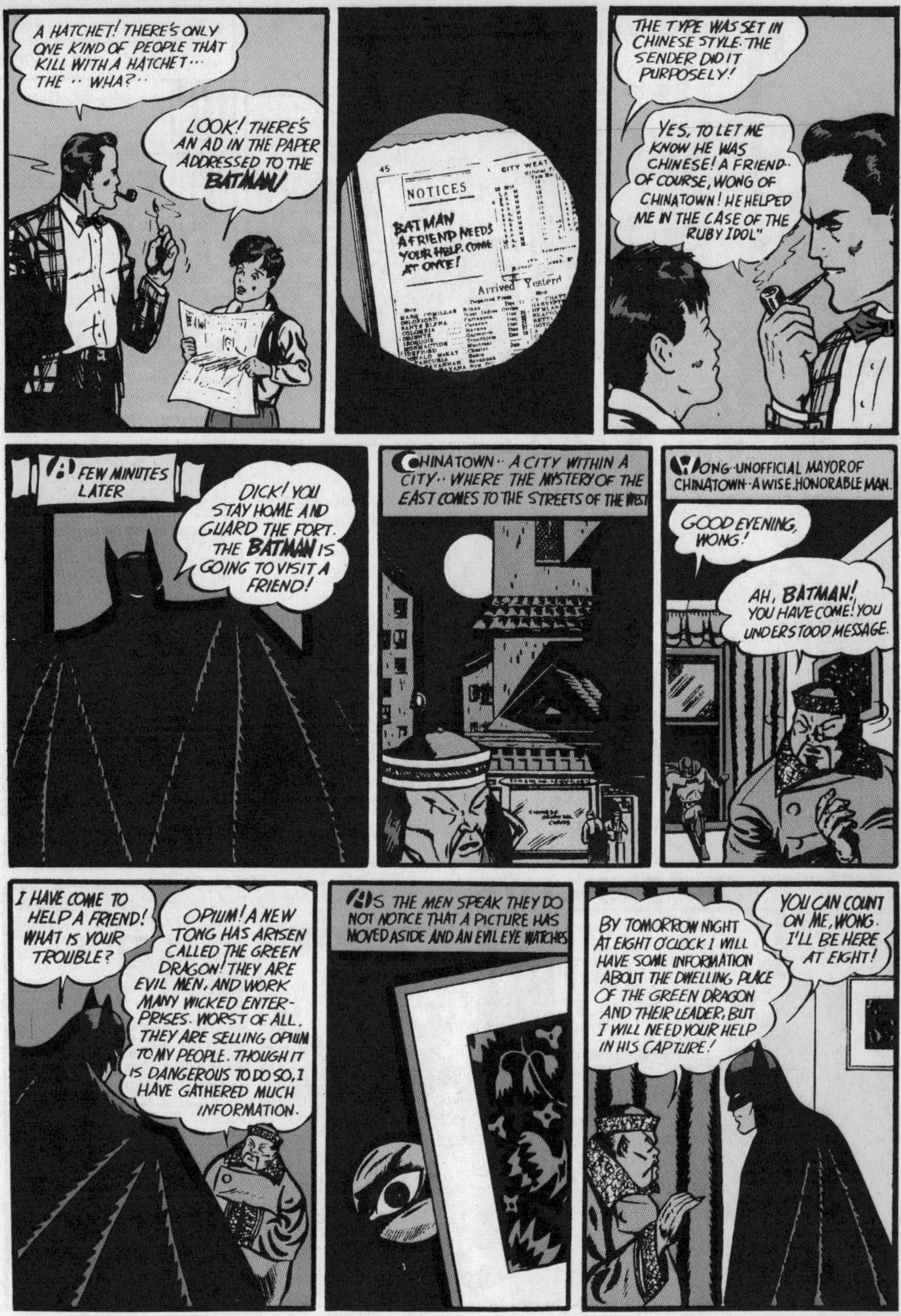

A HATCHET! THERE'S ONLY ONE KIND OF PEOPLE THAT KILL WITH A HATCHET... THE .. WHA?..
LOOK! THERE'S AN AD IN THE PAPER ADDRESSED TO THE BATMAN!
NOTICES
BATMAN A FRIEND NEEDS YOUR HELP. COME AT ONCE!
THE TYPE WAS SET IN CHINESE STYLE. THE SENDER DID IT PURPOSELY!
YES, TO LET ME KNOW HE WAS CHINESE! A FRIEND.. OF COURSE, WONG OF CHINATOWN! HE HELPED ME IN THE CASE OF THE RUBY IDOL"
A FEW MINUTES LATER
DICK! YOU STAY HOME AND GUARD THE FORT. THE BATMAN IS GOING TO VISIT A FRIEND!
CHINATOWN.. A CITY WITHIN A CITY.. WHERE THE MYSTERY OF THE EAST COMES TO THE STREETS OF THE WEST
WONG-UNOFFICIAL MAYOR OF CHINATOWN-A WISE, HONORABLE MAN.
GOOD EVENING, WONG!
AH, BATMAN! YOU HAVE COME! YOU UNDERSTOOD MESSAGE.
I HAVE COME TO HELP A FRIEND! WHAT IS YOUR TROUBLE?
OPIUM! A NEW TONG HAS ARISEN CALLED THE GREEN DRAGON! THEY ARE EVIL MEN, AND WORK MANY WICKED ENTER-PRISES. WORST OF ALL, THEY ARE SELLING OPIUM TO MY PEOPLE. THOUGH IT IS DANGEROUS TO DO SO, I HAVE GATHERED MUCH INFORMATION.
AS THE MEN SPEAK THEY DO NOT NOTICE THAT A PICTURE HAS MOVED ASIDE AND AN EVIL EYE WATCHES
BY TOMORROW NIGHT AT EIGHT O'CLOCK I WILL HAVE SOME INFORMATION ABOUT THE DWELLING PLACE OF THE GREEN DRAGON AND THEIR LEADER, BUT I WILL NEED YOUR HELP IN HIS CAPTURE!
YOU CAN COUNT ON ME, WONG. I'LL BE HERE AT EIGHT!

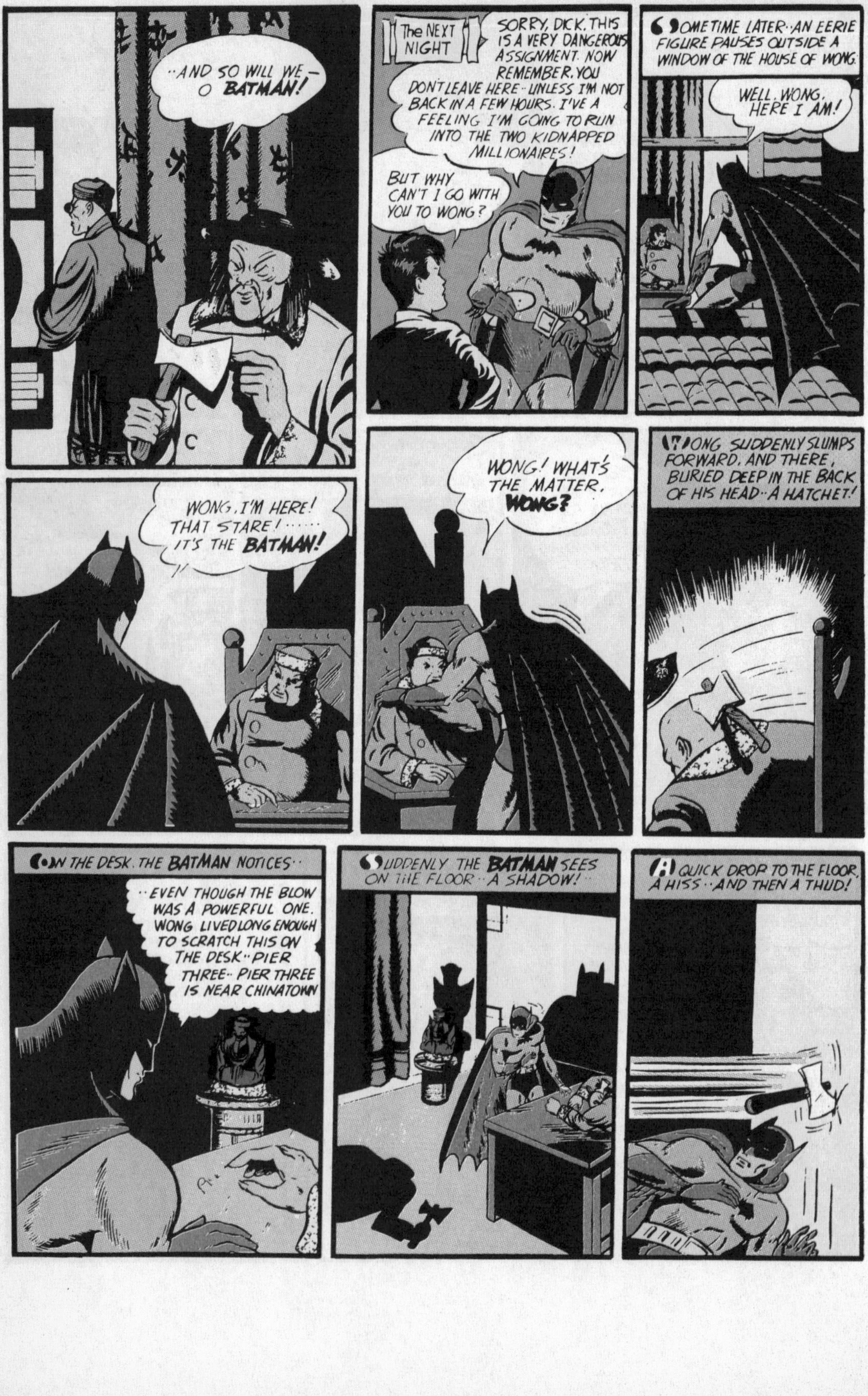

..AND SO WILL WE,— O BATMAN!
The NEXT NIGHT
SORRY, DICK. THIS IS A VERY DANGEROUS ASSIGNMENT. NOW REMEMBER. YOU DON'T LEAVE HERE -- UNLESS I'M NOT BACK IN A FEW HOURS. I'VE A FEELING I'M GOING TO RUN INTO THE TWO KIDNAPPED MILLIONAIRES!
BUT WHY CAN'T I GO WITH YOU TO WONG?
SOMETIME LATER--AN EERIE FIGURE PAUSES OUTSIDE A WINDOW OF THE HOUSE OF WONG.
WELL, WONG, HERE I AM!
WONG, I'M HERE! THAT STARE!...... IT'S THE BATMAN!
WONG! WHAT'S THE MATTER, WONG?
WONG SUDDENLY SLUMPS FORWARD, AND THERE, BURIED DEEP IN THE BACK OF HIS HEAD--A HATCHET!
ON THE DESK, THE BATMAN NOTICES--
..EVEN THOUGH THE BLOW WAS A POWERFUL ONE, WONG LIVED LONG ENOUGH TO SCRATCH THIS ON THE DESK--PIER THREE-- PIER THREE IS NEAR CHINATOWN
SUDDENLY THE BATMAN SEES ON THE FLOOR--A SHADOW!
A QUICK DROP TO THE FLOOR, A HISS--AND THEN A THUD!

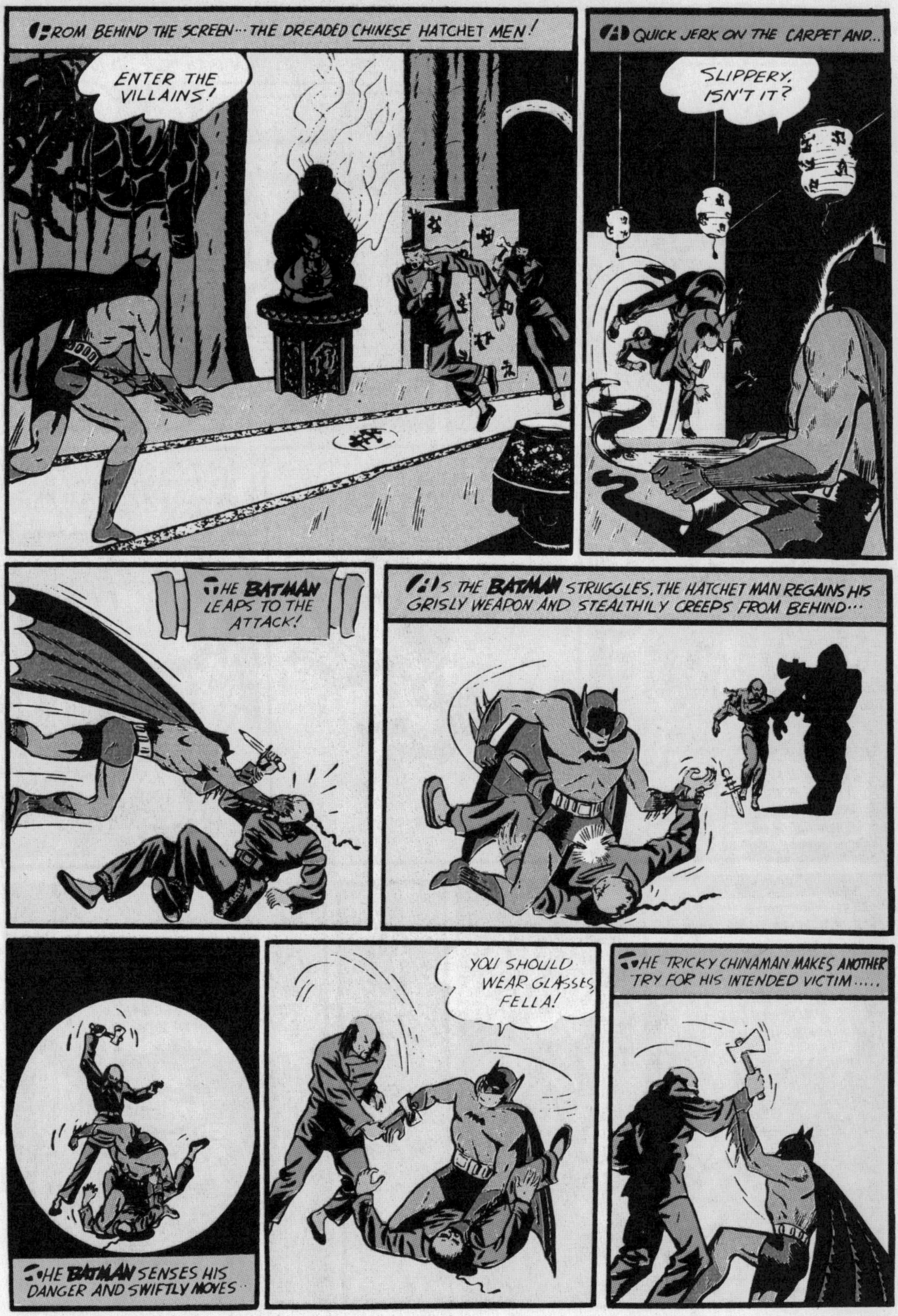
FROM BEHIND THE SCREEN... THE DREADED CHINESE HATCHET MEN!
ENTER THE VILLAINS!
A QUICK JERK ON THE CARPET AND...
SLIPPERY, ISN'T IT?
THE BATMAN LEAPS TO THE ATTACK!
AS THE BATMAN STRUGGLES, THE HATCHET MAN REGAINS HIS GRISLY WEAPON AND STEALTHILY CREEPS FROM BEHIND...
THE BATMAN SENSES HIS DANGER AND SWIFTLY MOVES..
YOU SHOULD WEAR GLASSES, FELLA!
THE TRICKY CHINAMAN MAKES ANOTHER TRY FOR HIS INTENDED VICTIM.....

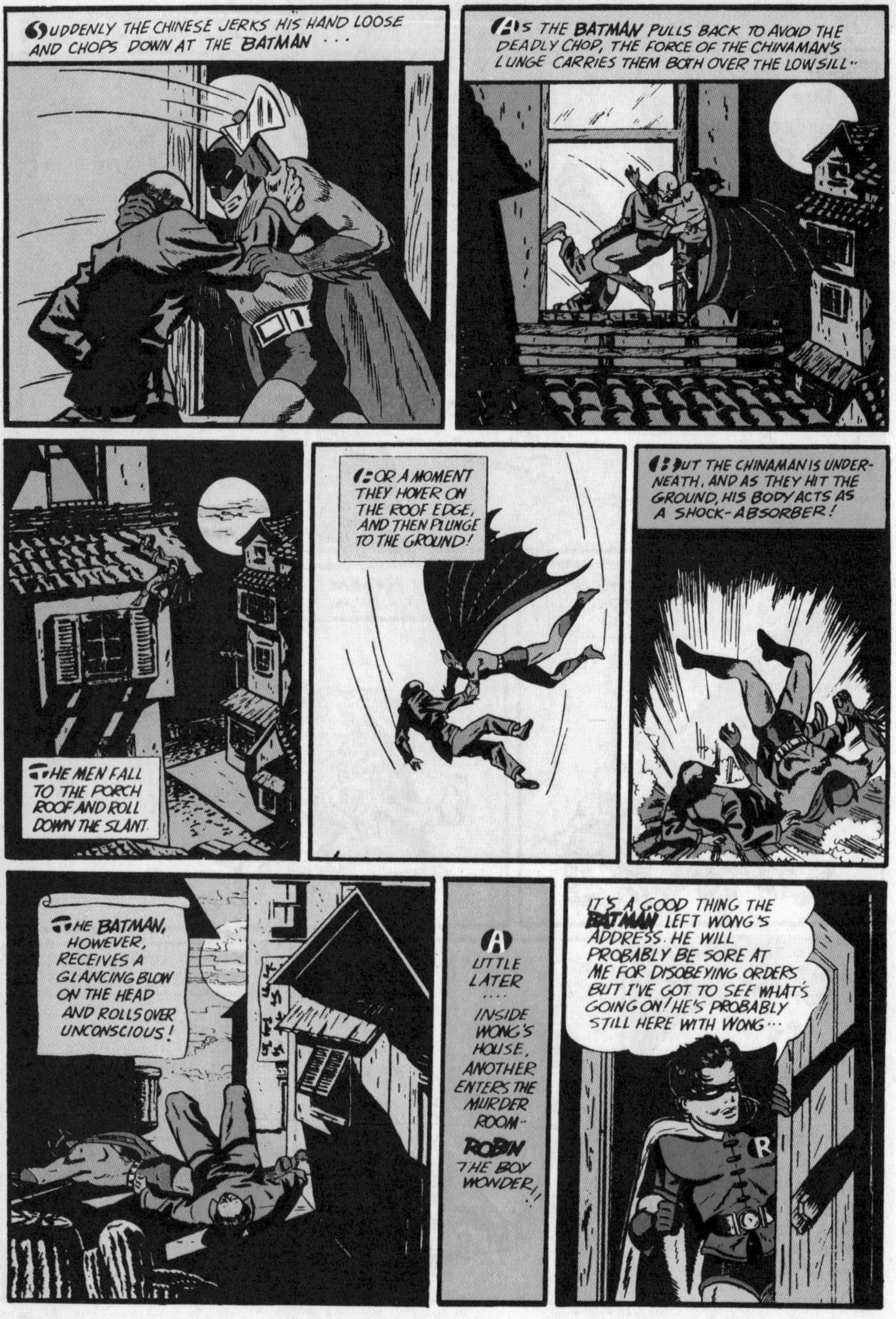
SUDDENLY THE CHINESE JERKS HIS HAND LOOSE AND CHOPS DOWN AT THE BATMAN . . .
AS THE BATMAN PULLS BACK TO AVOID THE DEADLY CHOP, THE FORCE OF THE CHINAMAN'S LUNGE CARRIES THEM BOTH OVER THE LOW SILL..
THE MEN FALL TO THE PORCH ROOF AND ROLL DOWN THE SLANT.
FOR A MOMENT THEY HOVER ON THE ROOF EDGE, AND THEN PLUNGE TO THE GROUND!
BUT THE CHINAMAN IS UNDERNEATH, AND AS THEY HIT THE GROUND, HIS BODY ACTS AS A SHOCK-ABSORBER!
THE BATMAN, HOWEVER, RECEIVES A GLANCING BLOW ON THE HEAD AND ROLLS OVER UNCONSCIOUS!
A LITTLE LATER .... INSIDE WONG'S HOUSE, ANOTHER ENTERS THE MURDER ROOM.. ROBIN THE BOY WONDER!!
IT'S A GOOD THING THE BATMAN LEFT WONG'S ADDRESS. HE WILL PROBABLY BE SORE AT ME FOR DISOBEYING ORDERS BUT I'VE GOT TO SEE WHAT'S GOING ON! HE'S PROBABLY STILL HERE WITH WONG...

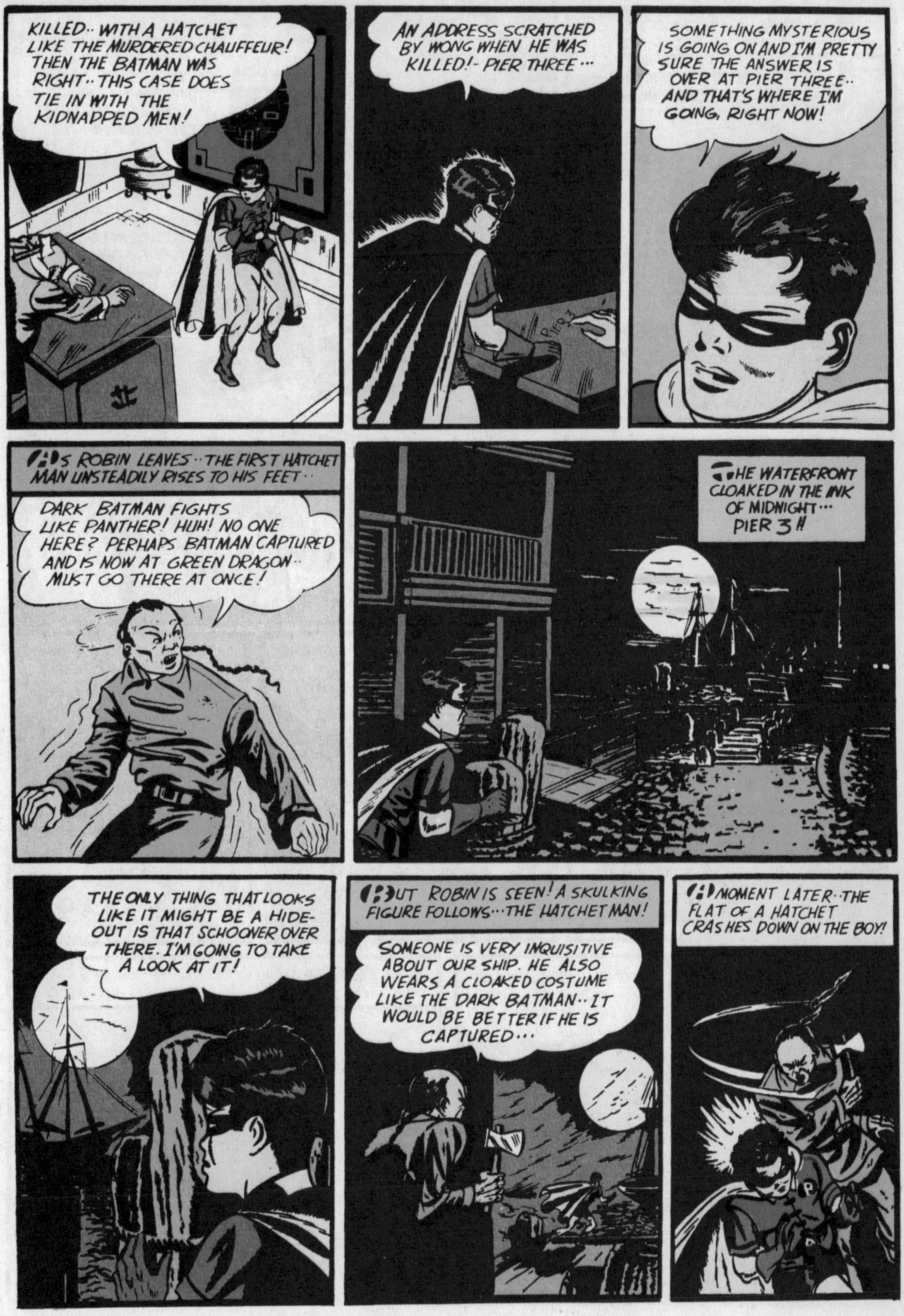

KILLED.. WITH A HATCHET LIKE THE MURDERED CHAUFFEUR! THEN THE BATMAN WAS RIGHT.. THIS CASE DOES TIE IN WITH THE KIDNAPPED MEN!
AN ADDRESS SCRATCHED BY WONG WHEN HE WAS KILLED! - PIER THREE...
PIER 3
SOMETHING MYSTERIOUS IS GOING ON AND I'M PRETTY SURE THE ANSWER IS OVER AT PIER THREE.. AND THAT'S WHERE I'M GOING, RIGHT NOW!
AS ROBIN LEAVES.. THE FIRST HATCHET MAN UNSTEADILY RISES TO HIS FEET..
DARK BATMAN FIGHTS LIKE PANTHER! HUH! NO ONE HERE? PERHAPS BATMAN CAPTURED AND IS NOW AT GREEN DRAGON.. MUST GO THERE AT ONCE!
THE WATERFRONT CLOAKED IN THE INK OF MIDNIGHT... PIER 3!!
THE ONLY THING THAT LOOKS LIKE IT MIGHT BE A HIDE-OUT IS THAT SCHOONER OVER THERE. I'M GOING TO TAKE A LOOK AT IT!
BUT ROBIN IS SEEN! A SKULKING FIGURE FOLLOWS... THE HATCHET MAN!
SOMEONE IS VERY INQUISITIVE ABOUT OUR SHIP. HE ALSO WEARS A CLOAKED COSTUME LIKE THE DARK BATMAN.. IT WOULD BE BETTER IF HE IS CAPTURED...
A MOMENT LATER.. THE FLAT OF A HATCHET CRASHES DOWN ON THE BOY!

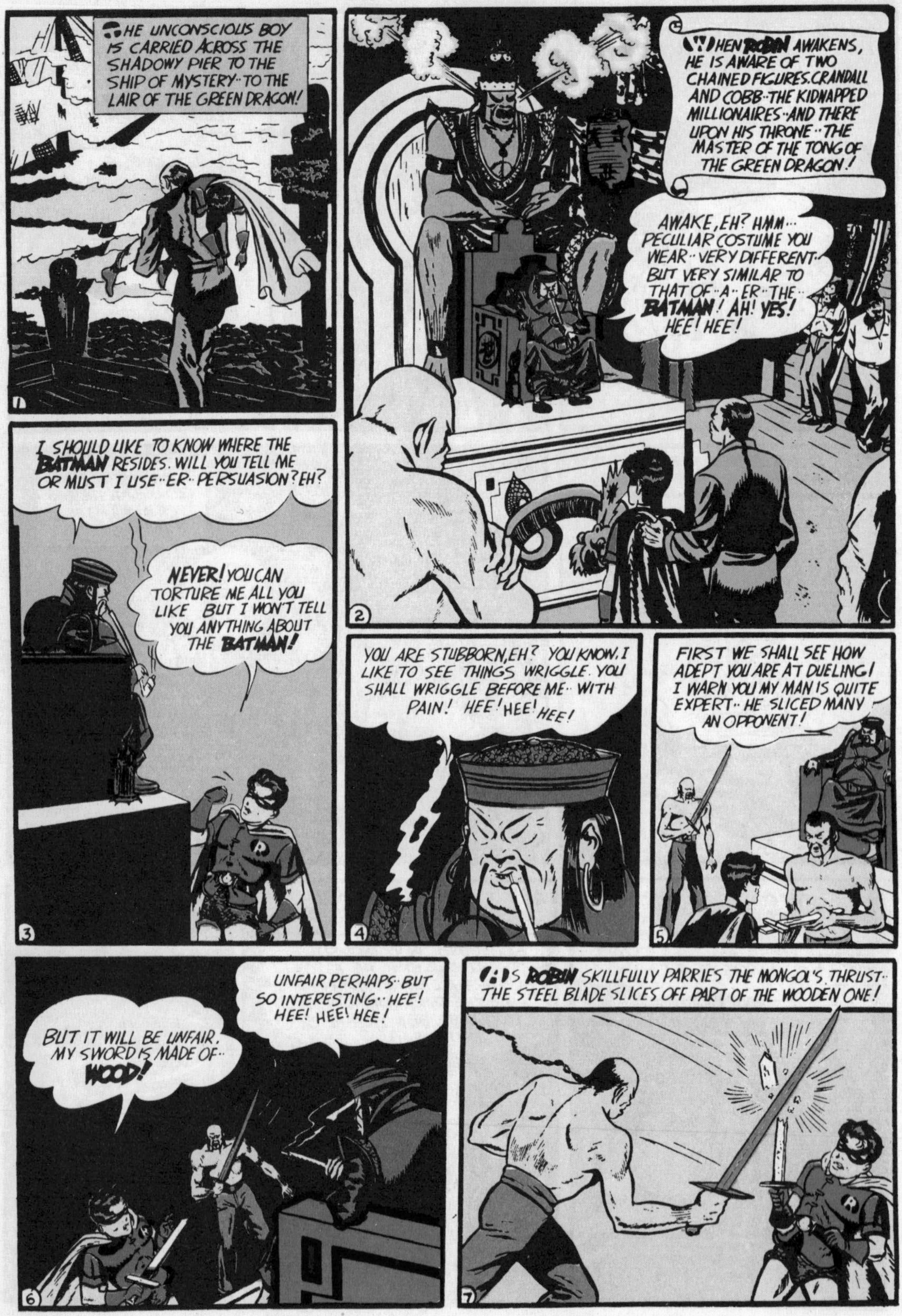
THE UNCONSCIOUS BOY IS CARRIED ACROSS THE SHADOWY PIER TO THE SHIP OF MYSTERY··TO THE LAIR OF THE GREEN DRAGON!
WHEN ROBIN AWAKENS, HE IS AWARE OF TWO CHAINED FIGURES. CRANDALL AND COBB··THE KIDNAPPED MILLIONAIRES··AND THERE UPON HIS THRONE··THE MASTER OF THE TONG OF THE GREEN DRAGON!
AWAKE, EH? HMM··· PECULIAR COSTUME YOU WEAR··VERY DIFFERENT· BUT VERY SIMILAR TO THAT OF··A··ER··THE·· BATMAN! AH! YES! HEE! HEE!
I SHOULD LIKE TO KNOW WHERE THE BATMAN RESIDES. WILL YOU TELL ME OR MUST I USE··ER··PERSUASION? EH?
NEVER! YOU CAN TORTURE ME ALL YOU LIKE BUT I WON'T TELL YOU ANYTHING ABOUT THE BATMAN!
YOU ARE STUBBORN, EH? YOU KNOW, I LIKE TO SEE THINGS WRIGGLE. YOU SHALL WRIGGLE BEFORE ME·· WITH PAIN! HEE! HEE! HEE!
FIRST WE SHALL SEE HOW ADEPT YOU ARE AT DUELING! I WARN YOU MY MAN IS QUITE EXPERT·· HE SLICED MANY AN OPPONENT!
BUT IT WILL BE UNFAIR. MY SWORD IS MADE OF·· WOOD!
UNFAIR PERHAPS·· BUT SO INTERESTING·· HEE! HEE! HEE! HEE!
AS ROBIN SKILLFULLY PARRIES THE MONGOL'S THRUST·· THE STEEL BLADE SLICES OFF PART OF THE WOODEN ONE!

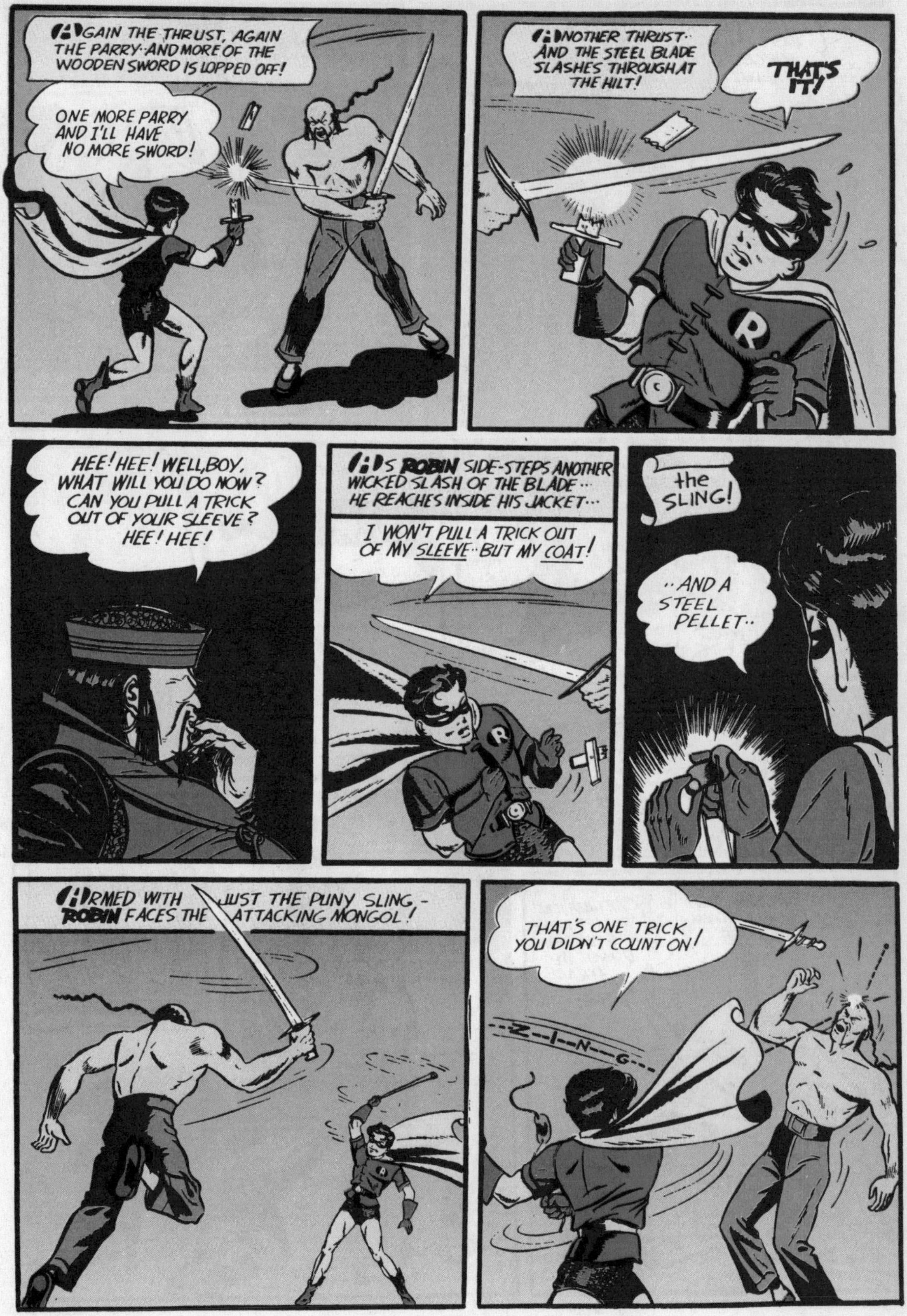
AGAIN THE THRUST, AGAIN THE PARRY--AND MORE OF THE WOODEN SWORD IS LOPPED OFF!
ONE MORE PARRY AND I'LL HAVE NO MORE SWORD!
ANOTHER THRUST-- AND THE STEEL BLADE SLASHES THROUGH AT THE HILT!
THAT'S IT!
HEE! HEE! WELL, BOY, WHAT WILL YOU DO NOW? CAN YOU PULL A TRICK OUT OF YOUR SLEEVE? HEE! HEE!
AS ROBIN SIDE-STEPS ANOTHER WICKED SLASH OF THE BLADE-- HE REACHES INSIDE HIS JACKET--
I WON'T PULL A TRICK OUT OF MY SLEEVE--BUT MY COAT!
the SLING!
--AND A STEEL PELLET--
ARMED WITH JUST THE PUNY SLING, - ROBIN FACES THE ATTACKING MONGOL!
THAT'S ONE TRICK YOU DIDN'T COUNT ON!
Z-I-N-G

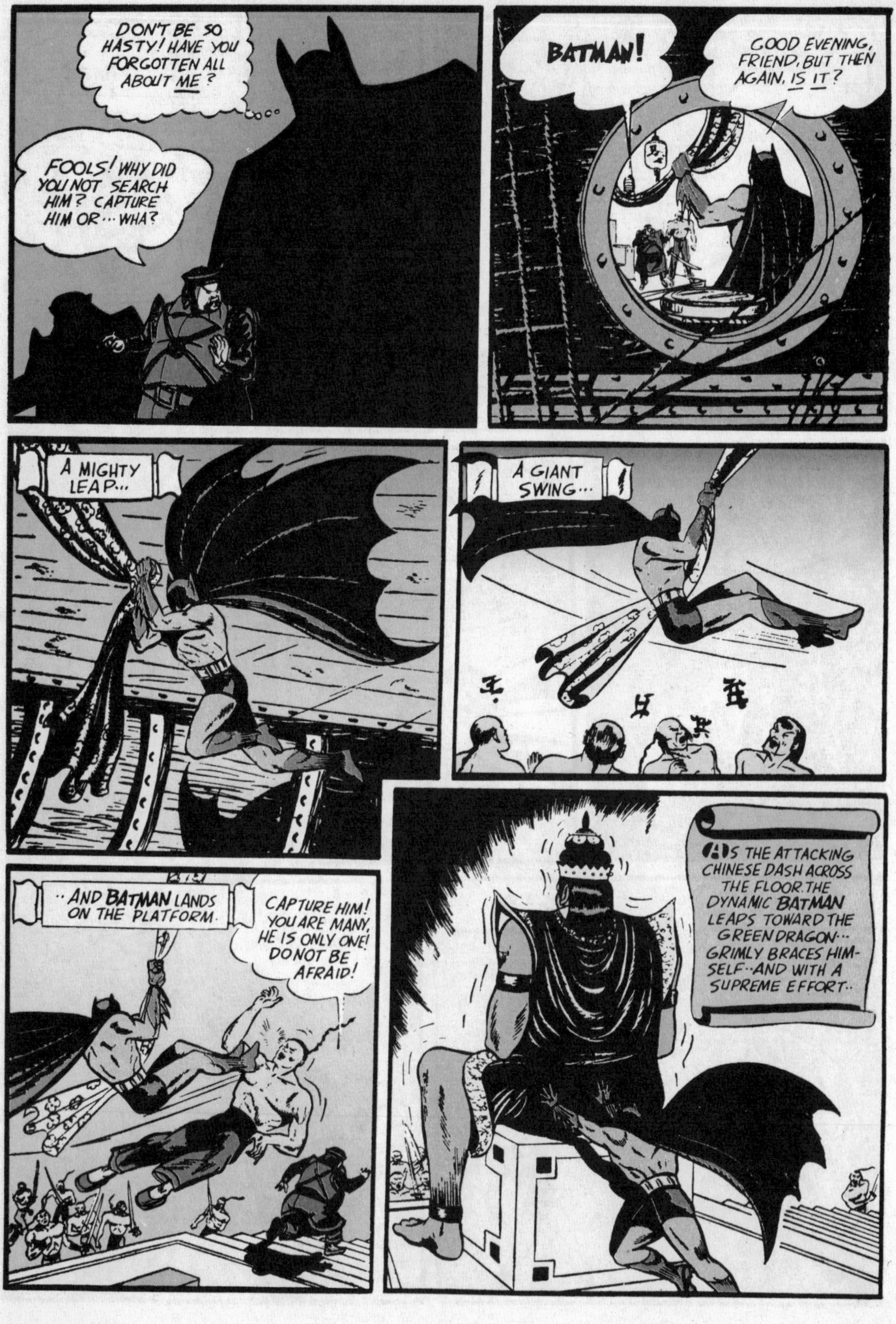

DON'T BE SO HASTY! HAVE YOU FORGOTTEN ALL ABOUT ME?
FOOLS! WHY DID YOU NOT SEARCH HIM? CAPTURE HIM OR ... WHA?
BATMAN!
GOOD EVENING, FRIEND, BUT THEN AGAIN, IS IT?
A MIGHTY LEAP...
A GIANT SWING...
..AND BATMAN LANDS ON THE PLATFORM.
CAPTURE HIM! YOU ARE MANY, HE IS ONLY ONE! DO NOT BE AFRAID!
AS THE ATTACKING CHINESE DASH ACROSS THE FLOOR. THE DYNAMIC BATMAN LEAPS TOWARD THE GREEN DRAGON... GRIMLY BRACES HIMSELF.. AND WITH A SUPREME EFFORT..

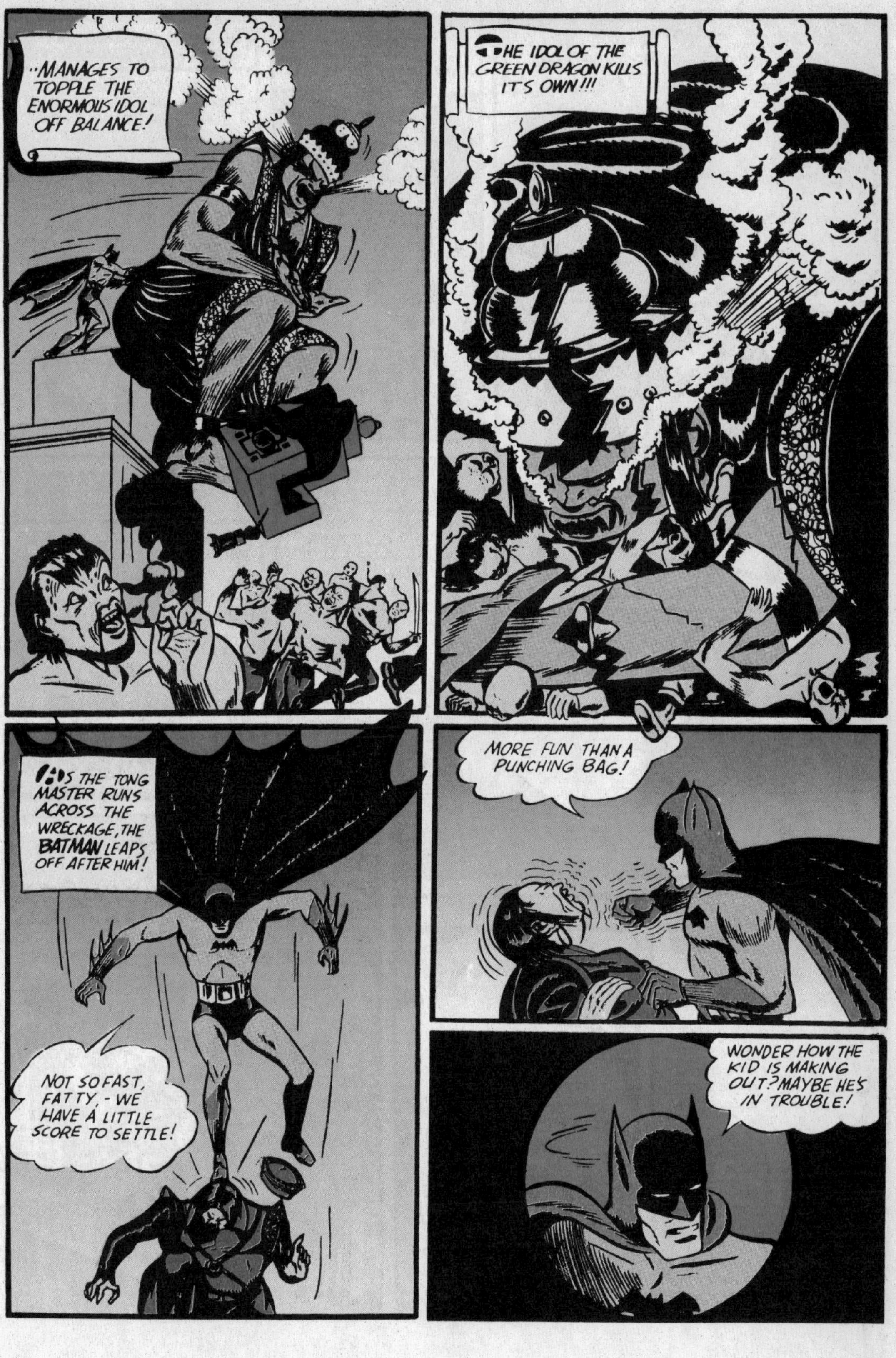
..MANAGES TO TOPPLE THE ENORMOUS IDOL OFF BALANCE!
THE IDOL OF THE GREEN DRAGON KILLS IT'S OWN!!!
AS THE TONG MASTER RUNS ACROSS THE WRECKAGE, THE BATMAN LEAPS OFF AFTER HIM!
NOT SO FAST, FATTY, - WE HAVE A LITTLE SCORE TO SETTLE!
MORE FUN THAN A PUNCHING BAG!
WONDER HOW THE KID IS MAKING OUT? MAYBE HE'S IN TROUBLE!

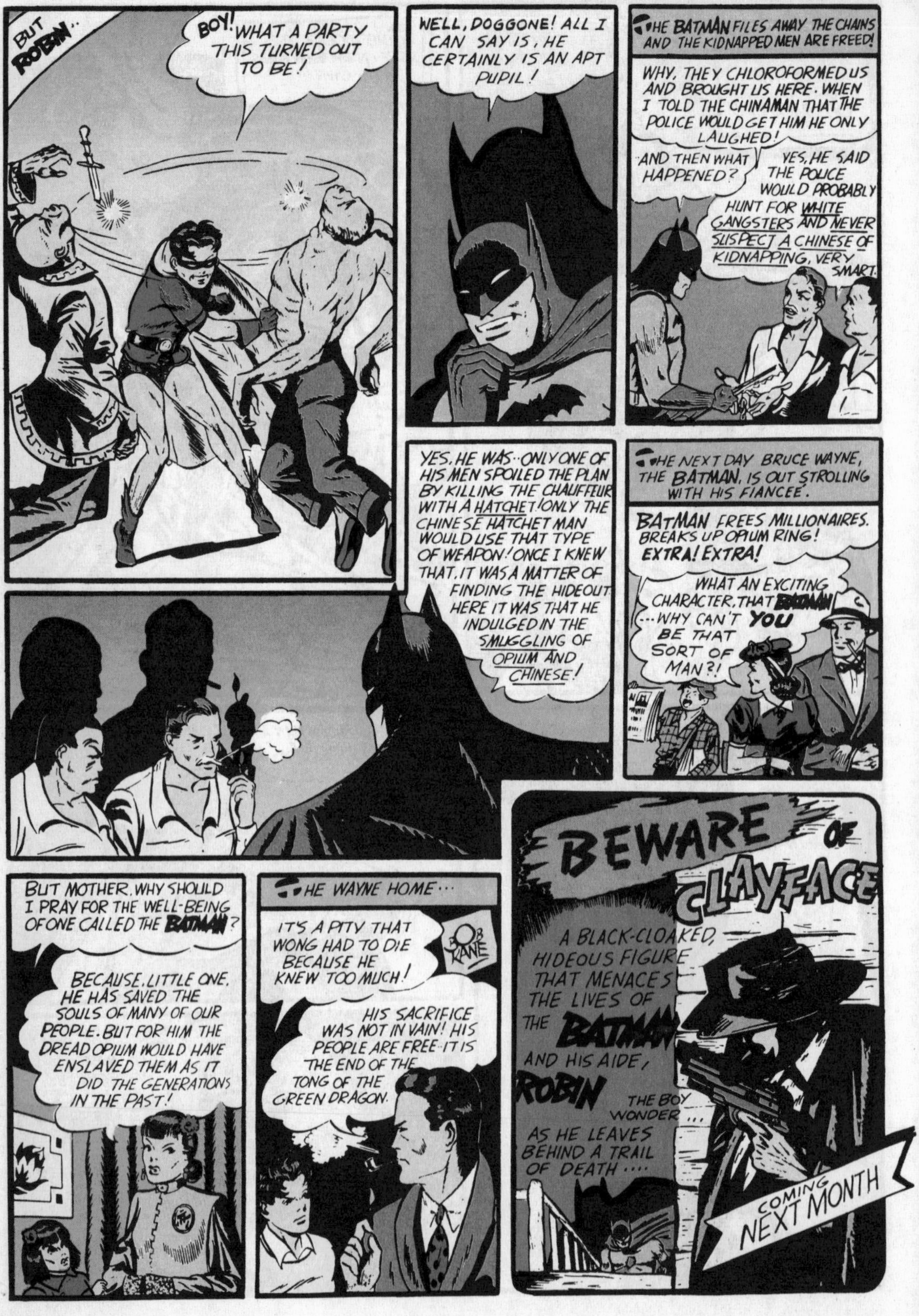
BUT ROBIN..
BOY! WHAT A PARTY THIS TURNED OUT TO BE!
WELL, DOGGONE! ALL I CAN SAY IS, HE CERTAINLY IS AN APT PUPIL!
THE BATMAN FILES AWAY THE CHAINS AND THE KIDNAPPED MEN ARE FREED!
WHY, THEY CHLOROFORMED US AND BROUGHT US HERE. WHEN I TOLD THE CHINAMAN THAT THE POLICE WOULD GET HIM HE ONLY LAUGHED!
AND THEN WHAT HAPPENED?
YES, HE SAID THE POLICE WOULD PROBABLY HUNT FOR WHITE GANGSTERS AND NEVER SUSPECT A CHINESE OF KIDNAPPING, VERY SMART.
YES, HE WAS--ONLY ONE OF HIS MEN SPOILED THE PLAN BY KILLING THE CHAUFFEUR WITH A HATCHET! ONLY THE CHINESE HATCHET MAN WOULD USE THAT TYPE OF WEAPON! ONCE I KNEW THAT, IT WAS A MATTER OF FINDING THE HIDEOUT. HERE IT WAS THAT HE INDULGED IN THE SMUGGLING OF OPIUM AND CHINESE!
THE NEXT DAY BRUCE WAYNE, THE BATMAN, IS OUT STROLLING WITH HIS FIANCEE.
BATMAN FREES MILLIONAIRES. BREAKS UP OPIUM RING! EXTRA! EXTRA!
WHAT AN EXCITING CHARACTER, THAT BATMAN --WHY CAN'T YOU BE THAT SORT OF MAN?!
BUT MOTHER, WHY SHOULD I PRAY FOR THE WELL-BEING OF ONE CALLED THE BATMAN?
BECAUSE, LITTLE ONE, HE HAS SAVED THE SOULS OF MANY OF OUR PEOPLE. BUT FOR HIM THE DREAD OPIUM WOULD HAVE ENSLAVED THEM AS IT DID THE GENERATIONS IN THE PAST!
THE WAYNE HOME...
IT'S A PITY THAT WONG HAD TO DIE BECAUSE HE KNEW TOO MUCH!
BOB KANE
HIS SACRIFICE WAS NOT IN VAIN! HIS PEOPLE ARE FREE--IT IS THE END OF THE TONG OF THE GREEN DRAGON.
BEWARE OF CLAYFACE
A BLACK-CLOAKED, HIDEOUS FIGURE THAT MENACES THE LIVES OF THE BATMAN AND HIS AIDE, ROBIN THE BOY WONDER... AS HE LEAVES BEHIND A TRAIL OF DEATH....
COMING NEXT MONTH

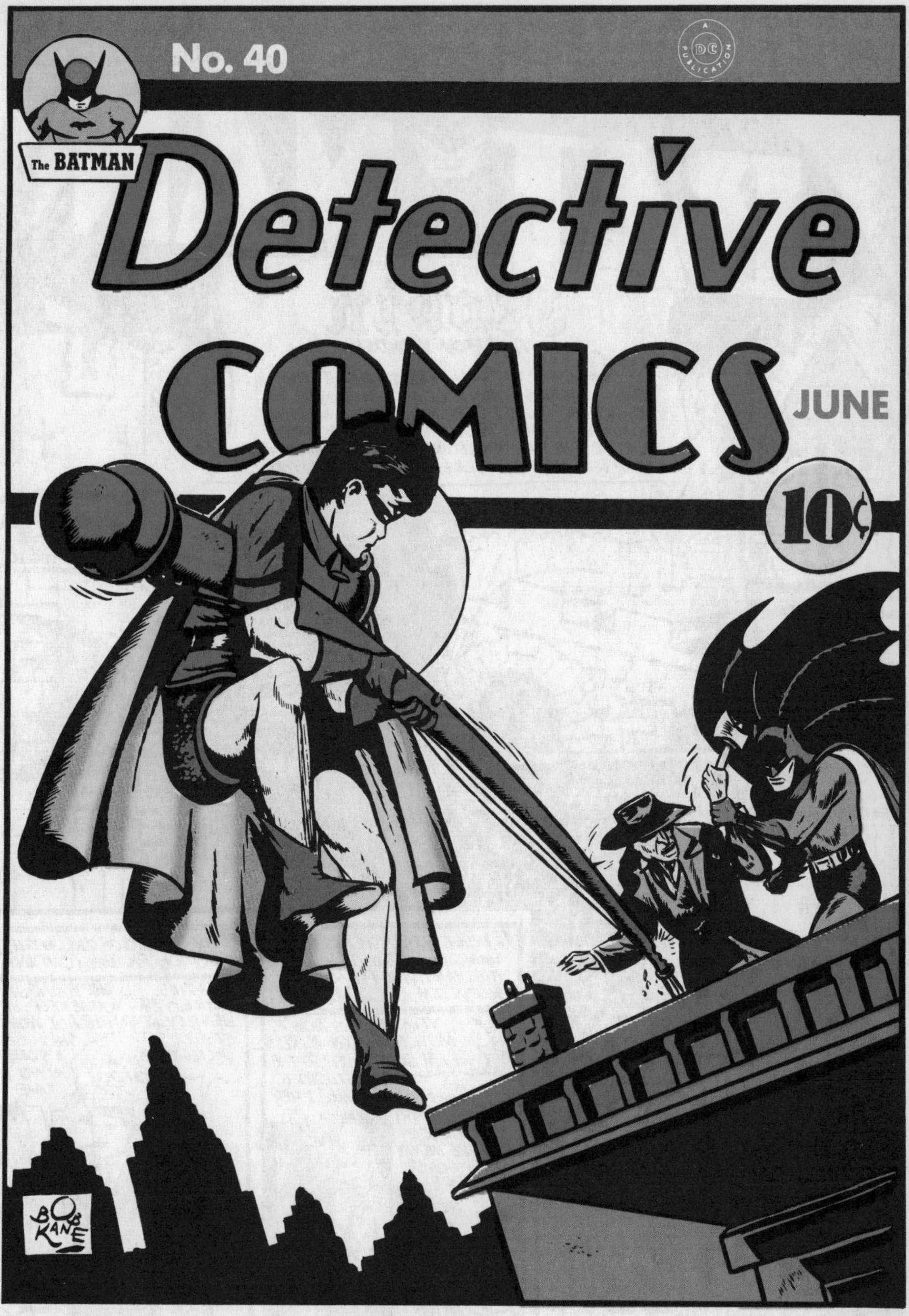
No. 40
A DC PUBLICATION
The BATMAN
Detective
COMICS
JUNE
10¢
BOB KANE

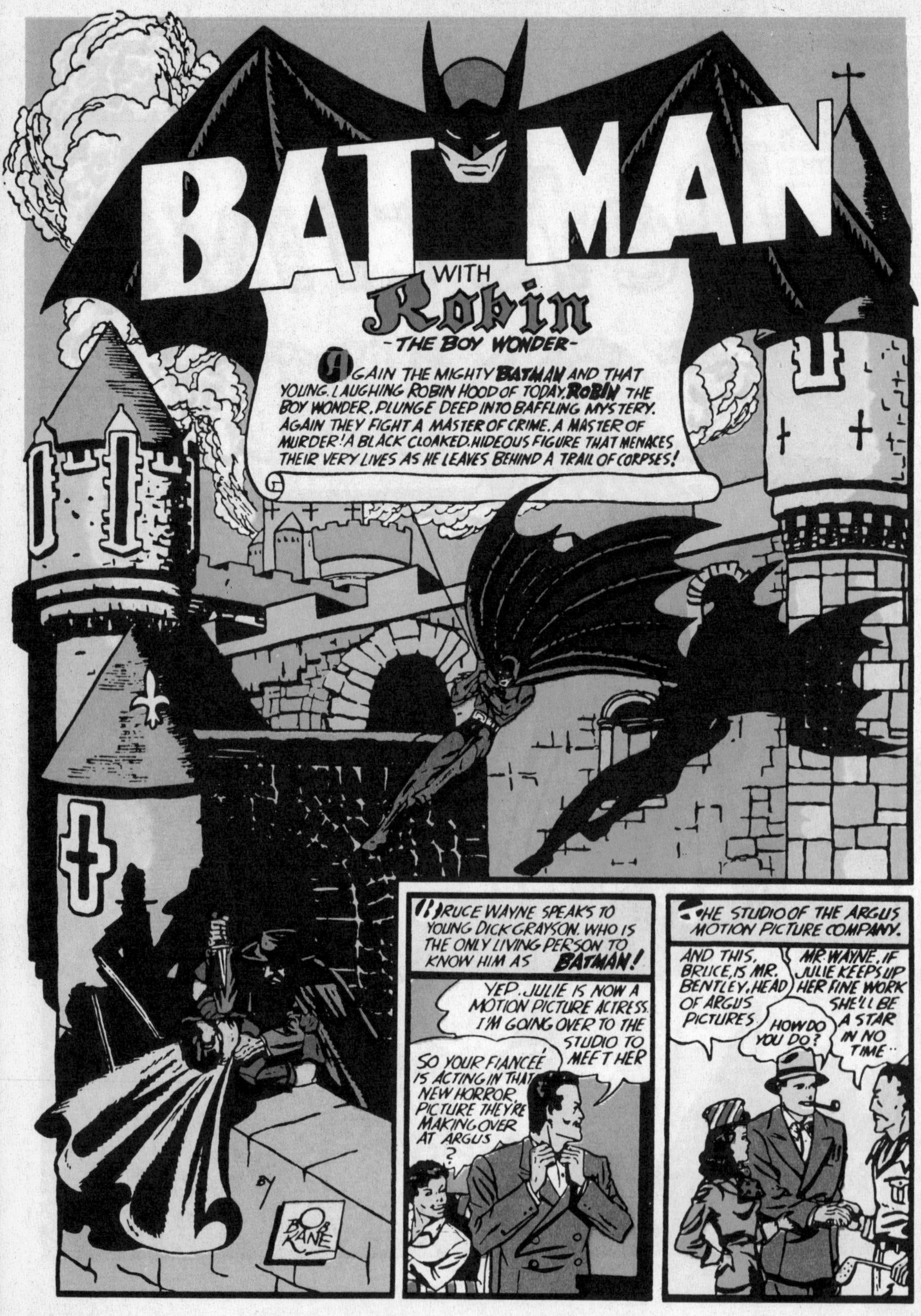
BATMAN
WITH
Robin
-THE BOY WONDER-
AGAIN THE MIGHTY BATMAN AND THAT YOUNG, LAUGHING ROBIN HOOD OF TODAY, ROBIN THE BOY WONDER, PLUNGE DEEP INTO BAFFLING MYSTERY. AGAIN THEY FIGHT A MASTER OF CRIME, A MASTER OF MURDER! A BLACK CLOAKED, HIDEOUS FIGURE THAT MENACES THEIR VERY LIVES AS HE LEAVES BEHIND A TRAIL OF CORPSES!
BY BOB KANE
BRUCE WAYNE SPEAKS TO YOUNG DICK GRAYSON, WHO IS THE ONLY LIVING PERSON TO KNOW HIM AS BATMAN!
SO YOUR FIANCÉE IS ACTING IN THAT NEW HORROR PICTURE THEY'RE MAKING OVER AT ARGUS?
YEP. JULIE IS NOW A MOTION PICTURE ACTRESS. I'M GOING OVER TO THE STUDIO TO MEET HER
THE STUDIO OF THE ARGUS MOTION PICTURE COMPANY.
AND THIS, BRUCE, IS MR. BENTLEY, HEAD OF ARGUS PICTURES.
HOW DO YOU DO?
MR. WAYNE, IF JULIE KEEPS UP HER FINE WORK SHE'LL BE A STAR IN NO TIME..

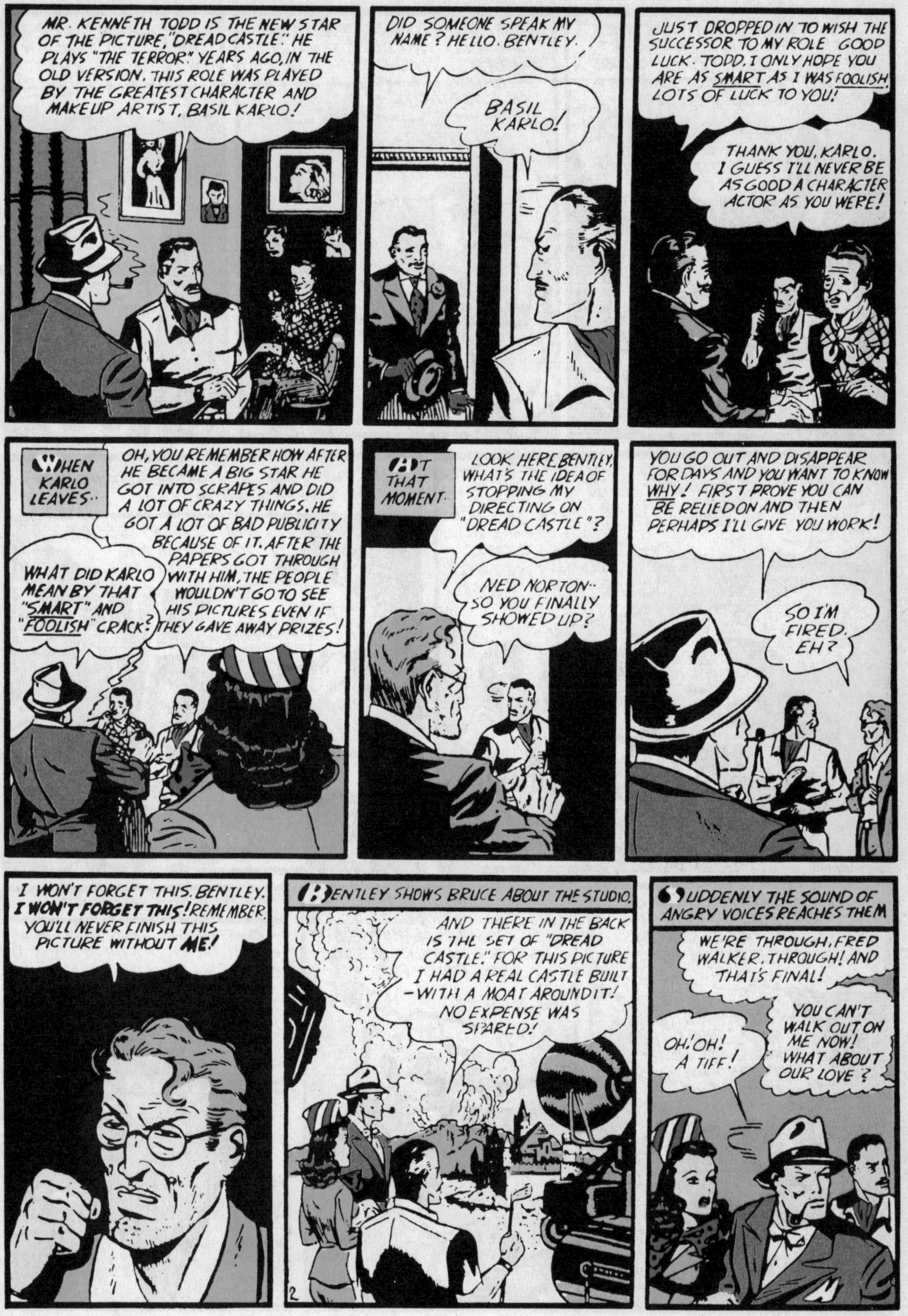
MR. KENNETH TODD IS THE NEW STAR OF THE PICTURE, "DREAD CASTLE." HE PLAYS "THE TERROR." YEARS AGO, IN THE OLD VERSION, THIS ROLE WAS PLAYED BY THE GREATEST CHARACTER AND MAKEUP ARTIST, BASIL KARLO!
DID SOMEONE SPEAK MY NAME? HELLO, BENTLEY.
BASIL KARLO!
JUST DROPPED IN TO WISH THE SUCCESSOR TO MY ROLE GOOD LUCK. TODD, I ONLY HOPE YOU ARE AS SMART AS I WAS FOOLISH. LOTS OF LUCK TO YOU!
THANK YOU, KARLO. I GUESS I'LL NEVER BE AS GOOD A CHARACTER ACTOR AS YOU WERE!
WHEN KARLO LEAVES..
WHAT DID KARLO MEAN BY THAT "SMART" AND "FOOLISH" CRACK?
OH, YOU REMEMBER HOW AFTER HE BECAME A BIG STAR HE GOT INTO SCRAPES AND DID A LOT OF CRAZY THINGS. HE GOT A LOT OF BAD PUBLICITY BECAUSE OF IT. AFTER THE PAPERS GOT THROUGH WITH HIM, THE PEOPLE WOULDN'T GO TO SEE HIS PICTURES EVEN IF THEY GAVE AWAY PRIZES!
AT THAT MOMENT..
LOOK HERE, BENTLEY, WHAT'S THE IDEA OF STOPPING MY DIRECTING ON "DREAD CASTLE"?
NED NORTON.. SO YOU FINALLY SHOWED UP?
YOU GO OUT AND DISAPPEAR FOR DAYS AND YOU WANT TO KNOW WHY! FIRST PROVE YOU CAN BE RELIED ON AND THEN PERHAPS I'LL GIVE YOU WORK!
SO I'M FIRED, EH?
I WON'T FORGET THIS, BENTLEY. I WON'T FORGET THIS! REMEMBER, YOU'LL NEVER FINISH THIS PICTURE WITHOUT ME!
BENTLEY SHOWS BRUCE ABOUT THE STUDIO.
AND THERE IN THE BACK IS THE SET OF "DREAD CASTLE." FOR THIS PICTURE I HAD A REAL CASTLE BUILT - WITH A MOAT AROUND IT! NO EXPENSE WAS SPARED!
2
SUDDENLY THE SOUND OF ANGRY VOICES REACHES THEM
WE'RE THROUGH, FRED WALKER, THROUGH! AND THAT'S FINAL!
YOU CAN'T WALK OUT ON ME NOW! WHAT ABOUT OUR LOVE?
OH! OH! A TIFF!

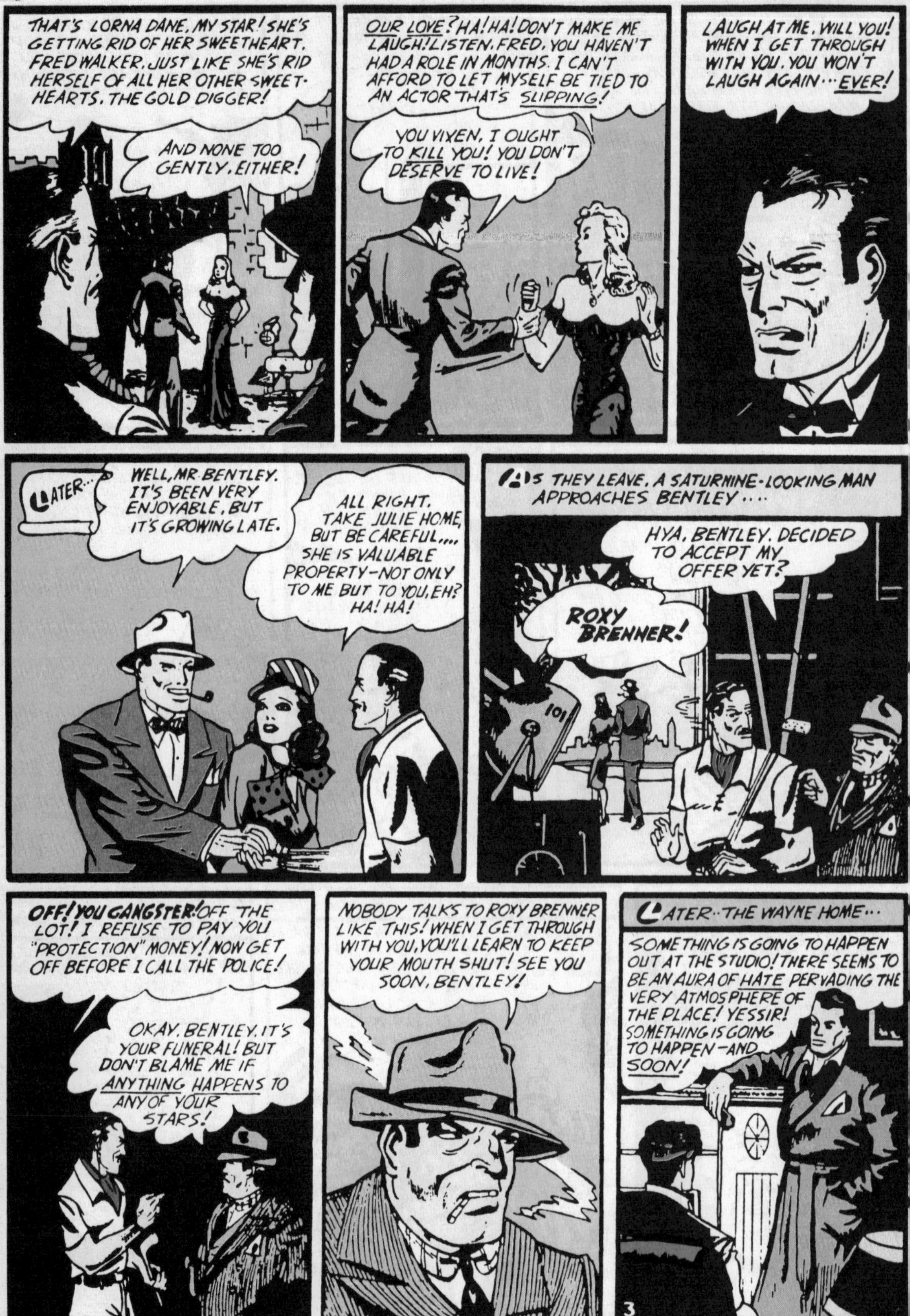
THAT'S LORNA DANE, MY STAR! SHE'S GETTING RID OF HER SWEETHEART, FRED WALKER, JUST LIKE SHE'S RID HERSELF OF ALL HER OTHER SWEET-HEARTS. THE GOLD DIGGER!
AND NONE TOO GENTLY, EITHER!
OUR LOVE? HA! HA! DON'T MAKE ME LAUGH! LISTEN, FRED, YOU HAVEN'T HAD A ROLE IN MONTHS. I CAN'T AFFORD TO LET MYSELF BE TIED TO AN ACTOR THAT'S SLIPPING!
YOU VIXEN, I OUGHT TO KILL YOU! YOU DON'T DESERVE TO LIVE!
LAUGH AT ME, WILL YOU! WHEN I GET THROUGH WITH YOU, YOU WON'T LAUGH AGAIN ... EVER!
LATER...
WELL, MR. BENTLEY. IT'S BEEN VERY ENJOYABLE, BUT IT'S GROWING LATE.
ALL RIGHT. TAKE JULIE HOME, BUT BE CAREFUL.... SHE IS VALUABLE PROPERTY-NOT ONLY TO ME BUT TO YOU, EH? HA! HA!
AS THEY LEAVE, A SATURNINE-LOOKING MAN APPROACHES BENTLEY...
HYA, BENTLEY. DECIDED TO ACCEPT MY OFFER YET?
ROXY BRENNER!
101
OFF! YOU GANGSTER! OFF THE LOT! I REFUSE TO PAY YOU "PROTECTION" MONEY! NOW GET OFF BEFORE I CALL THE POLICE!
OKAY, BENTLEY, IT'S YOUR FUNERAL! BUT DON'T BLAME ME IF ANYTHING HAPPENS TO ANY OF YOUR STARS!
NOBODY TALKS TO ROXY BRENNER LIKE THIS! WHEN I GET THROUGH WITH YOU, YOU'LL LEARN TO KEEP YOUR MOUTH SHUT! SEE YOU SOON, BENTLEY!
LATER.. THE WAYNE HOME...
SOMETHING IS GOING TO HAPPEN OUT AT THE STUDIO! THERE SEEMS TO BE AN AURA OF HATE PERVADING THE VERY ATMOSPHERE OF THE PLACE! YESSIR! SOMETHING IS GOING TO HAPPEN-AND SOON!
3

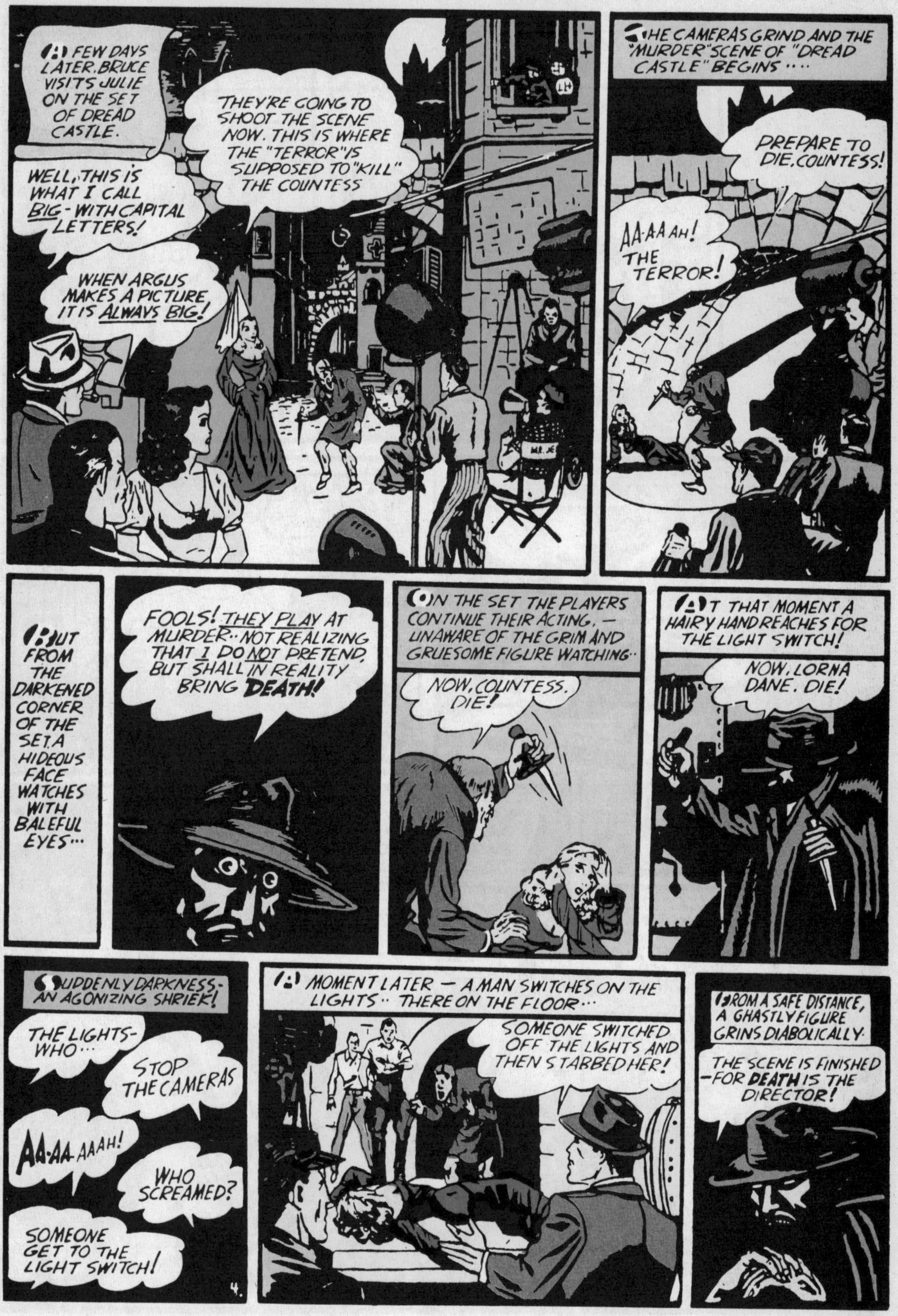
A FEW DAYS LATER. BRUCE VISITS JULIE ON THE SET OF DREAD CASTLE.
THEY'RE GOING TO SHOOT THE SCENE NOW. THIS IS WHERE THE "TERROR" IS SUPPOSED TO "KILL" THE COUNTESS
WELL, THIS IS WHAT I CALL BIG - WITH CAPITAL LETTERS!
WHEN ARGUS MAKES A PICTURE, IT IS ALWAYS BIG!
THE CAMERAS GRIND AND THE "MURDER" SCENE OF "DREAD CASTLE" BEGINS ....
PREPARE TO DIE, COUNTESS!
AA-AA AH! THE TERROR!
BUT FROM THE DARKENED CORNER OF THE SET, A HIDEOUS FACE WATCHES WITH BALEFUL EYES...
FOOLS! THEY PLAY AT MURDER.. NOT REALIZING THAT I DO NOT PRETEND, BUT SHALL IN REALITY BRING DEATH!
ON THE SET THE PLAYERS CONTINUE THEIR ACTING, — UNAWARE OF THE GRIM AND GRUESOME FIGURE WATCHING..
NOW, COUNTESS. DIE!
AT THAT MOMENT A HAIRY HAND REACHES FOR THE LIGHT SWITCH!
NOW, LORNA DANE. DIE!
SUDDENLY DARKNESS - AN AGONIZING SHRIEK!
THE LIGHTS - WHO...
STOP THE CAMERAS
AA-AA-AAAH!
WHO SCREAMED?
SOMEONE GET TO THE LIGHT SWITCH!
4.
A MOMENT LATER — A MAN SWITCHES ON THE LIGHTS.. THERE ON THE FLOOR...
SOMEONE SWITCHED OFF THE LIGHTS AND THEN STABBED HER!
FROM A SAFE DISTANCE, A GHASTLY FIGURE GRINS DIABOLICALLY.
THE SCENE IS FINISHED - FOR DEATH IS THE DIRECTOR!

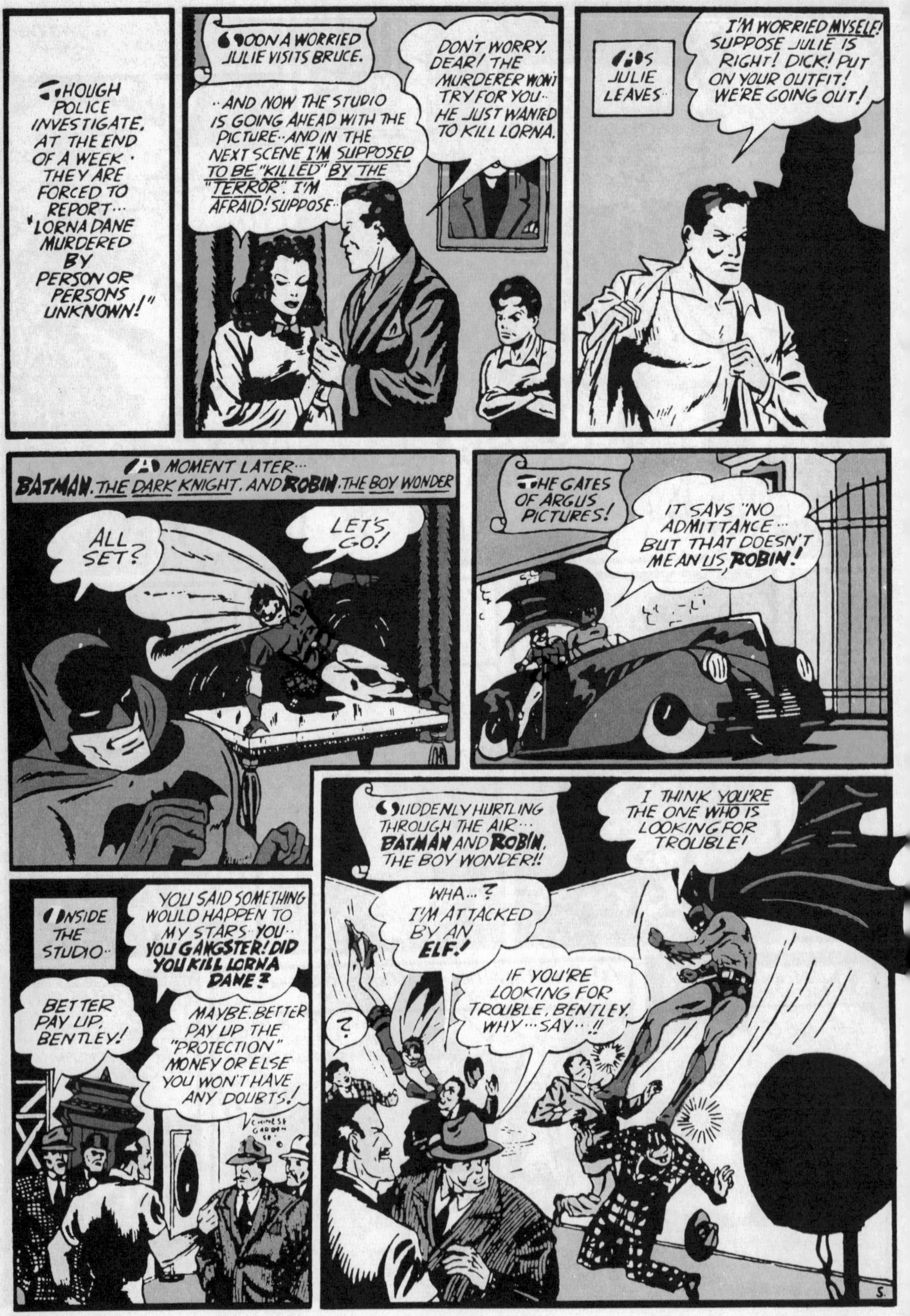
THOUGH POLICE INVESTIGATE, AT THE END OF A WEEK, THEY ARE FORCED TO REPORT... "LORNA DANE MURDERED BY PERSON OR PERSONS UNKNOWN!"
SOON A WORRIED JULIE VISITS BRUCE.
..AND NOW THE STUDIO IS GOING AHEAD WITH THE PICTURE..AND IN THE NEXT SCENE I'M SUPPOSED TO BE "KILLED" BY THE "TERROR". I'M AFRAID! SUPPOSE..
DON'T WORRY, DEAR! THE MURDERER WON'T TRY FOR YOU.. HE JUST WANTED TO KILL LORNA.
AS JULIE LEAVES..
I'M WORRIED MYSELF! SUPPOSE JULIE IS RIGHT! DICK! PUT ON YOUR OUTFIT! WE'RE GOING OUT!
A MOMENT LATER... BATMAN, THE DARK KNIGHT, AND ROBIN, THE BOY WONDER
ALL SET?
LET'S GO!
THE GATES OF ARGUS PICTURES!
IT SAYS "NO ADMITTANCE"... BUT THAT DOESN'T MEAN US, ROBIN!
INSIDE THE STUDIO..
YOU SAID SOMETHING WOULD HAPPEN TO MY STARS..YOU.. YOU GANGSTER! DID YOU KILL LORNA DANE?
BETTER PAY UP, BENTLEY!
MAYBE. BETTER PAY UP THE "PROTECTION" MONEY OR ELSE YOU WON'T HAVE ANY DOUBTS!
SUDDENLY HURTLING THROUGH THE AIR... BATMAN AND ROBIN, THE BOY WONDER!!
I THINK YOU'RE THE ONE WHO IS LOOKING FOR TROUBLE!
WHA...? I'M ATTACKED BY AN ELF!
IF YOU'RE LOOKING FOR TROUBLE, BENTLEY, WHY...SAY...!!
?

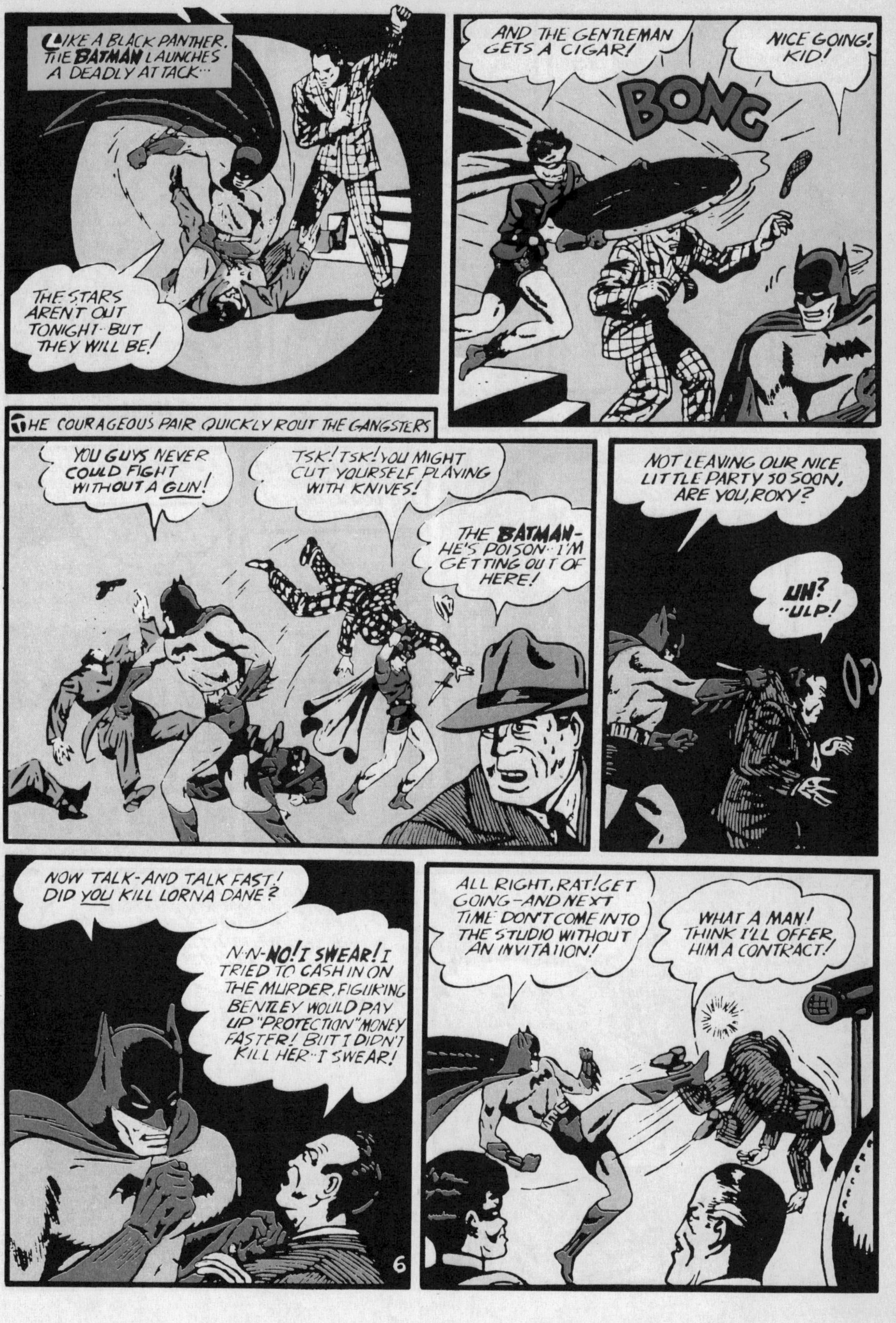
LIKE A BLACK PANTHER, THE BATMAN LAUNCHES A DEADLY ATTACK...
THE STARS AREN'T OUT TONIGHT.. BUT THEY WILL BE!
AND THE GENTLEMAN GETS A CIGAR!
NICE GOING! KID!
BONG
THE COURAGEOUS PAIR QUICKLY ROUT THE GANGSTERS
YOU GUYS NEVER COULD FIGHT WITHOUT A GUN!
TSK! TSK! YOU MIGHT CUT YOURSELF PLAYING WITH KNIVES!
THE BATMAN-HE'S POISON.. I'M GETTING OUT OF HERE!
NOT LEAVING OUR NICE LITTLE PARTY SO SOON, ARE YOU, ROXY?
UH? ..ULP!
NOW TALK-AND TALK FAST! DID YOU KILL LORNA DANE?
N-N-NO! I SWEAR! I TRIED TO CASH IN ON THE MURDER, FIGURING BENTLEY WOULD PAY UP "PROTECTION" MONEY FASTER! BUT I DIDN'T KILL HER.. I SWEAR!
6
ALL RIGHT, RAT! GET GOING-AND NEXT TIME DON'T COME INTO THE STUDIO WITHOUT AN INVITATION!
WHAT A MAN! THINK I'LL OFFER HIM A CONTRACT!

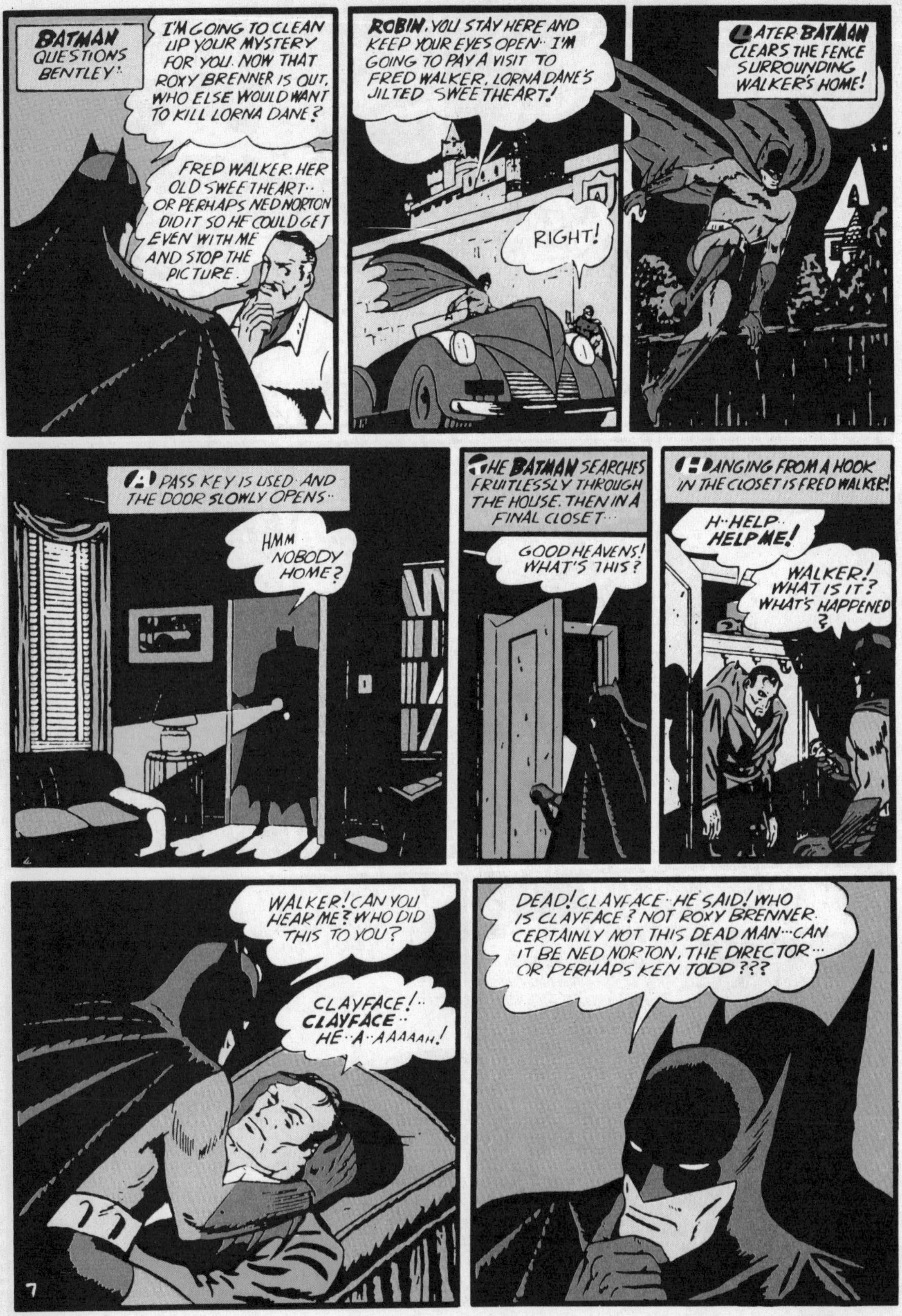
BATMAN QUESTIONS BENTLEY:
I'M GOING TO CLEAN UP YOUR MYSTERY FOR YOU. NOW THAT ROXY BRENNER IS OUT, WHO ELSE WOULD WANT TO KILL LORNA DANE?
FRED WALKER. HER OLD SWEETHEART.. OR PERHAPS NED NORTON DID IT SO HE COULD GET EVEN WITH ME AND STOP THE PICTURE.
ROBIN, YOU STAY HERE AND KEEP YOUR EYES OPEN.. I'M GOING TO PAY A VISIT TO FRED WALKER, LORNA DANE'S JILTED SWEETHEART!
RIGHT!
LATER BATMAN CLEARS THE FENCE SURROUNDING WALKER'S HOME!
A PASS KEY IS USED AND THE DOOR SLOWLY OPENS..
HMM NOBODY HOME?
THE BATMAN SEARCHES FRUITLESSLY THROUGH THE HOUSE. THEN IN A FINAL CLOSET...
GOOD HEAVENS! WHAT'S THIS?
HANGING FROM A HOOK IN THE CLOSET IS FRED WALKER!
H..HELP.. HELP ME!
WALKER! WHAT IS IT? WHAT'S HAPPENED?
WALKER! CAN YOU HEAR ME? WHO DID THIS TO YOU?
CLAYFACE!.. CLAYFACE.. HE..A..AAAAAH!
DEAD! CLAYFACE.. HE SAID! WHO IS CLAYFACE? NOT ROXY BRENNER. CERTAINLY NOT THIS DEAD MAN...CAN IT BE NED NORTON, THE DIRECTOR... OR PERHAPS KEN TODD???

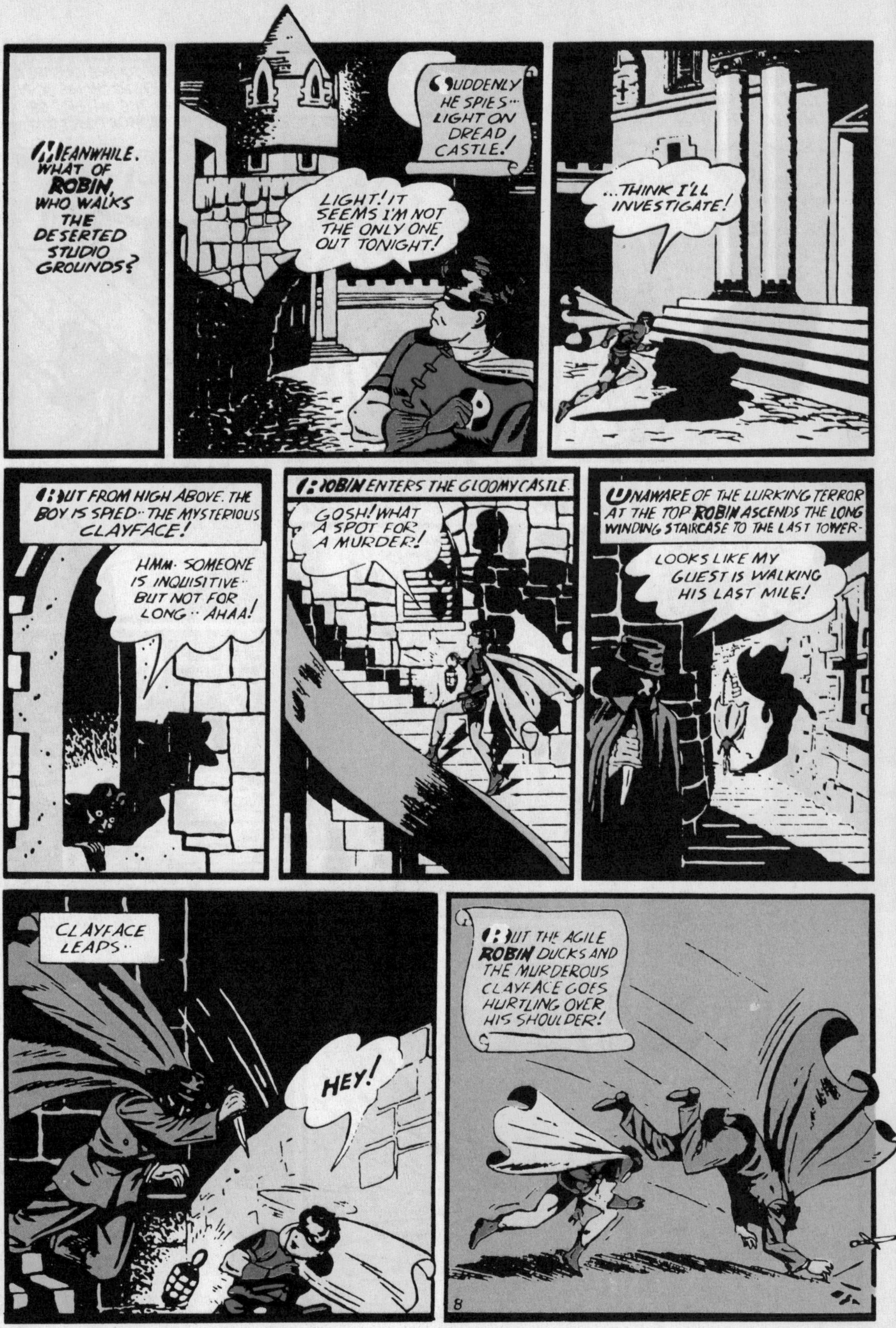
MEANWHILE, WHAT OF ROBIN, WHO WALKS THE DESERTED STUDIO GROUNDS?
SUDDENLY HE SPIES... LIGHT ON DREAD CASTLE!
LIGHT! IT SEEMS I'M NOT THE ONLY ONE OUT TONIGHT!
...THINK I'LL INVESTIGATE!
BUT FROM HIGH ABOVE, THE BOY IS SPIED.. THE MYSTERIOUS CLAYFACE!
HMM. SOMEONE IS INQUISITIVE.. BUT NOT FOR LONG.. AHAA!
ROBIN ENTERS THE GLOOMY CASTLE.
GOSH! WHAT A SPOT FOR A MURDER!
UNAWARE OF THE LURKING TERROR AT THE TOP ROBIN ASCENDS THE LONG WINDING STAIRCASE TO THE LAST TOWER-
LOOKS LIKE MY GUEST IS WALKING HIS LAST MILE!
CLAYFACE LEAPS..
HEY!
BUT THE AGILE ROBIN DUCKS AND THE MURDEROUS CLAYFACE GOES HURTLING OVER HIS SHOULDER!
8

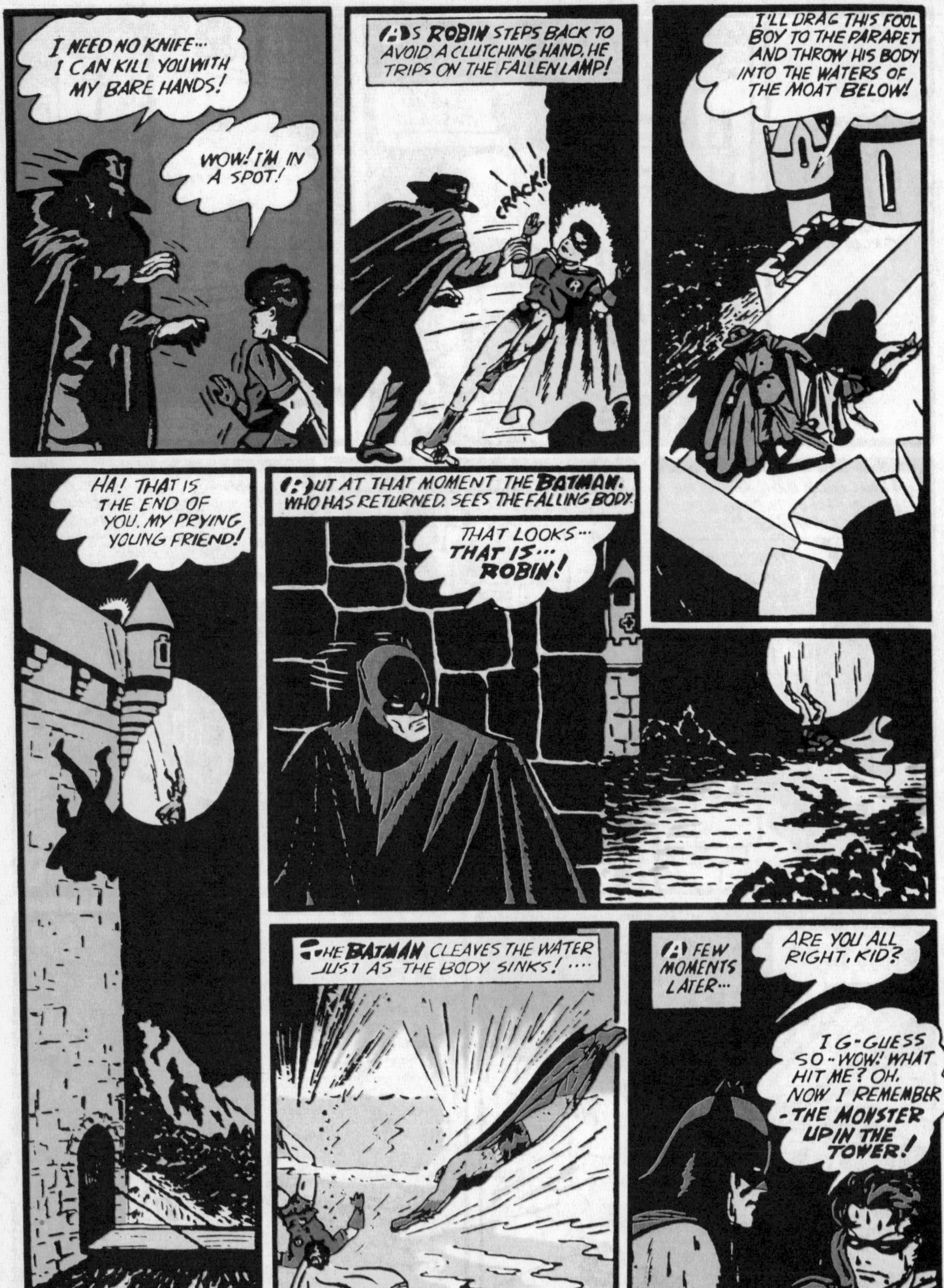
I NEED NO KNIFE... I CAN KILL YOU WITH MY BARE HANDS!
WOW! I'M IN A SPOT!
AS ROBIN STEPS BACK TO AVOID A CLUTCHING HAND, HE TRIPS ON THE FALLEN LAMP!
CRACK!
I'LL DRAG THIS FOOL BOY TO THE PARAPET AND THROW HIS BODY INTO THE WATERS OF THE MOAT BELOW!
HA! THAT IS THE END OF YOU, MY PRYING YOUNG FRIEND!
BUT AT THAT MOMENT THE BATMAN, WHO HAS RETURNED, SEES THE FALLING BODY.
THAT LOOKS... THAT IS... ROBIN!
THE BATMAN CLEAVES THE WATER JUST AS THE BODY SINKS! ....
A FEW MOMENTS LATER...
ARE YOU ALL RIGHT, KID?
I G-GUESS SO - WOW! WHAT HIT ME? OH, NOW I REMEMBER - THE MONSTER UP IN THE TOWER!

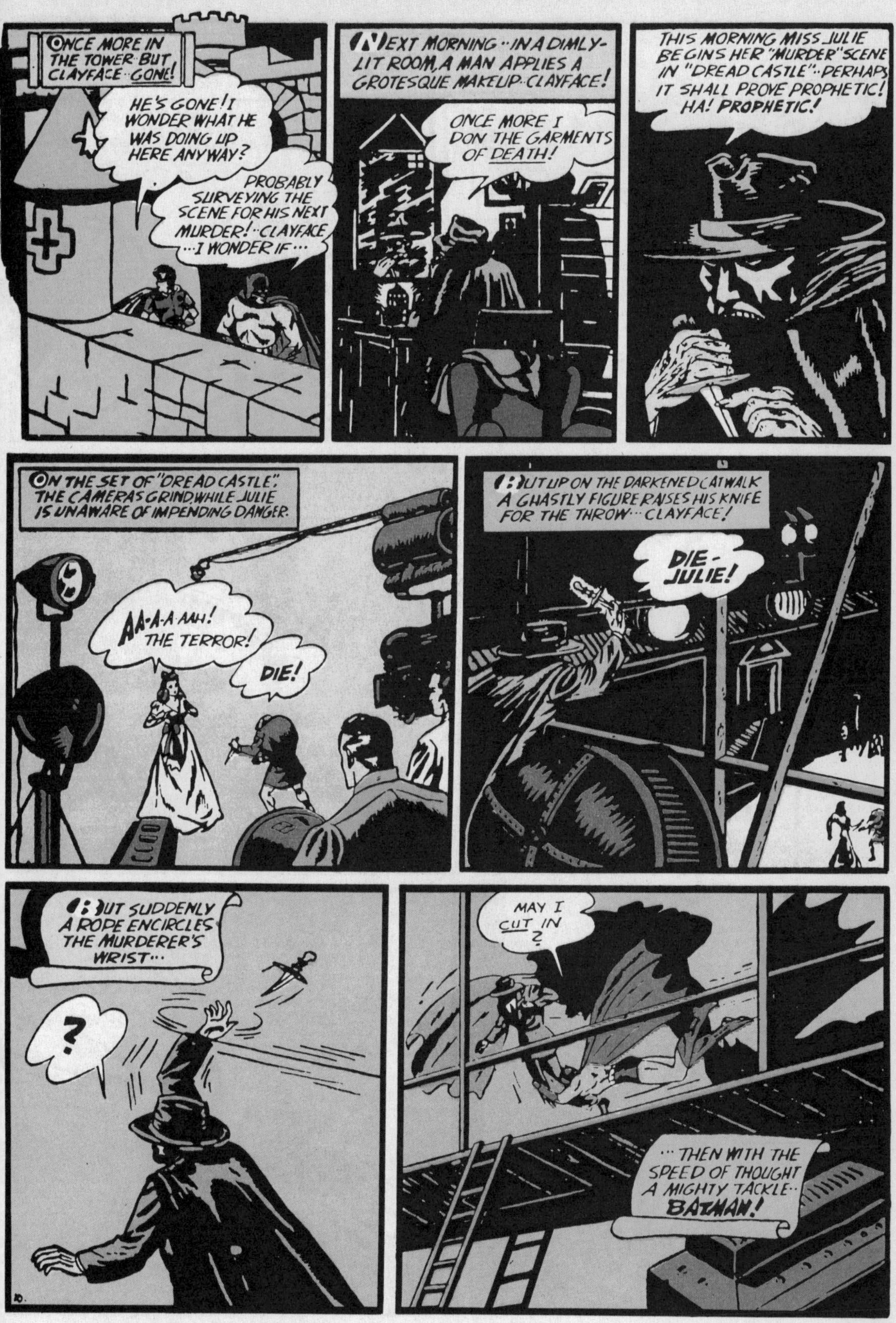
ONCE MORE IN THE TOWER BUT CLAYFACE GONE!
HE'S GONE! I WONDER WHAT HE WAS DOING UP HERE ANYWAY?
PROBABLY SURVEYING THE SCENE FOR HIS NEXT MURDER! -- CLAYFACE ... I WONDER IF ...
NEXT MORNING -- IN A DIMLY-LIT ROOM, A MAN APPLIES A GROTESQUE MAKEUP -- CLAYFACE!
ONCE MORE I DON THE GARMENTS OF DEATH!
THIS MORNING MISS JULIE BEGINS HER "MURDER" SCENE IN "DREAD CASTLE" -- PERHAPS IT SHALL PROVE PROPHETIC! HA! PROPHETIC!
ON THE SET OF "DREAD CASTLE", THE CAMERAS GRIND, WHILE JULIE IS UNAWARE OF IMPENDING DANGER.
AA-A-A-AAH! THE TERROR!
DIE!
BUT UP ON THE DARKENED CATWALK A GHASTLY FIGURE RAISES HIS KNIFE FOR THE THROW -- CLAYFACE!
DIE - JULIE!
BUT SUDDENLY A ROPE ENCIRCLES THE MURDERER'S WRIST ...
?
10.
MAY I CUT IN ?
... THEN WITH THE SPEED OF THOUGHT A MIGHTY TACKLE -- BATMAN!

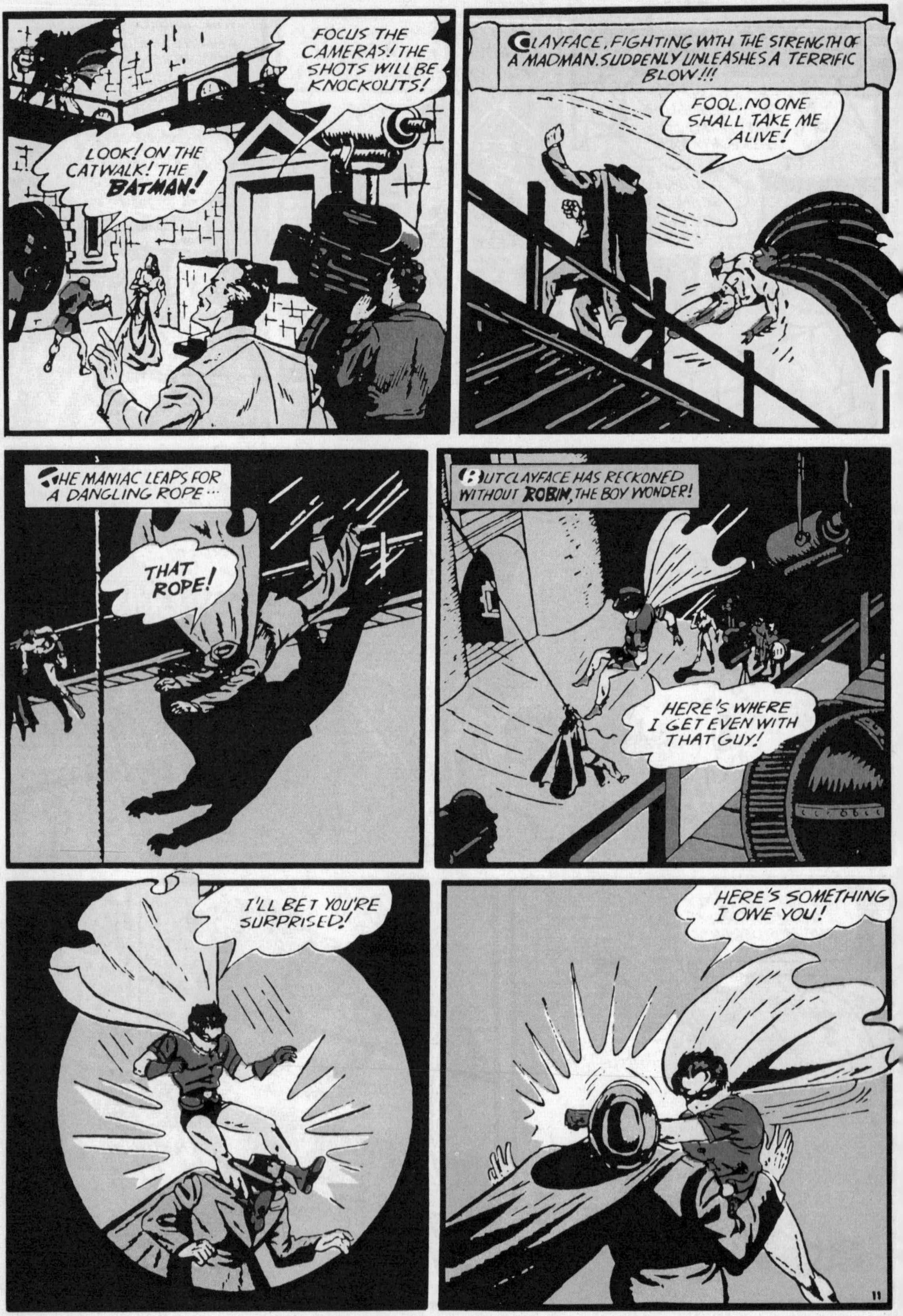
FOCUS THE CAMERAS! THE SHOTS WILL BE KNOCKOUTS!
LOOK! ON THE CATWALK! THE BATMAN!
CLAYFACE, FIGHTING WITH THE STRENGTH OF A MADMAN, SUDDENLY UNLEASHES A TERRIFIC BLOW!!!
FOOL, NO ONE SHALL TAKE ME ALIVE!
THE MANIAC LEAPS FOR A DANGLING ROPE...
THAT ROPE!
BUT CLAYFACE HAS RECKONED WITHOUT ROBIN, THE BOY WONDER!
HERE'S WHERE I GET EVEN WITH THAT GUY!
I'LL BET YOU'RE SURPRISED!
HERE'S SOMETHING I OWE YOU!
11

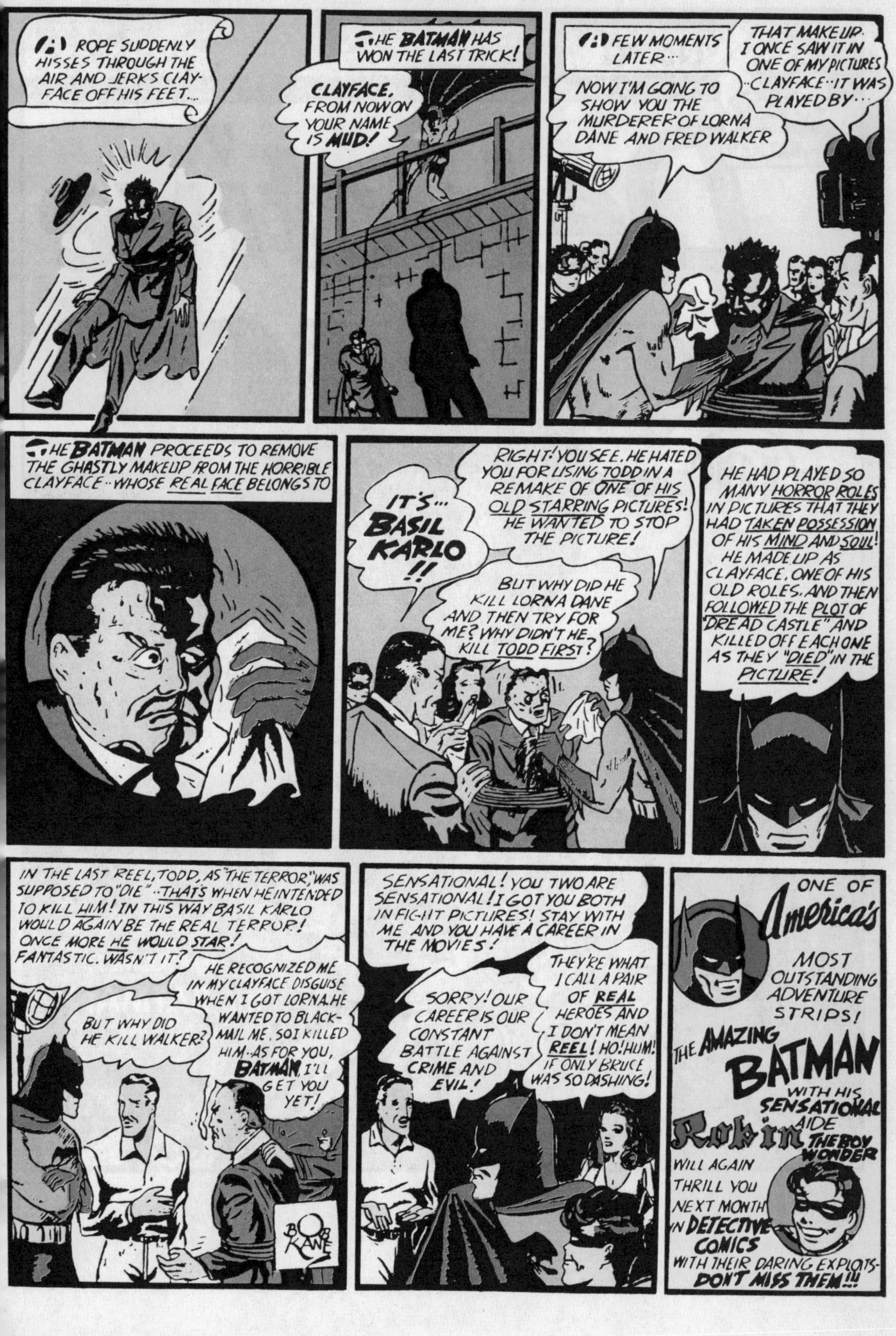
A ROPE SUDDENLY HISSES THROUGH THE AIR AND JERKS CLAYFACE OFF HIS FEET....
THE BATMAN HAS WON THE LAST TRICK!
CLAYFACE. FROM NOW ON YOUR NAME IS MUD!
A FEW MOMENTS LATER...
NOW I'M GOING TO SHOW YOU THE MURDERER OF LORNA DANE AND FRED WALKER
THAT MAKE UP. I ONCE SAW IT IN ONE OF MY PICTURES ..CLAYFACE..IT WAS PLAYED BY...
THE BATMAN PROCEEDS TO REMOVE THE GHASTLY MAKEUP FROM THE HORRIBLE CLAYFACE..WHOSE REAL FACE BELONGS TO
IT'S... BASIL KARLO !!
RIGHT! YOU SEE, HE HATED YOU FOR USING TODD IN A REMAKE OF ONE OF HIS OLD STARRING PICTURES! HE WANTED TO STOP THE PICTURE!
BUT WHY DID HE KILL LORNA DANE AND THEN TRY FOR ME? WHY DIDN'T HE KILL TODD FIRST?
HE HAD PLAYED SO MANY HORROR ROLES IN PICTURES THAT THEY HAD TAKEN POSSESSION OF HIS MIND AND SOUL! HE MADE UP AS CLAYFACE, ONE OF HIS OLD ROLES, AND THEN FOLLOWED THE PLOT OF "DREAD CASTLE" AND KILLED OFF EACH ONE AS THEY "DIED" IN THE PICTURE!
IN THE LAST REEL, TODD, AS "THE TERROR," WAS SUPPOSED TO "DIE"..THAT'S WHEN HE INTENDED TO KILL HIM! IN THIS WAY BASIL KARLO WOULD AGAIN BE THE REAL TERROR! ONCE MORE HE WOULD STAR! FANTASTIC, WASN'T IT?
BUT WHY DID HE KILL WALKER?
HE RECOGNIZED ME IN MY CLAYFACE DISGUISE WHEN I GOT LORNA.HE WANTED TO BLACKMAIL ME, SO I KILLED HIM..AS FOR YOU, BATMAN, I'LL GET YOU YET!
BOB KANE
SENSATIONAL! YOU TWO ARE SENSATIONAL! I GOT YOU BOTH IN FIGHT PICTURES! STAY WITH ME AND YOU HAVE A CAREER IN THE MOVIES!
SORRY! OUR CAREER IS OUR CONSTANT BATTLE AGAINST CRIME AND EVIL!
THEY'RE WHAT I CALL A PAIR OF REAL HEROES AND I DON'T MEAN REEL! HO! HUM! IF ONLY BRUCE WAS SO DASHING!
ONE OF America's MOST OUTSTANDING ADVENTURE STRIPS!
THE AMAZING BATMAN WITH HIS SENSATIONAL AIDE Robin THE BOY WONDER
WILL AGAIN THRILL YOU NEXT MONTH IN DETECTIVE COMICS WITH THEIR DARING EXPLOITS-
DON'T MISS THEM!!!

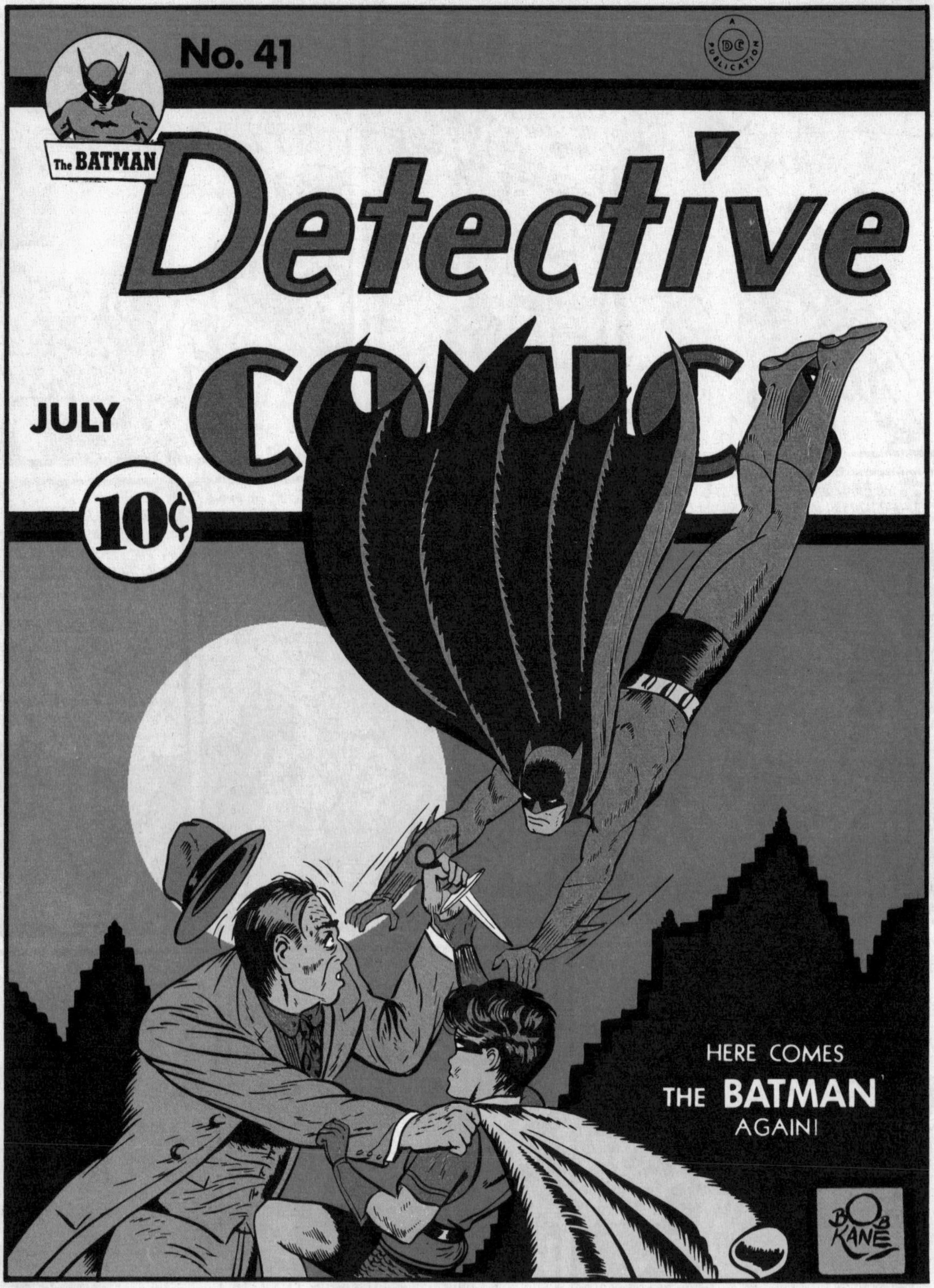
No. 41
A DC PUBLICATION
The BATMAN
Detective Comics
JULY
10¢
HERE COMES
THE BATMAN
AGAIN!
BOB KANE

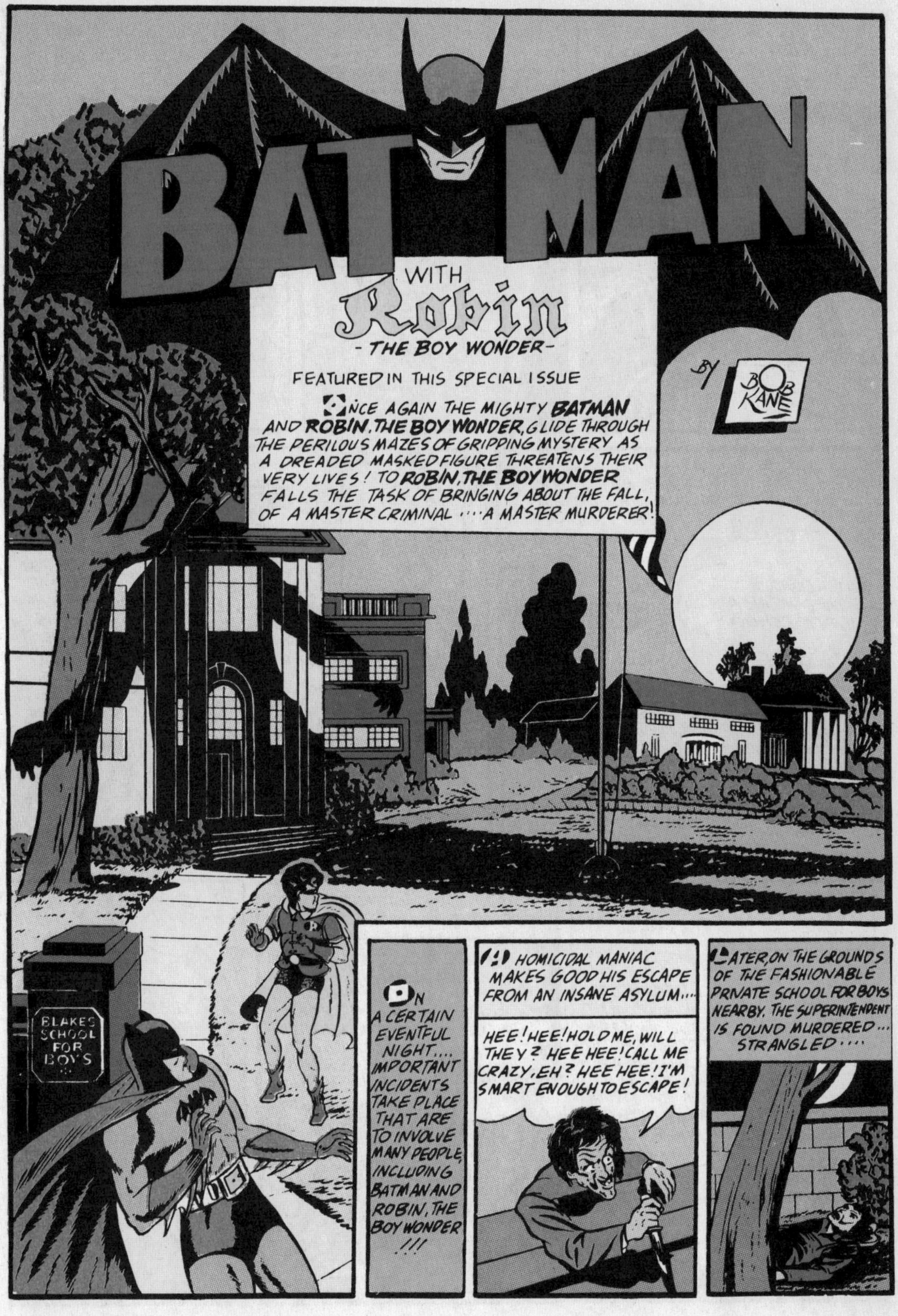
BATMAN
WITH Robin
-THE BOY WONDER-
FEATURED IN THIS SPECIAL ISSUE
ONCE AGAIN THE MIGHTY BATMAN AND ROBIN, THE BOY WONDER, GLIDE THROUGH THE PERILOUS MAZES OF GRIPPING MYSTERY AS A DREADED MASKED FIGURE THREATENS THEIR VERY LIVES! TO ROBIN, THE BOY WONDER FALLS THE TASK OF BRINGING ABOUT THE FALL, OF A MASTER CRIMINAL .... A MASTER MURDERER!
BY BOB KANE
BLAKES SCHOOL FOR BOYS
ON A CERTAIN EVENTFUL NIGHT,... IMPORTANT INCIDENTS TAKE PLACE THAT ARE TO INVOLVE MANY PEOPLE, INCLUDING BATMAN AND ROBIN, THE BOY WONDER !!!
A HOMICIDAL MANIAC MAKES GOOD HIS ESCAPE FROM AN INSANE ASYLUM....
HEE! HEE! HOLD ME, WILL THEY? HEE HEE! CALL ME CRAZY, EH? HEE HEE! I'M SMART ENOUGH TO ESCAPE!
LATER, ON THE GROUNDS OF THE FASHIONABLE PRIVATE SCHOOL FOR BOYS NEARBY, THE SUPERINTENDENT IS FOUND MURDERED... STRANGLED....

WHILE UP IN ONE OF THE DORMITORY ROOMS A BOY NAMED TED SPENCER OPENS HIS EYES TO SEE A FIGURE BEFORE HIM!

W...WHAT DO YOU WANT?

YOU!

"STARTLING NEWS HEADLINES THE NEWSPAPERS THE NEXT DAY..."

2 NEW YORK WORLD   MONDAY

YOUNG BOY DISAPPEARS FROM BLAKES BOYS' SCHOOL

ATTENDANT FOUND MURDERED ON GROUNDS MANIAC ESCAPED FROM A NEARBY ASYLUM IS SUSPECTED

POLICE ARE MYSTIFIED BY THE MURDER OF AN ATTENDANT OF THE WEALTHY AND FASHIONABLE BLAKE SCHOOL AND THE DISAPPEARANCE OF ONE OF ITS PUPILS

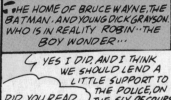

THE HOME OF BRUCE WAYNE, THE BATMAN, AND YOUNG DICK GRAYSON, WHO IS IN REALITY ROBIN...THE BOY WONDER...

DID YOU READ ABOUT THAT MURDER AND DISAPPEARANCE UP AT THAT BOYS' SCHOOL, BRUCE?

YES I DID, AND I THINK WE SHOULD LEND A LITTLE SUPPORT TO THE POLICE, ON THE SLY, OF COURSE.

SIMPLE! YOU DON'T KNOW IT YET, BUT YOU'RE BECOMING A PUPIL AT THE VERY FASHIONABLE SCHOOL FOR BOYS

BUT HOW DO WE GET NEAR A PRIVATE SCHOOL?

THE NEXT DAY DICK IS ENROLLED AS A PUPIL IN BLAKE SCHOOL

MR. WAYNE...YOUR REFERENCES ARE VERY FINE YOU MAY CONSIDER YOUR WARD DICK GRAYSON ENROLLED HERE AT SCHOOL!

THANK YOU, MR. BLAKE I THINK HE WILL PROVE A VERY APT PUPIL!...

YOU'D BE AMAZED IF YOU KNEW HOW APT HE IS!

AT THAT MOMENT...

IS IT TRUE ABOUT MY BEING DISCHARGED?

YES MR. GREER. IT IS! I CAN'T HAVE ANY OF MY TEACHERS FAILING A PUPIL BECAUSE HE MUDDLED A TEST. YOU SHOULD USE MORE DISCRETION... AFTER ALL...

GREER POUNDS THE DESK BEFORE THE CALM PRINCIPAL!

AFTER ALL, HE'S GOT A RICH FATHER WHO PAYS A NICE FEE AT THE SCHOOL. I GET IT! OKAY. BLAKE, I'LL GET OUT, BUT I'LL FIX YOU AND YOUR SNOBBISH SCHOOL. I'LL FIX YOU ALL!

IT LOOKS AS IF GREER HAS IT IN FOR YOU!

POPPYCOCK! HE'S HARMLESS! COME. NOW. I'LL INTRODUCE YOU TO THE REST OF THE STAFF! THEIR SLEEPING QUARTERS ARE IN THE HOUSE. YOU KNOW!

2

LATER

AND NOW I WANT YOU TO MEET MR. GRAVES, THE ART INSTRUCTOR.

HOW DO YOU DO!

AH! ANOTHER PUPIL TO ABSORB THE FINE POINTS OF ART! I SHALL MAKE A MASTER CRAFTSMAN OF YOU, MY BOY... A MASTER!

HOW DO YOU DO!

IT SEEMS YOU ARE A MASTER, MR. GRAVES. I NOTICE THESE FINE ENGRAVINGS HAVE YOUR NAME ON THEM!

THOSE ARE NOTHING! I WOULD LIKE TO SHOW YOU SOME REALLY FINE WORK I HAVE DONE. THEY ARE MASTERPIECES!

MODEST GUY!

ANOTHER MAN ENTERS...

THIS IS MR. HODGES, THE HISTORY INSTRUCTOR!

HOW DO YOU DO, MR. HODGES!

WELCOME TO BLAKE SCHOOL! AND NOW IF YOU'LL EXCUSE ME... GOOD DAY!

BRRR! DID WE GET THE COLD SHOULDER!

HODGES MAY BE A BIT RESERVED, BUT HE'S A FINE TEACHER!

HE KEEPS TO HIMSELF. NEVER TALKS TO ANOTHER! NO-ONE HERE LIKES HIM! I DON'T TRUST HIM!

HURRIED INSTRUCTIONS ARE GIVEN TO DICK BY BRUCE WAYNE...

POLICEMEN ALL OVER THE PLACE LOOKING FOR THE ESCAPED MANIAC AND THAT MISSING BOY!... LOOKS LIKE THERE WON'T BE MUCH PRIVACY FOR THE BATMAN TO WORK ABOUT HERE!

GUESS I'LL HAVE TO WORK ALONE, EH?

YES, BUT KEEP IN TOUCH WITH ME... YOU KNOW HOW! SEND ME DETAILS ON WHATEVER DEVELOPS! GOOD LUCK, AND WATCH YOURSELF!

RIGHT!

DICK IMMEDIATELY GETS TO WORK ON ONE OF HIS NEW FELLOW PUPILS

AND YOU SAY THAT THE POLICE SEARCHED TED SPENCER'S ROOM FOR A DIARY?

YES, THEY FIGURED HE MIGHT HAVE WRITTEN DOWN SOMETHING THAT HAD TO DO WITH HIS DISAPPEARANCE, BUT COULDN'T FIND IT!

THAT NIGHT A MANTLED FIGURE PROWLS THE DARK HALLWAY. ROBIN, THE BOY WONDER!

I'M GOING TO SEARCH TED SPENCER'S ROOM! I'D LIKE TO FIND THAT DIARY OF HIS!

3

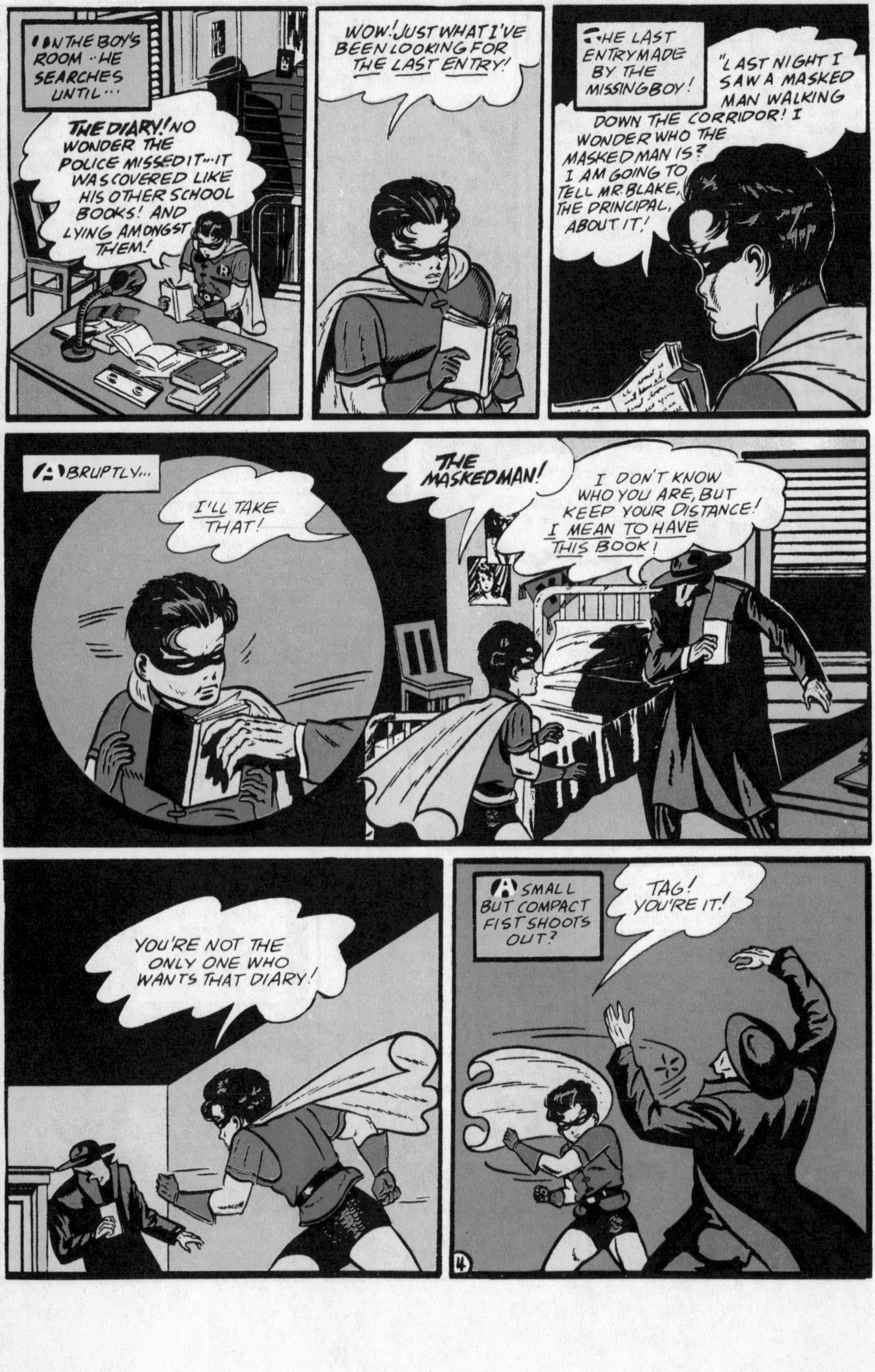
IN THE BOY'S ROOM .. HE SEARCHES UNTIL...
THE DIARY! NO WONDER THE POLICE MISSED IT...IT WAS COVERED LIKE HIS OTHER SCHOOL BOOKS! AND LYING AMONGST THEM!
WOW! JUST WHAT I'VE BEEN LOOKING FOR THE LAST ENTRY!
THE LAST ENTRY MADE BY THE MISSING BOY!
"LAST NIGHT I SAW A MASKED MAN WALKING DOWN THE CORRIDOR! I WONDER WHO THE MASKED MAN IS? I AM GOING TO TELL MR. BLAKE, THE PRINCIPAL, ABOUT IT!
ABRUPTLY...
I'LL TAKE THAT!
THE MASKED MAN!
I DON'T KNOW WHO YOU ARE, BUT KEEP YOUR DISTANCE! I MEAN TO HAVE THIS BOOK!
YOU'RE NOT THE ONLY ONE WHO WANTS THAT DIARY!
A SMALL BUT COMPACT FIST SHOOTS OUT?
TAG! YOU'RE IT!

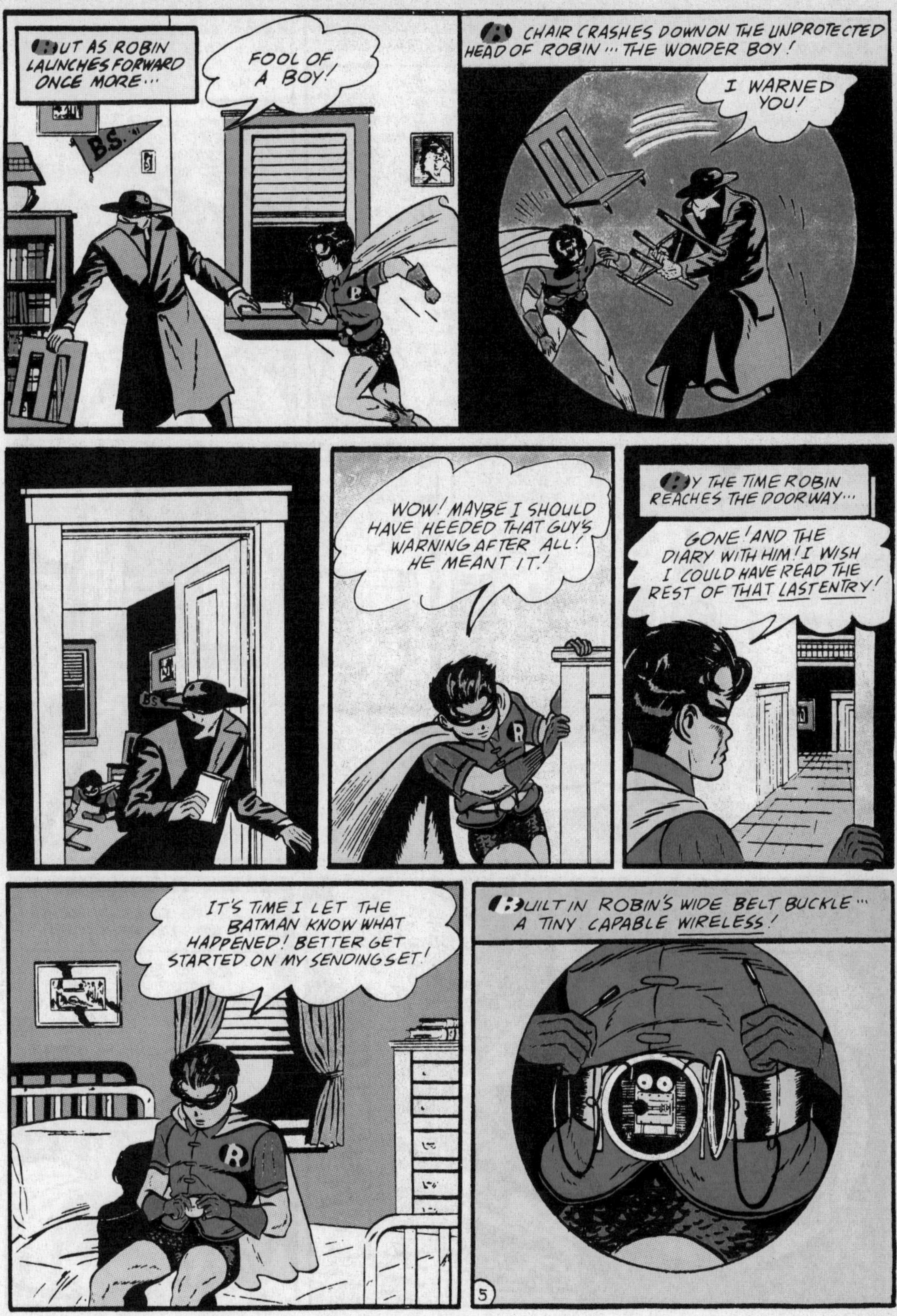
BUT AS ROBIN LAUNCHES FORWARD ONCE MORE...
FOOL OF A BOY!
B.S.
A CHAIR CRASHES DOWN ON THE UNPROTECTED HEAD OF ROBIN... THE WONDER BOY!
I WARNED YOU!
WOW! MAYBE I SHOULD HAVE HEEDED THAT GUY'S WARNING AFTER ALL! HE MEANT IT!
BY THE TIME ROBIN REACHES THE DOORWAY...
GONE! AND THE DIARY WITH HIM! I WISH I COULD HAVE READ THE REST OF THAT LAST ENTRY!
IT'S TIME I LET THE BATMAN KNOW WHAT HAPPENED! BETTER GET STARTED ON MY SENDING SET!
BUILT IN ROBIN'S WIDE BELT BUCKLE... A TINY CAPABLE WIRELESS!
5

OUTSIDE THE SCHOOL WALL, THE BATMAN IS CONTACTED!

THE PORTABLE PHONE... ROBIN HAS SOME NEWS FOR ME!

THE BATMAN IS INFORMED OF ALL THAT HAS TRANSPIRED!

AND THEN HE DISAPPEARED WITH THE DIARY!... WHAT SHALL I DO NOW?

THE MISSING BOY'S DIARY MENTIONED THE PRINCIPAL. MR. BLAKE... WHY NOT SEARCH HIS ROOMS... MAYBE HE KNOWS SOMETHING!

IN A LARGE GLOOMY ROOM A MAN STANDS READING BEFORE A ROARING FIRE... THE SINISTER MASKED MENACE!

HMM!... GOOD THING I SECURED THIS DIARY... MIGHT HAVE GIVEN THE POLICE A CLUE TO MY ACTIVITES HERE!

BETTER IF I RID MYSELF OF IT! NOTHING LIKE THE ALL-CONSUMING FLAME TO DEVOUR EVIDENCE... NOW I'M FREE TO CONTINUE MY WORK!

THE NEXT NIGHT, ROBIN IS ONCE MORE ON THE PROWL!

THAT'S BLAKE'S ROOM UP THERE! BEST I CLIMB THAT VINE AND ENTER THE OUTSIDE WINDOW INSTEAD OF THE DOOR!

AN AGONIZING SCREAM SUDDENLY SPLITS THE NIGHT AIR!

WHA.. SOMEONE IN TROUBLE!

AAGH! HELP! **HELP!**

IT CAME FROM AROUND THIS CORNER!

ROUNDING THE BUILDING, ROBIN STANDS TRANSFIXED WHEN HE SEES...

TRY TO TELL ME YOU'RE A JANITOR, EH! I KNOW YOU'RE A KEEPER LIKE THE OTHER ONE I KILLED!

⑥

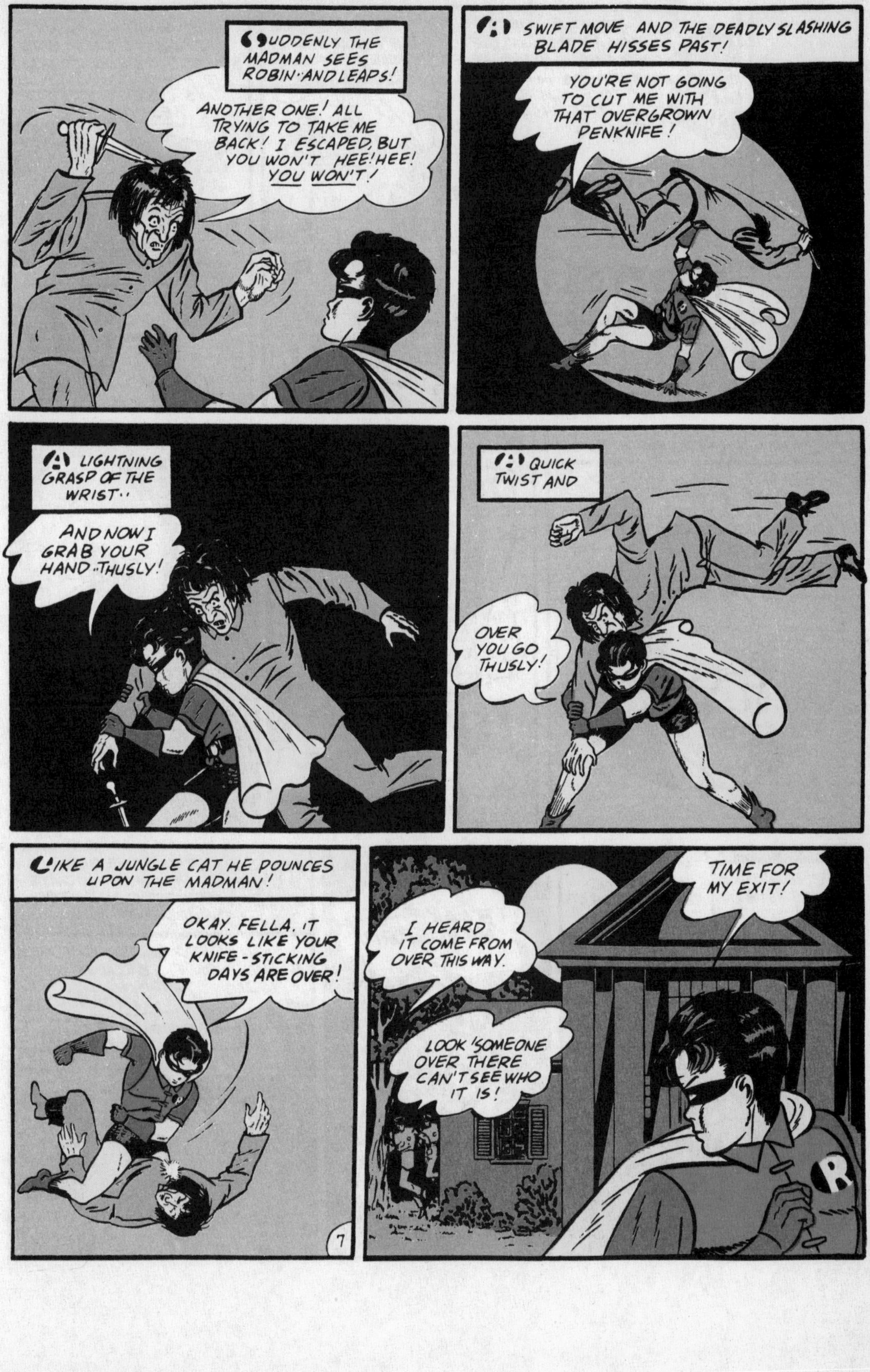
SUDDENLY THE MADMAN SEES ROBIN..AND LEAPS!
ANOTHER ONE! ALL TRYING TO TAKE ME BACK! I ESCAPED, BUT YOU WON'T HEE! HEE! YOU WON'T!
A SWIFT MOVE AND THE DEADLY SLASHING BLADE HISSES PAST!
YOU'RE NOT GOING TO CUT ME WITH THAT OVERGROWN PENKNIFE!
A LIGHTNING GRASP OF THE WRIST..
AND NOW I GRAB YOUR HAND..THUSLY!
A QUICK TWIST AND
OVER YOU GO THUSLY!
LIKE A JUNGLE CAT HE POUNCES UPON THE MADMAN!
OKAY. FELLA. IT LOOKS LIKE YOUR KNIFE-STICKING DAYS ARE OVER!
7
I HEARD IT COME FROM OVER THIS WAY.
TIME FOR MY EXIT!
LOOK! SOMEONE OVER THERE CAN'T SEE WHO IT IS!
R

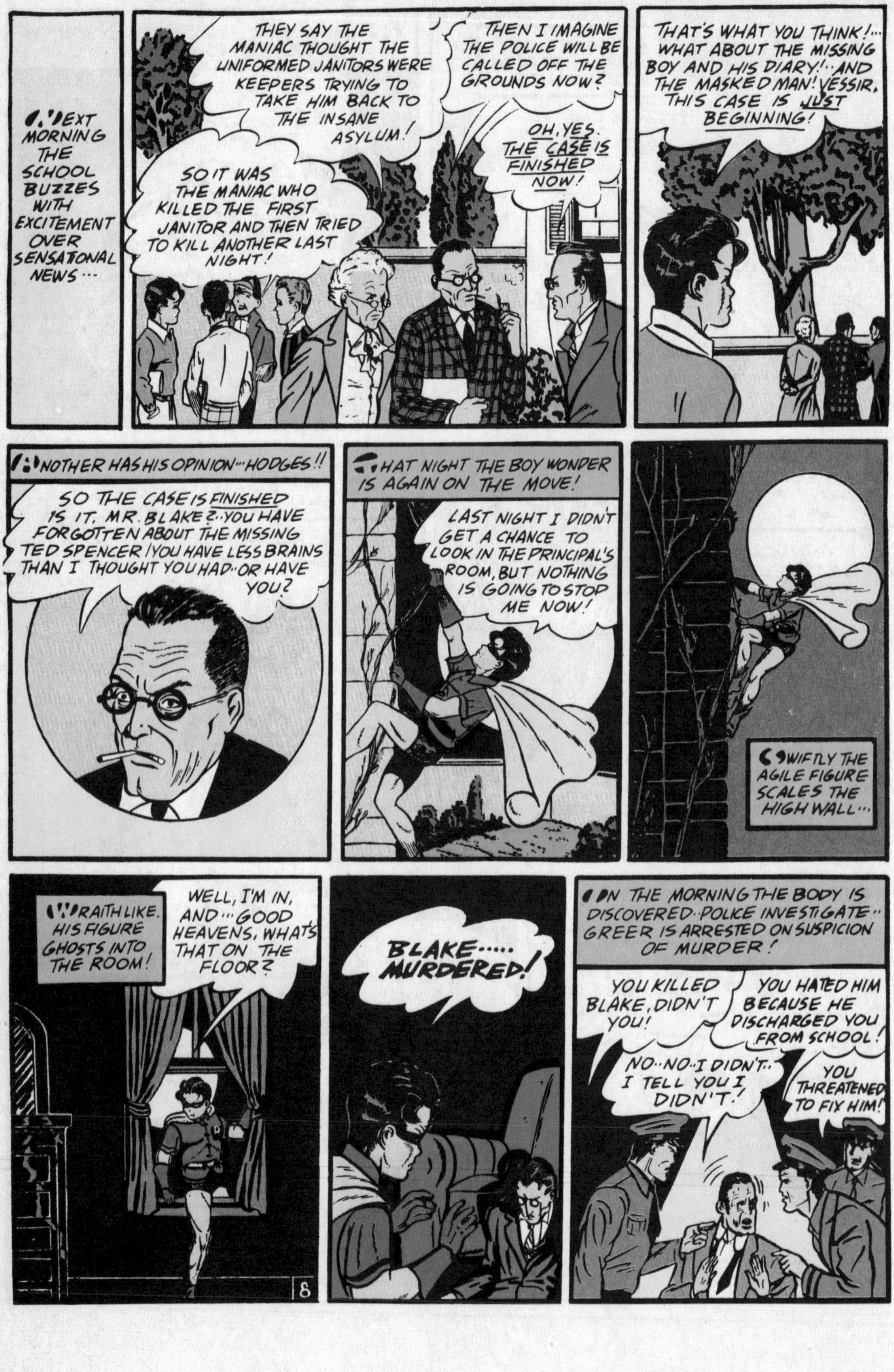
NEXT MORNING THE SCHOOL BUZZES WITH EXCITEMENT OVER SENSATIONAL NEWS...
THEY SAY THE MANIAC THOUGHT THE UNIFORMED JANITORS WERE KEEPERS TRYING TO TAKE HIM BACK TO THE INSANE ASYLUM!
SO IT WAS THE MANIAC WHO KILLED THE FIRST JANITOR AND THEN TRIED TO KILL ANOTHER LAST NIGHT!
THEN I IMAGINE THE POLICE WILL BE CALLED OFF THE GROUNDS NOW?
OH, YES. THE CASE IS FINISHED NOW!
THAT'S WHAT YOU THINK!... WHAT ABOUT THE MISSING BOY AND HIS DIARY!...AND THE MASKED MAN! YESSIR, THIS CASE IS JUST BEGINNING!
ANOTHER HAS HIS OPINION... HODGES!!
SO THE CASE IS FINISHED IS IT, MR. BLAKE?..YOU HAVE FORGOTTEN ABOUT THE MISSING TED SPENCER! YOU HAVE LESS BRAINS THAN I THOUGHT YOU HAD..OR HAVE YOU?
THAT NIGHT THE BOY WONDER IS AGAIN ON THE MOVE!
LAST NIGHT I DIDN'T GET A CHANCE TO LOOK IN THE PRINCIPAL'S ROOM, BUT NOTHING IS GOING TO STOP ME NOW!
SWIFTLY THE AGILE FIGURE SCALES THE HIGH WALL...
WRAITH LIKE, HIS FIGURE GHOSTS INTO THE ROOM!
WELL, I'M IN, AND... GOOD HEAVENS, WHAT'S THAT ON THE FLOOR?
8
BLAKE..... MURDERED!
ON THE MORNING THE BODY IS DISCOVERED..POLICE INVESTIGATE.. GREER IS ARRESTED ON SUSPICION OF MURDER!
YOU KILLED BLAKE, DIDN'T YOU!
YOU HATED HIM BECAUSE HE DISCHARGED YOU FROM SCHOOL!
NO..NO..I DIDN'T.. I TELL YOU I DIDN'T!
YOU THREATENED TO FIX HIM!

WHAT DID YOU DO WITH TED SPENCER, THE MISSING BOY?

YOU HATED HIM! YOU WANTED REVENGE! YOU KIDNAPPED HIM!

WE FOUND OUT THAT SPENCER WAS THE PUPIL WHO FAILED THAT TEST! IT WAS BECAUSE OF HIM THAT YOU WERE DISCHARGED!

NO..NO..NO..!!

YOU HATED BLAKE AND THE BOY!

YOU SATISFIED YOUR REVENGE. DIDN'T YOU? DIDN'T YOU?

YOU KILLED BLAKE AND PERHAPS HAVE ALREADY KILLED THE BOY!

NO.. NO..I'M INNOCENT!

WHO DO YOU THINK IS THE MYSTERY MURDERER? WHO DO YOU THINK IS THE MASKED MENACE? CHECK WHICH PERSON YOU THINK IS GUILTY!

GREER. ..THE SUSPECTED ONE?

BLAKE... THE PRINCIPAL..WAS HE THE MASKED MAN?

GRAVES.. ...THE ECCENTRIC ART TEACHER?

.THE ESCAPED MANIAC.. ...WAS HE THE MASKED MAN?

HODGES. THE MYSTERIOUS HISTORY TEACHER?

THAT NIGHT, ROBIN ONCE MORE CONTACTS THE BATMAN!

YES.. THE POLICE ARE OFF THE GROUNDS NOW BECAUSE THEY FEEL THE CASE IS CLOSED! WHY DO YOU ASK?

BECAUSE I STILL THINK THE CASE IS OPEN! TO-NIGHT I WANT YOU TO PATROL THE HOUSE WHILE I WATCH THE GROUNDS OUTSIDE THE SCHOOL WALL! I HAVE A HUNCH SOMETHING! IS GOING TO HAPPEN!

MIDNIGHT AND AS ROBIN FLITS SILENTLY ALONG THE DIMLY-LIT CORRIDOR...HE SEES..

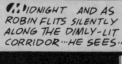

THE MASKED MAN!.. COMING FROM BLAKES ROOM!

THE WONDER BOY TRAILS THE MASKED MENACE!

THAT'S QUEER. WHAT'S HE WANT IN THIS CLASSROOM?

AS THE SHADOWY FIGURE PRESSES A SECRET PANEL THE BLACKBOARD SLIDES AWAY.

SWIFTLY THE PANEL ONCE MORE CLOSES THE MAN HAS DISAPPEARED!!

A SLIDING PANEL! THERE MUST BE SOME SORT OF TUNNEL BEHIND IT!

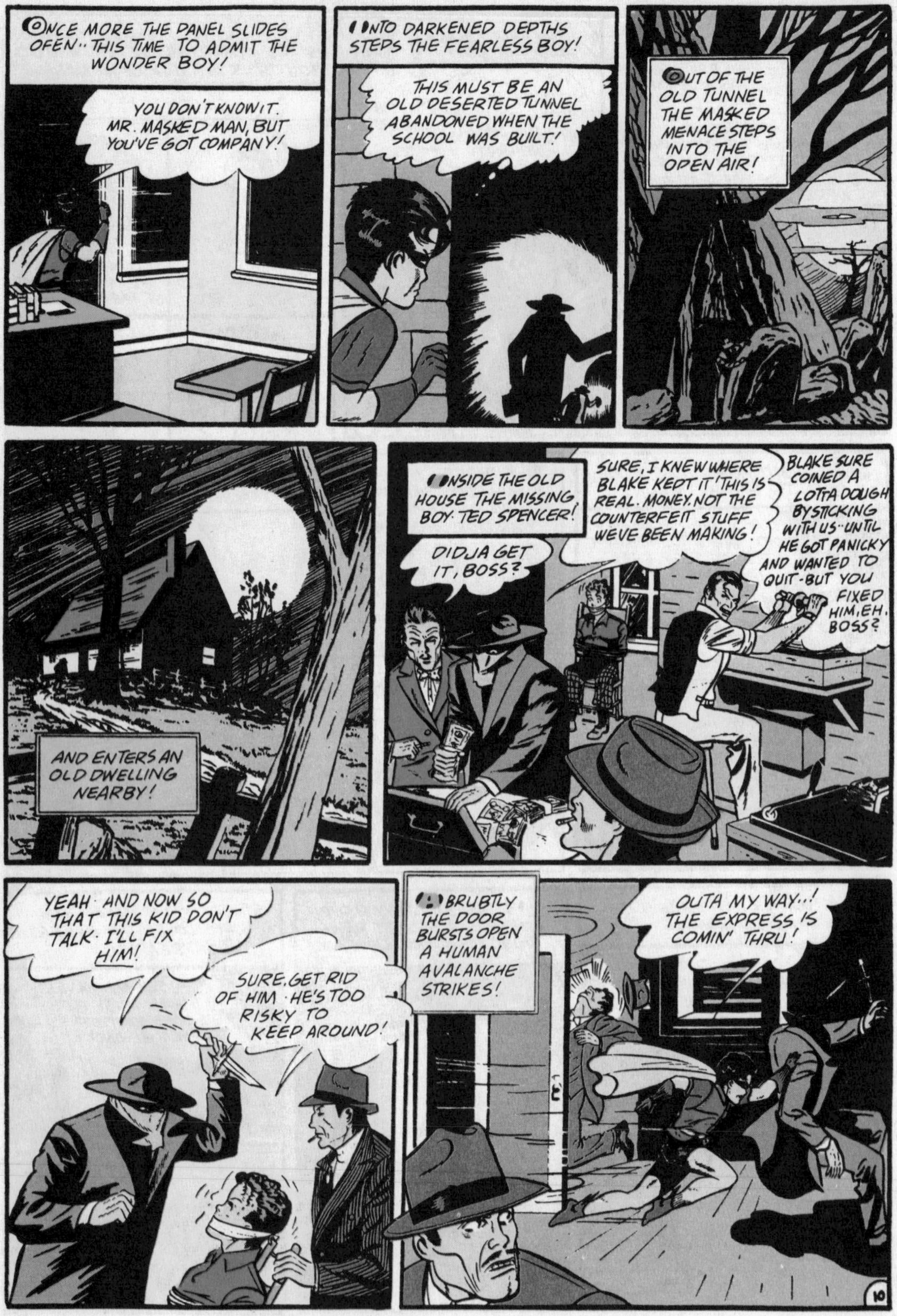
ONCE MORE THE PANEL SLIDES OPEN.. THIS TIME TO ADMIT THE WONDER BOY!
YOU DON'T KNOW IT. MR. MASKED MAN, BUT YOU'VE GOT COMPANY!
INTO DARKENED DEPTHS STEPS THE FEARLESS BOY!
THIS MUST BE AN OLD DESERTED TUNNEL ABANDONED WHEN THE SCHOOL WAS BUILT!
OUT OF THE OLD TUNNEL THE MASKED MENACE STEPS INTO THE OPEN AIR!
AND ENTERS AN OLD DWELLING NEARBY!
INSIDE THE OLD HOUSE THE MISSING BOY. TED SPENCER!
DIDJA GET IT, BOSS?
SURE, I KNEW WHERE BLAKE KEPT IT 'THIS IS REAL. MONEY. NOT THE COUNTERFEIT STUFF WE'VE BEEN MAKING!
BLAKE SURE COINED A LOTTA DOUGH BY STICKING WITH US.. UNTIL HE GOT PANICKY AND WANTED TO QUIT - BUT YOU FIXED HIM, EH, BOSS?
YEAH. AND NOW SO THAT THIS KID DON'T TALK. I'LL FIX HIM!
SURE. GET RID OF HIM. HE'S TOO RISKY TO KEEP AROUND!
ABRUBTLY THE DOOR BURSTS OPEN A HUMAN AVALANCHE STRIKES!
OUTA MY WAY..! THE EXPRESS IS COMIN' THRU!
10

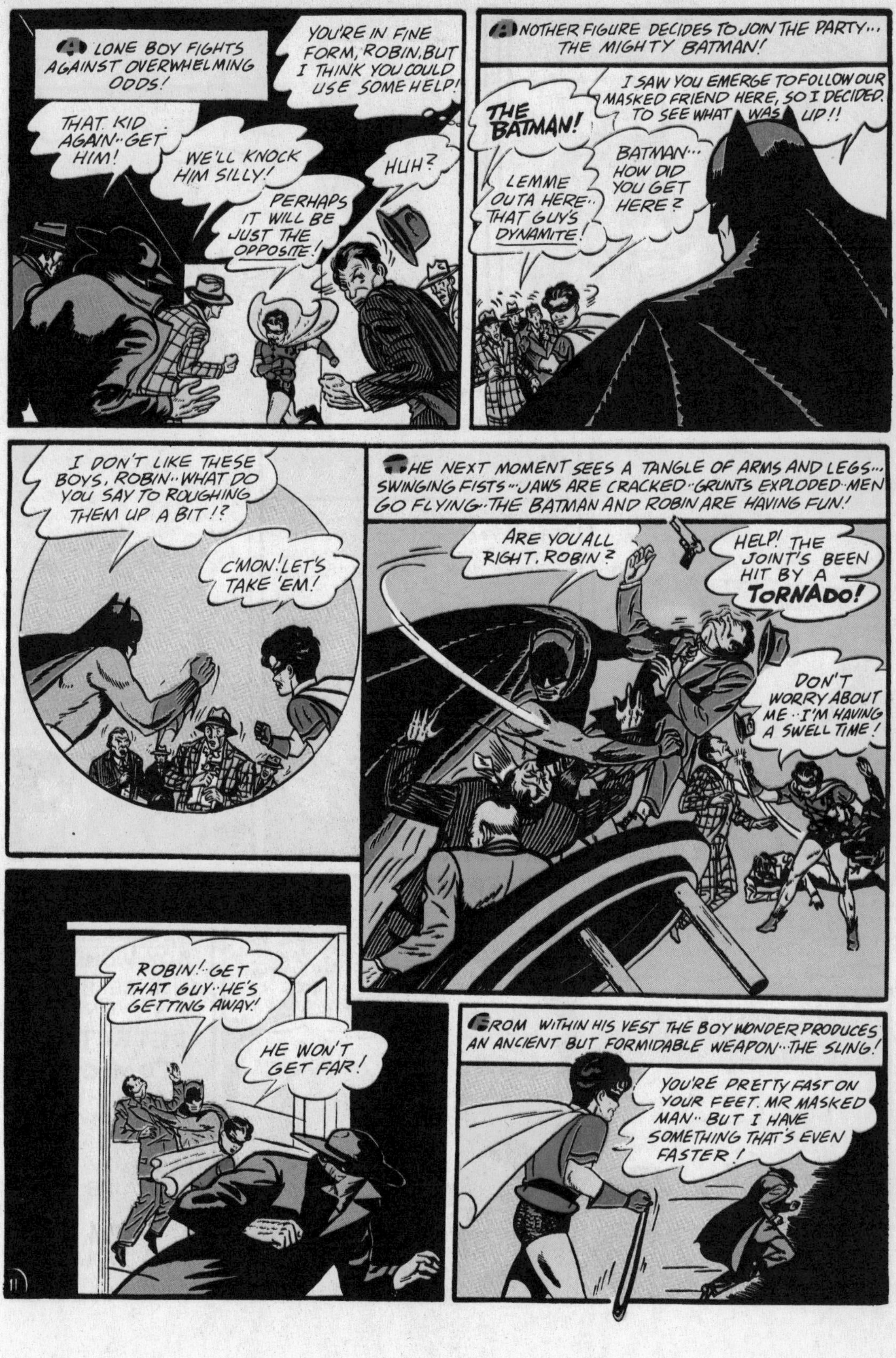
A LONE BOY FIGHTS AGAINST OVERWHELMING ODDS!
YOU'RE IN FINE FORM, ROBIN. BUT I THINK YOU COULD USE SOME HELP!
THAT KID AGAIN.. GET HIM!
WE'LL KNOCK HIM SILLY!
HUH?
PERHAPS IT WILL BE JUST THE OPPOSITE!
ANOTHER FIGURE DECIDES TO JOIN THE PARTY... THE MIGHTY BATMAN!
THE BATMAN!
I SAW YOU EMERGE TO FOLLOW OUR MASKED FRIEND HERE, SO I DECIDED TO SEE WHAT WAS UP!!
LEMME OUTA HERE.. THAT GUY'S DYNAMITE!
BATMAN... HOW DID YOU GET HERE?
I DON'T LIKE THESE BOYS, ROBIN.. WHAT DO YOU SAY TO ROUGHING THEM UP A BIT!?
C'MON! LET'S TAKE 'EM!
THE NEXT MOMENT SEES A TANGLE OF ARMS AND LEGS... SWINGING FISTS... JAWS ARE CRACKED.. GRUNTS EXPLODED.. MEN GO FLYING.. THE BATMAN AND ROBIN ARE HAVING FUN!
ARE YOU ALL RIGHT, ROBIN?
HELP! THE JOINT'S BEEN HIT BY A TORNADO!
DON'T WORRY ABOUT ME.. I'M HAVING A SWELL TIME!
ROBIN! GET THAT GUY.. HE'S GETTING AWAY!
HE WON'T GET FAR!
FROM WITHIN HIS VEST THE BOY WONDER PRODUCES AN ANCIENT BUT FORMIDABLE WEAPON.. THE SLING!
YOU'RE PRETTY FAST ON YOUR FEET. MR MASKED MAN.. BUT I HAVE SOMETHING THAT'S EVEN FASTER!
11

QUICKLY ROBIN UNFURLS HIS SLING...TWIRLS IT ABOUT HIS HEAD AND...

...THE MASKED MAN BECOMES A FALLEN MAN!

MISTER...YOUR HEADACHES ARE ONLY BEGINNING!

Z-T-N-G

GOOD SHOT, ROBIN. AND NOW WE'LL SEE WHO OUR MASKED MYSTERY MAN IS!

OOOH...MY HEAD!

AND THERE UNDER THE MASK... THE DEFIANT FACE OF...

GRAVES, THE ART TEACHER!!.... I DON'T UNDERSTAND ??

I THINK I DO! YOU REMEMBER GRAVES HERE IS A MASTER ENGRAVER! WHAT WOULD BE MORE SIMPLE THAN FOR HIM TO ENGRAVE MONEY...COUNTERFEIT MONEY!

GRAVES, AND THE PRINCIPAL WERE PARTNERS! GRAVES USED TO SNEAK OUT OF HIS ROOM AND USE THE TUNNEL TO GET HERE! ONE NIGHT HE WAS SPOTTED...BY THE BOY TED SPENCER!

I SEE, AND WHEN SPENCER TOLD BLAKE THAT HE SAW A MASKED MAN IN THE SCHOOL, BLAKE TOLD GRAVES, WHO KIDNAPPED HIM SO THAT HE WOULDN'T TELL ANYONE ELSE!

RIGHT! BUT BLAKE GOT PANICKY AND GRAVES KILLED HIM! THEN TONIGHT HE CAME BACK TO STEAL BLAKE'S HIDDEN MONEY!

WHAT A RACKET! USING THIS SCHOOL TO COVER UP A COUNTERFEITING RING! WELL, THE LAW WILL TAKE CARE OF THAT FROM NOW ON!

ONCE MORE THE WAYNE HOME!

ALL I'VE GOT TO SAY IS ...IF YOU'RE AS TERRIFIC, AS YOU ARE AS A KID... I PITY THE CRIMINALS WHEN YOU'RE A GROWN MAN!

WELL BRUCE, HOW DID I DO ON THIS CASE... OKAY?

BOB KANE

ROBIN, the ORIGINAL BOY WONDER, WILL BE BACK NEXT MONTH IN DETECTIVE COMICS TO THRILL YOU AGAIN IN ANOTHER EXCITING AND FAST-MOVING ADVENTURE WITH THE BATMAN!

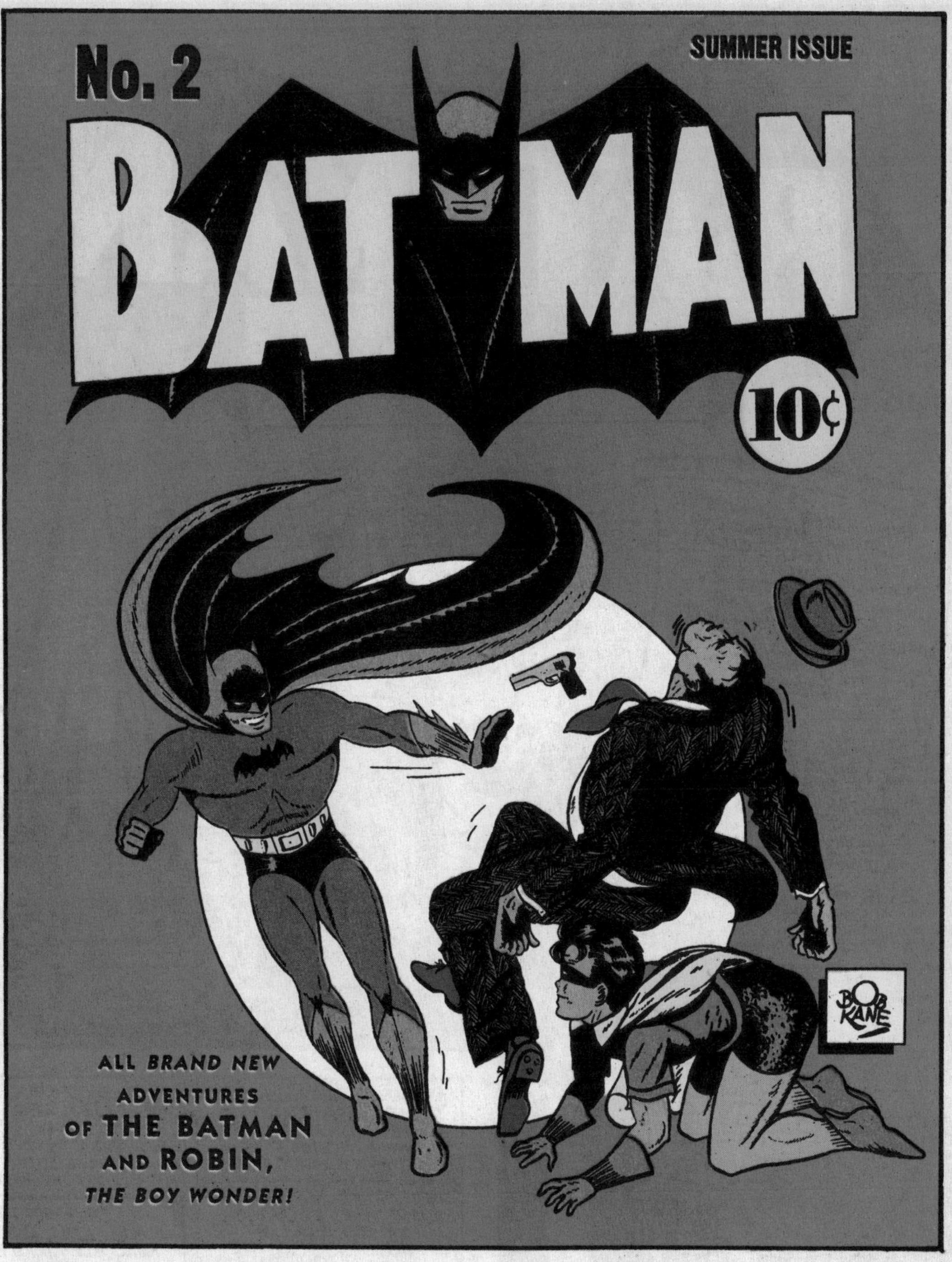
No. 2
SUMMER ISSUE
BATMAN
10¢
BOB KANE
ALL BRAND NEW
ADVENTURES
OF THE BATMAN
AND ROBIN,
THE BOY WONDER!

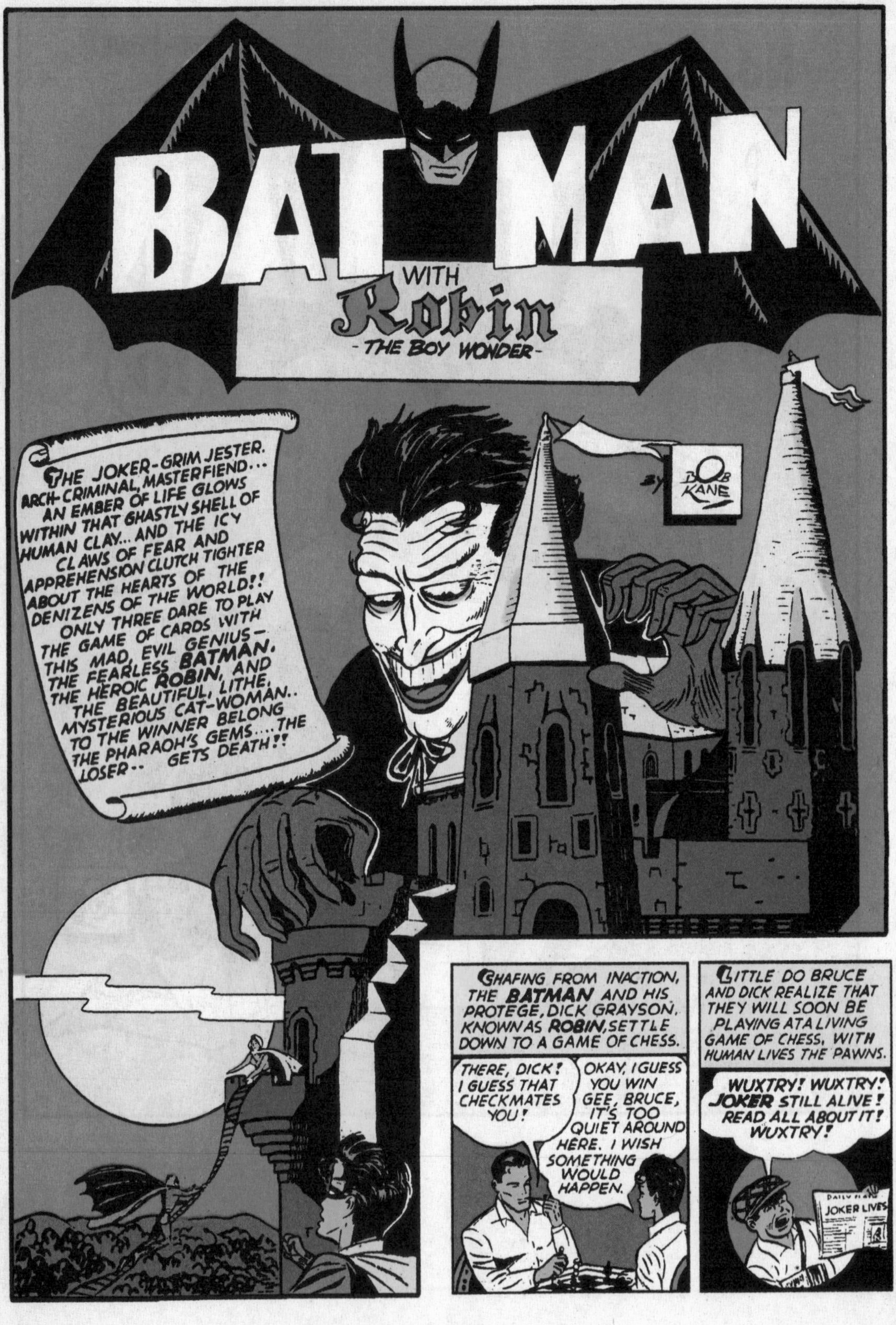
BATMAN
WITH Robin
-THE BOY WONDER-
BY BOB KANE
THE JOKER-GRIM JESTER. ARCH-CRIMINAL, MASTERFIEND... AN EMBER OF LIFE GLOWS WITHIN THAT GHASTLY SHELL OF HUMAN CLAY... AND THE ICY CLAWS OF FEAR AND APPREHENSION CLUTCH TIGHTER ABOUT THE HEARTS OF THE DENIZENS OF THE WORLD!! ONLY THREE DARE TO PLAY THE GAME OF CARDS WITH THIS MAD, EVIL GENIUS— THE FEARLESS BATMAN, THE HEROIC ROBIN, AND THE BEAUTIFUL, LITHE, MYSTERIOUS CAT-WOMAN.. TO THE WINNER BELONG THE PHARAOH'S GEMS.... THE LOSER-- GETS DEATH!!
CHAFING FROM INACTION, THE BATMAN AND HIS PROTEGE, DICK GRAYSON, KNOWN AS ROBIN, SETTLE DOWN TO A GAME OF CHESS.
THERE, DICK! I GUESS THAT CHECKMATES YOU!
OKAY, I GUESS YOU WIN GEE, BRUCE, IT'S TOO QUIET AROUND HERE. I WISH SOMETHING WOULD HAPPEN.
LITTLE DO BRUCE AND DICK REALIZE THAT THEY WILL SOON BE PLAYING AT A LIVING GAME OF CHESS, WITH HUMAN LIVES THE PAWNS.
WUXTRY! WUXTRY! JOKER STILL ALIVE! READ ALL ABOUT IT! WUXTRY!
JOKER LIVES

FATEFUL WORDS!

THE HERALD

VOL XII

JOKER LIVES!!

Joker found close to death after encounter with the Batman. Wound self-inflicted, rushed to Vesalius Hospital for emergency treatment.

E.S. Arthur to ship priceless Pharaoh gems to British Museum collection valued $10,000,00

THE STARTLING REVELATION THAT THE JOKER IS STILL ALIVE MOVES THE BATMAN TO PROMPT ACTION...

WHAT'S YOUR PLAN, BATMAN?

MY PLAN IS TO ABDUCT THE JOKER FROM THE HOSPITAL BEFORE HE BECOMES STRONG AND WILY ENOUGH TO SLIP THROUGH THE HANDS OF THE POLICE. THEN WE'LL TAKE HIM TO A FAMOUS BRAIN SPECIALIST FOR AN OPERATION, SO THAT HE CAN BE CURED AND TURNED INTO A VALUABLE CITIZEN.

MEANWHILE, IN A LUXURIOUS LAIR, THE MEMBERS OF CRIME SYNDICATE INC. MEET TO DISCUSS THEIR FUTURE ACTIVITIES....

I WONDER WHAT THAT NEWSY'S YELLIN' ABOUT OUTSIDE? HEY, JOHNNY! SEND UP A COPY OF THE EXTRA TO OUR ROOM.

WELL, BOYS! NOW THAT THE CHIEF'S DEAD WHADDA WE GONNA DO?

AIN'T THAT JUST LIKE THE CHIEF, WEASEL? ALWAYS DOIN' THE UNEXPECTED! GEE! ARE WE GONNA MISS 'IM!

HERE'S THE PAPER, NOW!

AS WEASEL RUNS HIS EYE DOWN THE PAGE, A DARING PLAN BEGINS TO FORMULATE INSIDE HIS SCHEMING MIND.

DAILY FLASH

VOL XX

JOKER AT VESALIUS HOSPITAL FOR EMERGENCY TREATMENT!

The Joker lies at the point of death in Vesalius Hospital. His chances for recovery are slim unless the medecossy operation is performed.

E.S. Arthur to ship priceless Pharaoh gems

THE CRIMINALS ARE BROUGHT TO THEIR FEET BY THE MOMENTOUS IMPLICATIONS OF THE NEWS STORY!

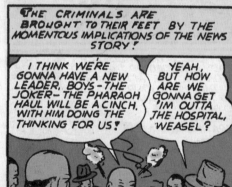

I THINK WE'RE GONNA HAVE A NEW LEADER, BOYS - THE JOKER - THE PHARAOH HAUL WILL BE A CINCH, WITH HIM DOING THE THINKING FOR US!

YEAH, BUT HOW ARE WE GONNA GET 'IM OUTTA THE HOSPITAL, WEASEL?

WITH GREAT CUNNING WEASEL RAPIDLY UNFOLDS HIS DARING SCHEME.

FIRST WE GET SOME OF US INTO THE HOSPITAL. THEN I GOT A PLAN FOR GETTIN' 'IM OUT AND PAST THE COPS. THAT'LL GROW HAIR BACK ON YOUR HEAD- NOW WHICH ONE OF YOU BIRDS THINKS HE CAN FLY-?

THE DIE IS CAST! ONCE MORE THE MACHINATIONS OF THE CRIME SYNDICATE WILL BE FELT! THIS TIME UNDER THE RUTHLESS LEADERSHIP OF THE JOKER!! WHAT IS THE CONNECTION BETWEEN THE PRICELESS PHARAOH GEMS AND WEASEL'S PLAN TO ABDUCT THE JOKER?

2

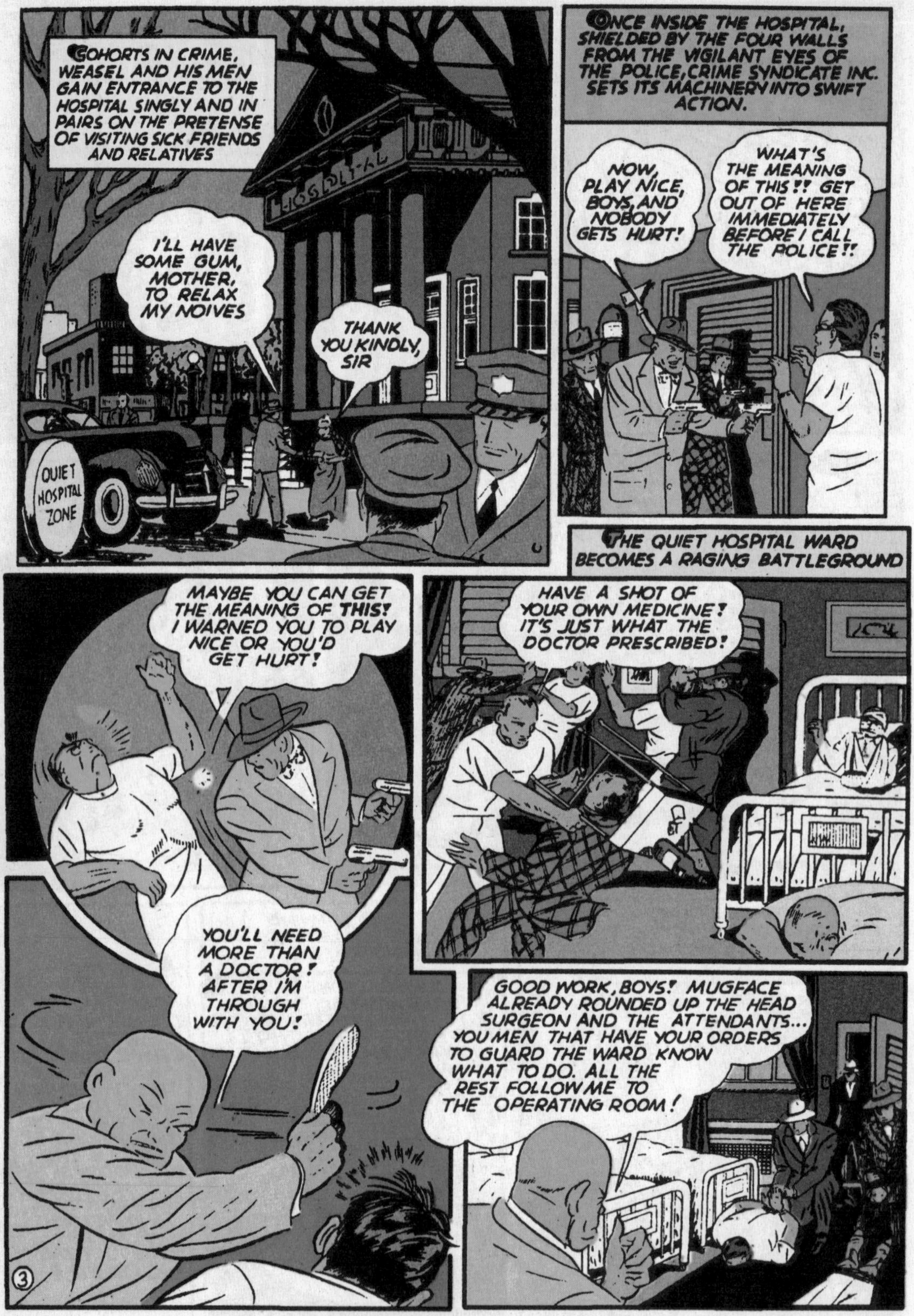
COHORTS IN CRIME, WEASEL AND HIS MEN GAIN ENTRANCE TO THE HOSPITAL SINGLY AND IN PAIRS ON THE PRETENSE OF VISITING SICK FRIENDS AND RELATIVES
I'LL HAVE SOME GUM, MOTHER, TO RELAX MY NOIVES
THANK YOU KINDLY, SIR
QUIET HOSPITAL ZONE
ONCE INSIDE THE HOSPITAL, SHIELDED BY THE FOUR WALLS FROM THE VIGILANT EYES OF THE POLICE, CRIME SYNDICATE INC. SETS ITS MACHINERY INTO SWIFT ACTION.
NOW, PLAY NICE, BOYS, AND NOBODY GETS HURT!
WHAT'S THE MEANING OF THIS!! GET OUT OF HERE IMMEDIATELY BEFORE I CALL THE POLICE!!
MAYBE YOU CAN GET THE MEANING OF THIS! I WARNED YOU TO PLAY NICE OR YOU'D GET HURT!
THE QUIET HOSPITAL WARD BECOMES A RAGING BATTLEGROUND
HAVE A SHOT OF YOUR OWN MEDICINE! IT'S JUST WHAT THE DOCTOR PRESCRIBED!
YOU'LL NEED MORE THAN A DOCTOR! AFTER I'M THROUGH WITH YOU!
3
GOOD WORK, BOYS! MUGFACE ALREADY ROUNDED UP THE HEAD SURGEON AND THE ATTENDANTS... YOU MEN THAT HAVE YOUR ORDERS TO GUARD THE WARD KNOW WHAT TO DO. ALL THE REST FOLLOW ME TO THE OPERATING ROOM!

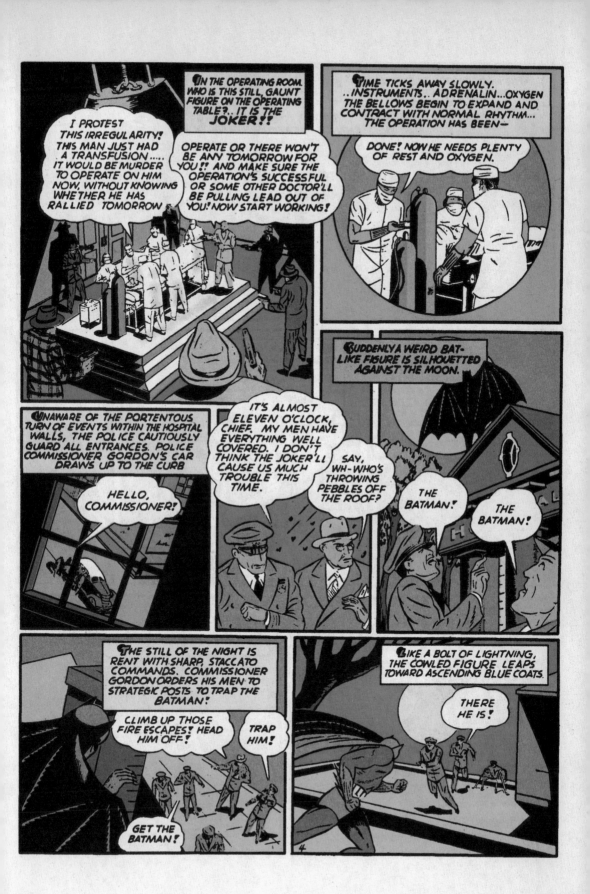

IN THE OPERATING ROOM, WHO IS THIS STILL, GAUNT FIGURE ON THE OPERATING TABLE?.. IT IS THE JOKER!!

I PROTEST THIS IRREGULARITY! THIS MAN JUST HAD A TRANSFUSION..... IT WOULD BE MURDER TO OPERATE ON HIM NOW, WITHOUT KNOWING WHETHER HE HAS RALLIED TOMORROW.

OPERATE OR THERE WON'T BE ANY TOMORROW FOR YOU!! AND MAKE SURE THE OPERATION'S SUCCESSFUL OR SOME OTHER DOCTOR'LL BE PULLING LEAD OUT OF YOU! NOW START WORKING!

TIME TICKS AWAY SLOWLY. ..INSTRUMENTS.. ADRENALIN...OXYGEN THE BELLOWS BEGIN TO EXPAND AND CONTRACT WITH NORMAL RHYTHM... THE OPERATION HAS BEEN—

DONE! NOW HE NEEDS PLENTY OF REST AND OXYGEN.

SUDDENLY A WEIRD BAT-LIKE FIGURE IS SILHOUETTED AGAINST THE MOON.

UNAWARE OF THE PORTENTOUS TURN OF EVENTS WITHIN THE HOSPITAL WALLS, THE POLICE CAUTIOUSLY GUARD ALL ENTRANCES. POLICE COMMISSIONER GORDON'S CAR DRAWS UP TO THE CURB

HELLO, COMMISSIONER!

IT'S ALMOST ELEVEN O'CLOCK, CHIEF. MY MEN HAVE EVERYTHING WELL COVERED. I DON'T THINK THE JOKER'LL CAUSE US MUCH TROUBLE THIS TIME.

SAY, WH–WHO'S THROWING PEBBLES OFF THE ROOF?

THE BATMAN!

THE BATMAN!

THE STILL OF THE NIGHT IS RENT WITH SHARP, STACCATO COMMANDS. COMMISSIONER GORDON ORDERS HIS MEN TO STRATEGIC POSTS TO TRAP THE BATMAN!

CLIMB UP THOSE FIRE ESCAPES! HEAD HIM OFF!

TRAP HIM!

GET THE BATMAN!

LIKE A BOLT OF LIGHTNING, THE COWLED FIGURE LEAPS TOWARD ASCENDING BLUE COATS.

THERE HE IS!

4

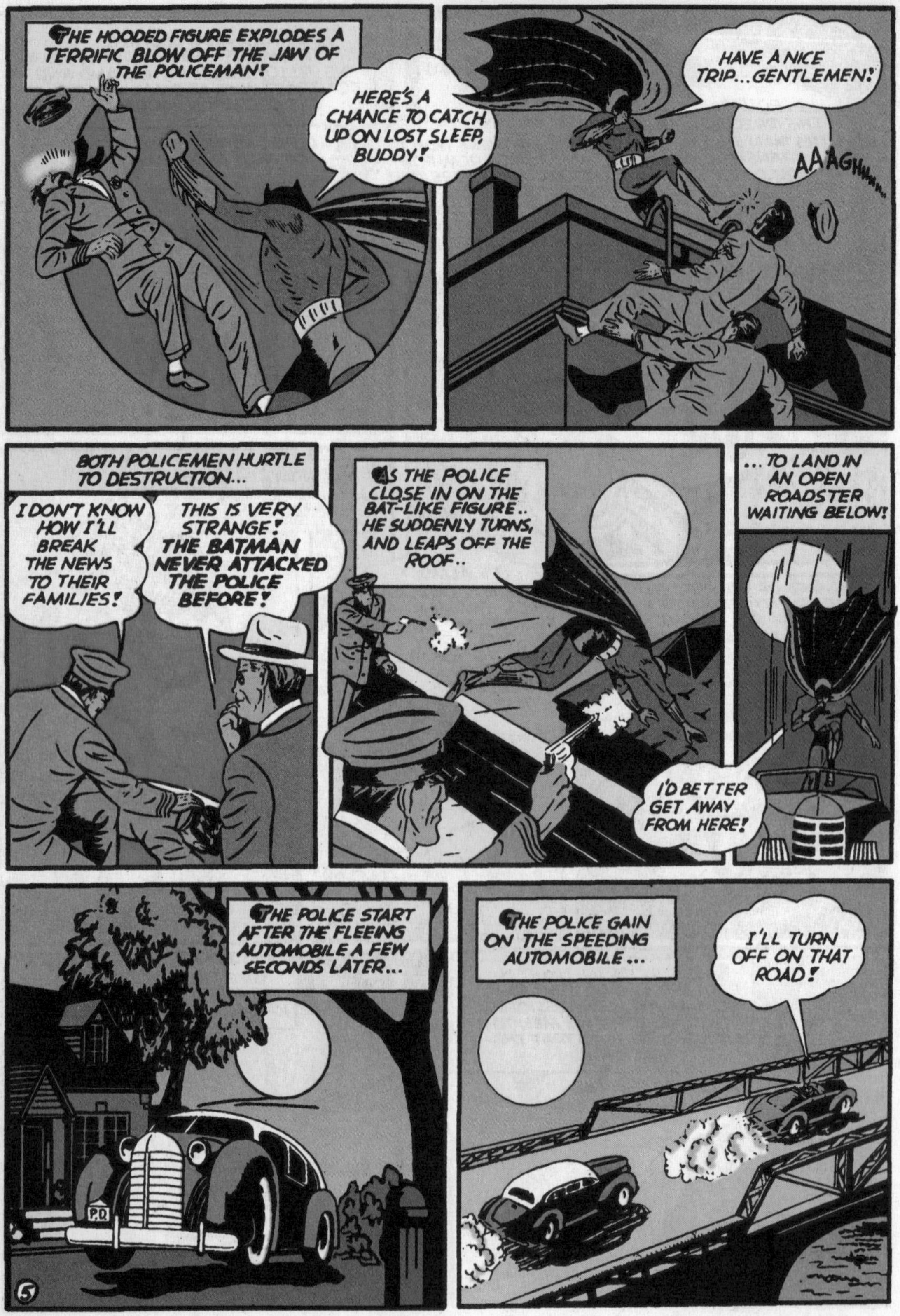
THE HOODED FIGURE EXPLODES A TERRIFIC BLOW OFF THE JAW OF THE POLICEMAN!
HERE'S A CHANCE TO CATCH UP ON LOST SLEEP, BUDDY!
HAVE A NICE TRIP... GENTLEMEN!
AAAGHHH...
BOTH POLICEMEN HURTLE TO DESTRUCTION...
I DON'T KNOW HOW I'LL BREAK THE NEWS TO THEIR FAMILIES!
THIS IS VERY STRANGE! THE BATMAN NEVER ATTACKED THE POLICE BEFORE!
AS THE POLICE CLOSE IN ON THE BAT-LIKE FIGURE.. HE SUDDENLY TURNS, AND LEAPS OFF THE ROOF..
...TO LAND IN AN OPEN ROADSTER WAITING BELOW!
I'D BETTER GET AWAY FROM HERE!
THE POLICE START AFTER THE FLEEING AUTOMOBILE A FEW SECONDS LATER...
P.D.
5
THE POLICE GAIN ON THE SPEEDING AUTOMOBILE...
I'LL TURN OFF ON THAT ROAD!

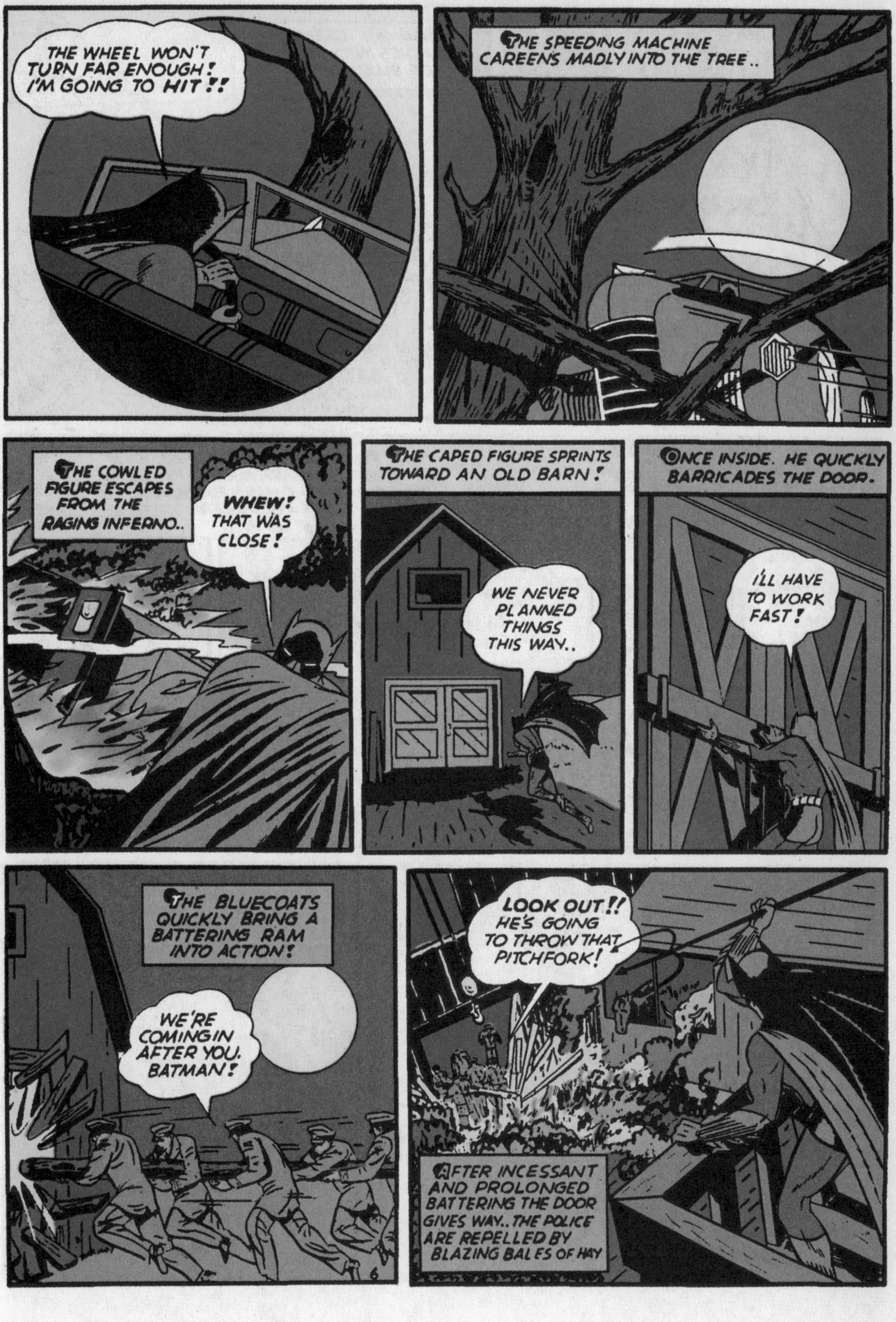
THE WHEEL WON'T TURN FAR ENOUGH! I'M GOING TO HIT!!
THE SPEEDING MACHINE CAREENS MADLY INTO THE TREE..
THE COWLED FIGURE ESCAPES FROM THE RAGING INFERNO..
WHEW! THAT WAS CLOSE!
THE CAPED FIGURE SPRINTS TOWARD AN OLD BARN!
WE NEVER PLANNED THINGS THIS WAY..
ONCE INSIDE. HE QUICKLY BARRICADES THE DOOR.
I'LL HAVE TO WORK FAST!
THE BLUECOATS QUICKLY BRING A BATTERING RAM INTO ACTION!
WE'RE COMING IN AFTER YOU. BATMAN!
6
LOOK OUT!! HE'S GOING TO THROW THAT PITCHFORK!
AFTER INCESSANT AND PROLONGED BATTERING THE DOOR GIVES WAY..THE POLICE ARE REPELLED BY BLAZING BALES OF HAY

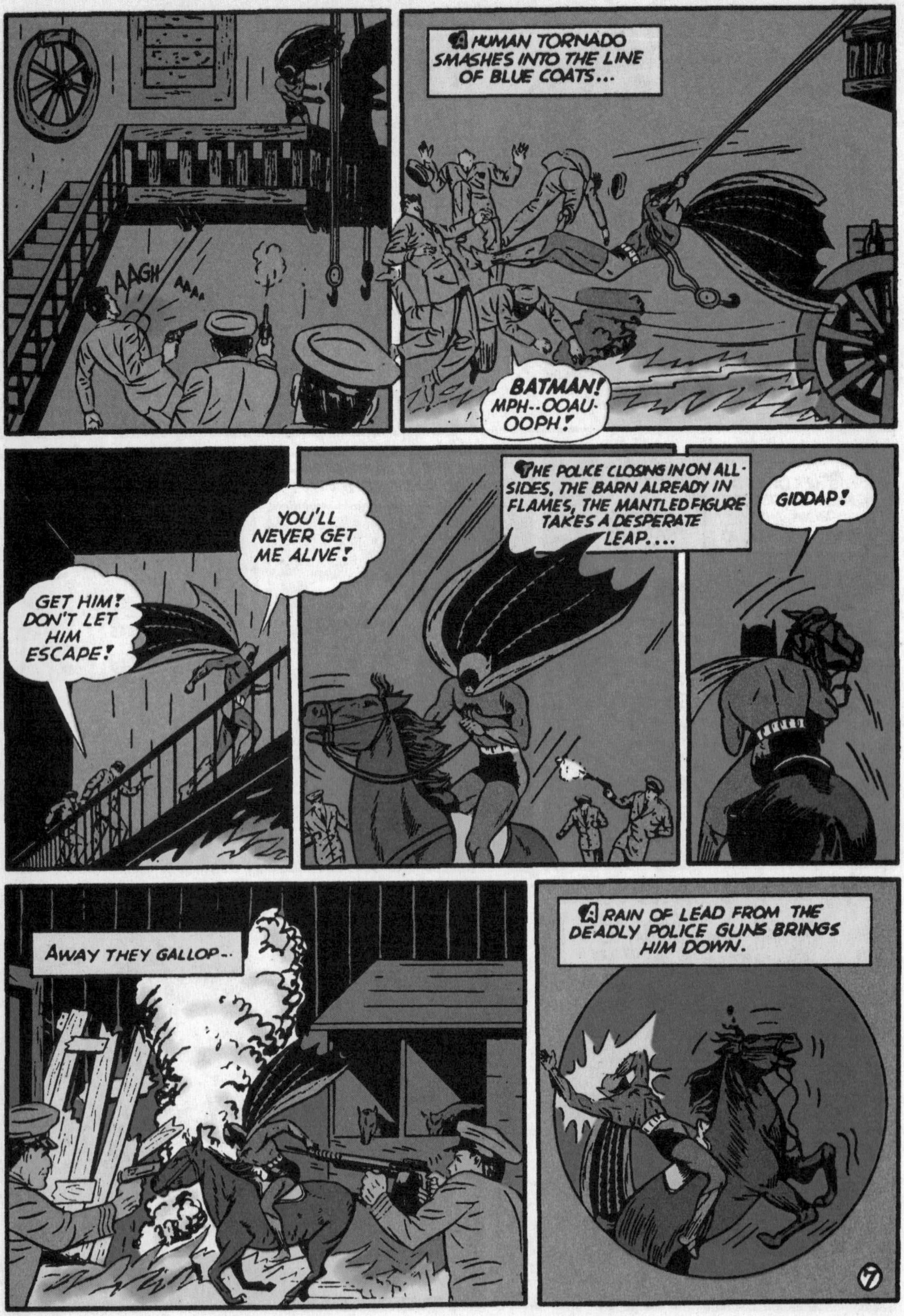
AAGH
AAAA
A HUMAN TORNADO SMASHES INTO THE LINE OF BLUE COATS...
BATMAN! MPH--OOAU-OOPH!
GET HIM! DON'T LET HIM ESCAPE!
YOU'LL NEVER GET ME ALIVE!
THE POLICE CLOSING IN ON ALL SIDES, THE BARN ALREADY IN FLAMES, THE MANTLED FIGURE TAKES A DESPERATE LEAP....
GIDDAP!
AWAY THEY GALLOP--
A RAIN OF LEAD FROM THE DEADLY POLICE GUNS BRINGS HIM DOWN.
7

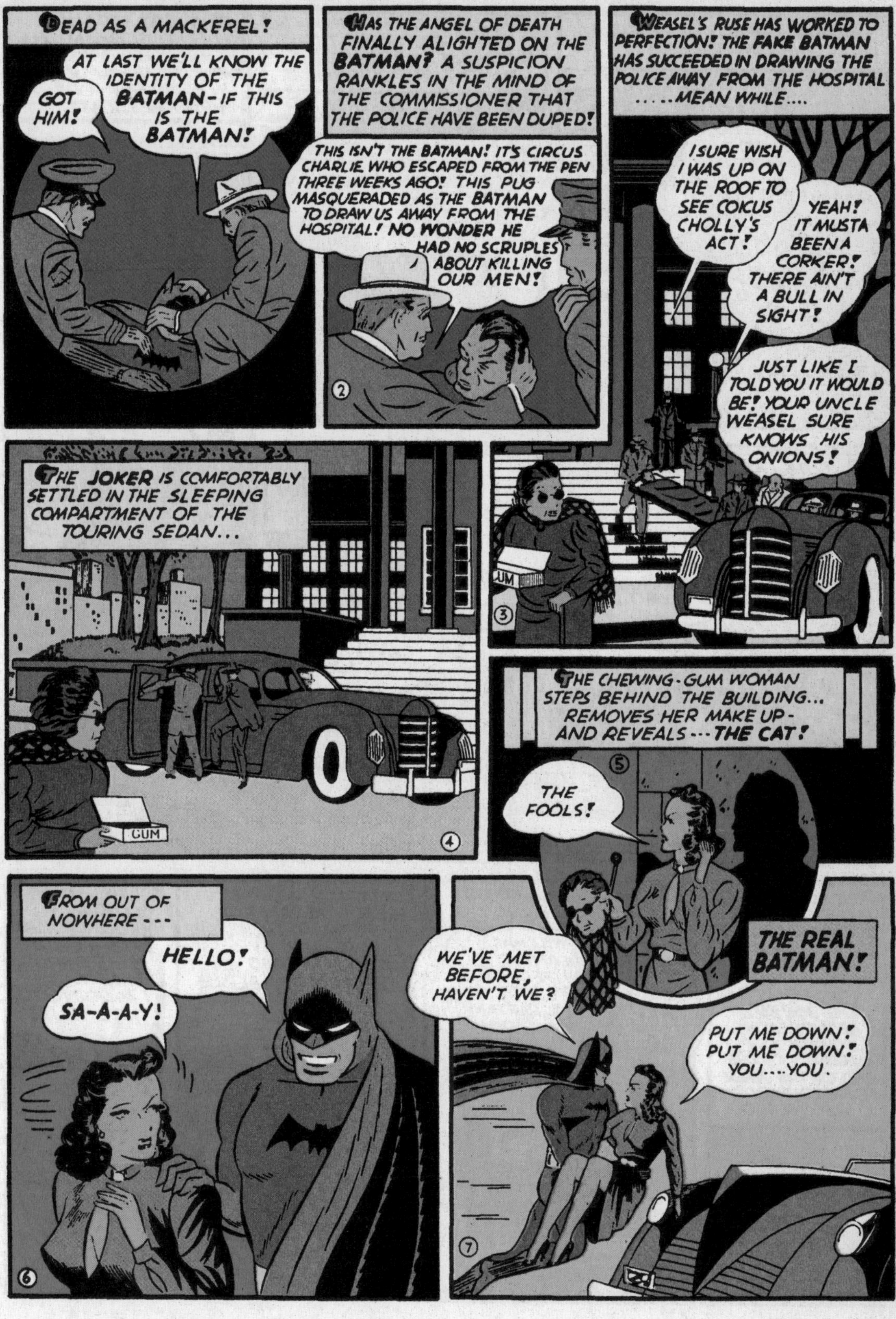
DEAD AS A MACKEREL!
AT LAST WE'LL KNOW THE IDENTITY OF THE BATMAN- IF THIS IS THE BATMAN!
GOT HIM!
HAS THE ANGEL OF DEATH FINALLY ALIGHTED ON THE BATMAN? A SUSPICION RANKLES IN THE MIND OF THE COMMISSIONER THAT THE POLICE HAVE BEEN DUPED!
THIS ISN'T THE BATMAN! IT'S CIRCUS CHARLIE WHO ESCAPED FROM THE PEN THREE WEEKS AGO! THIS PUG MASQUERADED AS THE BATMAN TO DRAW US AWAY FROM THE HOSPITAL! NO WONDER HE HAD NO SCRUPLES ABOUT KILLING OUR MEN!
WEASEL'S RUSE HAS WORKED TO PERFECTION! THE FAKE BATMAN HAS SUCCEEDED IN DRAWING THE POLICE AWAY FROM THE HOSPITAL .....MEAN WHILE....
I SURE WISH I WAS UP ON THE ROOF TO SEE CORCUS CHOLLY'S ACT!
YEAH! IT MUSTA BEEN A CORKER! THERE AIN'T A BULL IN SIGHT!
JUST LIKE I TOLD YOU IT WOULD BE! YOUR UNCLE WEASEL SURE KNOWS HIS ONIONS!
GUM
THE JOKER IS COMFORTABLY SETTLED IN THE SLEEPING COMPARTMENT OF THE TOURING SEDAN...
GUM
THE CHEWING-GUM WOMAN STEPS BEHIND THE BUILDING... REMOVES HER MAKE UP- AND REVEALS---THE CAT!
THE FOOLS!
FROM OUT OF NOWHERE ---
HELLO!
SA-A-A-Y!
WE'VE MET BEFORE, HAVEN'T WE?
THE REAL BATMAN!
PUT ME DOWN! PUT ME DOWN! YOU....YOU.

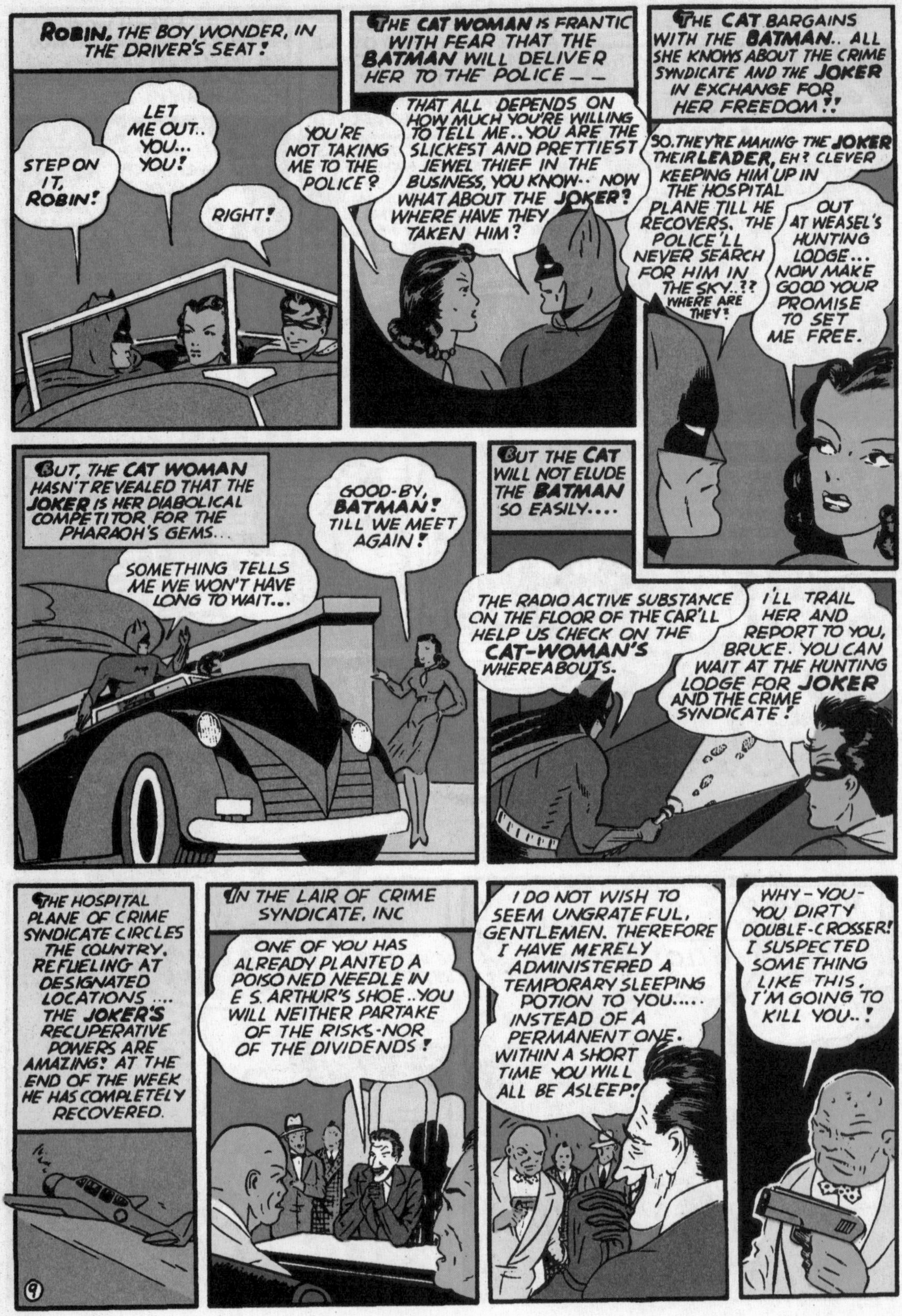
ROBIN, THE BOY WONDER, IN THE DRIVER'S SEAT!
STEP ON IT, ROBIN!
LET ME OUT.. YOU... YOU!
RIGHT!
THE CAT WOMAN IS FRANTIC WITH FEAR THAT THE BATMAN WILL DELIVER HER TO THE POLICE — —
YOU'RE NOT TAKING ME TO THE POLICE?
THAT ALL DEPENDS ON HOW MUCH YOU'RE WILLING TO TELL ME.. YOU ARE THE SLICKEST AND PRETTIEST JEWEL THIEF IN THE BUSINESS, YOU KNOW.. NOW WHAT ABOUT THE JOKER? WHERE HAVE THEY TAKEN HIM?
THE CAT BARGAINS WITH THE BATMAN.. ALL SHE KNOWS ABOUT THE CRIME SYNDICATE AND THE JOKER IN EXCHANGE FOR HER FREEDOM!!
OUT AT WEASEL'S HUNTING LODGE... NOW MAKE GOOD YOUR PROMISE TO SET ME FREE.
SO. THEY'RE MAKING THE JOKER THEIR LEADER, EH? CLEVER KEEPING HIM UP IN THE HOSPITAL PLANE TILL HE RECOVERS. THE POLICE'LL NEVER SEARCH FOR HIM IN THE SKY..?? WHERE ARE THEY?
BUT, THE CAT WOMAN HASN'T REVEALED THAT THE JOKER IS HER DIABOLICAL COMPETITOR FOR THE PHARAOH'S GEMS...
GOOD-BY, BATMAN! TILL WE MEET AGAIN!
SOMETHING TELLS ME WE WON'T HAVE LONG TO WAIT...
BUT THE CAT WILL NOT ELUDE THE BATMAN SO EASILY....
THE RADIO ACTIVE SUBSTANCE ON THE FLOOR OF THE CAR'LL HELP US CHECK ON THE CAT-WOMAN'S WHEREABOUTS.
I'LL TRAIL HER AND REPORT TO YOU, BRUCE. YOU CAN WAIT AT THE HUNTING LODGE FOR JOKER AND THE CRIME SYNDICATE!
THE HOSPITAL PLANE OF CRIME SYNDICATE CIRCLES THE COUNTRY, REFUELING AT DESIGNATED LOCATIONS .... THE JOKER'S RECUPERATIVE POWERS ARE AMAZING! AT THE END OF THE WEEK HE HAS COMPLETELY RECOVERED.
9
IN THE LAIR OF CRIME SYNDICATE, INC
ONE OF YOU HAS ALREADY PLANTED A POISONED NEEDLE IN E S. ARTHUR'S SHOE.. YOU WILL NEITHER PARTAKE OF THE RISKS-NOR OF THE DIVIDENDS!
I DO NOT WISH TO SEEM UNGRATEFUL, GENTLEMEN. THEREFORE I HAVE MERELY ADMINISTERED A TEMPORARY SLEEPING POTION TO YOU..... INSTEAD OF A PERMANENT ONE. WITHIN A SHORT TIME YOU WILL ALL BE ASLEEP!
WHY - YOU - YOU DIRTY DOUBLE-CROSSER! I SUSPECTED SOMETHING LIKE THIS, I'M GOING TO KILL YOU..!

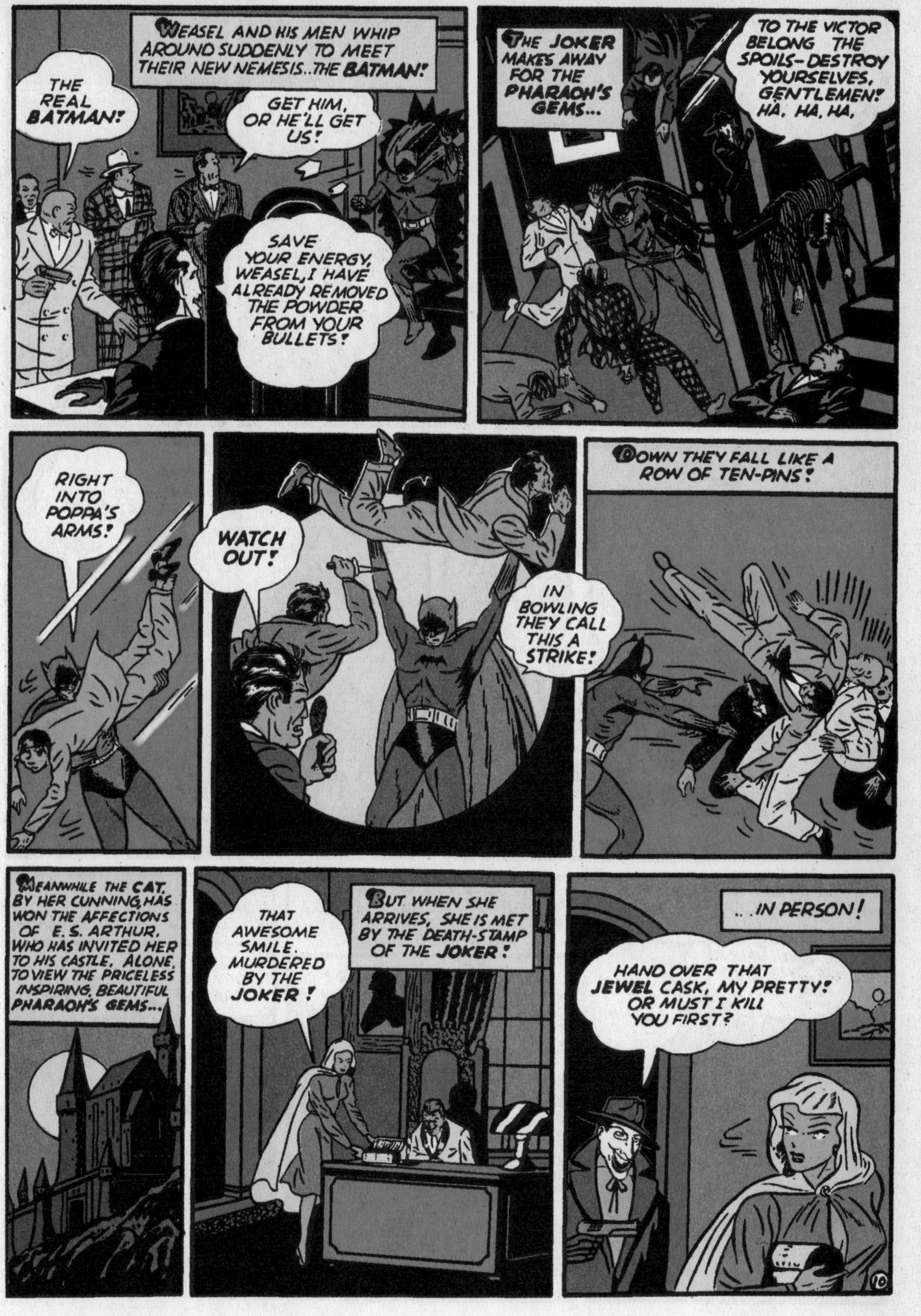
WEASEL AND HIS MEN WHIP AROUND SUDDENLY TO MEET THEIR NEW NEMESIS..THE BATMAN!
THE REAL BATMAN!
GET HIM, OR HE'LL GET US!
SAVE YOUR ENERGY, WEASEL, I HAVE ALREADY REMOVED THE POWDER FROM YOUR BULLETS!
THE JOKER MAKES AWAY FOR THE PHARAOH'S GEMS...
TO THE VICTOR BELONG THE SPOILS-DESTROY YOURSELVES, GENTLEMEN! HA, HA, HA,
RIGHT INTO POPPA'S ARMS!
WATCH OUT!
IN BOWLING THEY CALL THIS A STRIKE!
DOWN THEY FALL LIKE A ROW OF TEN-PINS!
MEANWHILE THE CAT, BY HER CUNNING, HAS WON THE AFFECTIONS OF E. S. ARTHUR, WHO HAS INVITED HER TO HIS CASTLE, ALONE, TO VIEW THE PRICELESS INSPIRING, BEAUTIFUL PHARAOH'S GEMS...
BUT WHEN SHE ARRIVES, SHE IS MET BY THE DEATH-STAMP OF THE JOKER!
THAT AWESOME SMILE. MURDERED BY THE JOKER!
...IN PERSON!
HAND OVER THAT JEWEL CASK, MY PRETTY! OR MUST I KILL YOU FIRST?
10

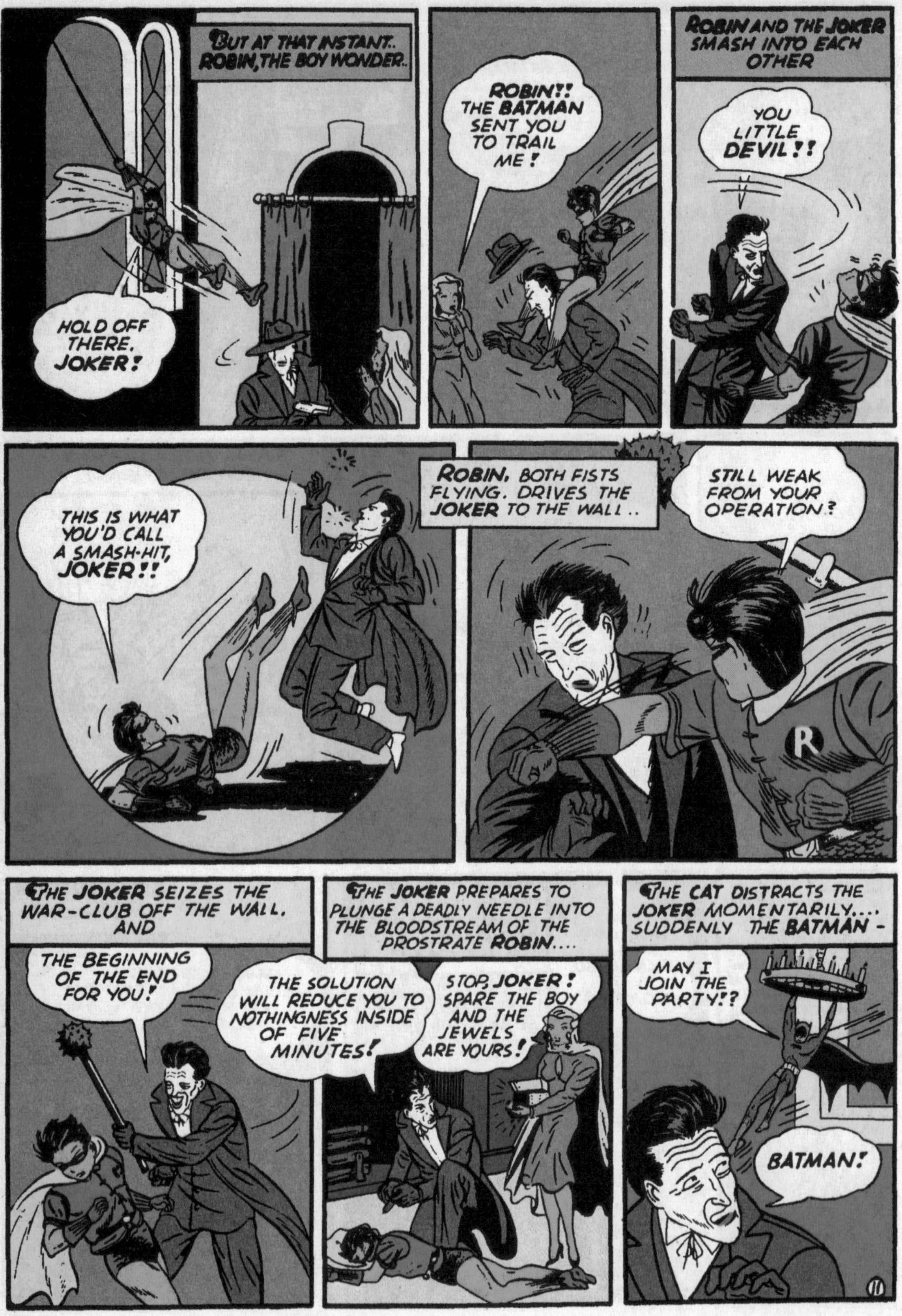
BUT AT THAT INSTANT.. ROBIN, THE BOY WONDER..
HOLD OFF THERE, JOKER!
ROBIN!! THE BATMAN SENT YOU TO TRAIL ME!
ROBIN AND THE JOKER SMASH INTO EACH OTHER
YOU LITTLE DEVIL!!
THIS IS WHAT YOU'D CALL A SMASH-HIT, JOKER!!
ROBIN, BOTH FISTS FLYING, DRIVES THE JOKER TO THE WALL..
STILL WEAK FROM YOUR OPERATION?
THE JOKER SEIZES THE WAR-CLUB OFF THE WALL, AND
THE BEGINNING OF THE END FOR YOU!
THE JOKER PREPARES TO PLUNGE A DEADLY NEEDLE INTO THE BLOODSTREAM OF THE PROSTRATE ROBIN....
THE SOLUTION WILL REDUCE YOU TO NOTHINGNESS INSIDE OF FIVE MINUTES!
STOP, JOKER! SPARE THE BOY AND THE JEWELS ARE YOURS!
THE CAT DISTRACTS THE JOKER MOMENTARILY.... SUDDENLY THE BATMAN -
MAY I JOIN THE PARTY!?
BATMAN!
11

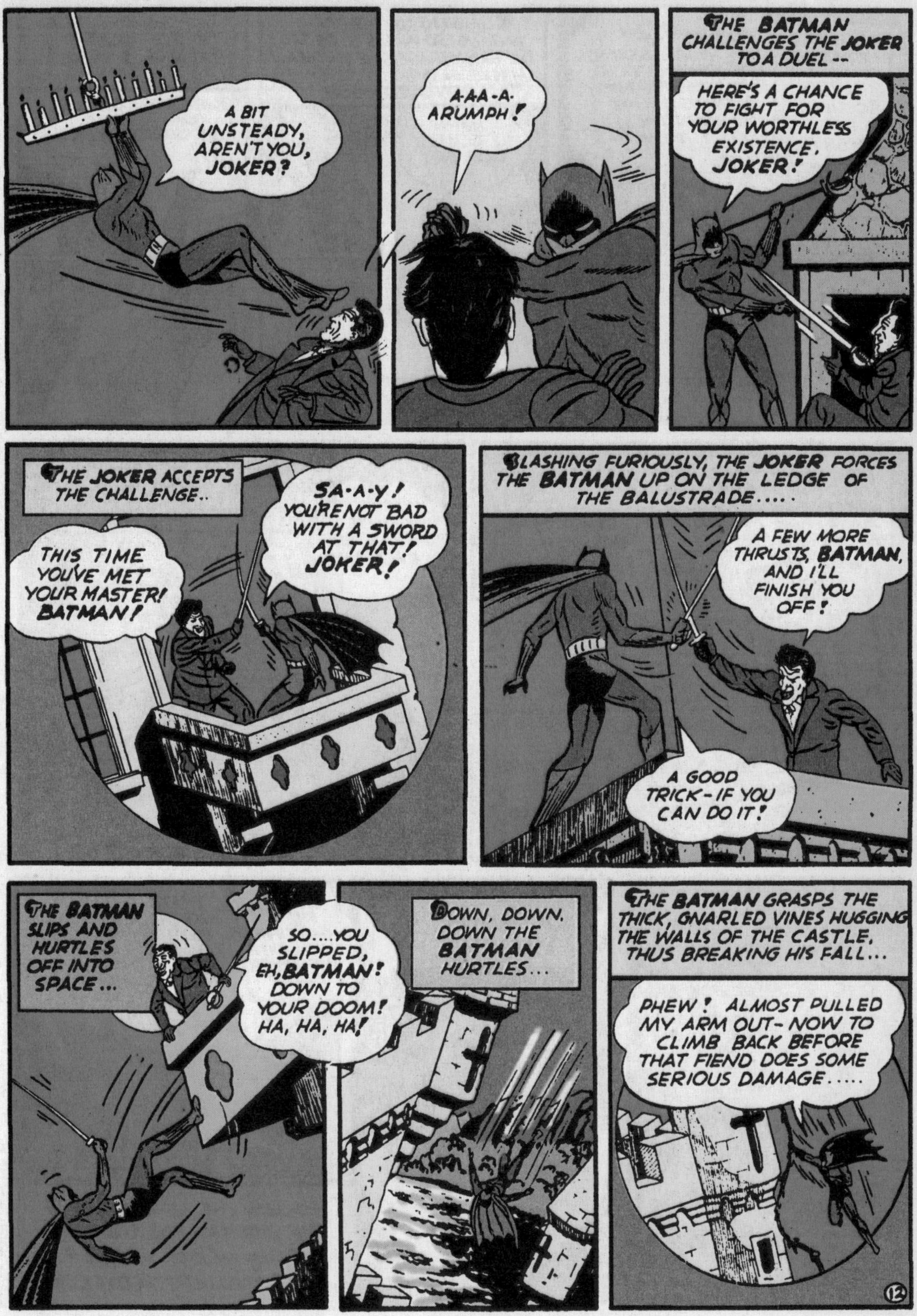
A BIT UNSTEADY, AREN'T YOU, JOKER?
A-A-A-A-ARUMPH!
THE BATMAN CHALLENGES THE JOKER TO A DUEL --
HERE'S A CHANCE TO FIGHT FOR YOUR WORTHLESS EXISTENCE, JOKER!
THE JOKER ACCEPTS THE CHALLENGE..
THIS TIME YOU'VE MET YOUR MASTER! BATMAN!
SA-A-Y! YOU'RE NOT BAD WITH A SWORD AT THAT! JOKER!
SLASHING FURIOUSLY, THE JOKER FORCES THE BATMAN UP ON THE LEDGE OF THE BALUSTRADE.....
A FEW MORE THRUSTS, BATMAN, AND I'LL FINISH YOU OFF!
A GOOD TRICK - IF YOU CAN DO IT!
THE BATMAN SLIPS AND HURTLES OFF INTO SPACE...
SO....YOU SLIPPED, EH, BATMAN! DOWN TO YOUR DOOM! HA, HA, HA!
DOWN, DOWN, DOWN THE BATMAN HURTLES...
THE BATMAN GRASPS THE THICK, GNARLED VINES HUGGING THE WALLS OF THE CASTLE, THUS BREAKING HIS FALL...
PHEW! ALMOST PULLED MY ARM OUT - NOW TO CLIMB BACK BEFORE THAT FIEND DOES SOME SERIOUS DAMAGE.....
12

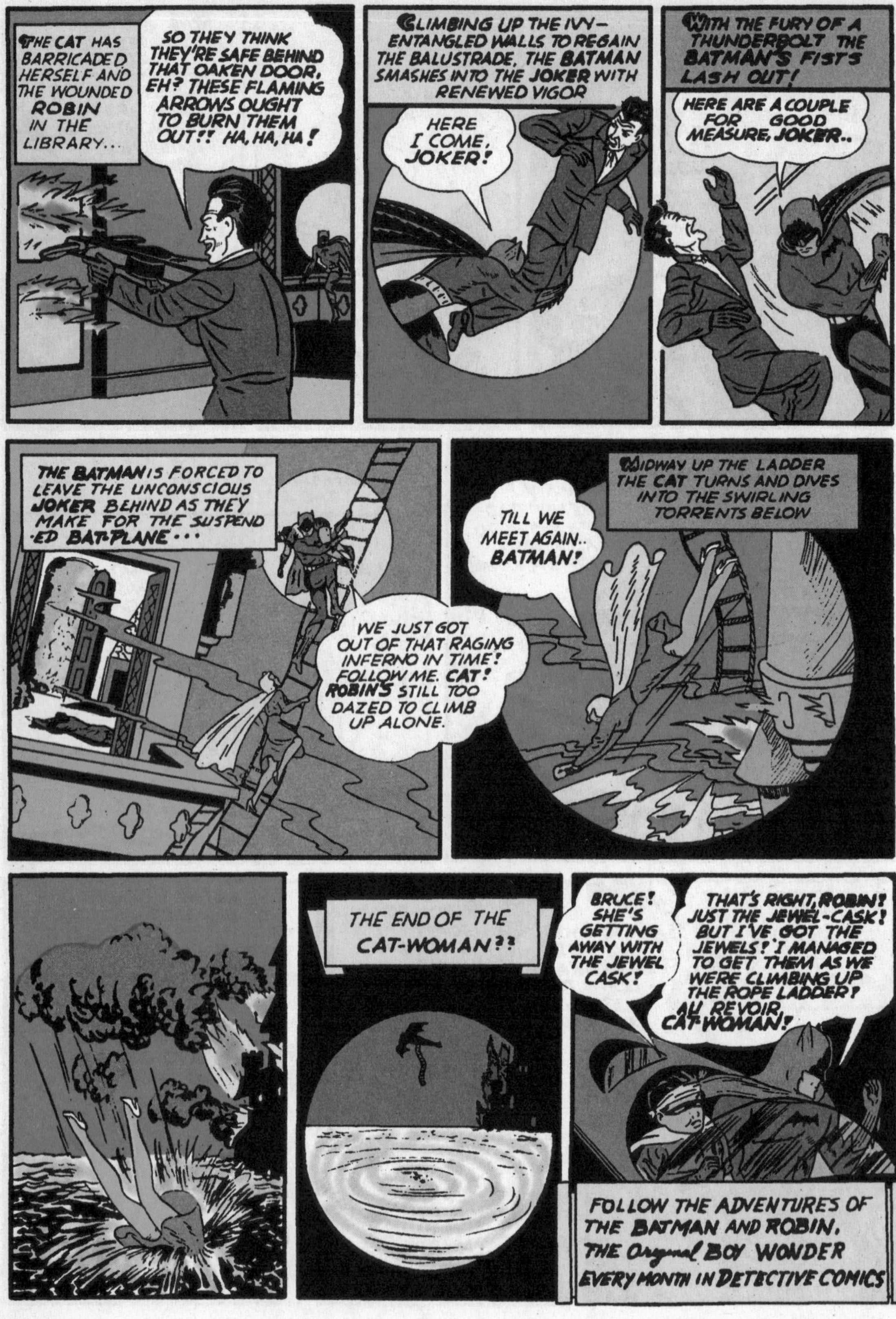
THE CAT HAS BARRICADED HERSELF AND THE WOUNDED ROBIN IN THE LIBRARY...
SO THEY THINK THEY'RE SAFE BEHIND THAT OAKEN DOOR, EH? THESE FLAMING ARROWS OUGHT TO BURN THEM OUT!! HA, HA, HA!
CLIMBING UP THE IVY-ENTANGLED WALLS TO REGAIN THE BALUSTRADE, THE BATMAN SMASHES INTO THE JOKER WITH RENEWED VIGOR
HERE I COME, JOKER!
WITH THE FURY OF A THUNDERBOLT THE BATMAN'S FISTS LASH OUT!
HERE ARE A COUPLE FOR GOOD MEASURE, JOKER..
THE BATMAN IS FORCED TO LEAVE THE UNCONSCIOUS JOKER BEHIND AS THEY MAKE FOR THE SUSPEND-ED BAT-PLANE...
WE JUST GOT OUT OF THAT RAGING INFERNO IN TIME! FOLLOW ME, CAT! ROBIN'S STILL TOO DAZED TO CLIMB UP ALONE.
MIDWAY UP THE LADDER THE CAT TURNS AND DIVES INTO THE SWIRLING TORRENTS BELOW
TILL WE MEET AGAIN.. BATMAN!
THE END OF THE CAT-WOMAN??
BRUCE! SHE'S GETTING AWAY WITH THE JEWEL CASK!
THAT'S RIGHT, ROBIN! JUST THE JEWEL-CASK! BUT I'VE GOT THE JEWELS! I MANAGED TO GET THEM AS WE WERE CLIMBING UP THE ROPE LADDER! AU REVOIR, CAT-WOMAN!
FOLLOW THE ADVENTURES OF THE BATMAN AND ROBIN, THE Original BOY WONDER EVERY MONTH IN DETECTIVE COMICS

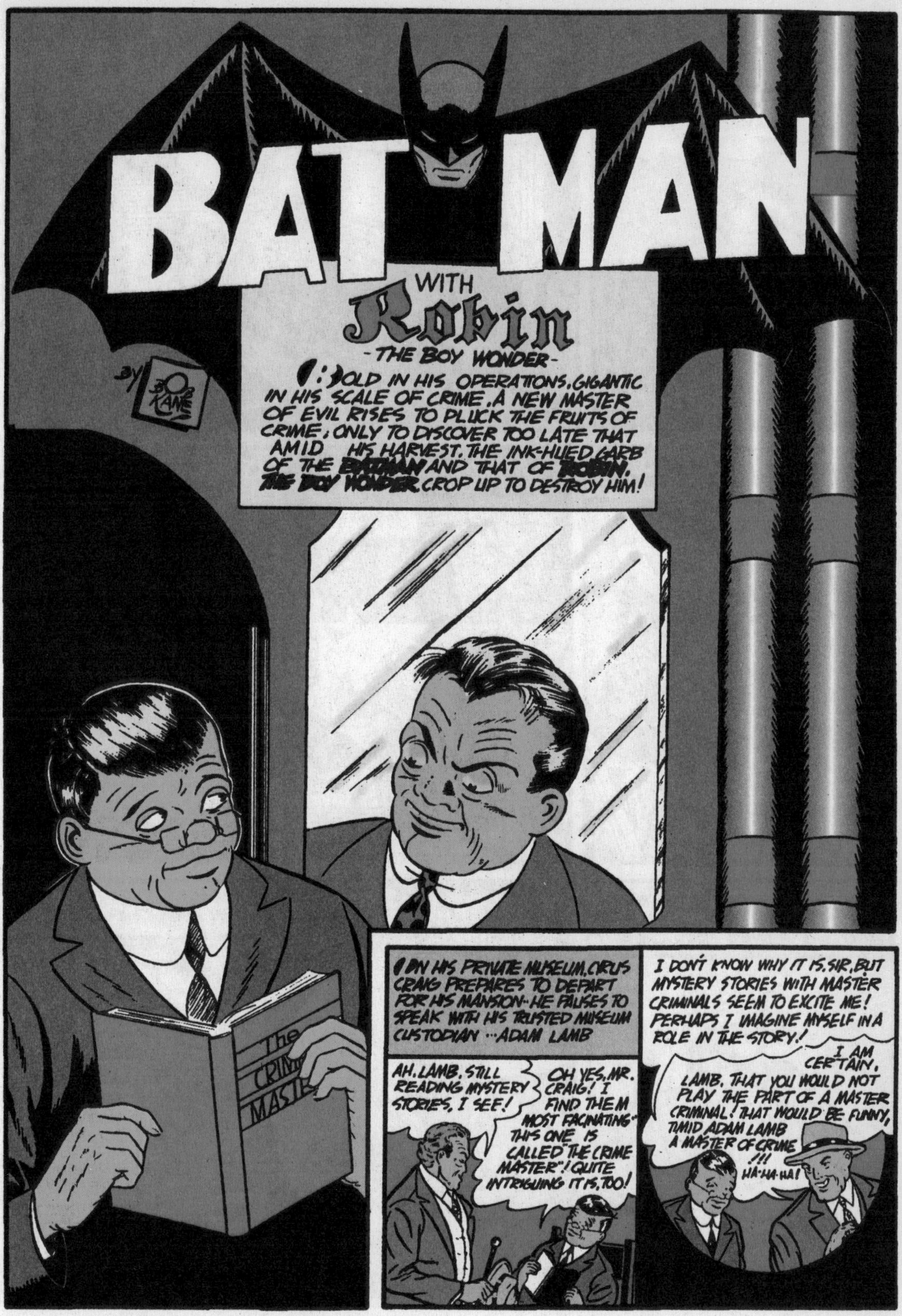
BATMAN
WITH Robin -THE BOY WONDER-
BY BOB KANE
BOLD IN HIS OPERATIONS, GIGANTIC IN HIS SCALE OF CRIME, A NEW MASTER OF EVIL RISES TO PLUCK THE FRUITS OF CRIME; ONLY TO DISCOVER TOO LATE THAT AMID HIS HARVEST, THE INK-HUED GARB OF THE BATMAN AND THAT OF ROBIN, THE BOY WONDER CROP UP TO DESTROY HIM!
The
IN HIS PRIVATE MUSEUM, CYRUS CRAIG PREPARES TO DEPART FOR HIS MANSION-- HE PAUSES TO SPEAK WITH HIS TRUSTED MUSEUM CUSTODIAN ... ADAM LAMB
AH, LAMB, STILL READING MYSTERY STORIES, I SEE!
OH YES, MR. CRAIG! I FIND THEM MOST FACINATING-- THIS ONE IS CALLED "THE CRIME MASTER"! QUITE INTRIGUING IT IS, TOO!
I DON'T KNOW WHY IT IS, SIR, BUT MYSTERY STORIES WITH MASTER CRIMINALS SEEM TO EXCITE ME! PERHAPS I IMAGINE MYSELF IN A ROLE IN THE STORY!
I AM CERTAIN, LAMB, THAT YOU WOULD NOT PLAY THE PART OF A MASTER CRIMINAL! THAT WOULD BE FUNNY, TIMID ADAM LAMB A MASTER OF CRIME !!! HA-HA-HA!

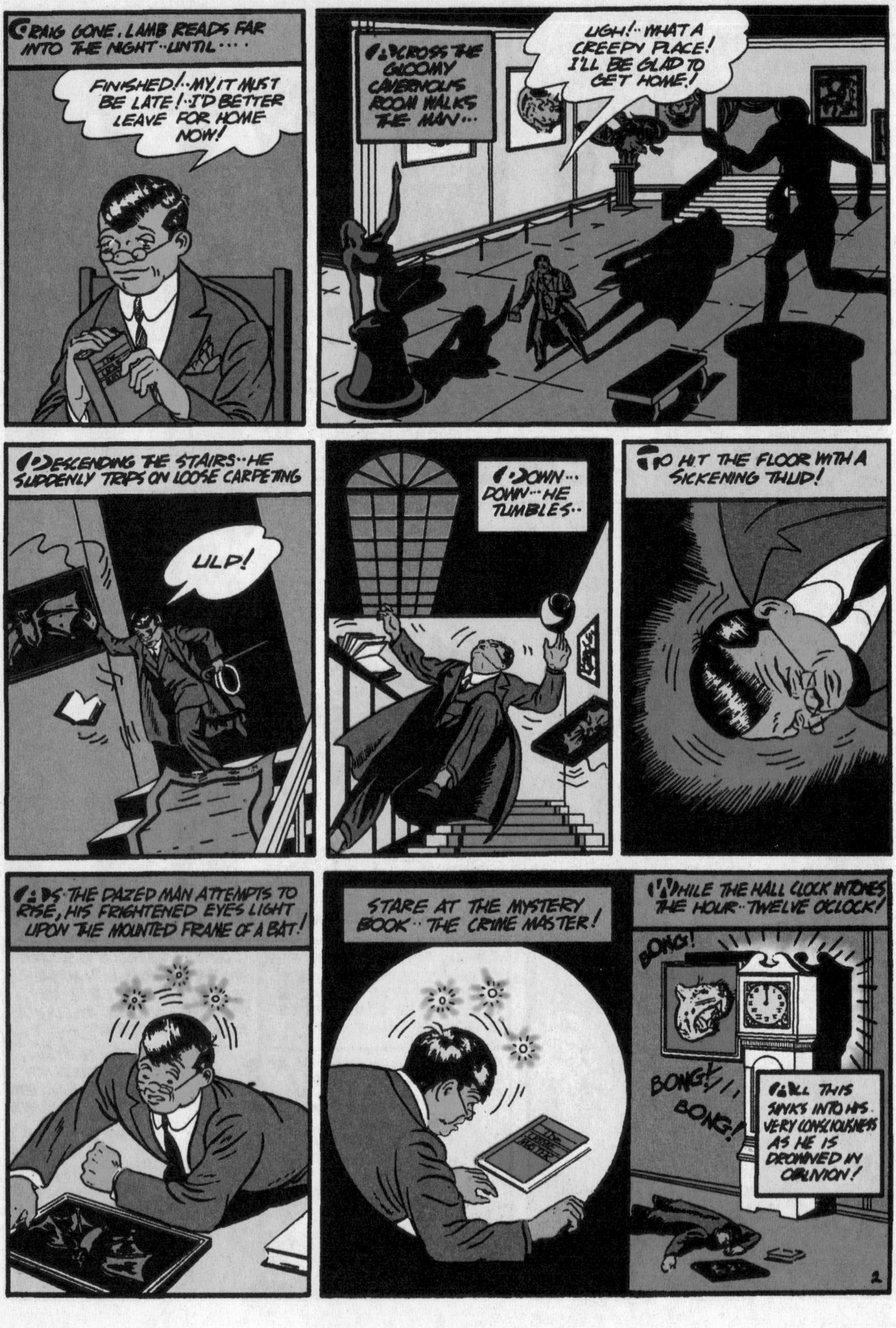
CRAIG GONE, LAMB READS FAR INTO THE NIGHT -- UNTIL ....
FINISHED! -- MY, IT MUST BE LATE! -- I'D BETTER LEAVE FOR HOME NOW!
ACROSS THE GLOOMY CAVERNOUS ROOM WALKS THE MAN...
UGH! -- WHAT A CREEPY PLACE! I'LL BE GLAD TO GET HOME!
DESCENDING THE STAIRS -- HE SUDDENLY TRIPS ON LOOSE CARPETING
ULP!
DOWN... DOWN -- HE TUMBLES..
TO HIT THE FLOOR WITH A SICKENING THUD!
AS THE DAZED MAN ATTEMPTS TO RISE, HIS FRIGHTENED EYES LIGHT UPON THE MOUNTED FRAME OF A BAT!
STARE AT THE MYSTERY BOOK -- THE CRIME MASTER!
WHILE THE HALL CLOCK INTONES THE HOUR -- TWELVE O'CLOCK!
BONG!
BONG!
BONG!
ALL THIS SINKS INTO HIS VERY CONSCIOUSNESS AS HE IS DROWNED IN OBLIVION!
2

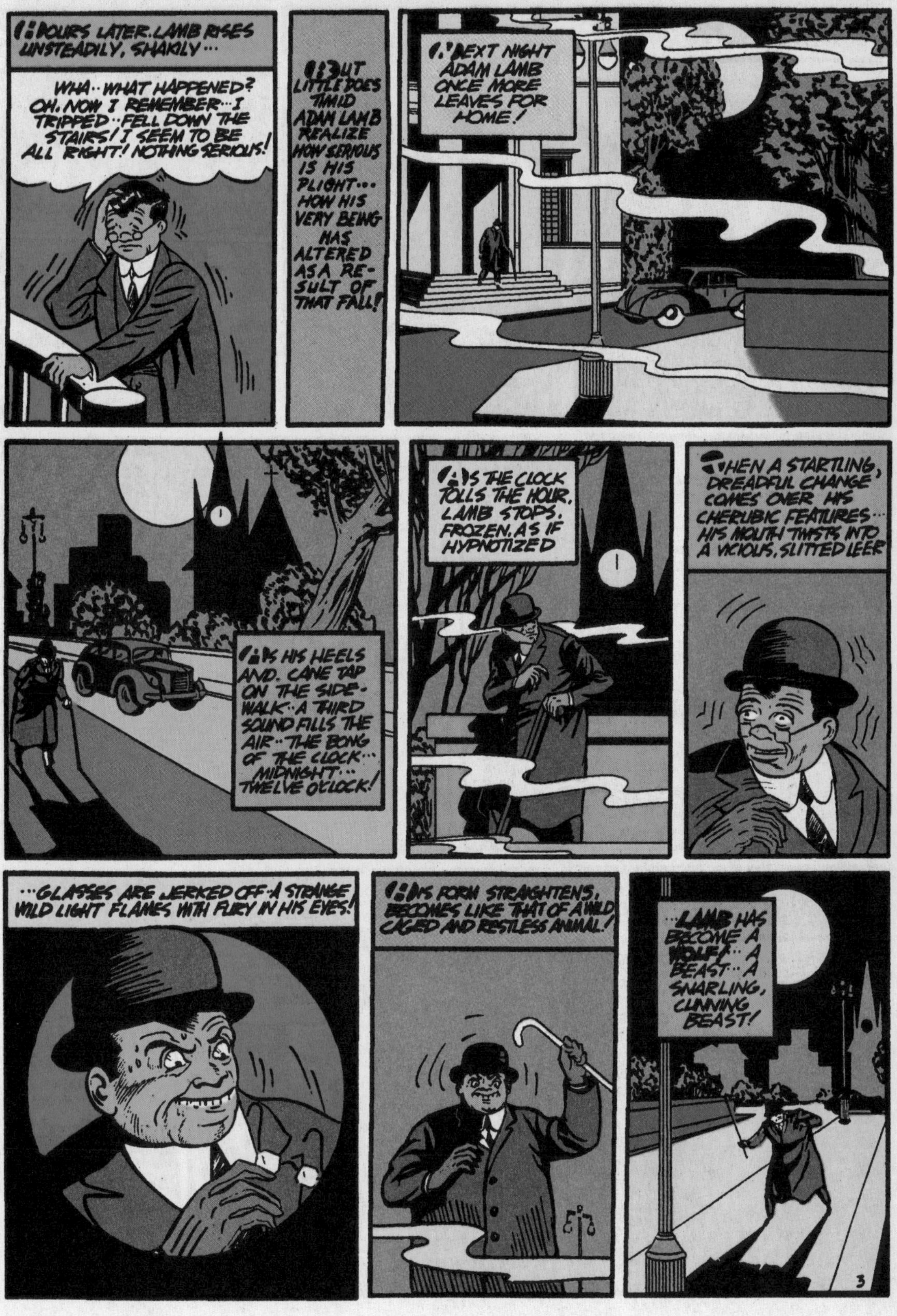
HOURS LATER, LAMB RISES UNSTEADILY, SHAKILY...
WHA.. WHAT HAPPENED? OH, NOW I REMEMBER... I TRIPPED.. FELL DOWN THE STAIRS! I SEEM TO BE ALL RIGHT! NOTHING SERIOUS!
BUT LITTLE DOES TIMID ADAM LAMB REALIZE HOW SERIOUS IS HIS PLIGHT... HOW HIS VERY BEING HAS ALTERED AS A RESULT OF THAT FALL!
NEXT NIGHT ADAM LAMB ONCE MORE LEAVES FOR HOME!
AS HIS HEELS AND CANE TAP ON THE SIDEWALK.. A THIRD SOUND FILLS THE AIR.. THE BONG OF THE CLOCK... MIDNIGHT... TWELVE O'CLOCK!
AS THE CLOCK TOLLS THE HOUR, LAMB STOPS, FROZEN, AS IF HYPNOTIZED
THEN A STARTLING, DREADFUL CHANGE COMES OVER HIS CHERUBIC FEATURES... HIS MOUTH TWISTS INTO A VICIOUS, SLITTED LEER
...GLASSES ARE JERKED OFF.. A STRANGE WILD LIGHT FLAMES WITH FURY IN HIS EYES!
HIS FORM STRAIGHTENS, BECOMES LIKE THAT OF A WILD CAGED AND RESTLESS ANIMAL!
...LAMB HAS BECOME A WOLF!.. A BEAST.. A SNARLING, CUNNING BEAST!
3

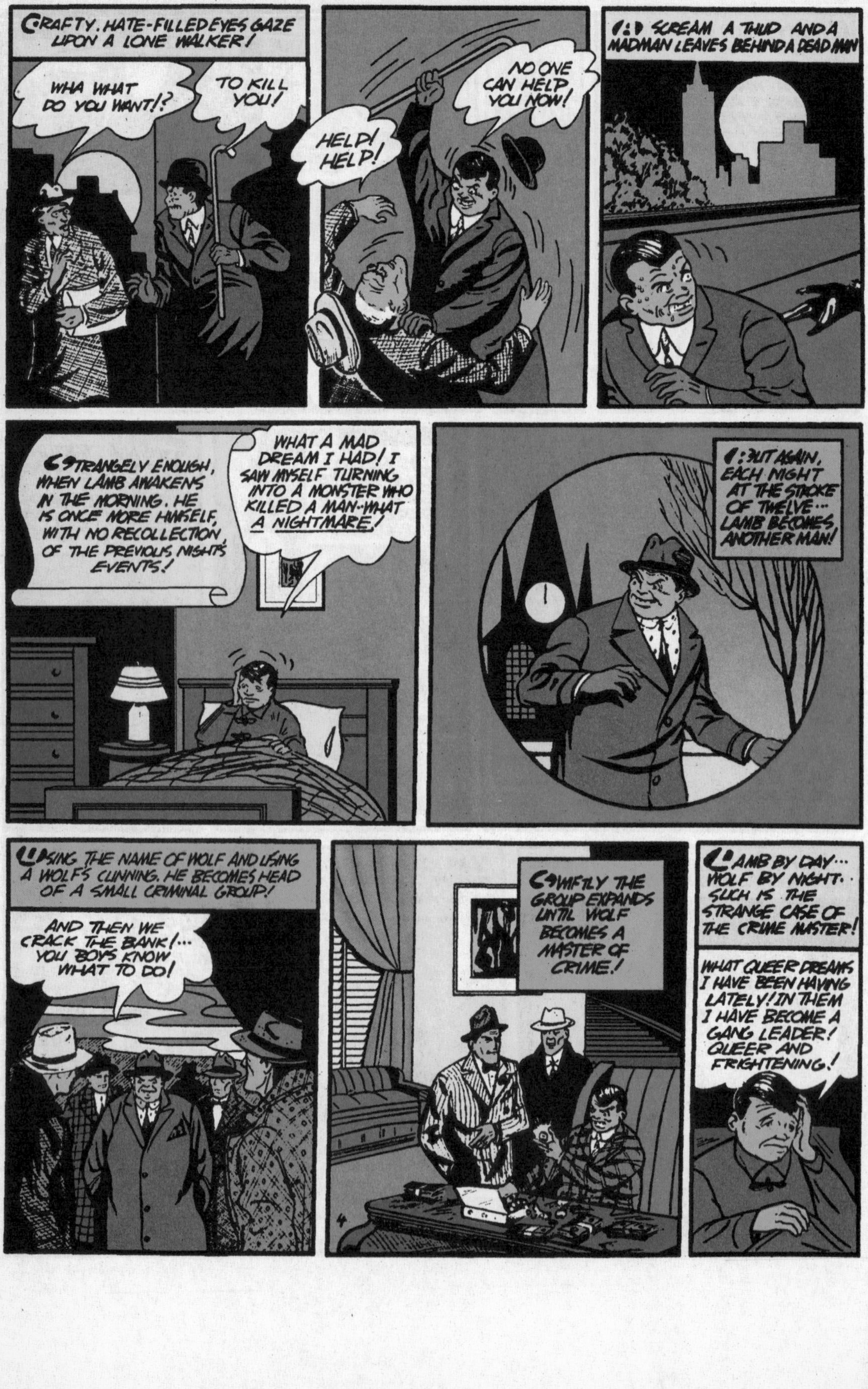
CRAFTY, HATE-FILLED EYES GAZE UPON A LONE WALKER!
WHA WHAT DO YOU WANT!?
TO KILL YOU!
NO ONE CAN HELP YOU NOW!
HELP! HELP!
A SCREAM A THUD AND A MADMAN LEAVES BEHIND A DEAD MAN
STRANGELY ENOUGH, WHEN LAMB AWAKENS IN THE MORNING, HE IS ONCE MORE HIMSELF, WITH NO RECOLLECTION OF THE PREVIOUS NIGHT'S EVENTS!
WHAT A MAD DREAM I HAD! I SAW MYSELF TURNING INTO A MONSTER WHO KILLED A MAN--WHAT A NIGHTMARE!
BUT AGAIN, EACH NIGHT AT THE STROKE OF TWELVE... LAMB BECOMES ANOTHER MAN!
USING THE NAME OF WOLF AND USING A WOLF'S CUNNING, HE BECOMES HEAD OF A SMALL CRIMINAL GROUP!
AND THEN WE CRACK THE BANK!... YOU BOYS KNOW WHAT TO DO!
SWIFTLY THE GROUP EXPANDS UNTIL WOLF BECOMES A MASTER OF CRIME!
LAMB BY DAY... WOLF BY NIGHT... SUCH IS THE STRANGE CASE OF THE CRIME MASTER!
WHAT QUEER DREAMS I HAVE BEEN HAVING LATELY! IN THEM I HAVE BECOME A GANG LEADER! QUEER AND FRIGHTENING!

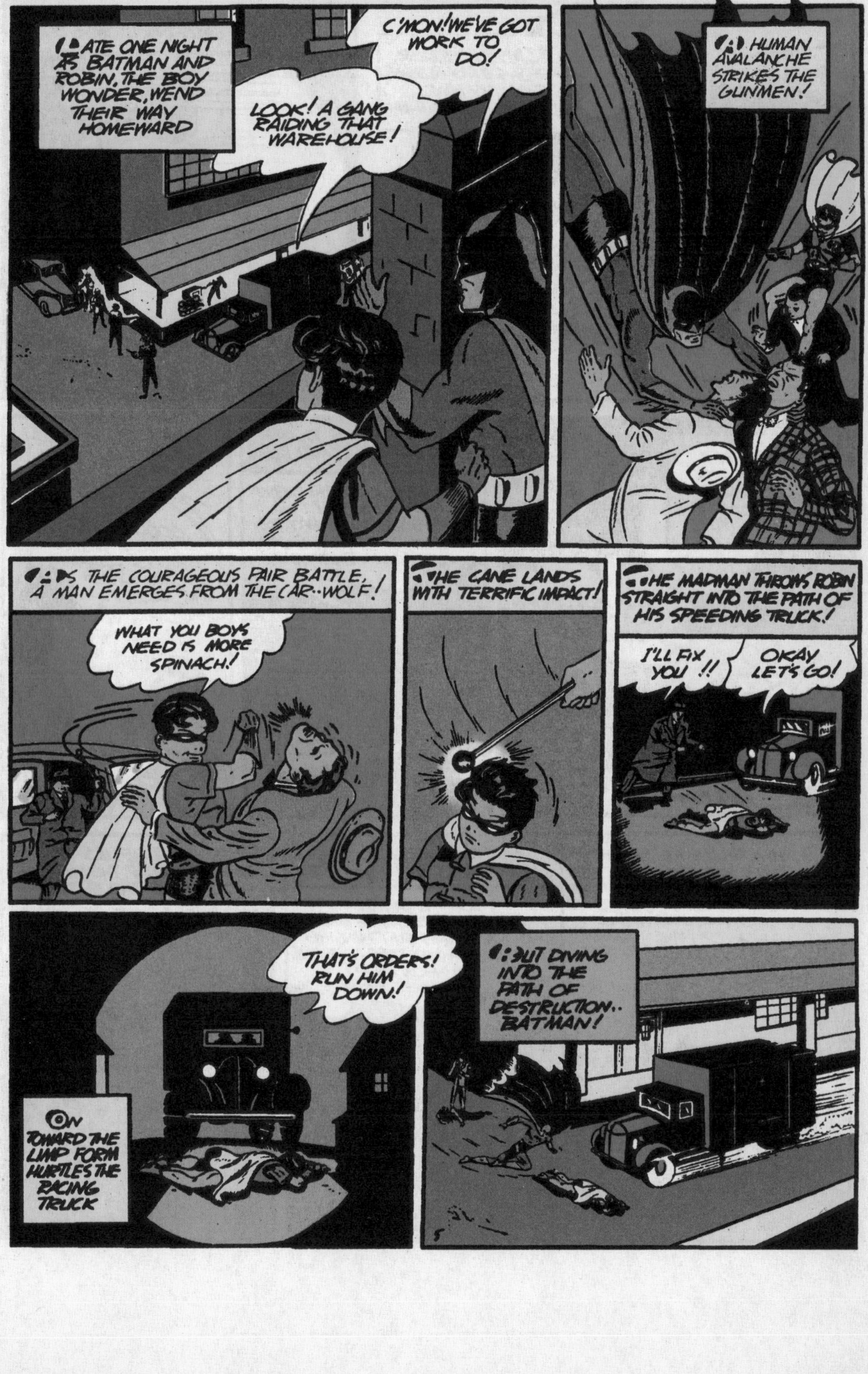
LATE ONE NIGHT AS BATMAN AND ROBIN, THE BOY WONDER, WEND THEIR WAY HOMEWARD
LOOK! A GANG RAIDING THAT WAREHOUSE!
C'MON! WE'VE GOT WORK TO DO!
A HUMAN AVALANCHE STRIKES THE GUNMEN!
AS THE COURAGEOUS PAIR BATTLE, A MAN EMERGES FROM THE CAR..WOLF!
WHAT YOU BOYS NEED IS MORE SPINACH!
THE CANE LANDS WITH TERRIFIC IMPACT!
THE MADMAN THROWS ROBIN STRAIGHT INTO THE PATH OF HIS SPEEDING TRUCK!
I'LL FIX YOU !!
OKAY LET'S GO!
ON TOWARD THE LIMP FORM HURTLES THE RACING TRUCK
THAT'S ORDERS! RUN HIM DOWN!
BUT DIVING INTO THE PATH OF DESTRUCTION.. BATMAN!

HIS SHOULDER PLOWS INTO ROBIN, ROLLING HIM TOWARD THE CURB!

..A QUICK SWERVE AND THE BATMAN ESCAPES THE CRUSHING, LOOMING DEATH!

OTHERS WERE ALSO MAKING GOOD THEIR ESCAPE...WOLF AND HIS MEN!

THE MURDERING RATS!..I'D LIKE TO...

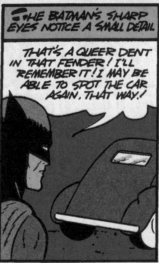

THE BATMAN'S SHARP EYES NOTICE A SMALL DETAIL

THAT'S A QUEER DENT IN THAT FENDER! I'LL REMEMBER IT! I MAY BE ABLE TO SPOT THE CAR AGAIN, THAT WAY!

WOW! WHAT HIT ME! THE EMPIRE STATE BUILDING?

GOOD THING YOU HAVE A THICK HEAD OF HAIR! IT CUSHIONED THE BLOW!

I THINK THAT'S THE NEW MOB THAT'S BEEN TROUBLING THE POLICE LATELY! BUT FROM NOW ON THEY'RE THE ONES WHO'LL HAVE TROUBLE! I'LL SEE TO THAT!

SAY, WHO IS THAT GANG, ANYWAY?

DAYS PASS, AND EACH MORNING LAMB AWAKES A PUZZLED MAN!

I DON'T UNDERSTAND IT THOSE DREAMS OF MINE AND THIS SUIT HANGING HERE!..WHO DOES IT BELONG TO...HOW DID IT GET HERE?

ONE NIGHT HE LIES AWAKE, PLANNING TO TRAP THE MYSTICAL OWNER OF THE SUIT!

I MUST SEE WHO IT IS THAT WEARS THE SUIT! I.... TWELVE O'CLOCK!

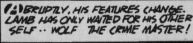

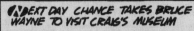
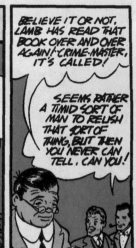

ABRUPTLY, HIS FEATURES CHANGE. LAMB HAS ONLY WAITED FOR HIS OTHER SELF.. WOLF THE CRIME MASTER!

NEXT DAY CHANCE TAKES BRUCE WAYNE TO VISIT CRAIG'S MUSEUM

SO YOU LIKE MY LITTLE COLLECTION, EH BRUCE?

IT'S VERY FINE! BY THE WAY I NOTICE YOUR KEEPER SEEMS QUITE ABSORBED IN HIS BOOK!

BELIEVE IT OR NOT, LAMB HAS READ THAT BOOK OVER AND OVER AGAIN! "CRIME-MASTER", IT'S CALLED!

SEEMS RATHER A TIMID SORT OF MAN TO RELISH THAT SORT OF THING, BUT THEN YOU NEVER CAN TELL, CAN YOU!

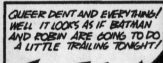

ON HIS WAY HOME BRUCE SUDDENLY HALTS, STOCK-STILL

THE BANDIT'S CAR OF LAST NIGHT!

QUEER DENT AND EVERYTHING! WELL IT LOOKS AS IF BATMAN AND ROBIN ARE GOING TO DO A LITTLE TRAILING TONIGHT!

NIGHTFALL ON THE WATERFRONT TWO FIGURES SLINK THROUGH THE SHADOWS. BATMAN AND THE WONDER BOY

WELL KID, TRAILING THIS CAR HAS CERTAINLY LED US TO THE MEN OF LAST NIGHT! LOOKS LIKE THEY'RE SET TO PULL ANOTHER WAREHOUSE JOB!

I SEE THE SMALL MAN WHO CLUBBED ME!

THEY'LL KILL HIM! WE'VE GOT TO SAVE HIM! LET'S GO, ROBIN!

LOOK! THEY'VE GOT THE WATCHMAN!

ACROSS THE LAST PIER LAUNCH THE TWO FIGURES WITH HURRICANE SPEED!

THEY'RE BACK AGAIN!

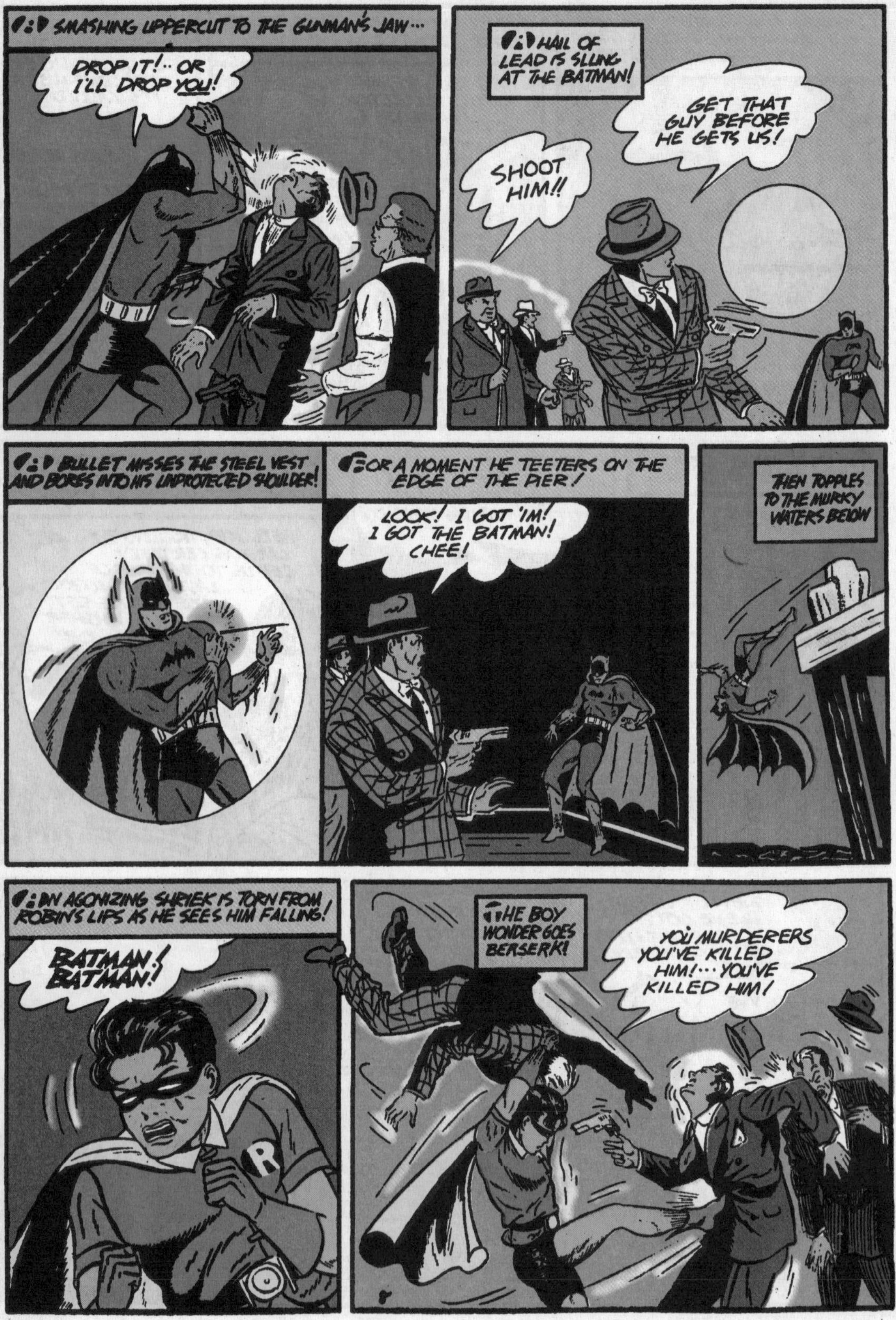
SMASHING UPPERCUT TO THE GUNMAN'S JAW...
DROP IT!.. OR I'LL DROP YOU!
HAIL OF LEAD IS SLUNG AT THE BATMAN!
GET THAT GUY BEFORE HE GETS US!
SHOOT HIM!!
BULLET MISSES THE STEEL VEST AND BORES INTO HIS UNPROTECTED SHOULDER!
FOR A MOMENT HE TEETERS ON THE EDGE OF THE PIER!
LOOK! I GOT 'IM! I GOT THE BATMAN! CHEE!
THEN TOPPLES TO THE MURKY WATERS BELOW
AGONIZING SHRIEK IS TORN FROM ROBIN'S LIPS AS HE SEES HIM FALLING!
BATMAN! BATMAN!
THE BOY WONDER GOES BERSERK!
YOU MURDERERS YOU'VE KILLED HIM!... YOU'VE KILLED HIM!

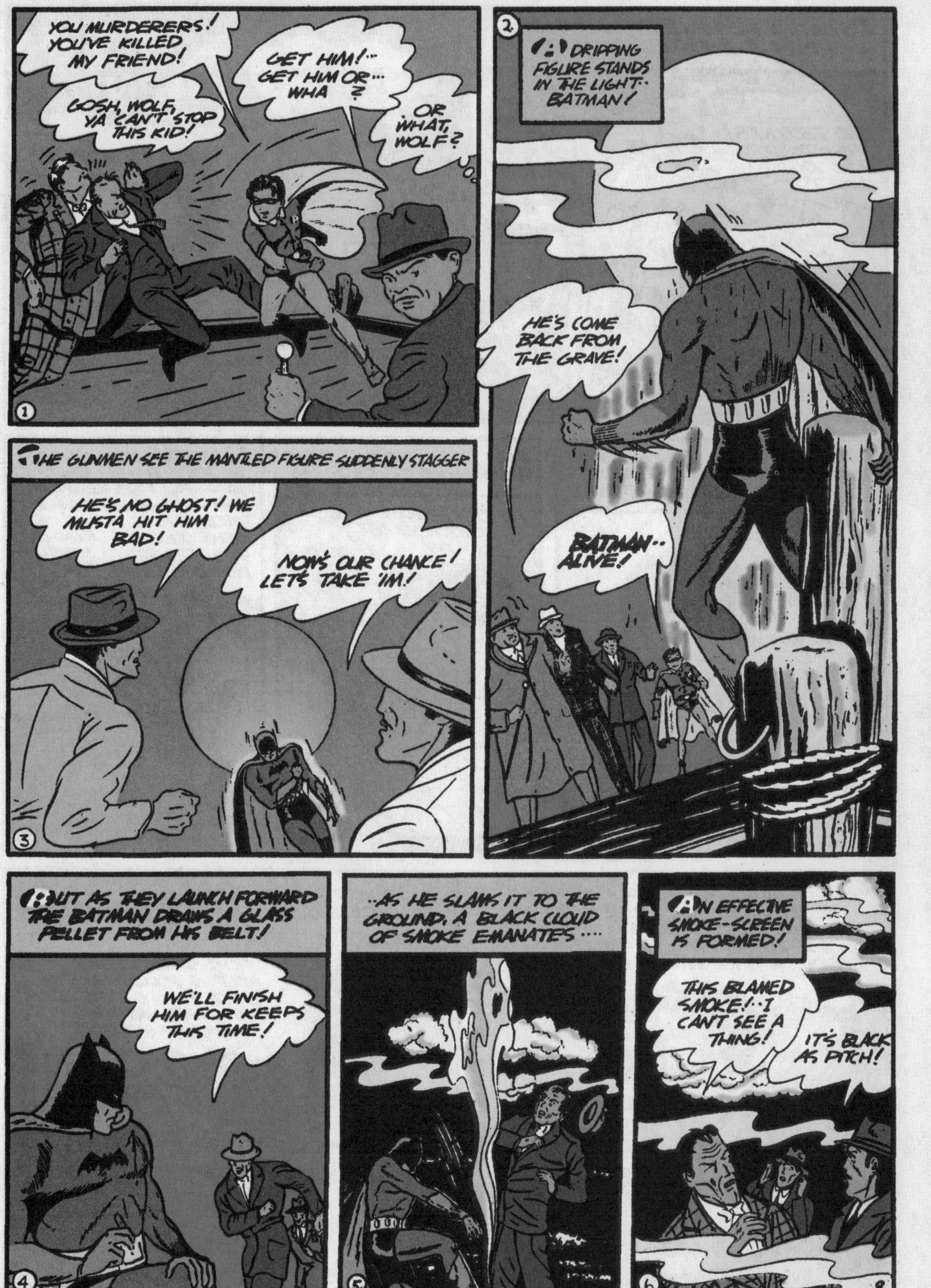
YOU MURDERERS! YOU'VE KILLED MY FRIEND!
GOSH, WOLF, YA CAN'T STOP THIS KID!
GET HIM!... GET HIM OR... WHA ?
...OR WHAT, WOLF?
A DRIPPING FIGURE STANDS IN THE LIGHT.. BATMAN!
HE'S COME BACK FROM THE GRAVE!
BATMAN.. ALIVE!
THE GUNMEN SEE THE MANTLED FIGURE SUDDENLY STAGGER
HE'S NO GHOST! WE MUSTA HIT HIM BAD!
NOW'S OUR CHANCE! LET'S TAKE 'IM!
BUT AS THEY LAUNCH FORWARD THE BATMAN DRAWS A GLASS PELLET FROM HIS BELT!
WE'LL FINISH HIM FOR KEEPS THIS TIME!
..AS HE SLAMS IT TO THE GROUND, A BLACK CLOUD OF SMOKE EMANATES....
AN EFFECTIVE SMOKE-SCREEN IS FORMED!
THIS BLAMED SMOKE!..I CAN'T SEE A THING!
IT'S BLACK AS PITCH!

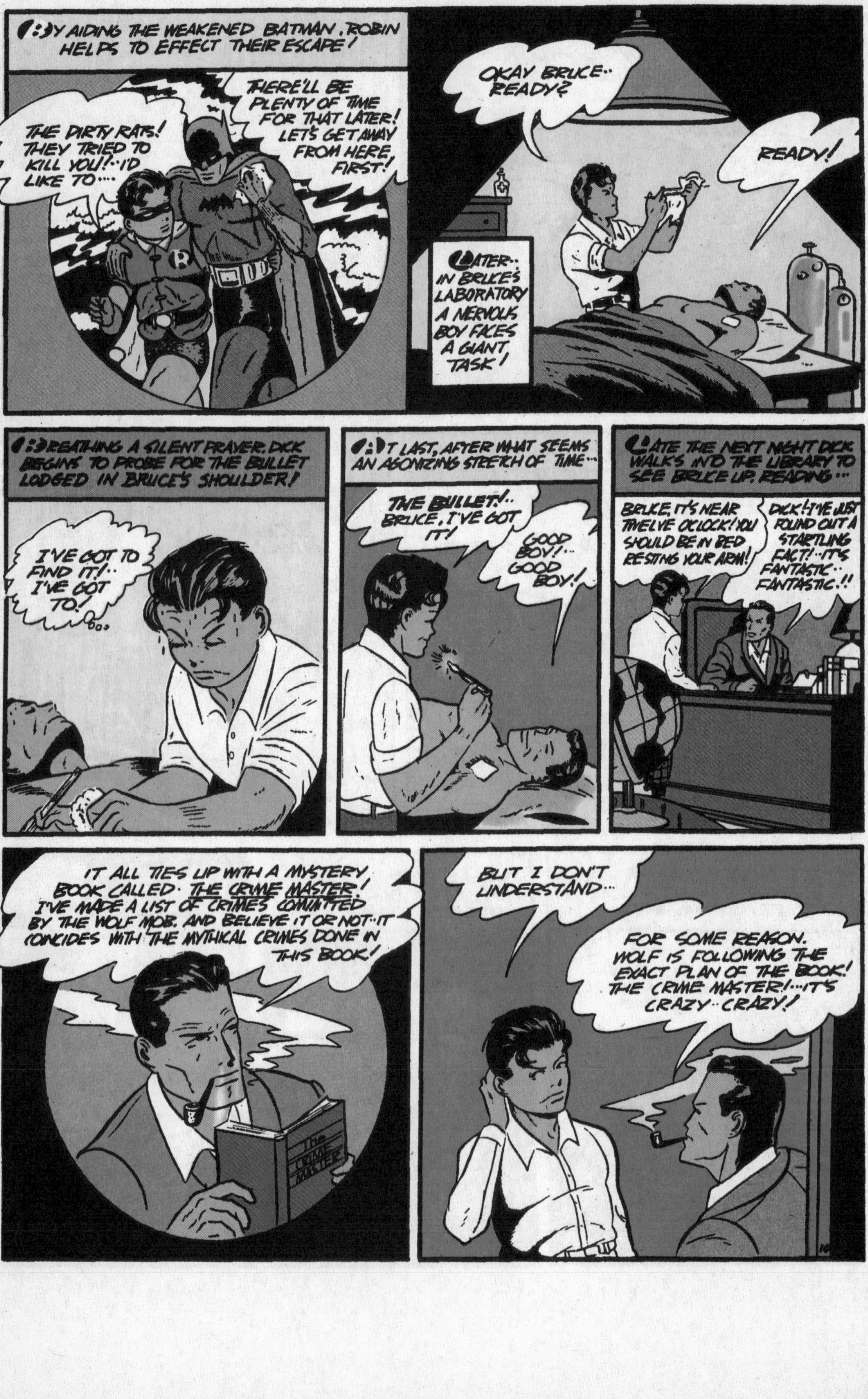
BY AIDING THE WEAKENED BATMAN, ROBIN HELPS TO EFFECT THEIR ESCAPE!
THE DIRTY RATS! THEY TRIED TO KILL YOU!..I'D LIKE TO....
THERE'LL BE PLENTY OF TIME FOR THAT LATER! LET'S GET AWAY FROM HERE, FIRST!
LATER.. IN BRUCE'S LABORATORY A NERVOUS BOY FACES A GIANT TASK!
OKAY BRUCE.. READY?
READY!
BREATHING A SILENT PRAYER, DICK BEGINS TO PROBE FOR THE BULLET LODGED IN BRUCE'S SHOULDER!
I'VE GOT TO FIND IT!.. I'VE GOT TO!
AT LAST, AFTER WHAT SEEMS AN AGONIZING STRETCH OF TIME...
THE BULLET!.. BRUCE, I'VE GOT IT!
GOOD BOY!.. GOOD BOY!
LATE THE NEXT NIGHT DICK WALKS INTO THE LIBRARY TO SEE BRUCE UP, READING...
BRUCE, IT'S NEAR TWELVE O'CLOCK! YOU SHOULD BE IN BED RESTING YOUR ARM!
DICK!-I'VE JUST FOUND OUT A STARTLING FACT!..IT'S FANTASTIC.. FANTASTIC.!!
IT ALL TIES UP WITH A MYSTERY BOOK CALLED THE CRIME MASTER! I'VE MADE A LIST OF CRIMES COMMITTED BY THE WOLF MOB, AND BELIEVE IT OR NOT..IT COINCIDES WITH THE MYTHICAL CRIMES DONE IN THIS BOOK!
The CRIME MASTER
BUT I DON'T UNDERSTAND...
FOR SOME REASON, WOLF IS FOLLOWING THE EXACT PLAN OF THE BOOK! THE CRIME MASTER!...IT'S CRAZY..CRAZY!

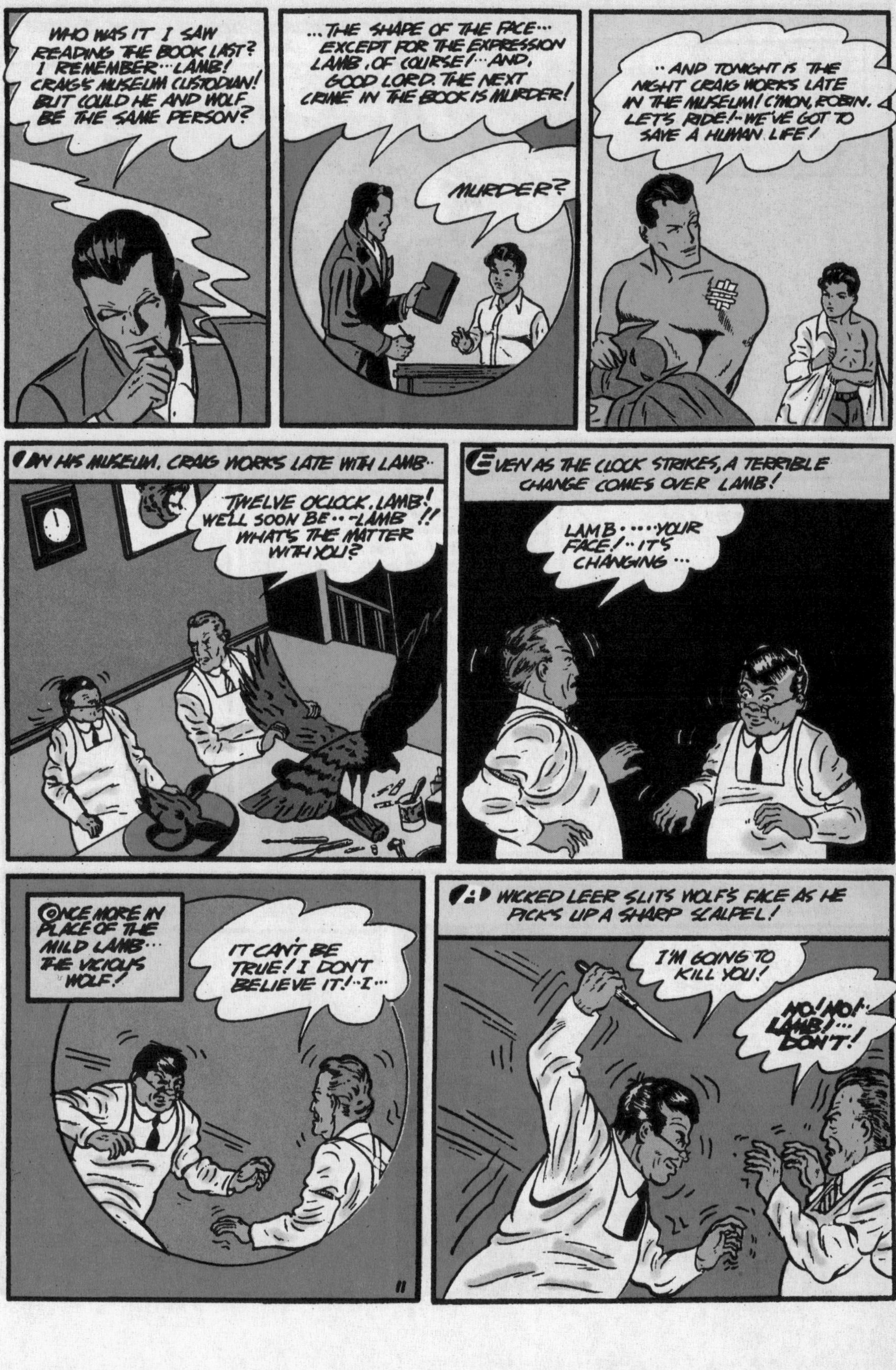
WHO WAS IT I SAW READING THE BOOK LAST? I REMEMBER···LAMB! CRAIG'S MUSEUM CUSTODIAN! BUT COULD HE AND WOLF BE THE SAME PERSON?
...THE SHAPE OF THE FACE··· EXCEPT FOR THE EXPRESSION LAMB, OF COURSE!···AND, GOOD LORD. THE NEXT CRIME IN THE BOOK IS MURDER!
MURDER?
··AND TONIGHT IS THE NIGHT CRAIG WORKS LATE IN THE MUSEUM! C'MON, ROBIN. LET'S RIDE!-WE'VE GOT TO SAVE A HUMAN LIFE!
IN HIS MUSEUM, CRAIG WORKS LATE WITH LAMB··
TWELVE O'CLOCK, LAMB! WE'LL SOON BE···LAMB!! WHAT'S THE MATTER WITH YOU?
EVEN AS THE CLOCK STRIKES, A TERRIBLE CHANGE COMES OVER LAMB!
LAMB·····YOUR FACE!··IT'S CHANGING···
ONCE MORE IN PLACE OF THE MILD LAMB··· THE VICIOUS WOLF!
IT CAN'T BE TRUE! I DON'T BELIEVE IT!··I···
A WICKED LEER SLITS WOLF'S FACE AS HE PICKS UP A SHARP SCALPEL!
I'M GOING TO KILL YOU!
NO! NO!· LAMB!··· DON'T!

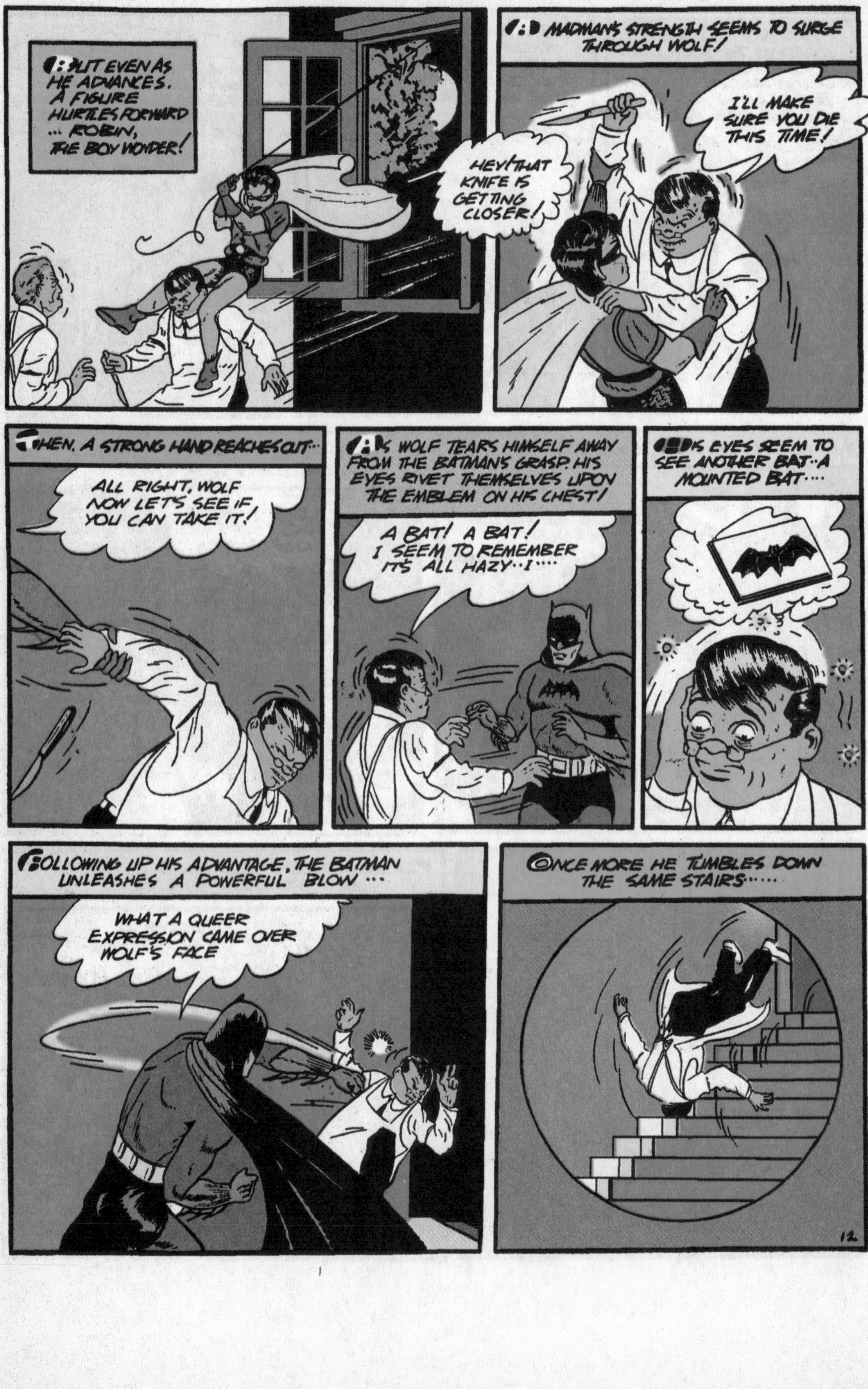
BUT EVEN AS HE ADVANCES. A FIGURE HURTLES FORWARD ... ROBIN, THE BOY WONDER!
A MADMAN'S STRENGTH SEEMS TO SURGE THROUGH WOLF!
HEY! THAT KNIFE IS GETTING CLOSER!
I'LL MAKE SURE YOU DIE THIS TIME!
THEN. A STRONG HAND REACHES OUT...
ALL RIGHT, WOLF NOW LET'S SEE IF, YOU CAN TAKE IT!
AS WOLF TEARS HIMSELF AWAY FROM THE BATMAN'S GRASP. HIS EYES RIVET THEMSELVES UPON THE EMBLEM ON HIS CHEST!
A BAT! A BAT! I SEEM TO REMEMBER IT'S ALL HAZY..I....
HIS EYES SEEM TO SEE ANOTHER BAT..A MOUNTED BAT....
FOLLOWING UP HIS ADVANTAGE. THE BATMAN UNLEASHES A POWERFUL BLOW ...
WHAT A QUEER EXPRESSION CAME OVER WOLF'S FACE
ONCE MORE HE TUMBLES DOWN THE SAME STAIRS.....
12

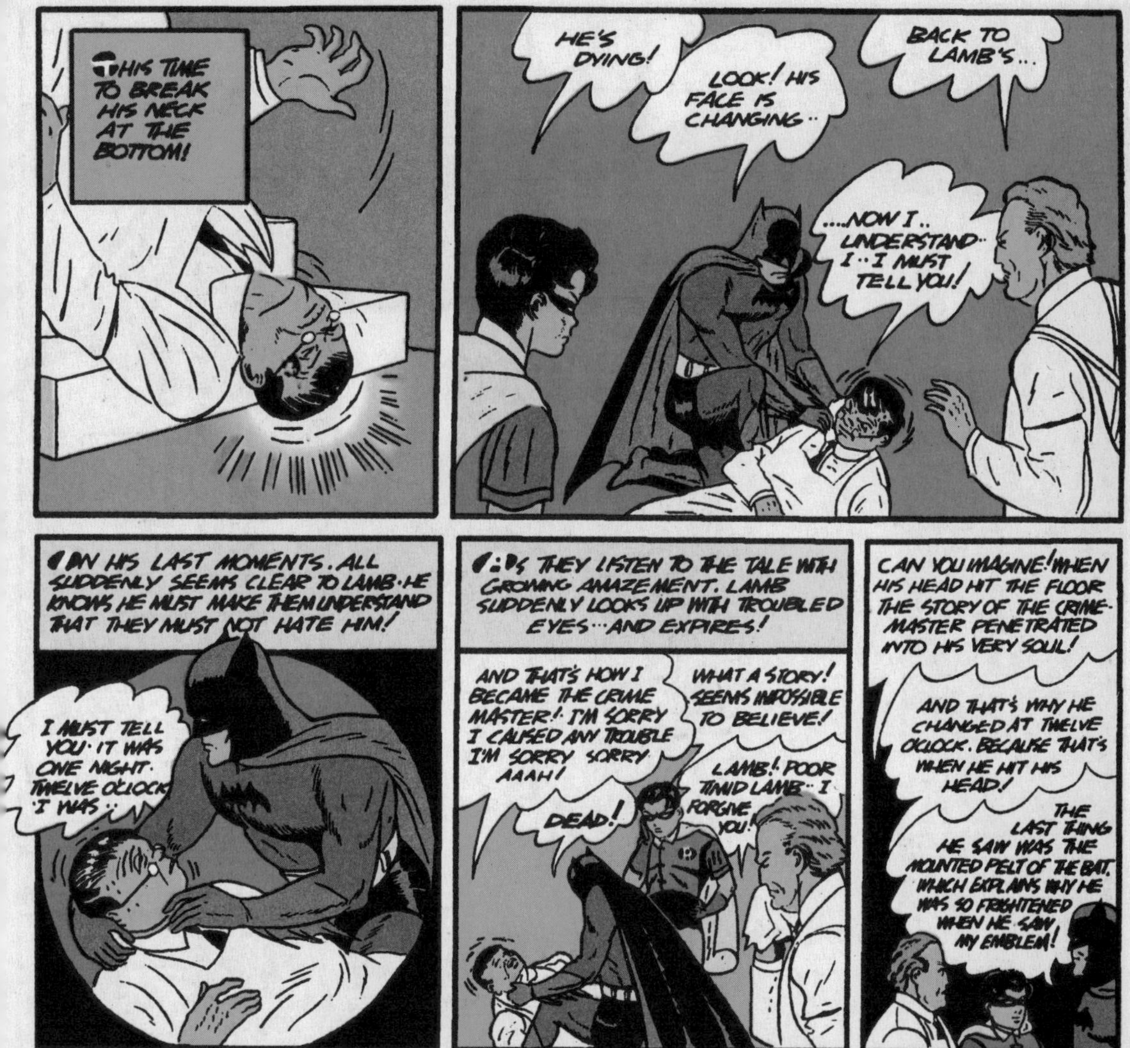
THIS TIME TO BREAK HIS NECK AT THE BOTTOM!
HE'S DYING!
LOOK! HIS FACE IS CHANGING..
BACK TO LAMB'S...
....NOW I.. UNDERSTAND.. I..I MUST TELL YOU!
IN HIS LAST MOMENTS, ALL SUDDENLY SEEMS CLEAR TO LAMB. HE KNOWS HE MUST MAKE THEM UNDERSTAND THAT THEY MUST NOT HATE HIM!
I MUST TELL YOU. IT WAS ONE NIGHT. TWELVE O'CLOCK 'I WAS..
AS THEY LISTEN TO THE TALE WITH GROWING AMAZEMENT, LAMB SUDDENLY LOOKS UP WITH TROUBLED EYES... AND EXPIRES!
AND THAT'S HOW I BECAME THE CRIME MASTER! I'M SORRY I CAUSED ANY TROUBLE I'M SORRY SORRY AAAH!
WHAT A STORY! SEEMS IMPOSSIBLE TO BELIEVE!
DEAD!
LAMB! POOR TIMID LAMB.. I FORGIVE YOU!
CAN YOU IMAGINE! WHEN HIS HEAD HIT THE FLOOR THE STORY OF THE CRIME-MASTER PENETRATED INTO HIS VERY SOUL!
AND THAT'S WHY HE CHANGED AT TWELVE O'CLOCK. BECAUSE THAT'S WHEN HE HIT HIS HEAD!
THE LAST THING HE SAW WAS THE MOUNTED PELT OF THE BAT, WHICH EXPLAINS WHY HE WAS SO FRIGHTENED WHEN HE SAW MY EMBLEM!
A BUMP ON THE HEAD CAUSED ALL THAT! THE BRAIN IS CERTAINLY A DELICATE THING!
LAMB WAS A PSYCHOLOGICAL JEKYLL AND HYDE! THIS IS THE ONLY TIME I WAS EVER SORRY TO SEE A CRIMINAL DIE! MEDICAL ATTENTION MIGHT HAVE CURED HIM!
Y'KNOW, I FEEL SORT OF SORRY FOR HIM!.. NOT FOR WOLF, BUT FOR LAMB!
BOB KANE
IT WAS OUR JOB! WE'VE GOT STEADY EMPLOYMENT ALL THE TIME IN THIS SORT OF THING!
BATMAN.. I DON'T KNOW HOW TO THANK YOU!
AS LONG AS THERE'S A CRIMINAL ABOUT, WE GO TO WORK ON HIM! YES, SIR, WORK AND HOW!
FOR a thrill a-minute
READ
THE AMAZING ADVENTURES OF
Batman
WITH
Robin
THE ORIGINAL BOY WONDER

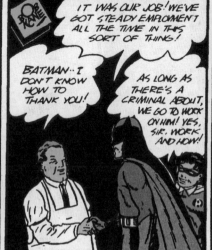

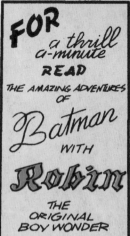

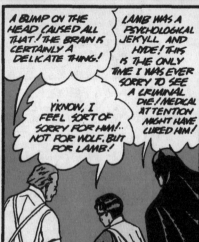

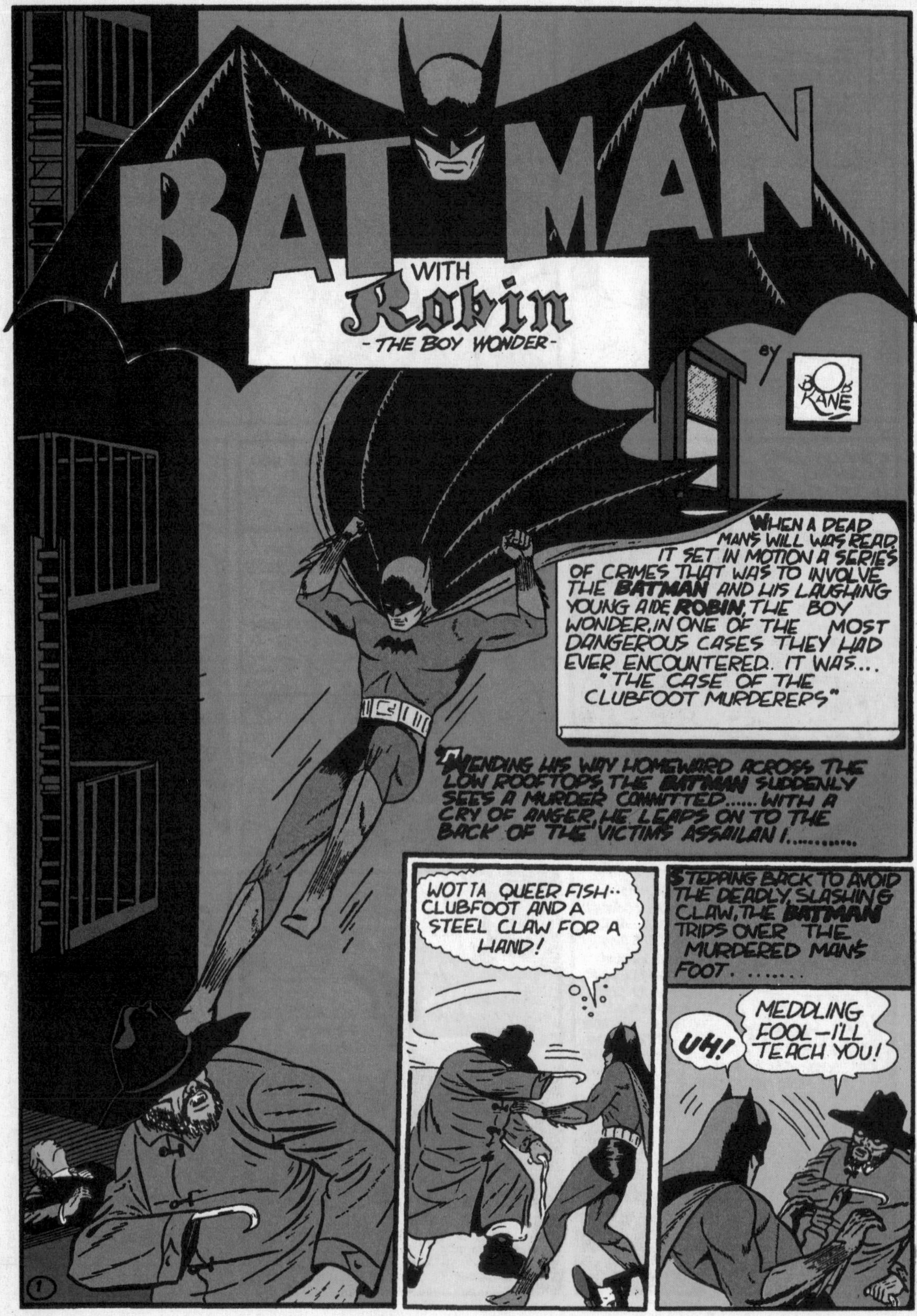
BATMAN
WITH Robin
-THE BOY WONDER-
BY BOB KANE
WHEN A DEAD MAN'S WILL WAS READ IT SET IN MOTION A SERIES OF CRIMES THAT WAS TO INVOLVE THE BATMAN AND HIS LAUGHING YOUNG AIDE, ROBIN, THE BOY WONDER, IN ONE OF THE MOST DANGEROUS CASES THEY HAD EVER ENCOUNTERED. IT WAS.... "THE CASE OF THE CLUBFOOT MURDERERS"
WENDING HIS WAY HOMEWARD ACROSS THE LOW ROOFTOPS THE BATMAN SUDDENLY SEES A MURDER COMMITTED...... WITH A CRY OF ANGER, HE LEAPS ON TO THE BACK OF THE VICTIM'S ASSAILANT!..........
WOTTA QUEER FISH.. CLUBFOOT AND A STEEL CLAW FOR A HAND!
STEPPING BACK TO AVOID THE DEADLY, SLASHING CLAW, THE BATMAN TRIPS OVER THE MURDERED MAN'S FOOT........
UH!
MEDDLING FOOL-I'LL TEACH YOU!

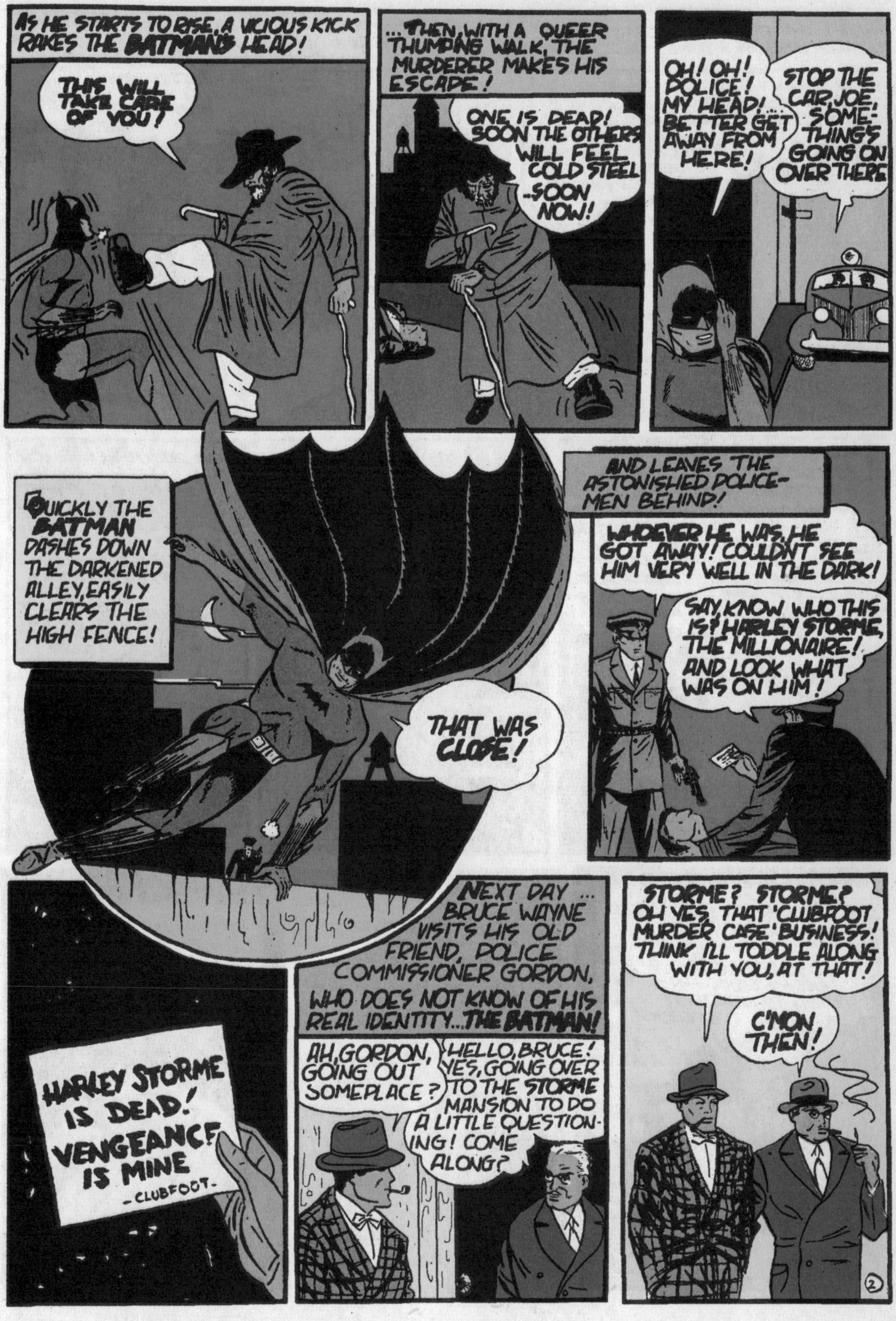
AS HE STARTS TO RISE, A VICIOUS KICK RAKES THE BATMAN'S HEAD!
THIS WILL TAKE CARE OF YOU!
...THEN, WITH A QUEER THUMPING WALK, THE MURDERER MAKES HIS ESCAPE!
ONE IS DEAD! SOON THE OTHERS WILL FEEL COLD STEEL --SOON NOW!
OH! OH! POLICE! MY HEAD!... BETTER GET AWAY FROM HERE!
STOP THE CAR JOE, SOME-THING'S GOING ON OVER THERE
QUICKLY THE BATMAN DASHES DOWN THE DARKENED ALLEY, EASILY CLEARS THE HIGH FENCE!
THAT WAS CLOSE!
AND LEAVES THE ASTONISHED POLICE-MEN BEHIND!
WHOEVER HE WAS, HE GOT AWAY! COULDN'T SEE HIM VERY WELL IN THE DARK!
SAY, KNOW WHO THIS IS? HARLEY STORME, THE MILLIONAIRE! AND LOOK WHAT WAS ON HIM!
HARLEY STORME IS DEAD! VENGEANCE IS MINE -CLUBFOOT-
NEXT DAY ... BRUCE WAYNE VISITS HIS OLD FRIEND, POLICE COMMISSIONER GORDON,
WHO DOES NOT KNOW OF HIS REAL IDENTITY...THE BATMAN!
AH, GORDON, GOING OUT SOMEPLACE?
HELLO, BRUCE! YES, GOING OVER TO THE STORME MANSION TO DO A LITTLE QUESTION-ING! COME ALONG?
STORME? STORME? OH YES, THAT 'CLUBFOOT MURDER CASE' BUSINESS! THINK I'LL TODDLE ALONG WITH YOU, AT THAT!
C'MON, THEN!
2

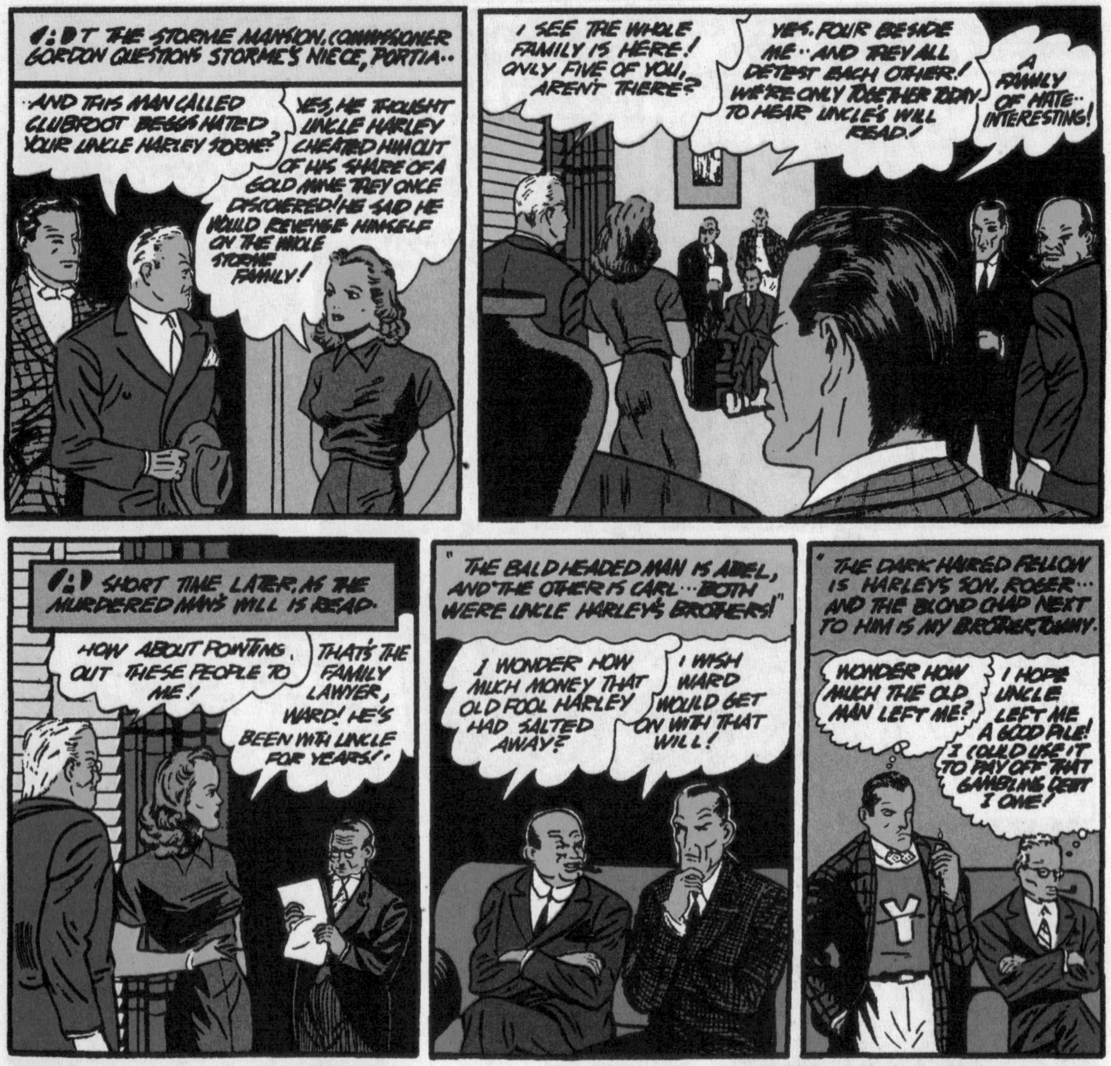
AT THE STORME MANSION, COMMISSIONER GORDON QUESTIONS STORME'S NIECE, PORTIA..
AND THIS MAN CALLED CLUBFOOT BEGGS HATED YOUR UNCLE HARLEY STORME?
YES, HE THOUGHT UNCLE HARLEY CHEATED HIM OUT OF HIS SHARE OF A GOLD MINE THEY ONCE DISCOVERED! HE SAID HE WOULD REVENGE HIMSELF ON THE WHOLE STORME FAMILY!
I SEE THE WHOLE FAMILY IS HERE! ONLY FIVE OF YOU, AREN'T THERE?
YES. FOUR BESIDE ME.. AND THEY ALL DETEST EACH OTHER! WE'RE ONLY TOGETHER TODAY TO HEAR UNCLE'S WILL READ!
A FAMILY OF HATE.. INTERESTING!
A SHORT TIME LATER, AS THE MURDERED MAN'S WILL IS READ.
HOW ABOUT POINTING OUT THESE PEOPLE TO ME!
THAT'S THE FAMILY LAWYER, WARD! HE'S BEEN WITH UNCLE FOR YEARS!
"THE BALD HEADED MAN IS ABEL, AND THE OTHER IS CARL...BOTH WERE UNCLE HARLEY'S BROTHERS!"
I WONDER HOW MUCH MONEY THAT OLD FOOL HARLEY HAD SALTED AWAY?
I WISH WARD WOULD GET ON WITH THAT WILL!
"THE DARK HAIRED FELLOW IS HARLEY'S SON, ROGER... AND THE BLOND CHAP NEXT TO HIM IS MY BROTHER, TOMMY.
WONDER HOW MUCH THE OLD MAN LEFT ME?
I HOPE UNCLE LEFT ME A GOOD PILE! I COULD USE IT TO PAY OFF THAT GAMBLING DEBT I OWE!
AT LAST THE END OF THE WILL IS REACHED..
"AND SO I LEAVE ALL MY EARTHLY GOODS HERE NOTED TO CHARITABLE INSTITUTIONS!
WHAT IS THIS,- A JOKE?
WHAT?
TO MY "BELOVED FAMILY AND FAMILY LAWYER. WARD. I LEAVE THE ENVELOPES IN THE BOX AND THEIR CONTENTS! PROFIT BY THEIR MESSAGE!
LETS HAVE THOSE ENVELOPES. WARD, THERE MUST BE MONEY IN THEM!
AND IN EACH ENVELOPE IS FOUND A PIECE OF GOLD WITH THE INSCRIPTION...
"UNITED WE STAND-DIVIDED WE FALL"
3

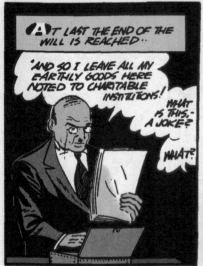

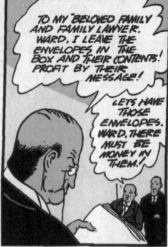

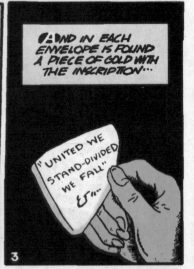

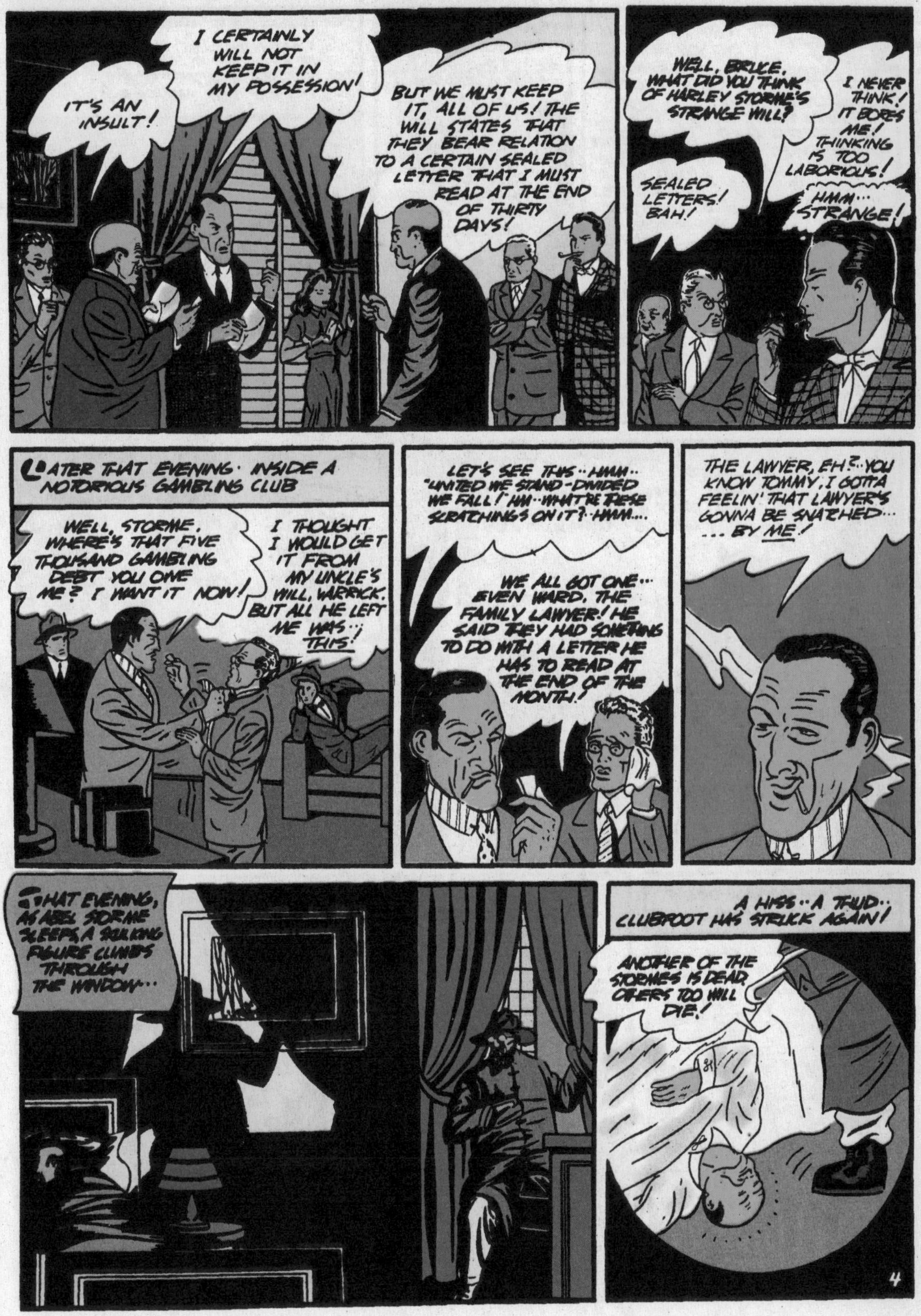
IT'S AN INSULT!
I CERTAINLY WILL NOT KEEP IT IN MY POSSESSION!
BUT WE MUST KEEP IT, ALL OF US! THE WILL STATES THAT THEY BEAR RELATION TO A CERTAIN SEALED LETTER THAT I MUST READ AT THE END OF THIRTY DAYS!
WELL, BRUCE, WHAT DID YOU THINK OF HARLEY STORME'S STRANGE WILL?
I NEVER THINK! IT BORES ME! THINKING IS TOO LABORIOUS!
SEALED LETTERS! BAH!
HMM... STRANGE!
LATER THAT EVENING · INSIDE A NOTORIOUS GAMBLING CLUB
WELL, STORME, WHERE'S THAT FIVE THOUSAND GAMBLING DEBT YOU OWE ME? I WANT IT NOW!
I THOUGHT I WOULD GET IT FROM MY UNCLE'S WILL, WARRICK. BUT ALL HE LEFT ME WAS... THIS!
LET'S SEE THIS · · HMM · · "UNITED WE STAND - DIVIDED WE FALL!" HM · · WHAT'RE THESE SCRATCHINGS ON IT? · · HMM....
WE ALL GOT ONE... EVEN WARD, THE FAMILY LAWYER! HE SAID THEY HAD SOMETHING TO DO WITH A LETTER HE HAS TO READ AT THE END OF THE MONTH!
THE LAWYER, EH? · · YOU KNOW TOMMY, I GOTTA FEELIN' THAT LAWYER'S GONNA BE SNATCHED... ... BY ME!
THAT EVENING, AS ABEL STORME SLEEPS, A SKULKING FIGURE CLIMBS THROUGH THE WINDOW...
A HISS · · A THUD · · CLUBFOOT HAS STRUCK AGAIN!
ANOTHER OF THE STORMES IS DEAD. OTHERS TOO WILL DIE!
4

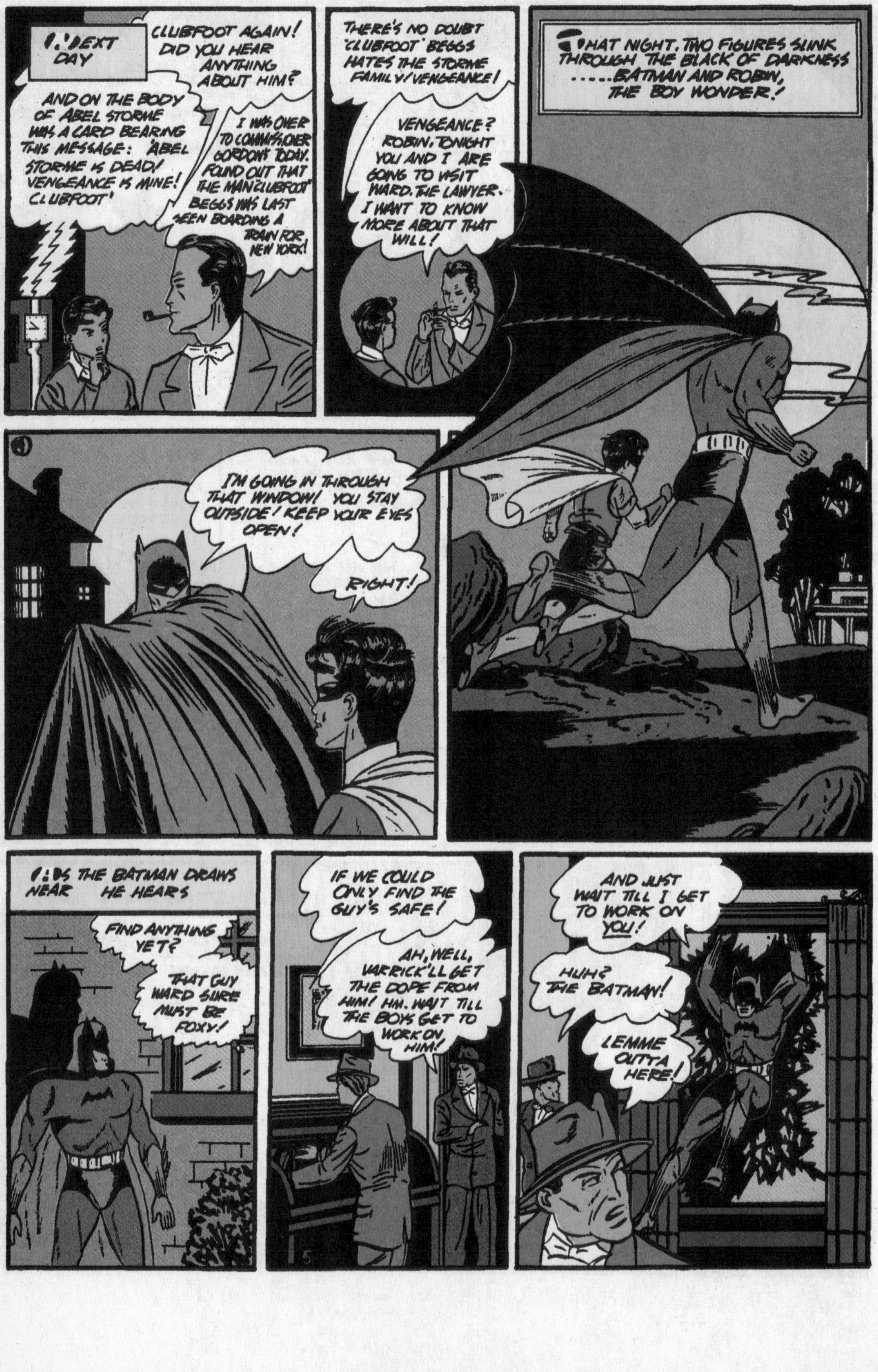
NEXT DAY
CLUBFOOT AGAIN! DID YOU HEAR ANYTHING ABOUT HIM?
AND ON THE BODY OF ABEL STORME WAS A CARD BEARING THIS MESSAGE: 'ABEL STORME IS DEAD! VENGEANCE IS MINE! CLUBFOOT'
I WAS OVER TO COMMISSIONER GORDON'S TODAY. FOUND OUT THAT THE MAN 'CLUBFOOT' BEGGS WAS LAST SEEN BOARDING A TRAIN FOR NEW YORK!
THERE'S NO DOUBT 'CLUBFOOT' BEGGS HATES THE STORME FAMILY! VENGEANCE!
VENGEANCE? ROBIN, TONIGHT YOU AND I ARE GOING TO VISIT WARD, THE LAWYER. I WANT TO KNOW MORE ABOUT THAT WILL!
THAT NIGHT, TWO FIGURES SLINK THROUGH THE BLACK OF DARKNESS .....BATMAN AND ROBIN, THE BOY WONDER!
I'M GOING IN THROUGH THAT WINDOW! YOU STAY OUTSIDE! KEEP YOUR EYES OPEN!
RIGHT!
AS THE BATMAN DRAWS NEAR HE HEARS
FIND ANYTHING YET?
THAT GUY WARD SURE MUST BE FOXY!
IF WE COULD ONLY FIND THE GUY'S SAFE!
AH, WELL, VARRICK'LL GET THE DOPE FROM HIM! HM. WAIT TILL THE BOYS GET TO WORK ON HIM!
AND JUST WAIT TILL I GET TO WORK ON YOU!
HUH? THE BATMAN!
LEMME OUTTA HERE!

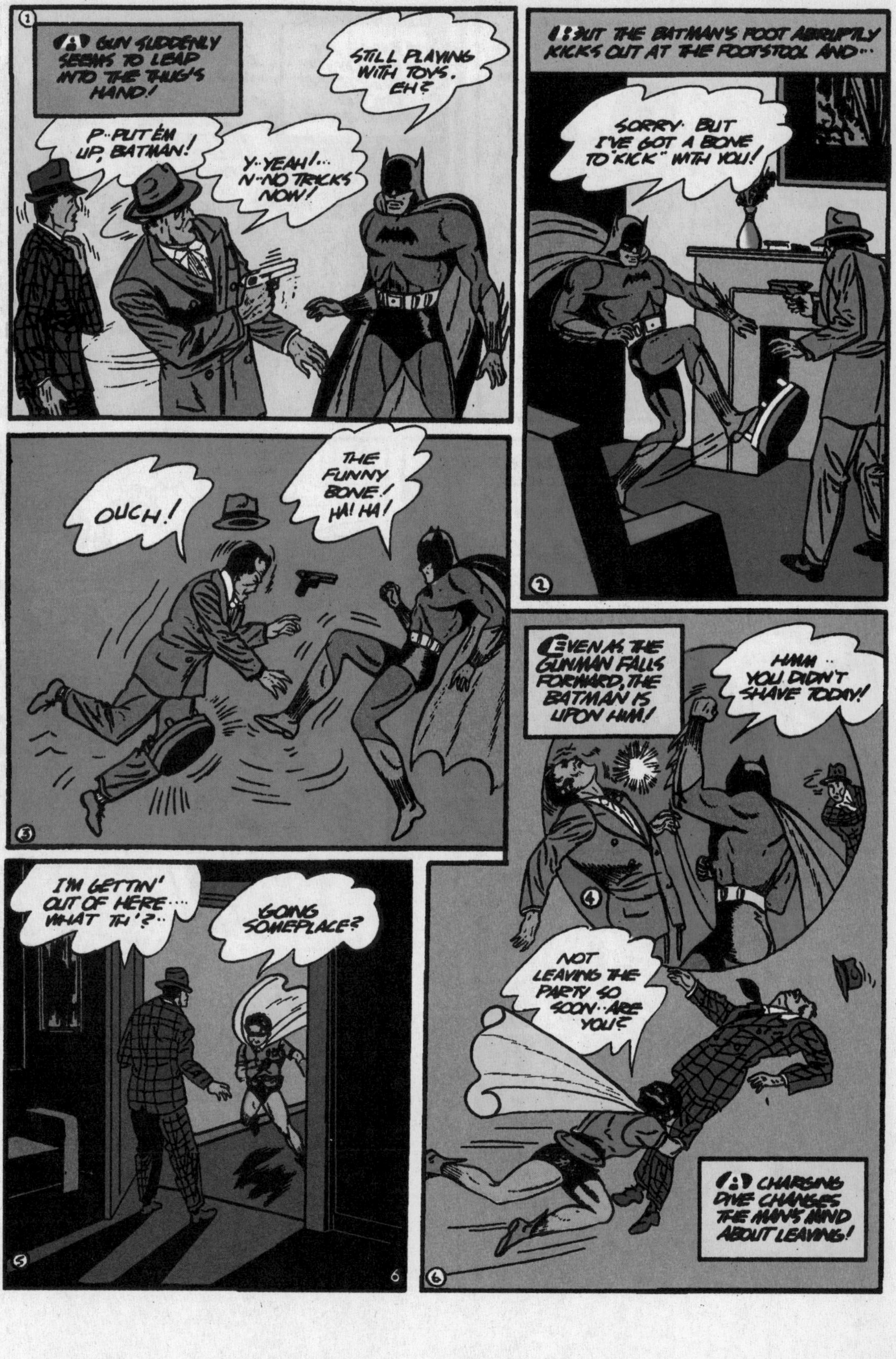
A GUN SUDDENLY SEEMS TO LEAP INTO THE THUG'S HAND!
P..PUT 'EM UP, BATMAN!
Y..YEAH!.. N..NO TRICKS NOW!
STILL PLAYING WITH TOYS, EH?
BUT THE BATMAN'S FOOT ABRUPTLY KICKS OUT AT THE FOOTSTOOL AND...
SORRY.. BUT I'VE GOT A BONE TO "KICK" WITH YOU!
OUCH!
THE FUNNY BONE! HA! HA!
EVEN AS THE GUNMAN FALLS FORWARD, THE BATMAN IS UPON HIM!
HMM.. YOU DIDN'T SHAVE TODAY!
I'M GETTIN' OUT OF HERE.... WHAT TH'?..
GOING SOMEPLACE?
NOT LEAVING THE PARTY SO SOON.. ARE YOU?
A CHARGING DIVE CHANGES THE MAN'S MIND ABOUT LEAVING!

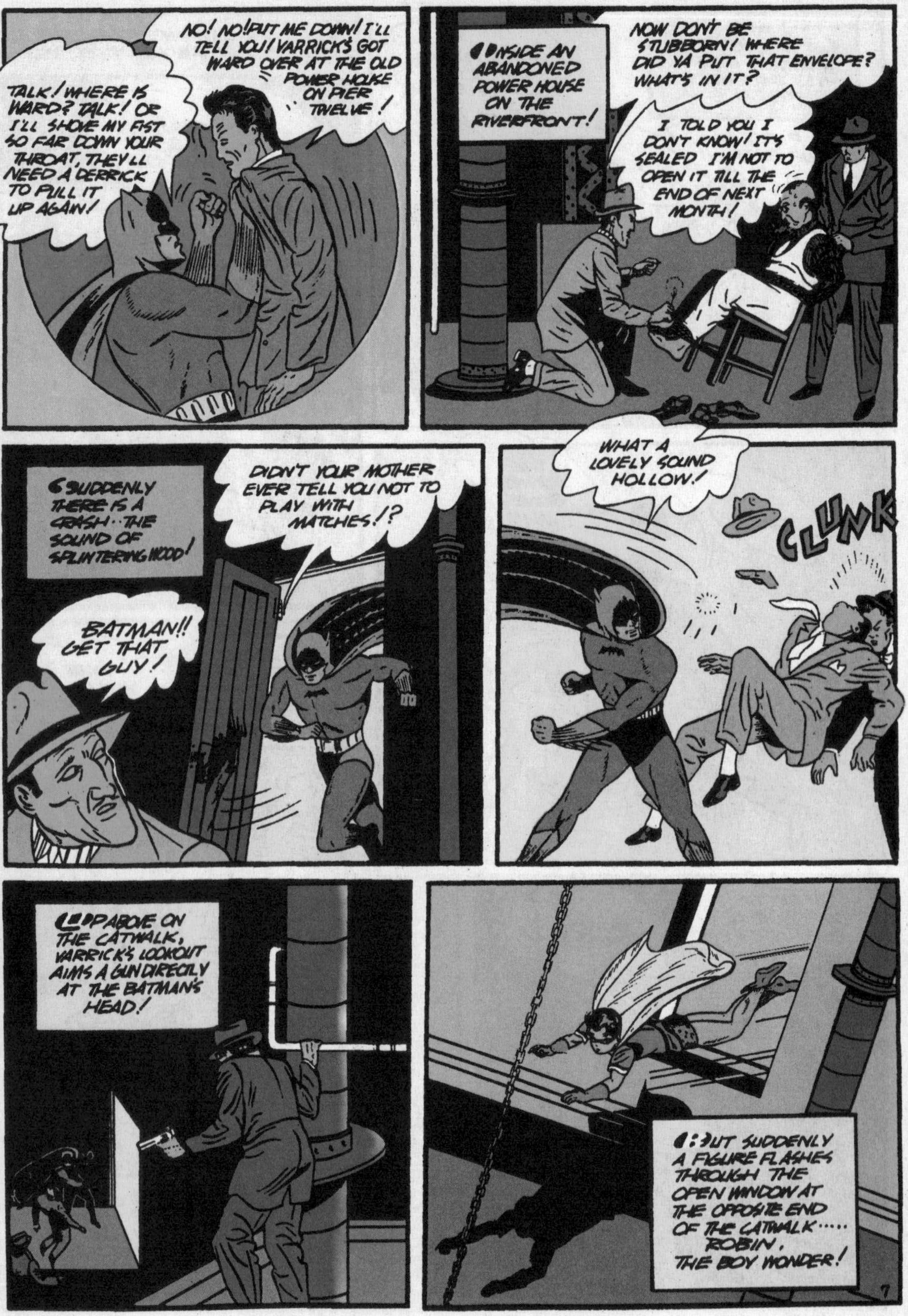
NO! NO! PUT ME DOWN! I'LL TELL YOU! VARRICK'S GOT WARD OVER AT THE OLD POWER HOUSE ON PIER TWELVE!
TALK! WHERE IS WARD? TALK! OR I'LL SHOVE MY FIST SO FAR DOWN YOUR THROAT, THEY'LL NEED A DERRICK TO PULL IT UP AGAIN!
INSIDE AN ABANDONED POWER HOUSE ON THE RIVERFRONT!
NOW DON'T BE STUBBORN! WHERE DID YA PUT THAT ENVELOPE? WHAT'S IN IT?
I TOLD YOU I DON'T KNOW! IT'S SEALED I'M NOT TO OPEN IT TILL THE END OF NEXT MONTH!
SUDDENLY THERE IS A CRASH.. THE SOUND OF SPLINTERING WOOD!
DIDN'T YOUR MOTHER EVER TELL YOU NOT TO PLAY WITH MATCHES!?
BATMAN!! GET THAT GUY!
WHAT A LOVELY SOUND HOLLOW!
CLUNK
UP ABOVE ON THE CATWALK, VARRICK'S LOOKOUT AIMS A GUN DIRECTLY AT THE BATMAN'S HEAD!
BUT SUDDENLY A FIGURE FLASHES THROUGH THE OPEN WINDOW AT THE OPPOSITE END OF THE CATWALK..... ROBIN, THE BOY WONDER!
7

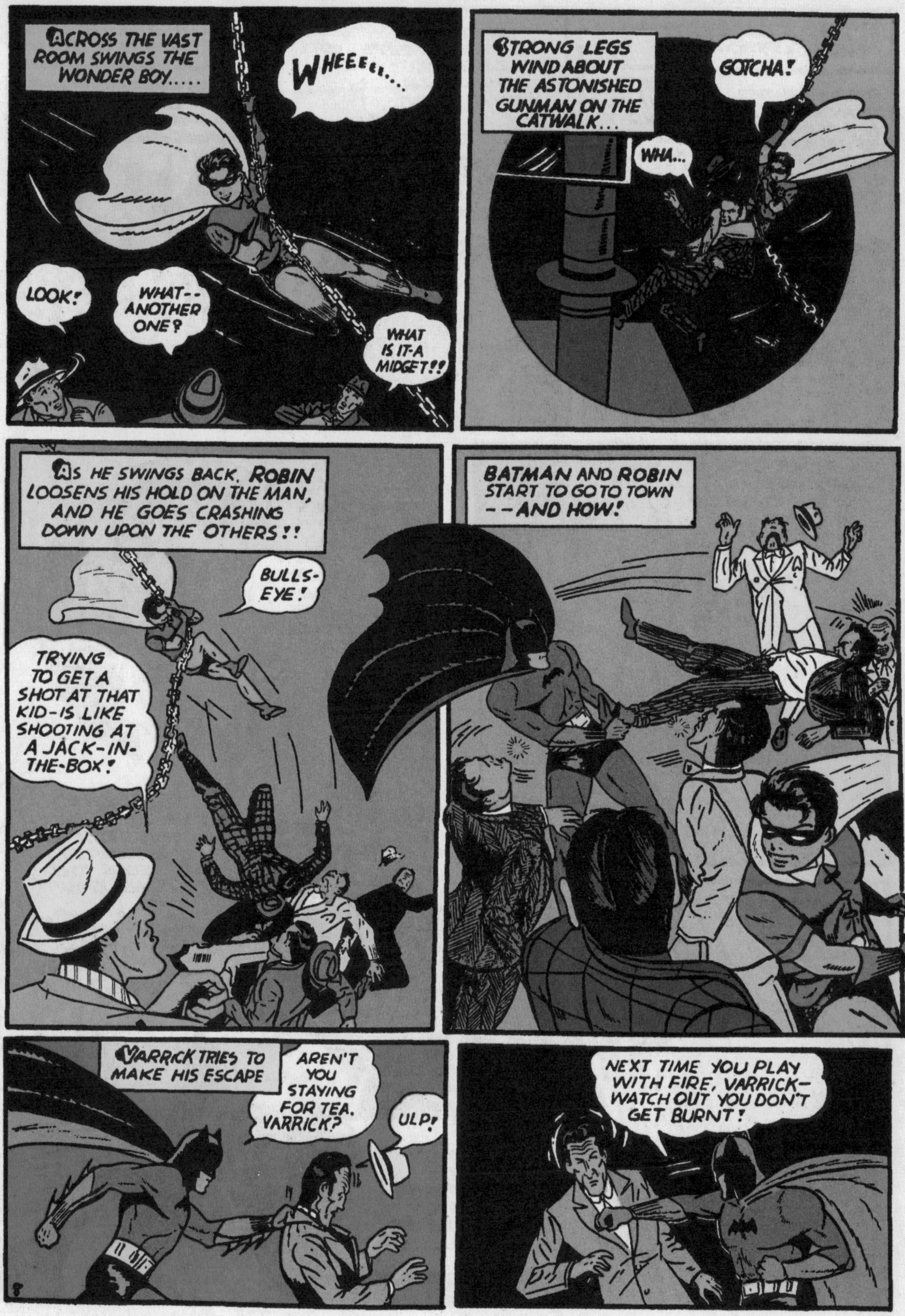
ACROSS THE VAST ROOM SWINGS THE WONDER BOY.....
WHEEEEE....
LOOK!
WHAT--ANOTHER ONE?
WHAT IS IT-A MIDGET!!
STRONG LEGS WIND ABOUT THE ASTONISHED GUNMAN ON THE CATWALK...
GOTCHA!
WHA...
AS HE SWINGS BACK, ROBIN LOOSENS HIS HOLD ON THE MAN, AND HE GOES CRASHING DOWN UPON THE OTHERS!!
BULLS-EYE!
TRYING TO GET A SHOT AT THAT KID-IS LIKE SHOOTING AT A JACK-IN-THE-BOX!
BATMAN AND ROBIN START TO GO TO TOWN --AND HOW!
VARRICK TRIES TO MAKE HIS ESCAPE
AREN'T YOU STAYING FOR TEA, VARRICK?
ULP!
NEXT TIME YOU PLAY WITH FIRE, VARRICK-WATCH OUT YOU DON'T GET BURNT!

Panel 1: "...WARD IS QUICKLY FREED... THEN QUESTIONED

VARRICK WANTED TO KNOW WHAT WAS IN THAT ENVELOPE... HE HAS SOME CRAZY IDEA THAT THE SCRATCHINGS ON THE TOKENS MEAN SOMETHING!

PERHAPS THEY DO!! YOU WOULDN'T KNOW WHAT WAS IN THE ENVELOPE, WOULD YOU?

Panel 2: OF COURSE NOT! THE ENVELOPE IS SEALED! YOU DON'T THINK I'D OPEN IT, DO YOU?

SORRY, JUST MY CURIOSITY!.. NOW, IF YOU'LL EXCUSE ME...

Panel 3: AT HOME, BRUCE PONDERS OVER A STRANGE PROBLEM...

VARRICK WAS SMART ENOUGH TO KNOW THERE WAS SOMETHING VALUABLE ABOUT THIS TOKEN THOUGH THE STORMES WERE TOO STUPID TO SEE IT!

Panel 4: THOSE FUNNY MARKINGS...AND THE MOTTO "UNITED WE STAND".. "DIVIDED WE FALL".. HMMM!

Panel 5: THE STORME'S ARE DIVIDED... AND THEY ALL RECEIVED A TOKEN- WHAT IF THEY WERE UNITED AND THE TOKENS UNITED? THAT'S IT.. OF COURSE! "UNITED WE STAND!"

Panel 6: YOU MEAN.. IF THE TOKENS WERE PUT TOGETHER THEY MIGHT MEAN SOMETHING?

..AND THAT SEALED LETTER AT WARD'S PLACE EXPLAINS IT ALL! I'VE GOT TO GET THAT LETTER TONIGHT!

ROBIN, YOU GO OVER TO ROGER STORME'S HOUSE JUST IN CASE "CLUBFOOT" SHOULD DECIDE TO GO PROWLING TONIGHT!

RIGHT!

Panel 7: THAT NIGHT.. BATMAN.. THE BLACK KNIGHT AND ROBIN, THE BOY WONDER!

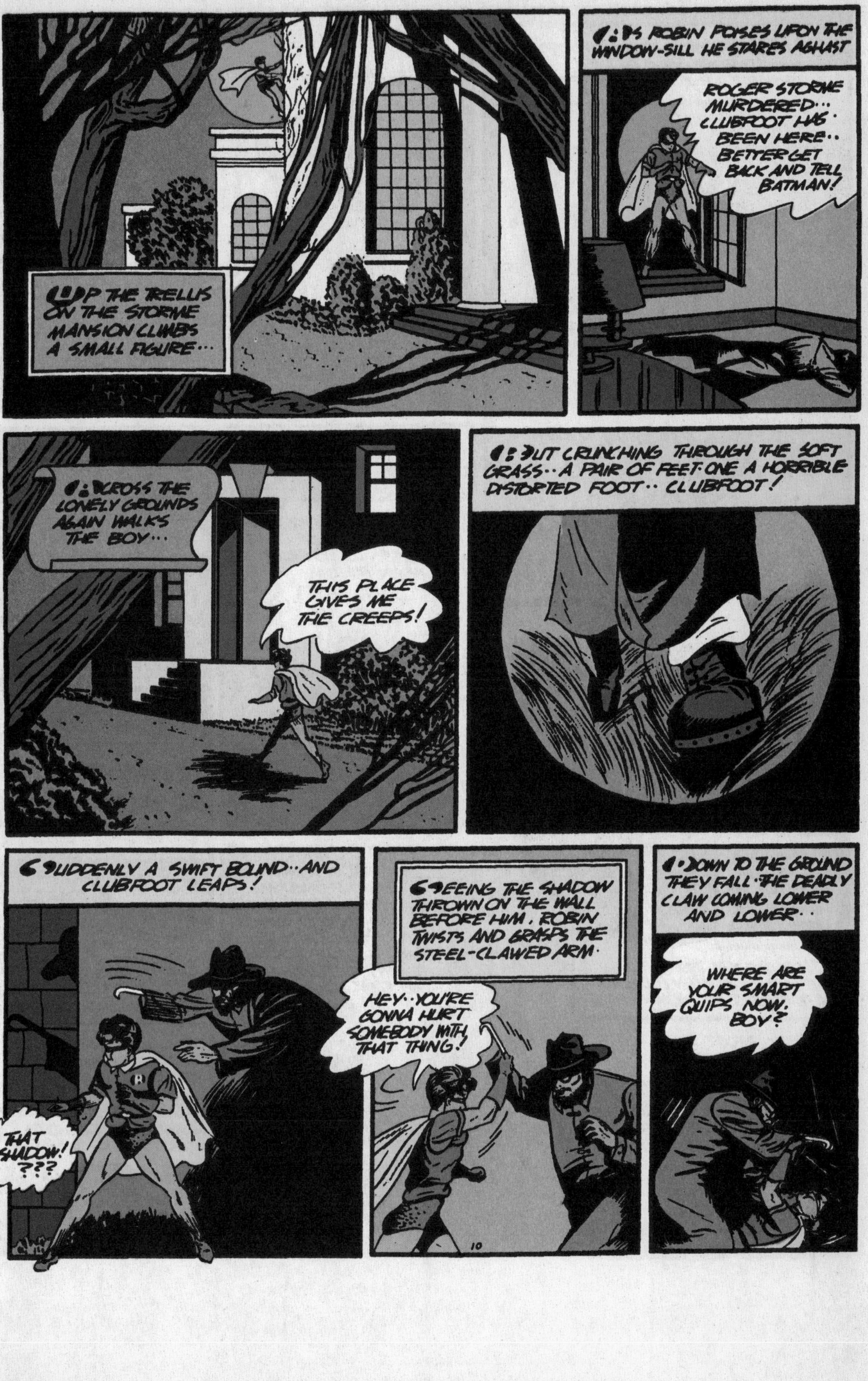
UP THE TRELLIS ON THE STORME MANSION CLIMBS A SMALL FIGURE...
AS ROBIN POISES UPON THE WINDOW-SILL HE STARES AGHAST
ROGER STORME MURDERED... CLUBFOOT HAS BEEN HERE.. BETTER GET BACK AND TELL BATMAN!
ACROSS THE LONELY GROUNDS AGAIN WALKS THE BOY...
THIS PLACE GIVES ME THE CREEPS!
BUT CRUNCHING THROUGH THE SOFT GRASS.. A PAIR OF FEET-ONE A HORRIBLE DISTORTED FOOT.. CLUBFOOT!
SUDDENLY A SWIFT BOUND..AND CLUBFOOT LEAPS!
THAT SHADOW! ???
SEEING THE SHADOW THROWN ON THE WALL BEFORE HIM, ROBIN TWISTS AND GRASPS THE STEEL-CLAWED ARM.
HEY.. YOU'RE GONNA HURT SOMEBODY WITH THAT THING!
DOWN TO THE GROUND THEY FALL-THE DEADLY CLAW COMING LOWER AND LOWER..
WHERE ARE YOUR SMART QUIPS NOW, BOY?
10

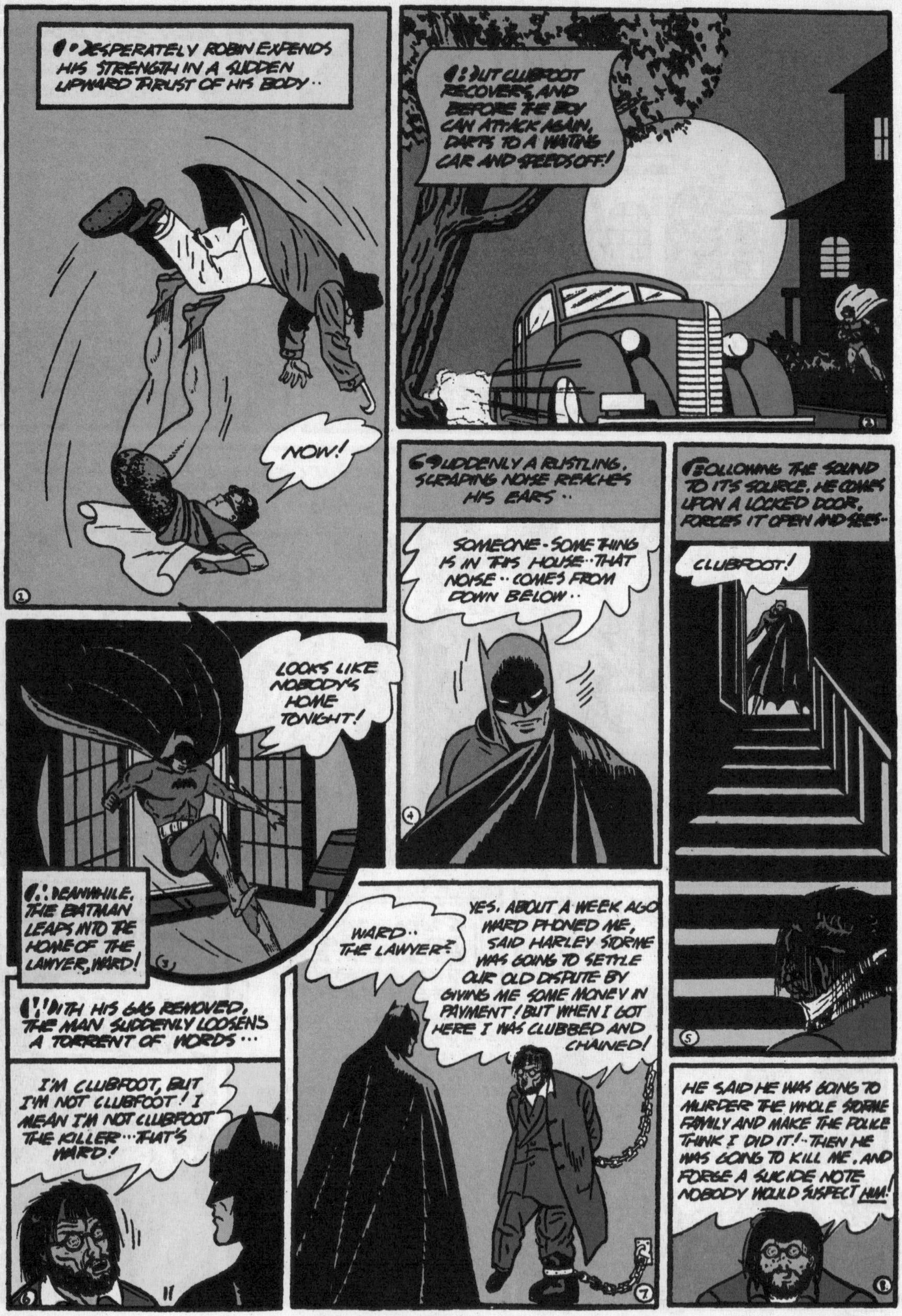
DESPERATELY ROBIN EXPENDS HIS STRENGTH IN A SUDDEN UPWARD THRUST OF HIS BODY..
NOW!
BUT CLUBFOOT RECOVERS, AND BEFORE THE BOY CAN ATTACK AGAIN, DARTS TO A WAITING CAR AND SPEEDS OFF!
LOOKS LIKE NOBODY'S HOME TONIGHT!
MEANWHILE, THE BATMAN LEAPS INTO THE HOME OF THE LAWYER, WARD!
SUDDENLY A RUSTLING, SCRAPING NOISE REACHES HIS EARS..
SOMEONE - SOME THING IS IN THIS HOUSE.. THAT NOISE.. COMES FROM DOWN BELOW..
FOLLOWING THE SOUND TO IT'S SOURCE, HE COMES UPON A LOCKED DOOR, FORCES IT OPEN AND SEES..
CLUBFOOT!
WITH HIS GAG REMOVED, THE MAN SUDDENLY LOOSENS A TORRENT OF WORDS...
I'M CLUBFOOT, BUT I'M NOT CLUBFOOT! I MEAN I'M NOT CLUBFOOT THE KILLER... THAT'S WARD!
WARD.. THE LAWYER?
YES. ABOUT A WEEK AGO WARD PHONED ME, SAID HARLEY STORME WAS GOING TO SETTLE OUR OLD DISPUTE BY GIVING ME SOME MONEY IN PAYMENT! BUT WHEN I GOT HERE I WAS CLUBBED AND CHAINED!
HE SAID HE WAS GOING TO MURDER THE WHOLE STORME FAMILY AND MAKE THE POLICE THINK I DID IT!.. THEN HE WAS GOING TO KILL ME, AND FORGE A SUICIDE NOTE NOBODY WOULD SUSPECT HIM!

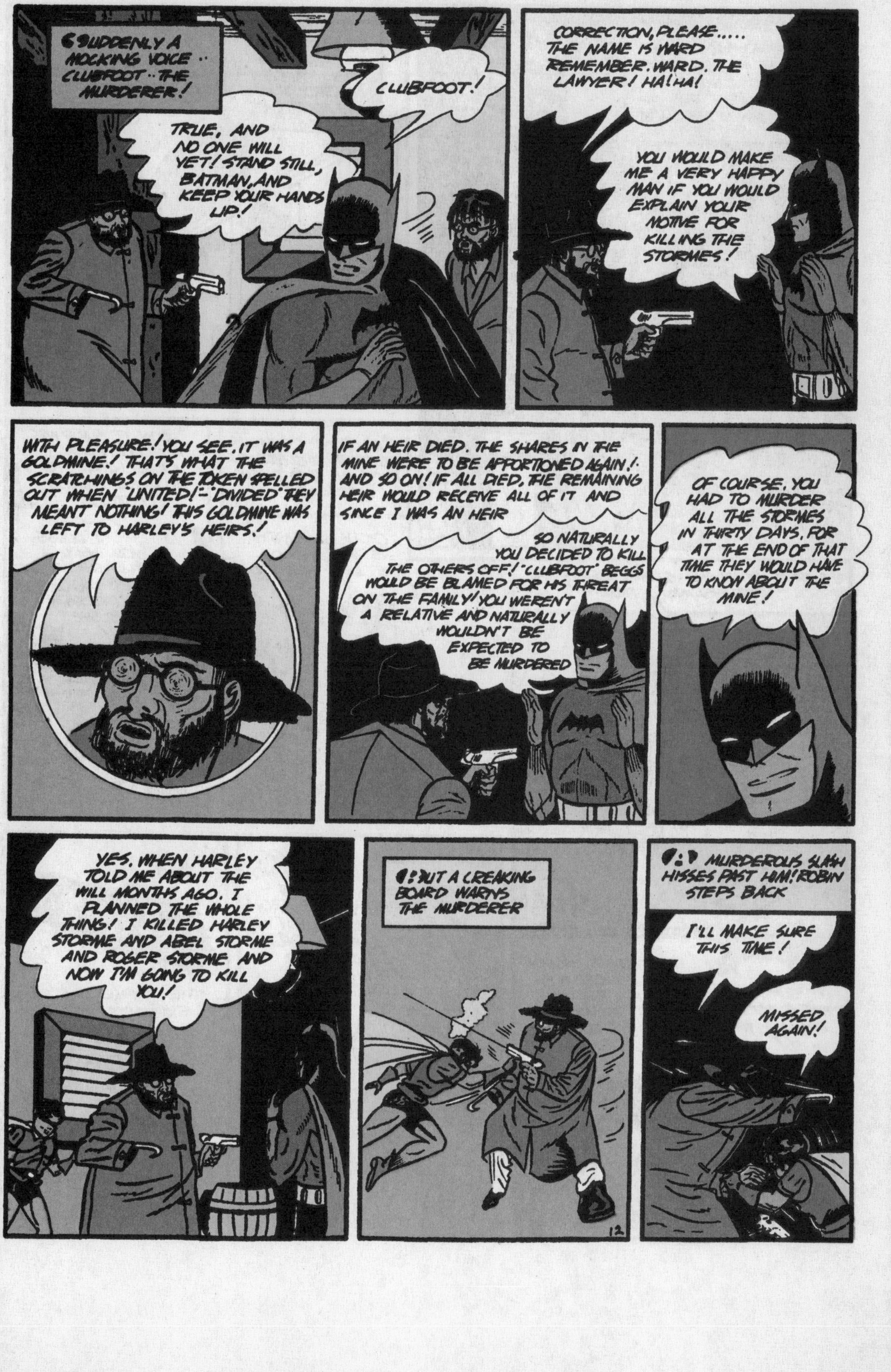
SUDDENLY A MOCKING VOICE .. CLUBFOOT .. THE MURDERER!
CLUBFOOT!
TRUE, AND NO ONE WILL YET! STAND STILL, BATMAN, AND KEEP YOUR HANDS UP!
CORRECTION, PLEASE..... THE NAME IS WARD REMEMBER. WARD. THE LAWYER! HA! HA!
YOU WOULD MAKE ME A VERY HAPPY MAN IF YOU WOULD EXPLAIN YOUR MOTIVE FOR KILLING THE STORMES!
WITH PLEASURE! YOU SEE, IT WAS A GOLDMINE! THAT'S WHAT THE SCRATCHINGS ON THE TOKEN SPELLED OUT WHEN "UNITED!"-"DIVIDED" THEY MEANT NOTHING! THIS GOLDMINE WAS LEFT TO HARLEY'S HEIRS!
IF AN HEIR DIED, THE SHARES IN THE MINE WERE TO BE APPORTIONED AGAIN!. AND SO ON! IF ALL DIED, THE REMAINING HEIR WOULD RECEIVE ALL OF IT AND SINCE I WAS AN HEIR
SO NATURALLY YOU DECIDED TO KILL THE OTHERS OFF! "CLUBFOOT" BEGGS WOULD BE BLAMED FOR HIS THREAT ON THE FAMILY! YOU WEREN'T A RELATIVE AND NATURALLY WOULDN'T BE EXPECTED TO BE MURDERED
OF COURSE, YOU HAD TO MURDER ALL THE STORMES IN THIRTY DAYS, FOR AT THE END OF THAT TIME THEY WOULD HAVE TO KNOW ABOUT THE MINE!
YES, WHEN HARLEY TOLD ME ABOUT THE WILL MONTHS AGO, I PLANNED THE WHOLE THING! I KILLED HARLEY STORME AND ABEL STORME AND ROGER STORME AND NOW I'M GOING TO KILL YOU!
BUT A CREAKING BOARD WARNS THE MURDERER
A MURDEROUS SLASH HISSES PAST HIM! ROBIN STEPS BACK
I'LL MAKE SURE THIS TIME!
MISSED AGAIN!

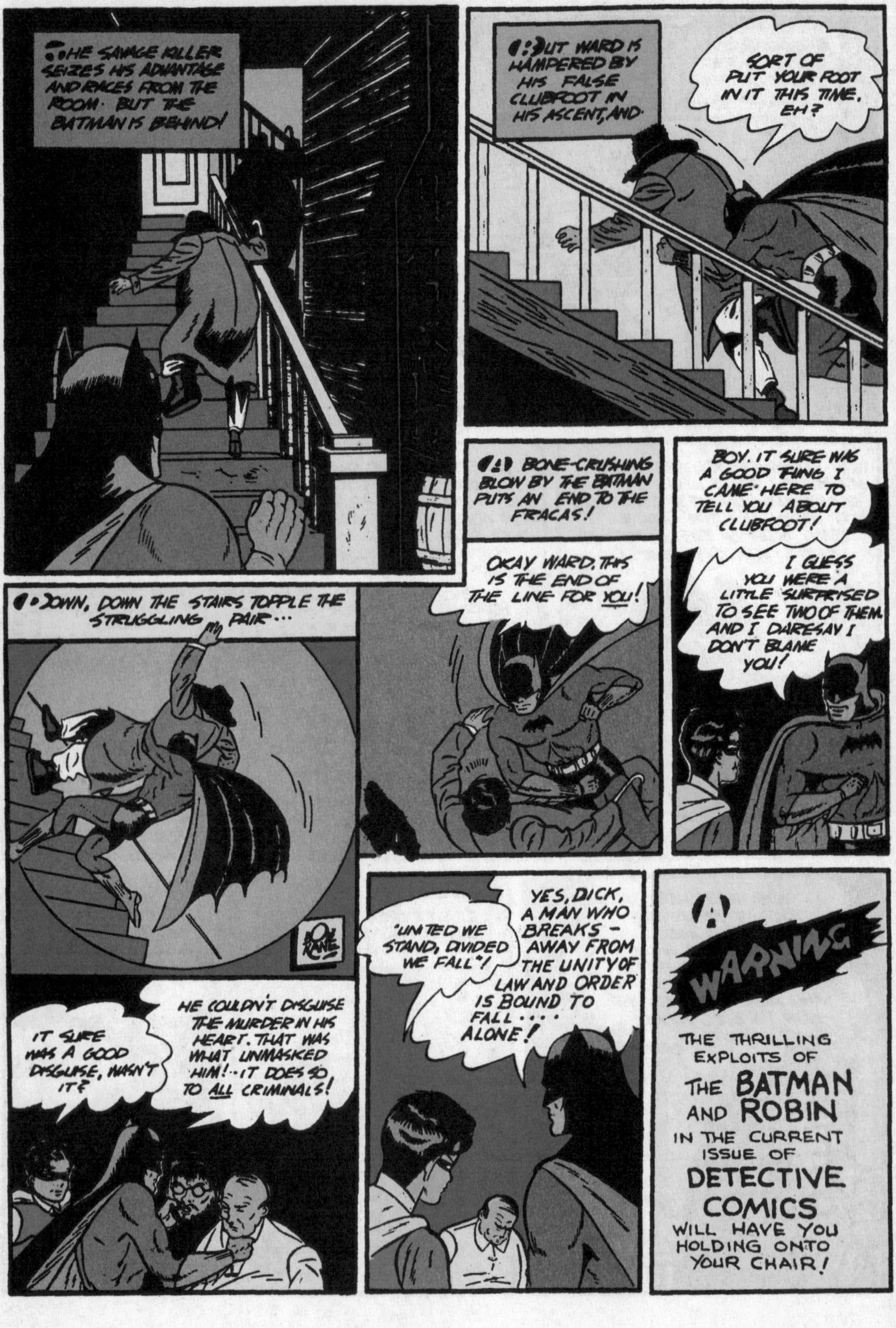
THE SAVAGE KILLER SEIZES HIS ADVANTAGE AND RACES FROM THE ROOM. BUT THE BATMAN IS BEHIND!
BUT WARD IS HAMPERED BY HIS FALSE CLUBFOOT IN HIS ASCENT, AND-
SORT OF PUT YOUR FOOT IN IT THIS TIME, EH?
DOWN, DOWN THE STAIRS TOPPLE THE STRUGGLING PAIR...
A BONE-CRUSHING BLOW BY THE BATMAN PUTS AN END TO THE FRACAS!
OKAY WARD, THIS IS THE END OF THE LINE FOR YOU!
BOY, IT SURE WAS A GOOD THING I CAME HERE TO TELL YOU ABOUT CLUBFOOT!
I GUESS YOU WERE A LITTLE SURPRISED TO SEE TWO OF THEM. AND I DARESAY I DON'T BLAME YOU!
IT SURE WAS A GOOD DISGUISE, WASN'T IT?
HE COULDN'T DISGUISE THE MURDER IN HIS HEART. THAT WAS WHAT UNMASKED HIM!.. IT DOES SO TO ALL CRIMINALS!
"UNITED WE STAND, DIVIDED WE FALL"!
YES, DICK, A MAN WHO BREAKS - AWAY FROM THE UNITY OF LAW AND ORDER IS BOUND TO FALL.... ALONE!
A WARNING
THE THRILLING EXPLOITS OF THE BATMAN AND ROBIN IN THE CURRENT ISSUE OF DETECTIVE COMICS WILL HAVE YOU HOLDING ONTO YOUR CHAIR!

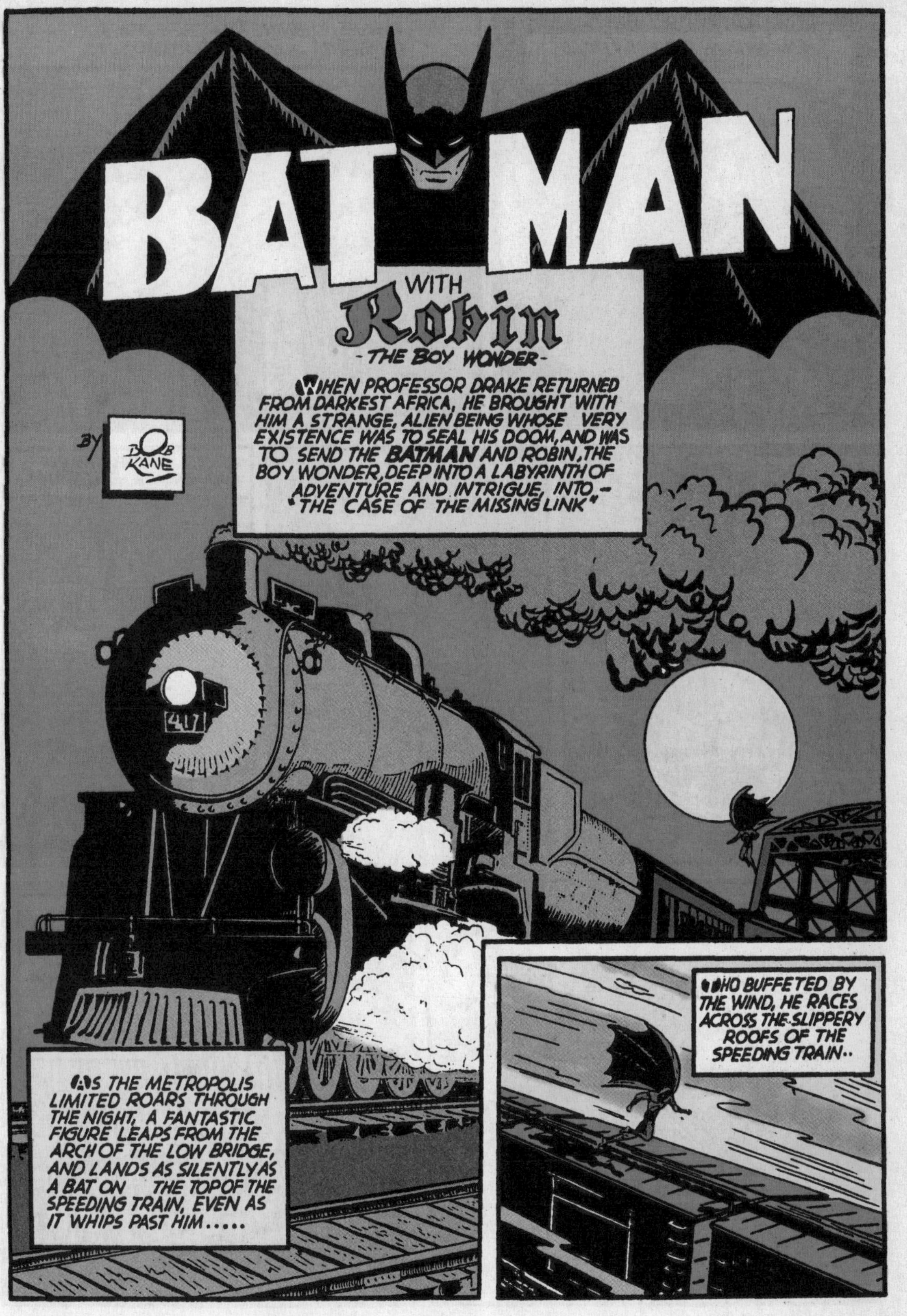
BATMAN
WITH
Robin
-THE BOY WONDER-
WHEN PROFESSOR DRAKE RETURNED FROM DARKEST AFRICA, HE BROUGHT WITH HIM A STRANGE, ALIEN BEING WHOSE VERY EXISTENCE WAS TO SEAL HIS DOOM, AND WAS TO SEND THE BATMAN AND ROBIN, THE BOY WONDER, DEEP INTO A LABYRINTH OF ADVENTURE AND INTRIGUE, INTO,- "THE CASE OF THE MISSING LINK"
BY BOB KANE
AS THE METROPOLIS LIMITED ROARS THROUGH THE NIGHT, A FANTASTIC FIGURE LEAPS FROM THE ARCH OF THE LOW BRIDGE, AND LANDS AS SILENTLY AS A BAT ON THE TOP OF THE SPEEDING TRAIN, EVEN AS IT WHIPS PAST HIM.....
WHO BUFFETED BY THE WIND, HE RACES ACROSS THE SLIPPERY ROOFS OF THE SPEEDING TRAIN..

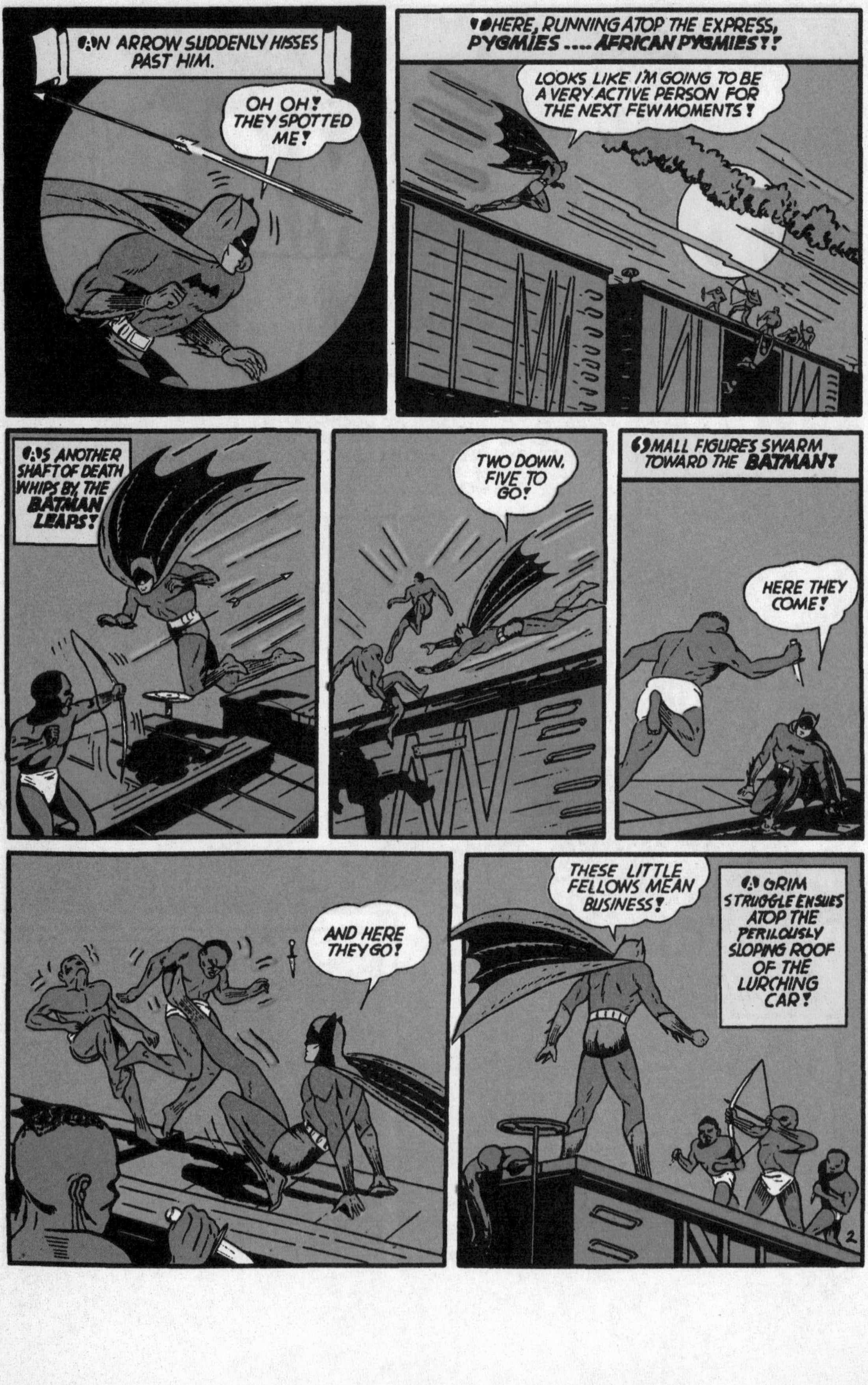
AN ARROW SUDDENLY HISSES PAST HIM.
OH OH! THEY SPOTTED ME!
THERE, RUNNING ATOP THE EXPRESS, PYGMIES .... AFRICAN PYGMIES!!
LOOKS LIKE I'M GOING TO BE A VERY ACTIVE PERSON FOR THE NEXT FEW MOMENTS!
AS ANOTHER SHAFT OF DEATH WHIPS BY, THE BATMAN LEAPS!
TWO DOWN, FIVE TO GO!
SMALL FIGURES SWARM TOWARD THE BATMAN!
HERE THEY COME!
AND HERE THEY GO!
THESE LITTLE FELLOWS MEAN BUSINESS!
A GRIM STRUGGLE ENSUES ATOP THE PERILOUSLY SLOPING ROOF OF THE LURCHING CAR!
2

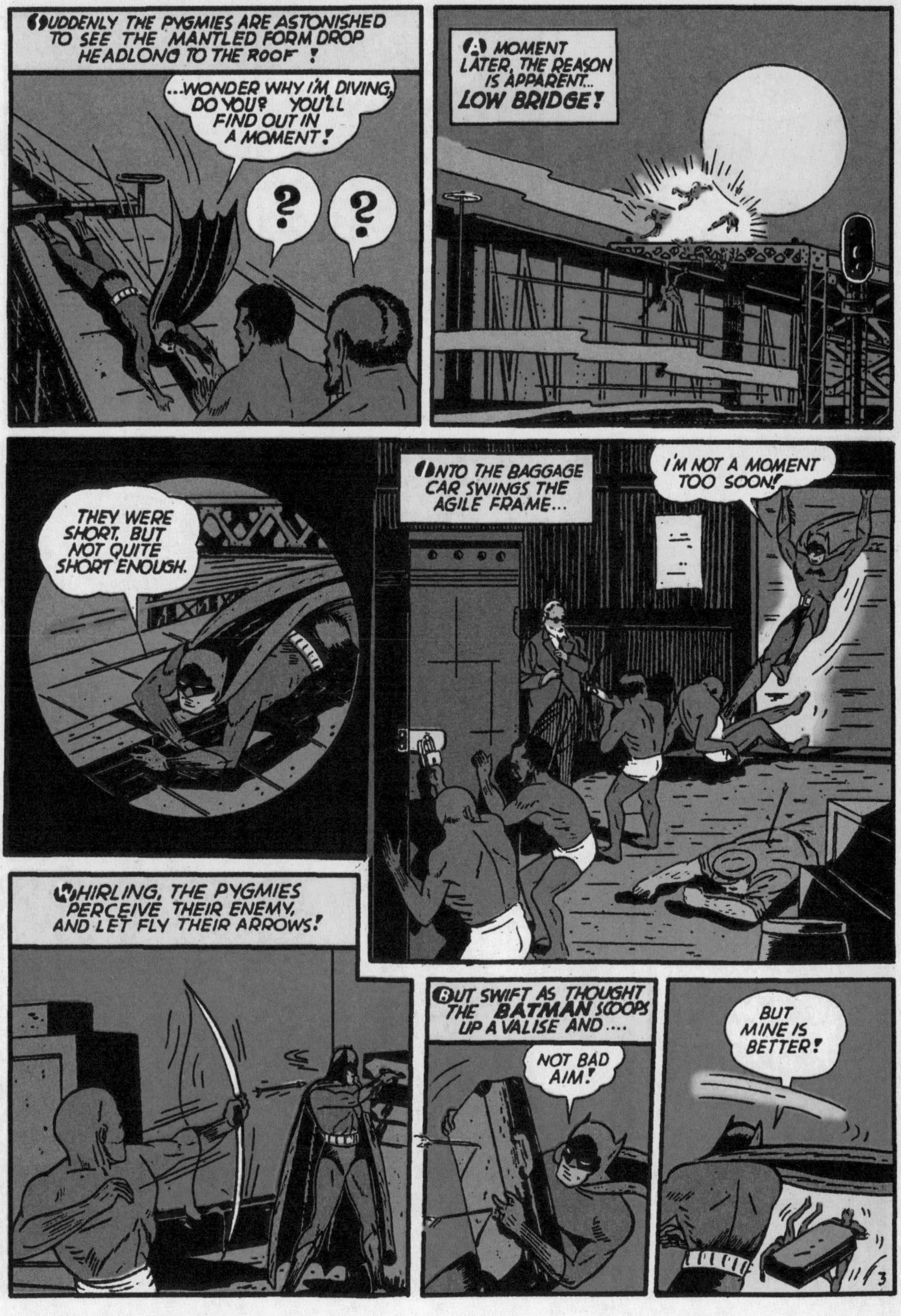
SUDDENLY THE PYGMIES ARE ASTONISHED TO SEE THE MANTLED FORM DROP HEADLONG TO THE ROOF !
...WONDER WHY I'M DIVING, DO YOU? YOU'LL FIND OUT IN A MOMENT!
?
?
A MOMENT LATER, THE REASON IS APPARENT... LOW BRIDGE!
THEY WERE SHORT, BUT NOT QUITE SHORT ENOUGH.
ONTO THE BAGGAGE CAR SWINGS THE AGILE FRAME...
I'M NOT A MOMENT TOO SOON!
WHIRLING, THE PYGMIES PERCEIVE THEIR ENEMY, AND LET FLY THEIR ARROWS!
BUT SWIFT AS THOUGHT THE BATMAN SCOOPS UP A VALISE AND....
NOT BAD AIM!
BUT MINE IS BETTER!
3

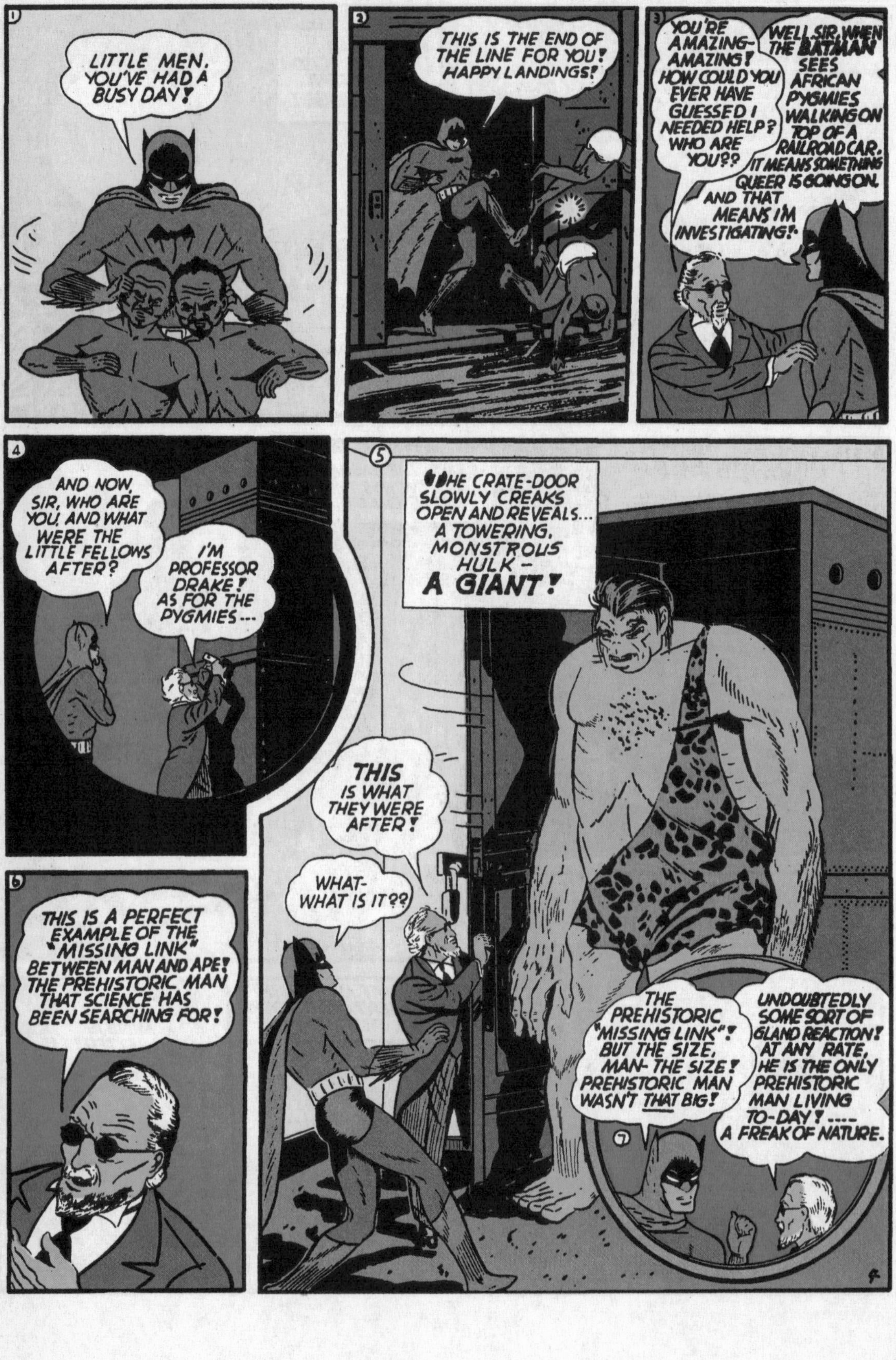
LITTLE MEN. YOU'VE HAD A BUSY DAY!
THIS IS THE END OF THE LINE FOR YOU! HAPPY LANDINGS!
YOU'RE AMAZING- AMAZING! HOW COULD YOU EVER HAVE GUESSED I NEEDED HELP? WHO ARE YOU??
WELL, SIR, WHEN THE BATMAN SEES AFRICAN PYGMIES WALKING ON TOP OF A RAILROAD CAR, IT MEANS SOMETHING QUEER IS GOING ON. AND THAT MEANS I'M INVESTIGATING!
AND NOW, SIR, WHO ARE YOU, AND WHAT WERE THE LITTLE FELLOWS AFTER?
I'M PROFESSOR DRAKE! AS FOR THE PYGMIES---
THE CRATE-DOOR SLOWLY CREAKS OPEN AND REVEALS... A TOWERING, MONSTROUS HULK - A GIANT!
THIS IS WHAT THEY WERE AFTER!
WHAT- WHAT IS IT??
THIS IS A PERFECT EXAMPLE OF THE "MISSING LINK" BETWEEN MAN AND APE! THE PREHISTORIC MAN THAT SCIENCE HAS BEEN SEARCHING FOR!
THE PREHISTORIC "MISSING LINK"? BUT THE SIZE, MAN- THE SIZE! PREHISTORIC MAN WASN'T THAT BIG!
UNDOUBTEDLY SOME SORT OF GLAND REACTION! AT ANY RATE, HE IS THE ONLY PREHISTORIC MAN LIVING TO-DAY! .... A FREAK OF NATURE.

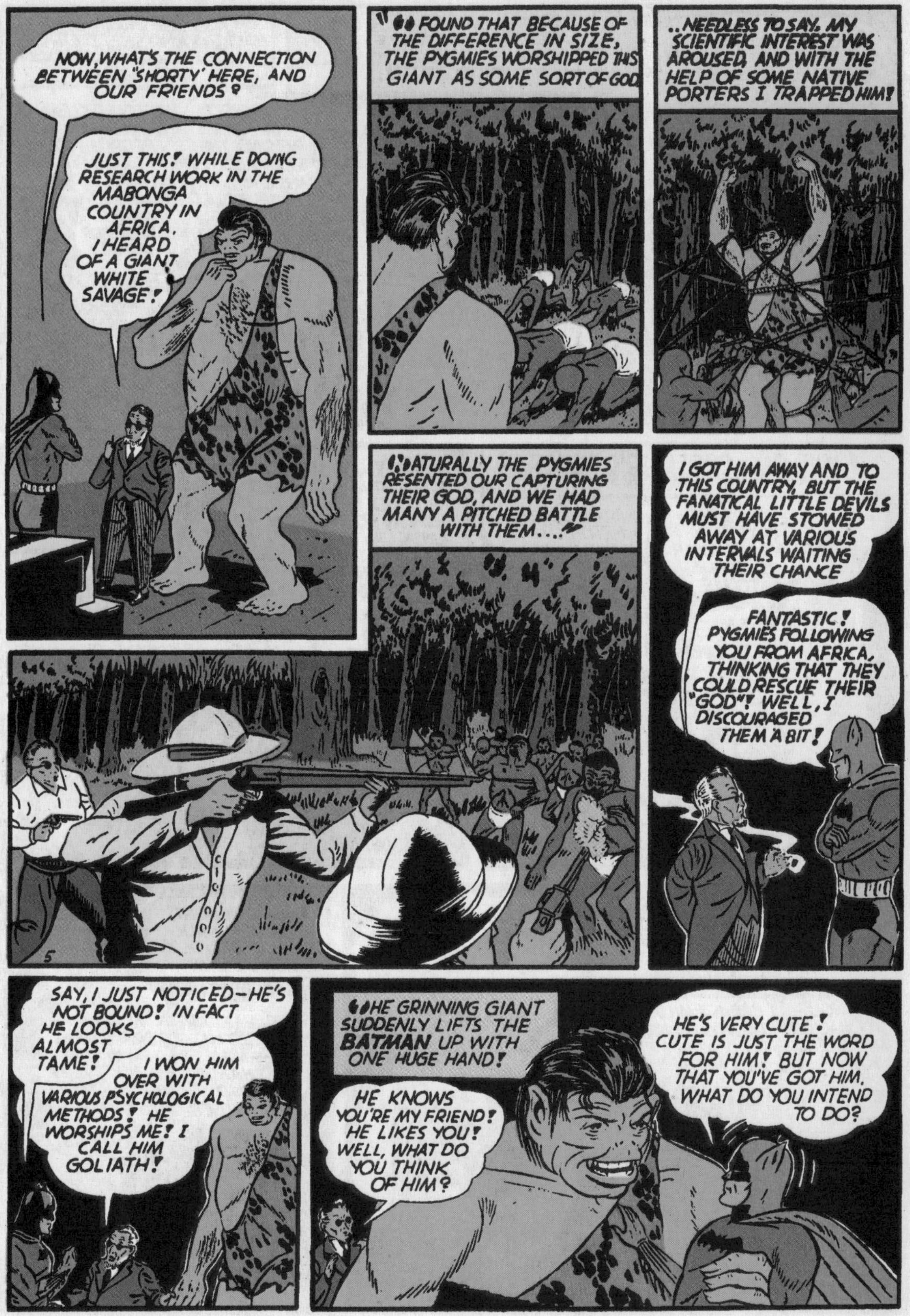
NOW, WHAT'S THE CONNECTION BETWEEN "SHORTY" HERE, AND OUR FRIENDS?
JUST THIS! WHILE DOING RESEARCH WORK IN THE MABONGA COUNTRY IN AFRICA, I HEARD OF A GIANT WHITE SAVAGE!
"I FOUND THAT BECAUSE OF THE DIFFERENCE IN SIZE, THE PYGMIES WORSHIPPED THIS GIANT AS SOME SORT OF GOD.
..NEEDLESS TO SAY, MY SCIENTIFIC INTEREST WAS AROUSED, AND WITH THE HELP OF SOME NATIVE PORTERS I TRAPPED HIM!
"NATURALLY THE PYGMIES RESENTED OUR CAPTURING THEIR GOD, AND WE HAD MANY A PITCHED BATTLE WITH THEM..."
I GOT HIM AWAY AND TO THIS COUNTRY, BUT THE FANATICAL LITTLE DEVILS MUST HAVE STOWED AWAY AT VARIOUS INTERVALS WAITING THEIR CHANCE
FANTASTIC! PYGMIES FOLLOWING YOU FROM AFRICA, THINKING THAT THEY COULD RESCUE THEIR "GOD"! WELL, I DISCOURAGED THEM A BIT!
SAY, I JUST NOTICED—HE'S NOT BOUND! IN FACT HE LOOKS ALMOST TAME!
I WON HIM OVER WITH VARIOUS PSYCHOLOGICAL METHODS! HE WORSHIPS ME! I CALL HIM GOLIATH!
THE GRINNING GIANT SUDDENLY LIFTS THE BATMAN UP WITH ONE HUGE HAND!
HE KNOWS YOU'RE MY FRIEND! HE LIKES YOU! WELL, WHAT DO YOU THINK OF HIM?
HE'S VERY CUTE! CUTE IS JUST THE WORD FOR HIM! BUT NOW THAT YOU'VE GOT HIM, WHAT DO YOU INTEND TO DO?

I'M GOING TO TRY TO CIVILIZE HIM! —TEACH HIM TO SPEAK ENGLISH! IMAGINE, A PREHISTORIC MAN LIVING IN THE WORLD OF TO-DAY—

YES, AND IMAGINE THE PUBLICITY WHEN THE POLICE LET THE NEWSPAPERS KNOW THE FACTS OF THIS CASE!!

THE BATMAN'S WORDS PROVE PROPHETIC, FOR THE NEXT DAY'S HEADLINES REVEAL THE STORY OF GOLIATH!...

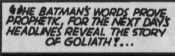

2¢ **DAILY STAR**

NO 8

GIANT 'MISSING LINK' DISCOVERED

PROFESSOR BRINGS BACK COLOSSUS FROM JUNGLE! MURDER OF BAGGAGEMA BY AFRICAN PYGMIES INVOLVES APE-MAN

THE POLICE WERE ASTONISHED TO-DAY TO DISCOVER A FIFTEEN FOOT GIANT.

ACROSS THE GROUNDS OF THE HACKETT AND SNEAD CIRCUS WALK TWO MEN.... HACKETT AND SNEAD...

HACKETT, I HAVE BEEN READING THE STORY ABOUT THE "MISSING LINK". IF WE COULD EXHIBIT HIM LIKE THAT CIRCUS EXHIBITS THAT GORILLA A...

WE COULD CLEAN UP A MILLION DOLLARS! PEOPLE WOULD FLOCK TO SEE HIM! I THINK WE OUGHT TO VISIT PROFESSOR DRAKE?

NEXT DAY, PROFESSOR DRAKE RECEIVES VISITORS...

YES, I'M PROFESSOR DRAKE! WHAT DID YOU WISH TO SPEAK TO ME ABOUT?

CHARMING FELLOW! PERFECTLY CHARMING!

WE ARE HACKETT AND SNEAD, THE CIRCUS OWNERS. IF YOU COULD LET US USE GOLIATH HERE FOR EXHIBITION PURPOSES, WE COULD ALL MAKE A LOT OF MONEY.

WHAT! YOU HAVE THE THE NERVE TO SUGGEST I PUT GOLIATH ON DISPLAY SO THE PUBLIC CAN GAPE AT HIM?? GET OUT! GET OUT!

NOW, NOW? BE CALM! BE CALM!

WE'RE GOING! WE'RE GOING! WE CAN TAKE A HINT.

BACK ON THE CIRCUS GROUNDS, HACKETT AND SNEAD THINK IN TERMS OF MONEY—AND MURDER?

A MILLION DOLLARS! IF WE CAN EXHIBIT THAT GIANT, WE COULD MAKE A MILLION DOLLARS!

I THINK WE OUGHT TO WEAR DOWN DRAKE'S RESISTANCE— PERMANENTLY? I'M GOING TO CALL IN THE BOYS? WE'LL STILL MAKE THAT MILLION

AT THE SAME MOMENT, DRAKE RECEIVES ANOTHER VISITOR... THE BATMAN! HE IS QUICKLY INFORMED OF LATEST DEVELOPMENTS!

AND YOU SAY HACKETT AND SNEAD HAVE BAD REPUTATIONS?

BAD IS A MILD WORD! THEY COULD MAKE QUITE A PILE OF MONEY WITH GOLIATH, AND MONEY IS THE ROOT OF ALL EVIL... ESPECIALLY WITH THEM!

I THINK YOU'RE GOING TO NEED A GUARD AROUND HERE, AND I KNOW JUST THE ONE...... ROBIN, THE BOY WONDER!!

THAT VERY NIGHT, FOUR MEN WALK STEALTHILY ACROSS THE DRAKE LAWN....

HEY, GRIMES, ARE YA SURE THAT APE-MAN AIN'T HANGIN' AROUND THE HOUSE?

DON'T WORRY. DRAKE LOCKS HIM IN THAT SHACK EVERY NIGHT JUST IN CASE HE MIGHT DECIDE TO GO ROAMING!

NOW ALL WE GOTTA DO IS GET RID OF DRAKE AND WE GET OUR DOUGH FROM HACKETT!

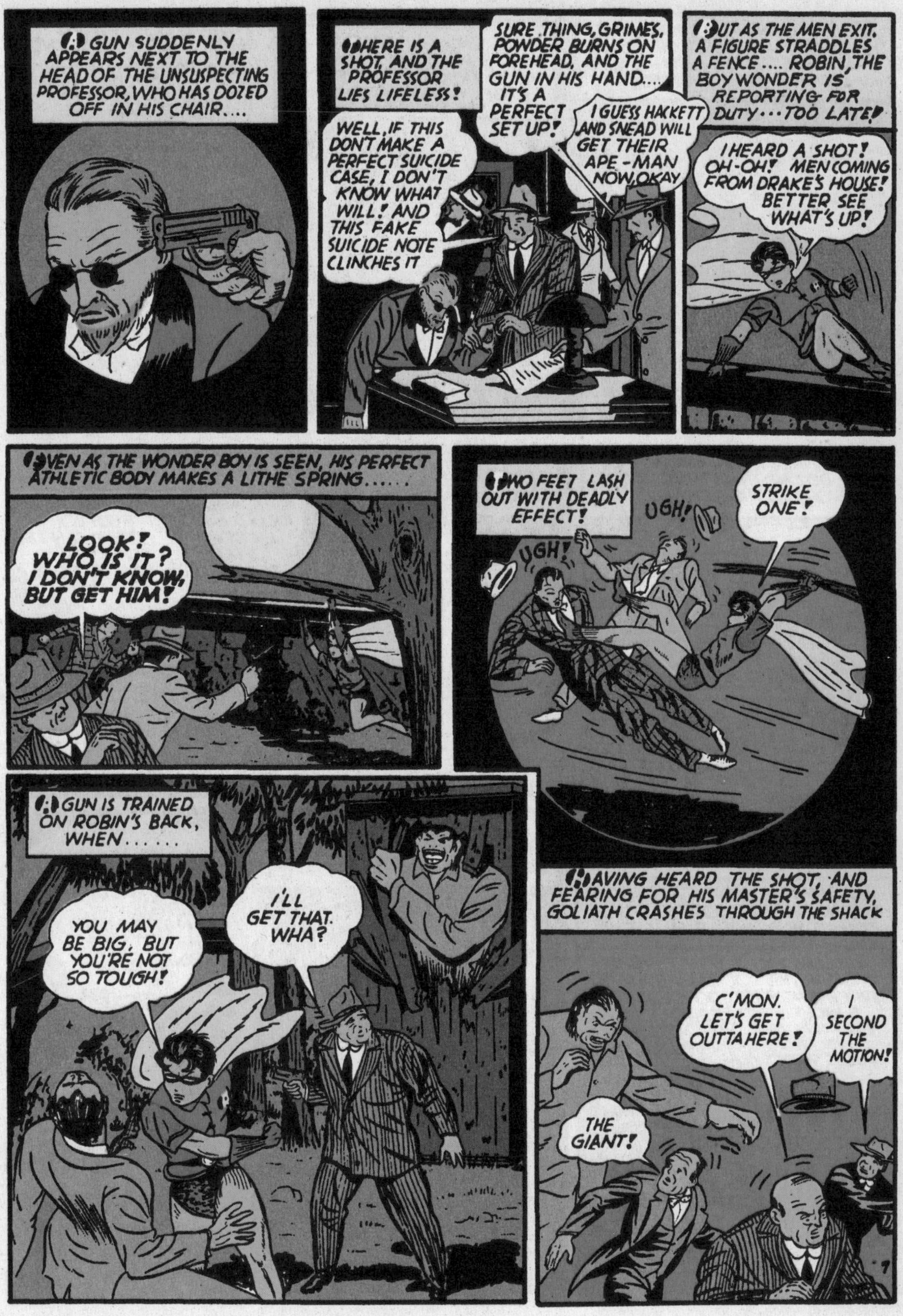
A GUN SUDDENLY APPEARS NEXT TO THE HEAD OF THE UNSUSPECTING PROFESSOR, WHO HAS DOZED OFF IN HIS CHAIR....
THERE IS A SHOT, AND THE PROFESSOR LIES LIFELESS!
WELL, IF THIS DON'T MAKE A PERFECT SUICIDE CASE, I DON'T KNOW WHAT WILL! AND THIS FAKE SUICIDE NOTE CLINCHES IT
SURE THING, GRIMES, POWDER BURNS ON FOREHEAD, AND THE GUN IN HIS HAND.... IT'S A PERFECT SET UP!
I GUESS HACKETT AND SNEAD WILL GET THEIR APE-MAN NOW, OKAY
BUT AS THE MEN EXIT, A FIGURE STRADDLES A FENCE.... ROBIN, THE BOY WONDER IS REPORTING FOR DUTY...TOO LATE!
I HEARD A SHOT! OH-OH! MEN COMING FROM DRAKE'S HOUSE! BETTER SEE WHAT'S UP!
EVEN AS THE WONDER BOY IS SEEN, HIS PERFECT ATHLETIC BODY MAKES A LITHE SPRING......
LOOK! WHO IS IT? I DON'T KNOW, BUT GET HIM!
TWO FEET LASH OUT WITH DEADLY EFFECT!
UGH!
UGH!
STRIKE ONE!
A GUN IS TRAINED ON ROBIN'S BACK, WHEN......
YOU MAY BE BIG, BUT YOU'RE NOT SO TOUGH!
I'LL GET THAT. WHA?
HAVING HEARD THE SHOT, AND FEARING FOR HIS MASTER'S SAFETY, GOLIATH CRASHES THROUGH THE SHACK
THE GIANT!
C'MON. LET'S GET OUTTA HERE!
I SECOND THE MOTION!

AS THE GIANT PLODS FORWARD, HE CATCHES A GLIMPSE OF A FACE THAT PENETRATES INTO HIS MIND...THAT FACE...GRIMES!

S-STEP ON IT!

ONE THOUGHT REMAINS IN THE PRIMITIVE'S MIND AS HE TRUDGES TO THE HOUSE... IS HIS MASTER SAFE?

INSTANTLY HE KNOWS THE AWFUL TRUTH—HIS BELOVED MASTER IS DEAD! THE SHOCK IS TOO MUCH FOR HIS FEEBLE MIND, AND THE APE-MAN BECOMES HARMLESS, A DODDERING FIGURE!

MEANWHILE ROBIN KNOWS HE MUST DO ONE THING IMMEDIATELY... ...REPORT TO THE BATMAN!

...AND THAT'S EXACTLY WHAT HAPPENED!

WE'LL HAVE TO BIDE OUR TIME AND SEE THE PAPERS IN THE MORNING!

NEXT MORNING:

OH, SO THAT'S IT!

DAILY STAR

PROFESSOR DRAKE A SUICIDE

WORRIED OVER "MISSING LINK'S" FUTURE, HE KILLS SELF, AND LEAVES APE-MAN TO HACKETT AND CIRCUS:

THEY FORGED THAT SUICIDE NOTE AND KILLED HIM! I'M GOING TO TELL THE POLICE!

...AND TELL THEM YOU WERE THERE AS ROBIN THE BOY WONDER? ...SORRY, CAN'T BE DONE! WELL HAVE TO DO A LITTLE MORE TIME-BIDING UNTIL THE RIGHT MOMENT!

MEANWHILE, HACKETT AND SNEAD LOSE NO TIME IN FLOODING THE COUNTRYSIDE WITH PUBLICITY!

IT SEEMS TO ME AS IF THIS TERRIFYING MONSTER IS ABOUT AS TERRIFYING AS A FLY! THE PUBLIC WON'T LIKE IT!

DON'T WORRY, ALL HE HAS TO DO IS LOOK AS FEROCIOUS AS HE DOES NOW AND THE PUBLIC WILL STILL EAT IT UP! THIS BABY IS BIG!—BIG!

AND HACKETT IS RIGHT, FOR AN OVERFLOWING CROWD COMES TO VIEW THE FAMED "MISSING LINK"...

AND NOTICE HOW HE DWARFS THESE OTHER WILD BEASTS.. EVEN THE MIGHTY ELEPHANT! HE IS LARGEST SPECIES OF...

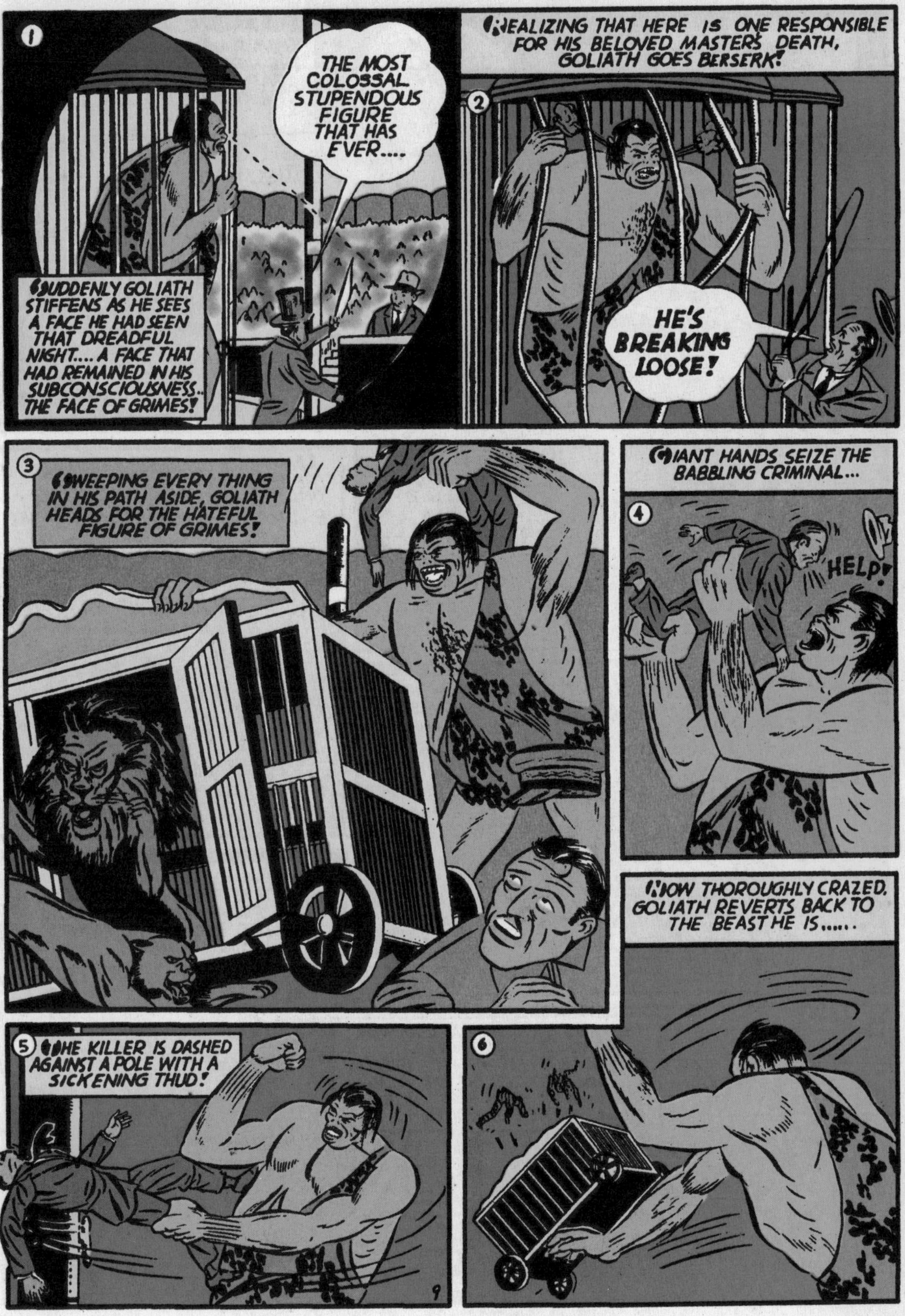
THE MOST COLOSSAL STUPENDOUS FIGURE THAT HAS EVER....
SUDDENLY GOLIATH STIFFENS AS HE SEES A FACE HE HAD SEEN THAT DREADFUL NIGHT.... A FACE THAT HAD REMAINED IN HIS SUBCONSCIOUSNESS.. THE FACE OF GRIMES!
REALIZING THAT HERE IS ONE RESPONSIBLE FOR HIS BELOVED MASTER'S DEATH, GOLIATH GOES BERSERK!
HE'S BREAKING LOOSE!
SWEEPING EVERY THING IN HIS PATH ASIDE, GOLIATH HEADS FOR THE HATEFUL FIGURE OF GRIMES!
GIANT HANDS SEIZE THE BABBLING CRIMINAL...
HELP!
NOW THOROUGHLY CRAZED, GOLIATH REVERTS BACK TO THE BEAST HE IS......
THE KILLER IS DASHED AGAINST A POLE WITH A SICKENING THUD!

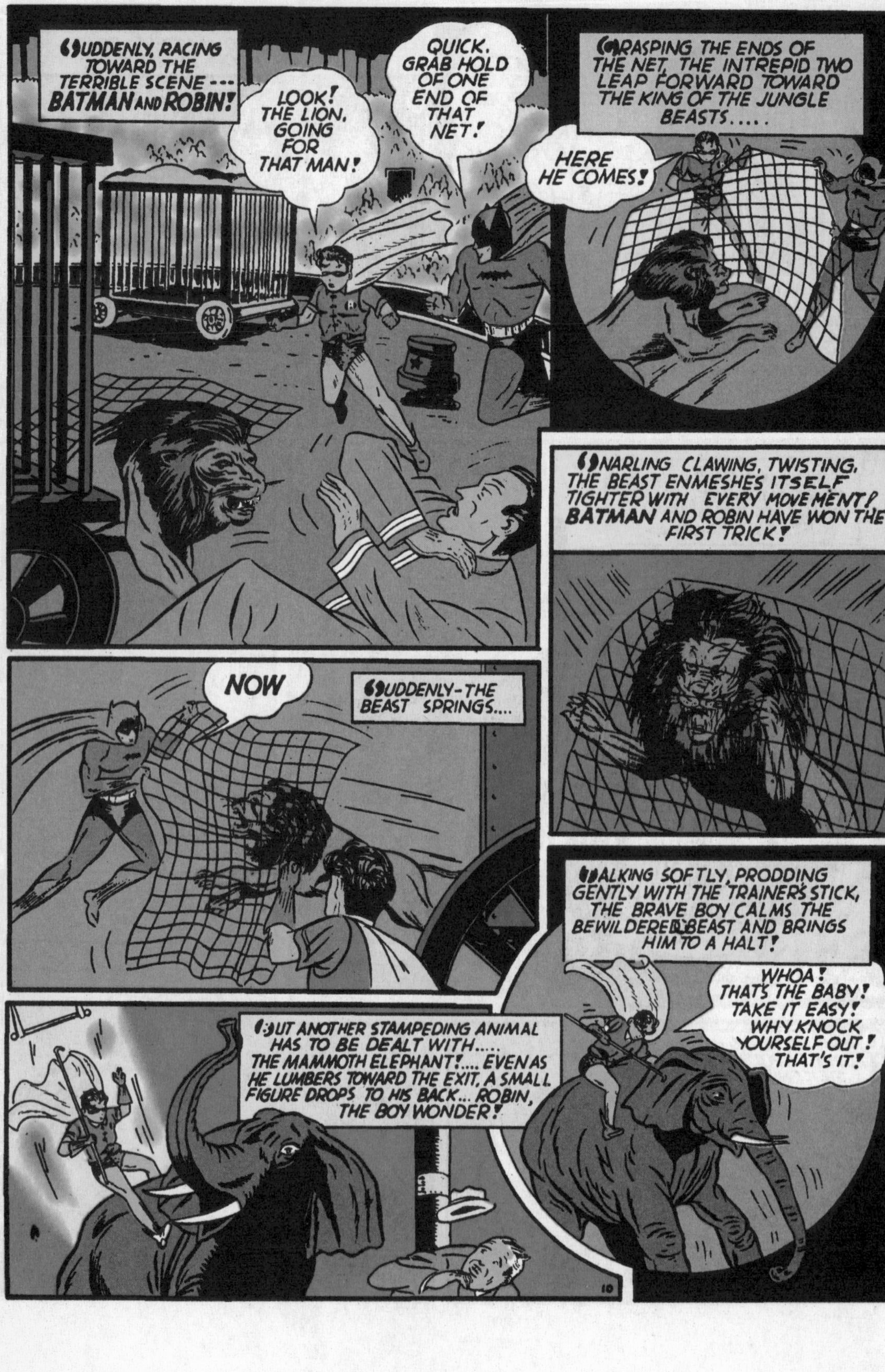
SUDDENLY, RACING TOWARD THE TERRIBLE SCENE --- BATMAN AND ROBIN!
LOOK! THE LION, GOING FOR THAT MAN!
QUICK. GRAB HOLD OF ONE END OF THAT NET!
GRASPING THE ENDS OF THE NET, THE INTREPID TWO LEAP FORWARD TOWARD THE KING OF THE JUNGLE BEASTS.....
HERE HE COMES!
SNARLING CLAWING, TWISTING, THE BEAST ENMESHES ITSELF TIGHTER WITH EVERY MOVEMENT! BATMAN AND ROBIN HAVE WON THE FIRST TRICK!
NOW
SUDDENLY-THE BEAST SPRINGS....
WALKING SOFTLY, PRODDING GENTLY WITH THE TRAINER'S STICK, THE BRAVE BOY CALMS THE BEWILDERED BEAST AND BRINGS HIM TO A HALT!
BUT ANOTHER STAMPEDING ANIMAL HAS TO BE DEALT WITH..... THE MAMMOTH ELEPHANT!.... EVEN AS HE LUMBERS TOWARD THE EXIT, A SMALL FIGURE DROPS TO HIS BACK... ROBIN, THE BOY WONDER!
WHOA! THAT'S THE BABY! TAKE IT EASY! WHY KNOCK YOURSELF OUT! THAT'S IT!

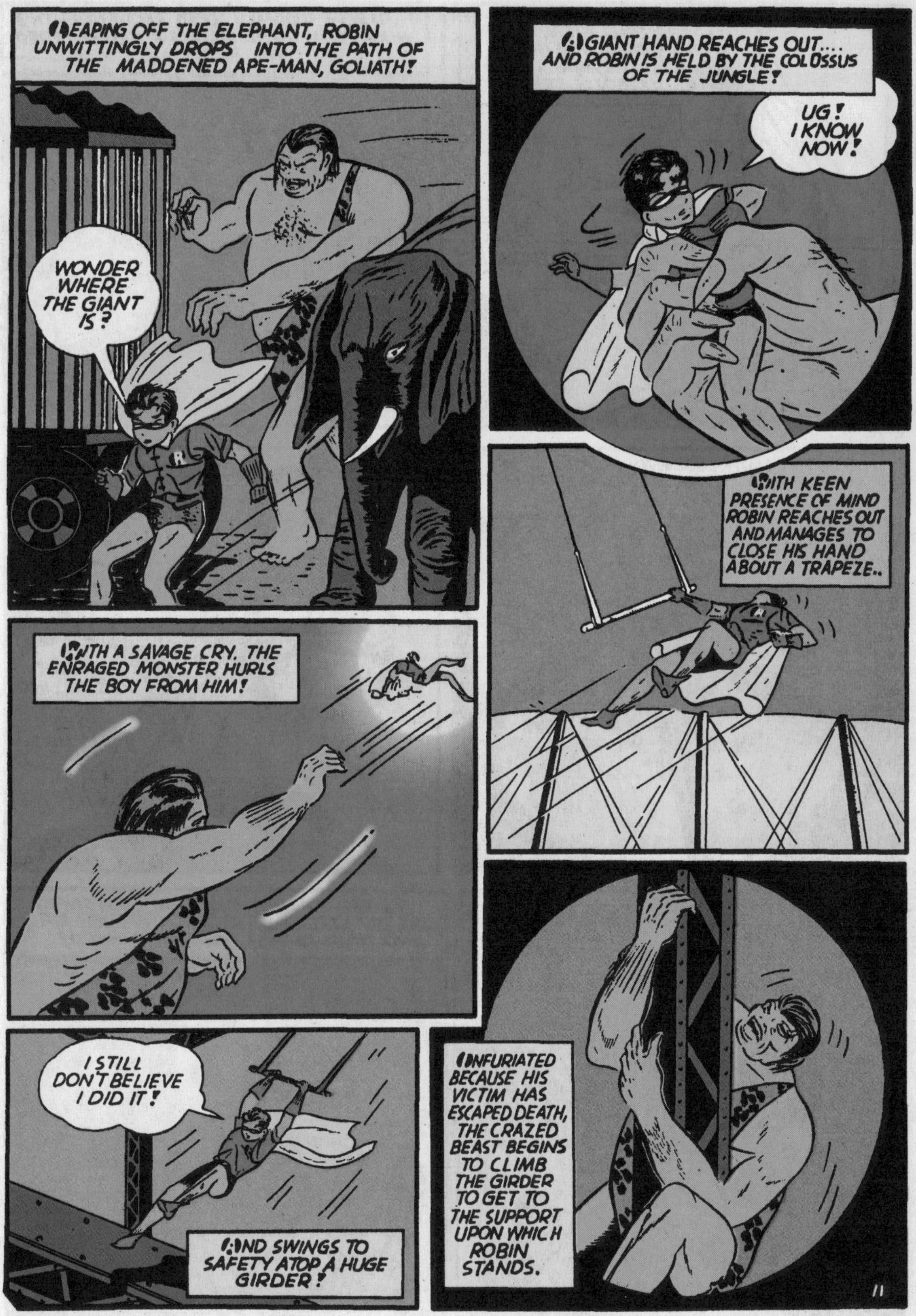
LEAPING OFF THE ELEPHANT, ROBIN UNWITTINGLY DROPS INTO THE PATH OF THE MADDENED APE-MAN, GOLIATH!
WONDER WHERE THE GIANT IS?
A GIANT HAND REACHES OUT.... AND ROBIN IS HELD BY THE COLOSSUS OF THE JUNGLE!
UG! I KNOW NOW!
WITH KEEN PRESENCE OF MIND ROBIN REACHES OUT AND MANAGES TO CLOSE HIS HAND ABOUT A TRAPEZE..
WITH A SAVAGE CRY, THE ENRAGED MONSTER HURLS THE BOY FROM HIM!
I STILL DON'T BELIEVE I DID IT!
AND SWINGS TO SAFETY ATOP A HUGE GIRDER!
INFURIATED BECAUSE HIS VICTIM HAS ESCAPED DEATH, THE CRAZED BEAST BEGINS TO CLIMB THE GIRDER TO GET TO THE SUPPORT UPON WHICH ROBIN STANDS.
11

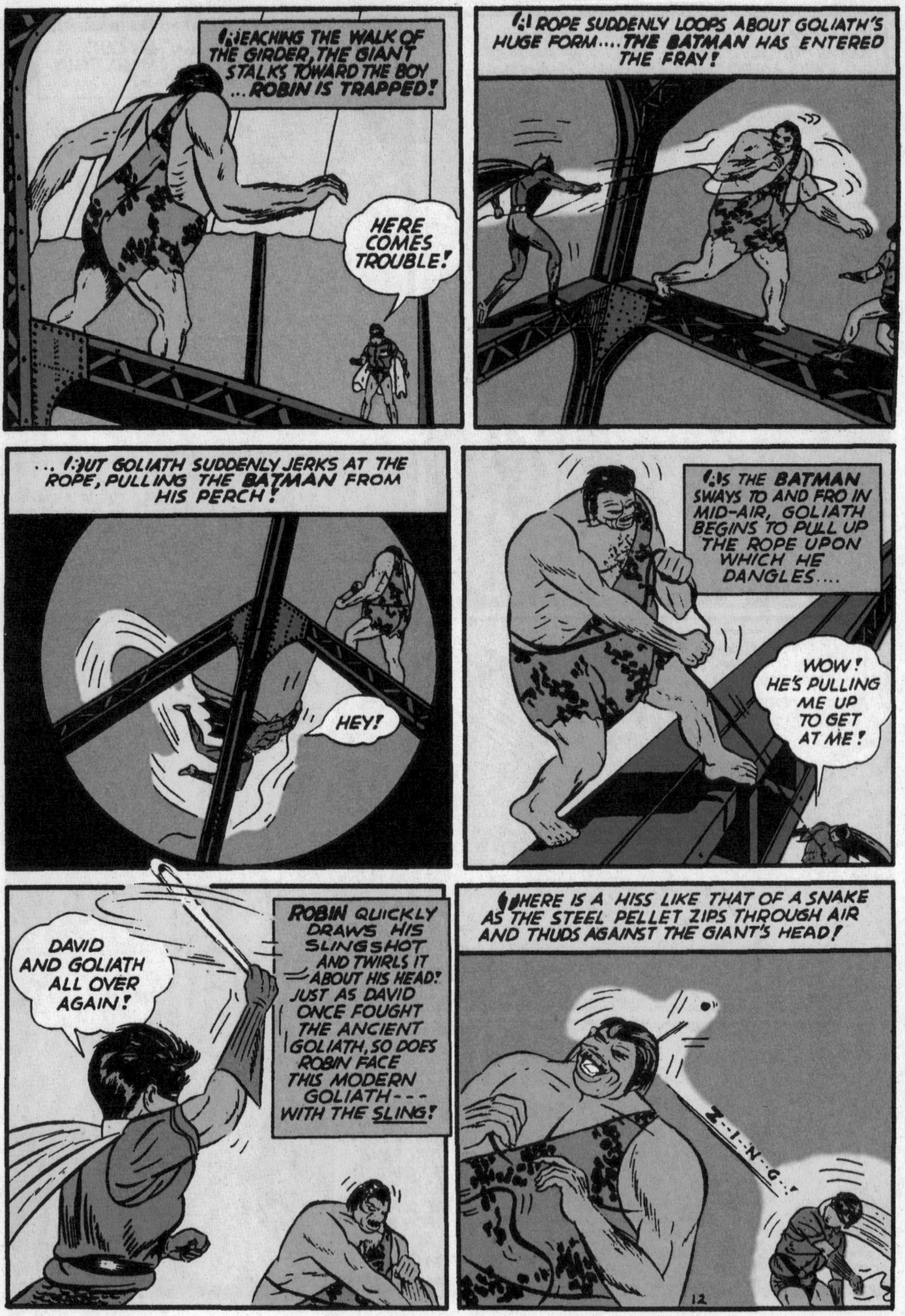
REACHING THE WALK OF THE GIRDER, THE GIANT STALKS TOWARD THE BOY ...ROBIN IS TRAPPED!
HERE COMES TROUBLE!
A ROPE SUDDENLY LOOPS ABOUT GOLIATH'S HUGE FORM....THE BATMAN HAS ENTERED THE FRAY!
... BUT GOLIATH SUDDENLY JERKS AT THE ROPE, PULLING THE BATMAN FROM HIS PERCH!
HEY!
AS THE BATMAN SWAYS TO AND FRO IN MID-AIR, GOLIATH BEGINS TO PULL UP THE ROPE UPON WHICH HE DANGLES....
WOW! HE'S PULLING ME UP TO GET AT ME!
DAVID AND GOLIATH ALL OVER AGAIN!
ROBIN QUICKLY DRAWS HIS SLINGSHOT AND TWIRLS IT ABOUT HIS HEAD! JUST AS DAVID ONCE FOUGHT THE ANCIENT GOLIATH, SO DOES ROBIN FACE THIS MODERN GOLIATH--- WITH THE SLING!
THERE IS A HISS LIKE THAT OF A SNAKE AS THE STEEL PELLET ZIPS THROUGH AIR AND THUDS AGAINST THE GIANT'S HEAD!
Z-I-N-G-!
12

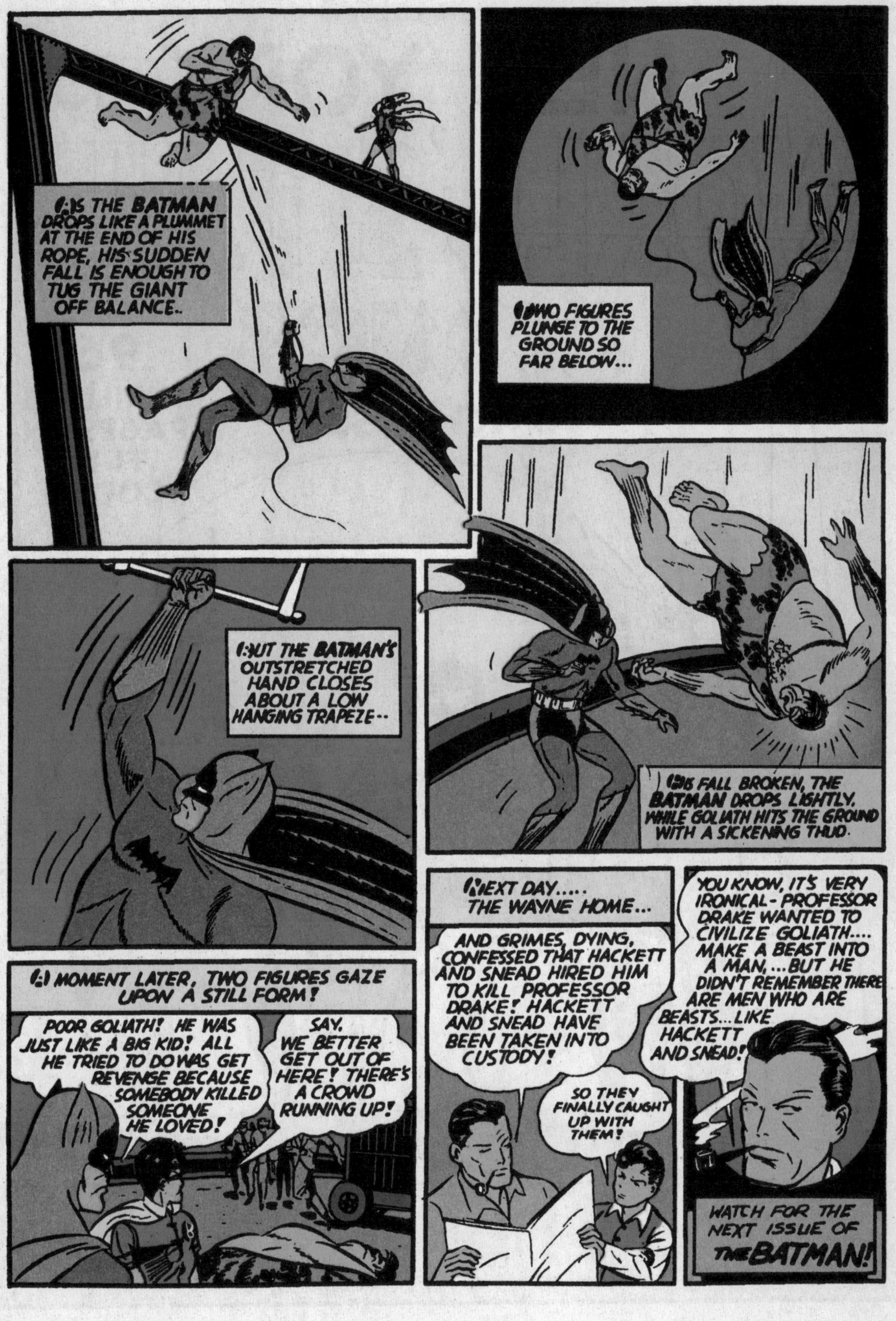
AS THE BATMAN DROPS LIKE A PLUMMET AT THE END OF HIS ROPE, HIS SUDDEN FALL IS ENOUGH TO TUG THE GIANT OFF BALANCE..
TWO FIGURES PLUNGE TO THE GROUND SO FAR BELOW...
BUT THE BATMAN'S OUTSTRETCHED HAND CLOSES ABOUT A LOW HANGING TRAPEZE--
HIS FALL BROKEN, THE BATMAN DROPS LIGHTLY, WHILE GOLIATH HITS THE GROUND WITH A SICKENING THUD.
A MOMENT LATER, TWO FIGURES GAZE UPON A STILL FORM!
POOR GOLIATH! HE WAS JUST LIKE A BIG KID! ALL HE TRIED TO DO WAS GET REVENGE BECAUSE SOMEBODY KILLED SOMEONE HE LOVED!
SAY, WE BETTER GET OUT OF HERE! THERE'S A CROWD RUNNING UP!
NEXT DAY..... THE WAYNE HOME...
AND GRIMES, DYING, CONFESSED THAT HACKETT AND SNEAD HIRED HIM TO KILL PROFESSOR DRAKE! HACKETT AND SNEAD HAVE BEEN TAKEN INTO CUSTODY!
SO THEY FINALLY CAUGHT UP WITH THEM!
YOU KNOW, IT'S VERY IRONICAL - PROFESSOR DRAKE WANTED TO CIVILIZE GOLIATH.... MAKE A BEAST INTO A MAN, ...BUT HE DIDN'T REMEMBER THERE ARE MEN WHO ARE BEASTS...LIKE HACKETT AND SNEAD!
WATCH FOR THE NEXT ISSUE OF THE BATMAN!

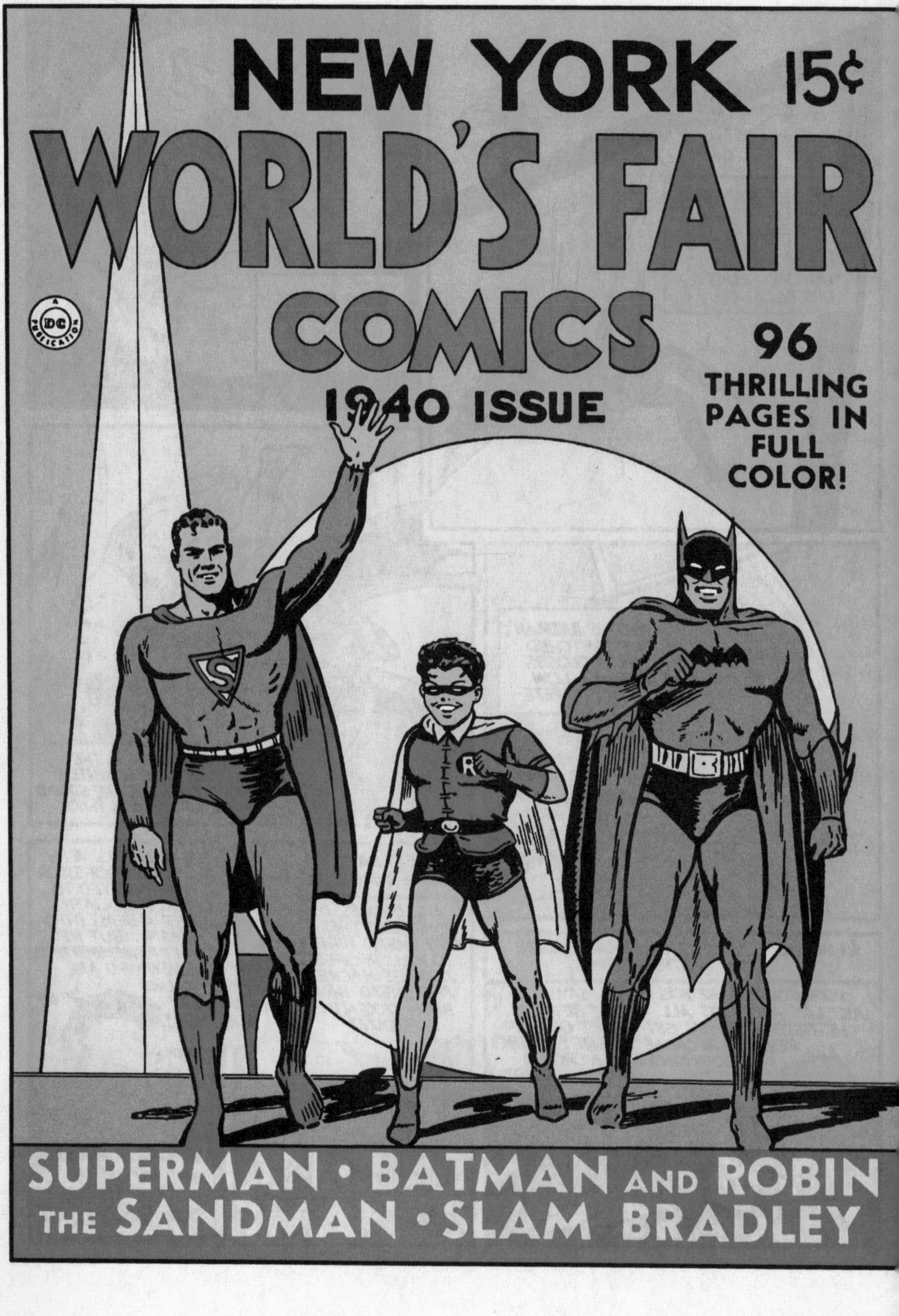
NEW YORK 15¢
WORLD'S FAIR
COMICS
1940 ISSUE
A DC PUBLICATION
96 THRILLING PAGES IN FULL COLOR!
SUPERMAN • BATMAN AND ROBIN
THE SANDMAN • SLAM BRADLEY

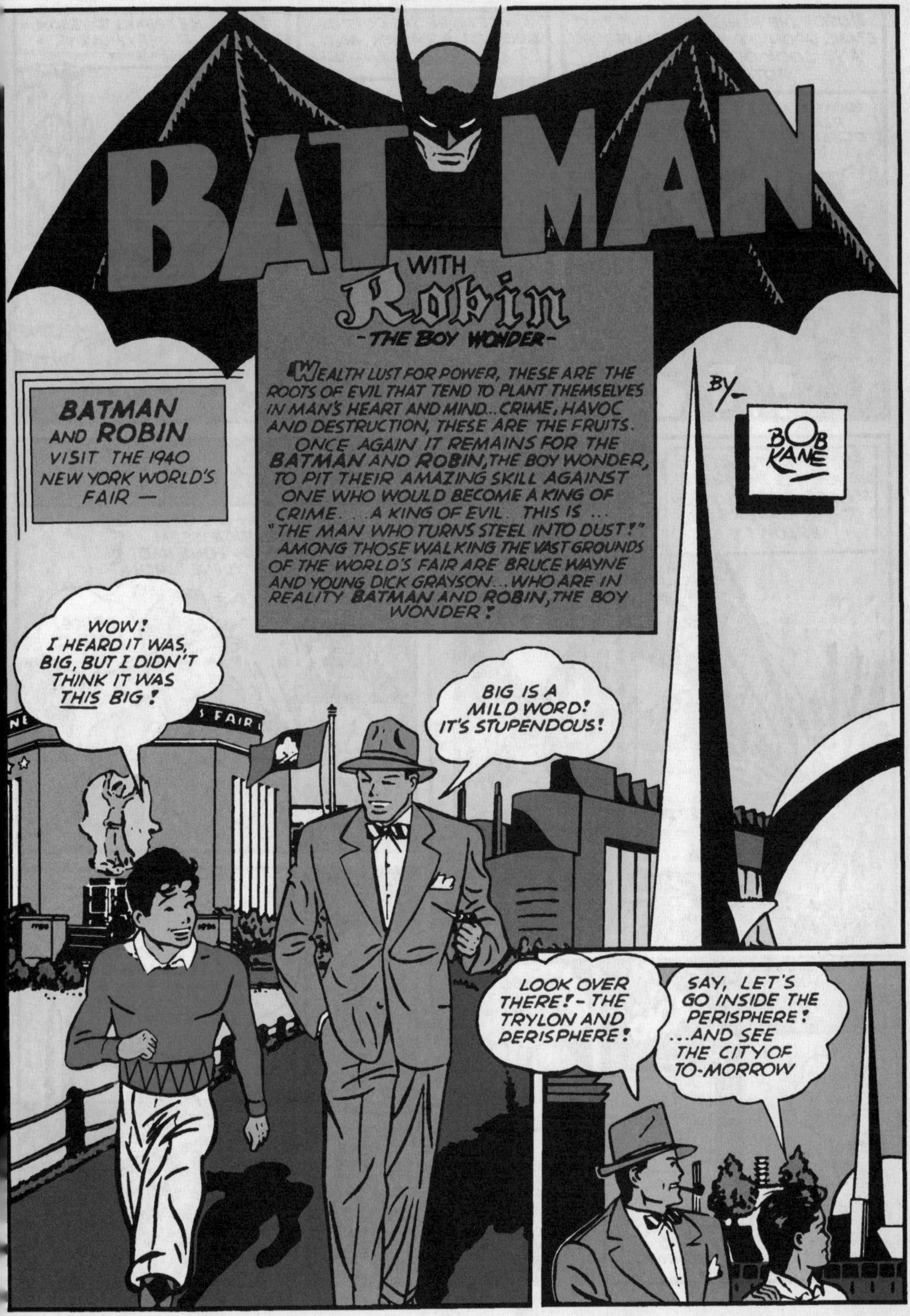
BATMAN
WITH
Robin
-THE BOY WONDER-
BATMAN AND ROBIN VISIT THE 1940 NEW YORK WORLD'S FAIR —
WEALTH LUST FOR POWER, THESE ARE THE ROOTS OF EVIL THAT TEND TO PLANT THEMSELVES IN MAN'S HEART AND MIND...CRIME, HAVOC AND DESTRUCTION, THESE ARE THE FRUITS. ONCE AGAIN IT REMAINS FOR THE BATMAN AND ROBIN, THE BOY WONDER, TO PIT THEIR AMAZING SKILL AGAINST ONE WHO WOULD BECOME A KING OF CRIME. . . A KING OF EVIL. THIS IS ... "THE MAN WHO TURNS STEEL INTO DUST!" AMONG THOSE WALKING THE VAST GROUNDS OF THE WORLD'S FAIR ARE BRUCE WAYNE AND YOUNG DICK GRAYSON...WHO ARE IN REALITY BATMAN AND ROBIN, THE BOY WONDER!
BY— BOB KANE
WOW! I HEARD IT WAS, BIG, BUT I DIDN'T THINK IT WAS THIS BIG!
BIG IS A MILD WORD! IT'S STUPENDOUS!
LOOK OVER THERE! - THE TRYLON AND PERISPHERE!
SAY, LET'S GO INSIDE THE PERISPHERE! ...AND SEE THE CITY OF TO-MORROW

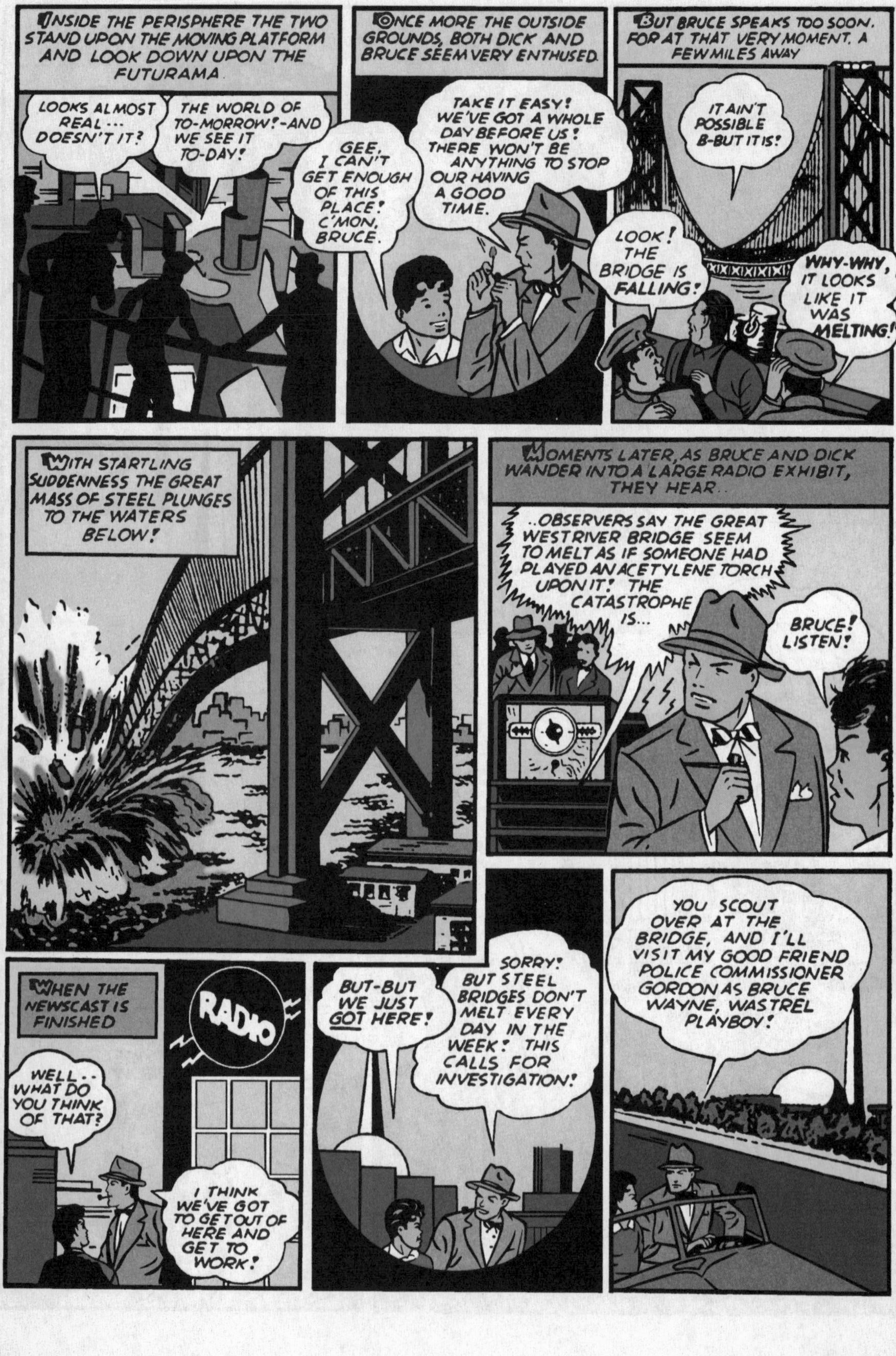
INSIDE THE PERISPHERE THE TWO STAND UPON THE MOVING PLATFORM AND LOOK DOWN UPON THE FUTURAMA.
LOOKS ALMOST REAL... DOESN'T IT?
THE WORLD OF TO-MORROW!-AND WE SEE IT TO-DAY!
ONCE MORE THE OUTSIDE GROUNDS, BOTH DICK AND BRUCE SEEM VERY ENTHUSED.
GEE, I CAN'T GET ENOUGH OF THIS PLACE! C'MON, BRUCE.
TAKE IT EASY! WE'VE GOT A WHOLE DAY BEFORE US! THERE WON'T BE ANYTHING TO STOP OUR HAVING A GOOD TIME.
BUT BRUCE SPEAKS TOO SOON. FOR AT THAT VERY MOMENT, A FEW MILES AWAY
IT AIN'T POSSIBLE B-BUT IT IS!
LOOK! THE BRIDGE IS FALLING!
WHY-WHY, IT LOOKS LIKE IT WAS MELTING!
WITH STARTLING SUDDENNESS THE GREAT MASS OF STEEL PLUNGES TO THE WATERS BELOW!
MOMENTS LATER, AS BRUCE AND DICK WANDER INTO A LARGE RADIO EXHIBIT, THEY HEAR..
..OBSERVERS SAY THE GREAT WESTRIVER BRIDGE SEEM TO MELT AS IF SOMEONE HAD PLAYED AN ACETYLENE TORCH UPON IT! THE CATASTROPHE IS...
BRUCE! LISTEN!
WHEN THE NEWSCAST IS FINISHED
RADIO
WELL.. WHAT DO YOU THINK OF THAT?
I THINK WE'VE GOT TO GET OUT OF HERE AND GET TO WORK!
BUT-BUT WE JUST GOT HERE!
SORRY! BUT STEEL BRIDGES DON'T MELT EVERY DAY IN THE WEEK! THIS CALLS FOR INVESTIGATION!
YOU SCOUT OVER AT THE BRIDGE, AND I'LL VISIT MY GOOD FRIEND POLICE COMMISSIONER GORDON AS BRUCE WAYNE, WASTREL PLAYBOY!

BRUCE WAYNE! FINALLY ROUSED YOURSELF ENOUGH TO TO PAY ME A VISIT, EH?

HELLO, GORDON!

WHILE PRETENDING IDLE CHATTER BRUCE CLEVERLY SWITCHES THE CONVERSATION

AND YOU MEAN TO SAY THE BRIDGE ACTUALLY MELTED AWAY?

ABSOLUTELY! JUST SEEMED TO CRUMPLE INTO DUST!

THE DOOR SUDDENLY BURSTS OPEN AND

MY NAME IS TRAVERS OF TRAVERS ENGINEERS! JUST READ THIS LETTER I RECEIVED!

WHO?

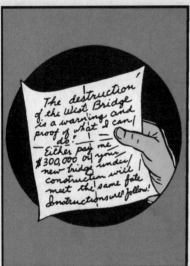

The destruction of the West Bridge is a warning and proof of what I can do! Either pay me $300,000 or your new bridge under construction will meet the same fate! Instructions will follow!

WE HAVE A NEW BRIDGE UNDER CONSTRUCTION! IF IT IS DESTROYED WE'LL LOSE HUNDREDS OF THOUSANDS OF DOLLARS! WHAT SHALL I DO?

IGNORE IT! PROBABLY A CRACKPOT TRYING TO CASH IN ON EASY MONEY! NOBODY CAN DESTROY A BRIDGE! THE STEEL WAS PROBABLY FAULTY, THAT'S ALL!

I WONDER GORDON, WHETHER YOU'RE WONDERING IF THE BRIDGE WAS REALLY DESTROYED BY THE WRITER OF THAT LETTER....

MEANWHILE, WHAT OF YOUNG DICK GRAYSON WHO IS INSPECTING THE SITE OF THE CATASTROPHE?

WELL, NOW I'LL SEE IF I CAN DIG UP ANYTHING IMPORTANT!

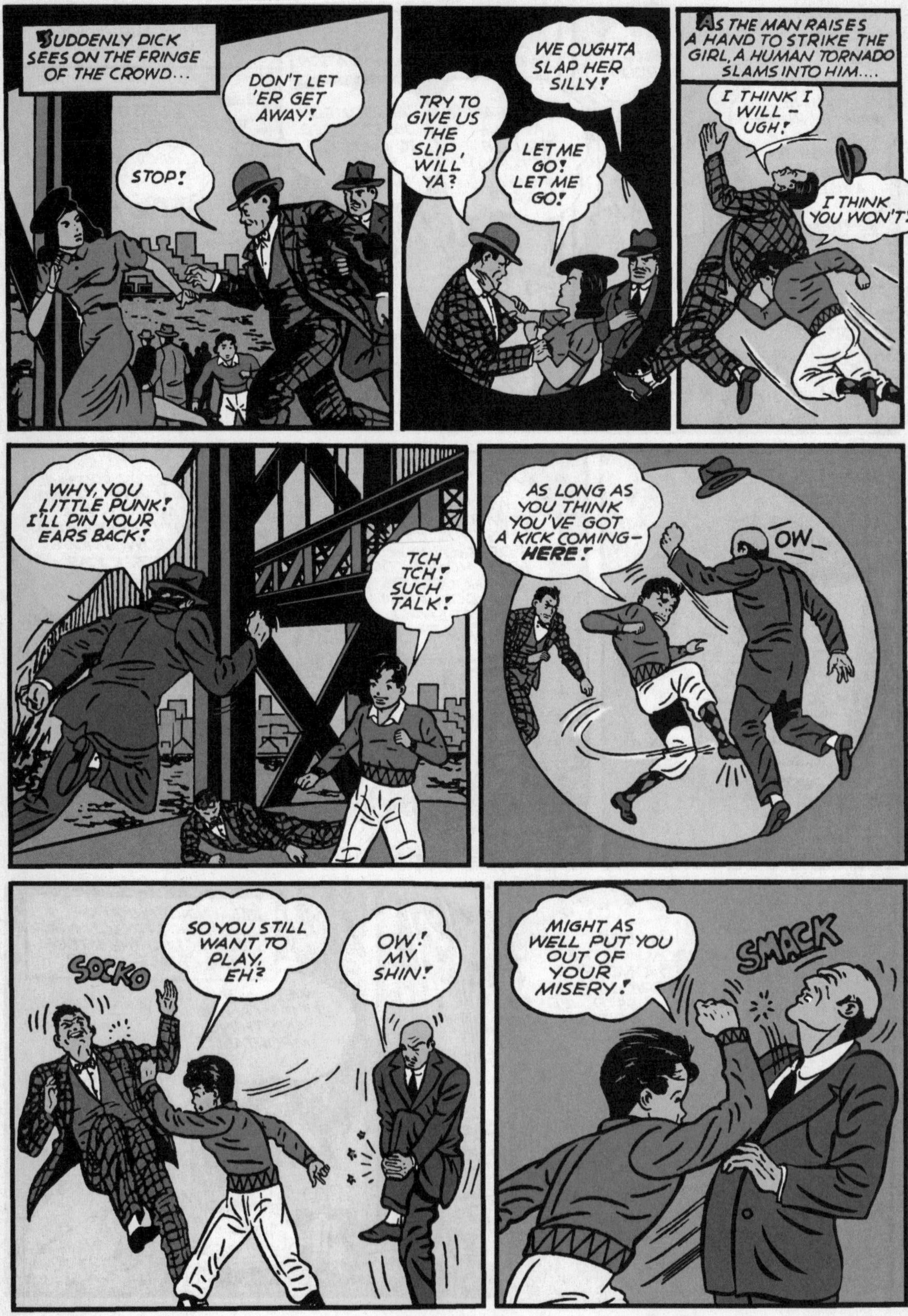
SUDDENLY DICK SEES ON THE FRINGE OF THE CROWD...
DON'T LET 'ER GET AWAY!
STOP!
TRY TO GIVE US THE SLIP, WILL YA?
WE OUGHTA SLAP HER SILLY!
LET ME GO! LET ME GO!
AS THE MAN RAISES A HAND TO STRIKE THE GIRL, A HUMAN TORNADO SLAMS INTO HIM....
I THINK I WILL -- UGH!
I THINK YOU WON'T!
WHY, YOU LITTLE PUNK! I'LL PIN YOUR EARS BACK!
TCH TCH! SUCH TALK!
AS LONG AS YOU THINK YOU'VE GOT A KICK COMING-- HERE!
OW--
SOCKO
SO YOU STILL WANT TO PLAY, EH?
OW! MY SHIN!
MIGHT AS WELL PUT YOU OUT OF YOUR MISERY!
SMACK

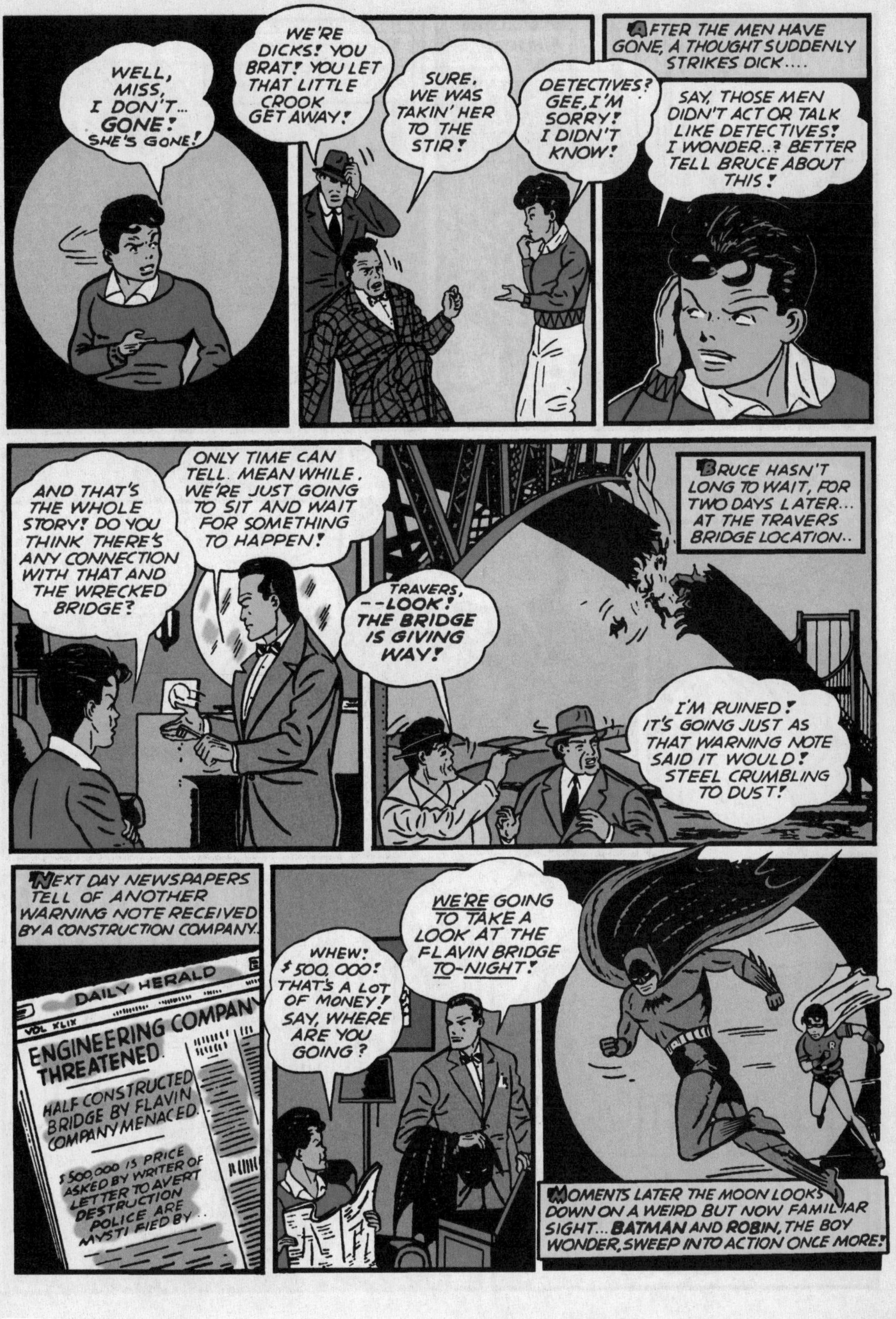

WELL, MISS, I DON'T... GONE! SHE'S GONE!
WE'RE DICKS! YOU BRAT! YOU LET THAT LITTLE CROOK GET AWAY!
SURE. WE WAS TAKIN' HER TO THE STIR!
DETECTIVES? GEE, I'M SORRY! I DIDN'T KNOW!
AFTER THE MEN HAVE GONE, A THOUGHT SUDDENLY STRIKES DICK....
SAY, THOSE MEN DIDN'T ACT OR TALK LIKE DETECTIVES! I WONDER..? BETTER TELL BRUCE ABOUT THIS!
AND THAT'S THE WHOLE STORY! DO YOU THINK THERE'S ANY CONNECTION WITH THAT AND THE WRECKED BRIDGE?
ONLY TIME CAN TELL. MEAN WHILE, WE'RE JUST GOING TO SIT AND WAIT FOR SOMETHING TO HAPPEN!
BRUCE HASN'T LONG TO WAIT, FOR TWO DAYS LATER... AT THE TRAVERS BRIDGE LOCATION..
TRAVERS, --LOOK! THE BRIDGE IS GIVING WAY!
I'M RUINED! IT'S GOING JUST AS THAT WARNING NOTE SAID IT WOULD! STEEL CRUMBLING TO DUST!
NEXT DAY NEWSPAPERS TELL OF ANOTHER WARNING NOTE RECEIVED BY A CONSTRUCTION COMPANY.
DAILY HERALD
VOL XLIX
ENGINEERING COMPANY THREATENED.
HALF CONSTRUCTED BRIDGE BY FLAVIN COMPANY MENACED.
$500,000 IS PRICE ASKED BY WRITER OF LETTER TO AVERT DESTRUCTION POLICE ARE MYSTI FIED BY ..
WHEW! $500,000! THAT'S A LOT OF MONEY! SAY, WHERE ARE YOU GOING?
WE'RE GOING TO TAKE A LOOK AT THE FLAVIN BRIDGE TO-NIGHT!
MOMENTS LATER THE MOON LOOKS DOWN ON A WEIRD BUT NOW FAMILIAR SIGHT... BATMAN AND ROBIN, THE BOY WONDER, SWEEP INTO ACTION ONCE MORE!

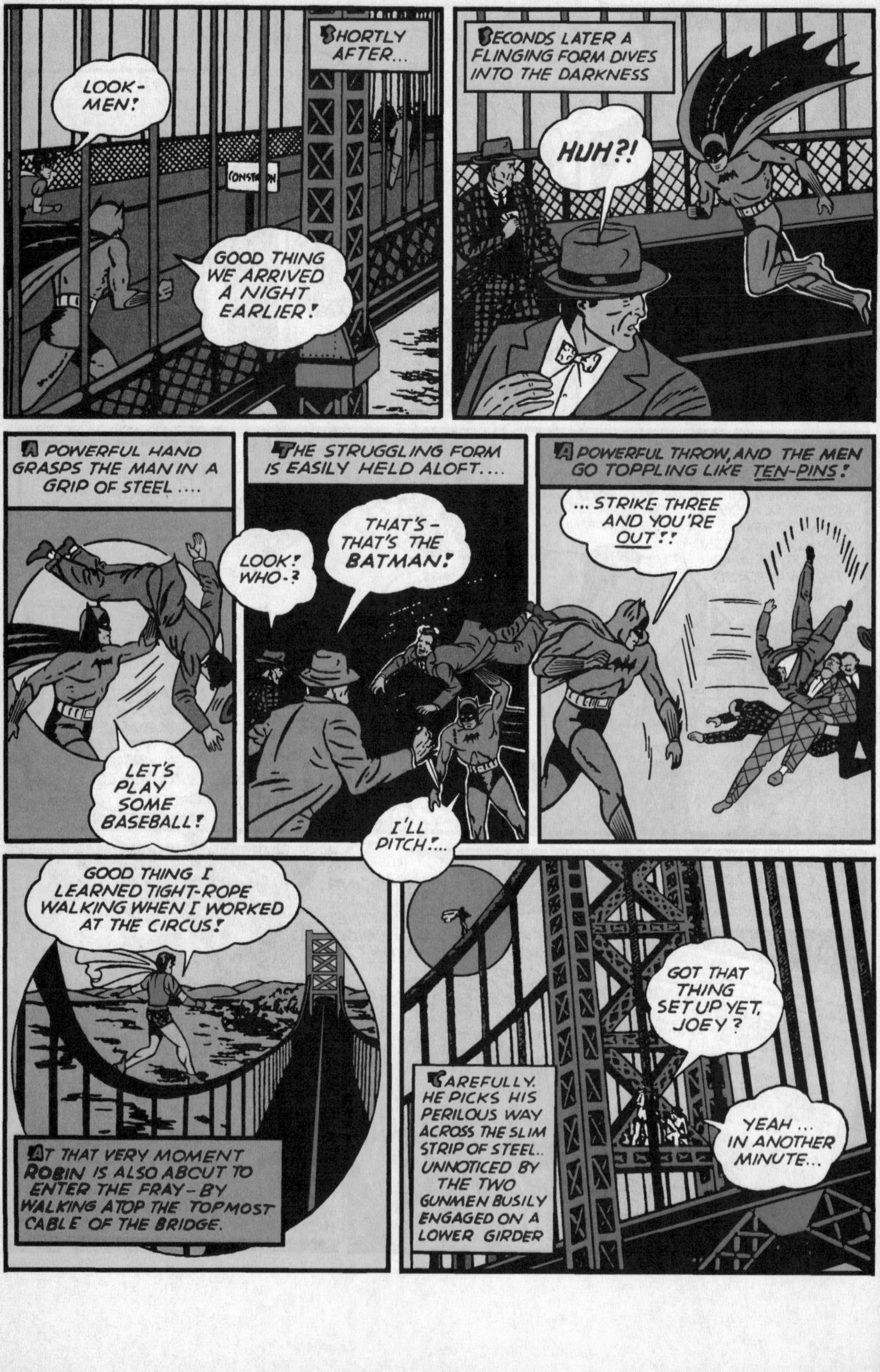
SHORTLY AFTER...
LOOK-MEN!
CONSTRUCTION
GOOD THING WE ARRIVED A NIGHT EARLIER!
SECONDS LATER A FLINGING FORM DIVES INTO THE DARKNESS
HUH?!
A POWERFUL HAND GRASPS THE MAN IN A GRIP OF STEEL....
LET'S PLAY SOME BASEBALL!
THE STRUGGLING FORM IS EASILY HELD ALOFT....
LOOK! WHO-?
THAT'S- THAT'S THE BATMAN!
I'LL PITCH!...
A POWERFUL THROW, AND THE MEN GO TOPPLING LIKE TEN-PINS!
...STRIKE THREE AND YOU'RE OUT!!
GOOD THING I LEARNED TIGHT-ROPE WALKING WHEN I WORKED AT THE CIRCUS!
AT THAT VERY MOMENT ROBIN IS ALSO ABOUT TO ENTER THE FRAY-BY WALKING ATOP THE TOPMOST CABLE OF THE BRIDGE.
CAREFULLY. HE PICKS HIS PERILOUS WAY ACROSS THE SLIM STRIP OF STEEL.. UNNOTICED BY THE TWO GUNMEN BUSILY ENGAGED ON A LOWER GIRDER
GOT THAT THING SET UP YET, JOEY?
YEAH ... IN ANOTHER MINUTE...

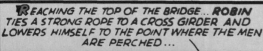

REACHING THE TOP OF THE BRIDGE... ROBIN TIES A STRONG ROPE TO A CROSS GIRDER AND LOWERS HIMSELF TO THE POINT WHERE THE MEN ARE PERCHED...

PEEK-A-BOO!

CATCH!

PICKING UP THE MAN, THE BOY WONDER DROPS HIM TOWARD THE BATMAN!

CAUGHT HIM...ON THE JAW!

AFTER DISPOSING OF THE OTHER GUNMAN, THE WONDERBOY SUDDENLY SEES DANGER MENACE THE BATMAN! --WITH A SWEEPING SWING.....

NOT NICE, TRYING TO SHOOT PEOPLE IN THE BACK!

THE WONDER BOY LANDS A WONDER PUNCH!

YOU MUST BE TIRED-LIE DOWN!

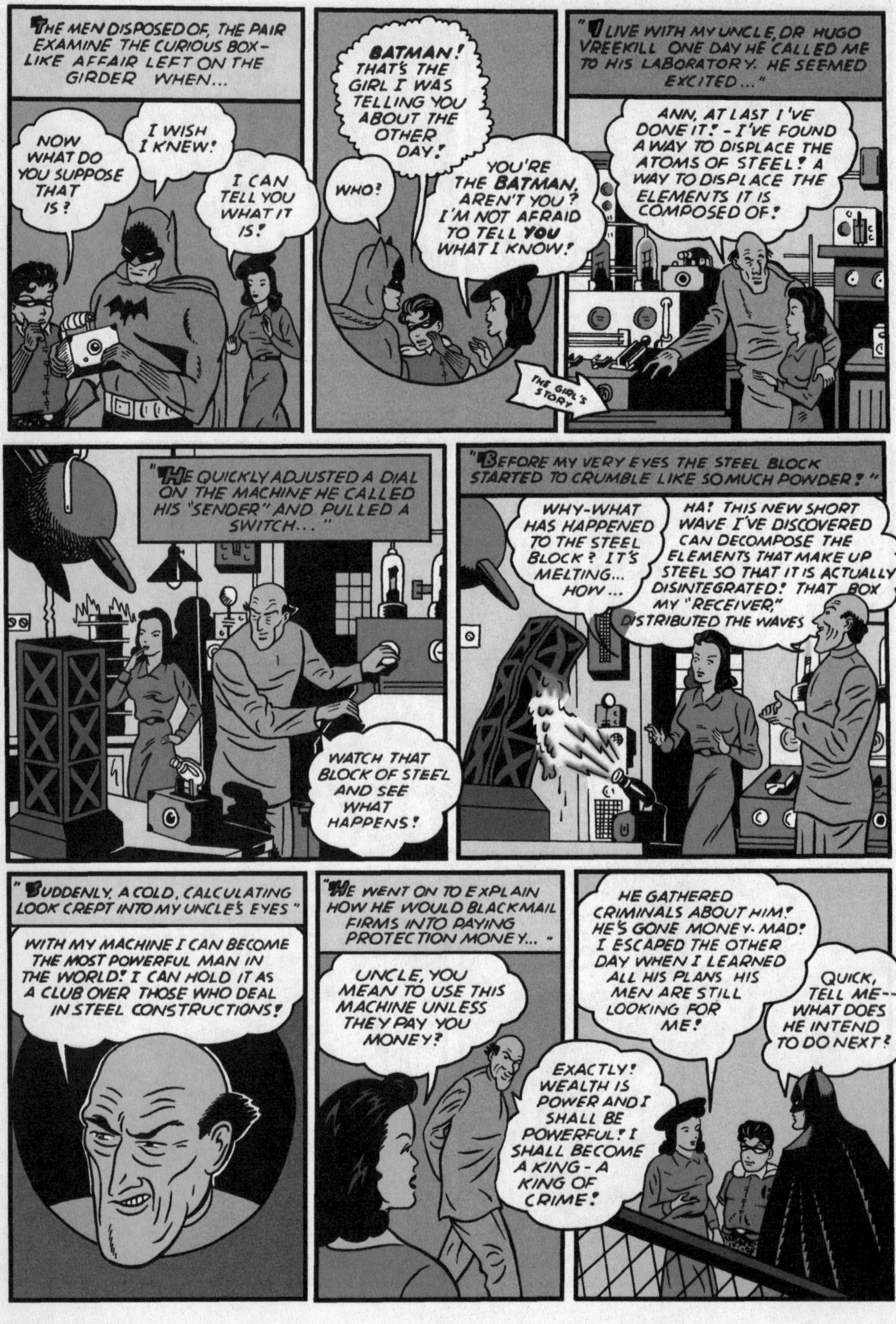
THE MEN DISPOSED OF, THE PAIR EXAMINE THE CURIOUS BOX-LIKE AFFAIR LEFT ON THE GIRDER WHEN...
NOW WHAT DO YOU SUPPOSE THAT IS?
I WISH I KNEW!
I CAN TELL YOU WHAT IT IS!
BATMAN! THAT'S THE GIRL I WAS TELLING YOU ABOUT THE OTHER DAY!
WHO?
YOU'RE THE BATMAN, AREN'T YOU? I'M NOT AFRAID TO TELL YOU WHAT I KNOW!
THE GIRL'S STORY
"I LIVE WITH MY UNCLE, DR HUGO VREEKILL ONE DAY HE CALLED ME TO HIS LABORATORY. HE SEEMED EXCITED..."
ANN, AT LAST I'VE DONE IT! - I'VE FOUND A WAY TO DISPLACE THE ATOMS OF STEEL! A WAY TO DISPLACE THE ELEMENTS IT IS COMPOSED OF!
"HE QUICKLY ADJUSTED A DIAL ON THE MACHINE HE CALLED HIS "SENDER" AND PULLED A SWITCH..."
WATCH THAT BLOCK OF STEEL AND SEE WHAT HAPPENS!
"BEFORE MY VERY EYES THE STEEL BLOCK STARTED TO CRUMBLE LIKE SO MUCH POWDER!"
WHY-WHAT HAS HAPPENED TO THE STEEL BLOCK? IT'S MELTING... HOW...
HA! THIS NEW SHORT WAVE I'VE DISCOVERED CAN DECOMPOSE THE ELEMENTS THAT MAKE UP STEEL SO THAT IT IS ACTUALLY DISINTEGRATED! THAT BOX MY "RECEIVER," DISTRIBUTED THE WAVES
"SUDDENLY, A COLD, CALCULATING LOOK CREPT INTO MY UNCLE'S EYES"
WITH MY MACHINE I CAN BECOME THE MOST POWERFUL MAN IN THE WORLD! I CAN HOLD IT AS A CLUB OVER THOSE WHO DEAL IN STEEL CONSTRUCTIONS!
"HE WENT ON TO EXPLAIN HOW HE WOULD BLACKMAIL FIRMS INTO PAYING PROTECTION MONEY..."
UNCLE, YOU MEAN TO USE THIS MACHINE UNLESS THEY PAY YOU MONEY?
EXACTLY! WEALTH IS POWER AND I SHALL BE POWERFUL! I SHALL BECOME A KING - A KING OF CRIME!
HE GATHERED CRIMINALS ABOUT HIM! HE'S GONE MONEY-MAD! I ESCAPED THE OTHER DAY WHEN I LEARNED ALL HIS PLANS HIS MEN ARE STILL LOOKING FOR ME!
QUICK, TELL ME-- WHAT DOES HE INTEND TO DO NEXT?

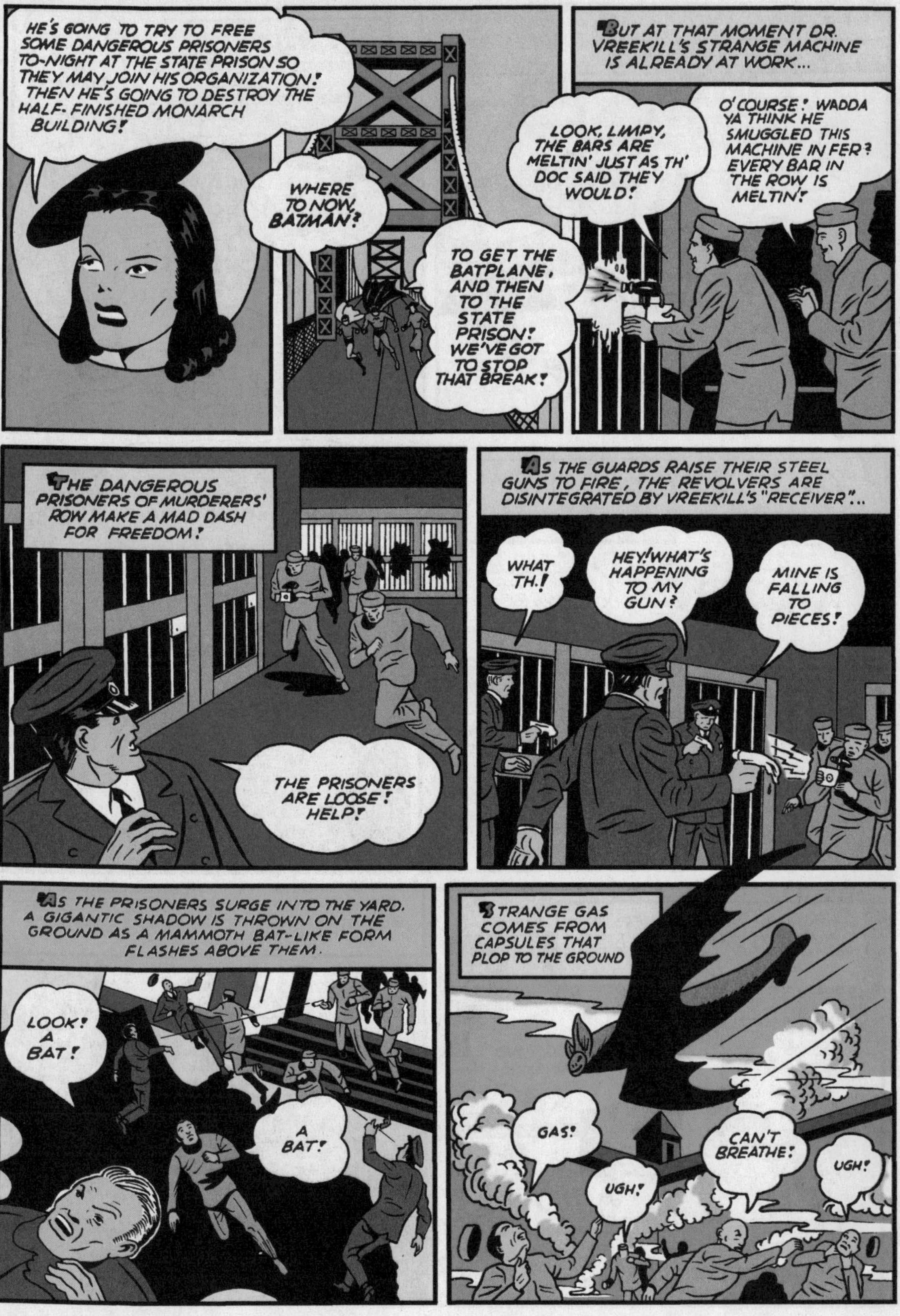

HE'S GOING TO TRY TO FREE SOME DANGEROUS PRISONERS TO-NIGHT AT THE STATE PRISON SO THEY MAY JOIN HIS ORGANIZATION! THEN HE'S GOING TO DESTROY THE HALF-FINISHED MONARCH BUILDING!
WHERE TO NOW, BATMAN?
TO GET THE BATPLANE, AND THEN TO THE STATE PRISON! WE'VE GOT TO STOP THAT BREAK!
BUT AT THAT MOMENT DR. VREEKILL'S STRANGE MACHINE IS ALREADY AT WORK...
LOOK, LIMPY, THE BARS ARE MELTIN' JUST AS TH' DOC SAID THEY WOULD!
O'COURSE! WADDA YA THINK HE SMUGGLED THIS MACHINE IN FER? EVERY BAR IN THE ROW IS MELTIN'!
THE DANGEROUS PRISONERS OF MURDERERS' ROW MAKE A MAD DASH FOR FREEDOM!
THE PRISONERS ARE LOOSE! HELP!
AS THE GUARDS RAISE THEIR STEEL GUNS TO FIRE, THE REVOLVERS ARE DISINTEGRATED BY VREEKILL'S "RECEIVER"...
WHAT TH.!
HEY! WHAT'S HAPPENING TO MY GUN?
MINE IS FALLING TO PIECES!
AS THE PRISONERS SURGE INTO THE YARD, A GIGANTIC SHADOW IS THROWN ON THE GROUND AS A MAMMOTH BAT-LIKE FORM FLASHES ABOVE THEM.
LOOK! A BAT!
A BAT!
STRANGE GAS COMES FROM CAPSULES THAT PLOP TO THE GROUND
GAS!
UGH!
CAN'T BREATHE!
UGH!

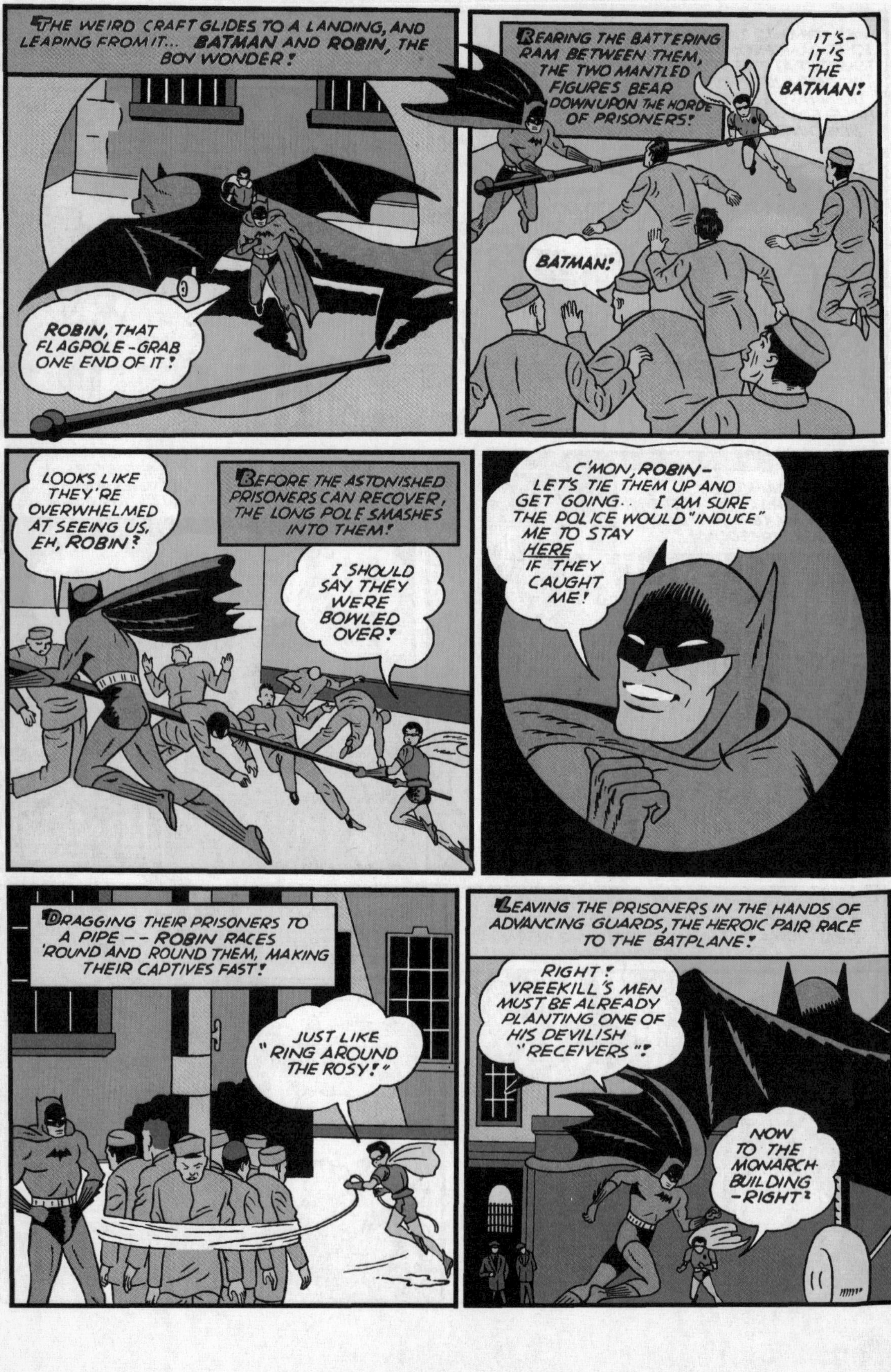
THE WEIRD CRAFT GLIDES TO A LANDING, AND LEAPING FROM IT... BATMAN AND ROBIN, THE BOY WONDER!
ROBIN, THAT FLAGPOLE-GRAB ONE END OF IT!
BEARING THE BATTERING RAM BETWEEN THEM, THE TWO MANTLED FIGURES BEAR DOWN UPON THE HORDE OF PRISONERS!
IT'S- IT'S THE BATMAN!
BATMAN!
LOOKS LIKE THEY'RE OVERWHELMED AT SEEING US, EH, ROBIN?
BEFORE THE ASTONISHED PRISONERS CAN RECOVER, THE LONG POLE SMASHES INTO THEM!
I SHOULD SAY THEY WERE BOWLED OVER!
C'MON, ROBIN- LET'S TIE THEM UP AND GET GOING.. I AM SURE THE POLICE WOULD "INDUCE" ME TO STAY HERE IF THEY CAUGHT ME!
DRAGGING THEIR PRISONERS TO A PIPE -- ROBIN RACES 'ROUND AND ROUND THEM, MAKING THEIR CAPTIVES FAST!
JUST LIKE "RING AROUND THE ROSY!"
LEAVING THE PRISONERS IN THE HANDS OF ADVANCING GUARDS, THE HEROIC PAIR RACE TO THE BATPLANE!
RIGHT! VREEKILL'S MEN MUST BE ALREADY PLANTING ONE OF HIS DEVILISH "RECEIVERS"!
NOW TO THE MONARCH BUILDING -RIGHT?

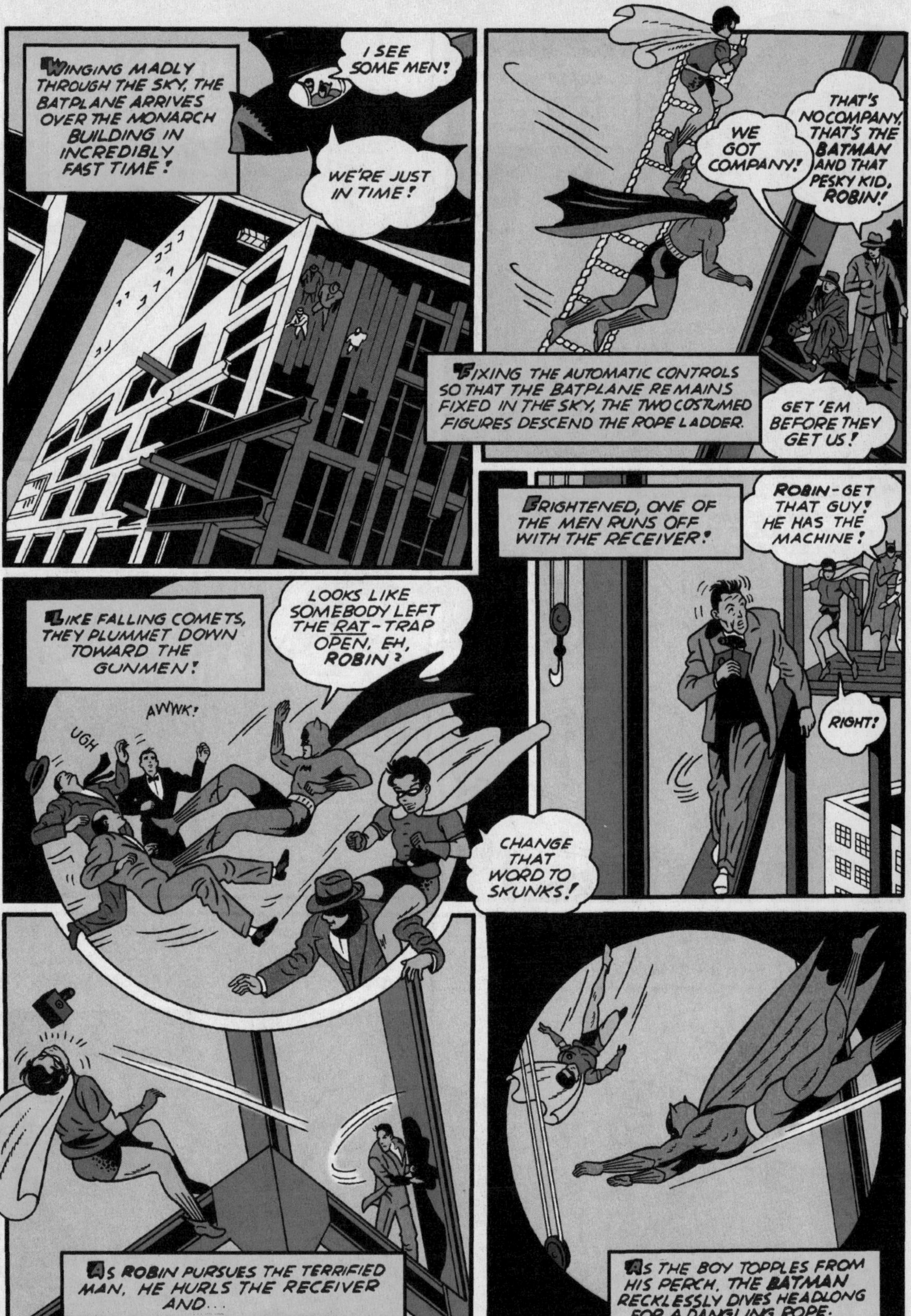
WINGING MADLY THROUGH THE SKY, THE BATPLANE ARRIVES OVER THE MONARCH BUILDING IN INCREDIBLY FAST TIME!
I SEE SOME MEN!
WE'RE JUST IN TIME!
THAT'S NO COMPANY, THAT'S THE BATMAN AND THAT PESKY KID, ROBIN!
WE GOT COMPANY!
FIXING THE AUTOMATIC CONTROLS SO THAT THE BATPLANE REMAINS FIXED IN THE SKY, THE TWO COSTUMED FIGURES DESCEND THE ROPE LADDER.
GET 'EM BEFORE THEY GET US!
LIKE FALLING COMETS, THEY PLUMMET DOWN TOWARD THE GUNMEN!
LOOKS LIKE SOMEBODY LEFT THE RAT-TRAP OPEN, EH, ROBIN?
AWWK!
UGH
CHANGE THAT WORD TO SKUNKS!
FRIGHTENED, ONE OF THE MEN RUNS OFF WITH THE RECEIVER!
ROBIN-GET THAT GUY! HE HAS THE MACHINE!
RIGHT!
AS ROBIN PURSUES THE TERRIFIED MAN, HE HURLS THE RECEIVER AND...
AS THE BOY TOPPLES FROM HIS PERCH, THE BATMAN RECKLESSLY DIVES HEADLONG FOR A DANGLING ROPE.

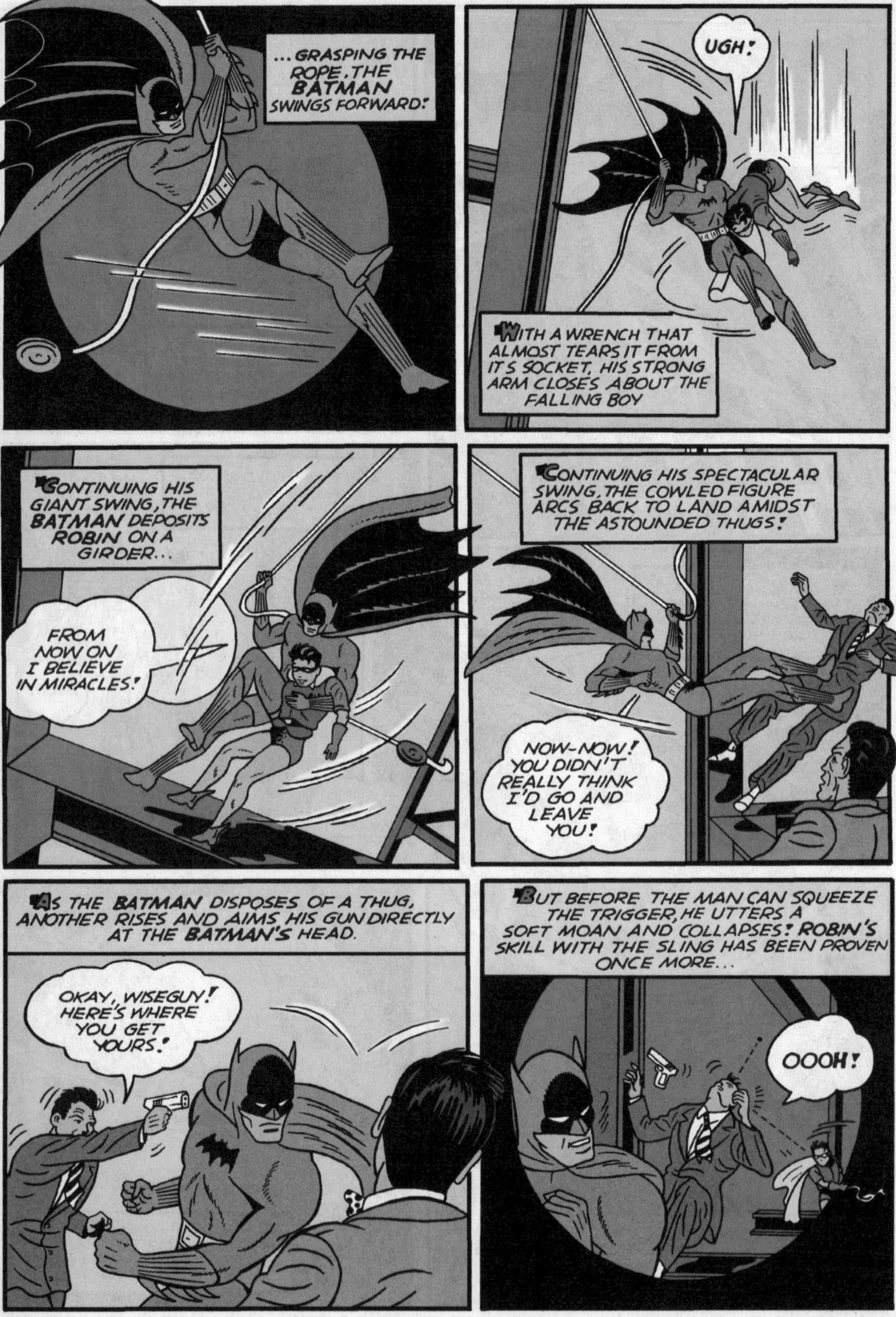
...GRASPING THE ROPE, THE BATMAN SWINGS FORWARD!
UGH!
WITH A WRENCH THAT ALMOST TEARS IT FROM IT'S SOCKET, HIS STRONG ARM CLOSES ABOUT THE FALLING BOY
CONTINUING HIS GIANT SWING, THE BATMAN DEPOSITS ROBIN ON A GIRDER...
FROM NOW ON I BELIEVE IN MIRACLES!
CONTINUING HIS SPECTACULAR SWING, THE COWLED FIGURE ARCS BACK TO LAND AMIDST THE ASTOUNDED THUGS!
NOW-NOW! YOU DIDN'T REALLY THINK I'D GO AND LEAVE YOU!
AS THE BATMAN DISPOSES OF A THUG, ANOTHER RISES AND AIMS HIS GUN DIRECTLY AT THE BATMAN'S HEAD.
OKAY, WISEGUY! HERE'S WHERE YOU GET YOURS!
BUT BEFORE THE MAN CAN SQUEEZE THE TRIGGER, HE UTTERS A SOFT MOAN AND COLLAPSES! ROBIN'S SKILL WITH THE SLING HAS BEEN PROVEN ONCE MORE...
OOOH!

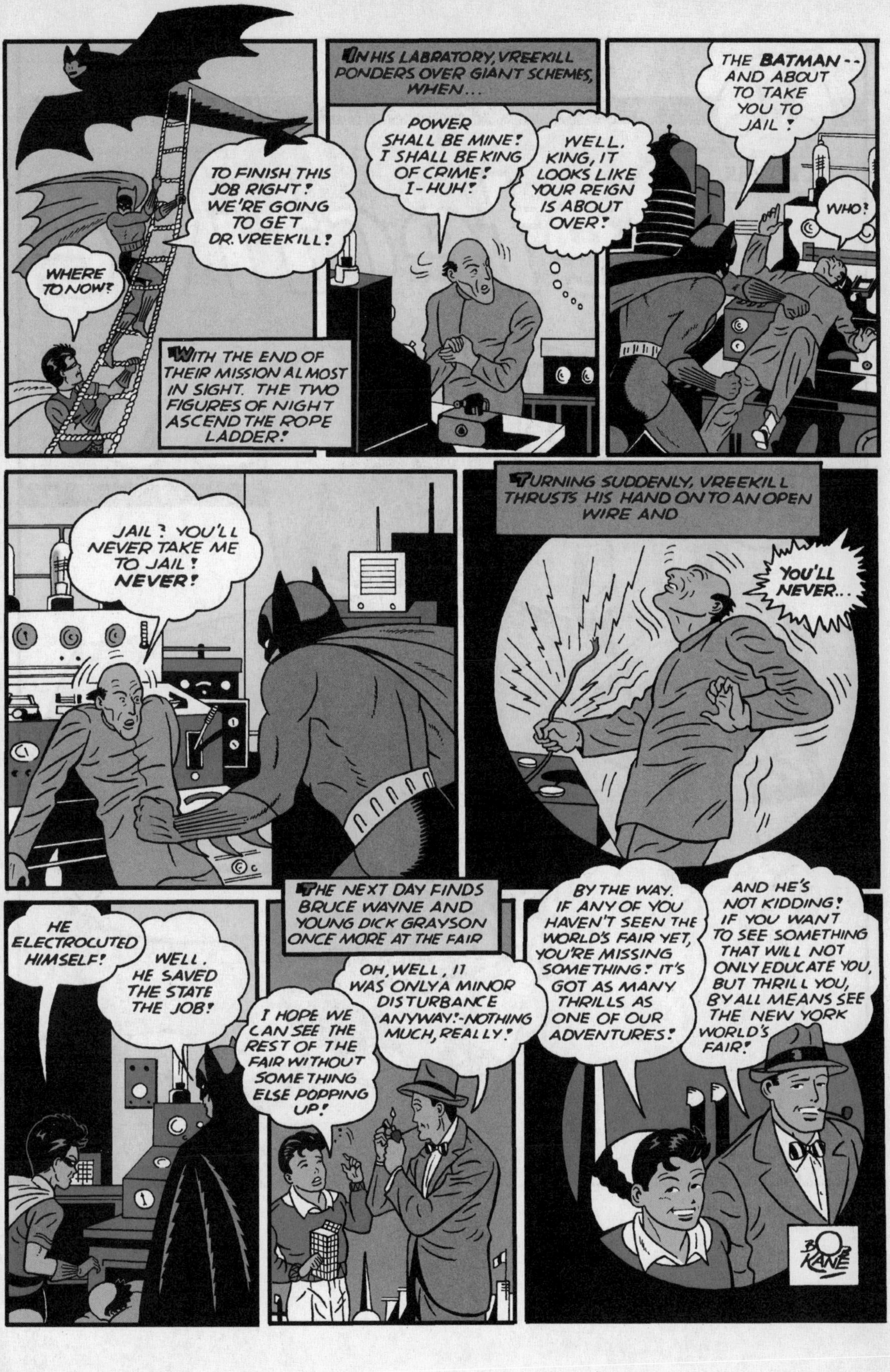
WITH THE END OF THEIR MISSION ALMOST IN SIGHT. THE TWO FIGURES OF NIGHT ASCEND THE ROPE LADDER!
WHERE TO NOW?
TO FINISH THIS JOB RIGHT! WE'RE GOING TO GET DR. VREEKILL!
IN HIS LABRATORY, VREEKILL PONDERS OVER GIANT SCHEMES, WHEN...
POWER SHALL BE MINE! I SHALL BE KING OF CRIME! I-HUH!
WELL, KING, IT LOOKS LIKE YOUR REIGN IS ABOUT OVER!
WHO?
THE BATMAN -- AND ABOUT TO TAKE YOU TO JAIL!
JAIL? YOU'LL NEVER TAKE ME TO JAIL! NEVER!
TURNING SUDDENLY, VREEKILL THRUSTS HIS HAND ON TO AN OPEN WIRE AND
YOU'LL NEVER...
HE ELECTROCUTED HIMSELF!
WELL. HE SAVED THE STATE THE JOB!
THE NEXT DAY FINDS BRUCE WAYNE AND YOUNG DICK GRAYSON ONCE MORE AT THE FAIR
I HOPE WE CAN SEE THE REST OF THE FAIR WITHOUT SOMETHING ELSE POPPING UP!
OH, WELL, IT WAS ONLY A MINOR DISTURBANCE ANYWAY!-NOTHING MUCH, REALLY!
BY THE WAY. IF ANY OF YOU HAVEN'T SEEN THE WORLD'S FAIR YET, YOU'RE MISSING SOMETHING! IT'S GOT AS MANY THRILLS AS ONE OF OUR ADVENTURES!
AND HE'S NOT KIDDING! IF YOU WANT TO SEE SOMETHING THAT WILL NOT ONLY EDUCATE YOU, BUT THRILL YOU, BY ALL MEANS SEE THE NEW YORK WORLD'S FAIR!
BOB KANE

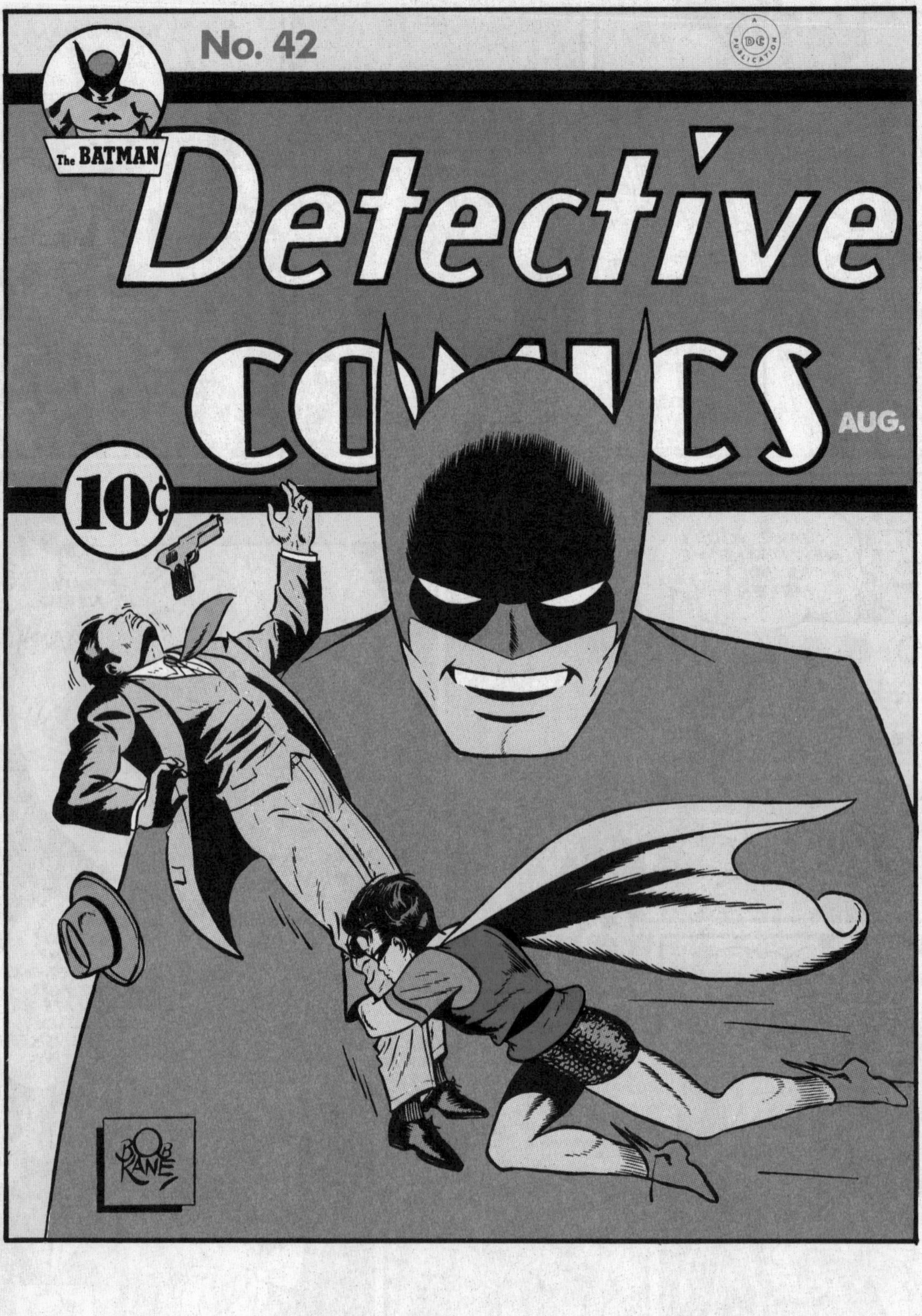

No. 42
A DC PUBLICATION
The BATMAN
Detective
COMICS
AUG.
10¢
BOB KANE

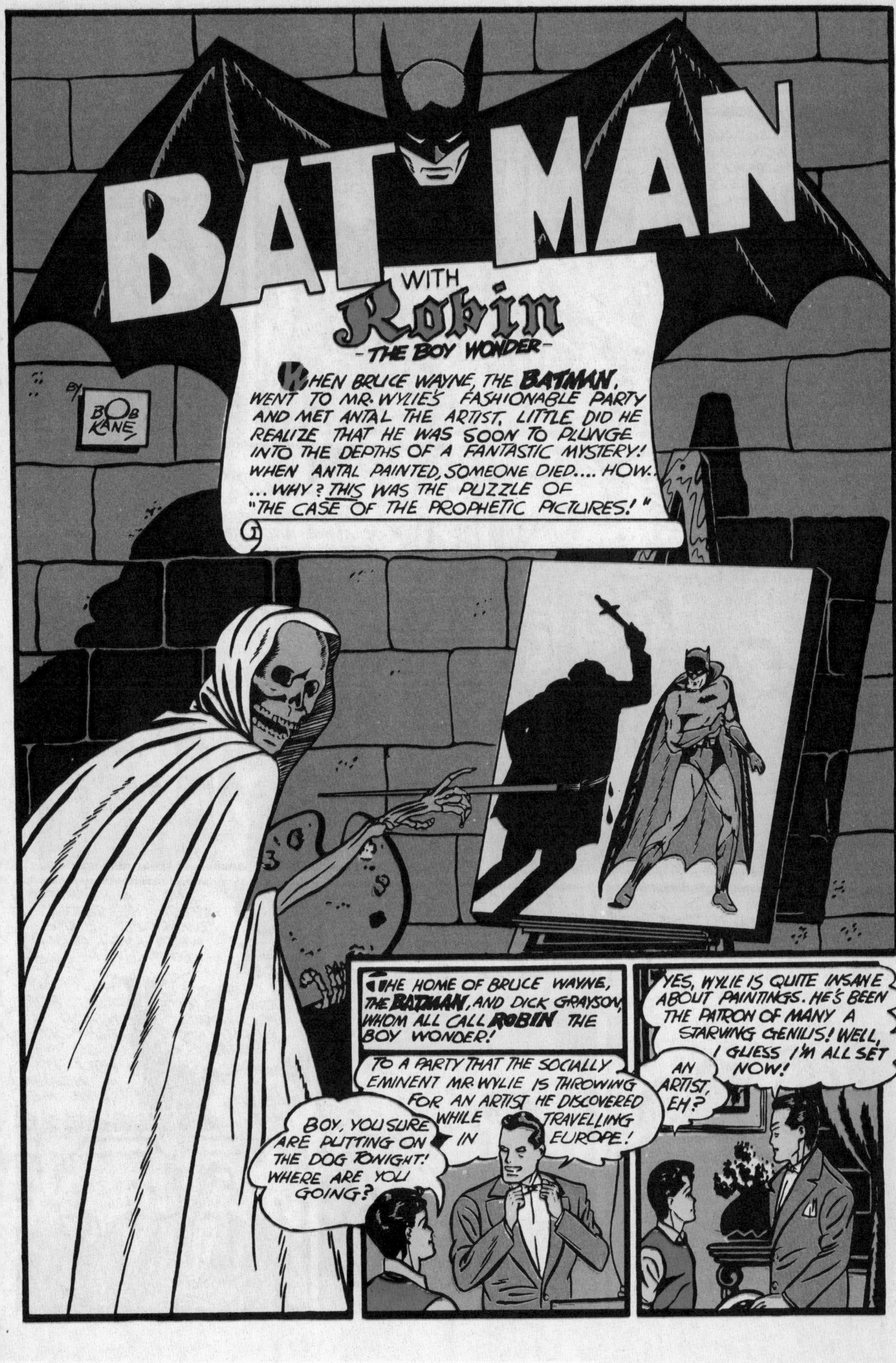

BATMAN
WITH Robin
-THE BOY WONDER-
BY BOB KANE
WHEN BRUCE WAYNE, THE BATMAN, WENT TO MR. WYLIE'S FASHIONABLE PARTY AND MET ANTAL THE ARTIST, LITTLE DID HE REALIZE THAT HE WAS SOON TO PLUNGE INTO THE DEPTHS OF A FANTASTIC MYSTERY! WHEN ANTAL PAINTED, SOMEONE DIED.... HOW... ...WHY? THIS WAS THE PUZZLE OF "THE CASE OF THE PROPHETIC PICTURES!"
THE HOME OF BRUCE WAYNE, THE BATMAN, AND DICK GRAYSON, WHOM ALL CALL ROBIN THE BOY WONDER!
BOY, YOU SURE ARE PUTTING ON THE DOG TONIGHT! WHERE ARE YOU GOING?
TO A PARTY THAT THE SOCIALLY EMINENT MR. WYLIE IS THROWING FOR AN ARTIST HE DISCOVERED WHILE IN TRAVELLING EUROPE!
AN ARTIST, EH?
YES, WYLIE IS QUITE INSANE ABOUT PAINTINGS. HE'S BEEN THE PATRON OF MANY A STARVING GENIUS! WELL, I GUESS I'M ALL SET NOW!

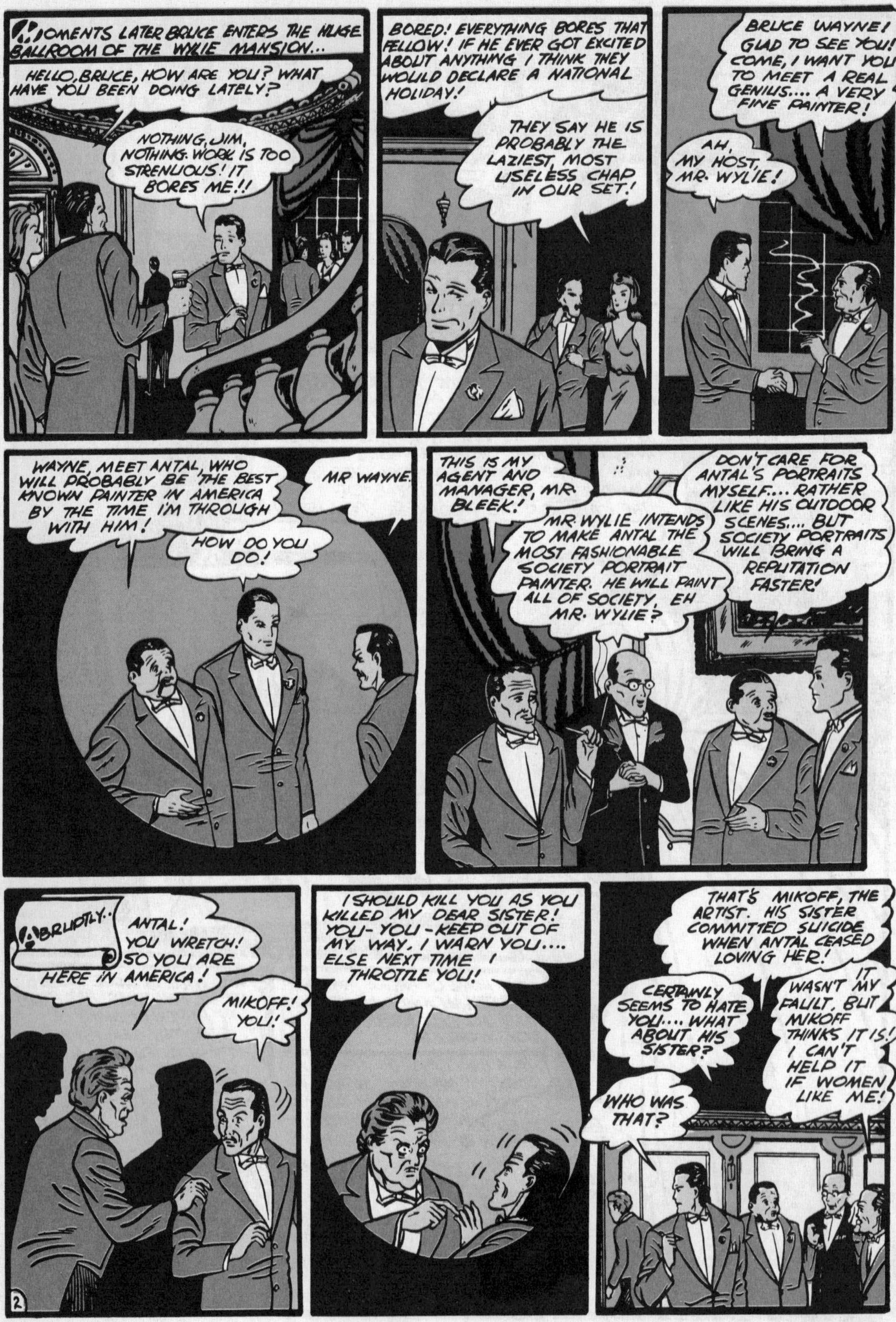
MOMENTS LATER BRUCE ENTERS THE HUGE BALLROOM OF THE WYLIE MANSION...
HELLO, BRUCE, HOW ARE YOU? WHAT HAVE YOU BEEN DOING LATELY?
NOTHING, JIM, NOTHING. WORK IS TOO STRENUOUS! IT BORES ME!!
BORED! EVERYTHING BORES THAT FELLOW! IF HE EVER GOT EXCITED ABOUT ANYTHING I THINK THEY WOULD DECLARE A NATIONAL HOLIDAY!
THEY SAY HE IS PROBABLY THE LAZIEST, MOST USELESS CHAP IN OUR SET!
BRUCE WAYNE! GLAD TO SEE YOU! COME, I WANT YOU TO MEET A REAL GENIUS.... A VERY FINE PAINTER!
AH, MY HOST, MR. WYLIE!
WAYNE, MEET ANTAL, WHO WILL PROBABLY BE THE BEST KNOWN PAINTER IN AMERICA BY THE TIME I'M THROUGH WITH HIM!
MR WAYNE.
HOW DO YOU DO!
THIS IS MY AGENT AND MANAGER, MR. BLEEK!
MR. WYLIE INTENDS TO MAKE ANTAL THE MOST FASHIONABLE SOCIETY PORTRAIT PAINTER. HE WILL PAINT ALL OF SOCIETY, EH MR. WYLIE?
DON'T CARE FOR ANTAL'S PORTRAITS MYSELF.... RATHER LIKE HIS OUTDOOR SCENES.... BUT SOCIETY PORTRAITS WILL BRING A REPUTATION FASTER!
ABRUPTLY..
ANTAL! YOU WRETCH! SO YOU ARE HERE IN AMERICA!
MIKOFF! YOU!
I SHOULD KILL YOU AS YOU KILLED MY DEAR SISTER! YOU- YOU -KEEP OUT OF MY WAY. I WARN YOU.... ELSE NEXT TIME I THROTTLE YOU!
WHO WAS THAT?
THAT'S MIKOFF, THE ARTIST. HIS SISTER COMMITTED SUICIDE WHEN ANTAL CEASED LOVING HER!
CERTAINLY SEEMS TO HATE YOU.... WHAT ABOUT HIS SISTER?
IT WASN'T MY FAULT, BUT MIKOFF THINKS IT IS! I CAN'T HELP IT IF WOMEN LIKE ME!
2

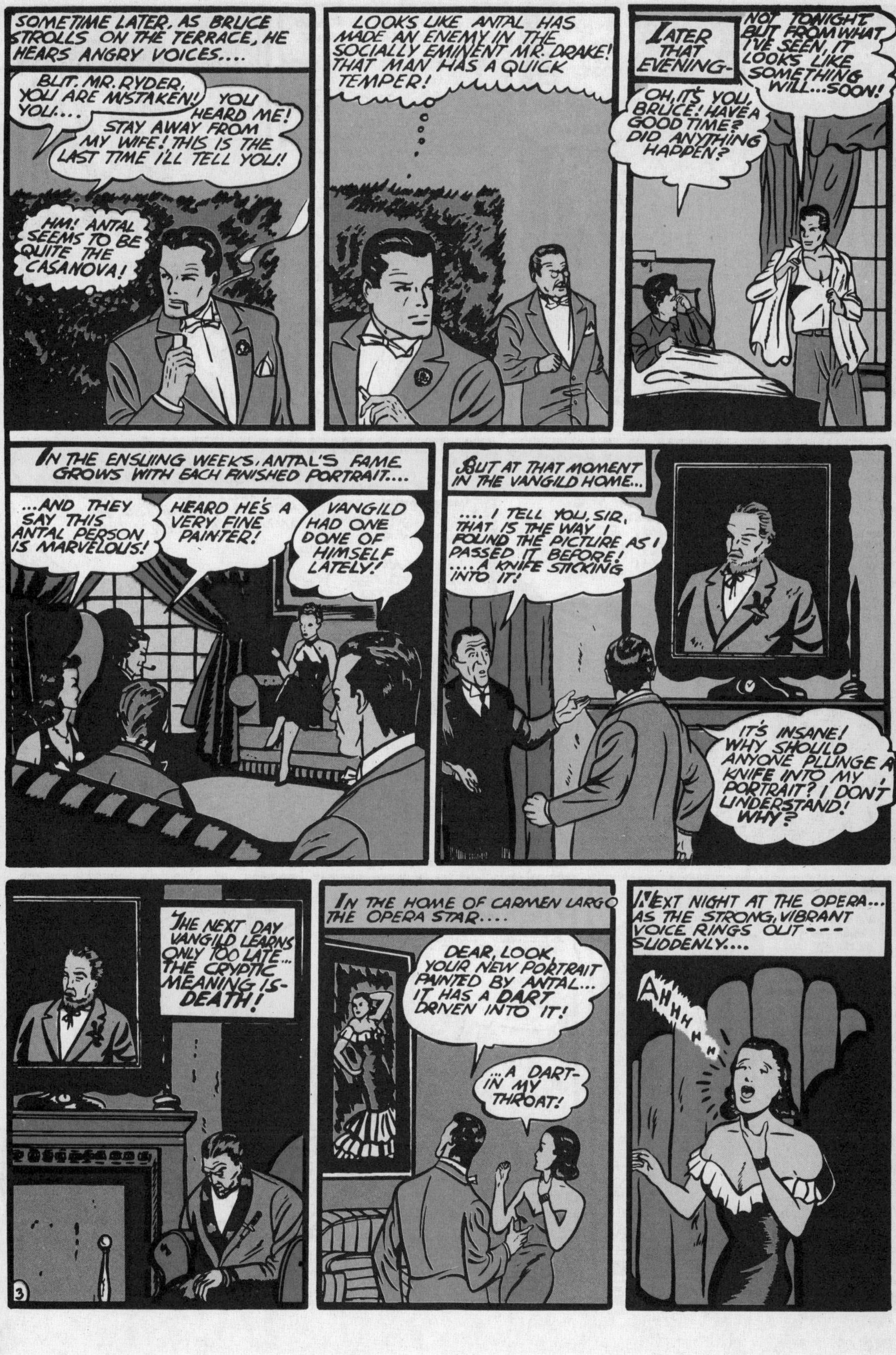

SOMETIME LATER, AS BRUCE STROLLS ON THE TERRACE, HE HEARS ANGRY VOICES....
BUT, MR. RYDER, YOU ARE MISTAKEN! YOU....
YOU HEARD ME! STAY AWAY FROM MY WIFE! THIS IS THE LAST TIME I'LL TELL YOU!
HM! ANTAL SEEMS TO BE QUITE THE CASANOVA!
LOOKS LIKE ANTAL HAS MADE AN ENEMY IN THE SOCIALLY EMINENT MR. DRAKE! THAT MAN HAS A QUICK TEMPER!
LATER THAT EVENING-
OH, IT'S YOU, BRUCE! HAVE A GOOD TIME? DID ANYTHING HAPPEN?
NOT TONIGHT, BUT FROM WHAT I'VE SEEN, IT LOOKS LIKE SOMETHING WILL...SOON!
IN THE ENSUING WEEKS, ANTAL'S FAME GROWS WITH EACH FINISHED PORTRAIT....
...AND THEY SAY THIS ANTAL PERSON IS MARVELOUS!
HEARD HE'S A VERY FINE PAINTER!
VANGILD HAD ONE DONE OF HIMSELF LATELY!
BUT AT THAT MOMENT IN THE VANGILD HOME...
.... I TELL YOU, SIR, THAT IS THE WAY I FOUND THE PICTURE AS I PASSED IT BEFORE! ....A KNIFE STICKING INTO IT!
IT'S INSANE! WHY SHOULD ANYONE PLUNGE A KNIFE INTO MY PORTRAIT? I DON'T UNDERSTAND! WHY?
THE NEXT DAY VANGILD LEARNS ONLY TOO LATE... THE CRYPTIC MEANING IS- DEATH!
3
IN THE HOME OF CARMEN LARGO THE OPERA STAR....
DEAR, LOOK, YOUR NEW PORTRAIT PAINTED BY ANTAL... IT HAS A DART DRIVEN INTO IT!
...A DART- IN MY THROAT!
NEXT NIGHT AT THE OPERA... AS THE STRONG, VIBRANT VOICE RINGS OUT--- SUDDENLY....
AHHHHH

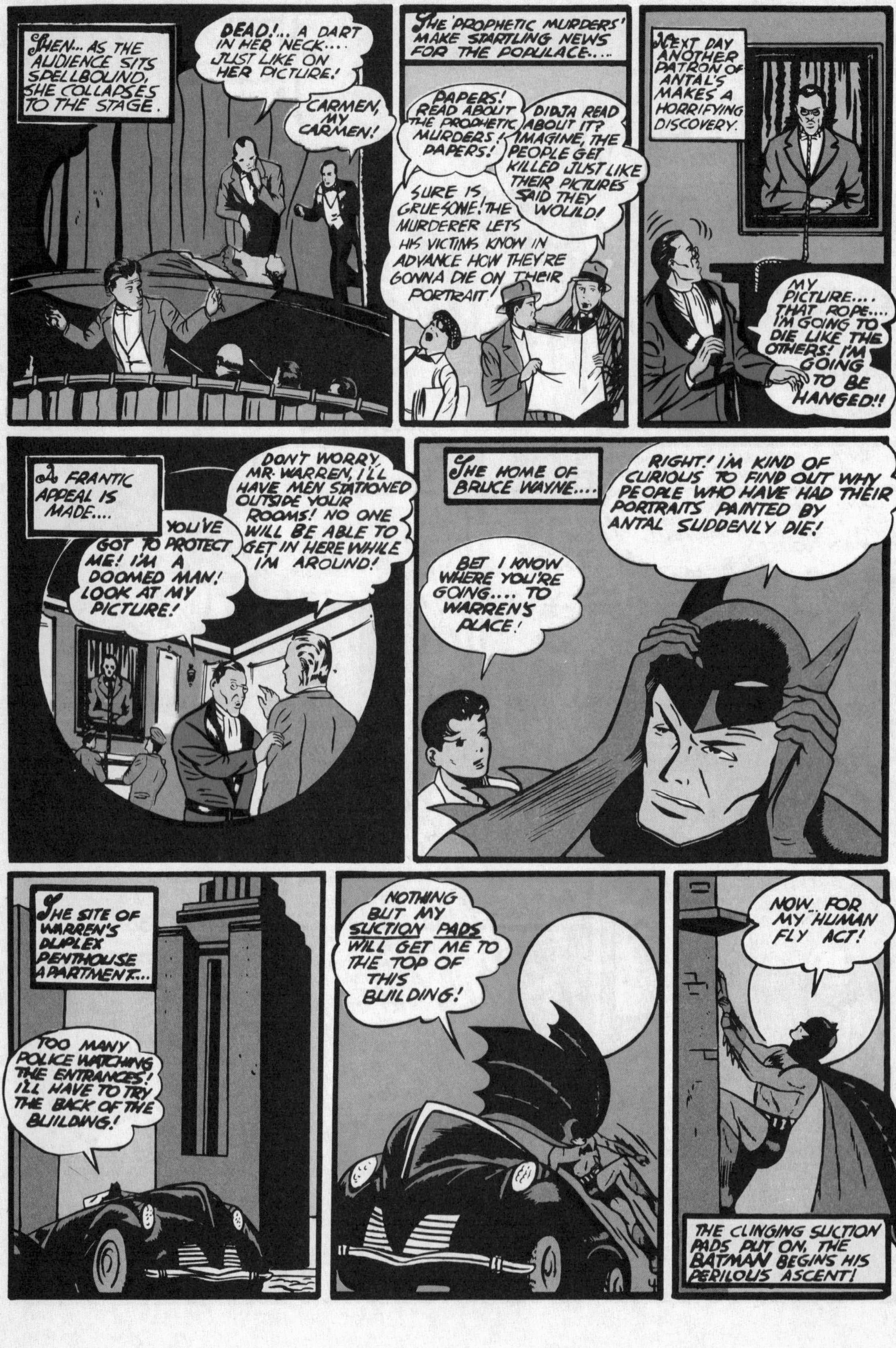
THEN... AS THE AUDIENCE SITS SPELLBOUND, SHE COLLAPSES TO THE STAGE.
DEAD!... A DART IN HER NECK.... JUST LIKE ON HER PICTURE!
CARMEN, MY CARMEN!
THE 'PROPHETIC MURDERS' MAKE STARTLING NEWS FOR THE POPULACE....
PAPERS! READ ABOUT THE PROPHETIC MURDERS! PAPERS!
DIDJA READ ABOUT IT? IMAGINE, THE PEOPLE GET KILLED JUST LIKE THEIR PICTURES SAID THEY WOULD!
SURE IS GRUESOME! THE MURDERER LETS HIS VICTIMS KNOW IN ADVANCE HOW THEY'RE GONNA DIE ON THEIR PORTRAIT!
NEXT DAY ANOTHER PATRON OF ANTAL'S MAKES A HORRIFYING DISCOVERY.
MY PICTURE.... THAT ROPE.... I'M GOING TO DIE LIKE THE OTHERS! I'M GOING TO BE HANGED!!
A FRANTIC APPEAL IS MADE....
YOU'VE GOT TO PROTECT ME! I'M A DOOMED MAN! LOOK AT MY PICTURE!
DON'T WORRY MR. WARREN, I'LL HAVE MEN STATIONED OUTSIDE YOUR ROOMS! NO ONE WILL BE ABLE TO GET IN HERE WHILE I'M AROUND!
THE HOME OF BRUCE WAYNE....
RIGHT! I'M KIND OF CURIOUS TO FIND OUT WHY PEOPLE WHO HAVE HAD THEIR PORTRAITS PAINTED BY ANTAL SUDDENLY DIE!
BET I KNOW WHERE YOU'RE GOING.... TO WARREN'S PLACE!
THE SITE OF WARREN'S DUPLEX PENTHOUSE APARTMENT...
TOO MANY POLICE WATCHING THE ENTRANCES! I'LL HAVE TO TRY THE BACK OF THE BUILDING!
NOTHING BUT MY SUCTION PADS WILL GET ME TO THE TOP OF THIS BUILDING!
NOW... FOR MY "HUMAN FLY ACT!
THE CLINGING SUCTION PADS PUT ON, THE BATMAN BEGINS HIS PERILOUS ASCENT!

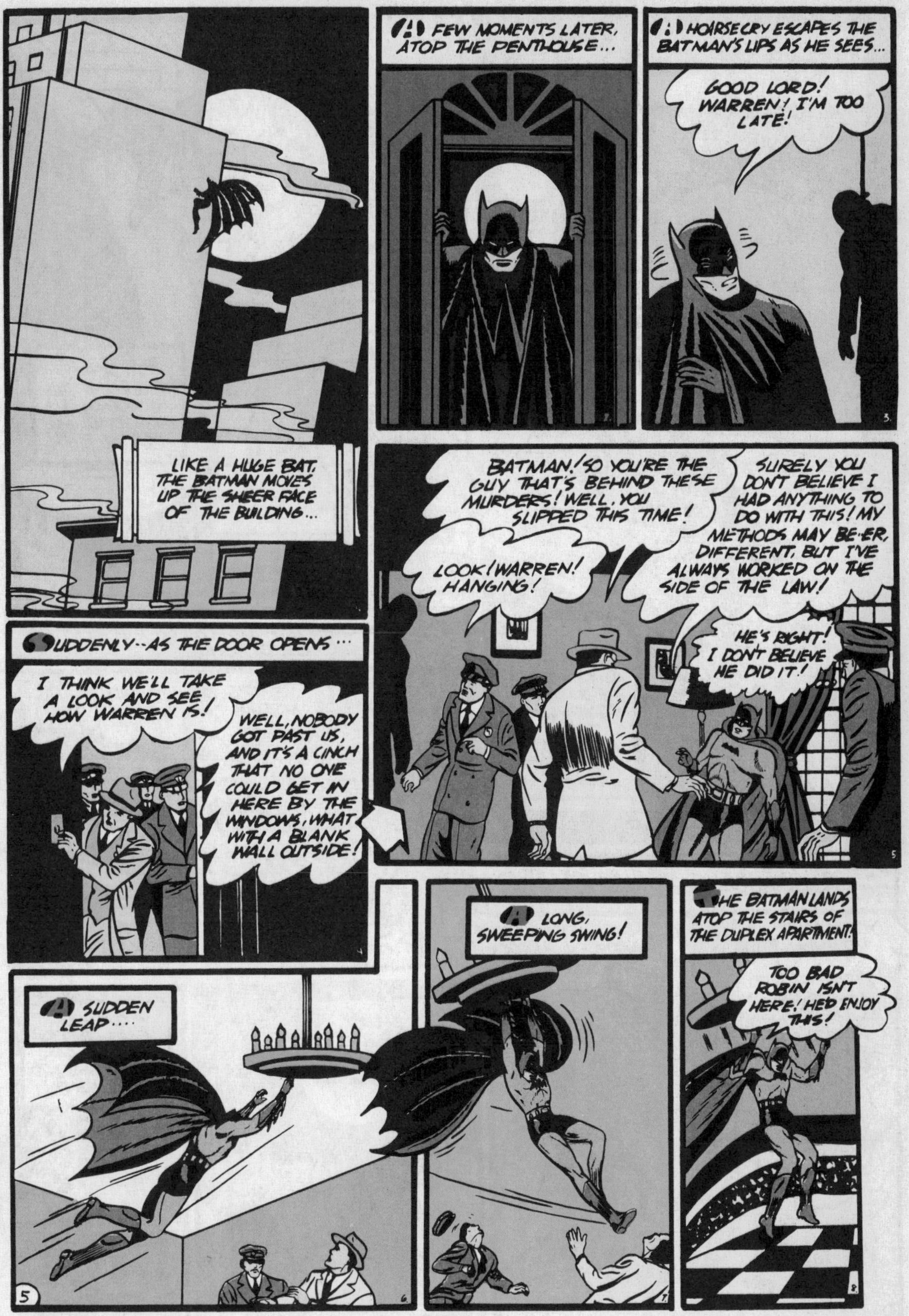

LIKE A HUGE BAT, THE BATMAN MOVES UP THE SHEER FACE OF THE BUILDING...
A FEW MOMENTS LATER, ATOP THE PENTHOUSE...
A HOARSE CRY ESCAPES THE BATMAN'S LIPS AS HE SEES...
GOOD LORD! WARREN! I'M TOO LATE!
SUDDENLY--AS THE DOOR OPENS...
I THINK WE'LL TAKE A LOOK AND SEE HOW WARREN IS!
WELL, NOBODY GOT PAST US, AND IT'S A CINCH THAT NO ONE COULD GET IN HERE BY THE WINDOWS, WHAT WITH A BLANK WALL OUTSIDE!
LOOK! WARREN! HANGING!
BATMAN! SO YOU'RE THE GUY THAT'S BEHIND THESE MURDERS! WELL, YOU SLIPPED THIS TIME!
SURELY YOU DON'T BELIEVE I HAD ANYTHING TO DO WITH THIS! MY METHODS MAY BE-ER, DIFFERENT, BUT I'VE ALWAYS WORKED ON THE SIDE OF THE LAW!
HE'S RIGHT! I DON'T BELIEVE HE DID IT!
A SUDDEN LEAP....
A LONG, SWEEPING SWING!
THE BATMAN LANDS ATOP THE STAIRS OF THE DUPLEX APARTMENT!
TOO BAD ROBIN ISN'T HERE! HE'D ENJOY THIS!

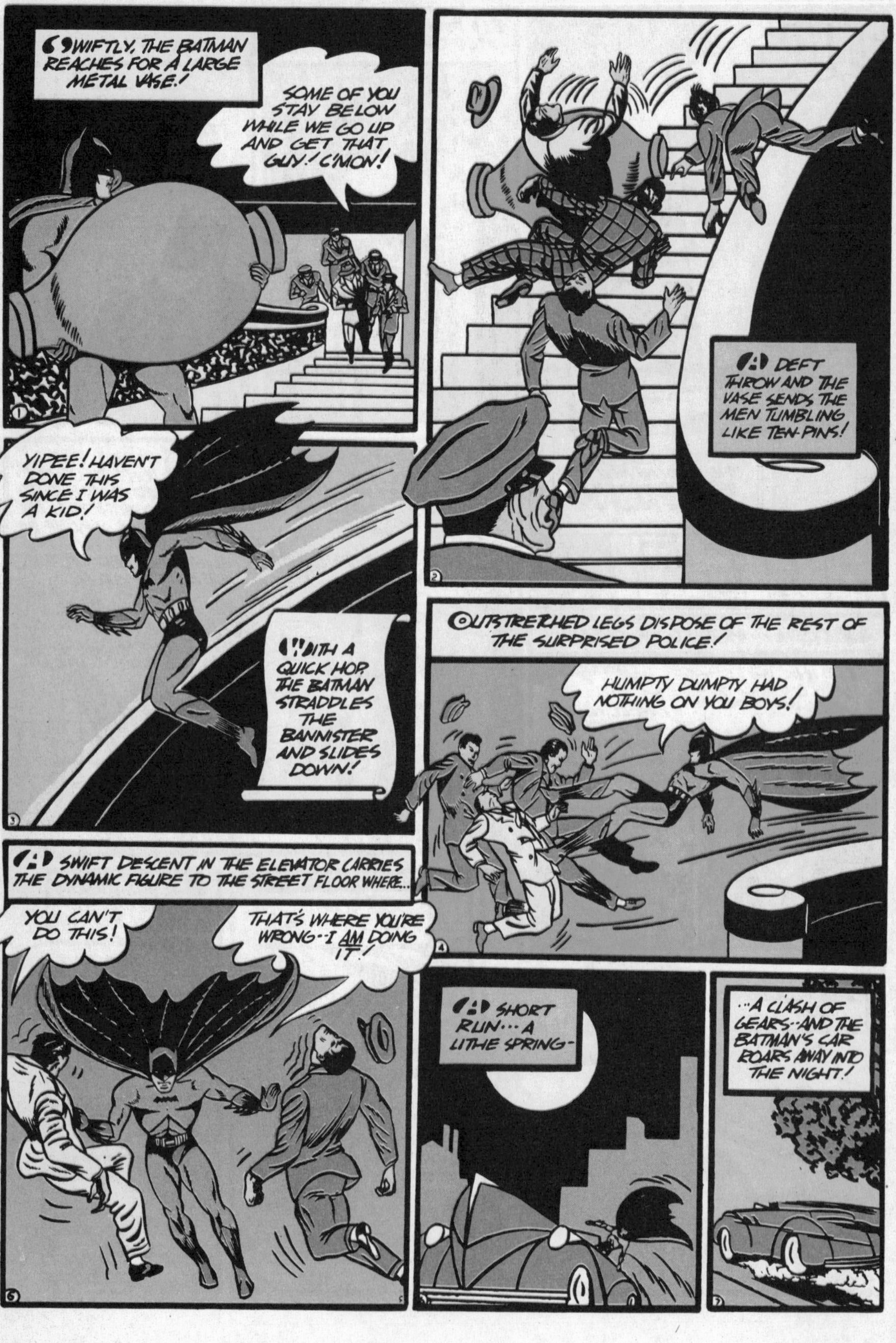
SWIFTLY, THE BATMAN REACHES FOR A LARGE METAL VASE!
SOME OF YOU STAY BELOW WHILE WE GO UP AND GET THAT GUY! C'MON!
A DEFT THROW AND THE VASE SENDS THE MEN TUMBLING LIKE TEN-PINS!
YIPEE! HAVEN'T DONE THIS SINCE I WAS A KID!
WITH A QUICK HOP, THE BATMAN STRADDLES THE BANNISTER AND SLIDES DOWN!
OUTSTRETCHED LEGS DISPOSE OF THE REST OF THE SURPRISED POLICE!
HUMPTY DUMPTY HAD NOTHING ON YOU BOYS!
A SWIFT DESCENT IN THE ELEVATOR CARRIES THE DYNAMIC FIGURE TO THE STREET FLOOR WHERE...
YOU CAN'T DO THIS!
THAT'S WHERE YOU'RE WRONG--I AM DOING IT!
A SHORT RUN... A LITHE SPRING-
...A CLASH OF GEARS--AND THE BATMAN'S CAR ROARS AWAY INTO THE NIGHT!

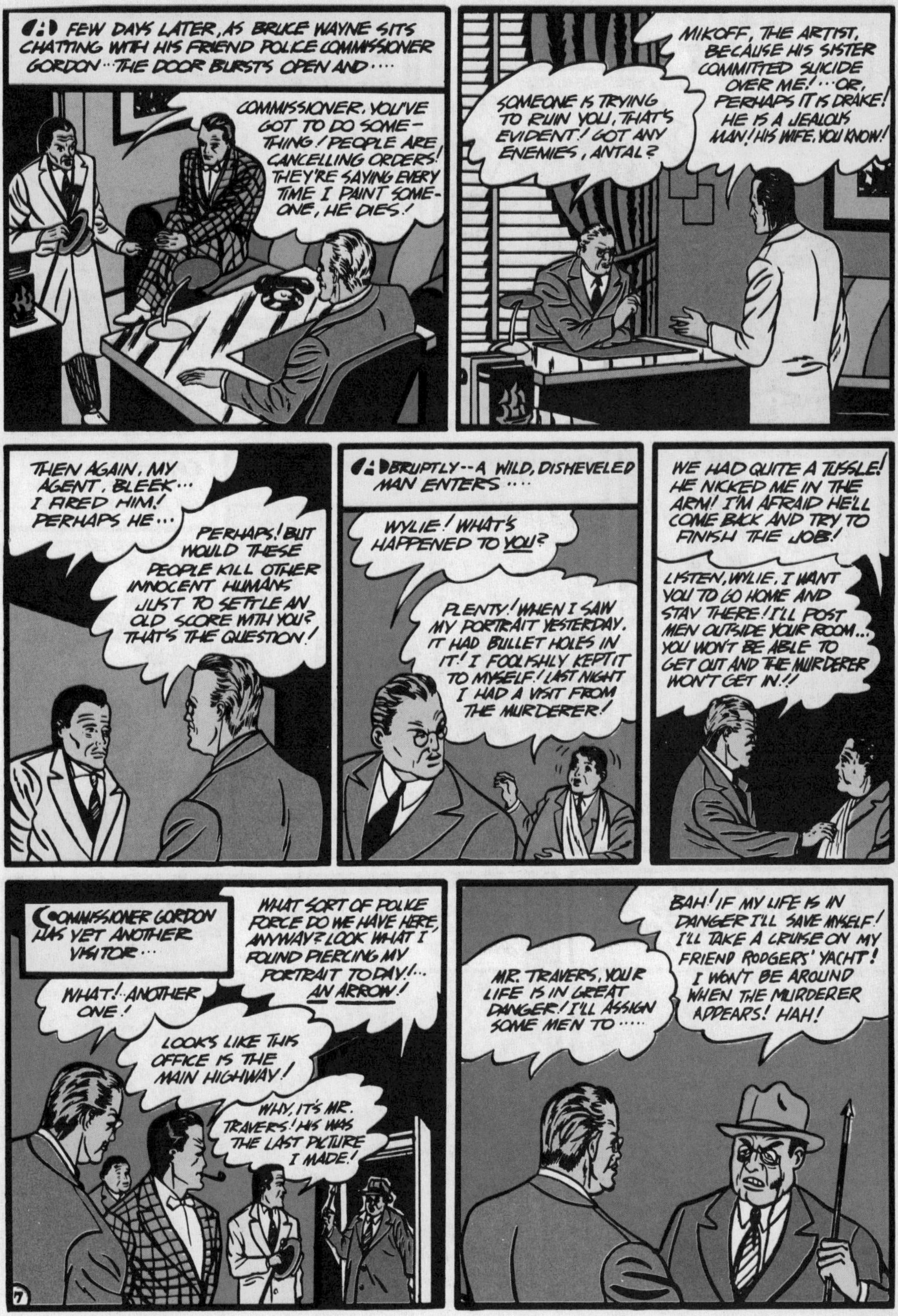
A FEW DAYS LATER, AS BRUCE WAYNE SITS CHATTING WITH HIS FRIEND POLICE COMMISSIONER GORDON···THE DOOR BURSTS OPEN AND····
COMMISSIONER, YOU'VE GOT TO DO SOME-THING! PEOPLE ARE CANCELLING ORDERS! THEY'RE SAYING EVERY TIME I PAINT SOME-ONE, HE DIES!
SOMEONE IS TRYING TO RUIN YOU, THAT'S EVIDENT! GOT ANY ENEMIES, ANTAL?
MIKOFF, THE ARTIST, BECAUSE HIS SISTER COMMITTED SUICIDE OVER ME!···OR, PERHAPS IT IS DRAKE! HE IS A JEALOUS MAN! HIS WIFE, YOU KNOW!
THEN AGAIN, MY AGENT, BLEEK··· I FIRED HIM! PERHAPS HE···
PERHAPS! BUT WOULD THESE PEOPLE KILL OTHER INNOCENT HUMANS JUST TO SETTLE AN OLD SCORE WITH YOU? THAT'S THE QUESTION!
ABRUPTLY--A WILD, DISHEVELED MAN ENTERS····
WYLIE! WHAT'S HAPPENED TO YOU?
PLENTY! WHEN I SAW MY PORTRAIT YESTERDAY, IT HAD BULLET HOLES IN IT! I FOOLISHLY KEPT IT TO MYSELF! LAST NIGHT I HAD A VISIT FROM THE MURDERER!
WE HAD QUITE A TUSSLE! HE NICKED ME IN THE ARM! I'M AFRAID HE'LL COME BACK AND TRY TO FINISH THE JOB!
LISTEN, WYLIE, I WANT YOU TO GO HOME AND STAY THERE! I'LL POST MEN OUTSIDE YOUR ROOM... YOU WON'T BE ABLE TO GET OUT AND THE MURDERER WON'T GET IN!!
COMMISSIONER GORDON HAS YET ANOTHER VISITOR···
WHAT SORT OF POLICE FORCE DO WE HAVE HERE, ANYWAY? LOOK WHAT I FOUND PIERCING MY PORTRAIT TODAY!... AN ARROW!
WHAT!·ANOTHER ONE!
LOOKS LIKE THIS OFFICE IS THE MAIN HIGHWAY!
WHY, IT'S MR. TRAVERS! HIS WAS THE LAST PICTURE I MADE!
7
MR. TRAVERS, YOUR LIFE IS IN GREAT DANGER! I'LL ASSIGN SOME MEN TO·····
BAH! IF MY LIFE IS IN DANGER I'LL SAVE MYSELF! I'LL TAKE A CRUISE ON MY FRIEND RODGERS' YACHT! I WON'T BE AROUND WHEN THE MURDERER APPEARS! HAH!

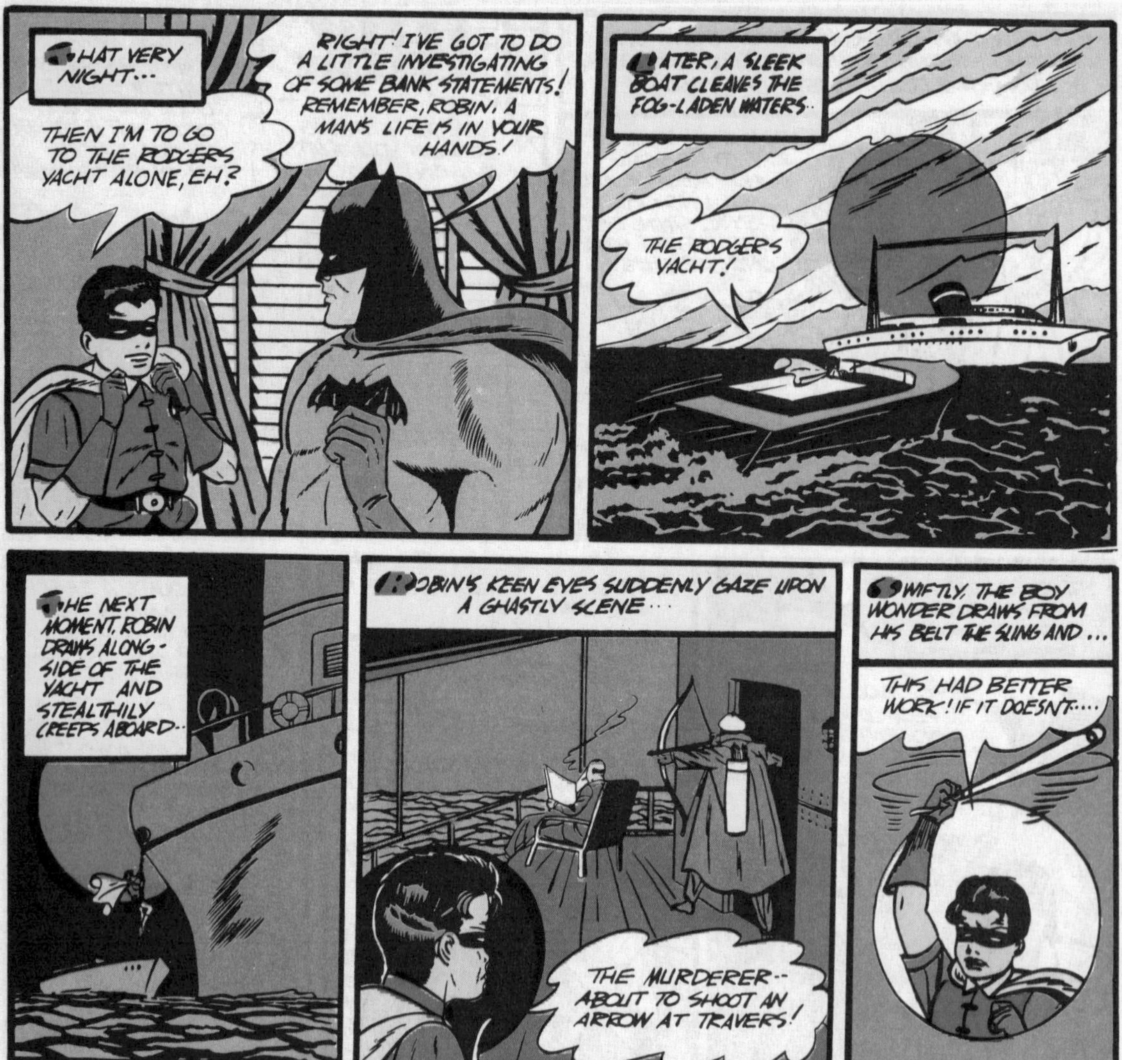
THAT VERY NIGHT...
THEN I'M TO GO TO THE RODGERS YACHT ALONE, EH?
RIGHT! I'VE GOT TO DO A LITTLE INVESTIGATING OF SOME BANK STATEMENTS! REMEMBER, ROBIN, A MAN'S LIFE IS IN YOUR HANDS!
LATER, A SLEEK BOAT CLEAVES THE FOG-LADEN WATERS..
THE RODGERS YACHT!
THE NEXT MOMENT, ROBIN DRAWS ALONG-SIDE OF THE YACHT AND STEALTHILY CREEPS ABOARD..
ROBIN'S KEEN EYES SUDDENLY GAZE UPON A GHASTLY SCENE...
THE MURDERER-- ABOUT TO SHOOT AN ARROW AT TRAVERS!
SWIFTLY, THE BOY WONDER DRAWS FROM HIS BELT THE SLING AND ...
THIS HAD BETTER WORK! IF IT DOESN'T....
EVEN AS THE ARROW BOLTS FROM THE TAUT STRING, SO DOES THE STEEL PELLET STREAK FORWARD, STRIKING IT IN MID-AIR!
Z-I-N-G
8
THE BOY WONDER LEAPS AT THE GHASTLY MURDERER!
AN INTRUDER, EH?.. I'LL TAKE CARE OF YOU!

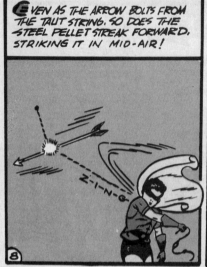

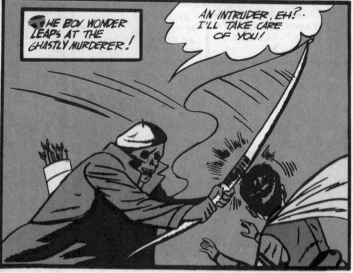

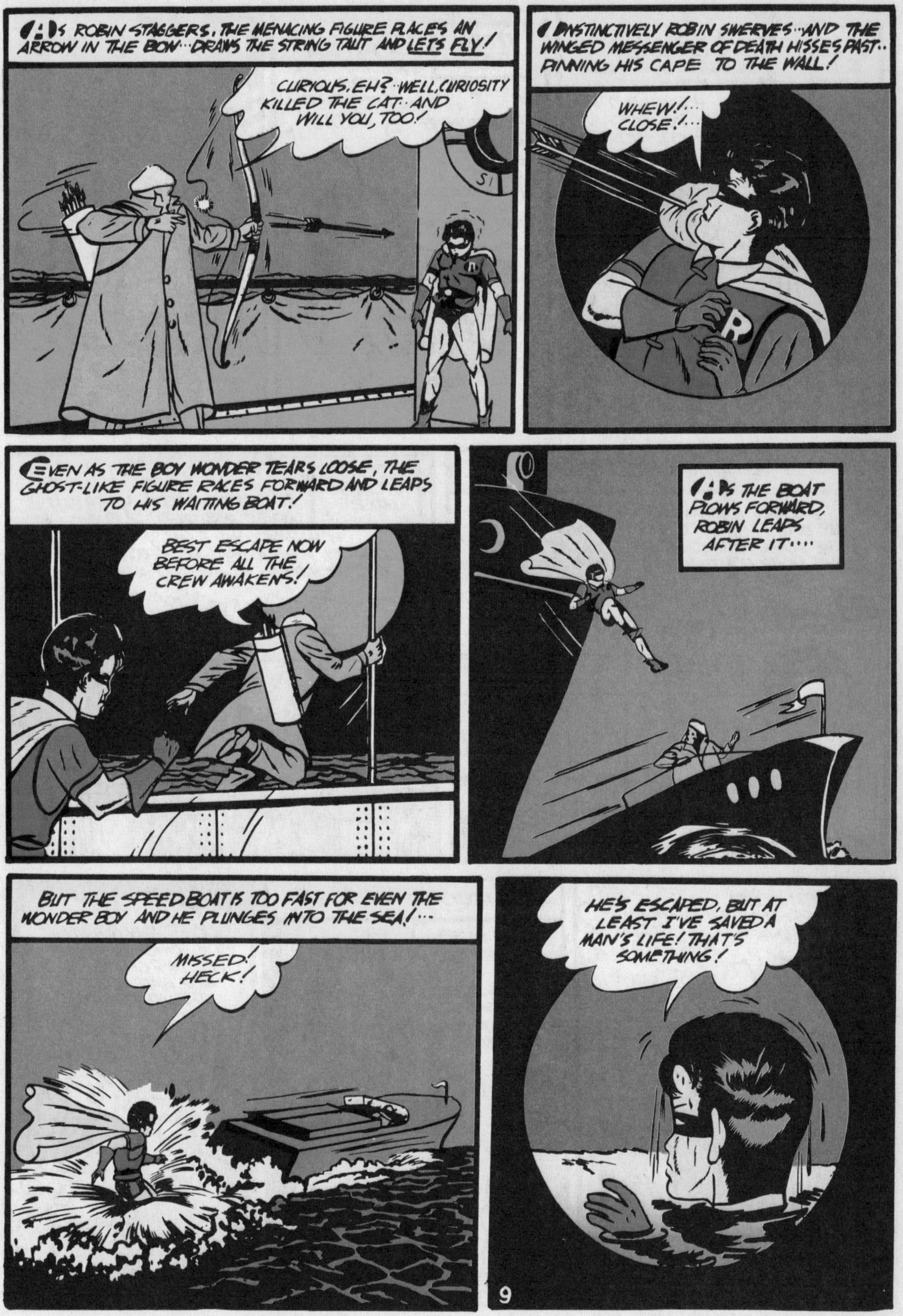
AS ROBIN STAGGERS, THE MENACING FIGURE PLACES AN ARROW IN THE BOW...DRAWS THE STRING TAUT AND LETS FLY!
CURIOUS, EH? ..WELL, CURIOSITY KILLED THE CAT..AND WILL YOU, TOO!
INSTINCTIVELY ROBIN SWERVES...AND THE WINGED MESSENGER OF DEATH HISSES PAST.. PINNING HIS CAPE TO THE WALL!
WHEW!... CLOSE!...
EVEN AS THE BOY WONDER TEARS LOOSE, THE GHOST-LIKE FIGURE RACES FORWARD AND LEAPS TO HIS WAITING BOAT!
BEST ESCAPE NOW BEFORE ALL THE CREW AWAKENS!
AS THE BOAT PLOWS FORWARD, ROBIN LEAPS AFTER IT....
BUT THE SPEEDBOAT IS TOO FAST FOR EVEN THE WONDER BOY AND HE PLUNGES INTO THE SEA!...
MISSED! HECK!
HE'S ESCAPED, BUT AT LEAST I'VE SAVED A MAN'S LIFE! THAT'S SOMETHING!
9

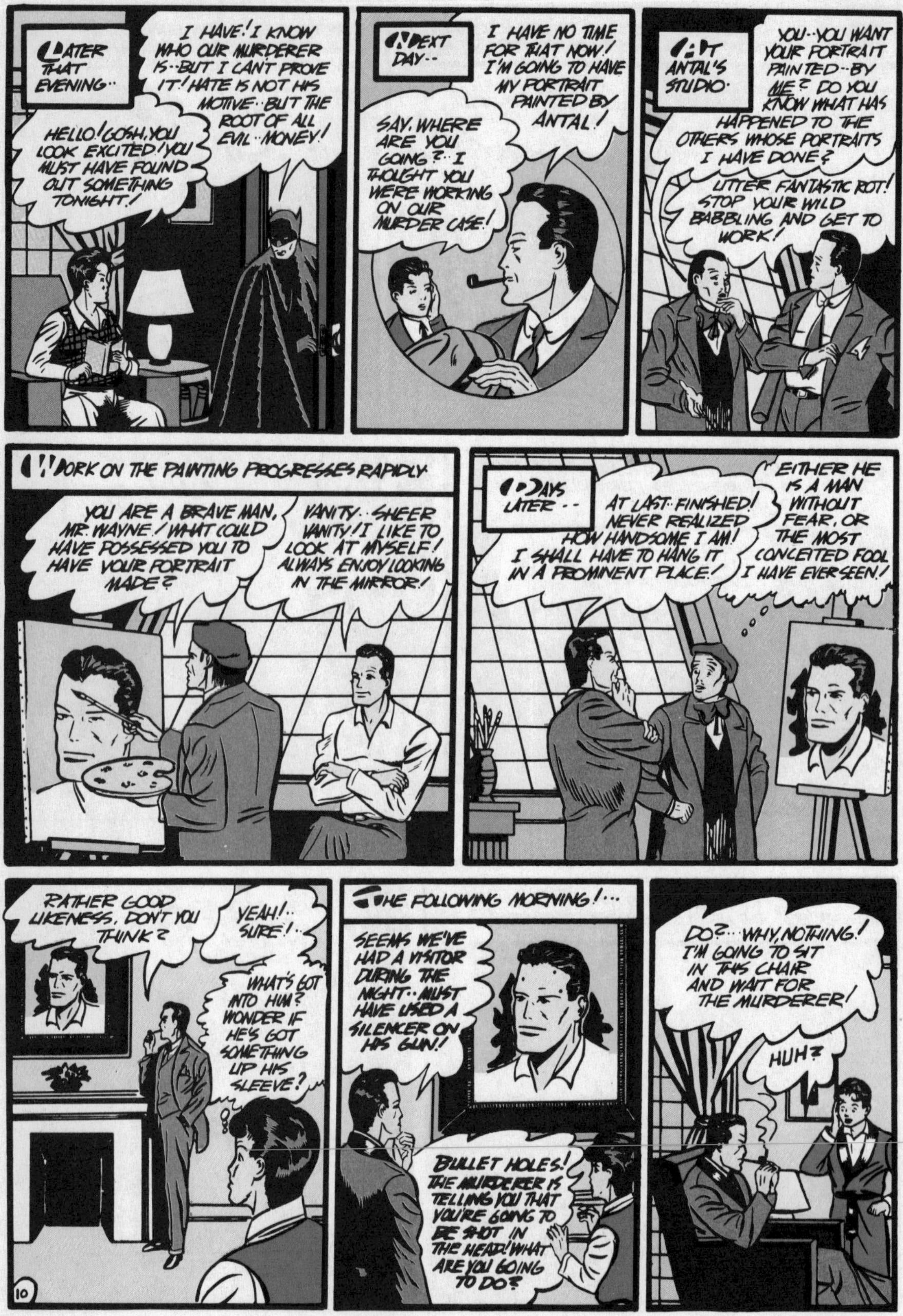
LATER THAT EVENING..
I HAVE! I KNOW WHO OUR MURDERER IS..BUT I CAN'T PROVE IT! HATE IS NOT HIS MOTIVE..BUT THE ROOT OF ALL EVIL..MONEY!
HELLO! GOSH, YOU LOOK EXCITED! YOU MUST HAVE FOUND OUT SOMETHING TONIGHT!
NEXT DAY--
I HAVE NO TIME FOR THAT NOW! I'M GOING TO HAVE MY PORTRAIT PAINTED BY ANTAL!
SAY, WHERE ARE YOU GOING?..I THOUGHT YOU WERE WORKING ON OUR MURDER CASE!
AT ANTAL'S STUDIO.
YOU..YOU WANT YOUR PORTRAIT PAINTED..BY ME? DO YOU KNOW WHAT HAS HAPPENED TO THE OTHERS WHOSE PORTRAITS I HAVE DONE?
UTTER FANTASTIC ROT! STOP YOUR WILD BABBLING AND GET TO WORK!
WORK ON THE PAINTING PROGRESSES RAPIDLY.
YOU ARE A BRAVE MAN, MR. WAYNE! WHAT COULD HAVE POSSESSED YOU TO HAVE YOUR PORTRAIT MADE?
VANITY..SHEER VANITY! I LIKE TO LOOK AT MYSELF! ALWAYS ENJOY LOOKING IN THE MIRROR!
DAYS LATER--
AT LAST FINISHED! NEVER REALIZED HOW HANDSOME I AM! I SHALL HAVE TO HANG IT IN A PROMINENT PLACE!
EITHER HE IS A MAN WITHOUT FEAR, OR THE MOST CONCEITED FOOL I HAVE EVER SEEN!
RATHER GOOD LIKENESS, DON'T YOU THINK?
YEAH!.. SURE!..
WHAT'S GOT INTO HIM? WONDER IF HE'S GOT SOMETHING UP HIS SLEEVE?
10
THE FOLLOWING MORNING!...
SEEMS WE'VE HAD A VISITOR DURING THE NIGHT..MUST HAVE USED A SILENCER ON HIS GUN!
BULLET HOLES! THE MURDERER IS TELLING YOU THAT YOU'RE GOING TO BE SHOT IN THE HEAD! WHAT ARE YOU GOING TO DO?
DO?...WHY, NOTHING! I'M GOING TO SIT IN THIS CHAIR AND WAIT FOR THE MURDERER!
HUH?

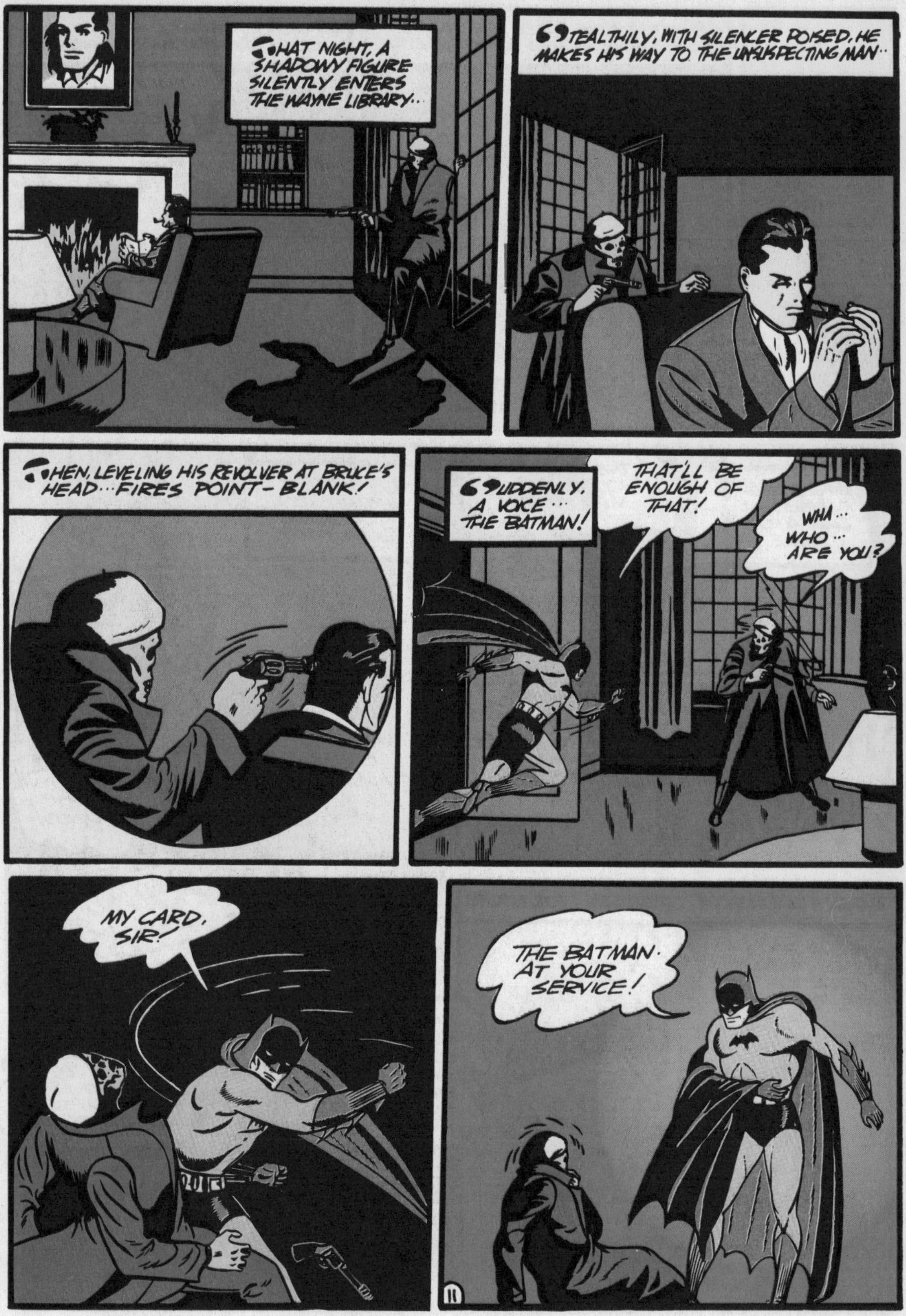
THAT NIGHT, A SHADOWY FIGURE SILENTLY ENTERS THE WAYNE LIBRARY...
STEALTHILY, WITH SILENCER POISED, HE MAKES HIS WAY TO THE UNSUSPECTING MAN...
THEN, LEVELING HIS REVOLVER AT BRUCE'S HEAD...FIRES POINT-BLANK!
SUDDENLY, A VOICE... THE BATMAN!
THAT'LL BE ENOUGH OF THAT!
WHA... WHO... ARE YOU?
MY CARD, SIR!
THE BATMAN. AT YOUR SERVICE!
11

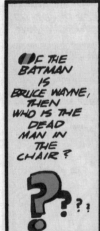

IF THE BATMAN IS BRUCE WAYNE, THEN WHO IS THE DEAD MAN IN THE CHAIR?

?? ??!

SUDDENLY, THE FALLEN MAN LUNGES FORWARD, A MURDEROUS GLEAM IN HIS EYES--

YOU -- YOU!

STRONG, POWERFUL HANDS CLOSE ABOUT THE BATMAN'S THROAT!

I'VE KILLED SO MANY, ONE MORE OR LESS DOESN'T MATTER TO ME! YOU SHALL DIE!

THE STRUGGLING FIGURES FALL BACK ACROSS A TABLE!

THIS IS WHERE YOU TAKE A RIDE, BUDDY!

A SUDDEN UPWARD SURGE OF THE BATMAN'S MUSCULAR LEGS--

HAPPY LANDINGS!

THEN A FINAL BLOW THAT EXPLODES OFF THE KILLER'S JAW!

YESSIR, FELLA, YOU'RE NUMBER ONE ON THE **HIT** PARADE!

OKAY, DICK, IT'S ALL OVER! WELL, WHAT DO YOU THINK OF MY IDEA OF HAVING A DUMMY PUT OVER YOU?

IT WORKED SWELL! WHEN I WORKED MY HANDS IN THE SLEEVES, IT REALLY LOOKED ALIVE! AND SINCE I'M TOO SMALL TO REACH THE TOP OF THE DUMMY, THE SHOTS WENT OVER MY HEAD INTO THE DUMMY'S HEAD!

NOW HOW ABOUT SHOWING ME WHO IS UNDER THAT MASK?

WITH PLEASURE, DICK!

THE MASK OFF, A FAMILIAR FACE IS REVEALED IN THE LIGHT··MR·WYLIE!

WYLIE!··WHY··YOU SAID THE MOTIVE WAS MONEY! WYLIE IS A RICH MAN! WHY, HE WOULDN'T··

THE NIGHT ROBIN WAS OVER AT THE RODGERS YACHT I BROKE INTO WYLIE'S OFFICE AND EXAMINED HIS BOOKS! THEY SHOWED HE WAS HEAVILY IN DEBT!

WYLIE HAD BOUGHT A LOT OF ANTAL'S PICTURES WHILE IN EUROPE! HE GOT THEM CHEAPLY, FOR ANTAL WAS NOT WELL KNOWN! HE KNEW, HOWEVER, THAT HE COULD GET FABULOUS PRICES FOR THEM IF...

...IF ANTAL SUDDENLY BECAME NOTORIOUSLY FAMOUS! HE CONCEIVED THE IDEA FOR THESE "PROPHETIC" MURDERS. HE KNEW THE CURIOUS PUBLIC WOULD ASK FOR ANTAL'S PICTURES!

YOU DEVIL! I WOULD HAVE MADE A FORTUNE IF IT HADN'T BEEN FOR YOU!

BUT I THOUGHT HE WAS SUPPOSED TO BE WOUNDED BY THE MURDERER?

WYLIE SHOT HIMSELF IN THE ARM TO DIVERT SUSPICION! TELL ME, WYLIE, HOW DID YOU EVADE THE POLICE WHO WERE SUPPOSED TO BE GUARDING YOUR LIFE AT HOME?

A CLOSET IN MY ROOM WAS IN REALITY AN OPENING TO A SECRET PASSAGE THAT LED TO THE OUTSIDE! I COULD WALK IN AND OUT AT WILL!

ABRUPTLY··WYLIE TEARS LOOSE··PLUCKS THE FALLEN PISTOL OFF THE FLOOR···

YOU'RE NOT GOING TO HAND ME TO THE POLICE!

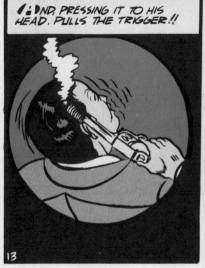

AND, PRESSING IT TO HIS HEAD, PULLS THE TRIGGER!!

HE COULDN'T STAND THE DISGRACE!

MUCH BETTER THIS WAY! NOW I THINK WE'D BETTER CALL THE POLICE AND TELL THEM THAT MR. BRUCE WAYNE'S LIFE WAS SAVED BY THE BATMAN!

THE END.

THE amazing Batman

THE ADVENTURE STRIP THAT HAS EVERYTHING!

FAST MOVING, ACTION-PACKED ADVENTURE MYSTERY AND INTRIGUE

WITH

Robin THE original BOY WONDER

WHOSE ASTOUNDING EXPLOITS WILL THRILL YOU EACH AND EVERY MONTH IN DETECTIVE COMICS

13

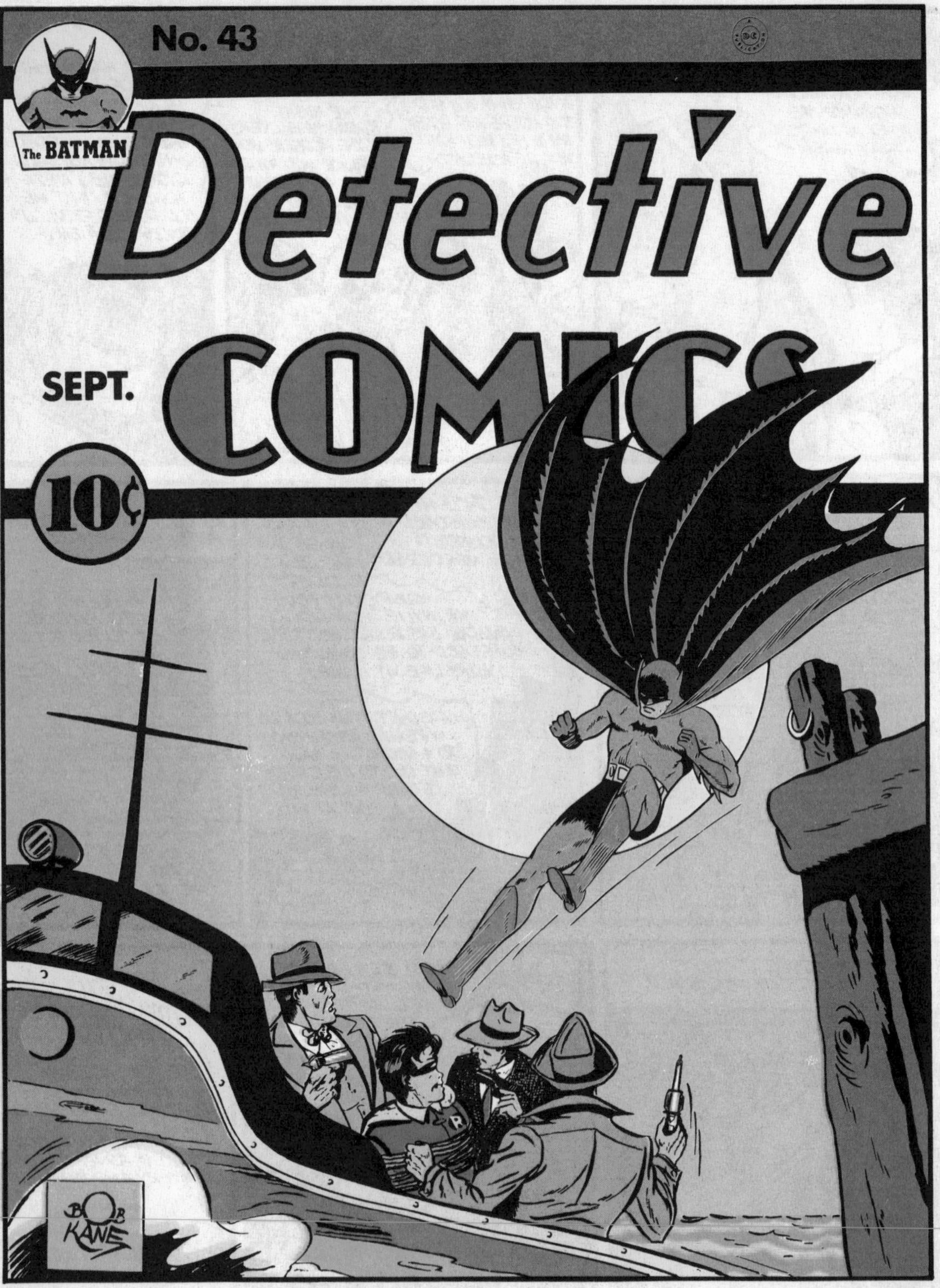

No. 43
The BATMAN
Detective
COMICS
SEPT.
10¢
BOB KANE

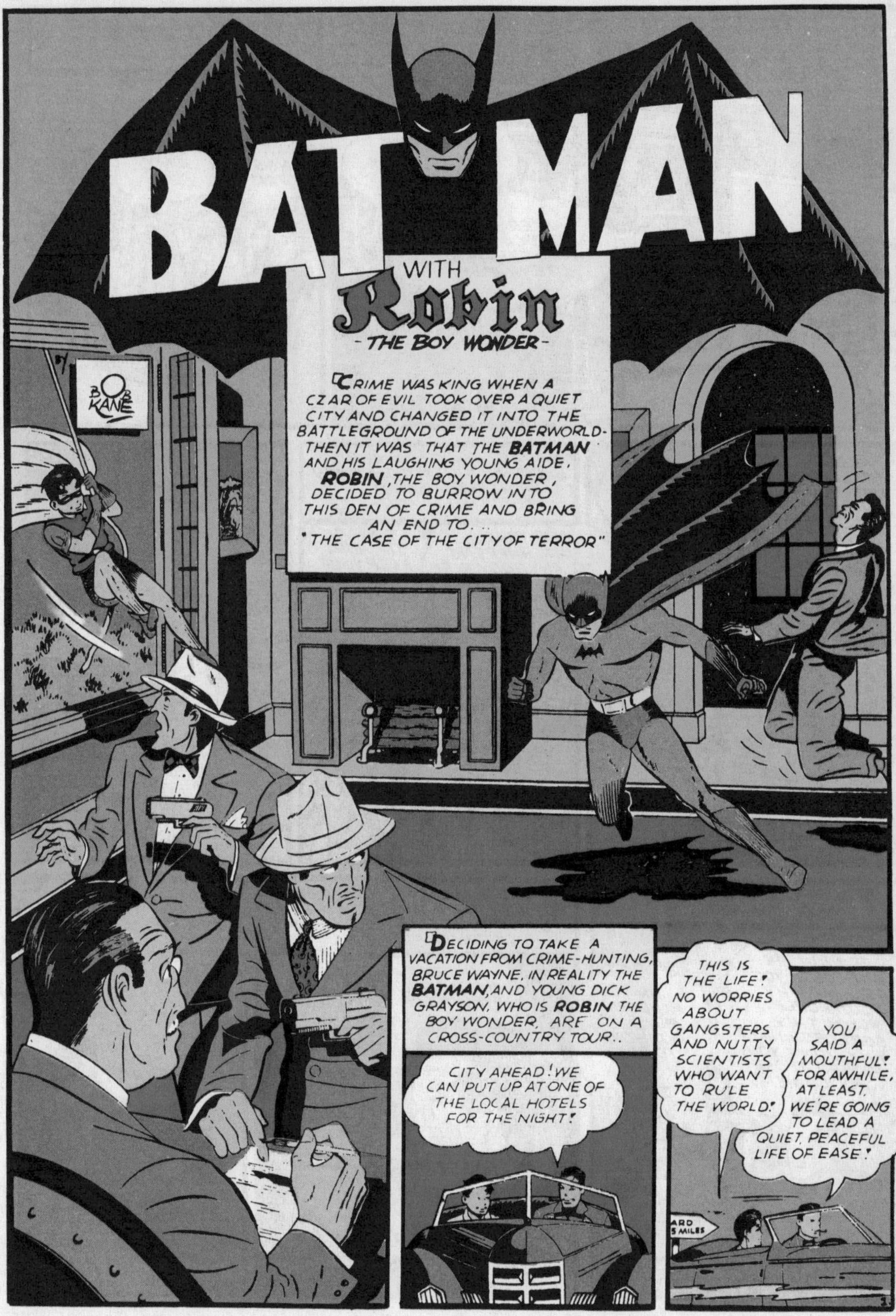
BATMAN
WITH
Robin
-THE BOY WONDER-
BOB KANE
"CRIME WAS KING WHEN A CZAR OF EVIL TOOK OVER A QUIET CITY AND CHANGED IT INTO THE BATTLEGROUND OF THE UNDERWORLD- THEN IT WAS THAT THE BATMAN AND HIS LAUGHING YOUNG AIDE, ROBIN, THE BOY WONDER, DECIDED TO BURROW INTO THIS DEN OF CRIME AND BRING AN END TO... "THE CASE OF THE CITY OF TERROR"
"DECIDING TO TAKE A VACATION FROM CRIME-HUNTING, BRUCE WAYNE, IN REALITY THE BATMAN, AND YOUNG DICK GRAYSON, WHO IS ROBIN THE BOY WONDER, ARE ON A CROSS-COUNTRY TOUR..
CITY AHEAD! WE CAN PUT UP AT ONE OF THE LOCAL HOTELS FOR THE NIGHT!
THIS IS THE LIFE! NO WORRIES ABOUT GANGSTERS AND NUTTY SCIENTISTS WHO WANT TO RULE THE WORLD!
YOU SAID A MOUTHFUL! FOR AWHILE, AT LEAST, WE'RE GOING TO LEAD A QUIET, PEACEFUL LIFE OF EASE!

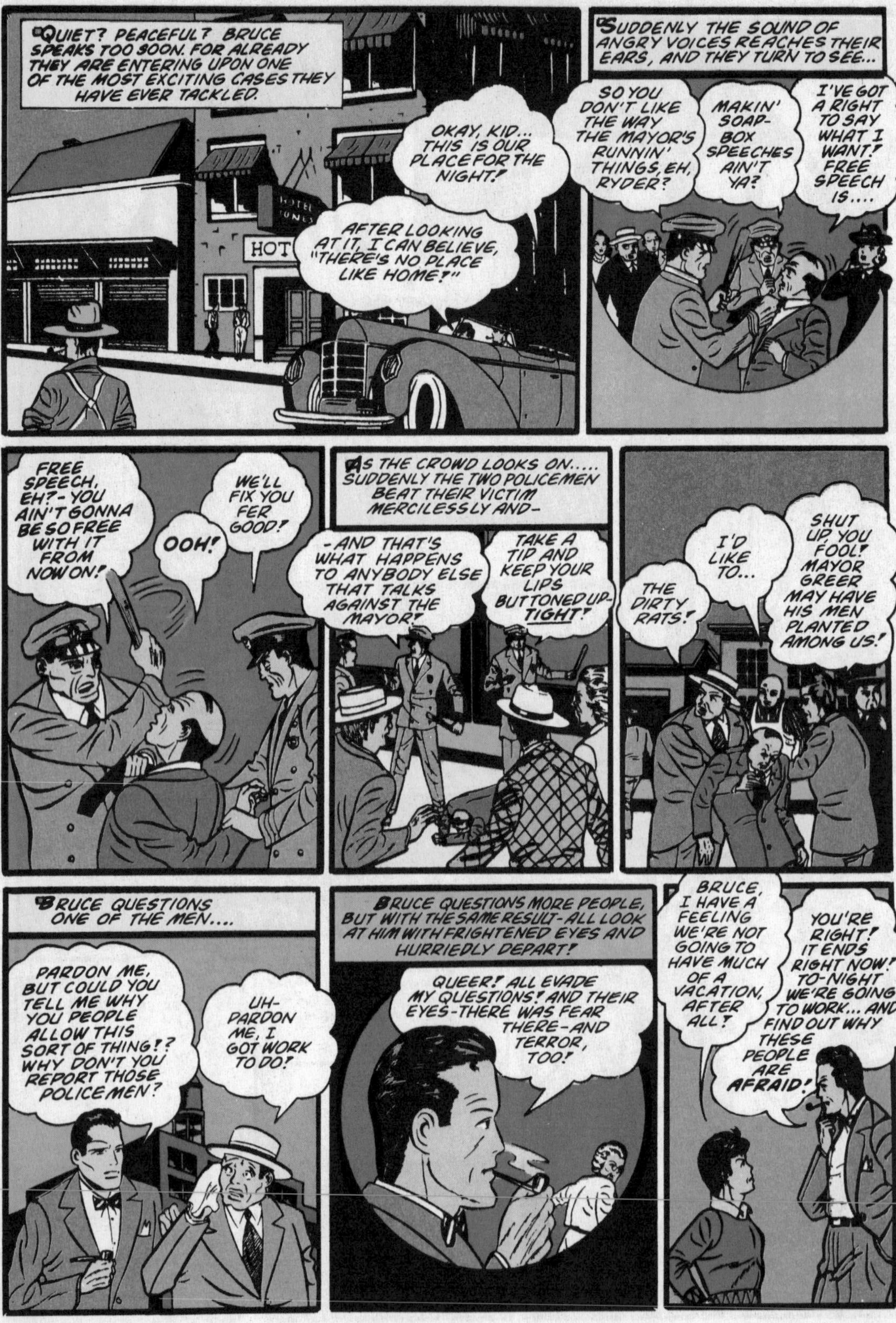
QUIET? PEACEFUL? BRUCE SPEAKS TOO SOON. FOR ALREADY THEY ARE ENTERING UPON ONE OF THE MOST EXCITING CASES THEY HAVE EVER TACKLED.
OKAY, KID... THIS IS OUR PLACE FOR THE NIGHT!
AFTER LOOKING AT IT, I CAN BELIEVE, "THERE'S NO PLACE LIKE HOME!"
HOT
SUDDENLY THE SOUND OF ANGRY VOICES REACHES THEIR EARS, AND THEY TURN TO SEE...
SO YOU DON'T LIKE THE WAY THE MAYOR'S RUNNIN' THINGS, EH, RYDER?
MAKIN' SOAP-BOX SPEECHES AIN'T YA?
I'VE GOT A RIGHT TO SAY WHAT I WANT! FREE SPEECH IS....
FREE SPEECH, EH?- YOU AIN'T GONNA BE SO FREE WITH IT FROM NOW ON!
OOH!
WE'LL FIX YOU FER GOOD!
AS THE CROWD LOOKS ON..... SUDDENLY THE TWO POLICEMEN BEAT THEIR VICTIM MERCILESSLY AND-
-AND THAT'S WHAT HAPPENS TO ANYBODY ELSE THAT TALKS AGAINST THE MAYOR!
TAKE A TIP AND KEEP YOUR LIPS BUTTONED UP- TIGHT!
THE DIRTY RATS!
I'D LIKE TO...
SHUT UP, YOU FOOL! MAYOR GREER MAY HAVE HIS MEN PLANTED AMONG US!
BRUCE QUESTIONS ONE OF THE MEN....
PARDON ME, BUT COULD YOU TELL ME WHY YOU PEOPLE ALLOW THIS SORT OF THING!? WHY DON'T YOU REPORT THOSE POLICEMEN?
UH- PARDON ME, I GOT WORK TO DO!
BRUCE QUESTIONS MORE PEOPLE, BUT WITH THE SAME RESULT- ALL LOOK AT HIM WITH FRIGHTENED EYES AND HURRIEDLY DEPART!
QUEER! ALL EVADE MY QUESTIONS! AND THEIR EYES- THERE WAS FEAR THERE- AND TERROR, TOO!
BRUCE, I HAVE A FEELING WE'RE NOT GOING TO HAVE MUCH OF A VACATION, AFTER ALL!
YOU'RE RIGHT! IT ENDS RIGHT NOW! TO-NIGHT WE'RE GOING TO WORK... AND FIND OUT WHY THESE PEOPLE ARE AFRAID!

LATER THAT NIGHT...... BRUCE WAYNE DONS A FANTASTIC GARB...

WHERE ARE YOU GOING?

I'M GOING TO PAY A VISIT TO A MR. CARTER, THE MOST RESPECTED MAN IN TOWN! HE'S RICH AND HAS A LOT OF INFLUENCE!

DOWN THE SHEER FACE OF THE BUILDING CLAMBERS HIS LITHE FIGURE...THE BATMAN TAKES TO A TRAIL OF CRIME ONCE AGAIN.

A POLICE CAR! CARTER HAS VISITORS!

MOMENTS LATER THE PERFECTLY TRAINED BODY CLEARS THE HIGH FENCE SURROUNDING THE CARTER HOME.

INSIDE THE HOUSE.....

YOU CAN'T ARREST ME! WHAT SORT OF TRUMPED UP CHARGE HAVE...

YOU BEEN SHOOTIN' YOUR MOUTH OFF AGAINST THE MAYOR!

YEAH, THAT'S LIBEL!

.....THEN A MOCKING VOICE...

WE'RE TAKIN' YOU TO JAIL AND... HUH?

SPEAKING OF JAIL--- HOW LONG HAVE YOU BEEN OUT?

WHA?

IT'S... IT'S THE BATMAN!

YOU'LL HAVE TO BE QUICKER THAN THAT!

WITH THE SWIFTNESS OF THOUGHT, A HAND REACHES OUT FOR THE NEARBY FLOOR LAMP, AND..

GET HIM! GET-UGH!

BEFORE THE MEN CAN RECOVER, THE BATMAN IS TWISTING AMONG THEM LIKE AN ANGRY CYCLONE!

MUCH BETTER THAN SLEEPING POWDER AND GETS THE SAME EFFECT!

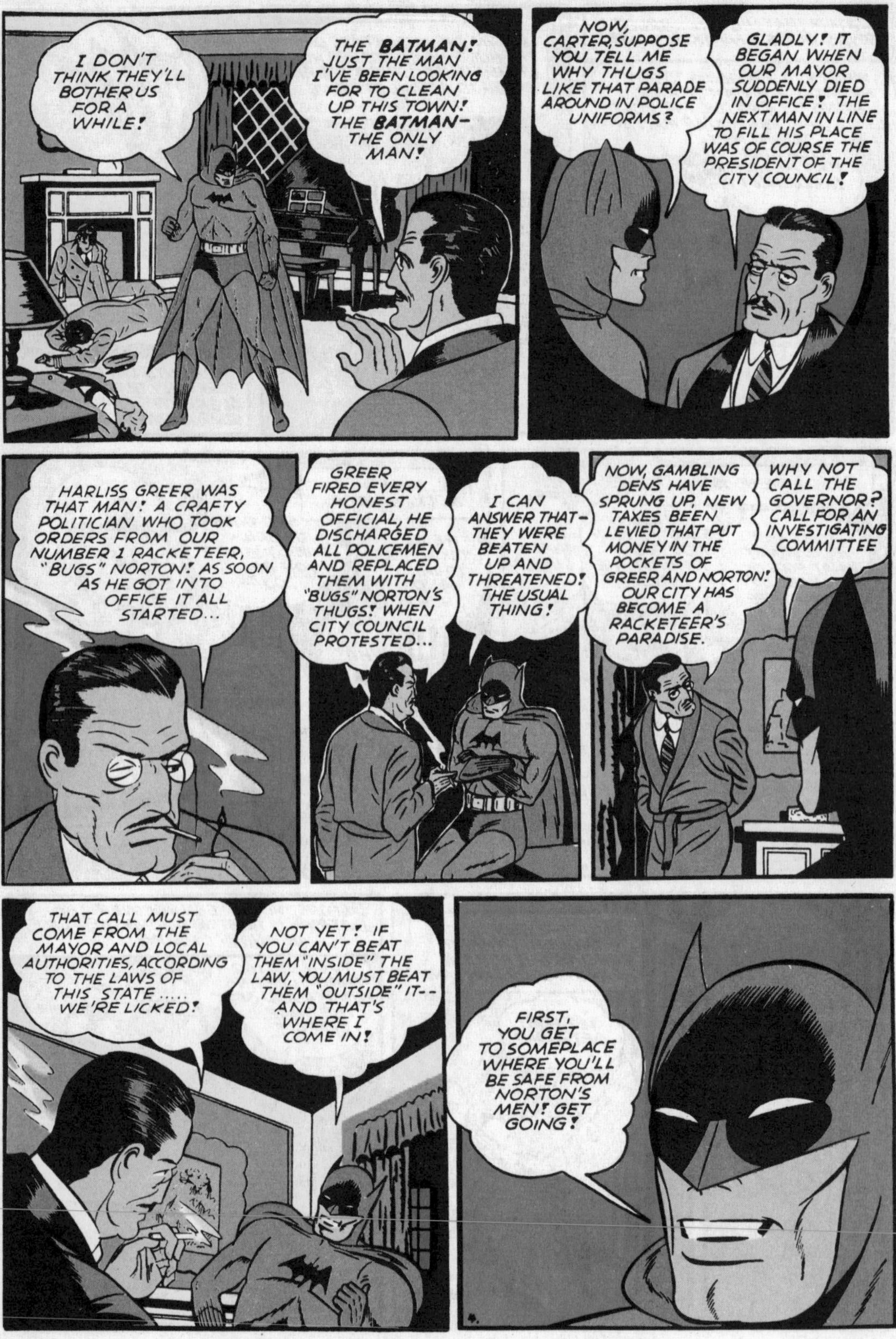
I DON'T THINK THEY'LL BOTHER US FOR A WHILE!
THE BATMAN! JUST THE MAN I'VE BEEN LOOKING FOR TO CLEAN UP THIS TOWN! THE BATMAN— THE ONLY MAN!
NOW, CARTER, SUPPOSE YOU TELL ME WHY THUGS LIKE THAT PARADE AROUND IN POLICE UNIFORMS?
GLADLY! IT BEGAN WHEN OUR MAYOR SUDDENLY DIED IN OFFICE! THE NEXT MAN IN LINE TO FILL HIS PLACE WAS OF COURSE THE PRESIDENT OF THE CITY COUNCIL!
HARLISS GREER WAS THAT MAN! A CRAFTY POLITICIAN WHO TOOK ORDERS FROM OUR NUMBER 1 RACKETEER, "BUGS" NORTON! AS SOON AS HE GOT INTO OFFICE IT ALL STARTED...
GREER FIRED EVERY HONEST OFFICIAL, HE DISCHARGED ALL POLICEMEN AND REPLACED THEM WITH "BUGS" NORTON'S THUGS! WHEN CITY COUNCIL PROTESTED...
I CAN ANSWER THAT- THEY WERE BEATEN UP AND THREATENED! THE USUAL THING!
NOW, GAMBLING DENS HAVE SPRUNG UP, NEW TAXES BEEN LEVIED THAT PUT MONEY IN THE POCKETS OF GREER AND NORTON! OUR CITY HAS BECOME A RACKETEER'S PARADISE.
WHY NOT CALL THE GOVERNOR? CALL FOR AN INVESTIGATING COMMITTEE
THAT CALL MUST COME FROM THE MAYOR AND LOCAL AUTHORITIES, ACCORDING TO THE LAWS OF THIS STATE ..... WE'RE LICKED!
NOT YET! IF YOU CAN'T BEAT THEM "INSIDE" THE LAW, YOU MUST BEAT THEM "OUTSIDE" IT-- AND THAT'S WHERE I COME IN!
FIRST, YOU GET TO SOMEPLACE WHERE YOU'LL BE SAFE FROM NORTON'S MEN! GET GOING!

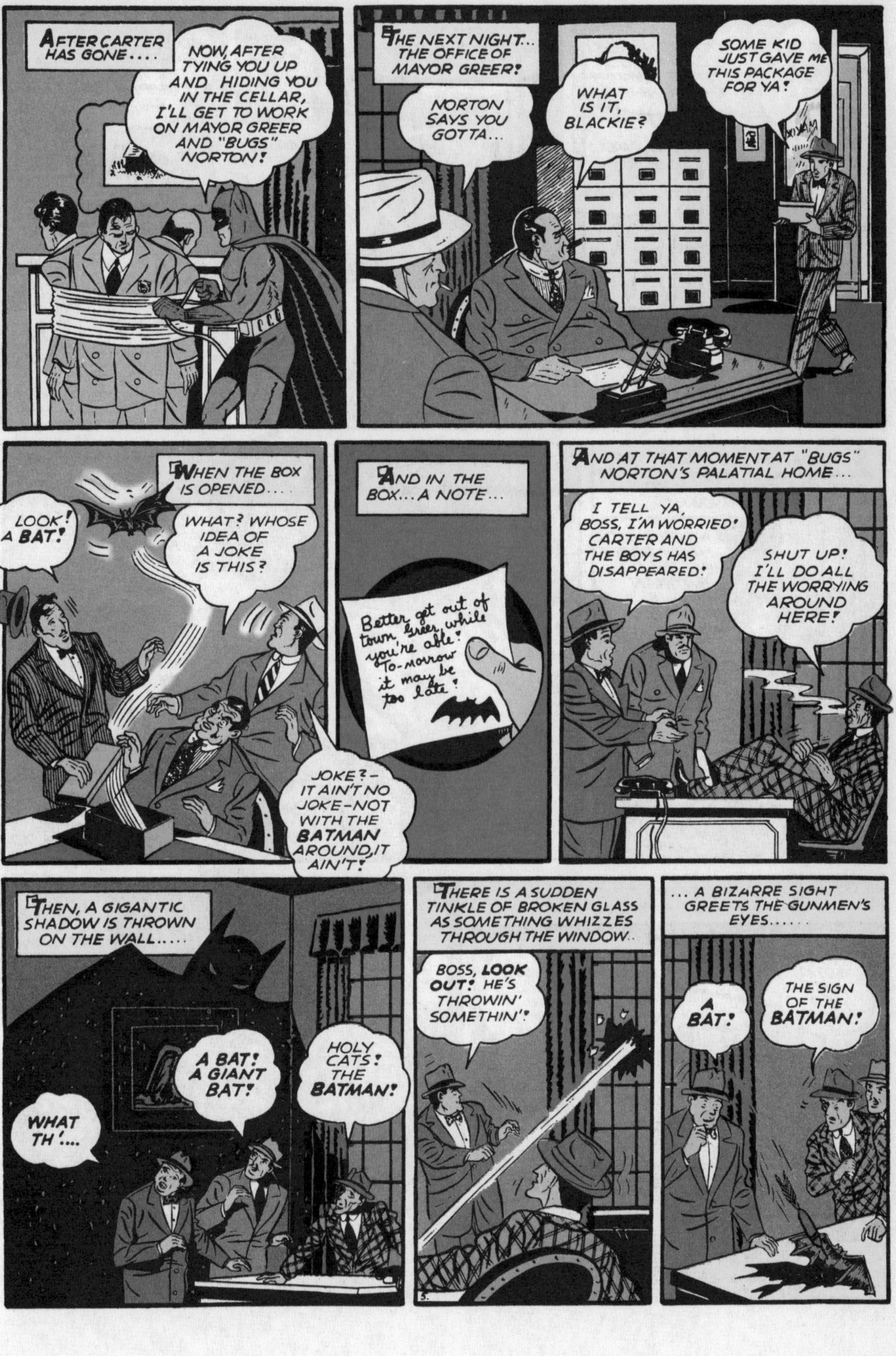
AFTER CARTER HAS GONE....
NOW, AFTER TYING YOU UP AND HIDING YOU IN THE CELLAR, I'LL GET TO WORK ON MAYOR GREER AND "BUGS" NORTON!
THE NEXT NIGHT... THE OFFICE OF MAYOR GREER!
NORTON SAYS YOU GOTTA...
WHAT IS IT, BLACKIE?
SOME KID JUST GAVE ME THIS PACKAGE FOR YA!
WHEN THE BOX IS OPENED....
LOOK! A BAT!
WHAT? WHOSE IDEA OF A JOKE IS THIS?
JOKE?- IT AIN'T NO JOKE-NOT WITH THE BATMAN AROUND, IT AIN'T!
AND IN THE BOX... A NOTE...
Better get out of town, Greer, while you're able! To-morrow it may be too late!
AND AT THAT MOMENT AT "BUGS" NORTON'S PALATIAL HOME...
I TELL YA, BOSS, I'M WORRIED! CARTER AND THE BOYS HAS DISAPPEARED!
SHUT UP! I'LL DO ALL THE WORRYING AROUND HERE!
THEN, A GIGANTIC SHADOW IS THROWN ON THE WALL.....
WHAT TH'....
A BAT! A GIANT BAT!
HOLY CATS! THE BATMAN!
THERE IS A SUDDEN TINKLE OF BROKEN GLASS AS SOMETHING WHIZZES THROUGH THE WINDOW..
BOSS, LOOK OUT! HE'S THROWIN' SOMETHIN'!
... A BIZARRE SIGHT GREETS THE GUNMEN'S EYES......
A BAT!
THE SIGN OF THE BATMAN!

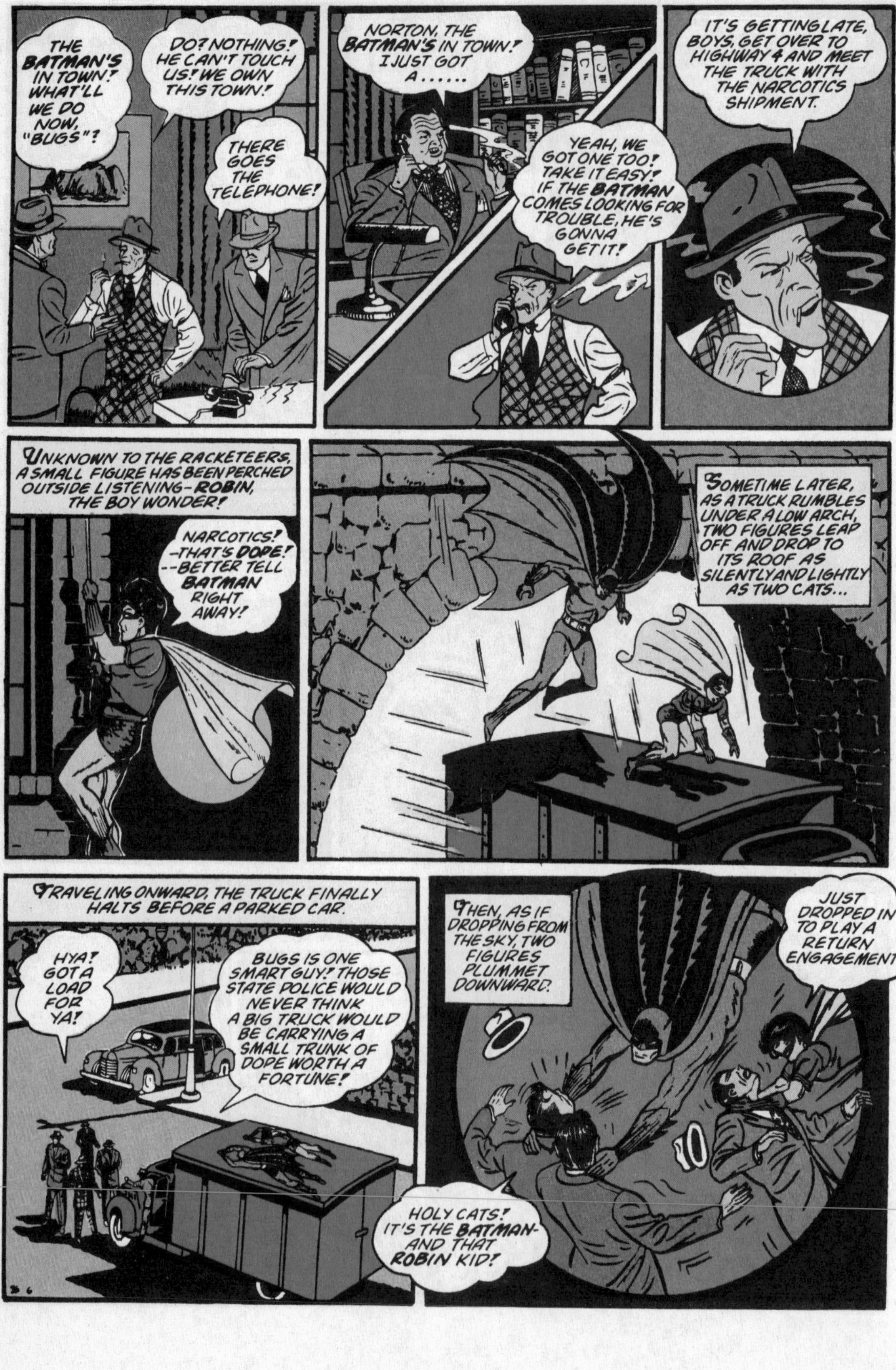
THE BATMAN'S IN TOWN! WHAT'LL WE DO NOW, "BUGS"?
DO? NOTHING! HE CAN'T TOUCH US! WE OWN THIS TOWN!
THERE GOES THE TELEPHONE!
NORTON, THE BATMAN'S IN TOWN! I JUST GOT A......
YEAH, WE GOT ONE TOO! TAKE IT EASY! IF THE BATMAN COMES LOOKING FOR TROUBLE, HE'S GONNA GET IT!
IT'S GETTING LATE, BOYS, GET OVER TO HIGHWAY 4 AND MEET THE TRUCK WITH THE NARCOTICS SHIPMENT.
UNKNOWN TO THE RACKETEERS, A SMALL FIGURE HAS BEEN PERCHED OUTSIDE LISTENING- ROBIN, THE BOY WONDER!
NARCOTICS! -THAT'S DOPE! --BETTER TELL BATMAN RIGHT AWAY!
SOMETIME LATER, AS A TRUCK RUMBLES UNDER A LOW ARCH, TWO FIGURES LEAP OFF AND DROP TO ITS ROOF AS SILENTLY AND LIGHTLY AS TWO CATS...
TRAVELING ONWARD, THE TRUCK FINALLY HALTS BEFORE A PARKED CAR.
HYA! GOT A LOAD FOR YA!
BUGS IS ONE SMART GUY! THOSE STATE POLICE WOULD NEVER THINK A BIG TRUCK WOULD BE CARRYING A SMALL TRUNK OF DOPE WORTH A FORTUNE!
THEN, AS IF DROPPING FROM THE SKY, TWO FIGURES PLUMMET DOWNWARD.
JUST DROPPED IN TO PLAY A RETURN ENGAGEMENT!
HOLY CATS! IT'S THE BATMAN- AND THAT ROBIN KID!

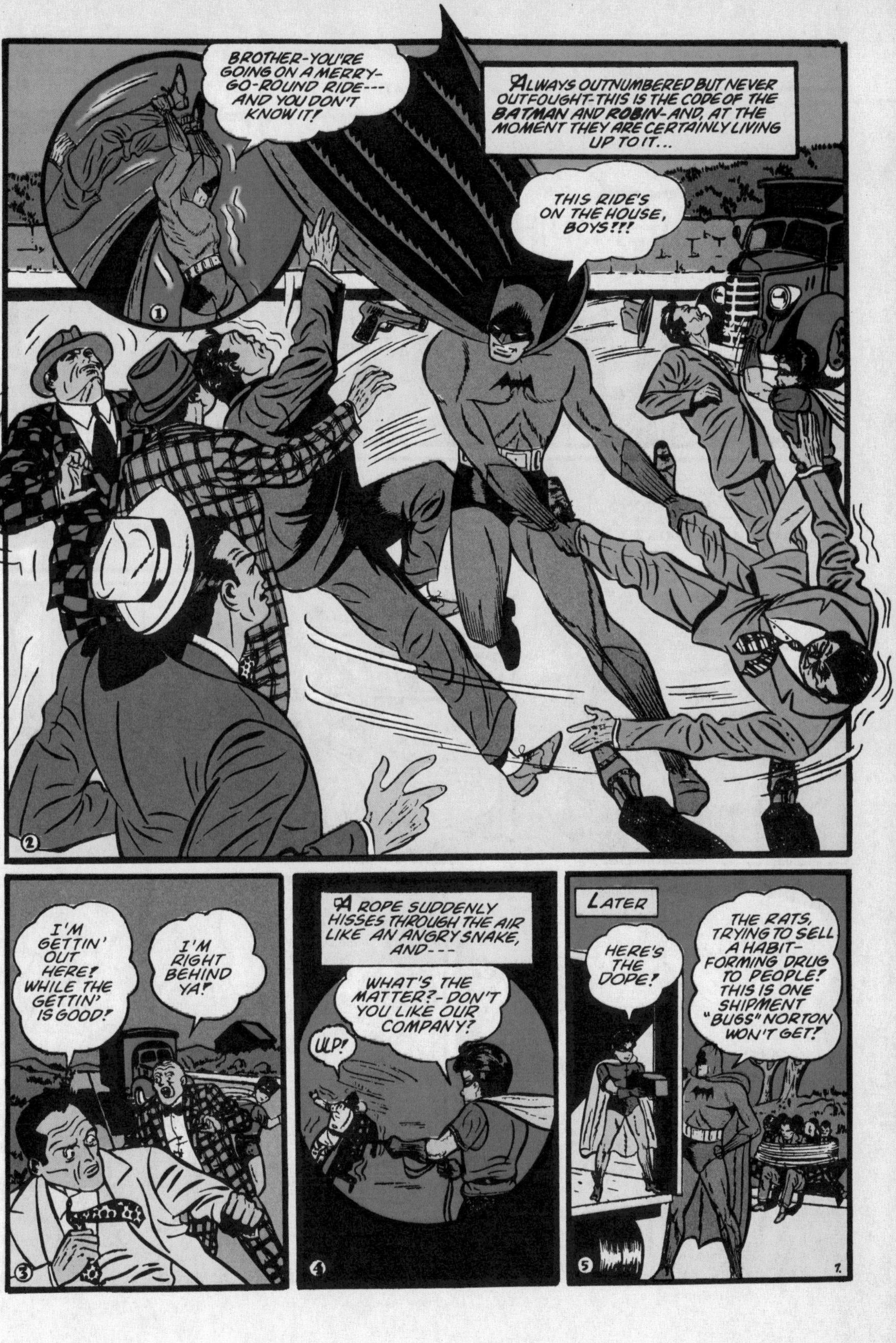
BROTHER-YOU'RE GOING ON A MERRY-GO-ROUND RIDE--- AND YOU DON'T KNOW IT!
ALWAYS OUTNUMBERED BUT NEVER OUTFOUGHT-THIS IS THE CODE OF THE BATMAN AND ROBIN-AND, AT THE MOMENT THEY ARE CERTAINLY LIVING UP TO IT...
THIS RIDE'S ON THE HOUSE, BOYS???
I'M GETTIN' OUT HERE! WHILE THE GETTIN' IS GOOD!
I'M RIGHT BEHIND YA!
A ROPE SUDDENLY HISSES THROUGH THE AIR LIKE AN ANGRY SNAKE, AND---
WHAT'S THE MATTER?-DON'T YOU LIKE OUR COMPANY?
ULP!
LATER
HERE'S THE DOPE!
THE RATS, TRYING TO SELL A HABIT-FORMING DRUG TO PEOPLE! THIS IS ONE SHIPMENT "BUGS" NORTON WON'T GET!
7.

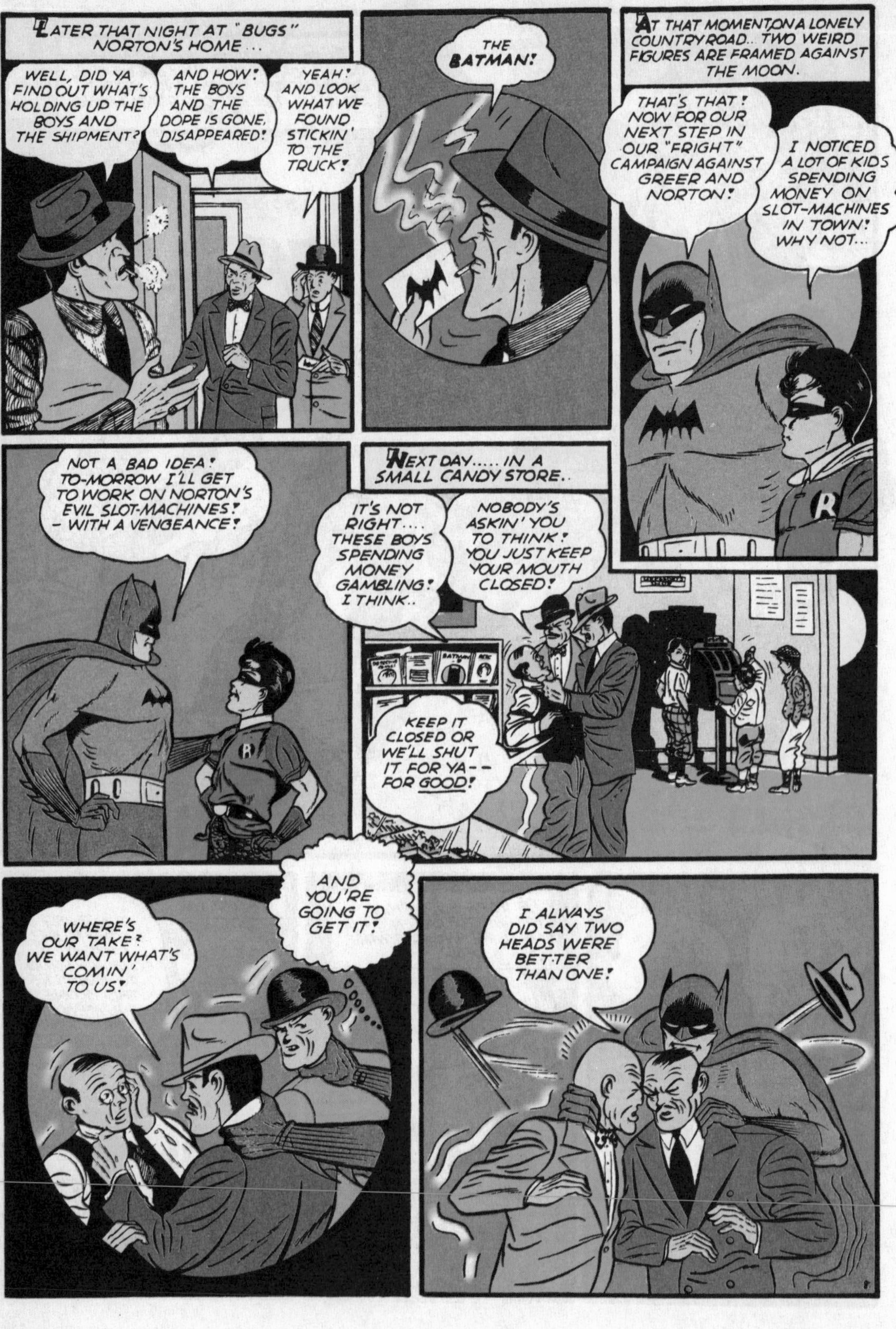
LATER THAT NIGHT AT "BUGS" NORTON'S HOME...
WELL, DID YA FIND OUT WHAT'S HOLDING UP THE BOYS AND THE SHIPMENT?
AND HOW! THE BOYS AND THE DOPE IS GONE. DISAPPEARED!
YEAH! AND LOOK WHAT WE FOUND STICKIN' TO THE TRUCK!
THE BATMAN!
AT THAT MOMENT, ON A LONELY COUNTRY ROAD.. TWO WEIRD FIGURES ARE FRAMED AGAINST THE MOON.
THAT'S THAT! NOW FOR OUR NEXT STEP IN OUR "FRIGHT" CAMPAIGN AGAINST GREER AND NORTON!
I NOTICED A LOT OF KIDS SPENDING MONEY ON SLOT-MACHINES IN TOWN! WHY NOT...
NOT A BAD IDEA! TO-MORROW I'LL GET TO WORK ON NORTON'S EVIL SLOT-MACHINES! - WITH A VENGEANCE!
NEXT DAY..... IN A SMALL CANDY STORE..
IT'S NOT RIGHT.... THESE BOYS SPENDING MONEY GAMBLING! I THINK..
NOBODY'S ASKIN' YOU TO THINK! YOU JUST KEEP YOUR MOUTH CLOSED!
KEEP IT CLOSED OR WE'LL SHUT IT FOR YA-- FOR GOOD!
WHERE'S OUR TAKE? WE WANT WHAT'S COMIN' TO US!
AND YOU'RE GOING TO GET IT!
I ALWAYS DID SAY TWO HEADS WERE BET-TER THAN ONE!

YES! AND IF YOU WANT TO KEEP MY RESPECT YOU'LL STOP PLAYING THE MACHINES! *ROBIN* DOESN'T, SO WHY SHOULD YOU?

GEE, IF *ROBIN* THE BOY WONDER DON'T, I GUESS THAT'S GOOD ENOUGH FOR US! WE'LL TELL ALL THE KIDS!

ALL OVER THE CITY, STORE OWNERS ARE AMAZED TO SEE A MANTLED, MUSCULAR FIGURE STRIDE IN, SEIZE SLOT-MACHINES, AND CALMLY PROCEED TO SMASH THEM ...

WHEN YOU SEE NORTON'S MEN TELL THEM THE *BATMAN* DECIDED TO PLAY THE MACHINES HIS OWN WAY!

TH—THE *BATMAN!*

BOSS, THE *BATMAN'S* RUNNIN' ALL AROUND THE TOWN WRECKIN' OUR SLOT-MACHINES

THERE AIN'T ONE LEFT IN GOOD CONDITION!

THE *BATMAN* AGAIN!

THEN A SERIES OF STRANGE EVENTS TAKE PLACE.... MAYOR GREER'S "POLICEMEN" START TO DISAPPEAR.... A "POLICEMAN" MIGHT BE WALKING HIS BEAT WHEN....

...A COWLED SHADOW MIGHT DROP UPON A MAN.

OR A SMALL AGILE FIGURE MIGHT SUDDENLY FLASH THROUGH THE AIR..

THE DISAPPEARANCES BEGIN TO TAKE EFFECT

I CAN'T UNDERSTAND IT! TWENTY OF OUR MEN HAVE VANISHED DURING A FEW NIGHTS! WHO....

IT'S THE *BATMAN!* — THAT'S WHO! I DON'T LIKE IT! THE TOWNSPEOPLE ARE BEGINNING TO LAUGH AT US!.... A MAN AND A BOY AGAINST OUR "MOB" ...BAH!

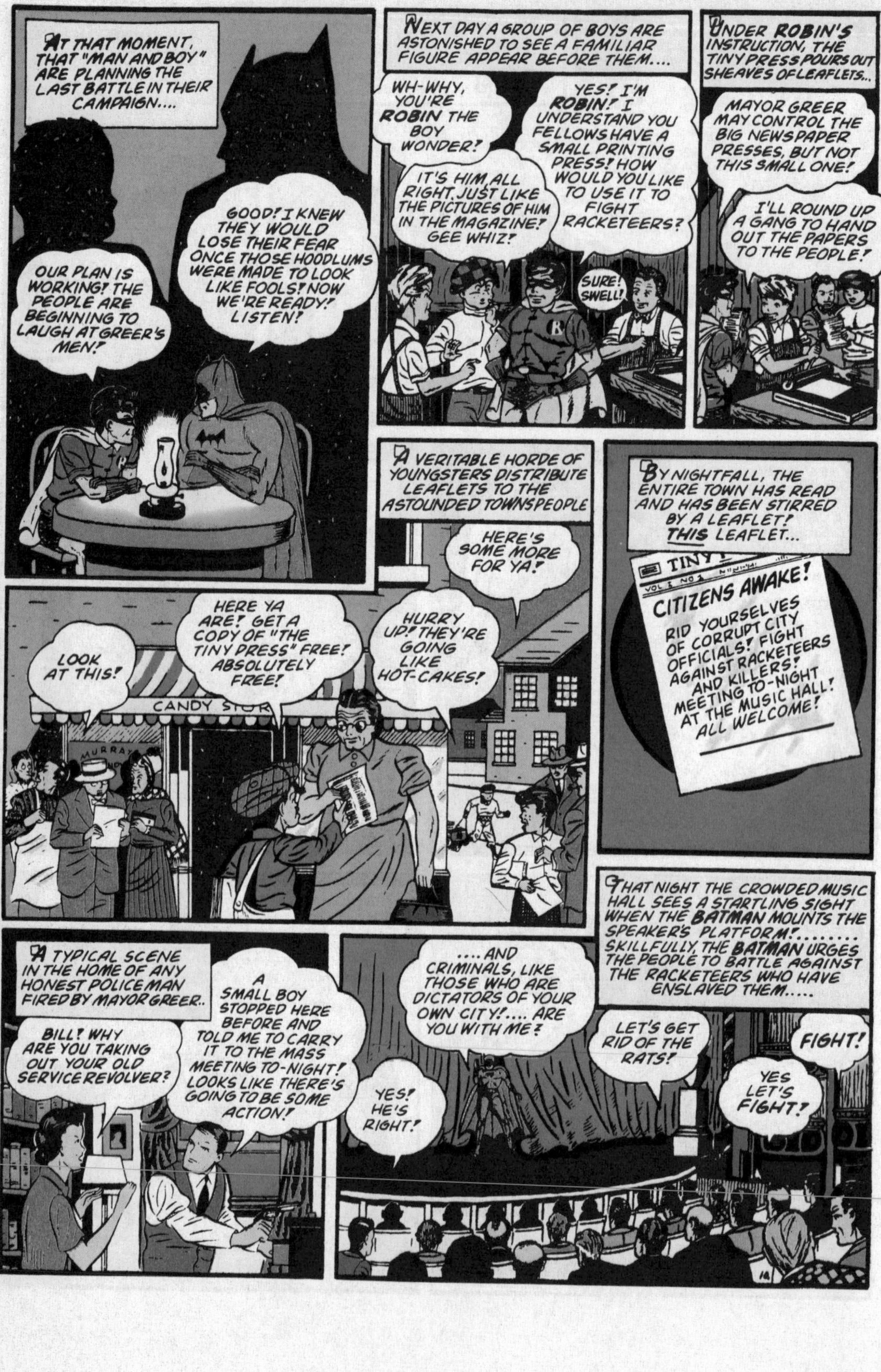
AT THAT MOMENT, THAT "MAN AND BOY" ARE PLANNING THE LAST BATTLE IN THEIR CAMPAIGN....
OUR PLAN IS WORKING! THE PEOPLE ARE BEGINNING TO LAUGH AT GREER'S MEN!
GOOD! I KNEW THEY WOULD LOSE THEIR FEAR ONCE THOSE HOODLUMS WERE MADE TO LOOK LIKE FOOLS! NOW WE'RE READY! LISTEN!
NEXT DAY A GROUP OF BOYS ARE ASTONISHED TO SEE A FAMILIAR FIGURE APPEAR BEFORE THEM....
WH-WHY, YOU'RE ROBIN THE BOY WONDER!
YES! I'M ROBIN! I UNDERSTAND YOU FELLOWS HAVE A SMALL PRINTING PRESS! HOW WOULD YOU LIKE TO USE IT TO FIGHT RACKETEERS?
IT'S HIM ALL RIGHT, JUST LIKE THE PICTURES OF HIM IN THE MAGAZINE! GEE WHIZ!
SURE! SWELL!
UNDER ROBIN'S INSTRUCTION, THE TINY PRESS POURS OUT SHEAVES OF LEAFLETS...
MAYOR GREER MAY CONTROL THE BIG NEWSPAPER PRESSES, BUT NOT THIS SMALL ONE!
I'LL ROUND UP A GANG TO HAND OUT THE PAPERS TO THE PEOPLE!
A VERITABLE HORDE OF YOUNGSTERS DISTRIBUTE LEAFLETS TO THE ASTOUNDED TOWNSPEOPLE
HERE'S SOME MORE FOR YA!
LOOK AT THIS!
HERE YA ARE! GET A COPY OF "THE TINY PRESS" FREE! ABSOLUTELY FREE!
HURRY UP! THEY'RE GOING LIKE HOT-CAKES!
CANDY STOR
BY NIGHTFALL, THE ENTIRE TOWN HAS READ AND HAS BEEN STIRRED BY A LEAFLET! THIS LEAFLET...
CITIZENS AWAKE!
RID YOURSELVES OF CORRUPT CITY OFFICIALS! FIGHT AGAINST RACKETEERS AND KILLERS! MEETING TO-NIGHT AT THE MUSIC HALL! ALL WELCOME!
A TYPICAL SCENE IN THE HOME OF ANY HONEST POLICE MAN FIRED BY MAYOR GREER..
BILL! WHY ARE YOU TAKING OUT YOUR OLD SERVICE REVOLVER?
A SMALL BOY STOPPED HERE BEFORE AND TOLD ME TO CARRY IT TO THE MASS MEETING TO-NIGHT! LOOKS LIKE THERE'S GOING TO BE SOME ACTION!
THAT NIGHT THE CROWDED MUSIC HALL SEES A STARTLING SIGHT WHEN THE BATMAN MOUNTS THE SPEAKER'S PLATFORM!........ SKILLFULLY, THE BATMAN URGES THE PEOPLE TO BATTLE AGAINST THE RACKETEERS WHO HAVE ENSLAVED THEM.....
....AND CRIMINALS, LIKE THOSE WHO ARE DICTATORS OF YOUR OWN CITY!.... ARE YOU WITH ME?
YES! HE'S RIGHT!
LET'S GET RID OF THE RATS!
FIGHT!
YES LET'S FIGHT!

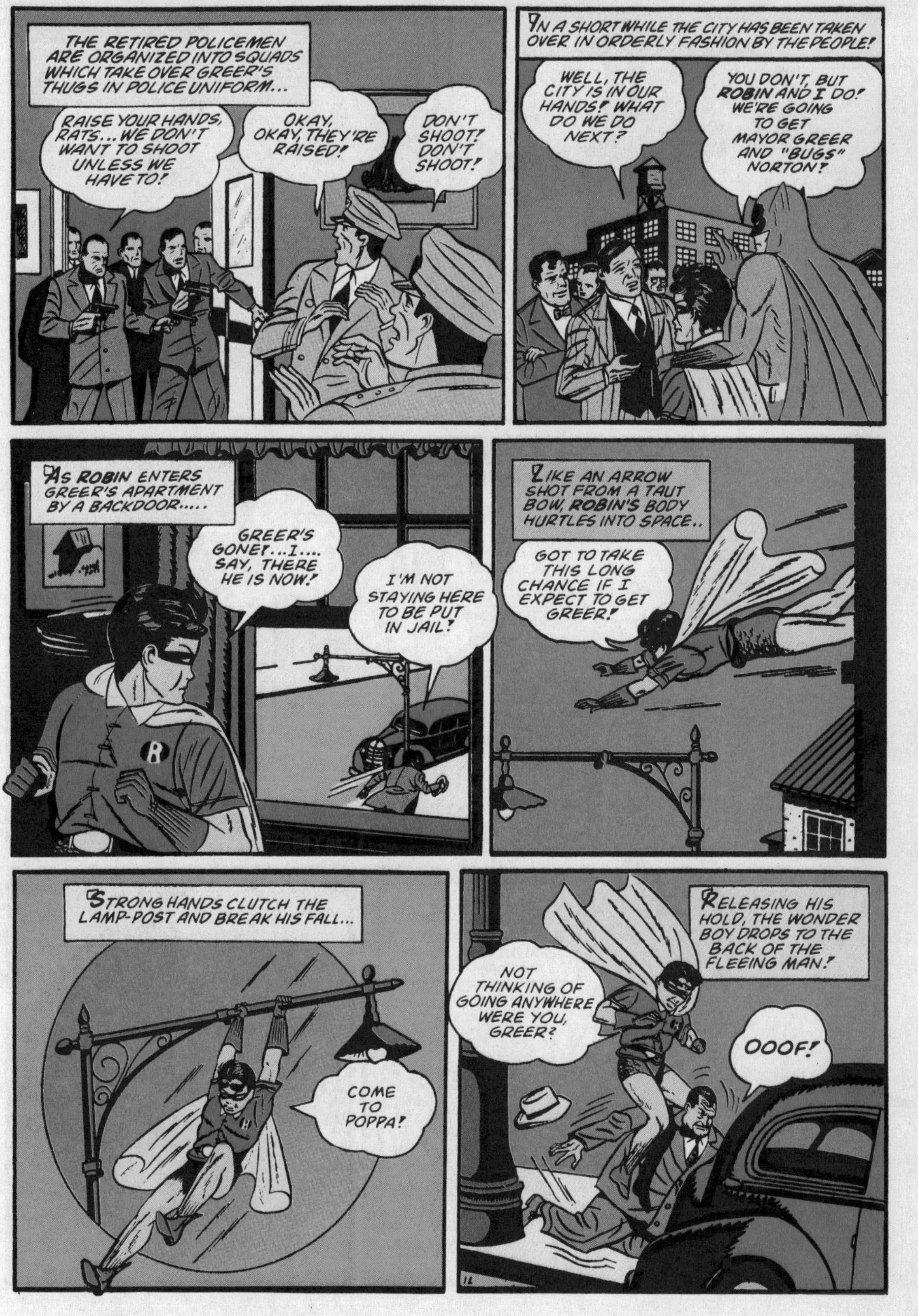
THE RETIRED POLICEMEN ARE ORGANIZED INTO SQUADS WHICH TAKE OVER GREER'S THUGS IN POLICE UNIFORM...
RAISE YOUR HANDS, RATS... WE DON'T WANT TO SHOOT UNLESS WE HAVE TO!
OKAY, OKAY, THEY'RE RAISED!
DON'T SHOOT! DON'T SHOOT!
IN A SHORT WHILE THE CITY HAS BEEN TAKEN OVER IN ORDERLY FASHION BY THE PEOPLE!
WELL, THE CITY IS IN OUR HANDS! WHAT DO WE DO NEXT?
YOU DON'T, BUT ROBIN AND I DO! WE'RE GOING TO GET MAYOR GREER AND "BUGS" NORTON!
AS ROBIN ENTERS GREER'S APARTMENT BY A BACKDOOR.....
GREER'S GONE!...I.... SAY, THERE HE IS NOW!
I'M NOT STAYING HERE TO BE PUT IN JAIL!
LIKE AN ARROW SHOT FROM A TAUT BOW, ROBIN'S BODY HURTLES INTO SPACE..
GOT TO TAKE THIS LONG CHANCE IF I EXPECT TO GET GREER!
STRONG HANDS CLUTCH THE LAMP-POST AND BREAK HIS FALL...
COME TO POPPA!
RELEASING HIS HOLD, THE WONDER BOY DROPS TO THE BACK OF THE FLEEING MAN!
NOT THINKING OF GOING ANYWHERE WERE YOU, GREER?
OOOF!

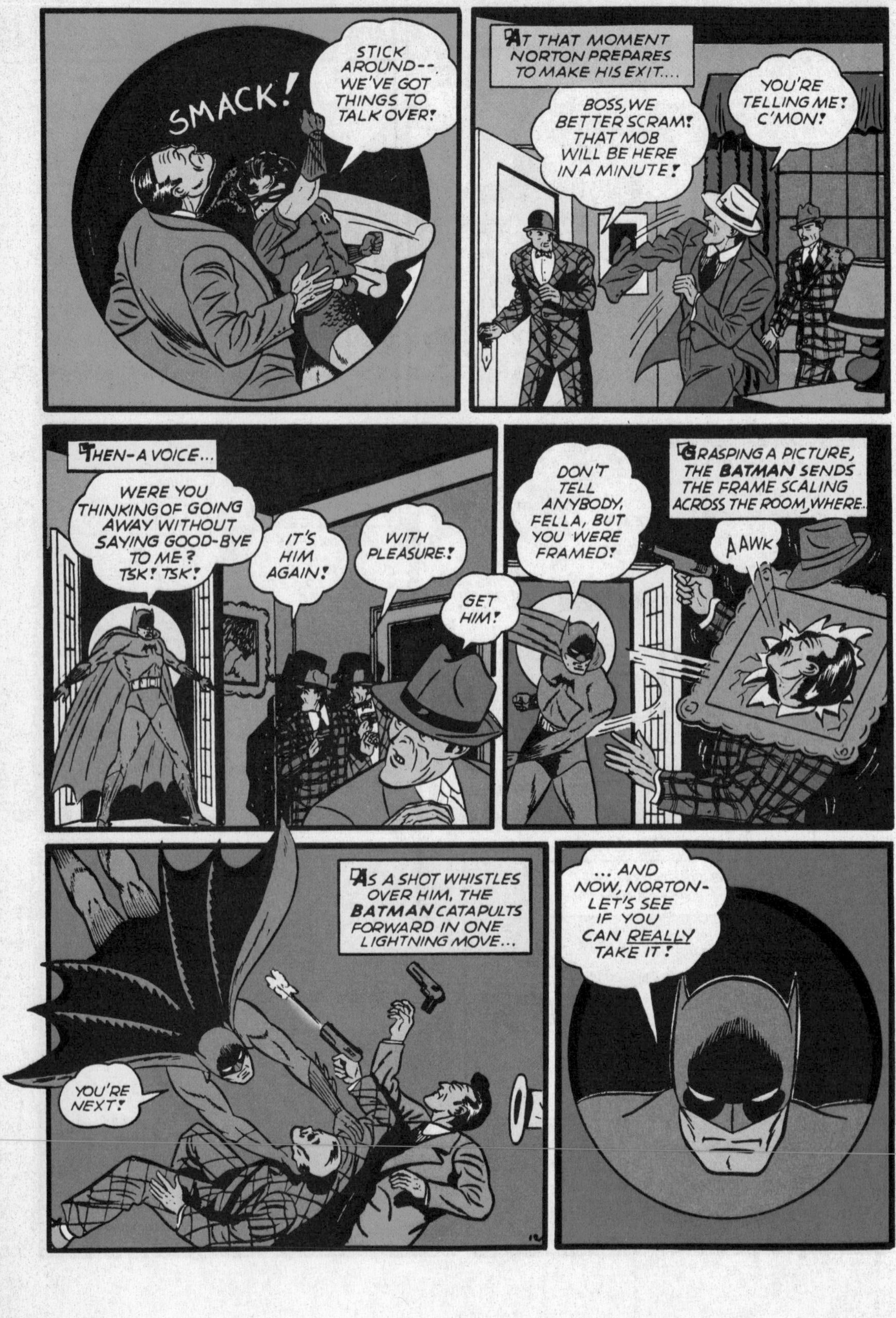
SMACK!
STICK AROUND--. WE'VE GOT THINGS TO TALK OVER!
AT THAT MOMENT NORTON PREPARES TO MAKE HIS EXIT....
BOSS, WE BETTER SCRAM! THAT MOB WILL BE HERE IN A MINUTE!
YOU'RE TELLING ME! C'MON!
THEN-A VOICE...
WERE YOU THINKING OF GOING AWAY WITHOUT SAYING GOOD-BYE TO ME? TSK! TSK!
IT'S HIM AGAIN!
WITH PLEASURE!
GET HIM!
GRASPING A PICTURE, THE BATMAN SENDS THE FRAME SCALING ACROSS THE ROOM, WHERE..
DON'T TELL ANYBODY, FELLA, BUT YOU WERE FRAMED!
AAWK
AS A SHOT WHISTLES OVER HIM, THE BATMAN CATAPULTS FORWARD IN ONE LIGHTNING MOVE...
YOU'RE NEXT!
... AND NOW, NORTON- LET'S SEE IF YOU CAN REALLY TAKE IT!

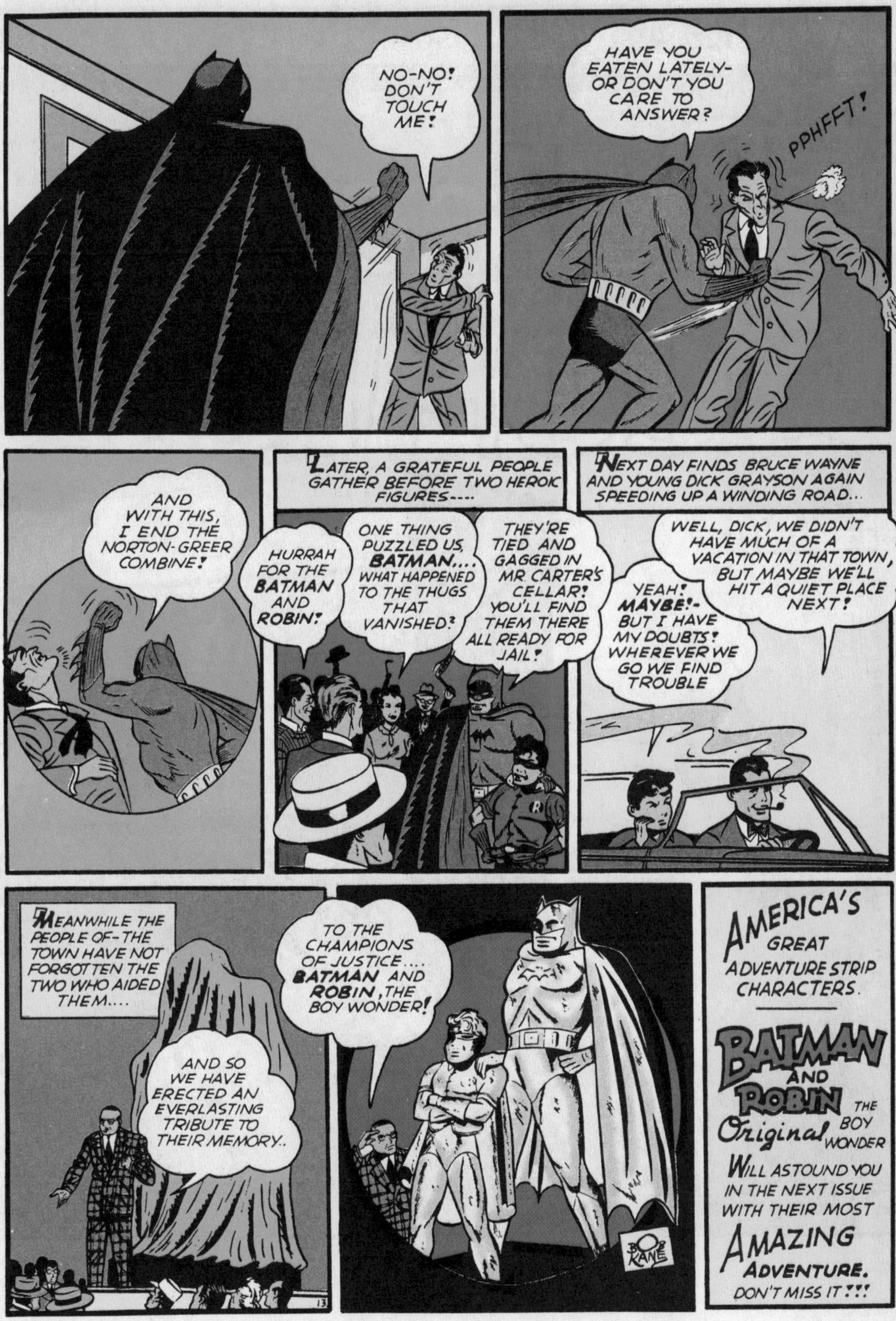
NO-NO! DON'T TOUCH ME!
HAVE YOU EATEN LATELY- OR DON'T YOU CARE TO ANSWER?
PPHFFT!
AND WITH THIS, I END THE NORTON-GREER COMBINE!
LATER, A GRATEFUL PEOPLE GATHER BEFORE TWO HEROIC FIGURES----
HURRAH FOR THE BATMAN AND ROBIN!
ONE THING PUZZLED US, BATMAN.... WHAT HAPPENED TO THE THUGS THAT VANISHED?
THEY'RE TIED AND GAGGED IN MR. CARTER'S CELLAR! YOU'LL FIND THEM THERE ALL READY FOR JAIL!
NEXT DAY FINDS BRUCE WAYNE AND YOUNG DICK GRAYSON AGAIN SPEEDING UP A WINDING ROAD...
WELL, DICK, WE DIDN'T HAVE MUCH OF A VACATION IN THAT TOWN, BUT MAYBE WE'LL HIT A QUIET PLACE NEXT!
YEAH! MAYBE!- BUT I HAVE MY DOUBTS! WHEREVER WE GO WE FIND TROUBLE
MEANWHILE THE PEOPLE OF-THE TOWN HAVE NOT FORGOTTEN THE TWO WHO AIDED THEM....
AND SO WE HAVE ERECTED AN EVERLASTING TRIBUTE TO THEIR MEMORY..
13
TO THE CHAMPIONS OF JUSTICE.... BATMAN AND ROBIN, THE BOY WONDER!
BOB KANE
AMERICA'S GREAT ADVENTURE STRIP CHARACTERS.
BATMAN AND ROBIN THE BOY WONDER
Original
WILL ASTOUND YOU IN THE NEXT ISSUE WITH THEIR MOST AMAZING ADVENTURE.
DON'T MISS IT!!!

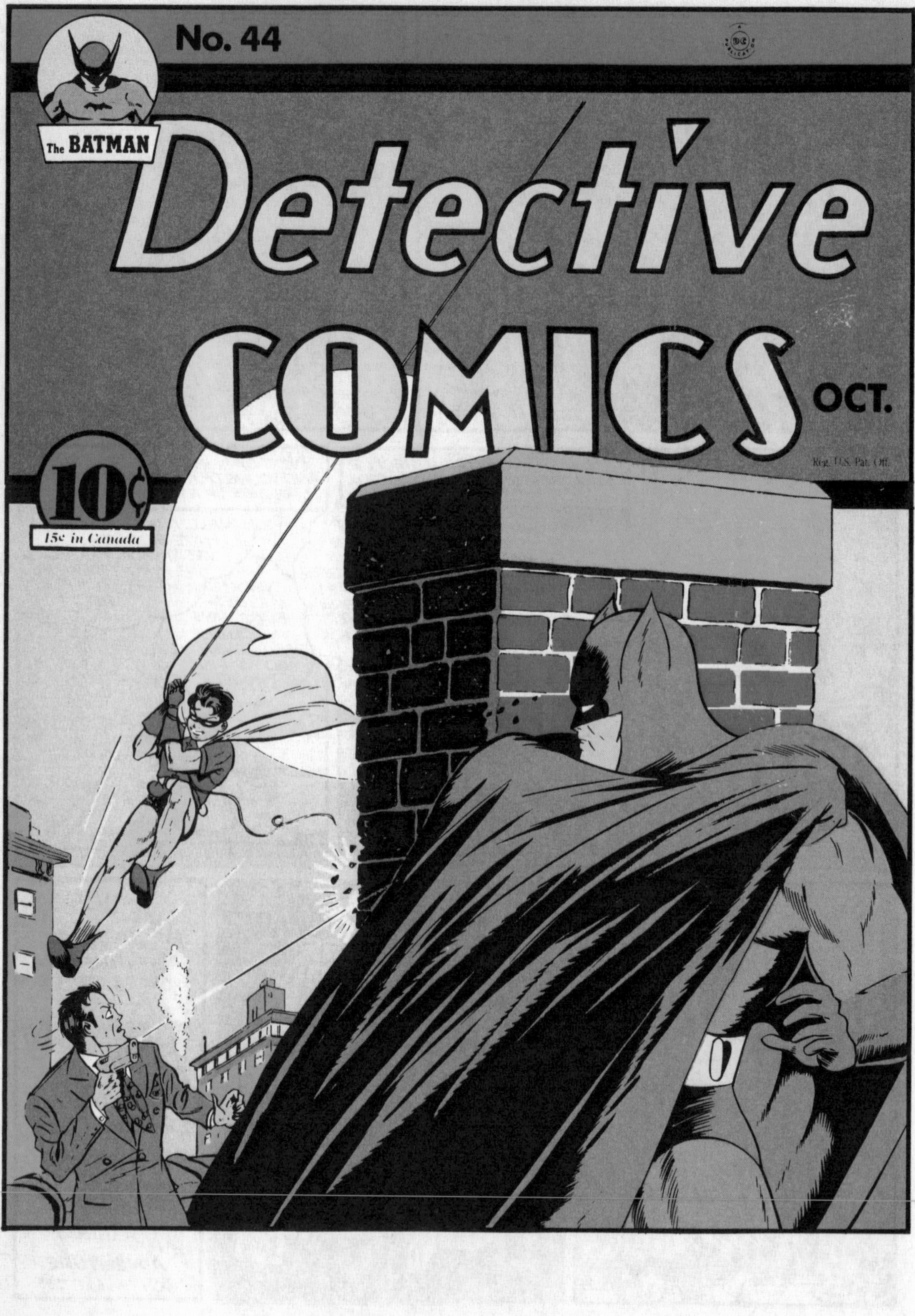
No. 44
The BATMAN
Detective
COMICS
OCT.
Reg. U.S. Pat. Off.
10¢
15¢ in Canada

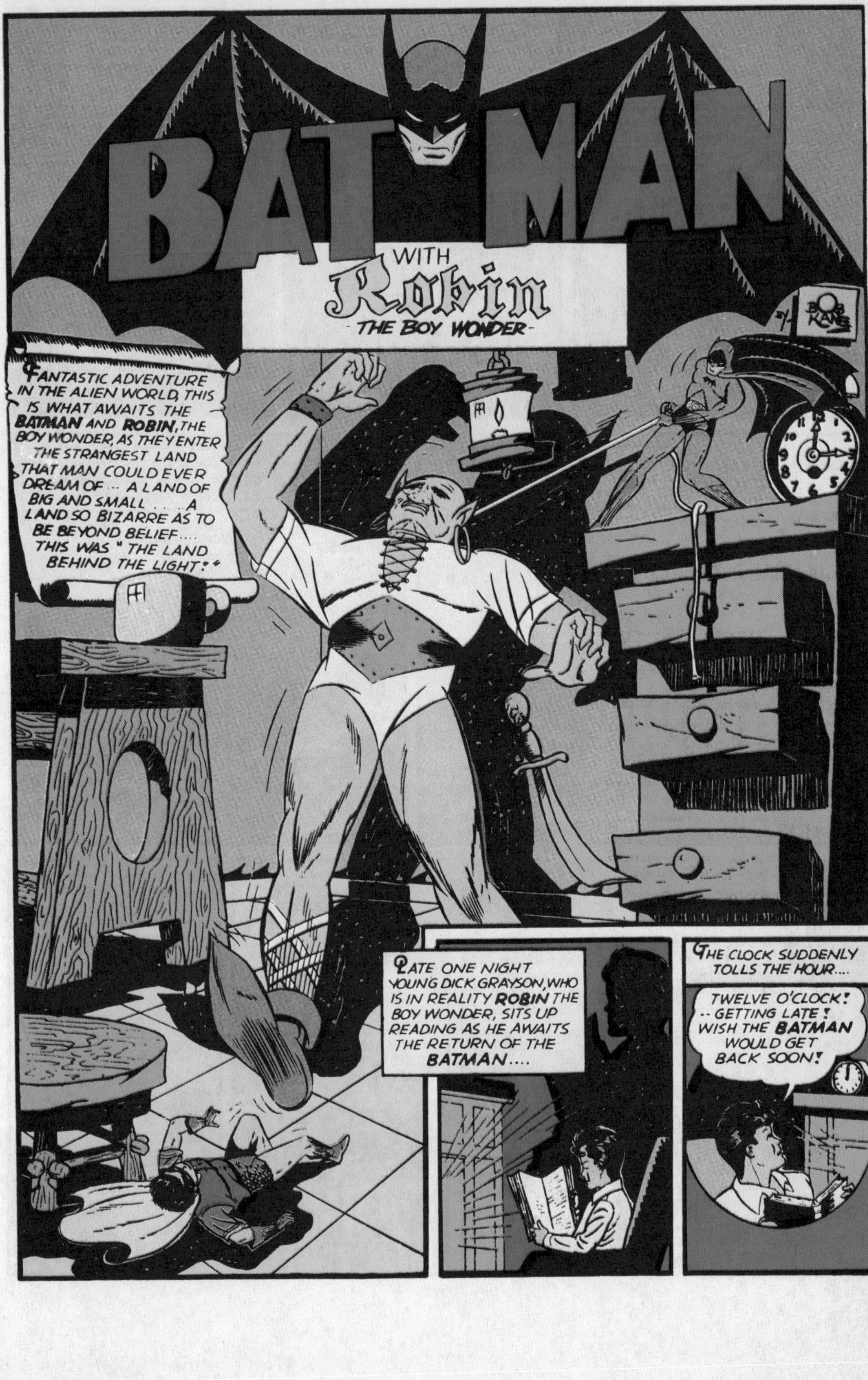
BATMAN
WITH Robin
-THE BOY WONDER-
BY BOB KANE
FANTASTIC ADVENTURE IN THE ALIEN WORLD, THIS IS WHAT AWAITS THE BATMAN AND ROBIN, THE BOY WONDER, AS THEY ENTER THE STRANGEST LAND THAT MAN COULD EVER DREAM OF ... A LAND OF BIG AND SMALL .... A LAND SO BIZARRE AS TO BE BEYOND BELIEF.... THIS WAS "THE LAND BEHIND THE LIGHT!"
LATE ONE NIGHT YOUNG DICK GRAYSON, WHO IS IN REALITY ROBIN THE BOY WONDER, SITS UP READING AS HE AWAITS THE RETURN OF THE BATMAN....
THE CLOCK SUDDENLY TOLLS THE HOUR....
TWELVE O'CLOCK! -- GETTING LATE! WISH THE BATMAN WOULD GET BACK SOON!

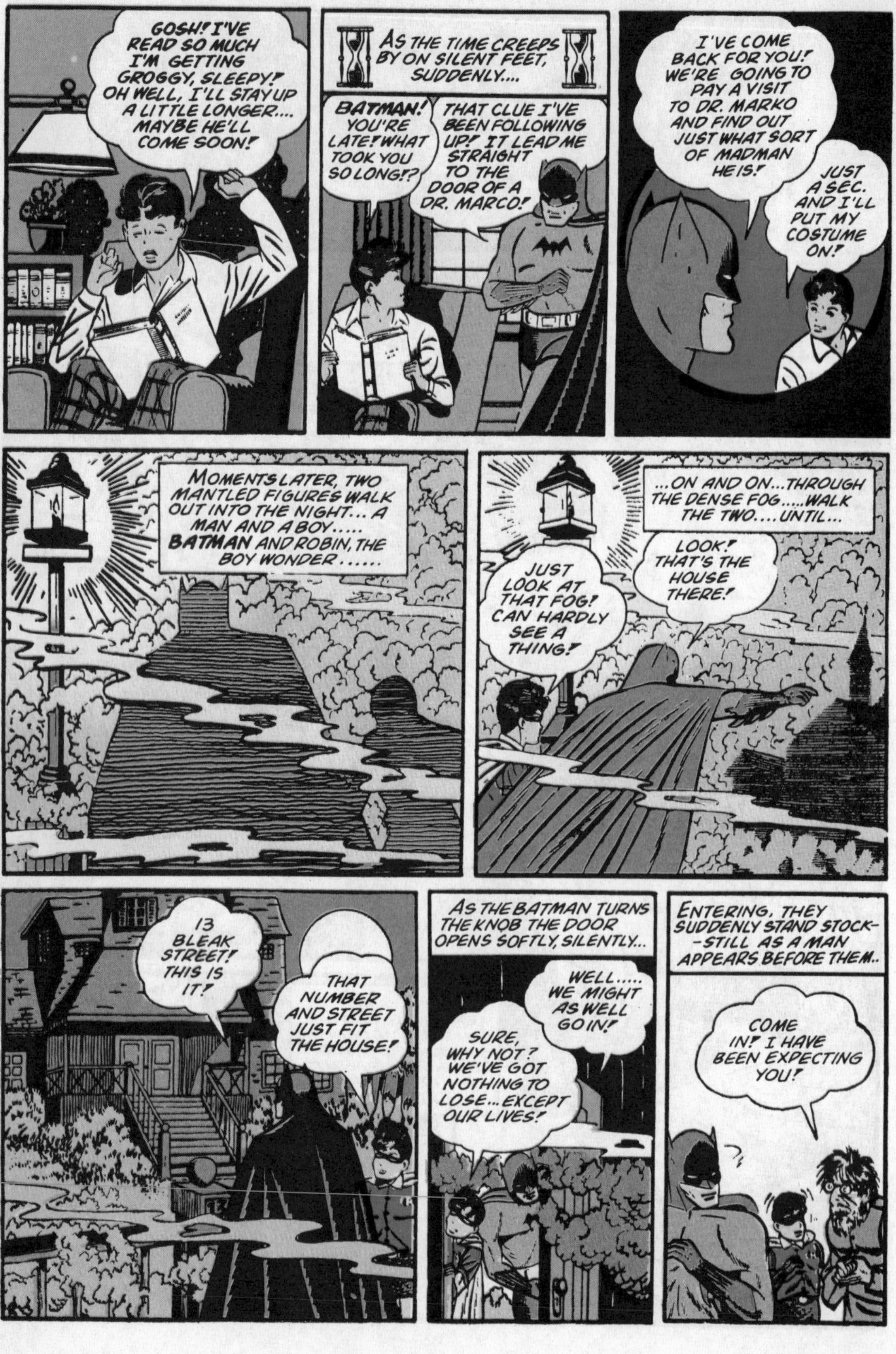
GOSH! I'VE READ SO MUCH I'M GETTING GROGGY, SLEEPY! OH WELL, I'LL STAY UP A LITTLE LONGER.... MAYBE HE'LL COME SOON!
AS THE TIME CREEPS BY ON SILENT FEET, SUDDENLY....
BATMAN! YOU'RE LATE! WHAT TOOK YOU SO LONG!?
THAT CLUE I'VE BEEN FOLLOWING UP! IT LEAD ME STRAIGHT TO THE DOOR OF A DR. MARCO!
I'VE COME BACK FOR YOU! WE'RE GOING TO PAY A VISIT TO DR. MARKO AND FIND OUT JUST WHAT SORT OF MADMAN HE IS!
JUST A SEC. AND I'LL PUT MY COSTUME ON!
MOMENTS LATER, TWO MANTLED FIGURES WALK OUT INTO THE NIGHT... A MAN AND A BOY..... BATMAN AND ROBIN, THE BOY WONDER......
...ON AND ON...THROUGH THE DENSE FOG.....WALK THE TWO....UNTIL...
JUST LOOK AT THAT FOG! CAN HARDLY SEE A THING!
LOOK! THAT'S THE HOUSE THERE!
13 BLEAK STREET! THIS IS IT!
THAT NUMBER AND STREET JUST FIT THE HOUSE!
AS THE BATMAN TURNS THE KNOB THE DOOR OPENS SOFTLY, SILENTLY...
WELL..... WE MIGHT AS WELL GO IN!
SURE, WHY NOT? WE'VE GOT NOTHING TO LOSE... EXCEPT OUR LIVES!
ENTERING, THEY SUDDENLY STAND STOCK-STILL AS A MAN APPEARS BEFORE THEM..
COME IN! I HAVE BEEN EXPECTING YOU!

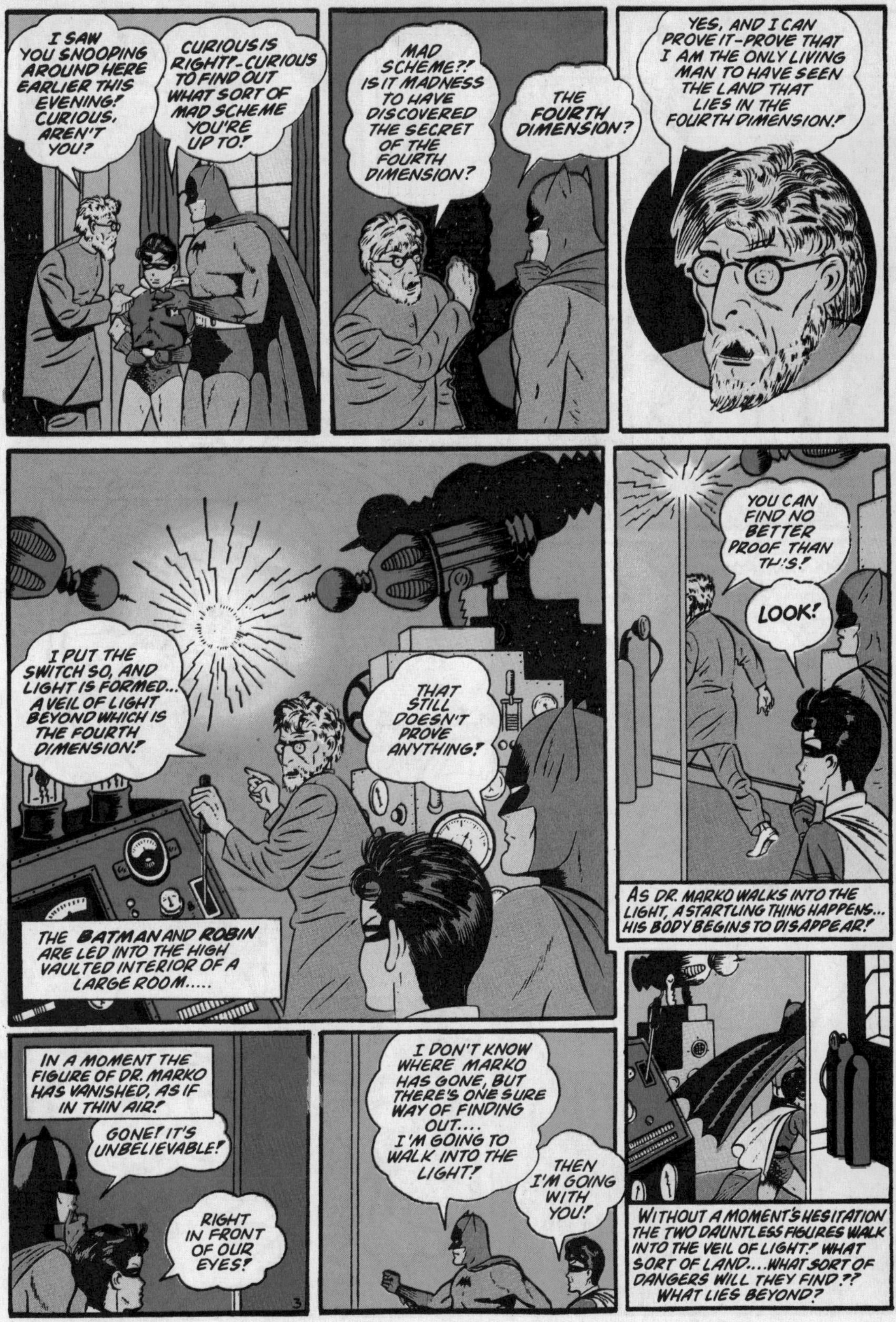

I SAW YOU SNOOPING AROUND HERE EARLIER THIS EVENING! CURIOUS, AREN'T YOU?
CURIOUS IS RIGHT!-CURIOUS TO FIND OUT WHAT SORT OF MAD SCHEME YOU'RE UP TO!
MAD SCHEME?! IS IT MADNESS TO HAVE DISCOVERED THE SECRET OF THE FOURTH DIMENSION?
THE FOURTH DIMENSION?
YES, AND I CAN PROVE IT-PROVE THAT I AM THE ONLY LIVING MAN TO HAVE SEEN THE LAND THAT LIES IN THE FOURTH DIMENSION!
THE BATMAN AND ROBIN ARE LED INTO THE HIGH VAULTED INTERIOR OF A LARGE ROOM.....
I PUT THE SWITCH SO, AND LIGHT IS FORMED... A VEIL OF LIGHT BEYOND WHICH IS THE FOURTH DIMENSION!
THAT STILL DOESN'T PROVE ANYTHING!
YOU CAN FIND NO BETTER PROOF THAN THIS!
LOOK!
AS DR. MARKO WALKS INTO THE LIGHT, A STARTLING THING HAPPENS... HIS BODY BEGINS TO DISAPPEAR!
IN A MOMENT THE FIGURE OF DR. MARKO HAS VANISHED, AS IF IN THIN AIR!
GONE! IT'S UNBELIEVABLE!
RIGHT IN FRONT OF OUR EYES!
3
I DON'T KNOW WHERE MARKO HAS GONE, BUT THERE'S ONE SURE WAY OF FINDING OUT.... I'M GOING TO WALK INTO THE LIGHT!
THEN I'M GOING WITH YOU!
WITHOUT A MOMENT'S HESITATION THE TWO DAUNTLESS FIGURES WALK INTO THE VEIL OF LIGHT! WHAT SORT OF LAND... WHAT SORT OF DANGERS WILL THEY FIND?? WHAT LIES BEYOND?

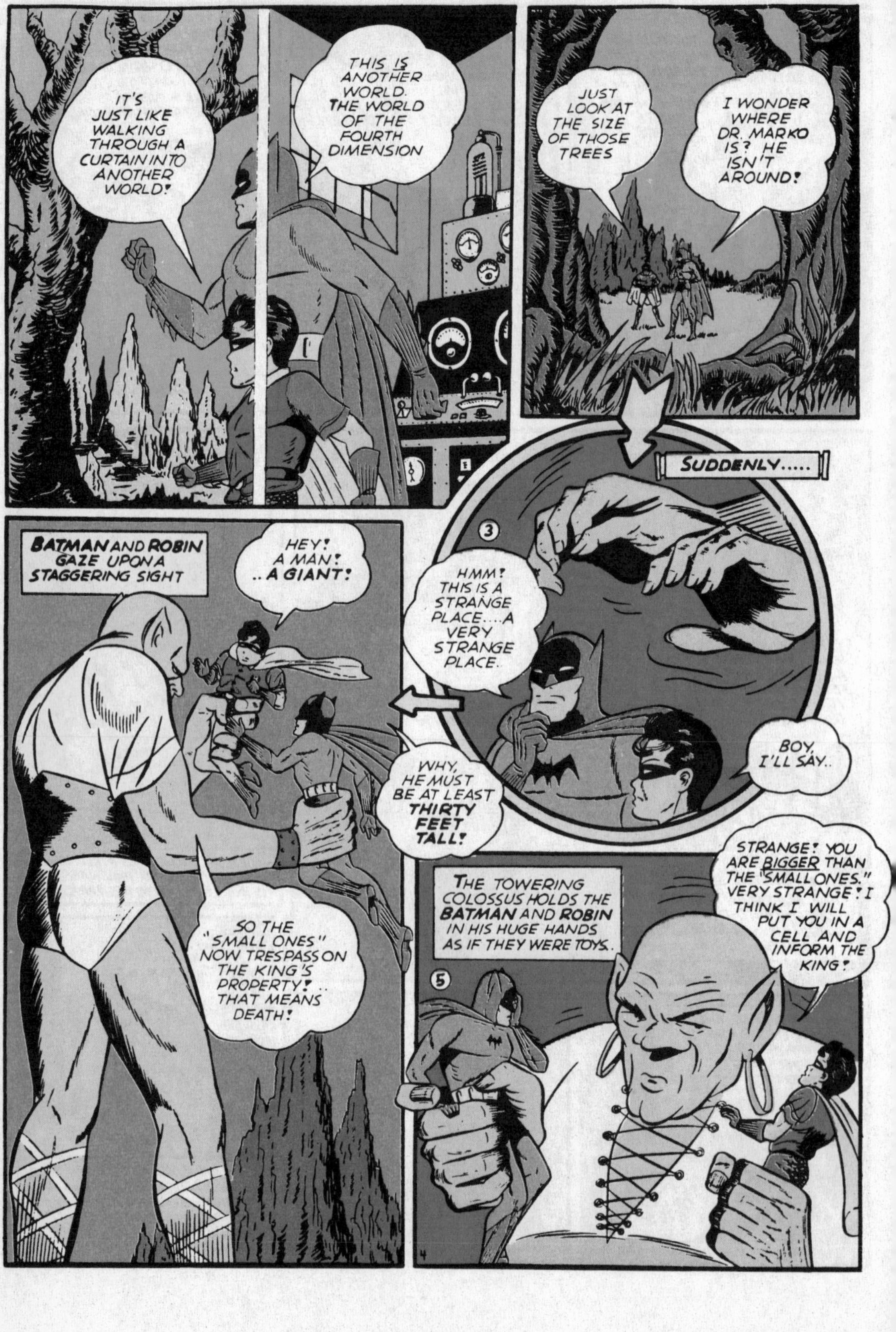
IT'S JUST LIKE WALKING THROUGH A CURTAIN INTO ANOTHER WORLD!
THIS IS ANOTHER WORLD. THE WORLD OF THE FOURTH DIMENSION
JUST LOOK AT THE SIZE OF THOSE TREES
I WONDER WHERE DR. MARKO IS? HE ISN'T AROUND!
SUDDENLY.....
3
HMM! THIS IS A STRANGE PLACE....A VERY STRANGE PLACE.
BOY, I'LL SAY..
BATMAN AND ROBIN GAZE UPON A STAGGERING SIGHT
HEY! A MAN! ..A GIANT!
WHY, HE MUST BE AT LEAST THIRTY FEET TALL!
SO THE "SMALL ONES" NOW TRESPASS ON THE KING'S PROPERTY! .. THAT MEANS DEATH!
THE TOWERING COLOSSUS HOLDS THE BATMAN AND ROBIN IN HIS HUGE HANDS AS IF THEY WERE TOYS.
5
STRANGE! YOU ARE BIGGER THAN THE "SMALL ONES." VERY STRANGE! I THINK I WILL PUT YOU IN A CELL AND INFORM THE KING!

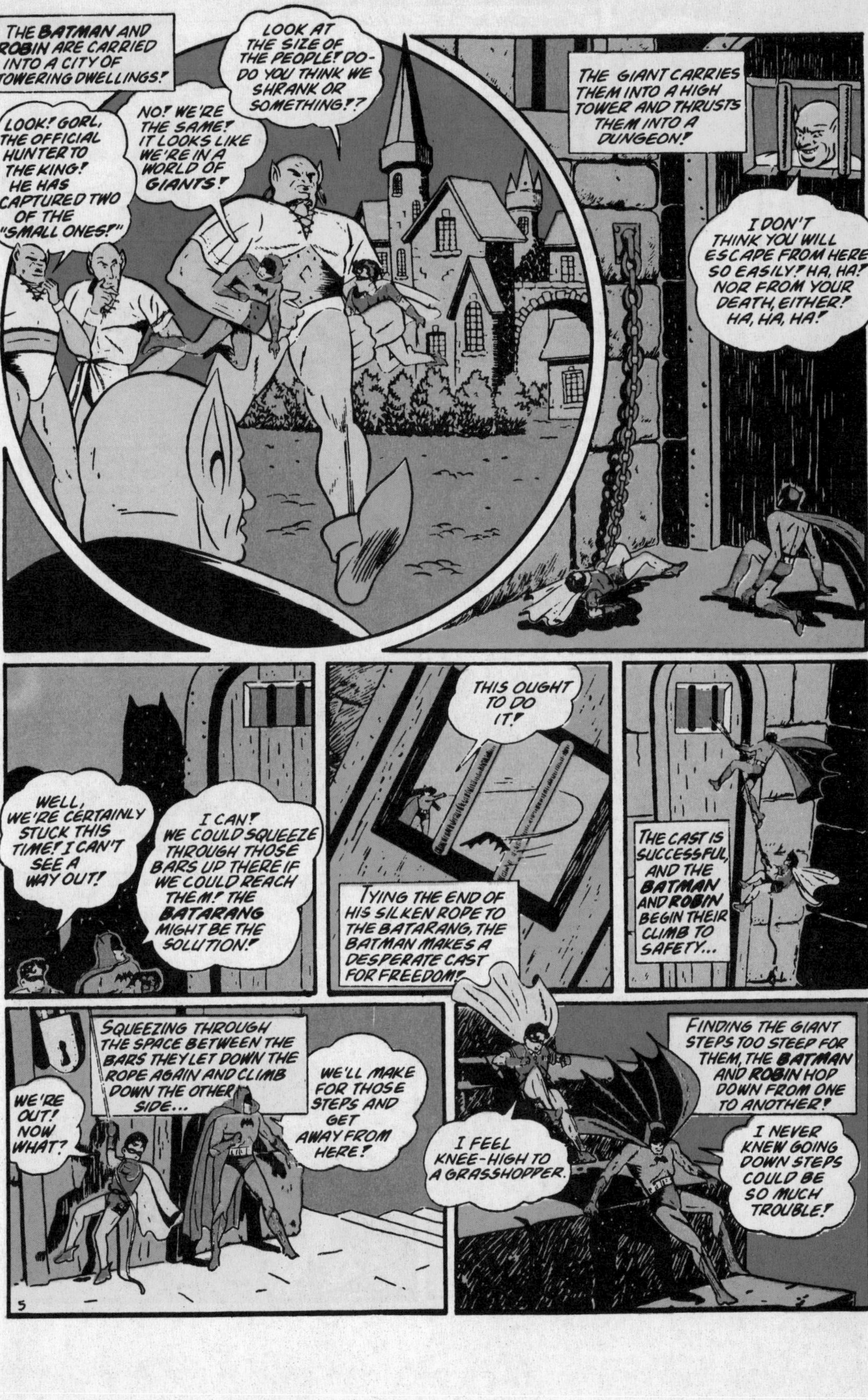
THE BATMAN AND ROBIN ARE CARRIED INTO A CITY OF TOWERING DWELLINGS!
LOOK AT THE SIZE OF THE PEOPLE! DO-DO YOU THINK WE SHRANK OR SOMETHING!?
NO! WE'RE THE SAME! IT LOOKS LIKE WE'RE IN A WORLD OF GIANTS!
LOOK! GORL, THE OFFICIAL HUNTER TO THE KING! HE HAS CAPTURED TWO OF THE "SMALL ONES!"
THE GIANT CARRIES THEM INTO A HIGH TOWER AND THRUSTS THEM INTO A DUNGEON!
I DON'T THINK YOU WILL ESCAPE FROM HERE SO EASILY! HA, HA! NOR FROM YOUR DEATH, EITHER! HA, HA, HA!
WELL, WE'RE CERTAINLY STUCK THIS TIME! I CAN'T SEE A WAY OUT!
I CAN! WE COULD SQUEEZE THROUGH THOSE BARS UP THERE IF WE COULD REACH THEM! THE BATARANG MIGHT BE THE SOLUTION!
THIS OUGHT TO DO IT!
TYING THE END OF HIS SILKEN ROPE TO THE BATARANG, THE BATMAN MAKES A DESPERATE CAST FOR FREEDOM!
THE CAST IS SUCCESSFUL, AND THE BATMAN AND ROBIN BEGIN THEIR CLIMB TO SAFETY...
SQUEEZING THROUGH THE SPACE BETWEEN THE BARS THEY LET DOWN THE ROPE AGAIN AND CLIMB DOWN THE OTHER SIDE...
WE'RE OUT! NOW WHAT?
WE'LL MAKE FOR THOSE STEPS AND GET AWAY FROM HERE!
FINDING THE GIANT STEPS TOO STEEP FOR THEM, THE BATMAN AND ROBIN HOP DOWN FROM ONE TO ANOTHER!
I FEEL KNEE-HIGH TO A GRASSHOPPER.
I NEVER KNEW GOING DOWN STEPS COULD BE SO MUCH TROUBLE!
5

TWO DOORS!

YOU LOOK THROUGH ONE AND I THE OTHER AND WE'LL SEE IF ANYONE IS ABOUT!

As ROBIN WALKS CAUTIOUSLY TOWARD THE DOOR, A CAT SOFTLY, SILENTLY, STALKS BEHIND A NORMAL SIZE HOUSE-CAT.... BUT NOW AS LARGE AS A TIGER!

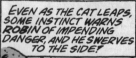

EVEN AS THE CAT LEAPS, SOME INSTINCT WARNS ROBIN OF IMPENDING DANGER, AND HE SWERVES TO THE SIDE!

HUH?

FURIOUS, THE CAT MAKES ANOTHER BOUND TO ITS INTENDED VICTIM, WHEN A MANTLED FIGURE LAUNCHES FORWARD TO LAND UPON ITS BACK... BATMAN!

NOT SO FAST PUSSY!

FLAILING OUT WITH SHARP CLAWS THE CAT TRIES TO SHAKE HIM OFF, BUT THE BATMAN HOLDS ON LIKE GRIM DEATH....

NOW'S MY CUE TO SING "HOLD THAT TIGER!"

..... HIS MUSCLES BUNCHING FROM THE STRAIN, THE BATMAN DRAWS HIS ARM TIGHTER...TIGHTER... UNTIL HE FEELS THE BODY GO LIMP BENEATH HIM.

NOW I KNOW HOW A MOUSE FEELS! THE SIZE OF THAT CAT!

DON'T FORGET WE'RE IN A LAND OF GIANTS, SO THAT EVERYTHING IS LARGE COMPARED TO US!

6

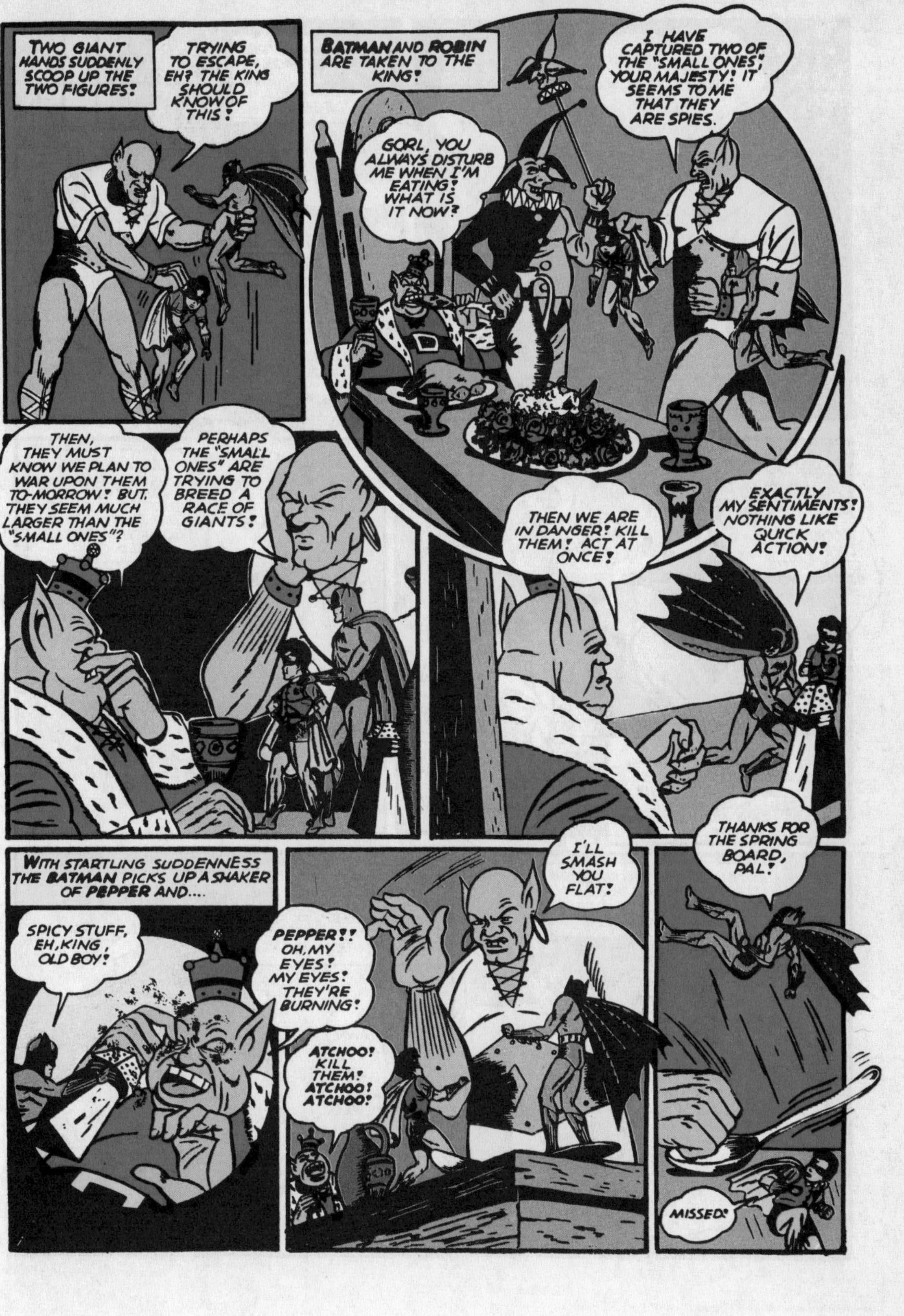
TWO GIANT HANDS SUDDENLY SCOOP UP THE TWO FIGURES!
TRYING TO ESCAPE, EH? THE KING SHOULD KNOW OF THIS!
BATMAN AND ROBIN ARE TAKEN TO THE KING!
I HAVE CAPTURED TWO OF THE "SMALL ONES", YOUR MAJESTY! IT SEEMS TO ME THAT THEY ARE SPIES.
GORL, YOU ALWAYS DISTURB ME WHEN I'M EATING! WHAT IS IT NOW?
THEN, THEY MUST KNOW WE PLAN TO WAR UPON THEM TO-MORROW! BUT, THEY SEEM MUCH LARGER THAN THE "SMALL ONES"?
PERHAPS THE "SMALL ONES" ARE TRYING TO BREED A RACE OF GIANTS!
THEN WE ARE IN DANGER! KILL THEM! ACT AT ONCE!
EXACTLY MY SENTIMENTS! NOTHING LIKE QUICK ACTION!
WITH STARTLING SUDDENNESS THE BATMAN PICKS UP A SHAKER OF PEPPER AND....
SPICY STUFF, EH, KING, OLD BOY!
PEPPER!! OH, MY EYES! MY EYES! THEY'RE BURNING!
ATCHOO! KILL THEM! ATCHOO! ATCHOO!
I'LL SMASH YOU FLAT!
THANKS FOR THE SPRING BOARD, PAL!
MISSED!

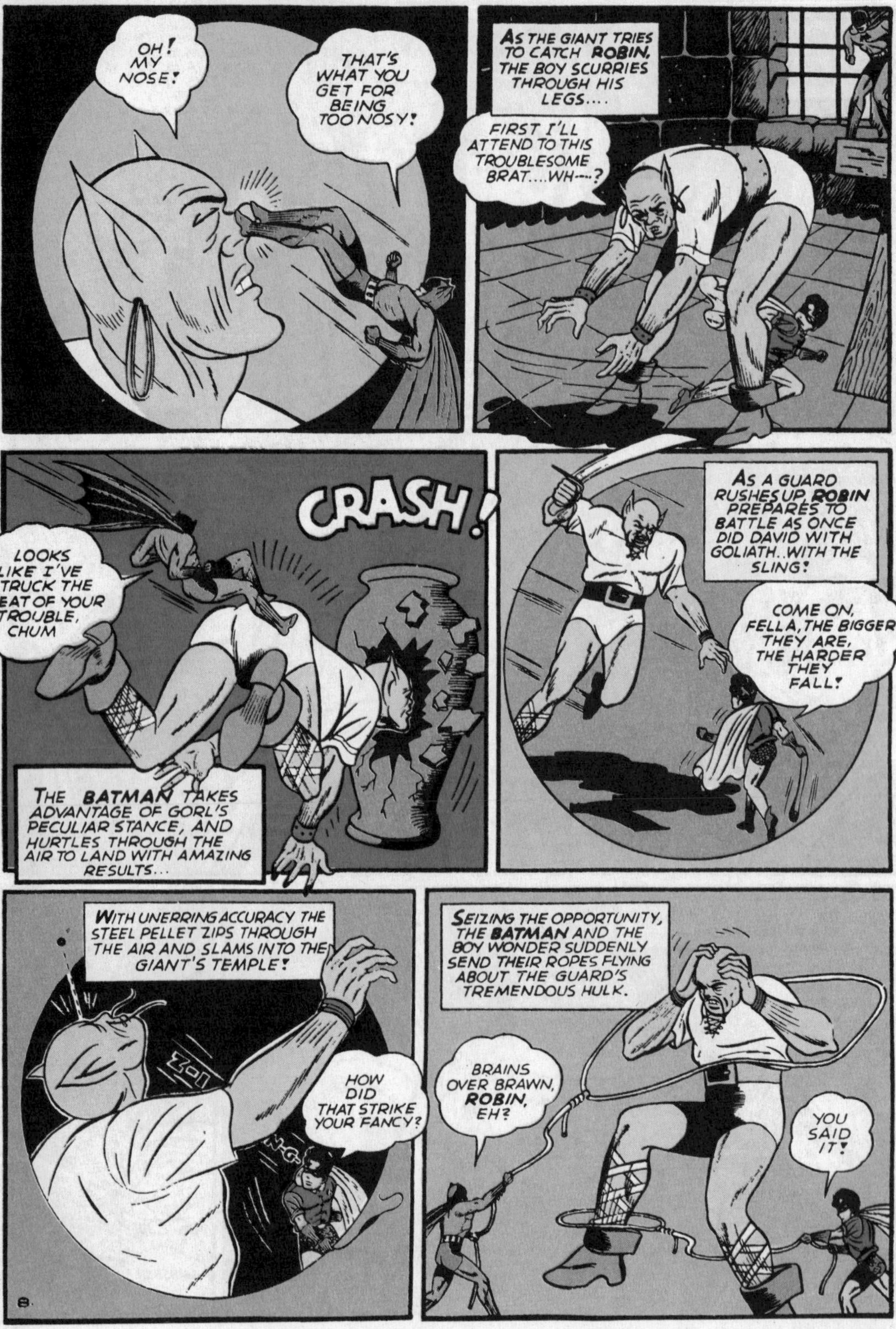

OH! MY NOSE!
THAT'S WHAT YOU GET FOR BEING TOO NOSY!
AS THE GIANT TRIES TO CATCH ROBIN, THE BOY SCURRIES THROUGH HIS LEGS....
FIRST I'LL ATTEND TO THIS TROUBLESOME BRAT....WH---?
CRASH!
LOOKS LIKE I'VE STRUCK THE SEAT OF YOUR TROUBLE, CHUM
THE BATMAN TAKES ADVANTAGE OF GORL'S PECULIAR STANCE, AND HURTLES THROUGH THE AIR TO LAND WITH AMAZING RESULTS...
AS A GUARD RUSHES UP, ROBIN PREPARES TO BATTLE AS ONCE DID DAVID WITH GOLIATH..WITH THE SLING!
COME ON, FELLA, THE BIGGER THEY ARE, THE HARDER THEY FALL!
WITH UNERRING ACCURACY THE STEEL PELLET ZIPS THROUGH THE AIR AND SLAMS INTO THE GIANT'S TEMPLE!
HOW DID THAT STRIKE YOUR FANCY?
8.
SEIZING THE OPPORTUNITY, THE BATMAN AND THE BOY WONDER SUDDENLY SEND THEIR ROPES FLYING ABOUT THE GUARD'S TREMENDOUS HULK.
BRAINS OVER BRAWN, ROBIN, EH?
YOU SAID IT!

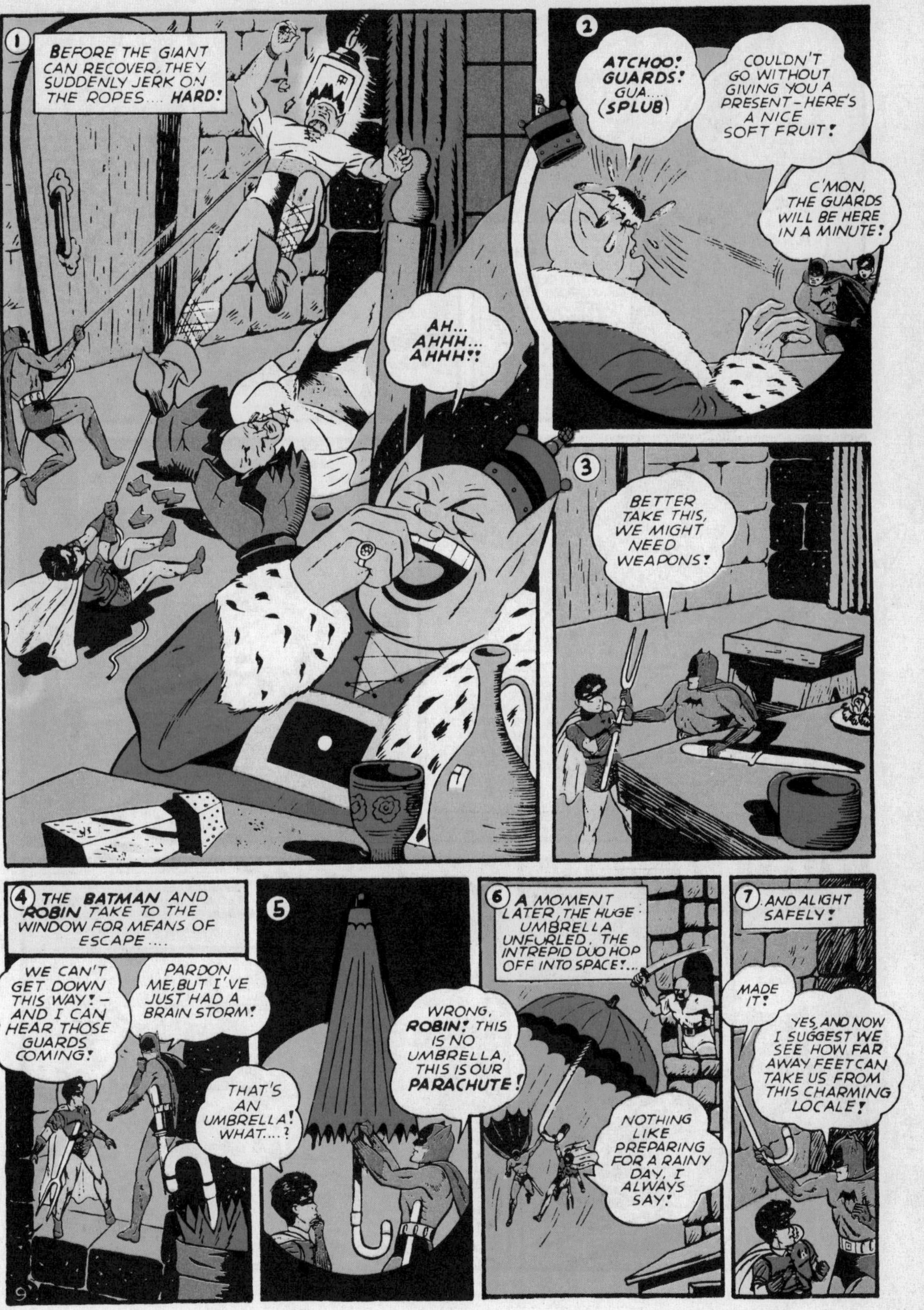
BEFORE THE GIANT CAN RECOVER, THEY SUDDENLY JERK ON THE ROPES.... HARD!
AH... AHHH... AHHH!!
ATCHOO! GUARDS! GUA.... (SPLUB)
COULDN'T GO WITHOUT GIVING YOU A PRESENT—HERE'S A NICE SOFT FRUIT!
C'MON, THE GUARDS WILL BE HERE IN A MINUTE!
BETTER TAKE THIS, WE MIGHT NEED WEAPONS!
THE BATMAN AND ROBIN TAKE TO THE WINDOW FOR MEANS OF ESCAPE....
WE CAN'T GET DOWN THIS WAY!— AND I CAN HEAR THOSE GUARDS COMING!
PARDON ME, BUT I'VE JUST HAD A BRAIN STORM!
THAT'S AN UMBRELLA! WHAT....?
WRONG, ROBIN! THIS IS NO UMBRELLA, THIS IS OUR PARACHUTE!
A MOMENT LATER, THE HUGE UMBRELLA UNFURLED, THE INTREPID DUO HOP OFF INTO SPACE!...
NOTHING LIKE PREPARING FOR A RAINY DAY, I ALWAYS SAY!
.AND ALIGHT SAFELY!
MADE IT!
YES, AND NOW I SUGGEST WE SEE HOW FAR AWAY FEET CAN TAKE US FROM THIS CHARMING LOCALE!

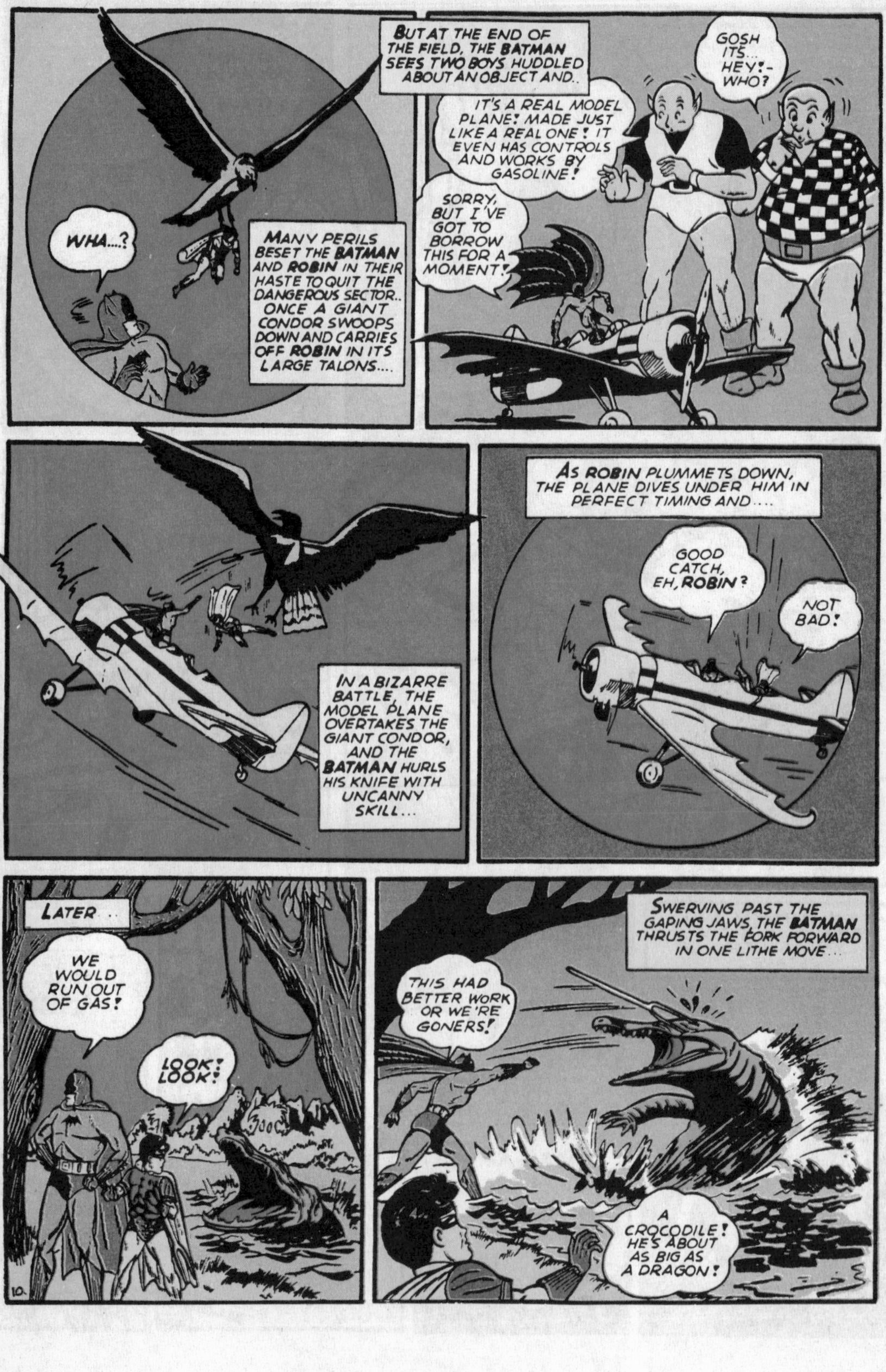
MANY PERILS BESET THE BATMAN AND ROBIN IN THEIR HASTE TO QUIT THE DANGEROUS SECTOR.. ONCE A GIANT CONDOR SWOOPS DOWN AND CARRIES OFF ROBIN IN ITS LARGE TALONS....
WHA...?
BUT AT THE END OF THE FIELD, THE BATMAN SEES TWO BOYS HUDDLED ABOUT AN OBJECT AND..
IT'S A REAL MODEL PLANE! MADE JUST LIKE A REAL ONE! IT EVEN HAS CONTROLS AND WORKS BY GASOLINE!
GOSH ITS... HEY!- WHO?
SORRY, BUT I'VE GOT TO BORROW THIS FOR A MOMENT!
IN A BIZARRE BATTLE, THE MODEL PLANE OVERTAKES THE GIANT CONDOR, AND THE BATMAN HURLS HIS KNIFE WITH UNCANNY SKILL...
AS ROBIN PLUMMETS DOWN, THE PLANE DIVES UNDER HIM IN PERFECT TIMING AND....
GOOD CATCH, EH, ROBIN?
NOT BAD!
LATER..
WE WOULD RUN OUT OF GAS!
LOOK! LOOK!
10.
SWERVING PAST THE GAPING JAWS, THE BATMAN THRUSTS THE FORK FORWARD IN ONE LITHE MOVE...
THIS HAD BETTER WORK OR WE'RE GONERS!
A CROCODILE! HE'S ABOUT AS BIG AS A DRAGON!

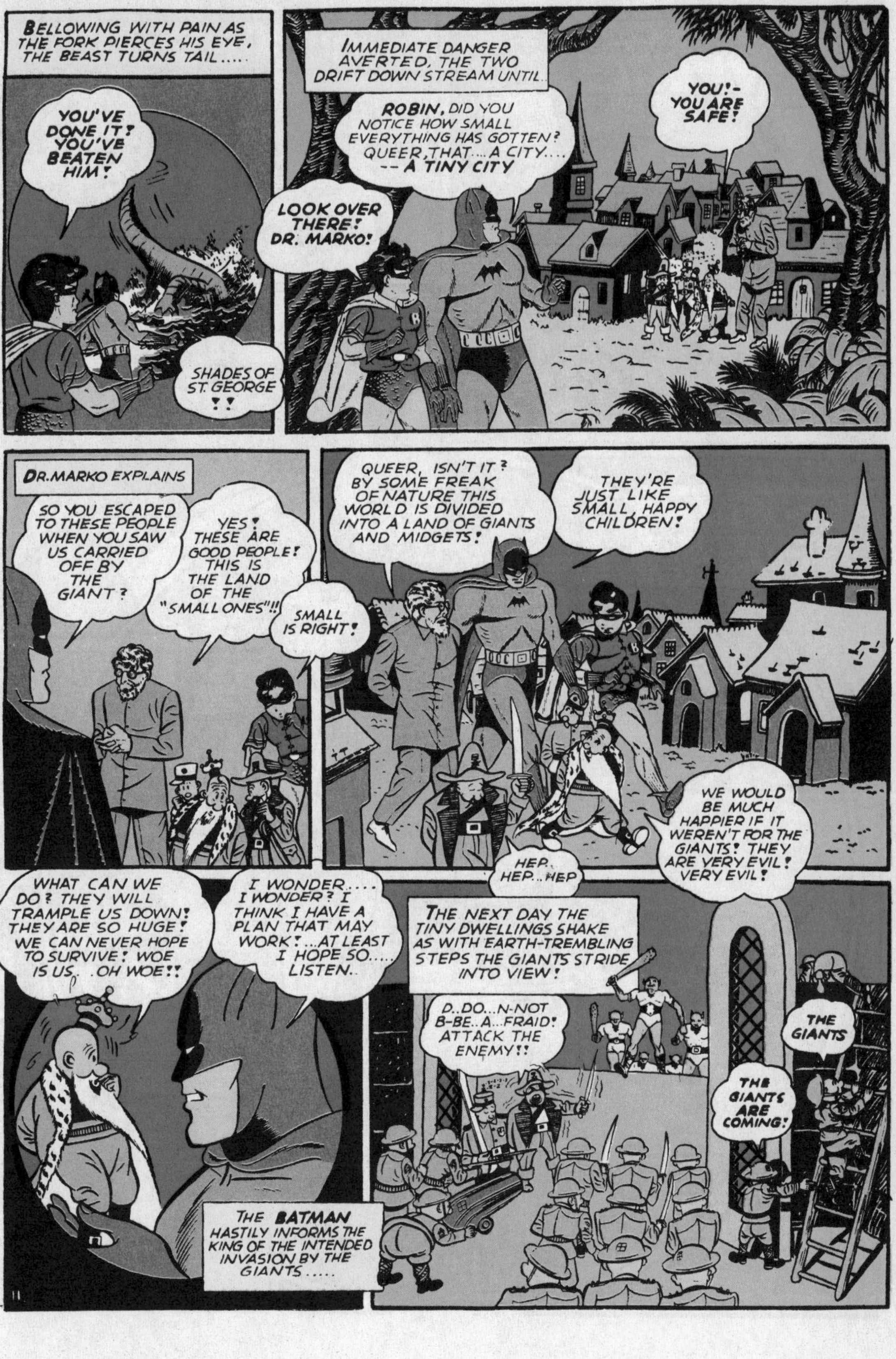
BELLOWING WITH PAIN AS THE FORK PIERCES HIS EYE, THE BEAST TURNS TAIL.....
YOU'VE DONE IT? YOU'VE BEATEN HIM!
SHADES OF ST. GEORGE !!
IMMEDIATE DANGER AVERTED, THE TWO DRIFT DOWN STREAM UNTIL..
ROBIN, DID YOU NOTICE HOW SMALL EVERYTHING HAS GOTTEN? QUEER, THAT.... A CITY.... -- A TINY CITY
LOOK OVER THERE! DR. MARKO!
YOU!- YOU ARE SAFE!
DR. MARKO EXPLAINS
SO YOU ESCAPED TO THESE PEOPLE WHEN YOU SAW US CARRIED OFF BY THE GIANT?
YES! THESE ARE GOOD PEOPLE! THIS IS THE LAND OF THE "SMALL ONES"!!
SMALL IS RIGHT!
QUEER, ISN'T IT? BY SOME FREAK OF NATURE THIS WORLD IS DIVIDED INTO A LAND OF GIANTS AND MIDGETS!
THEY'RE JUST LIKE SMALL, HAPPY CHILDREN!
HEP.. HEP...HEP
WE WOULD BE MUCH HAPPIER IF IT WEREN'T FOR THE GIANTS! THEY ARE VERY EVIL! VERY EVIL!
WHAT CAN WE DO? THEY WILL TRAMPLE US DOWN! THEY ARE SO HUGE! WE CAN NEVER HOPE TO SURVIVE! WOE IS US.. ..OH WOE!!
I WONDER.... I WONDER? I THINK I HAVE A PLAN THAT MAY WORK! ...AT LEAST I HOPE SO..... LISTEN..
THE BATMAN HASTILY INFORMS THE KING OF THE INTENDED INVASION BY THE GIANTS.....
THE NEXT DAY THE TINY DWELLINGS SHAKE AS WITH EARTH-TREMBLING STEPS THE GIANTS STRIDE INTO VIEW!
D..DO...N-NOT B-BE...A...FRAID! ATTACK THE ENEMY!!
THE GIANTS
THE GIANTS ARE COMING!

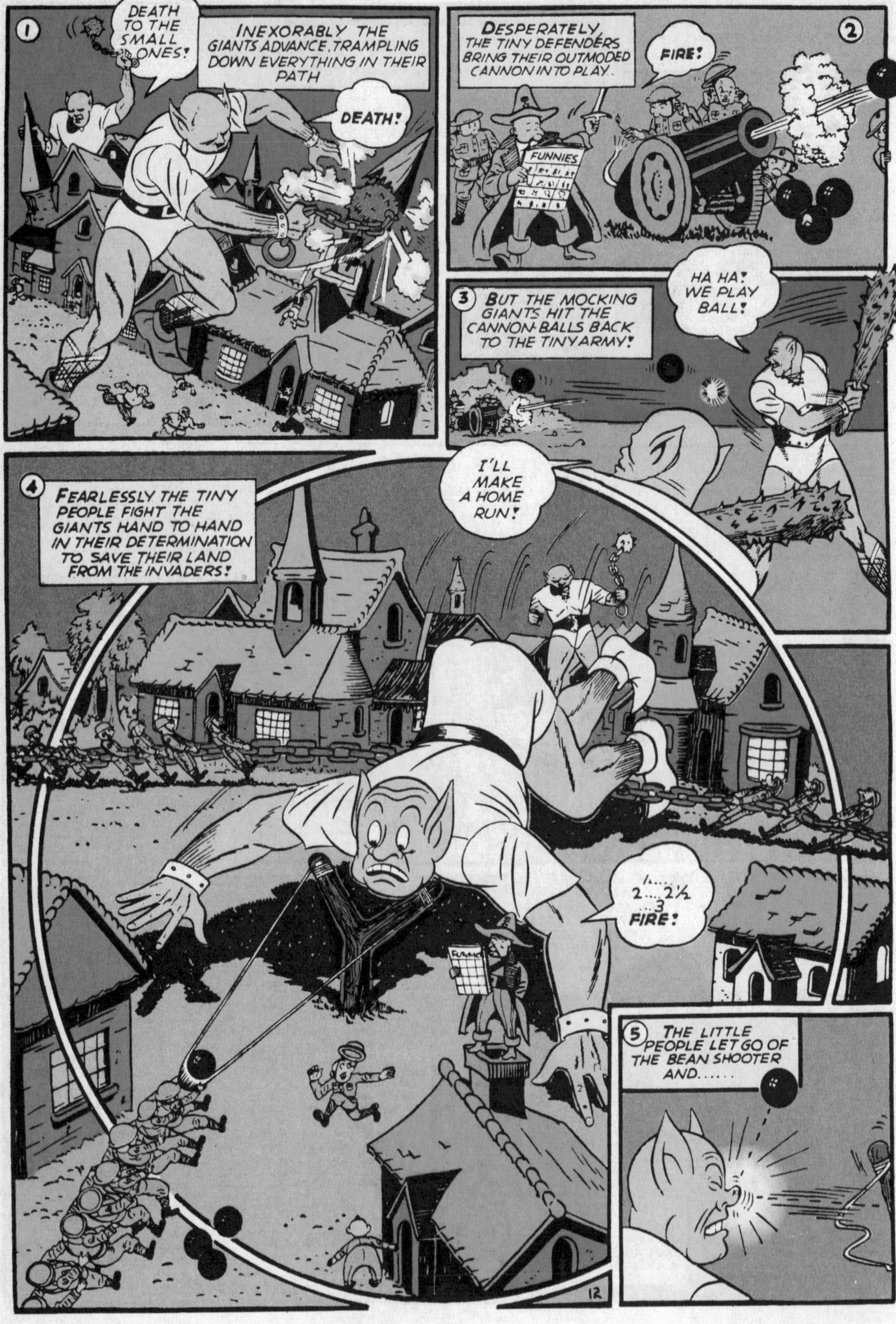
1
DEATH TO THE SMALL ONES!
INEXORABLY THE GIANTS ADVANCE, TRAMPLING DOWN EVERYTHING IN THEIR PATH
DEATH!
DESPERATELY, THE TINY DEFENDERS BRING THEIR OUTMODED CANNON INTO PLAY.
FIRE!
2
FUNNIES
3
BUT THE MOCKING GIANTS HIT THE CANNON-BALLS BACK TO THE TINY ARMY!
HA HA! WE PLAY BALL!
4
FEARLESSLY THE TINY PEOPLE FIGHT THE GIANTS HAND TO HAND IN THEIR DETERMINATION TO SAVE THEIR LAND FROM THE INVADERS!
I'LL MAKE A HOME RUN!
1.... 2.... 2½ ....3 FIRE!
5
THE LITTLE PEOPLE LET GO OF THE BEAN SHOOTER AND......
12

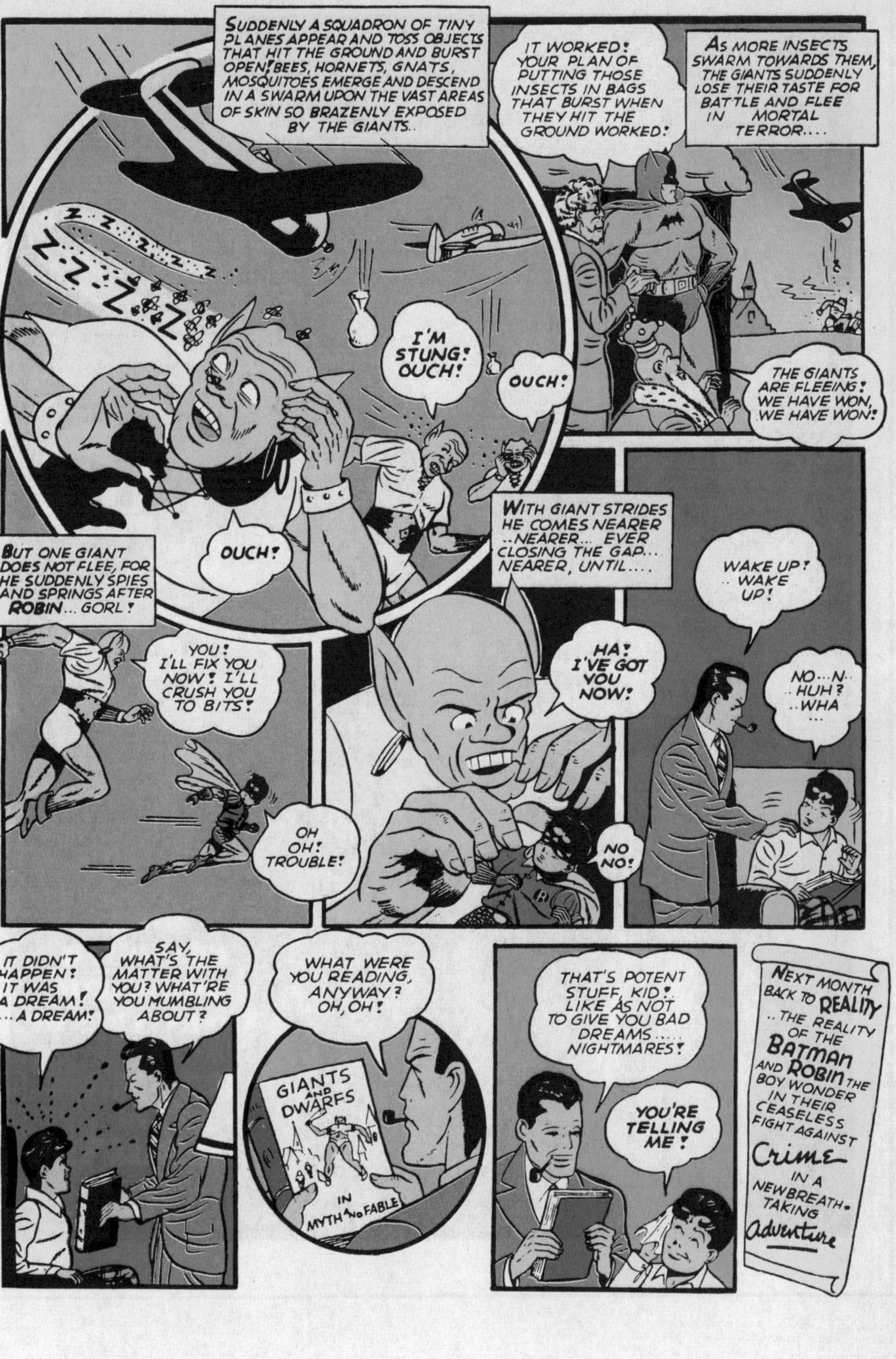

SUDDENLY A SQUADRON OF TINY PLANES APPEAR AND TOSS OBJECTS THAT HIT THE GROUND AND BURST OPEN! BEES, HORNETS, GNATS, MOSQUITOES EMERGE AND DESCEND IN A SWARM UPON THE VAST AREAS OF SKIN SO BRAZENLY EXPOSED BY THE GIANTS..
I'M STUNG! OUCH!
OUCH!
OUCH!
IT WORKED! YOUR PLAN OF PUTTING THOSE INSECTS IN BAGS THAT BURST WHEN THEY HIT THE GROUND WORKED!
AS MORE INSECTS SWARM TOWARDS THEM, THE GIANTS SUDDENLY LOSE THEIR TASTE FOR BATTLE AND FLEE IN MORTAL TERROR....
THE GIANTS ARE FLEEING! WE HAVE WON, WE HAVE WON!
BUT ONE GIANT DOES NOT FLEE, FOR HE SUDDENLY SPIES AND SPRINGS AFTER ROBIN... GORL!
YOU! I'LL FIX YOU NOW! I'LL CRUSH YOU TO BITS!
OH OH! TROUBLE!
WITH GIANT STRIDES HE COMES NEARER ..NEARER... EVER CLOSING THE GAP... NEARER, UNTIL....
HA! I'VE GOT YOU NOW!
NO NO!
WAKE UP! .. WAKE UP!
NO...N.. ..HUH? ..WHA ...
IT DIDN'T HAPPEN! IT WAS A DREAM! ...A DREAM!
SAY, WHAT'S THE MATTER WITH YOU? WHAT'RE YOU MUMBLING ABOUT?
WHAT WERE YOU READING, ANYWAY? OH, OH!
GIANTS AND DWARFS IN MYTH AND FABLE
THAT'S POTENT STUFF, KID! LIKE AS NOT TO GIVE YOU BAD DREAMS..... NIGHTMARES!
YOU'RE TELLING ME!
NEXT MONTH BACK TO REALITY ..THE REALITY OF THE BATMAN AND ROBIN THE BOY WONDER IN THEIR CEASELESS FIGHT AGAINST Crime IN A NEW BREATH-TAKING Adventure

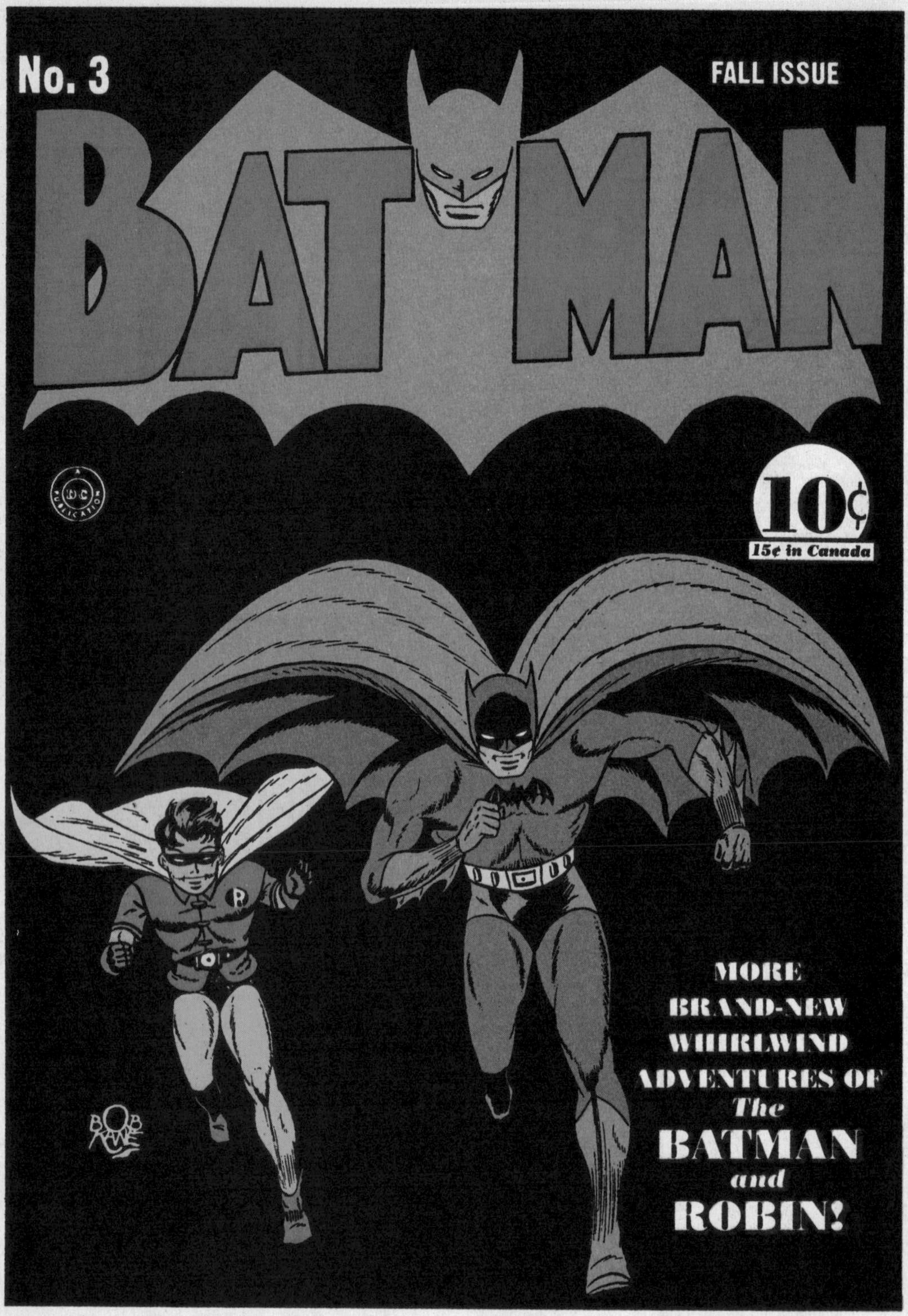
No. 3
FALL ISSUE
BATMAN
10¢
15¢ in Canada
MORE
BRAND-NEW
WHIRLWIND
ADVENTURES OF
The
BATMAN
and
ROBIN!

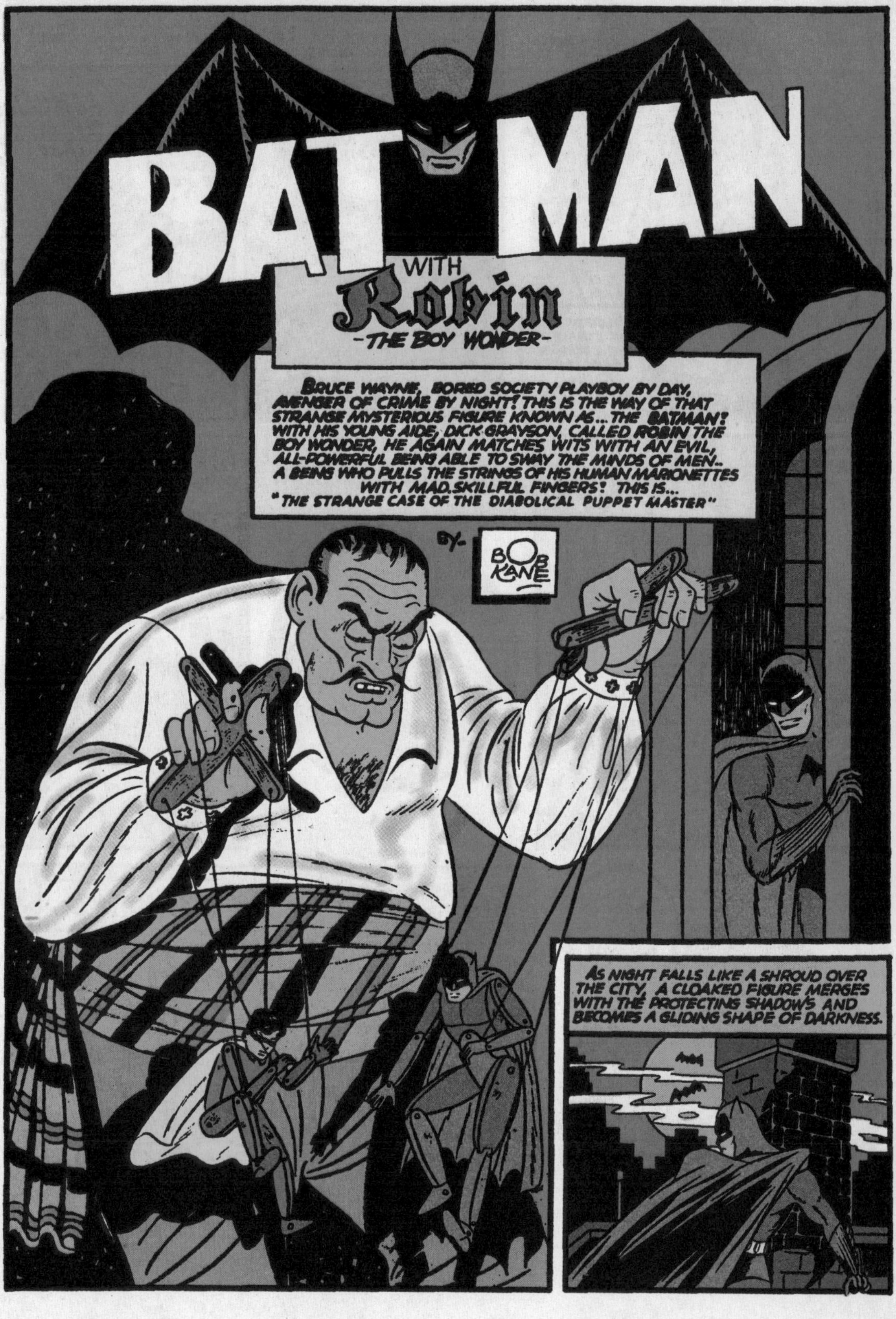
BAT MAN
WITH Robin -THE BOY WONDER-
BRUCE WAYNE, BORED SOCIETY PLAYBOY BY DAY, AVENGER OF CRIME BY NIGHT! THIS IS THE WAY OF THAT STRANGE MYSTERIOUS FIGURE KNOWN AS...THE BATMAN! WITH HIS YOUNG AIDE, DICK GRAYSON, CALLED ROBIN THE BOY WONDER, HE AGAIN MATCHES WITS WITH AN EVIL, ALL-POWERFUL BEING ABLE TO SWAY THE MINDS OF MEN.. A BEING WHO PULLS THE STRINGS OF HIS HUMAN MARIONETTES WITH MAD, SKILLFUL FINGERS! THIS IS... "THE STRANGE CASE OF THE DIABOLICAL PUPPET MASTER"
BY- BOB KANE
AS NIGHT FALLS LIKE A SHROUD OVER THE CITY, A CLOAKED FIGURE MERGES WITH THE PROTECTING SHADOWS AND BECOMES A GLIDING SHAPE OF DARKNESS.

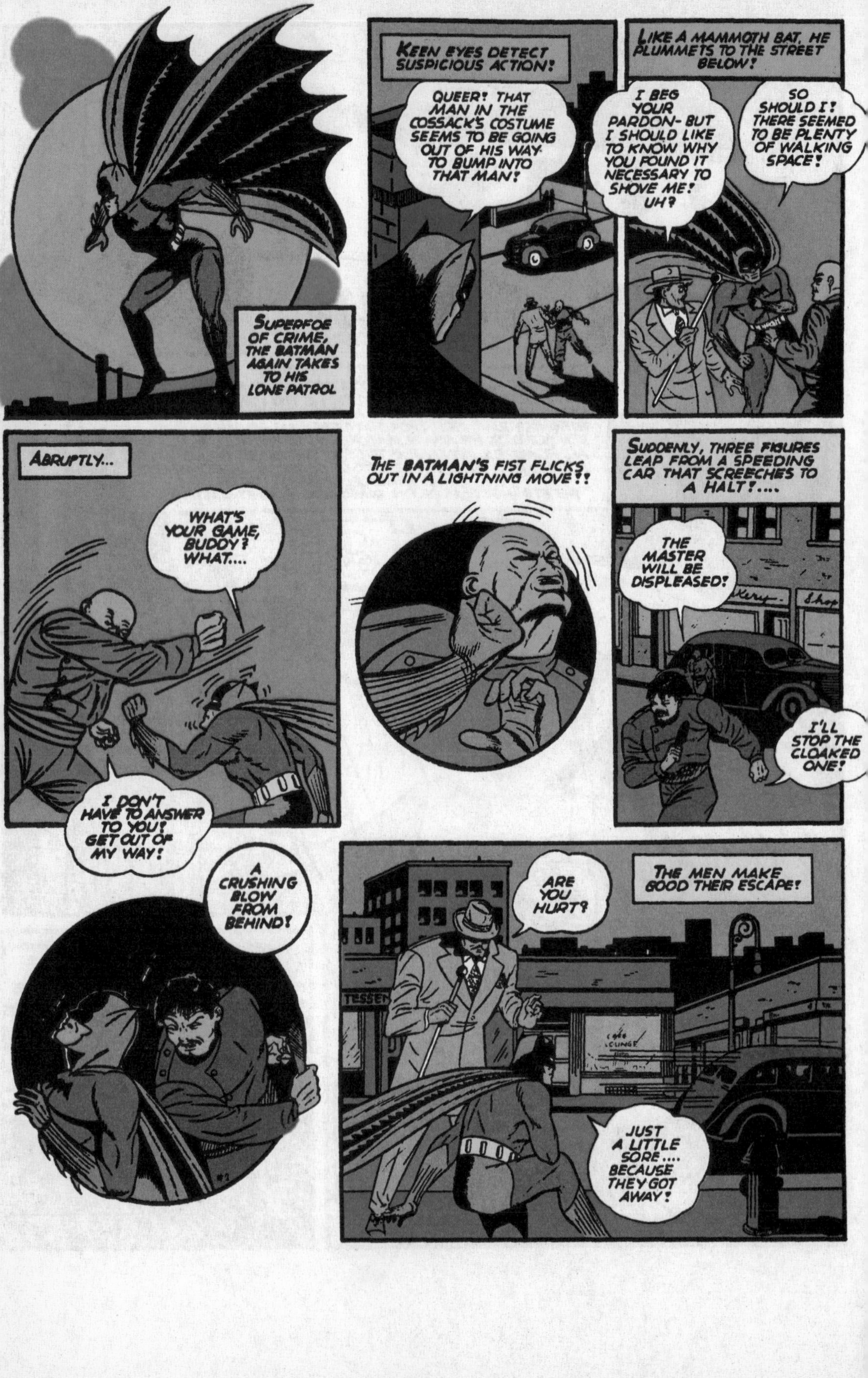
SUPERFOE OF CRIME, THE BATMAN AGAIN TAKES TO HIS LONE PATROL
KEEN EYES DETECT SUSPICIOUS ACTION!
QUEER! THAT MAN IN THE COSSACK'S COSTUME SEEMS TO BE GOING OUT OF HIS WAY TO BUMP INTO THAT MAN!
LIKE A MAMMOTH BAT, HE PLUMMETS TO THE STREET BELOW!
I BEG YOUR PARDON- BUT I SHOULD LIKE TO KNOW WHY YOU FOUND IT NECESSARY TO SHOVE ME! UH?
SO SHOULD I! THERE SEEMED TO BE PLENTY OF WALKING SPACE!
ABRUPTLY...
WHAT'S YOUR GAME, BUDDY? WHAT....
I DON'T HAVE TO ANSWER TO YOU! GET OUT OF MY WAY!
THE BATMAN'S FIST FLICKS OUT IN A LIGHTNING MOVE!!
SUDDENLY, THREE FIGURES LEAP FROM A SPEEDING CAR THAT SCREECHES TO A HALT!....
THE MASTER WILL BE DISPLEASED!
I'LL STOP THE CLOAKED ONE!
A CRUSHING BLOW FROM BEHIND!
ARE YOU HURT?
THE MEN MAKE GOOD THEIR ESCAPE!
JUST A LITTLE SORE.... BECAUSE THEY GOT AWAY!

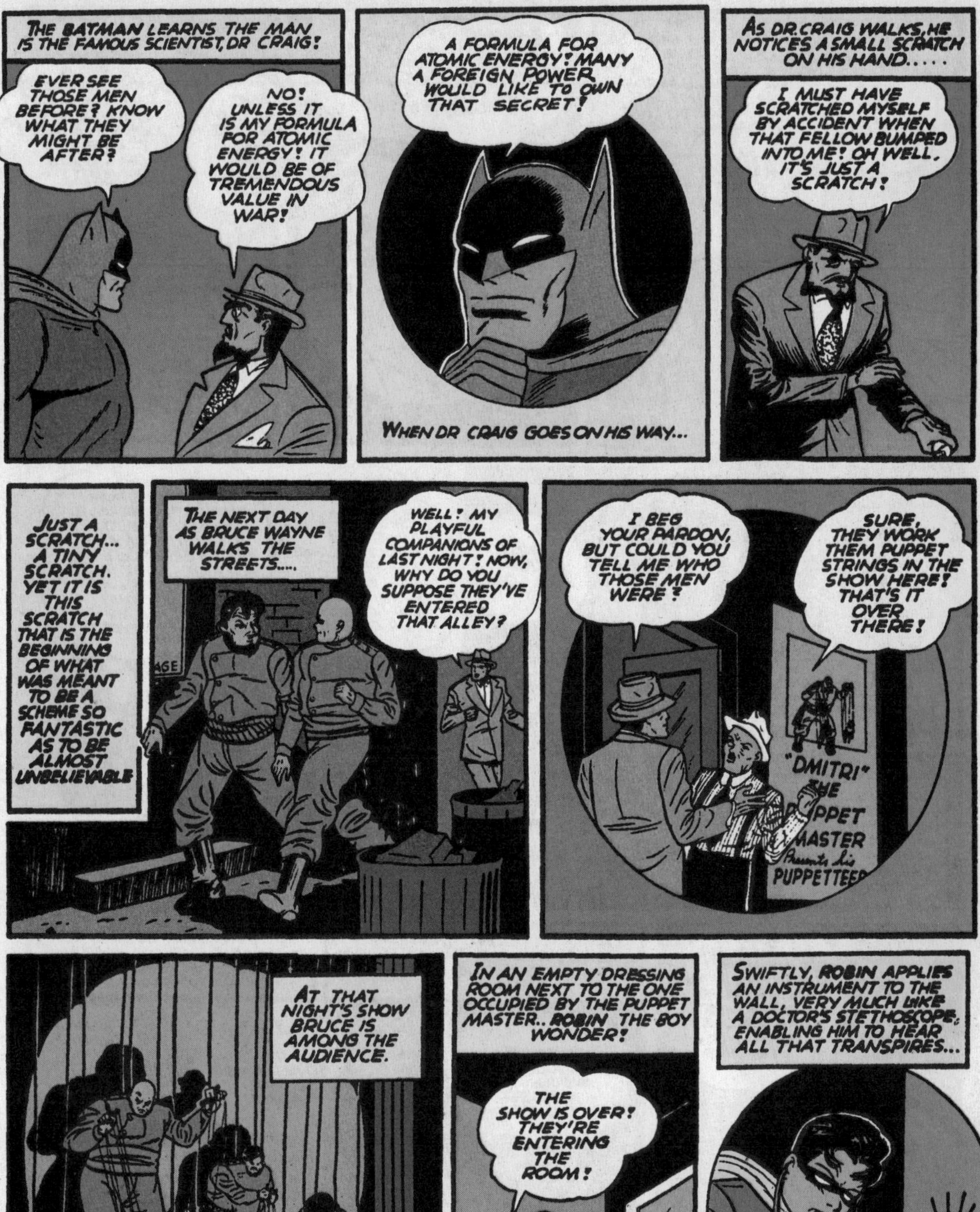
THE BATMAN LEARNS THE MAN IS THE FAMOUS SCIENTIST, DR CRAIG!
EVER SEE THOSE MEN BEFORE? KNOW WHAT THEY MIGHT BE AFTER?
NO! UNLESS IT IS MY FORMULA FOR ATOMIC ENERGY! IT WOULD BE OF TREMENDOUS VALUE IN WAR!
A FORMULA FOR ATOMIC ENERGY! MANY A FOREIGN POWER WOULD LIKE TO OWN THAT SECRET!
WHEN DR CRAIG GOES ON HIS WAY...
AS DR. CRAIG WALKS, HE NOTICES A SMALL SCRATCH ON HIS HAND.....
I MUST HAVE SCRATCHED MYSELF BY ACCIDENT WHEN THAT FELLOW BUMPED INTO ME! OH WELL, IT'S JUST A SCRATCH!
JUST A SCRATCH... A TINY SCRATCH. YET IT IS THIS SCRATCH THAT IS THE BEGINNING OF WHAT WAS MEANT TO BE A SCHEME SO FANTASTIC AS TO BE ALMOST UNBELIEVABLE
THE NEXT DAY AS BRUCE WAYNE WALKS THE STREETS....
WELL! MY PLAYFUL COMPANIONS OF LAST NIGHT! NOW, WHY DO YOU SUPPOSE THEY'VE ENTERED THAT ALLEY?
I BEG YOUR PARDON, BUT COULD YOU TELL ME WHO THOSE MEN WERE?
SURE, THEY WORK THEM PUPPET STRINGS IN THE SHOW HERE! THAT'S IT OVER THERE!
"DMITRI" THE
MASTER
AT THAT NIGHT'S SHOW BRUCE IS AMONG THE AUDIENCE.
THAT'S THEM ALL RIGHT! PERHAPS ROBIN WILL FIND OUT WHAT THIS IS ALL ABOUT!
IN AN EMPTY DRESSING ROOM NEXT TO THE ONE OCCUPIED BY THE PUPPET MASTER.. ROBIN THE BOY WONDER!
THE SHOW IS OVER! THEY'RE ENTERING THE ROOM!
SWIFTLY, ROBIN APPLIES AN INSTRUMENT TO THE WALL, VERY MUCH LIKE A DOCTOR'S STETHOSCOPE, ENABLING HIM TO HEAR ALL THAT TRANSPIRES...

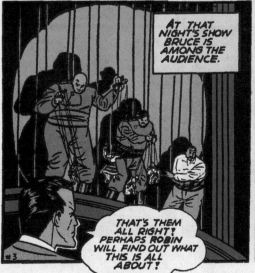

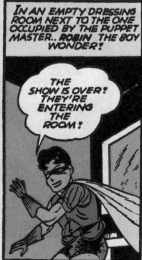

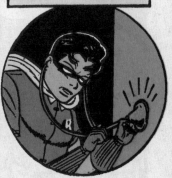

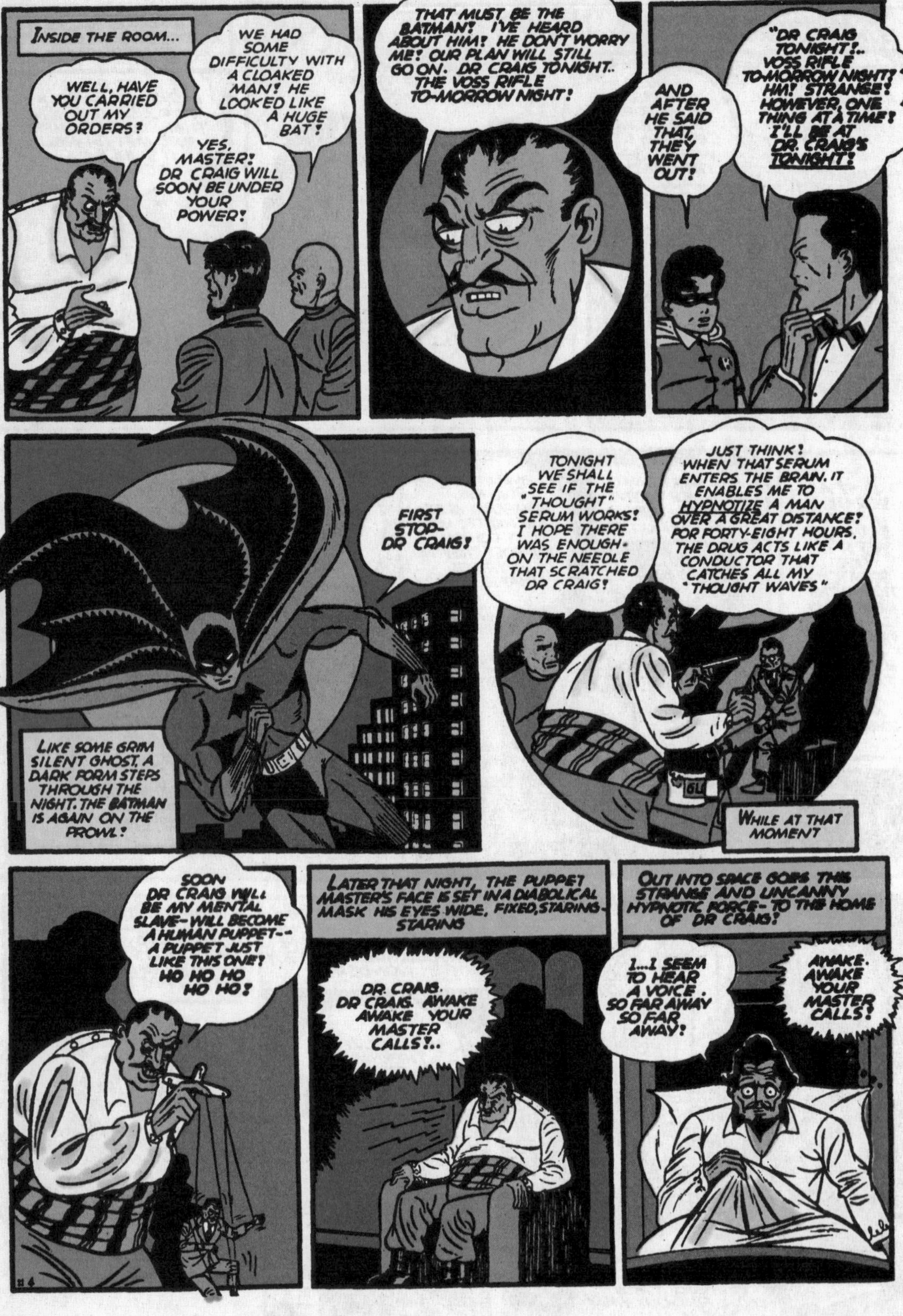
INSIDE THE ROOM...
WELL, HAVE YOU CARRIED OUT MY ORDERS?
YES, MASTER! DR CRAIG WILL SOON BE UNDER YOUR POWER!
WE HAD SOME DIFFICULTY WITH A CLOAKED MAN! HE LOOKED LIKE A HUGE BAT!
THAT MUST BE THE BATMAN! I'VE HEARD ABOUT HIM! HE DON'T WORRY ME! OUR PLAN WILL STILL GO ON. DR CRAIG TONIGHT.. THE VOSS RIFLE TO-MORROW NIGHT!
AND AFTER HE SAID THAT, THEY WENT OUT!
"DR CRAIG TONIGHT!.. VOSS RIFLE TO-MORROW NIGHT!" HM! STRANGE! HOWEVER, ONE THING AT A TIME! I'LL BE AT DR. CRAIG'S TONIGHT!
FIRST STOP- DR CRAIG!
LIKE SOME GRIM SILENT GHOST, A DARK FORM STEPS THROUGH THE NIGHT. THE BATMAN IS AGAIN ON THE PROWL!
TONIGHT WE SHALL SEE IF THE "THOUGHT" SERUM WORKS! I HOPE THERE WAS ENOUGH ON THE NEEDLE THAT SCRATCHED DR CRAIG!
JUST THINK! WHEN THAT SERUM ENTERS THE BRAIN, IT ENABLES ME TO HYPNOTIZE A MAN OVER A GREAT DISTANCE! FOR FORTY-EIGHT HOURS, THE DRUG ACTS LIKE A CONDUCTOR THAT CATCHES ALL MY "THOUGHT WAVES"
WHILE AT THAT MOMENT
SOON DR CRAIG WILL BE MY MENTAL SLAVE- WILL BECOME A HUMAN PUPPET-- A PUPPET JUST LIKE THIS ONE! HO HO HO HO HO!
LATER THAT NIGHT, THE PUPPET MASTER'S FACE IS SET IN A DIABOLICAL MASK HIS EYES WIDE, FIXED, STARING- STARING
DR. CRAIG. DR CRAIG. AWAKE AWAKE YOUR MASTER CALLS!..
OUT INTO SPACE GOES THIS STRANGE AND UNCANNY HYPNOTIC FORCE- TO THE HOME OF DR CRAIG!
I...I SEEM TO HEAR A VOICE. SO FAR AWAY SO FAR AWAY!
AWAKE. AWAKE YOUR MASTER CALLS!

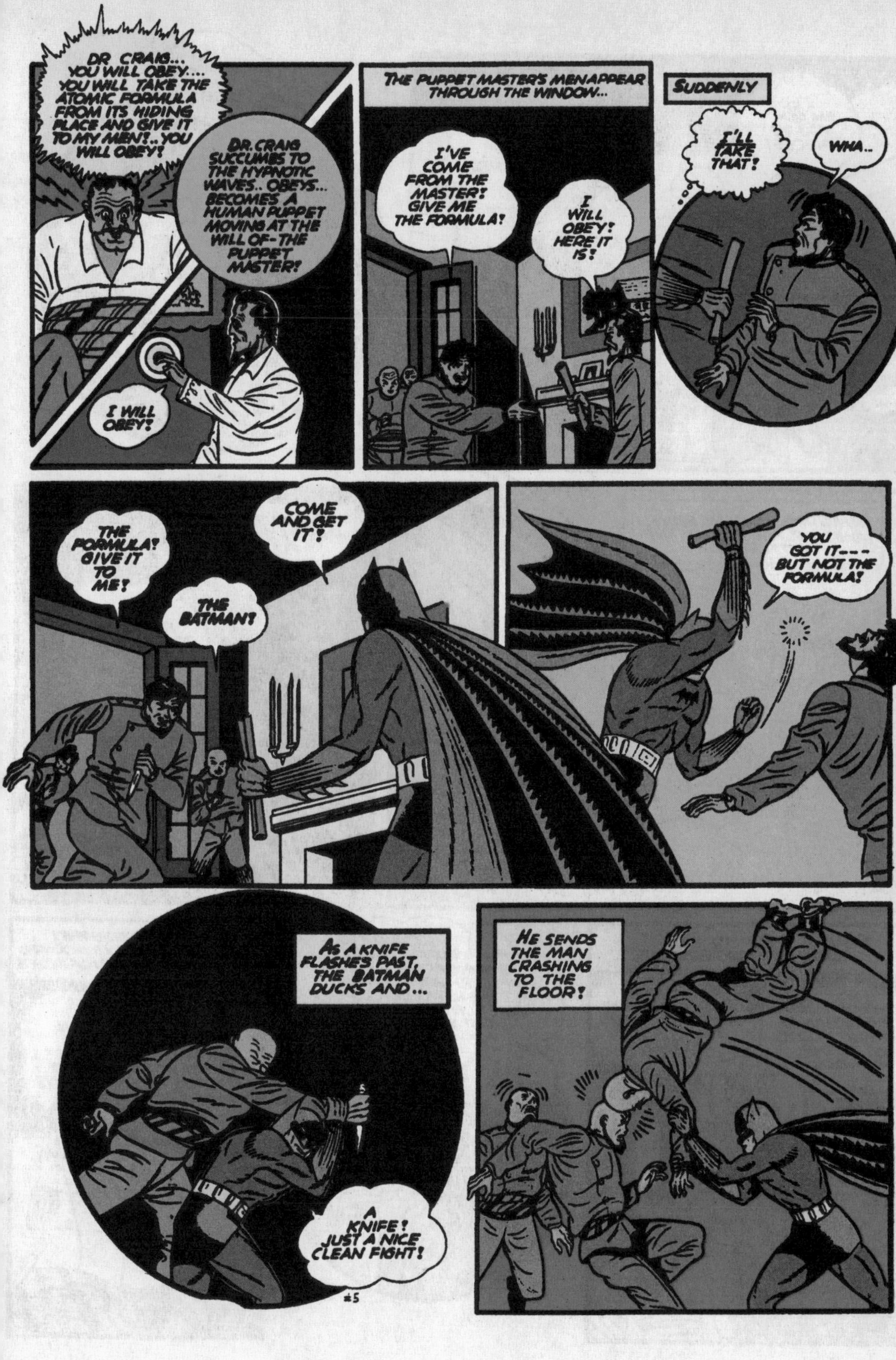
DR. CRAIG... YOU WILL OBEY.... YOU WILL TAKE THE ATOMIC FORMULA FROM ITS HIDING PLACE AND GIVE IT TO MY MEN!.. YOU WILL OBEY!
DR. CRAIG SUCCUMBS TO THE HYPNOTIC WAVES.. OBEYS... BECOMES A HUMAN PUPPET MOVING AT THE WILL OF THE PUPPET MASTER!
I WILL OBEY!
THE PUPPET MASTER'S MEN APPEAR THROUGH THE WINDOW...
I'VE COME FROM THE MASTER! GIVE ME THE FORMULA!
I WILL OBEY! HERE IT IS!
SUDDENLY
I'LL TAKE THAT!
WHA..
THE FORMULA! GIVE IT TO ME!
THE BATMAN!
COME AND GET IT!
YOU GOT IT--- BUT NOT THE FORMULA!
AS A KNIFE FLASHES PAST, THE BATMAN DUCKS AND...
A KNIFE! JUST A NICE CLEAN FIGHT!
HE SENDS THE MAN CRASHING TO THE FLOOR!

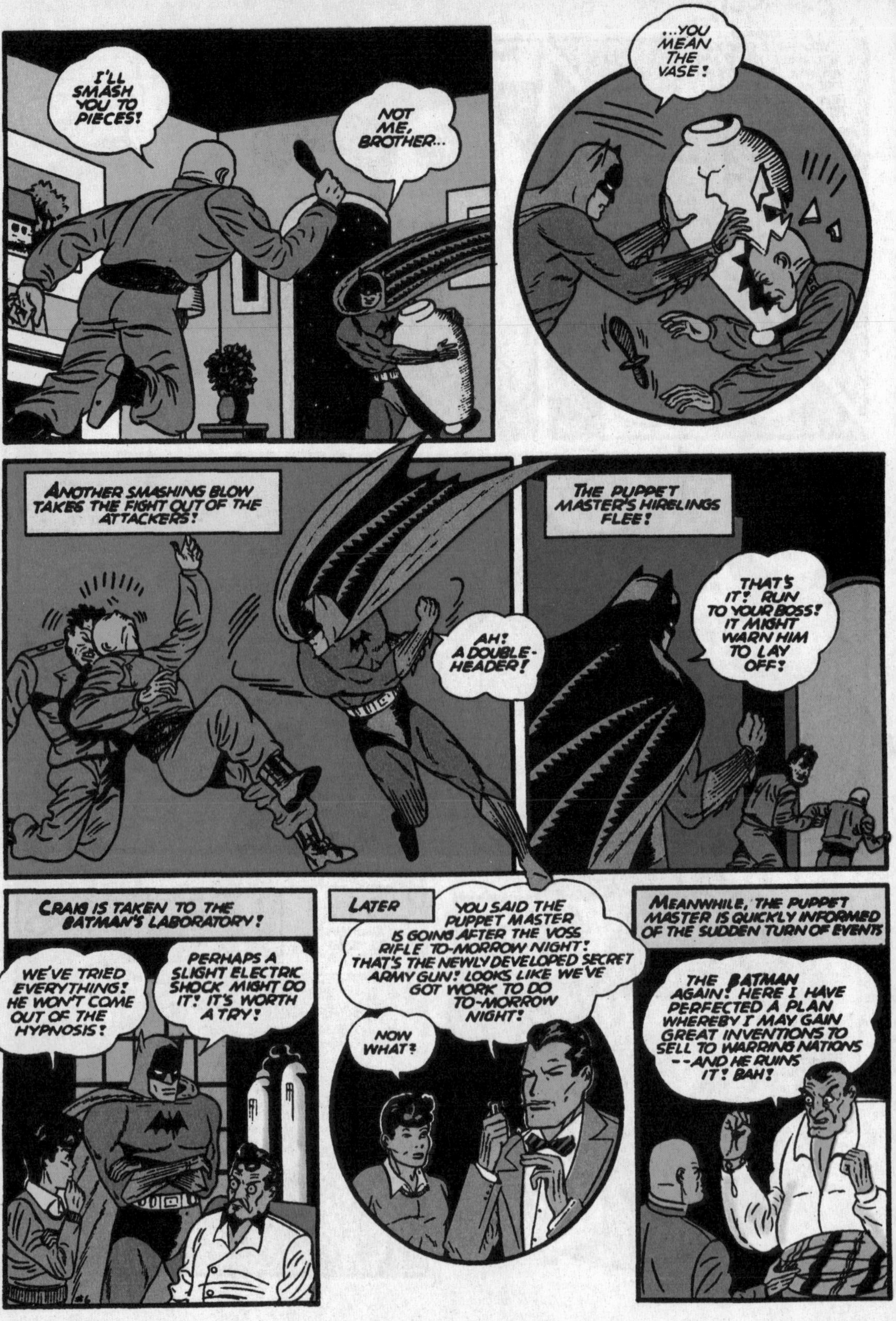
I'LL SMASH YOU TO PIECES!
NOT ME, BROTHER...
...YOU MEAN THE VASE!
ANOTHER SMASHING BLOW TAKES THE FIGHT OUT OF THE ATTACKERS!
AH! A DOUBLE-HEADER!
THE PUPPET MASTER'S HIRELINGS FLEE!
THAT'S IT! RUN TO YOUR BOSS! IT MIGHT WARN HIM TO LAY OFF!
CRAIG IS TAKEN TO THE BATMAN'S LABORATORY!
WE'VE TRIED EVERYTHING! HE WON'T COME OUT OF THE HYPNOSIS!
PERHAPS A SLIGHT ELECTRIC SHOCK MIGHT DO IT! IT'S WORTH A TRY!
LATER
YOU SAID THE PUPPET MASTER IS GOING AFTER THE VOSS RIFLE TO-MORROW NIGHT! THAT'S THE NEWLY DEVELOPED SECRET ARMY GUN! LOOKS LIKE WE'VE GOT WORK TO DO TO-MORROW NIGHT!
NOW WHAT?
MEANWHILE, THE PUPPET MASTER IS QUICKLY INFORMED OF THE SUDDEN TURN OF EVENTS
THE BATMAN AGAIN! HERE I HAVE PERFECTED A PLAN WHEREBY I MAY GAIN GREAT INVENTIONS TO SELL TO WARRING NATIONS --AND HE RUINS IT! BAH!

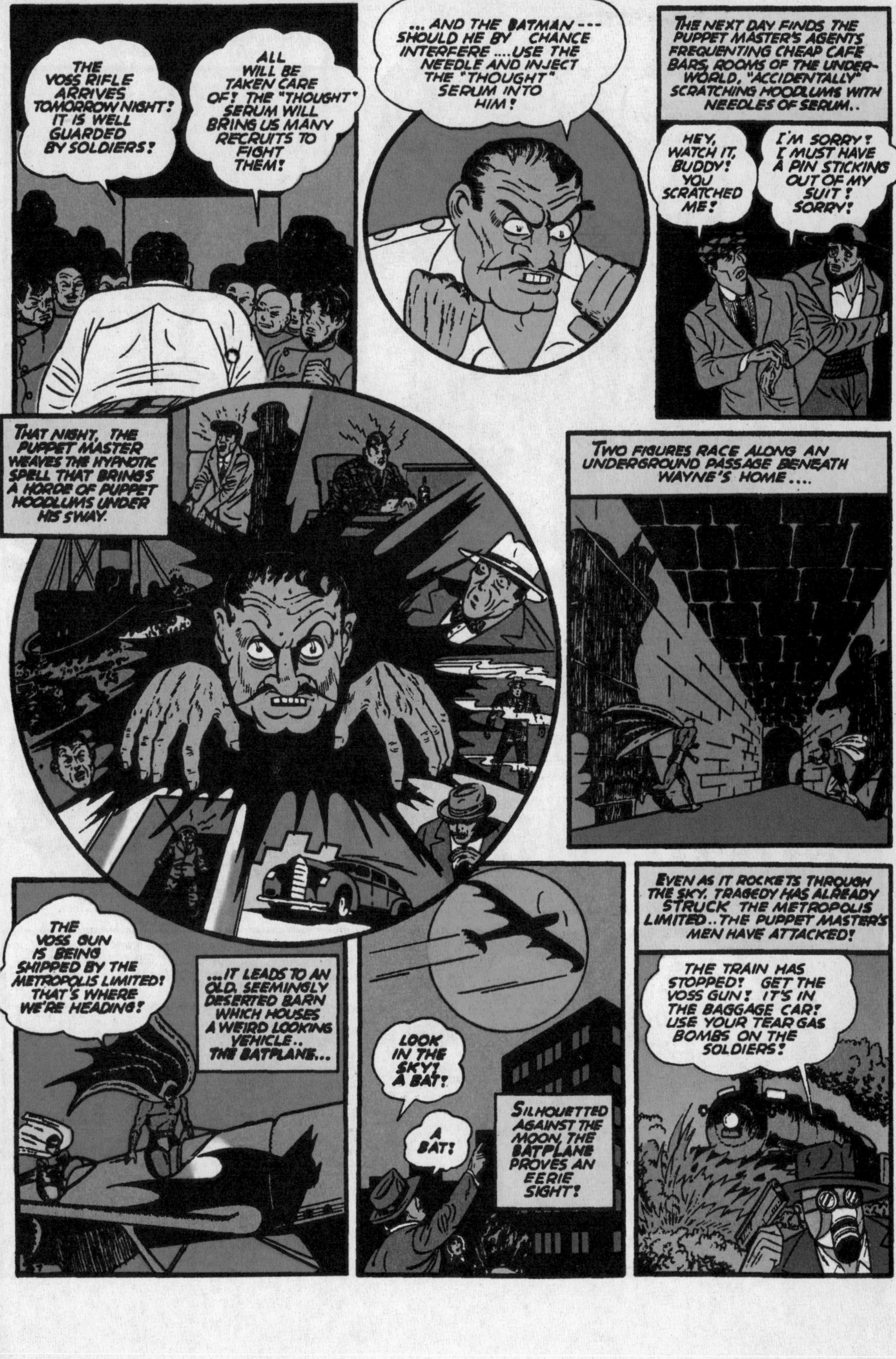
THE VOSS RIFLE ARRIVES TOMORROW NIGHT! IT IS WELL GUARDED BY SOLDIERS!
ALL WILL BE TAKEN CARE OF! THE "THOUGHT" SERUM WILL BRING US MANY RECRUITS TO FIGHT THEM!
... AND THE BATMAN --- SHOULD HE BY CHANCE INTERFERE ....USE THE NEEDLE AND INJECT THE "THOUGHT" SERUM INTO HIM!
THE NEXT DAY FINDS THE PUPPET MASTER'S AGENTS FREQUENTING CHEAP CAFE BARS, ROOMS OF THE UNDER-WORLD, "ACCIDENTALLY" SCRATCHING HOODLUMS WITH NEEDLES OF SERUM..
HEY, WATCH IT, BUDDY! YOU SCRATCHED ME!
I'M SORRY! I MUST HAVE A PIN STICKING OUT OF MY SUIT! SORRY!
THAT NIGHT, THE PUPPET MASTER WEAVES THE HYPNOTIC SPELL THAT BRINGS A HORDE OF PUPPET HOODLUMS UNDER HIS SWAY.
TWO FIGURES RACE ALONG AN UNDERGROUND PASSAGE BENEATH WAYNE'S HOME....
THE VOSS GUN IS BEING SHIPPED BY THE METROPOLIS LIMITED! THAT'S WHERE WE'RE HEADING!
...IT LEADS TO AN OLD, SEEMINGLY DESERTED BARN WHICH HOUSES A WEIRD LOOKING VEHICLE.. THE BATPLANE...
LOOK IN THE SKY! A BAT!
A BAT!
SILHOUETTED AGAINST THE MOON, THE BATPLANE PROVES AN EERIE SIGHT!
EVEN AS IT ROCKETS THROUGH THE SKY, TRAGEDY HAS ALREADY STRUCK THE METROPOLIS LIMITED..THE PUPPET MASTER'S MEN HAVE ATTACKED!
THE TRAIN HAS STOPPED! GET THE VOSS GUN! IT'S IN THE BAGGAGE CAR! USE YOUR TEAR GAS BOMBS ON THE SOLDIERS!

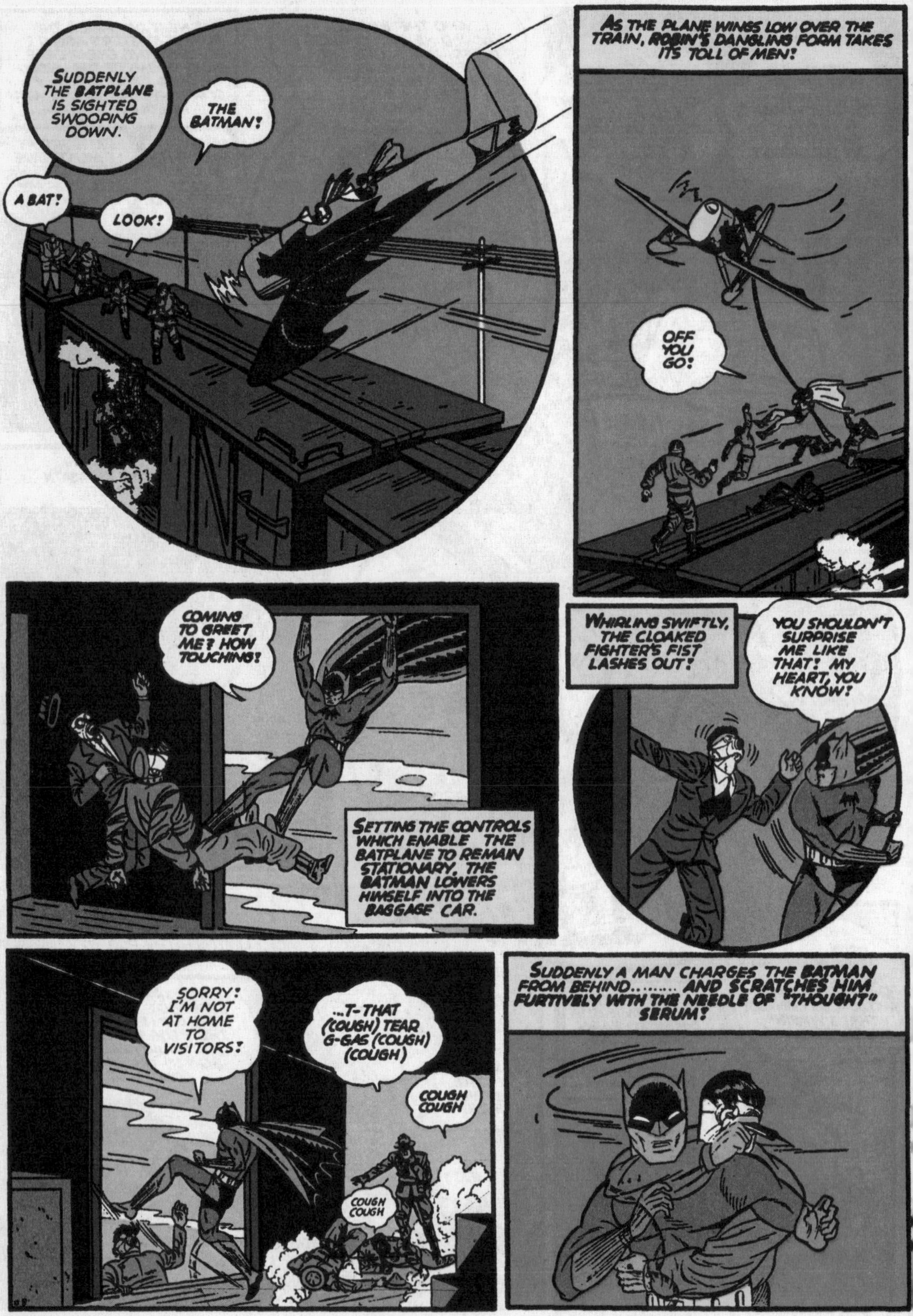
SUDDENLY THE BATPLANE IS SIGHTED SWOOPING DOWN.
THE BATMAN!
A BAT!
LOOK!
AS THE PLANE WINGS LOW OVER THE TRAIN, ROBIN'S DANGLING FORM TAKES ITS TOLL OF MEN!
OFF YOU GO!
COMING TO GREET ME? HOW TOUCHING!
SETTING THE CONTROLS WHICH ENABLE THE BATPLANE TO REMAIN STATIONARY, THE BATMAN LOWERS HIMSELF INTO THE BAGGAGE CAR.
WHIRLING SWIFTLY, THE CLOAKED FIGHTER'S FIST LASHES OUT!
YOU SHOULDN'T SURPRISE ME LIKE THAT! MY HEART, YOU KNOW!
SORRY! I'M NOT AT HOME TO VISITORS!
...T-THAT (COUGH) TEAR G-GAS (COUGH) (COUGH)
COUGH COUGH
COUGH COUGH
SUDDENLY A MAN CHARGES THE BATMAN FROM BEHIND........ AND SCRATCHES HIM FURTIVELY WITH THE NEEDLE OF "THOUGHT" SERUM!

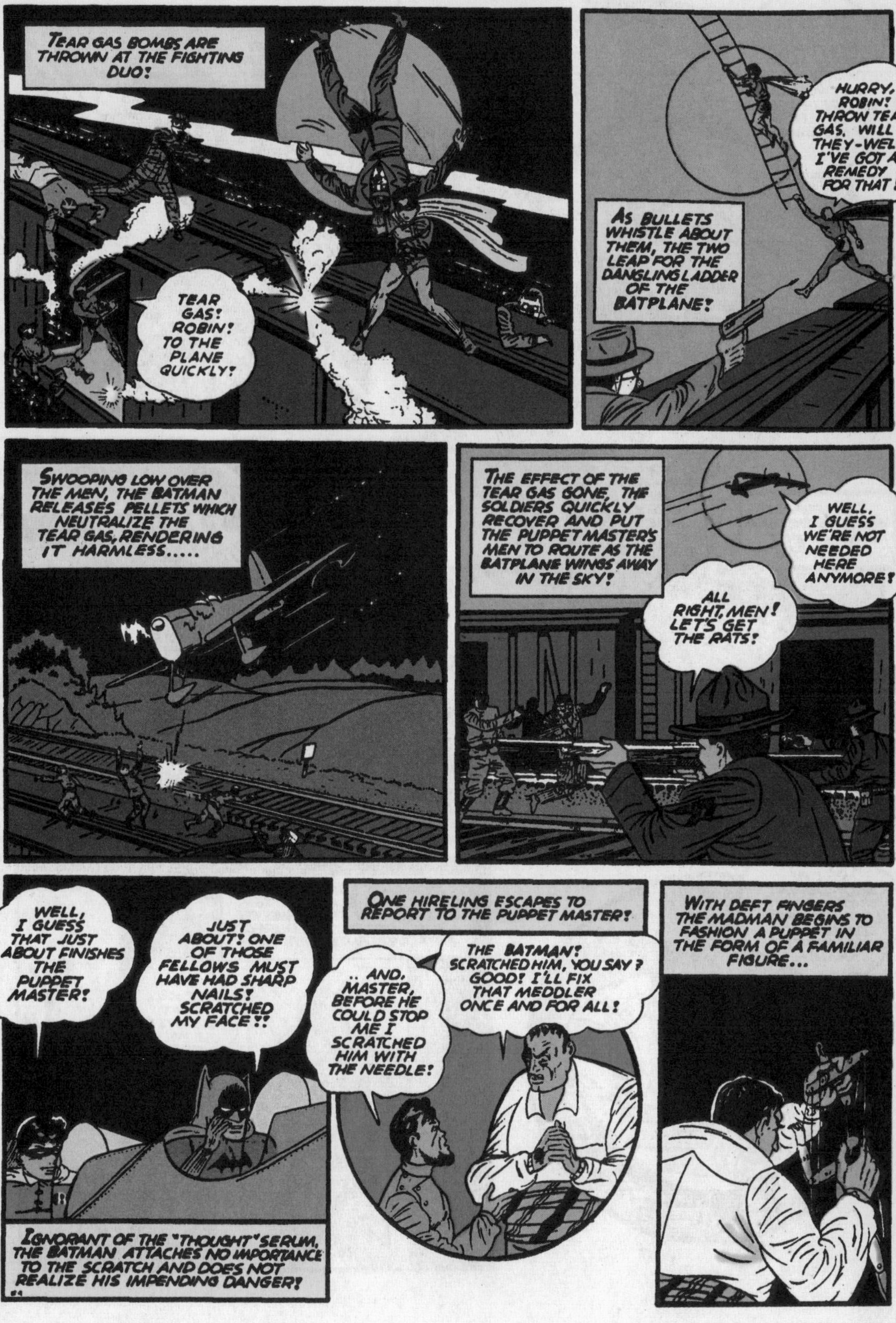
TEAR GAS BOMBS ARE THROWN AT THE FIGHTING DUO!
TEAR GAS! ROBIN! TO THE PLANE QUICKLY!
AS BULLETS WHISTLE ABOUT THEM, THE TWO LEAP FOR THE DANGLING LADDER OF THE BATPLANE!
HURRY, ROBIN! THROW TEAR GAS, WILL THEY-WELL, I'VE GOT A REMEDY FOR THAT!
SWOOPING LOW OVER THE MEN, THE BATMAN RELEASES PELLETS WHICH NEUTRALIZE THE TEAR GAS, RENDERING IT HARMLESS.....
THE EFFECT OF THE TEAR GAS GONE, THE SOLDIERS QUICKLY RECOVER AND PUT THE PUPPET MASTER'S MEN TO ROUTE AS THE BATPLANE WINGS AWAY IN THE SKY!
WELL, I GUESS WE'RE NOT NEEDED HERE ANYMORE!
ALL RIGHT, MEN! LET'S GET THE RATS!
WELL, I GUESS THAT JUST ABOUT FINISHES THE PUPPET MASTER!
JUST ABOUT! ONE OF THOSE FELLOWS MUST HAVE HAD SHARP NAILS! SCRATCHED MY FACE!!
IGNORANT OF THE "THOUGHT" SERUM, THE BATMAN ATTACHES NO IMPORTANCE TO THE SCRATCH AND DOES NOT REALIZE HIS IMPENDING DANGER!
ONE HIRELING ESCAPES TO REPORT TO THE PUPPET MASTER!
.. AND, MASTER, BEFORE HE COULD STOP ME I SCRATCHED HIM WITH THE NEEDLE!
THE BATMAN! SCRATCHED HIM, YOU SAY? GOOD! I'LL FIX THAT MEDDLER ONCE AND FOR ALL!
WITH DEFT FINGERS THE MADMAN BEGINS TO FASHION A PUPPET IN THE FORM OF A FAMILIAR FIGURE...

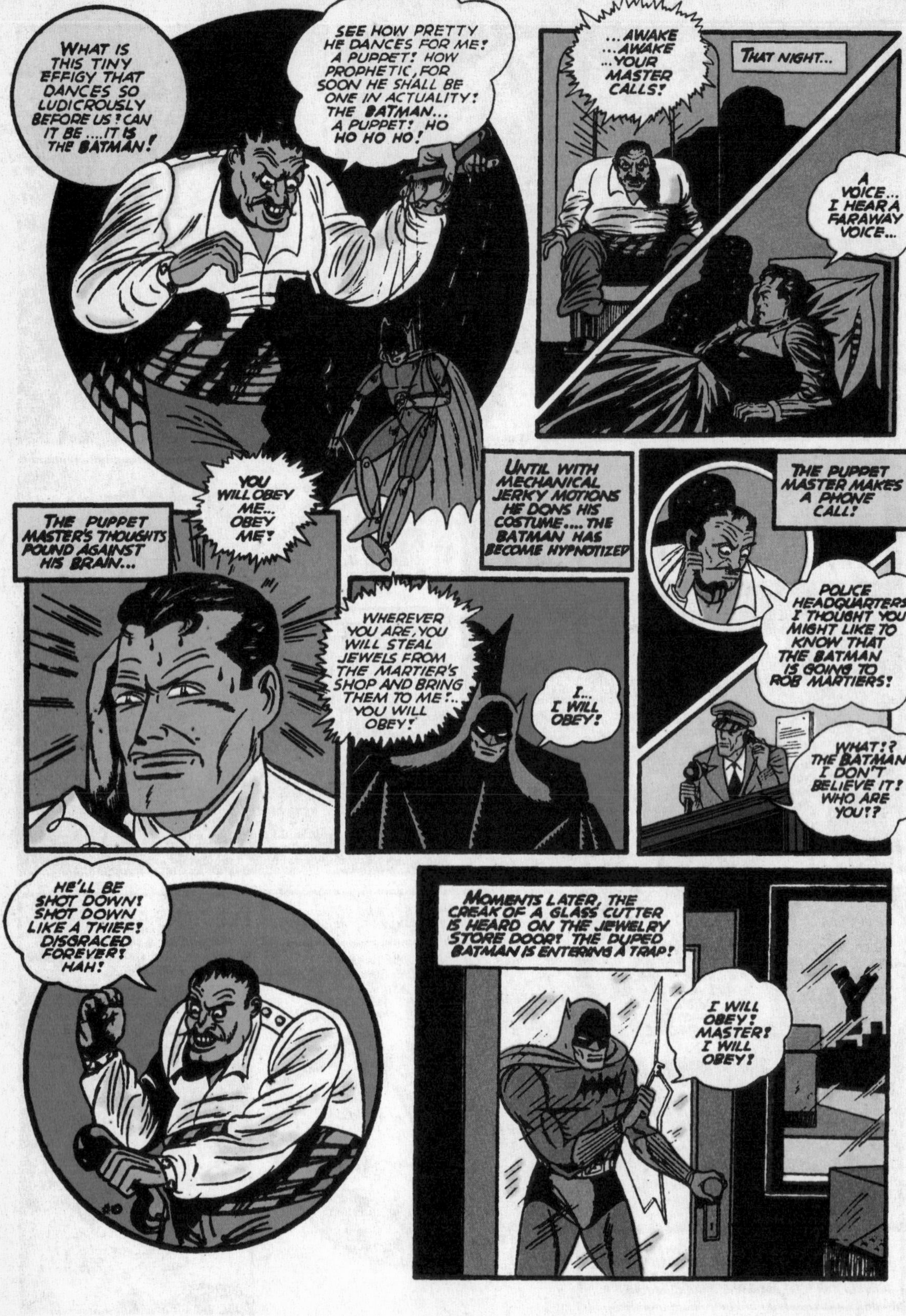
WHAT IS THIS TINY EFFIGY THAT DANCES SO LUDICROUSLY BEFORE US? CAN IT BE ....IT IS THE BATMAN!
SEE HOW PRETTY HE DANCES FOR ME! A PUPPET! HOW PROPHETIC, FOR SOON HE SHALL BE ONE IN ACTUALITY! THE BATMAN... A PUPPET! HO HO HO HO!
...AWAKE ...AWAKE ...YOUR MASTER CALLS!
THAT NIGHT...
A VOICE... I HEAR A FARAWAY VOICE...
YOU WILL OBEY ME... OBEY ME!
THE PUPPET MASTER'S THOUGHTS POUND AGAINST HIS BRAIN...
UNTIL WITH MECHANICAL JERKY MOTIONS HE DONS HIS COSTUME.... THE BATMAN HAS BECOME HYPNOTIZED
WHEREVER YOU ARE, YOU WILL STEAL JEWELS FROM THE MARTIER'S SHOP AND BRING THEM TO ME!.. YOU WILL OBEY!
I... I WILL OBEY!
THE PUPPET MASTER MAKES A PHONE CALL!
POLICE HEADQUARTERS I THOUGHT YOU MIGHT LIKE TO KNOW THAT THE BATMAN IS GOING TO ROB MARTIERS!
WHAT!? THE BATMAN I DON'T BELIEVE IT! WHO ARE YOU!?
HE'LL BE SHOT DOWN! SHOT DOWN LIKE A THIEF! DISGRACED FOREVER! HAH!
MOMENTS LATER, THE CREAK OF A GLASS CUTTER IS HEARD ON THE JEWELRY STORE DOOR! THE DUPED BATMAN IS ENTERING A TRAP!
I WILL OBEY! MASTER! I WILL OBEY!

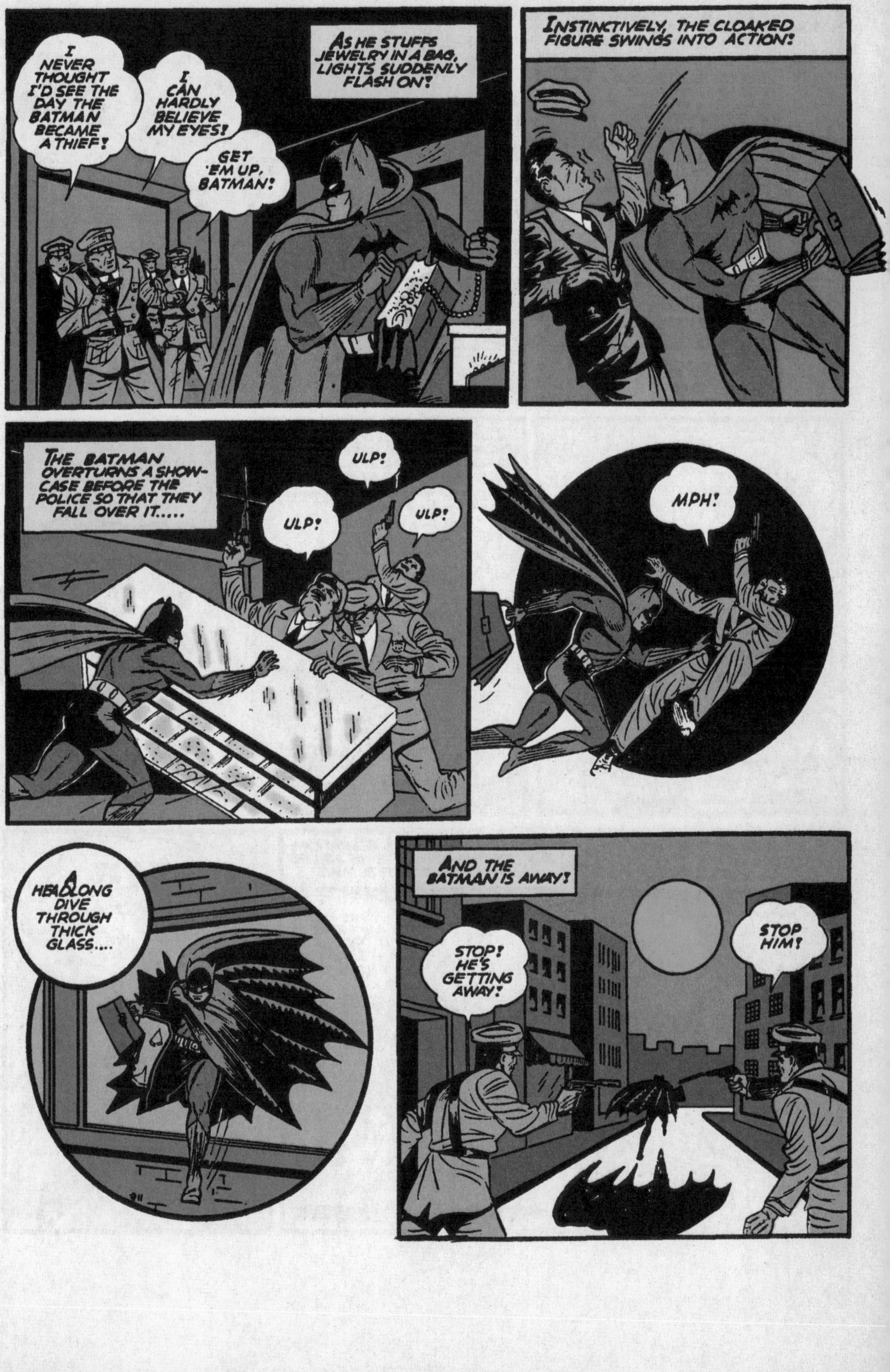

As he stuffs jewelry in a bag, lights suddenly flash on!
I never thought I'd see the day the Batman became a thief!
I can hardly believe my eyes!
Get 'em up, Batman!
Instinctively, the cloaked figure swings into action!
The Batman overturns a show-case before the police so that they fall over it.....
Ulp!
Ulp!
Ulp!
Mph!
A headlong dive through thick glass....
And the Batman is away!
Stop! He's getting away!
Stop him!

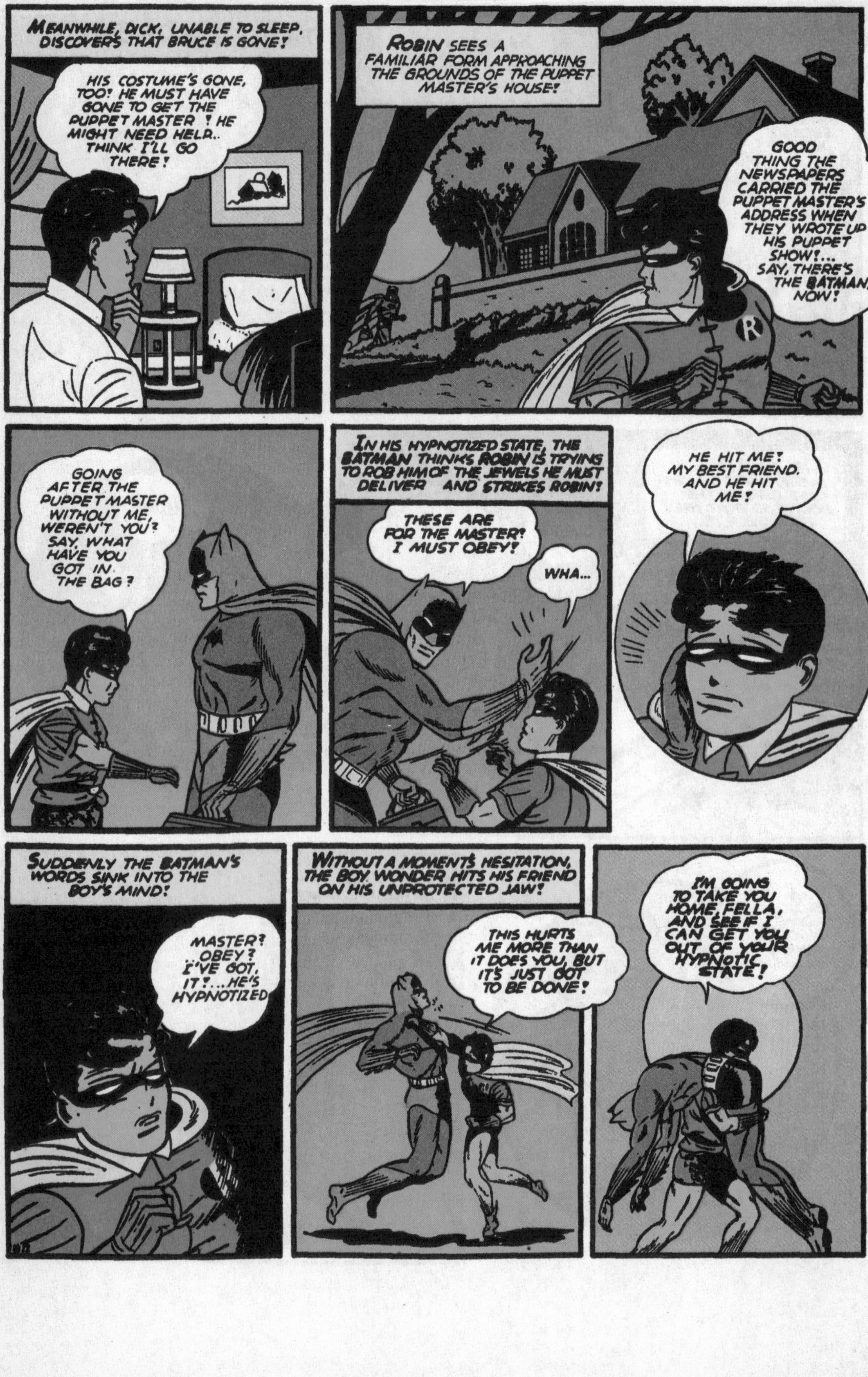
MEANWHILE, DICK, UNABLE TO SLEEP, DISCOVERS THAT BRUCE IS GONE!
HIS COSTUME'S GONE, TOO! HE MUST HAVE GONE TO GET THE PUPPET MASTER ! HE MIGHT NEED HELP.. THINK I'LL GO THERE!
ROBIN SEES A FAMILIAR FORM APPROACHING THE GROUNDS OF THE PUPPET MASTER'S HOUSE!
GOOD THING THE NEWSPAPERS CARRIED THE PUPPET MASTER'S ADDRESS WHEN THEY WROTE UP HIS PUPPET SHOW!... SAY, THERE'S THE BATMAN, NOW!
GOING AFTER THE PUPPET MASTER WITHOUT ME, WEREN'T YOU? SAY, WHAT HAVE YOU GOT IN THE BAG?
IN HIS HYPNOTIZED STATE, THE BATMAN THINKS ROBIN IS TRYING TO ROB HIM OF THE JEWELS HE MUST DELIVER AND STRIKES ROBIN!
THESE ARE FOR THE MASTER! I MUST OBEY!
WHA...
HE HIT ME! MY BEST FRIEND. AND HE HIT ME!
SUDDENLY THE BATMAN'S WORDS SINK INTO THE BOY'S MIND!
MASTER? ..OBEY? I'VE GOT IT!...HE'S HYPNOTIZED
WITHOUT A MOMENT'S HESITATION, THE BOY WONDER HITS HIS FRIEND ON HIS UNPROTECTED JAW!
THIS HURTS ME MORE THAN IT DOES YOU, BUT IT'S JUST GOT TO BE DONE!
I'M GOING TO TAKE YOU HOME, FELLA, AND SEE IF I CAN GET YOU OUT OF YOUR HYPNOTIC STATE!

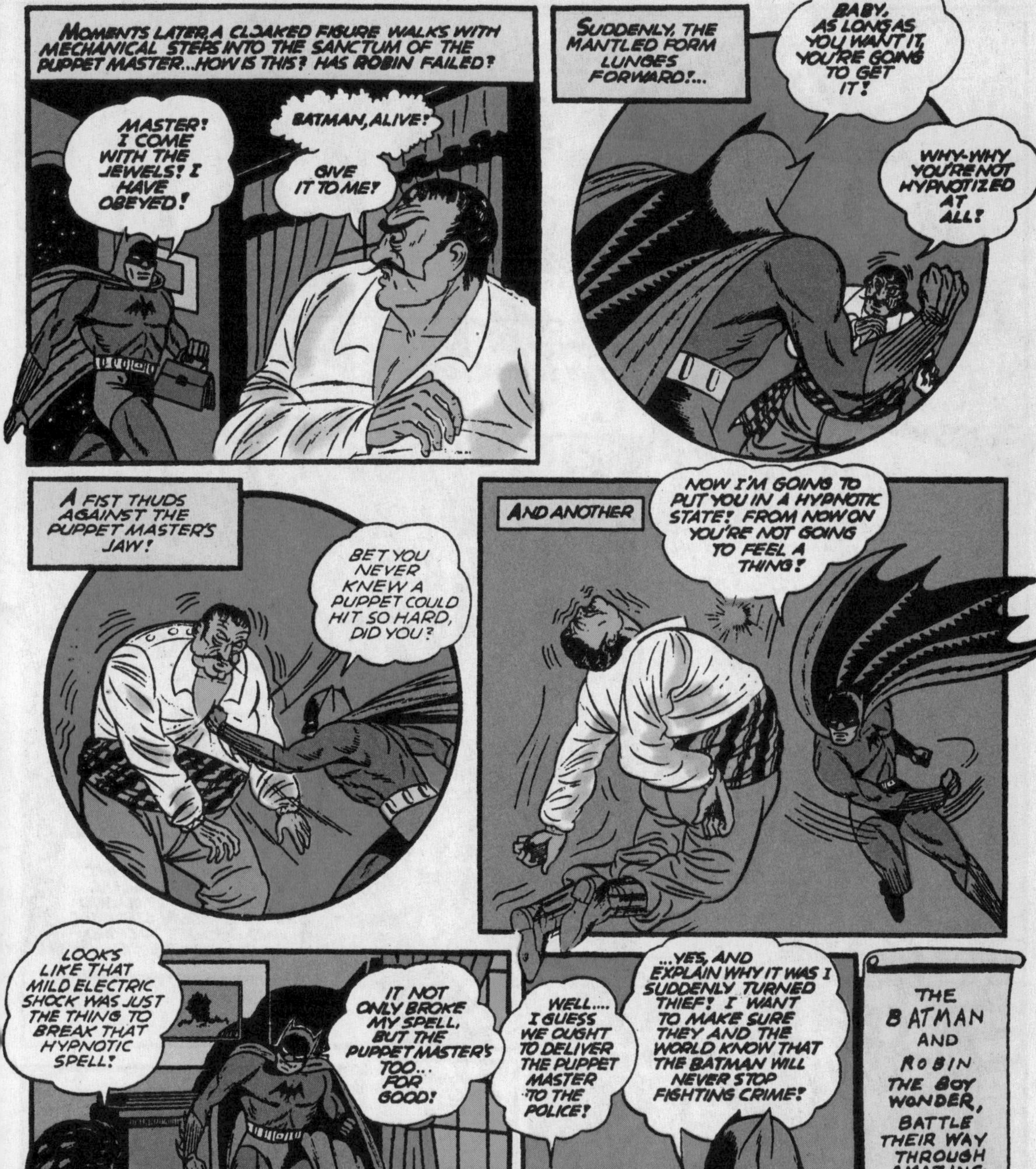
MOMENTS LATER A CLOAKED FIGURE WALKS WITH MECHANICAL STEPS INTO THE SANCTUM OF THE PUPPET MASTER...HOW IS THIS? HAS ROBIN FAILED?
MASTER! I COME WITH THE JEWELS! I HAVE OBEYED!
BATMAN, ALIVE?
GIVE IT TO ME!
SUDDENLY, THE MANTLED FORM LUNGES FORWARD!...
BABY, AS LONG AS YOU WANT IT, YOU'RE GOING TO GET IT!
WHY-WHY YOU'RE NOT HYPNOTIZED AT ALL!
A FIST THUDS AGAINST THE PUPPET MASTER'S JAW!
BET YOU NEVER KNEW A PUPPET COULD HIT SO HARD, DID YOU?
AND ANOTHER
NOW I'M GOING TO PUT YOU IN A HYPNOTIC STATE! FROM NOW ON YOU'RE NOT GOING TO FEEL A THING!
LOOKS LIKE THAT MILD ELECTRIC SHOCK WAS JUST THE THING TO BREAK THAT HYPNOTIC SPELL!
IT NOT ONLY BROKE MY SPELL, BUT THE PUPPET MASTER'S TOO... FOR GOOD!
WELL.... I GUESS WE OUGHT TO DELIVER THE PUPPET MASTER TO THE POLICE!
...YES, AND EXPLAIN WHY IT WAS I SUDDENLY TURNED THIEF! I WANT TO MAKE SURE THEY AND THE WORLD KNOW THAT THE BATMAN WILL NEVER STOP FIGHTING CRIME!
THE BATMAN AND ROBIN THE BOY WONDER, BATTLE THEIR WAY THROUGH AMAZING ADVENTURES EVERY MONTH IN DETECTIVE COMICS
DON'T MISS IT!

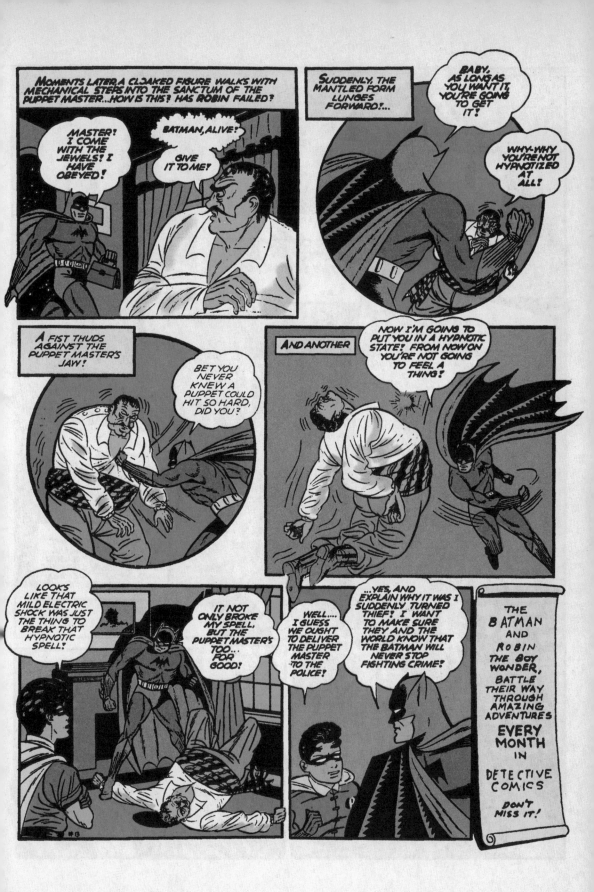

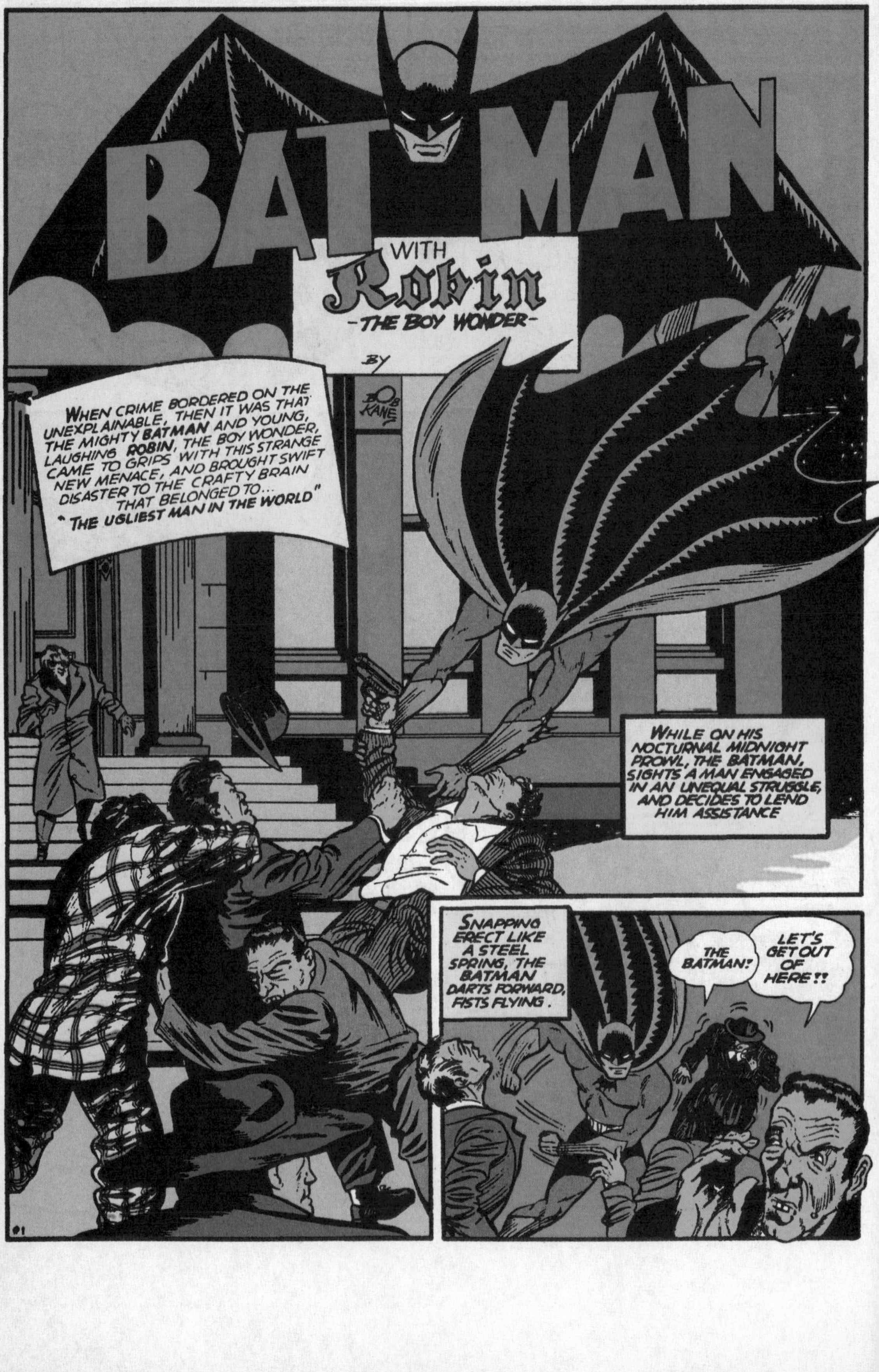
BATMAN
WITH Robin
-THE BOY WONDER-
BY BOB KANE
WHEN CRIME BORDERED ON THE UNEXPLAINABLE, THEN IT WAS THAT THE MIGHTY BATMAN AND YOUNG, LAUGHING ROBIN, THE BOY WONDER, CAME TO GRIPS WITH THIS STRANGE NEW MENACE, AND BROUGHT SWIFT DISASTER TO THE CRAFTY BRAIN THAT BELONGED TO... "THE UGLIEST MAN IN THE WORLD"
WHILE ON HIS NOCTURNAL MIDNIGHT PROWL, THE BATMAN, SIGHTS A MAN ENGAGED IN AN UNEQUAL STRUGGLE, AND DECIDES TO LEND HIM ASSISTANCE
SNAPPING ERECT LIKE A STEEL SPRING, THE BATMAN DARTS FORWARD, FISTS FLYING.
THE BATMAN!
LET'S GET OUT OF HERE!!

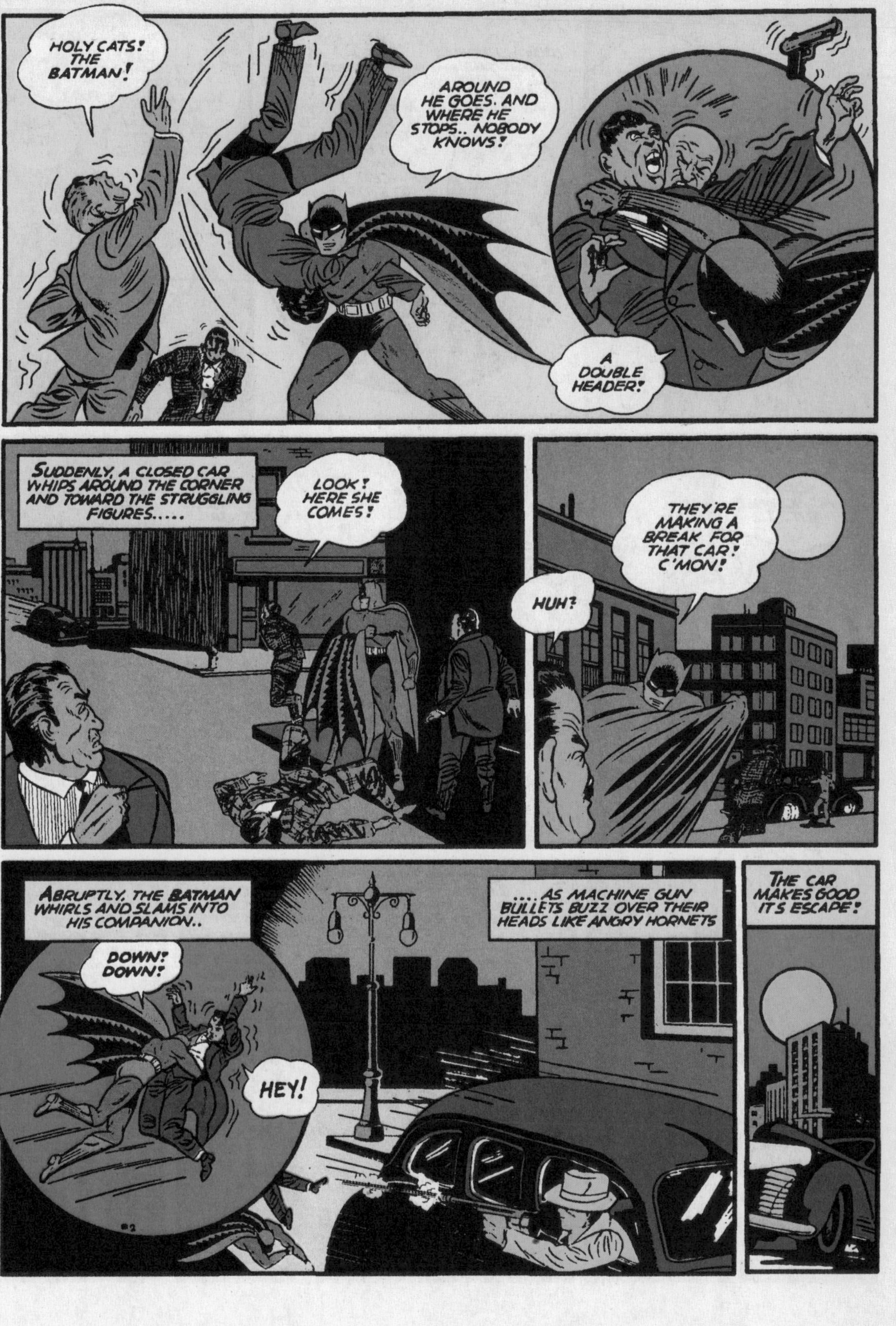
HOLY CATS! THE BATMAN!
AROUND HE GOES. AND WHERE HE STOPS.. NOBODY KNOWS!
A DOUBLE HEADER!
SUDDENLY, A CLOSED CAR WHIPS AROUND THE CORNER AND TOWARD THE STRUGGLING FIGURES.....
LOOK! HERE SHE COMES!
THEY'RE MAKING A BREAK FOR THAT CAR! C'MON!
HUH?
ABRUPTLY, THE BATMAN WHIRLS AND SLAMS INTO HIS COMPANION..
DOWN! DOWN!
HEY!
....AS MACHINE GUN BULLETS BUZZ OVER THEIR HEADS LIKE ANGRY HORNETS
THE CAR MAKES GOOD ITS ESCAPE!

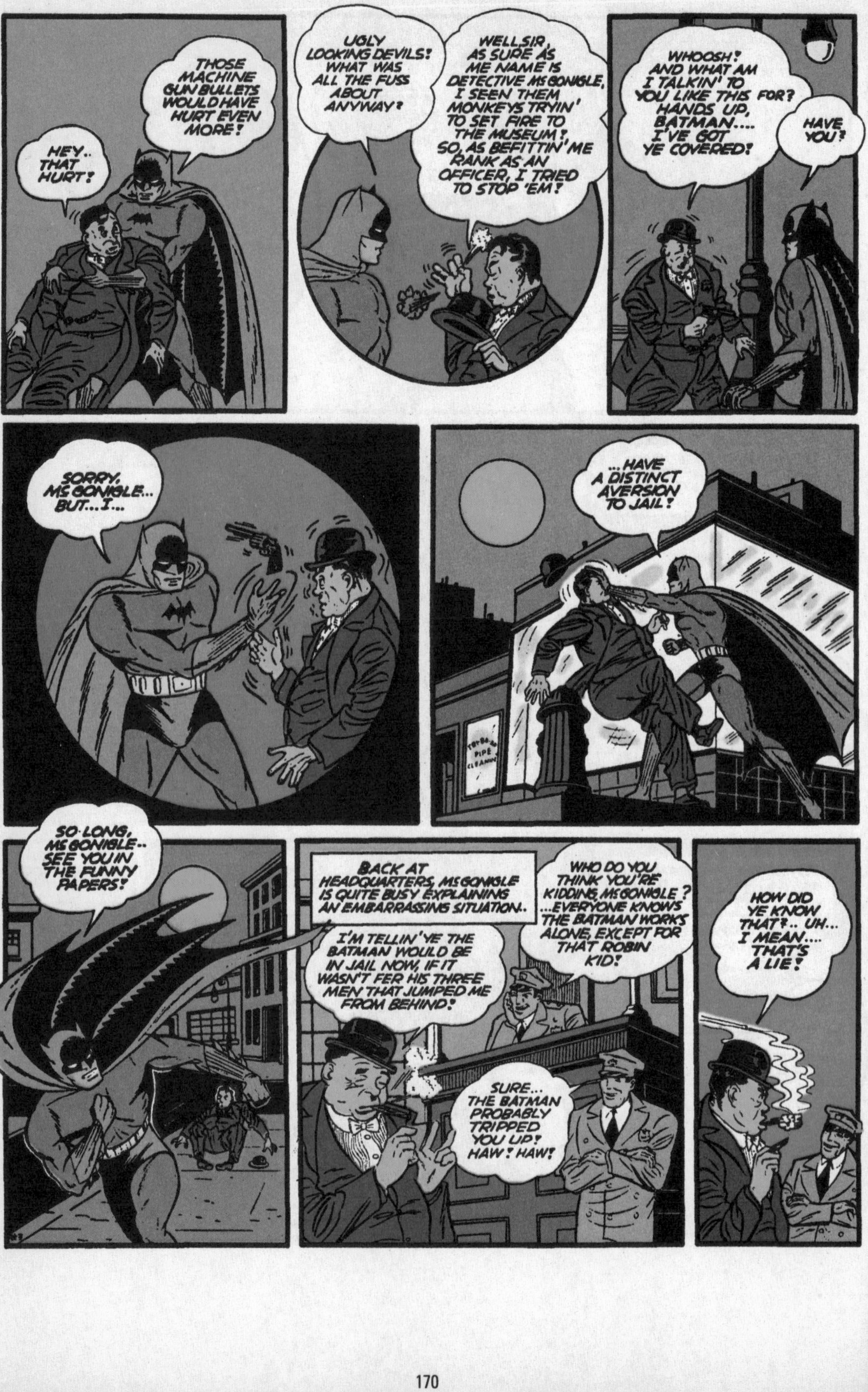
THOSE MACHINE GUN BULLETS WOULD HAVE HURT EVEN MORE!
HEY.. THAT HURT!
UGLY LOOKING DEVILS! WHAT WAS ALL THE FUSS ABOUT ANYWAY?
WELL SIR, AS SURE AS ME NAME IS DETECTIVE McGONIGLE, I SEEN THEM MONKEYS TRYIN' TO SET FIRE TO THE MUSEUM! SO, AS BEFITTIN' ME RANK AS AN OFFICER, I TRIED TO STOP 'EM!
WHOOSH! AND WHAT AM I TALKIN' TO YOU LIKE THIS FOR? HANDS UP, BATMAN.... I'VE GOT YE COVERED!
HAVE YOU?
SORRY, McGONIGLE... BUT...I...
...HAVE A DISTINCT AVERSION TO JAIL!
SO LONG, McGONIGLE.. SEE YOU IN THE FUNNY PAPERS!
BACK AT HEADQUARTERS, McGONIGLE IS QUITE BUSY EXPLAINING AN EMBARRASSING SITUATION..
I'M TELLIN' YE THE BATMAN WOULD BE IN JAIL NOW, IF IT WASN'T FER HIS THREE MEN THAT JUMPED ME FROM BEHIND!
WHO DO YOU THINK YOU'RE KIDDING, McGONIGLE? ...EVERYONE KNOWS THE BATMAN WORKS ALONE, EXCEPT FOR THAT ROBIN KID!
SURE... THE BATMAN PROBABLY TRIPPED YOU UP! HAW! HAW!
HOW DID YE KNOW THAT?.. UH... I MEAN.... THAT'S A LIE!

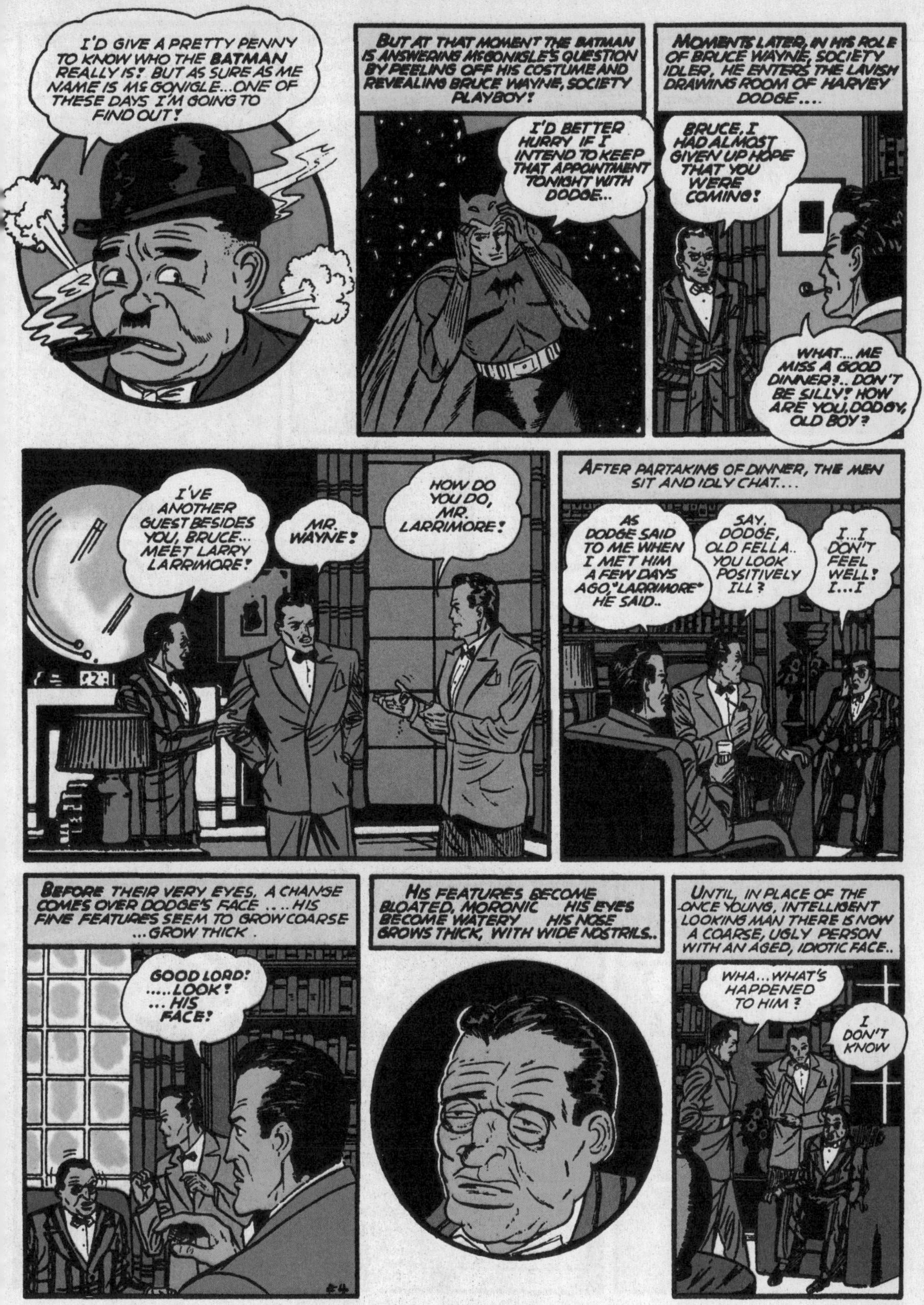
I'D GIVE A PRETTY PENNY TO KNOW WHO THE BATMAN REALLY IS! BUT AS SURE AS ME NAME IS MC GONIGLE...ONE OF THESE DAYS I'M GOING TO FIND OUT!
BUT AT THAT MOMENT THE BATMAN IS ANSWERING MCGONIGLE'S QUESTION BY PEELING OFF HIS COSTUME AND REVEALING BRUCE WAYNE, SOCIETY PLAYBOY!
I'D BETTER HURRY IF I INTEND TO KEEP THAT APPOINTMENT TONIGHT WITH DODGE...
MOMENTS LATER, IN HIS ROLE OF BRUCE WAYNE, SOCIETY IDLER, HE ENTERS THE LAVISH DRAWING ROOM OF HARVEY DODGE....
BRUCE, I HAD ALMOST GIVEN UP HOPE THAT YOU WERE COMING!
WHAT.... ME MISS A GOOD DINNER?.. DON'T BE SILLY! HOW ARE YOU, DODGY, OLD BOY?
I'VE ANOTHER GUEST BESIDES YOU, BRUCE... MEET LARRY LARRIMORE!
MR. WAYNE!
HOW DO YOU DO, MR. LARRIMORE!
AFTER PARTAKING OF DINNER, THE MEN SIT AND IDLY CHAT....
AS DODGE SAID TO ME WHEN I MET HIM A FEW DAYS AGO, "LARRIMORE" HE SAID..
SAY, DODGE, OLD FELLA.. YOU LOOK POSITIVELY ILL?
I...I DON'T FEEL WELL! I...I
BEFORE THEIR VERY EYES, A CHANGE COMES OVER DODGE'S FACE ....HIS FINE FEATURES SEEM TO GROW COARSE ...GROW THICK .
GOOD LORD! .....LOOK! ... HIS FACE!
HIS FEATURES BECOME BLOATED, MORONIC HIS EYES BECOME WATERY HIS NOSE GROWS THICK, WITH WIDE NOSTRILS..
UNTIL, IN PLACE OF THE ONCE YOUNG, INTELLIGENT LOOKING MAN THERE IS NOW A COARSE, UGLY PERSON WITH AN AGED, IDIOTIC FACE..
WHA...WHAT'S HAPPENED TO HIM?
I DON'T KNOW

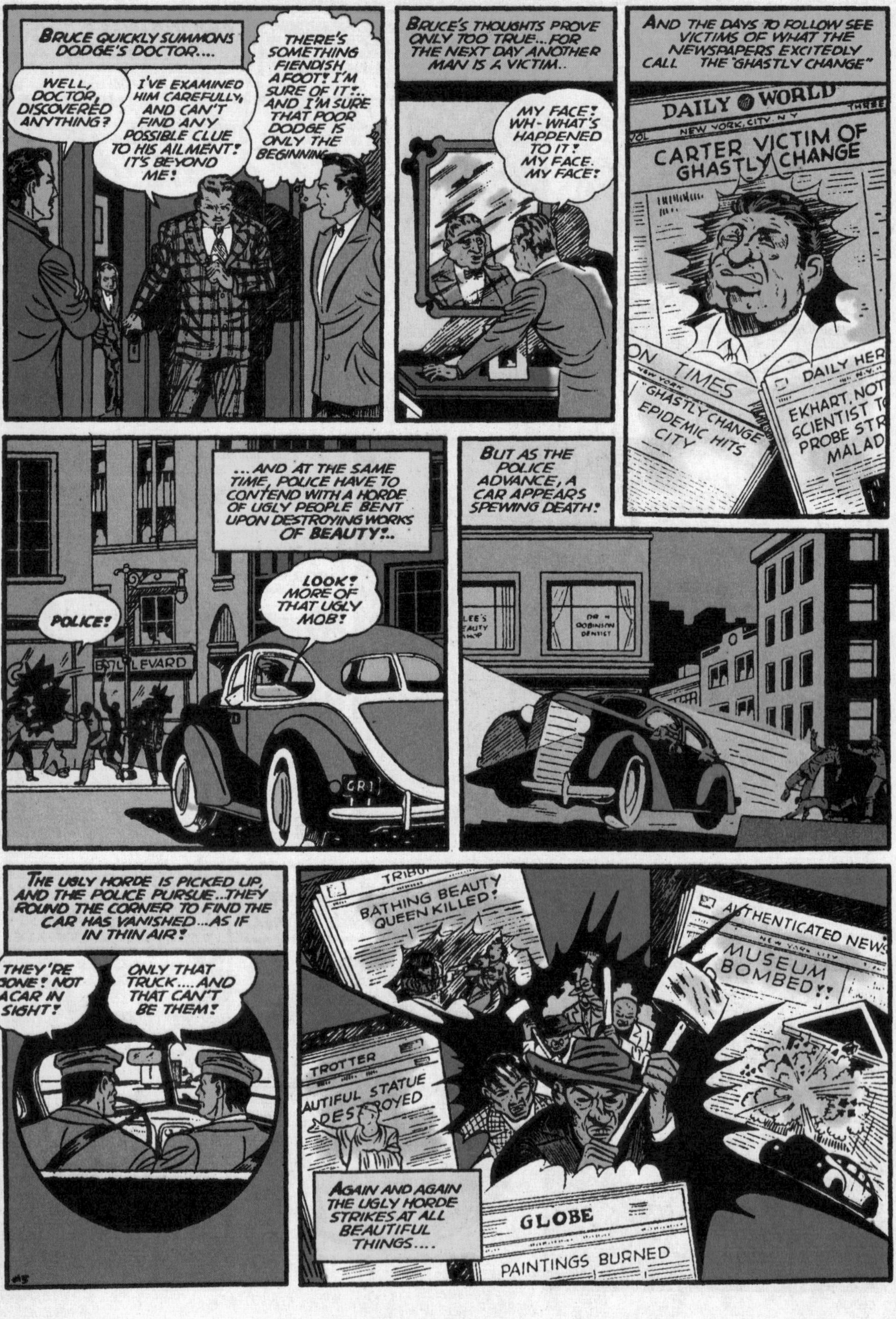
BRUCE QUICKLY SUMMONS DODGE'S DOCTOR....
WELL, DOCTOR, DISCOVERED ANYTHING?
I'VE EXAMINED HIM CAREFULLY, AND CAN'T FIND ANY POSSIBLE CLUE TO HIS AILMENT! IT'S BEYOND ME!
THERE'S SOMETHING FIENDISH AFOOT! I'M SURE OF IT!.. AND I'M SURE THAT POOR DODGE IS ONLY THE BEGINNING..
BRUCE'S THOUGHTS PROVE ONLY TOO TRUE...FOR THE NEXT DAY ANOTHER MAN IS A VICTIM..
MY FACE! WH-WHAT'S HAPPENED TO IT! MY FACE. MY FACE!
AND THE DAYS TO FOLLOW SEE VICTIMS OF WHAT THE NEWSPAPERS EXCITEDLY CALL THE "GHASTLY CHANGE"
DAILY WORLD
NEW YORK CITY N.Y.
CARTER VICTIM OF GHASTLY CHANGE
TIMES
"GHASTLY CHANGE" EPIDEMIC HITS CITY
DAILY HER
EKHART, NOT SCIENTIST TO PROBE STR MALAD
...AND AT THE SAME TIME, POLICE HAVE TO CONTEND WITH A HORDE OF UGLY PEOPLE BENT UPON DESTROYING WORKS OF BEAUTY!..
POLICE!
BOULEVARD
LOOK! MORE OF THAT UGLY MOB!
GR1
BUT AS THE POLICE ADVANCE, A CAR APPEARS SPEWING DEATH!
DR. H. ROBINSON DENTIST
THE UGLY HORDE IS PICKED UP, AND THE POLICE PURSUE...THEY ROUND THE CORNER TO FIND THE CAR HAS VANISHED...AS IF IN THIN AIR!
THEY'RE GONE! NOT A CAR IN SIGHT!
ONLY THAT TRUCK....AND THAT CAN'T BE THEM!
BATHING BEAUTY QUEEN KILLED!
AUTHENTICATED NEWS
MUSEUM BOMBED!!
TROTTER
AUTIFUL STATUE DESTROYED
AGAIN AND AGAIN THE UGLY HORDE STRIKES AT ALL BEAUTIFUL THINGS....
GLOBE
PAINTINGS BURNED

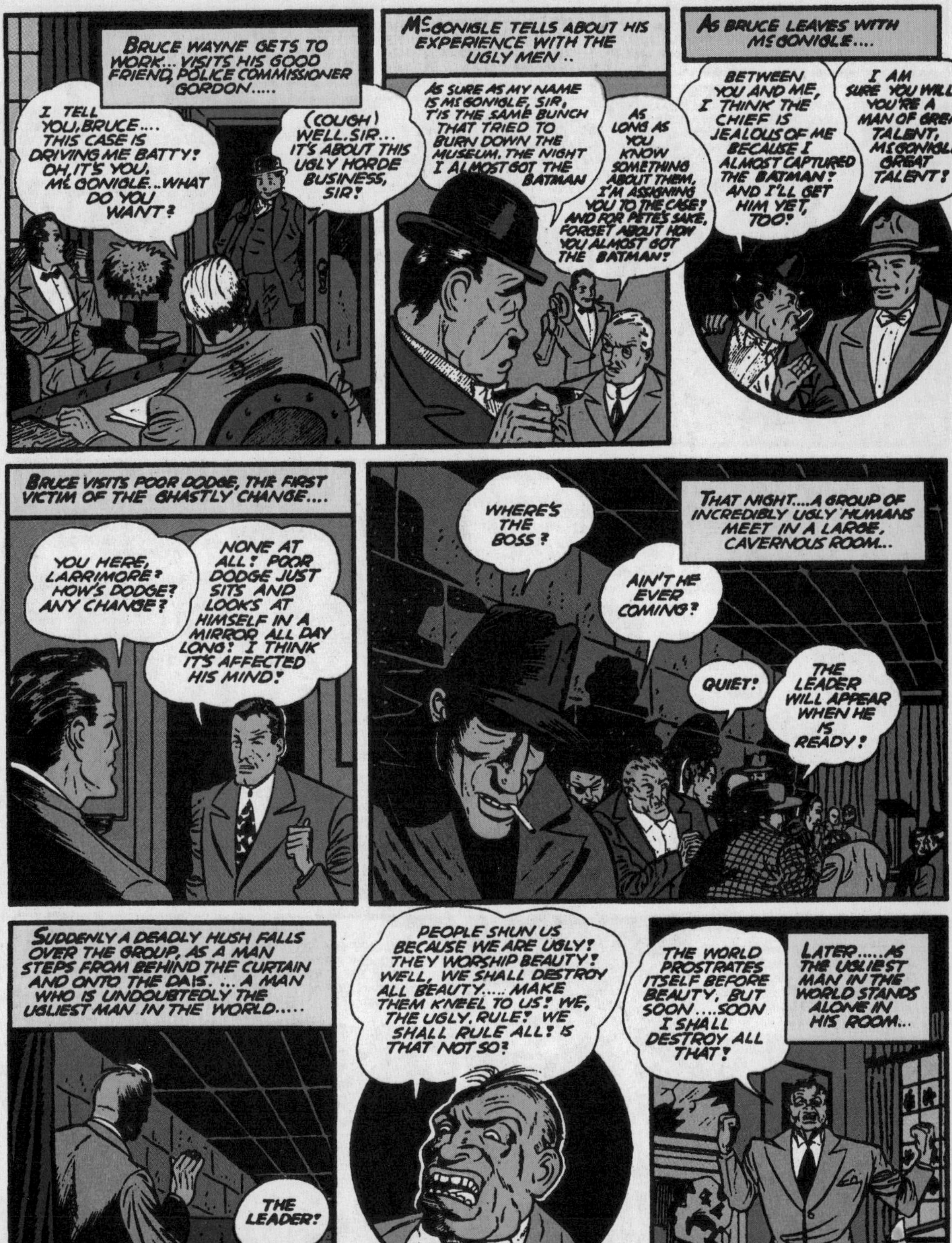
BRUCE WAYNE GETS TO WORK... VISITS HIS GOOD FRIEND, POLICE COMMISSIONER GORDON.....
I TELL YOU, BRUCE.... THIS CASE IS DRIVING ME BATTY! OH, IT'S YOU, MC GONIGLE...WHAT DO YOU WANT?
(COUGH) WELL, SIR... IT'S ABOUT THIS UGLY HORDE BUSINESS, SIR!
MC GONIGLE TELLS ABOUT HIS EXPERIENCE WITH THE UGLY MEN ..
AS SURE AS MY NAME IS MC GONIGLE, SIR, T'IS THE SAME BUNCH THAT TRIED TO BURN DOWN THE MUSEUM, THE NIGHT I ALMOST GOT THE BATMAN
AS LONG AS YOU KNOW SOMETHING ABOUT THEM, I'M ASSIGNING YOU TO THE CASE! AND FOR PETE'S SAKE, FORGET ABOUT HOW YOU ALMOST GOT THE BATMAN!
AS BRUCE LEAVES WITH MC GONIGLE....
BETWEEN YOU AND ME, I THINK THE CHIEF IS JEALOUS OF ME BECAUSE I ALMOST CAPTURED THE BATMAN! AND I'LL GET HIM YET, TOO!
I AM SURE YOU WILL! YOU'RE A MAN OF GREAT TALENT, MC GONIGLE.. GREAT TALENT!
BRUCE VISITS POOR DODGE, THE FIRST VICTIM OF THE GHASTLY CHANGE....
YOU HERE, LARRIMORE? HOW'S DODGE? ANY CHANGE?
NONE AT ALL! POOR DODGE JUST SITS AND LOOKS AT HIMSELF IN A MIRROR ALL DAY LONG! I THINK IT'S AFFECTED HIS MIND!
THAT NIGHT....A GROUP OF INCREDIBLY UGLY HUMANS MEET IN A LARGE, CAVERNOUS ROOM...
WHERE'S THE BOSS?
AIN'T HE EVER COMING?
QUIET!
THE LEADER WILL APPEAR WHEN HE IS READY!
SUDDENLY A DEADLY HUSH FALLS OVER THE GROUP, AS A MAN STEPS FROM BEHIND THE CURTAIN AND ONTO THE DAIS. ... A MAN WHO IS UNDOUBTEDLY THE UGLIEST MAN IN THE WORLD.....
THE LEADER!
PEOPLE SHUN US BECAUSE WE ARE UGLY! THEY WORSHIP BEAUTY! WELL, WE SHALL DESTROY ALL BEAUTY..... MAKE THEM KNEEL TO US! WE, THE UGLY, RULE! WE SHALL RULE ALL! IS THAT NOT SO?
THE DEFORMED MEN FALL UNDER THE SPELL OF THE ALMOST HYPNOTIC, BRILLIANT SPEECH OF THEIR LEADER....
LATER.....AS THE UGLIEST MAN IN THE WORLD STANDS ALONE IN HIS ROOM...
THE WORLD PROSTRATES ITSELF BEFORE BEAUTY, BUT SOON....SOON I SHALL DESTROY ALL THAT!

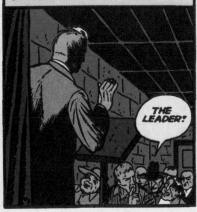

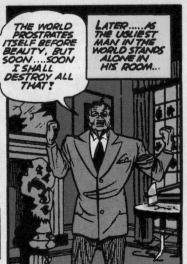

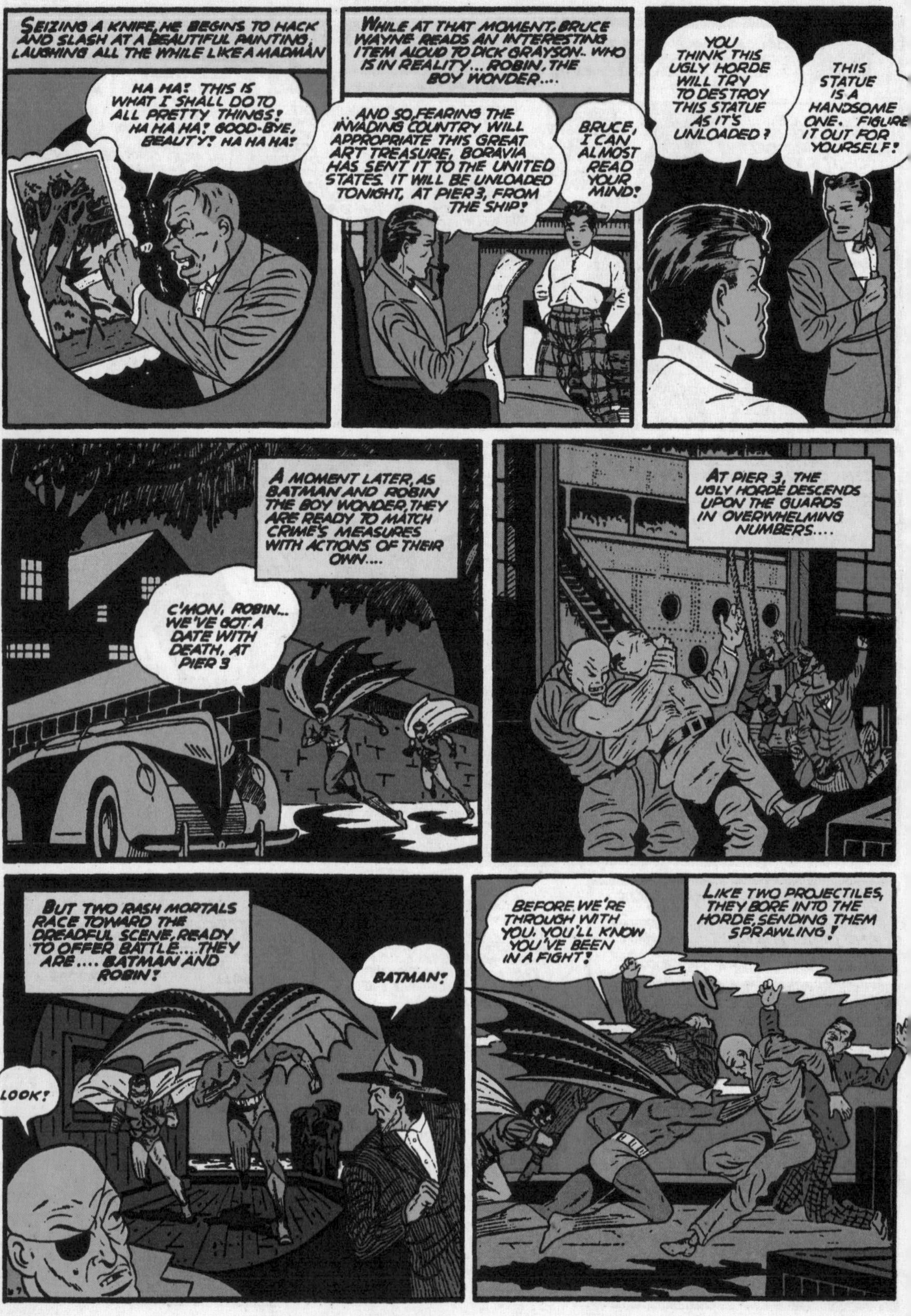
SEIZING A KNIFE, HE BEGINS TO HACK AND SLASH AT A BEAUTIFUL PAINTING, LAUGHING ALL THE WHILE LIKE A MADMAN
HA HA! THIS IS WHAT I SHALL DO TO ALL PRETTY THINGS! HA HA HA! GOOD-BYE, BEAUTY! HA HA HA!
WHILE AT THAT MOMENT, BRUCE WAYNE READS AN INTERESTING ITEM ALOUD TO DICK GRAYSON.. WHO IS IN REALITY... ROBIN, THE BOY WONDER....
...AND SO, FEARING THE INVADING COUNTRY WILL APPROPRIATE THIS GREAT ART TREASURE, BORAVIA HAS SENT IT TO THE UNITED STATES. IT WILL BE UNLOADED TONIGHT, AT PIER 3, FROM THE SHIP!
BRUCE, I CAN ALMOST READ YOUR MIND!
YOU THINK THIS UGLY HORDE WILL TRY TO DESTROY THIS STATUE AS IT'S UNLOADED?
THIS STATUE IS A HANDSOME ONE. FIGURE IT OUT FOR YOURSELF!
A MOMENT LATER, AS BATMAN AND ROBIN THE BOY WONDER, THEY ARE READY TO MATCH CRIME'S MEASURES WITH ACTIONS OF THEIR OWN....
C'MON, ROBIN... WE'VE GOT A DATE WITH DEATH, AT PIER 3
AT PIER 3, THE UGLY HORDE DESCENDS UPON THE GUARDS IN OVERWHELMING NUMBERS....
BUT TWO RASH MORTALS RACE TOWARD THE DREADFUL SCENE, READY TO OFFER BATTLE.... THEY ARE.... BATMAN AND ROBIN!
BATMAN!
LOOK!
LIKE TWO PROJECTILES, THEY BORE INTO THE HORDE, SENDING THEM SPRAWLING!
BEFORE WE'RE THROUGH WITH YOU, YOU'LL KNOW YOU'VE BEEN IN A FIGHT!

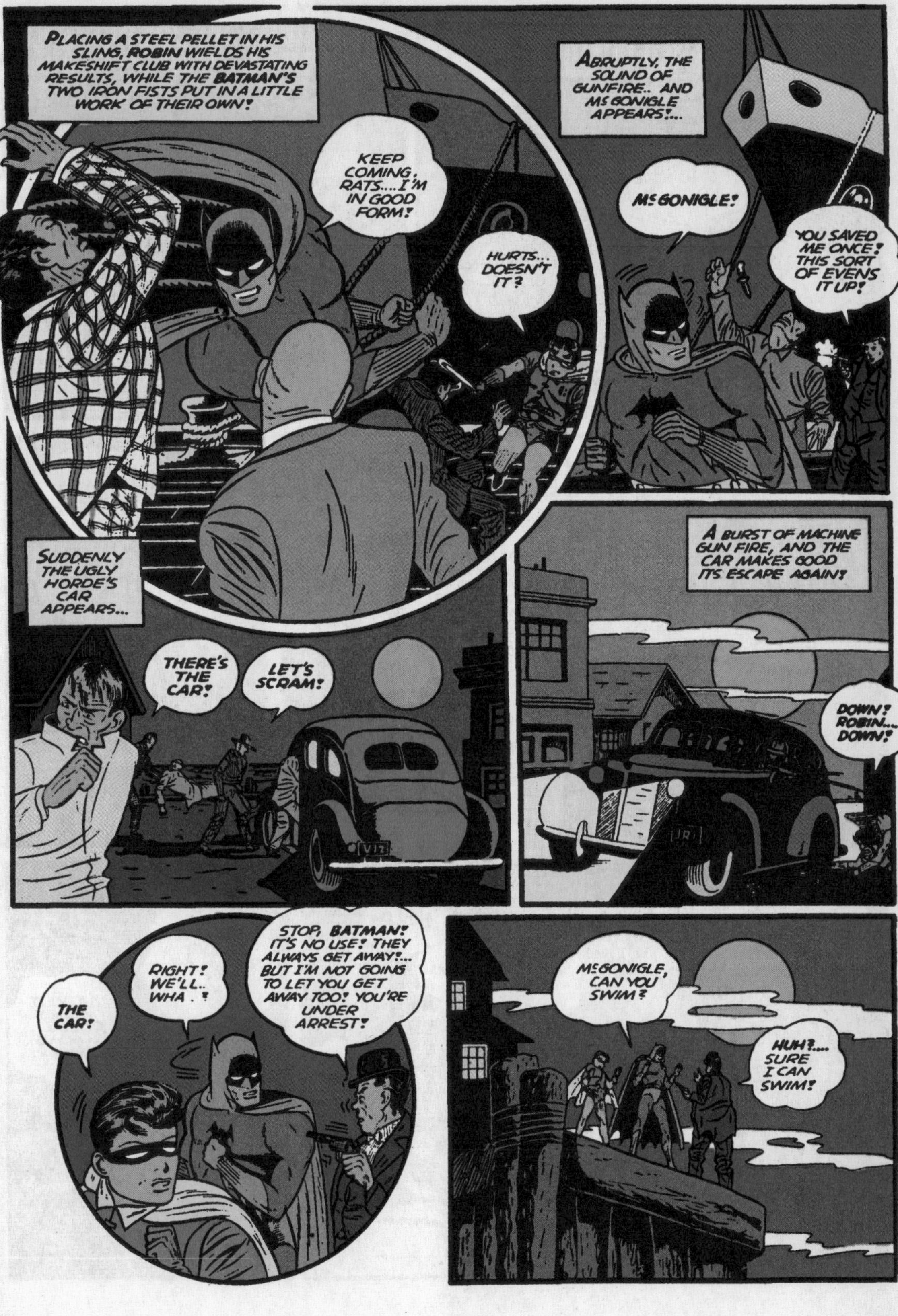
PLACING A STEEL PELLET IN HIS SLING, ROBIN WIELDS HIS MAKESHIFT CLUB WITH DEVASTATING RESULTS, WHILE THE BATMAN'S TWO IRON FISTS PUT IN A LITTLE WORK OF THEIR OWN!
KEEP COMING, RATS....I'M IN GOOD FORM!
HURTS... DOESN'T IT?
ABRUPTLY, THE SOUND OF GUNFIRE.. AND MCGONIGLE APPEARS!...
MCGONIGLE!
YOU SAVED ME ONCE! THIS SORT OF EVENS IT UP!
SUDDENLY THE UGLY HORDE'S CAR APPEARS...
THERE'S THE CAR!
LET'S SCRAM!
A BURST OF MACHINE GUN FIRE, AND THE CAR MAKES GOOD ITS ESCAPE AGAIN!
DOWN! ROBIN.... DOWN!
THE CAR!
RIGHT! WE'LL.. WHA.. !
STOP, BATMAN! IT'S NO USE! THEY ALWAYS GET AWAY!... BUT I'M NOT GOING TO LET YOU GET AWAY TOO! YOU'RE UNDER ARREST!
MCGONIGLE, CAN YOU SWIM?
HUH?.... SURE I CAN SWIM!

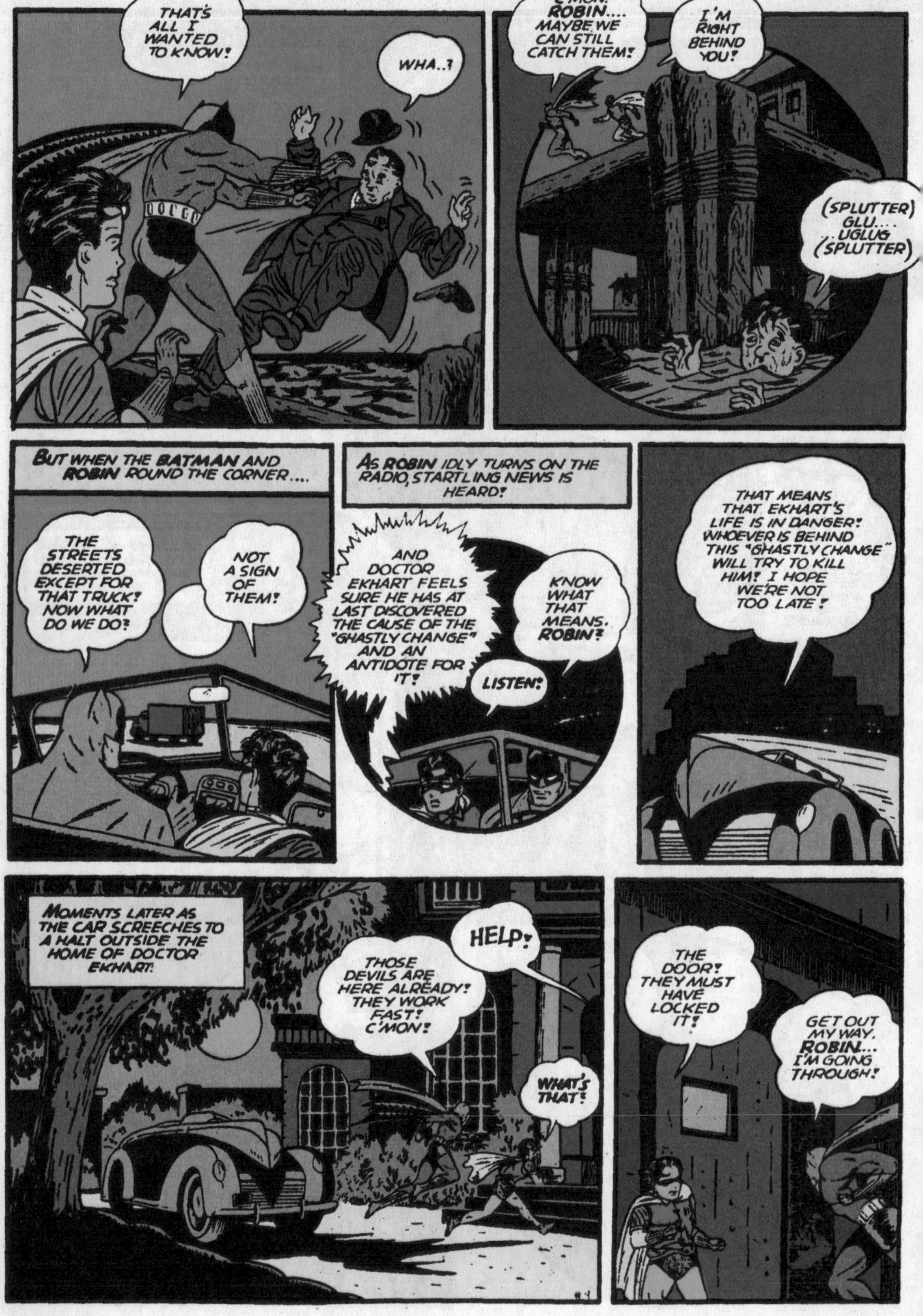

THAT'S ALL I WANTED TO KNOW!
WHA..?
C'MON. ROBIN.... MAYBE WE CAN STILL CATCH THEM!
I'M RIGHT BEHIND YOU!
(SPLUTTER) GLU... ..UGLUG (SPLUTTER)
BUT WHEN THE BATMAN AND ROBIN ROUND THE CORNER....
THE STREETS DESERTED EXCEPT FOR THAT TRUCK! NOW WHAT DO WE DO?
NOT A SIGN OF THEM!
AS ROBIN IDLY TURNS ON THE RADIO, STARTLING NEWS IS HEARD!
AND DOCTOR EKHART FEELS SURE HE HAS AT LAST DISCOVERED THE CAUSE OF THE "GHASTLY CHANGE" AND AN ANTIDOTE FOR IT!
KNOW WHAT THAT MEANS. ROBIN?
LISTEN!
THAT MEANS THAT EKHART'S LIFE IS IN DANGER! WHOEVER IS BEHIND THIS "GHASTLY CHANGE" WILL TRY TO KILL HIM! I HOPE WE'RE NOT TOO LATE!
MOMENTS LATER AS THE CAR SCREECHES TO A HALT OUTSIDE THE HOME OF DOCTOR EKHART:
HELP!
THOSE DEVILS ARE HERE ALREADY! THEY WORK FAST! C'MON!
WHAT'S THAT!
THE DOOR! THEY MUST HAVE LOCKED IT!
GET OUT MY WAY. ROBIN... I'M GOING THROUGH!

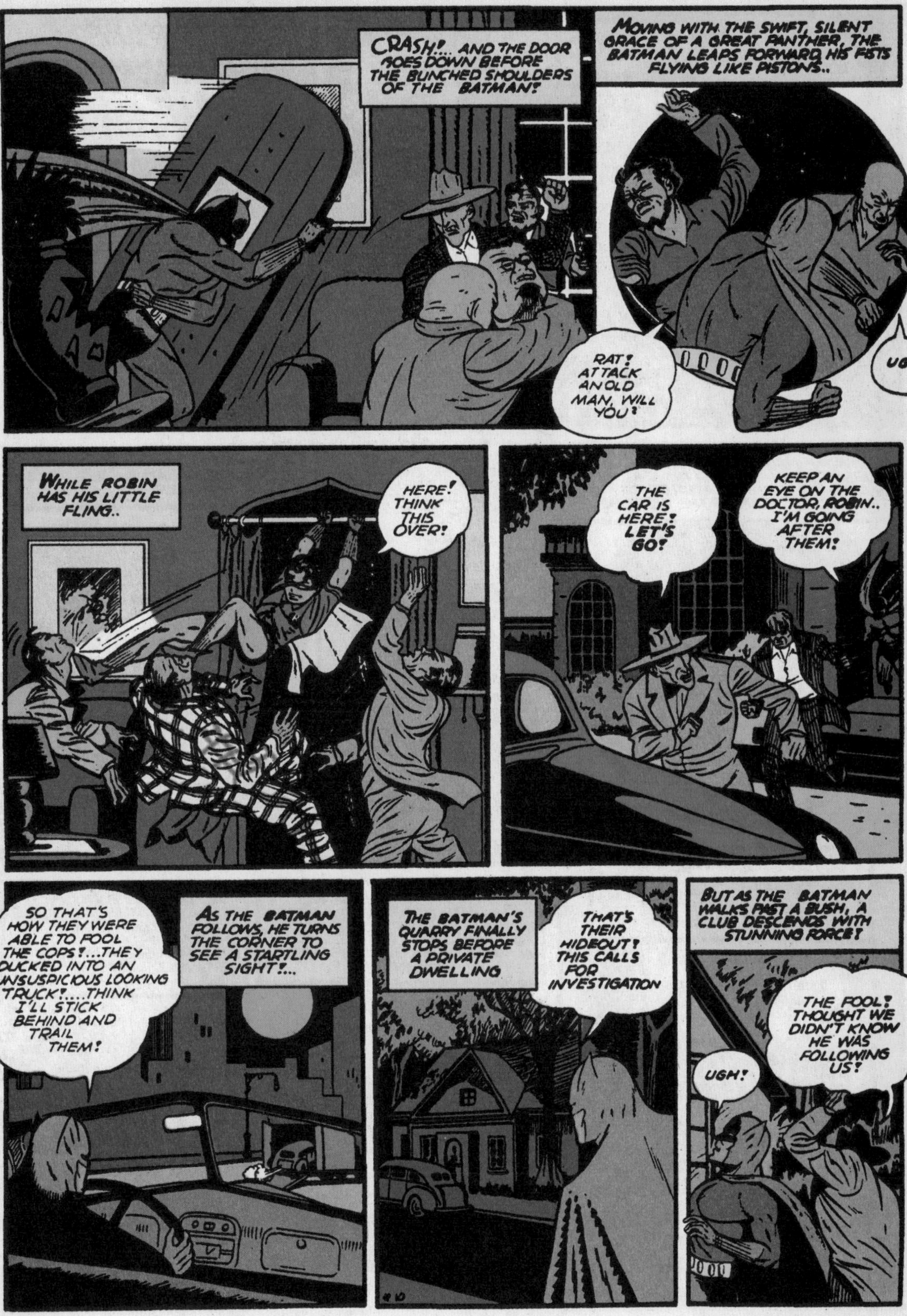
CRASH!.. AND THE DOOR GOES DOWN BEFORE THE BUNCHED SHOULDERS OF THE BATMAN!
MOVING WITH THE SWIFT, SILENT GRACE OF A GREAT PANTHER, THE BATMAN LEAPS FORWARD, HIS FISTS FLYING LIKE PISTONS..
RAT! ATTACK AN OLD MAN, WILL YOU?
UGH!
WHILE ROBIN HAS HIS LITTLE FLING..
HERE! THINK THIS OVER!
THE CAR IS HERE! LET'S GO!
KEEP AN EYE ON THE DOCTOR, ROBIN.. I'M GOING AFTER THEM!
SO THAT'S HOW THEY WERE ABLE TO FOOL THE COPS!...THEY DUCKED INTO AN UNSUSPICIOUS LOOKING TRUCK!....THINK I'LL STICK BEHIND AND TRAIL THEM!
AS THE BATMAN FOLLOWS, HE TURNS THE CORNER TO SEE A STARTLING SIGHT!...
THE BATMAN'S QUARRY FINALLY STOPS BEFORE A PRIVATE DWELLING
THAT'S THEIR HIDEOUT! THIS CALLS FOR INVESTIGATION
BUT AS THE BATMAN WALKS PAST A BUSH, A CLUB DESCENDS WITH STUNNING FORCE!
UGH!
THE FOOL! THOUGHT WE DIDN'T KNOW HE WAS FOLLOWING US!

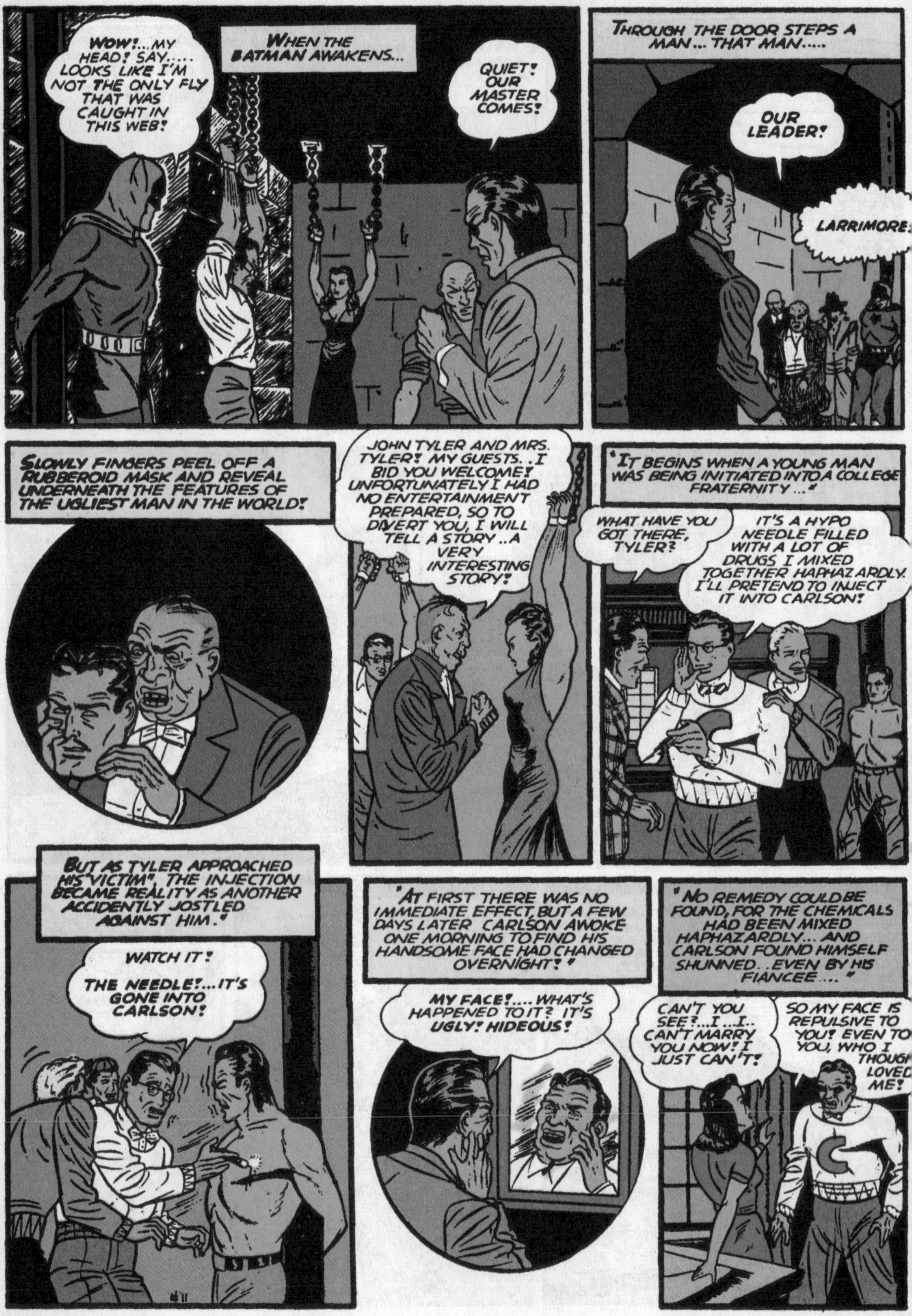
WOW!...MY HEAD! SAY..... LOOKS LIKE I'M NOT THE ONLY FLY THAT WAS CAUGHT IN THIS WEB!
WHEN THE BATMAN AWAKENS...
QUIET! OUR MASTER COMES!
THROUGH THE DOOR STEPS A MAN... THAT MAN.....
OUR LEADER!
LARRIMORE
SLOWLY FINGERS PEEL OFF A RUBBEROID MASK AND REVEAL UNDERNEATH THE FEATURES OF THE UGLIEST MAN IN THE WORLD!
JOHN TYLER AND MRS. TYLER! MY GUESTS..I BID YOU WELCOME! UNFORTUNATELY I HAD NO ENTERTAINMENT PREPARED, SO TO DIVERT YOU, I WILL TELL A STORY..A VERY INTERESTING STORY!
"IT BEGINS WHEN A YOUNG MAN WAS BEING INITIATED INTO A COLLEGE FRATERNITY..."
WHAT HAVE YOU GOT THERE, TYLER?
IT'S A HYPO NEEDLE FILLED WITH A LOT OF DRUGS I MIXED TOGETHER HAPHAZARDLY. I'LL PRETEND TO INJECT IT INTO CARLSON!
BUT AS TYLER APPROACHED HIS "VICTIM", THE INJECTION BECAME REALITY AS ANOTHER ACCIDENTLY JOSTLED AGAINST HIM."
WATCH IT!
THE NEEDLE!...IT'S GONE INTO CARLSON!
"AT FIRST THERE WAS NO IMMEDIATE EFFECT, BUT A FEW DAYS LATER CARLSON AWOKE ONE MORNING TO FIND HIS HANDSOME FACE HAD CHANGED OVERNIGHT!"
MY FACE!....WHAT'S HAPPENED TO IT? IT'S UGLY! HIDEOUS!
"NO REMEDY COULD BE FOUND, FOR THE CHEMICALS HAD BEEN MIXED HAPHAZARDLY... AND CARLSON FOUND HIMSELF SHUNNED..EVEN BY HIS FIANCEE...."
CAN'T YOU SEE?...I...I.. CAN'T MARRY YOU NOW! I JUST CAN'T!
SO MY FACE IS REPULSIVE TO YOU! EVEN TO YOU, WHO I THOUGH LOVED ME!

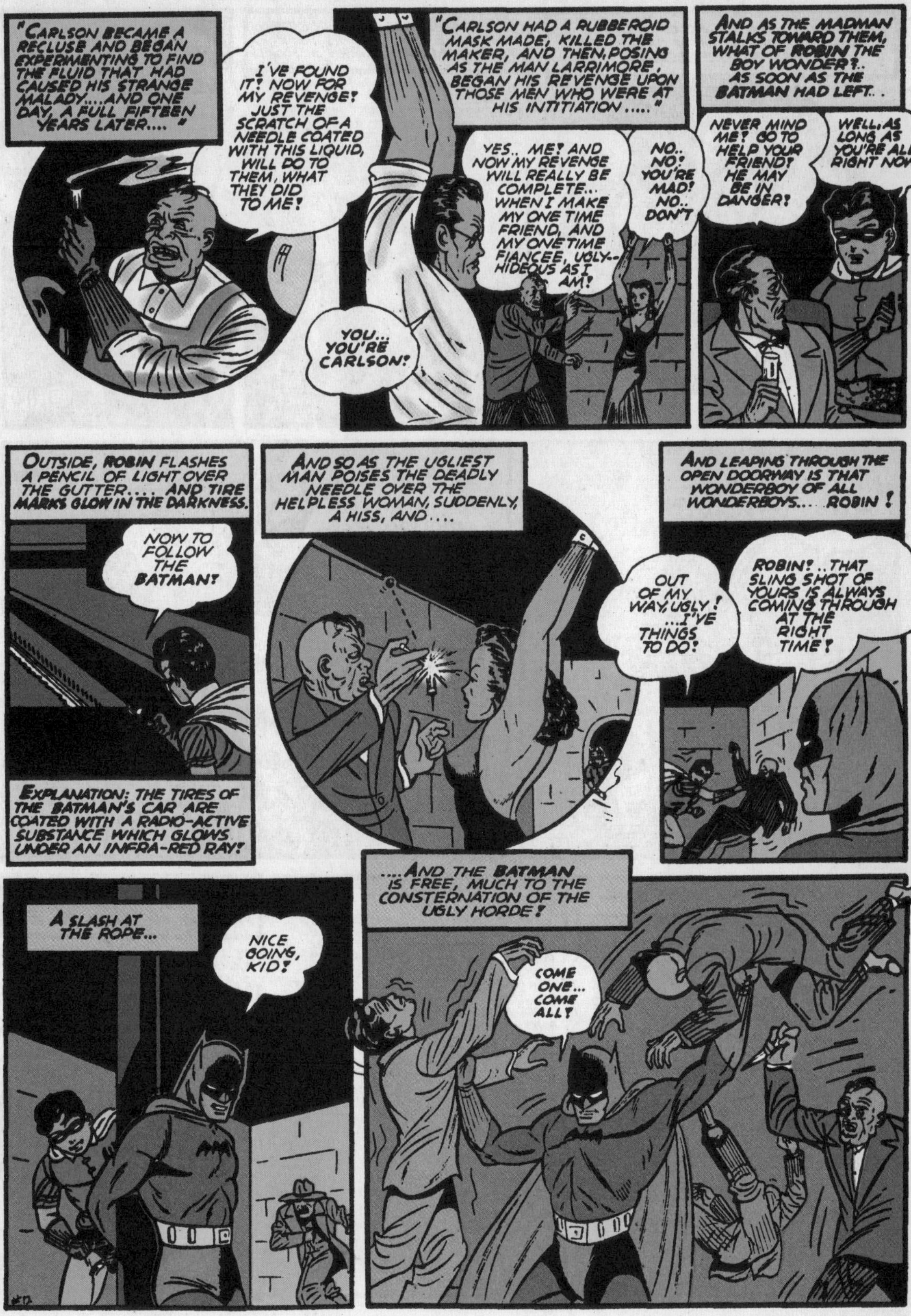
"CARLSON BECAME A RECLUSE AND BEGAN EXPERIMENTING TO FIND THE FLUID THAT HAD CAUSED HIS STRANGE MALADY....AND ONE DAY, A FULL FIFTEEN YEARS LATER.... "
I'VE FOUND IT! NOW FOR MY REVENGE! JUST THE SCRATCH OF A NEEDLE COATED WITH THIS LIQUID, WILL DO TO THEM, WHAT THEY DID TO ME!
"CARLSON HAD A RUBBEROID MASK MADE, KILLED THE MAKER, AND THEN, POSING AS THE MAN LARRIMORE, BEGAN HIS REVENGE UPON THOSE MEN WHO WERE AT HIS INTITIATION ..... "
YOU... YOU'RE CARLSON!
YES.. ME! AND NOW MY REVENGE WILL REALLY BE COMPLETE... WHEN I MAKE MY ONE TIME FRIEND, AND MY ONE TIME FIANCEE, UGLY-- HIDEOUS AS I AM!
NO.. NO! YOU'RE MAD! NO.. DON'T
AND AS THE MADMAN STALKS TOWARD THEM, WHAT OF ROBIN THE BOY WONDER?.. AS SOON AS THE BATMAN HAD LEFT. . .
NEVER MIND ME! GO TO HELP YOUR FRIEND! HE MAY BE IN DANGER!
WELL, AS LONG AS YOU'RE ALL RIGHT NOW..
OUTSIDE, ROBIN FLASHES A PENCIL OF LIGHT OVER THE GUTTER.... AND TIRE MARKS GLOW IN THE DARKNESS.
NOW TO FOLLOW THE BATMAN!
EXPLANATION: THE TIRES OF THE BATMAN'S CAR ARE COATED WITH A RADIO-ACTIVE SUBSTANCE WHICH GLOWS UNDER AN INFRA-RED RAY!
AND SO AS THE UGLIEST MAN POISES THE DEADLY NEEDLE OVER THE HELPLESS WOMAN, SUDDENLY, A HISS, AND....
AND LEAPING THROUGH THE OPEN DOORWAY IS THAT WONDERBOY OF ALL WONDERBOYS.... ROBIN !
OUT OF MY WAY, UGLY ! ...I'VE THINGS TO DO!
ROBIN! ..THAT SLING SHOT OF YOURS IS ALWAYS COMING THROUGH AT THE RIGHT TIME!
A SLASH AT THE ROPE...
NICE GOING, KID!
....AND THE BATMAN IS FREE, MUCH TO THE CONSTERNATION OF THE UGLY HORDE!
COME ONE... COME ALL!

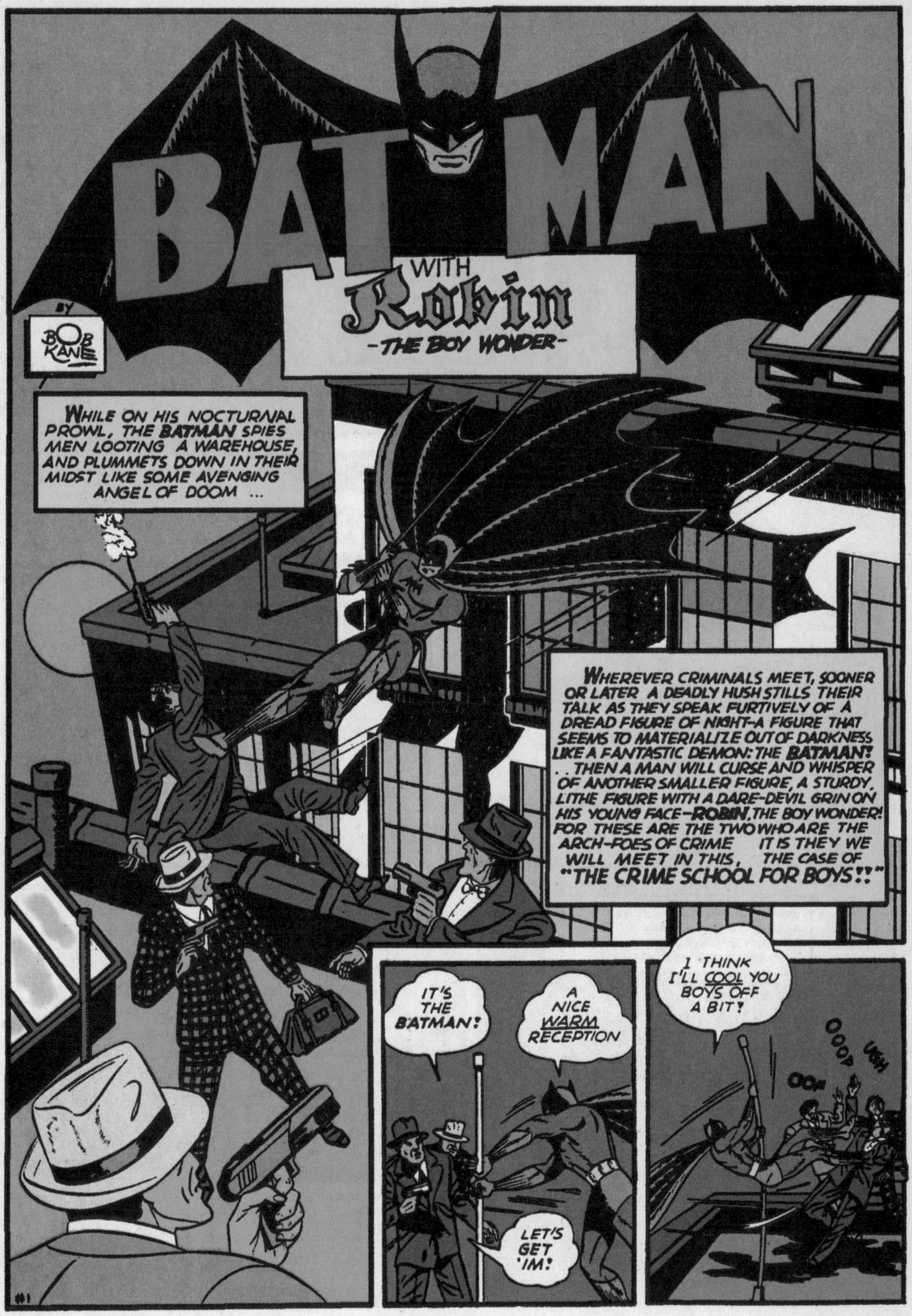
BATMAN
WITH Robin -THE BOY WONDER-
BY BOB KANE
WHILE ON HIS NOCTURNAL PROWL, THE BATMAN SPIES MEN LOOTING A WAREHOUSE, AND PLUMMETS DOWN IN THEIR MIDST LIKE SOME AVENGING ANGEL OF DOOM ...
WHEREVER CRIMINALS MEET, SOONER OR LATER A DEADLY HUSH STILLS THEIR TALK AS THEY SPEAK FURTIVELY OF A DREAD FIGURE OF NIGHT-A FIGURE THAT SEEMS TO MATERIALIZE OUT OF DARKNESS LIKE A FANTASTIC DEMON: THE BATMAN! . . THEN A MAN WILL CURSE AND WHISPER OF ANOTHER SMALLER FIGURE, A STURDY, LITHE FIGURE WITH A DARE-DEVIL GRIN ON HIS YOUNG FACE-ROBIN, THE BOY WONDER! FOR THESE ARE THE TWO WHO ARE THE ARCH-FOES OF CRIME. IT IS THEY WE WILL MEET IN THIS, THE CASE OF "THE CRIME SCHOOL FOR BOYS!!"
IT'S THE BATMAN!
A NICE WARM RECEPTION
LET'S GET 'IM!
I THINK I'LL COOL YOU BOYS OFF A BIT!
OOOP
UGH
OOF

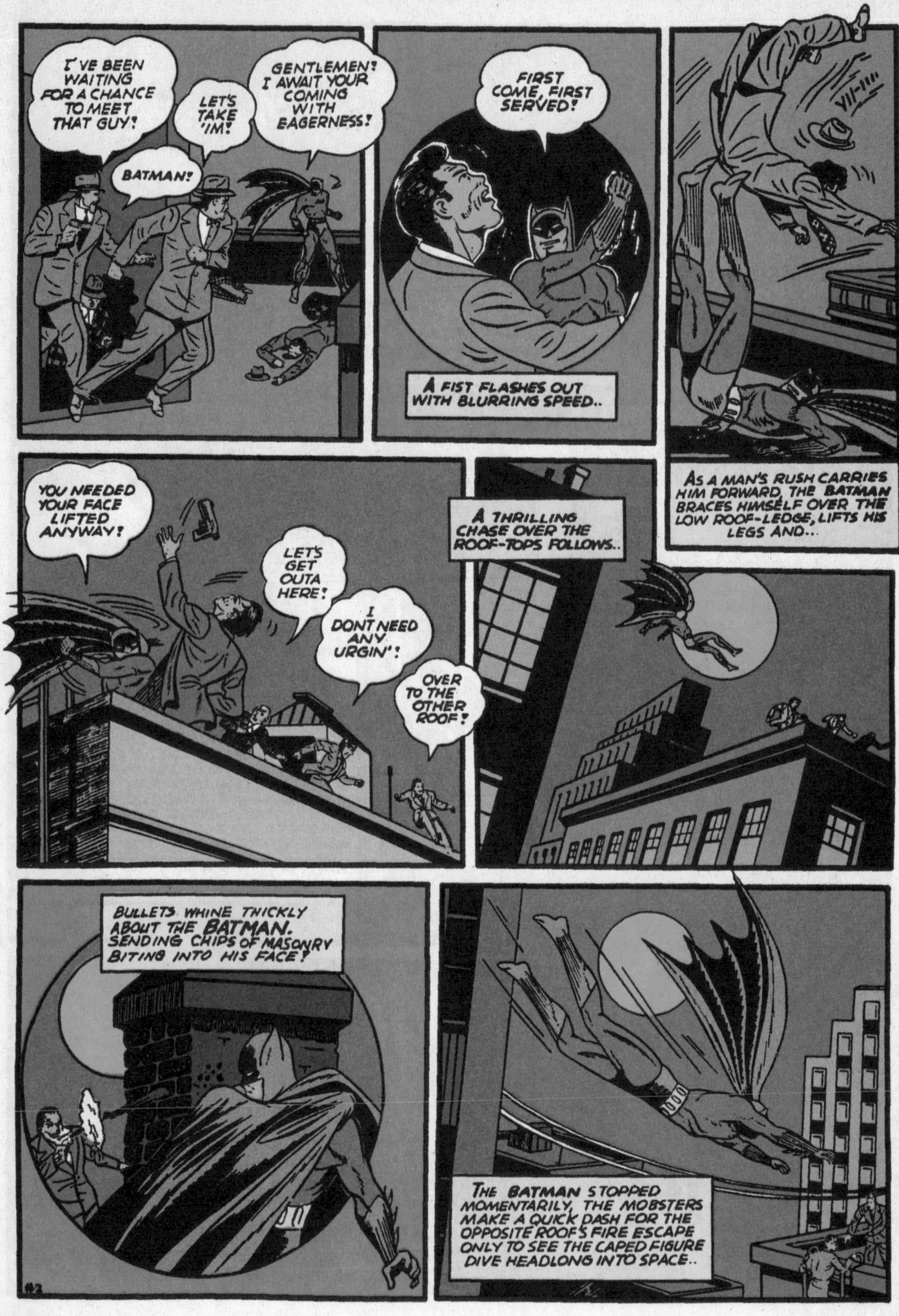
I'VE BEEN WAITING FOR A CHANCE TO MEET THAT GUY!
LET'S TAKE 'IM!
GENTLEMEN! I AWAIT YOUR COMING WITH EAGERNESS!
BATMAN!
FIRST COME, FIRST SERVED!
A FIST FLASHES OUT WITH BLURRING SPEED..
YI-I-I!
AS A MAN'S RUSH CARRIES HIM FORWARD, THE BATMAN BRACES HIMSELF OVER THE LOW ROOF-LEDGE, LIFTS HIS LEGS AND...
YOU NEEDED YOUR FACE LIFTED ANYWAY!
LET'S GET OUTA HERE!
I DONT NEED ANY URGIN'!
OVER TO THE OTHER ROOF!
A THRILLING CHASE OVER THE ROOF-TOPS FOLLOWS..
BULLETS WHINE THICKLY ABOUT THE BATMAN. SENDING CHIPS OF MASONRY BITING INTO HIS FACE!
THE BATMAN STOPPED MOMENTARILY, THE MOBSTERS MAKE A QUICK DASH FOR THE OPPOSITE ROOF'S FIRE ESCAPE ONLY TO SEE THE CAPED FIGURE DIVE HEADLONG INTO SPACE..

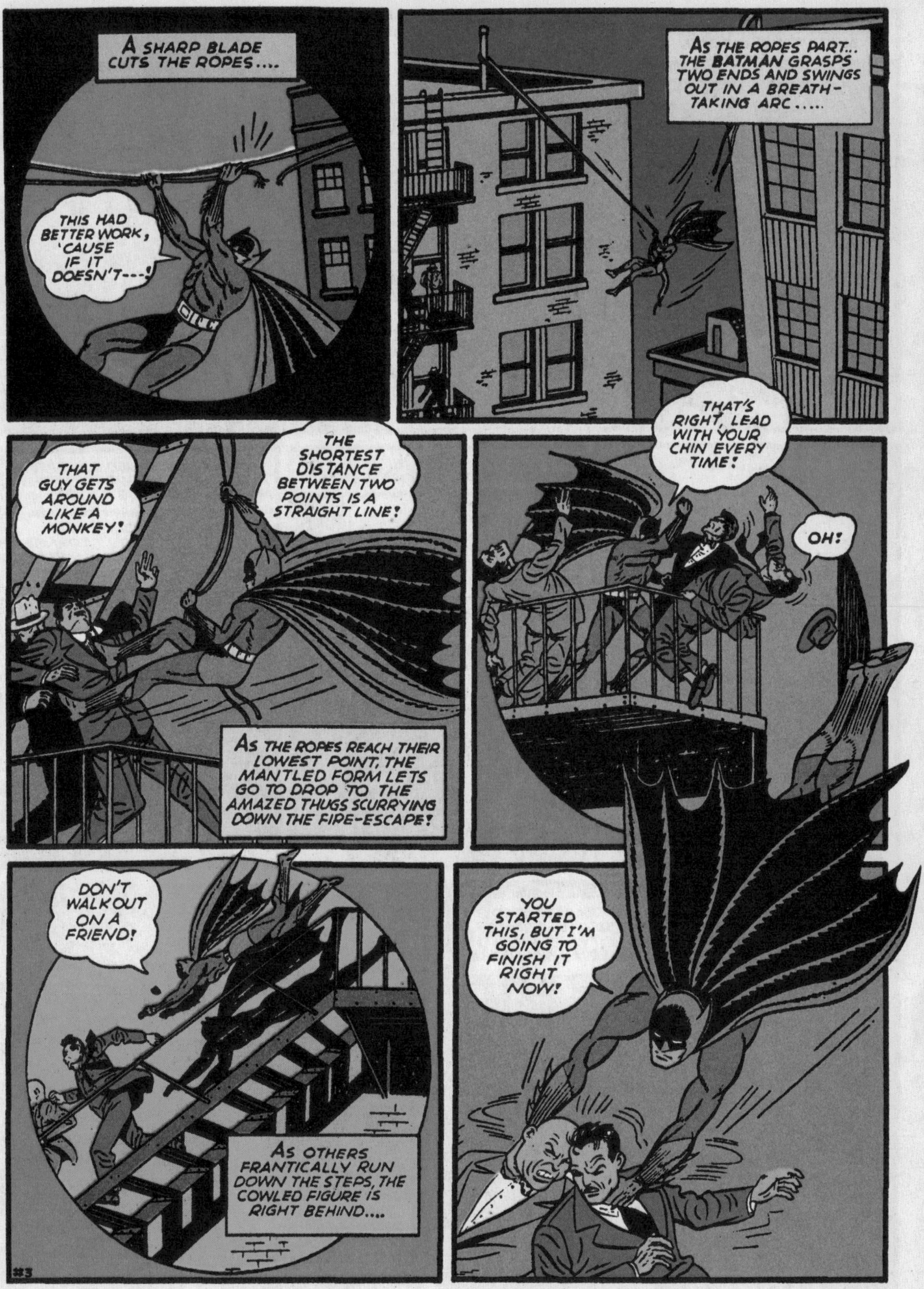
A SHARP BLADE CUTS THE ROPES....
THIS HAD BETTER WORK, 'CAUSE IF IT DOESN'T---!
AS THE ROPES PART... THE BATMAN GRASPS TWO ENDS AND SWINGS OUT IN A BREATH-TAKING ARC.....
THAT GUY GETS AROUND LIKE A MONKEY!
THE SHORTEST DISTANCE BETWEEN TWO POINTS IS A STRAIGHT LINE!
AS THE ROPES REACH THEIR LOWEST POINT, THE MANTLED FORM LETS GO TO DROP TO THE AMAZED THUGS SCURRYING DOWN THE FIRE-ESCAPE!
THAT'S RIGHT, LEAD WITH YOUR CHIN EVERY TIME!
OH!
DON'T WALK OUT ON A FRIEND!
AS OTHERS FRANTICALLY RUN DOWN THE STEPS, THE COWLED FIGURE IS RIGHT BEHIND....
#3
YOU STARTED THIS, BUT I'M GOING TO FINISH IT RIGHT NOW!

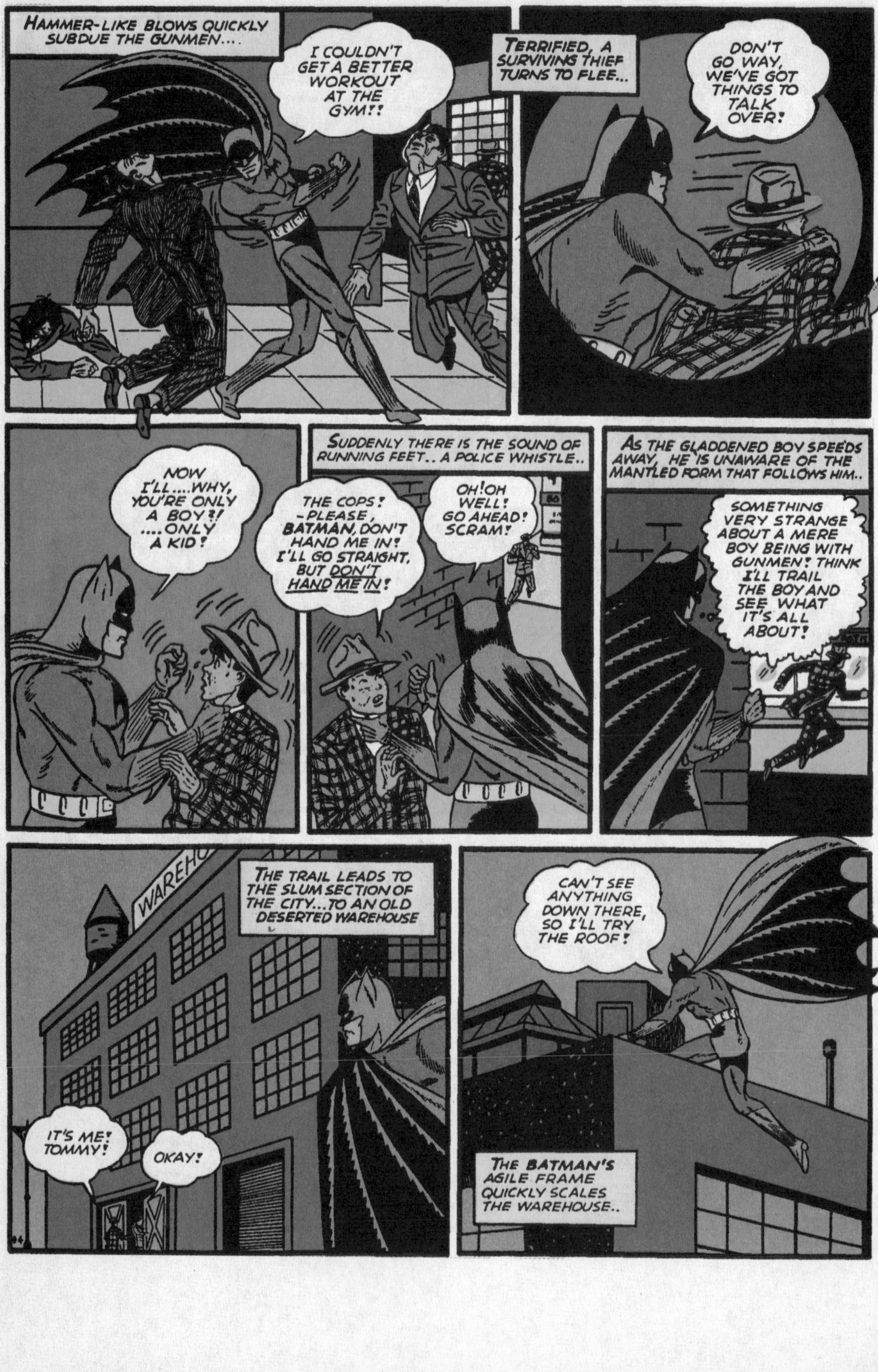

HAMMER-LIKE BLOWS QUICKLY SUBDUE THE GUNMEN...
I COULDN'T GET A BETTER WORKOUT AT THE GYM!!
TERRIFIED, A SURVIVING THIEF TURNS TO FLEE...
DON'T GO WAY, WE'VE GOT THINGS TO TALK OVER!
NOW I'LL....WHY, YOU'RE ONLY A BOY?! ....ONLY A KID!
SUDDENLY THERE IS THE SOUND OF RUNNING FEET.. A POLICE WHISTLE..
THE COPS! -PLEASE, BATMAN, DON'T HAND ME IN! I'LL GO STRAIGHT, BUT DON'T HAND ME IN!
OH! OH WELL! GO AHEAD! SCRAM!
AS THE GLADDENED BOY SPEEDS AWAY, HE IS UNAWARE OF THE MANTLED FORM THAT FOLLOWS HIM..
SOMETHING VERY STRANGE ABOUT A MERE BOY BEING WITH GUNMEN! THINK I'LL TRAIL THE BOY AND SEE WHAT IT'S ALL ABOUT!
THE TRAIL LEADS TO THE SLUM SECTION OF THE CITY...TO AN OLD DESERTED WAREHOUSE
WAREHO
IT'S ME! TOMMY!
OKAY!
CAN'T SEE ANYTHING DOWN THERE, SO I'LL TRY THE ROOF!
THE BATMAN'S AGILE FRAME QUICKLY SCALES THE WAREHOUSE..

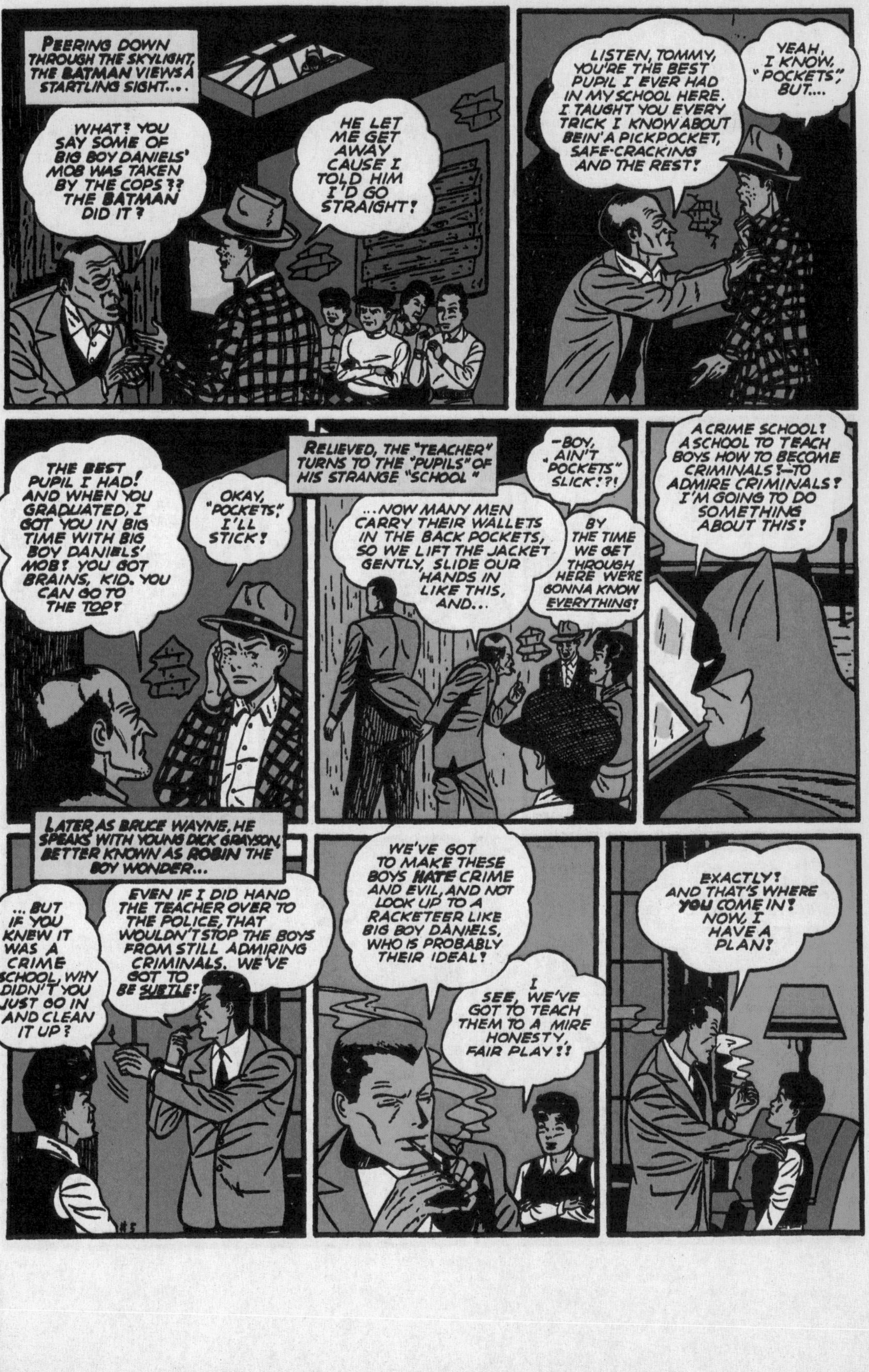

PEERING DOWN THROUGH THE SKYLIGHT, THE BATMAN VIEWS A STARTLING SIGHT....
WHAT? YOU SAY SOME OF BIG BOY DANIELS' MOB WAS TAKEN BY THE COPS?? THE BATMAN DID IT?
HE LET ME GET AWAY CAUSE I TOLD HIM I'D GO STRAIGHT!
LISTEN, TOMMY, YOU'RE THE BEST PUPIL I EVER HAD IN MY SCHOOL HERE. I TAUGHT YOU EVERY TRICK I KNOW ABOUT BEIN' A PICKPOCKET, SAFE-CRACKING AND THE REST!
YEAH, I KNOW, "POCKETS," BUT....
THE BEST PUPIL I HAD! AND WHEN YOU GRADUATED, I GOT YOU IN BIG TIME WITH BIG BOY DANIELS' MOB! YOU GOT BRAINS, KID. YOU CAN GO TO THE TOP!
OKAY, "POCKETS," I'LL STICK!
RELIEVED, THE "TEACHER" TURNS TO THE "PUPILS" OF HIS STRANGE "SCHOOL"
...NOW MANY MEN CARRY THEIR WALLETS IN THE BACK POCKETS, SO WE LIFT THE JACKET GENTLY, SLIDE OUR HANDS IN LIKE THIS, AND...
-BOY, AIN'T "POCKETS" SLICK!?!
BY THE TIME WE GET THROUGH HERE WE'RE GONNA KNOW EVERYTHING!
A CRIME SCHOOL! A SCHOOL TO TEACH BOYS HOW TO BECOME CRIMINALS!—TO ADMIRE CRIMINALS! I'M GOING TO DO SOMETHING ABOUT THIS!
LATER AS BRUCE WAYNE, HE SPEAKS WITH YOUNG DICK GRAYSON, BETTER KNOWN AS ROBIN THE BOY WONDER...
...BUT IF YOU KNEW IT WAS A CRIME SCHOOL, WHY DIDN'T YOU JUST GO IN AND CLEAN IT UP?
EVEN IF I DID HAND THE TEACHER OVER TO THE POLICE, THAT WOULDN'T STOP THE BOYS FROM STILL ADMIRING CRIMINALS. WE'VE GOT TO BE SUBTLE!
WE'VE GOT TO MAKE THESE BOYS HATE CRIME AND EVIL, AND NOT LOOK UP TO A RACKETEER LIKE BIG BOY DANIELS, WHO IS PROBABLY THEIR IDEAL!
I SEE, WE'VE GOT TO TEACH THEM TO A MIRE HONESTY, FAIR PLAY!!
EXACTLY! AND THAT'S WHERE YOU COME IN! NOW, I HAVE A PLAN!

BRUCE BEGINS THE FIRST STEP IN HIS CAMPAIGN BY RENTING AN OLD BARN IN THE SLUM SECTION....

I'M GOING TO MAKE A GYMNASIUM HERE FOR THE UNDERPRIVILEGED CHILDREN OF THIS NEIGHBORHOOD!

YES, I CAN LET YOU HAVE THIS PLACE! WHAT DO YOU INTEND TO DO WITH IT?

HEY, PIPE THE NEW KID ON THE BLOCK!

I AIN'T EVER SEEN HIM BEFORE!

A FEW DAYS LATER, A NEW BOY MAKES HIS APPEARANCE IN THE NEIGHBORHOOD...

COME ON-- LET'S HAVE SOME FUN WID HIM!

NEW KID AROUND HERE, AIN'T CHA? WELL, I'M BUTCH, AND I'M THE BOSS O' THE BLOCK!

SO WHAT?

SO THIS.. I'M GONNA PUSH YOUR FACE IN!

THEN I'D BETTER MOVE IT!

HAPPY DAZE!

THEN, AS THE BOY RUSHES FORWARD ONCE MORE...DICK SIDESTEPS, AND....

YOU CAN'T DO THIS TO ME! I'LL..

WELL, IF I CAN'T DO THAT!

...I CAN DO THIS!

HEY! DID YA SEE THAT?!?

HOLY CATS!

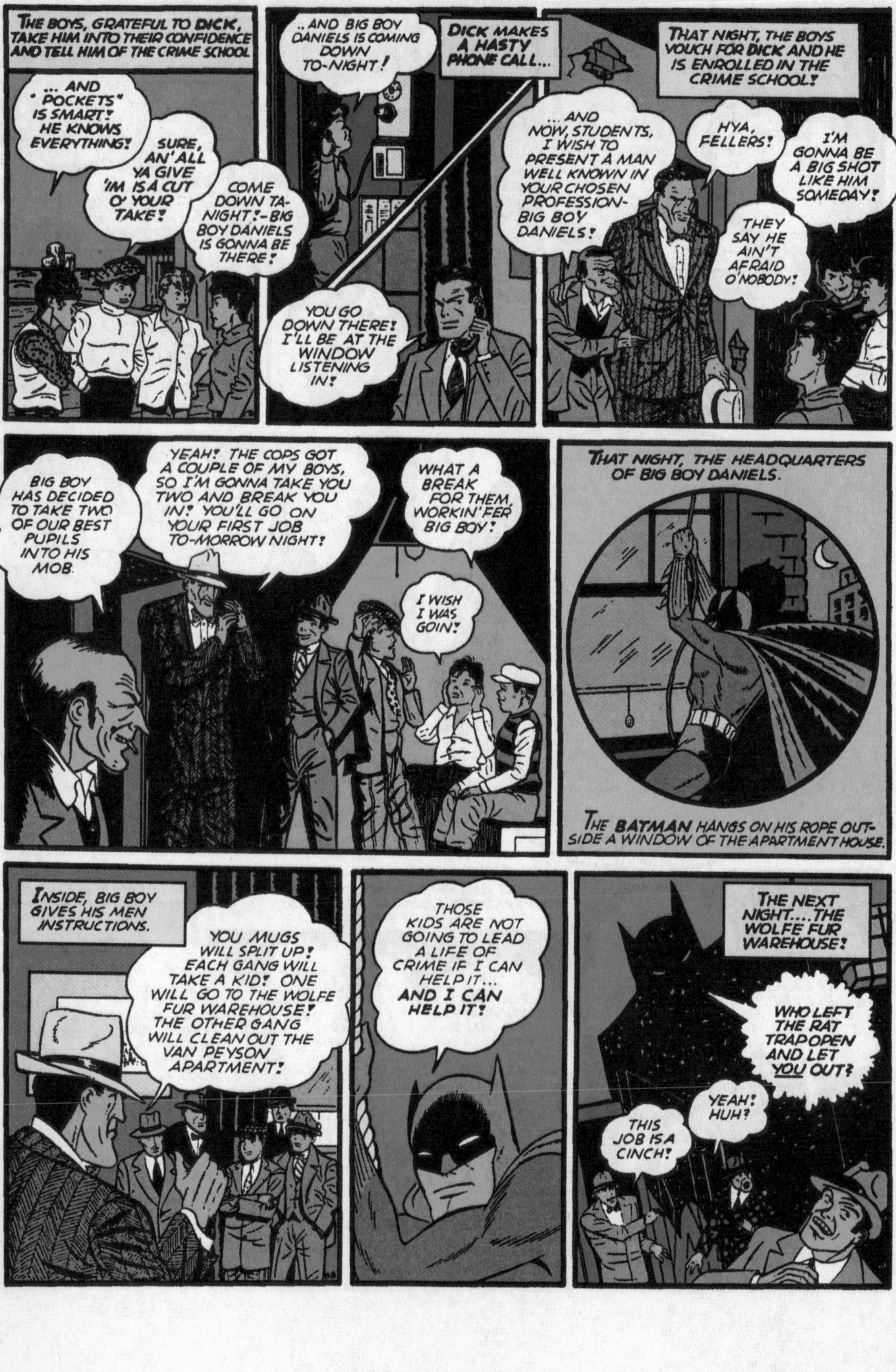
THE BOYS, GRATEFUL TO DICK, TAKE HIM INTO THEIR CONFIDENCE AND TELL HIM OF THE CRIME SCHOOL
... AND "POCKETS" IS SMART! HE KNOWS EVERYTHING!
SURE, AN' ALL YA GIVE 'IM IS A CUT O' YOUR TAKE!
COME DOWN TA-NIGHT!- BIG BOY DANIELS IS GONNA BE THERE!
.. AND BIG BOY DANIELS IS COMING DOWN TO-NIGHT!
DICK MAKES A HASTY PHONE CALL...
YOU GO DOWN THERE! I'LL BE AT THE WINDOW LISTENING IN!
THAT NIGHT, THE BOYS VOUCH FOR DICK AND HE IS ENROLLED IN THE CRIME SCHOOL!
... AND NOW, STUDENTS, I WISH TO PRESENT A MAN WELL KNOWN IN YOUR CHOSEN PROFESSION- BIG BOY DANIELS!
HYA, FELLERS!
I'M GONNA BE A BIG SHOT LIKE HIM SOMEDAY!
THEY SAY HE AIN'T AFRAID O'NOBODY!
BIG BOY HAS DECIDED TO TAKE TWO OF OUR BEST PUPILS INTO HIS MOB.
YEAH! THE COPS GOT A COUPLE OF MY BOYS, SO I'M GONNA TAKE YOU TWO AND BREAK YOU IN! YOU'LL GO ON YOUR FIRST JOB TO-MORROW NIGHT!
WHAT A BREAK FOR THEM, WORKIN' FER BIG BOY!
I WISH I WAS GOIN!
THAT NIGHT, THE HEADQUARTERS OF BIG BOY DANIELS.
THE BATMAN HANGS ON HIS ROPE OUTSIDE A WINDOW OF THE APARTMENT HOUSE.
INSIDE, BIG BOY GIVES HIS MEN INSTRUCTIONS.
YOU MUGS WILL SPLIT UP! EACH GANG WILL TAKE A KID! ONE WILL GO TO THE WOLFE FUR WAREHOUSE! THE OTHER GANG WILL CLEAN OUT THE VAN PEYSON APARTMENT!
THOSE KIDS ARE NOT GOING TO LEAD A LIFE OF CRIME IF I CAN HELP IT... AND I CAN HELP IT!
THE NEXT NIGHT.... THE WOLFE FUR WAREHOUSE!
WHO LEFT THE RAT TRAP OPEN AND LET YOU OUT?
YEAH! HUH?
THIS JOB IS A CINCH!

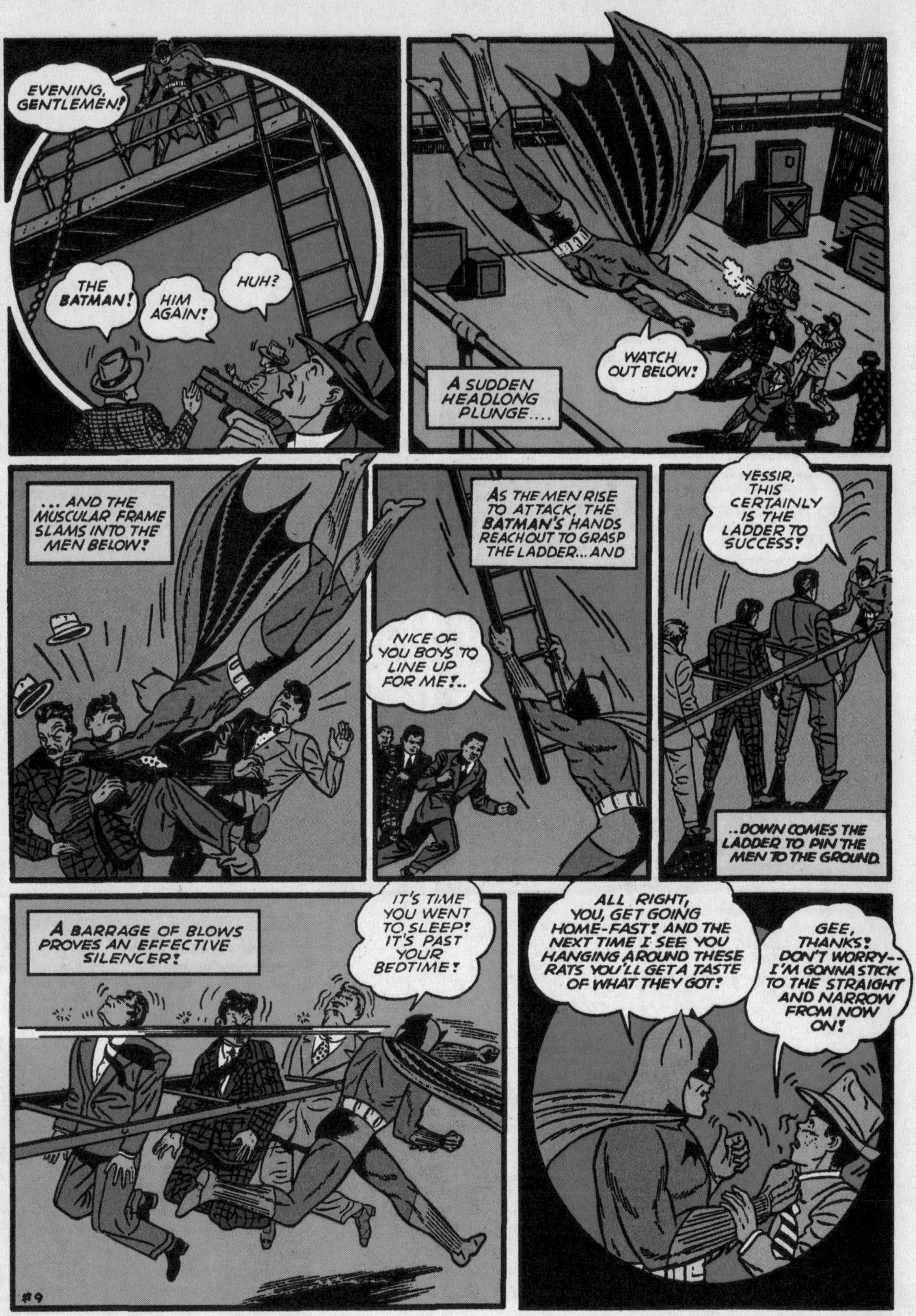
EVENING, GENTLEMEN!
THE BATMAN!
HIM AGAIN!
HUH?
A SUDDEN HEADLONG PLUNGE....
WATCH OUT BELOW!
... AND THE MUSCULAR FRAME SLAMS INTO THE MEN BELOW!
AS THE MEN RISE TO ATTACK, THE BATMAN'S HANDS REACH OUT TO GRASP THE LADDER... AND
NICE OF YOU BOYS TO LINE UP FOR ME!..
YESSIR, THIS CERTAINLY IS THE LADDER TO SUCCESS!
..DOWN COMES THE LADDER TO PIN THE MEN TO THE GROUND.
A BARRAGE OF BLOWS PROVES AN EFFECTIVE SILENCER!
IT'S TIME YOU WENT TO SLEEP! IT'S PAST YOUR BEDTIME!
#9
ALL RIGHT, YOU, GET GOING HOME-FAST! AND THE NEXT TIME I SEE YOU HANGING AROUND THESE RATS YOU'LL GET A TASTE OF WHAT THEY GOT!
GEE, THANKS! DON'T WORRY-- I'M GONNA STICK TO THE STRAIGHT AND NARROW FROM NOW ON!

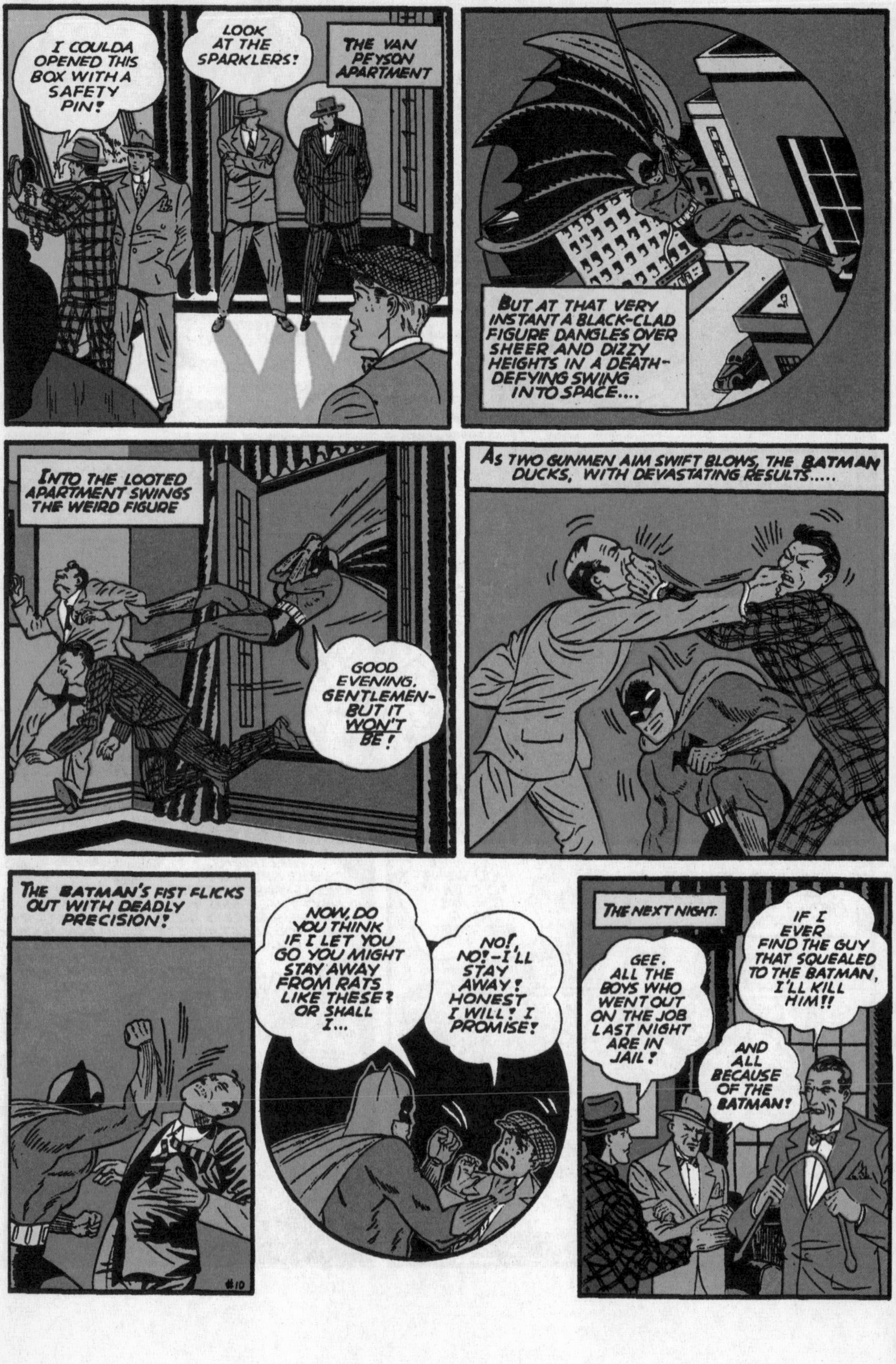
I COULDA OPENED THIS BOX WITH A SAFETY PIN!
LOOK AT THE SPARKLERS!
THE VAN PEYSON APARTMENT
BUT AT THAT VERY INSTANT A BLACK-CLAD FIGURE DANGLES OVER SHEER AND DIZZY HEIGHTS IN A DEATH-DEFYING SWING INTO SPACE....
INTO THE LOOTED APARTMENT SWINGS THE WEIRD FIGURE
GOOD EVENING, GENTLEMEN- BUT IT WON'T BE!
AS TWO GUNMEN AIM SWIFT BLOWS, THE BATMAN DUCKS, WITH DEVASTATING RESULTS.....
THE BATMAN'S FIST FLICKS OUT WITH DEADLY PRECISION!
NOW, DO YOU THINK IF I LET YOU GO YOU MIGHT STAY AWAY FROM RATS LIKE THESE? OR SHALL I...
NO!, NO!-I'LL STAY AWAY! HONEST I WILL! I PROMISE!
THE NEXT NIGHT.
GEE. ALL THE BOYS WHO WENT OUT ON THE JOB LAST NIGHT ARE IN JAIL!
IF I EVER FIND THE GUY THAT SQUEALED TO THE BATMAN, I'LL KILL HIM!!
AND ALL BECAUSE OF THE BATMAN!

YES, THIS IS THE BATMAN!--AND I'M WARNING YOU TO CLOSE UP THAT CRIME SCHOOL THAT "POCKETS" RUNS FOR YOU!

"POCKETS," EH? I BET HE'S THE RAT THAT LET INFORMATION LEAK OUT TO THE BATMAN!

AT THAT MOMENT THE BATMAN PUTS THROUGH A CALL....

NO- I DIDN'T! NO-NO! A..AGH!

SO YA RATTED TO THE BATMAN, EH, "POCKETS"? DOUBLE-CROSS ME, WILL YA?

BIG BOY PAYS A 'SOCIAL' VISIT!

THEN, LEAPING THROUGH THE SKYLIGHT ...THE BATMAN!

THAT'S MURDER, BIG BOY!

BATMAN!

HUH?

THAT GUY!

BIG BOY'S MEN QUICKLY DRAW GUNS TO "COVER" THE HOODED FIGURE!

BIG BOY, IF I WEREN'T COVERED BY THESE GUNS, I'D MOP THE FLOOR WITH YOU! BUT OF COURSE YOU'RE TOO YELLOW TO...

YELLOW, EH? IT'LL BE A PLEASURE TO PUSH YOU AROUND! C'MON!

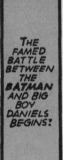

THE FAMED BATTLE BETWEEN THE BATMAN AND BIG BOY DANIELS BEGINS!

AS THE BURLY THUG SWINGS WITH A PONDEROUS FIST, THE BATMAN NIMBLY DUCKS....

CLUMSY!

SEE WHAT EASY LIVING DOES TO YOU? MAKES YOU SOFT!

UGH!

YOU'RE GOING TO START PAYING YOUR DEBT TO SOCIETY RIGHT NOW, BIG BOY!

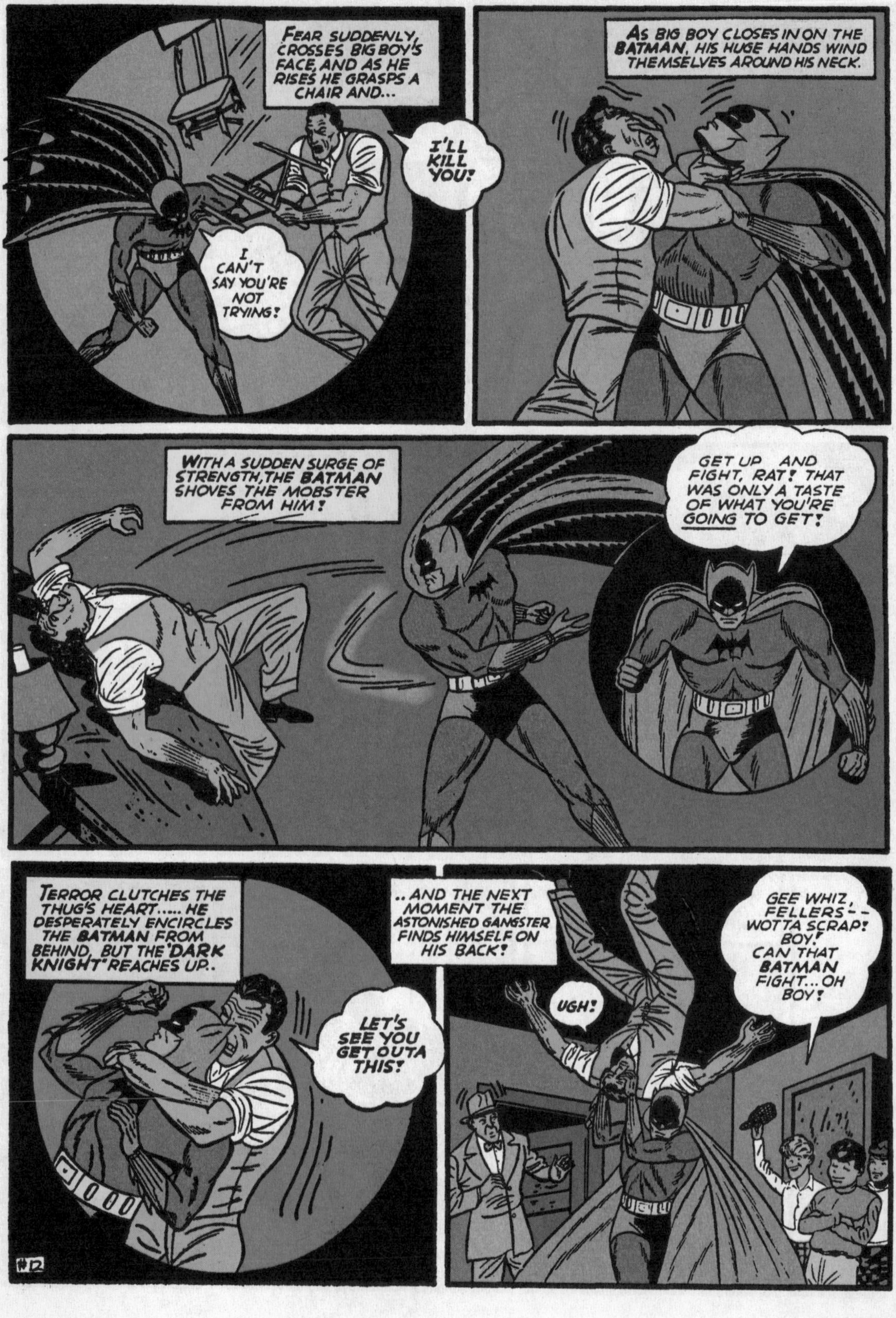
FEAR SUDDENLY, CROSSES BIG BOY'S FACE, AND AS HE RISES HE GRASPS A CHAIR AND...
I'LL KILL YOU!
I CAN'T SAY YOU'RE NOT TRYING!
AS BIG BOY CLOSES IN ON THE BATMAN, HIS HUGE HANDS WIND THEMSELVES AROUND HIS NECK.
WITH A SUDDEN SURGE OF STRENGTH, THE BATMAN SHOVES THE MOBSTER FROM HIM!
GET UP AND FIGHT, RAT! THAT WAS ONLY A TASTE OF WHAT YOU'RE GOING TO GET!
TERROR CLUTCHES THE THUG'S HEART..... HE DESPERATELY ENCIRCLES THE BATMAN FROM BEHIND, BUT THE 'DARK KNIGHT' REACHES UP..
LET'S SEE YOU GET OUTA THIS!
#12
..AND THE NEXT MOMENT THE ASTONISHED GANGSTER FINDS HIMSELF ON HIS BACK!
UGH!
GEE WHIZ, FELLERS-- WOTTA SCRAP! BOY! CAN THAT BATMAN FIGHT...OH BOY!

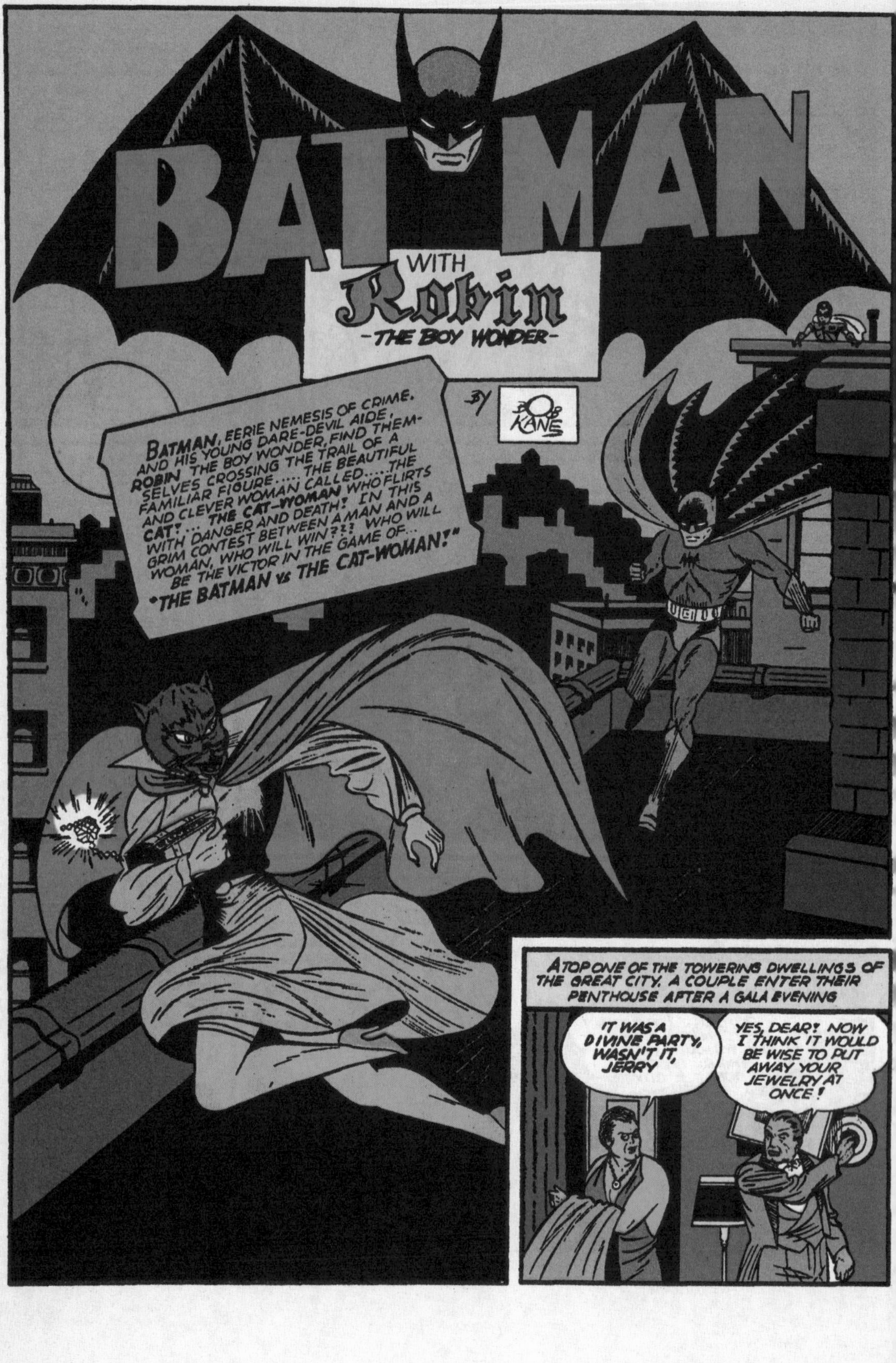
BATMAN
WITH Robin
-THE BOY WONDER-
BY BOB KANE
BATMAN, EERIE NEMESIS OF CRIME, AND HIS YOUNG DARE-DEVIL AIDE, ROBIN THE BOY WONDER, FIND THEMSELVES CROSSING THE TRAIL OF A FAMILIAR FIGURE..... THE BEAUTIFUL AND CLEVER WOMAN CALLED.....THE CAT!... THE CAT-WOMAN WHO FLIRTS WITH DANGER AND DEATH! IN THIS GRIM CONTEST BETWEEN A MAN AND A WOMAN, WHO WILL WIN??? WHO WILL BE THE VICTOR IN THE GAME OF...
"THE BATMAN vs THE CAT-WOMAN!"
ATOP ONE OF THE TOWERING DWELLINGS OF THE GREAT CITY, A COUPLE ENTER THEIR PENTHOUSE AFTER A GALA EVENING
IT WAS A DIVINE PARTY, WASN'T IT, JERRY
YES, DEAR! NOW I THINK IT WOULD BE WISE TO PUT AWAY YOUR JEWELRY AT ONCE!

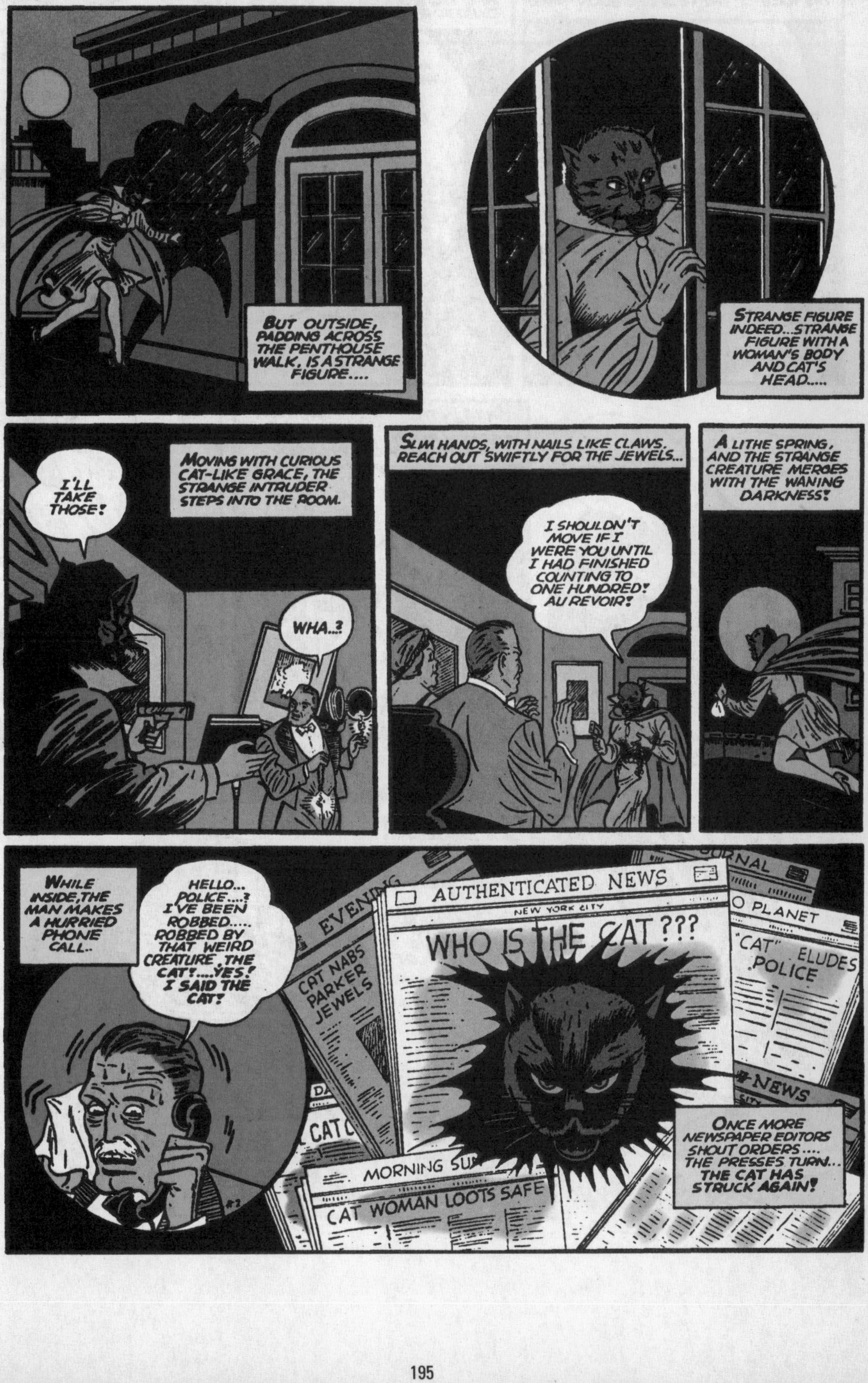

BUT OUTSIDE, PADDING ACROSS THE PENTHOUSE WALK, IS A STRANGE FIGURE....
STRANGE FIGURE INDEED...STRANGE FIGURE WITH A WOMAN'S BODY AND CAT'S HEAD.....
MOVING WITH CURIOUS CAT-LIKE GRACE, THE STRANGE INTRUDER STEPS INTO THE ROOM.
I'LL TAKE THOSE!
WHA..?
SLIM HANDS, WITH NAILS LIKE CLAWS, REACH OUT SWIFTLY FOR THE JEWELS...
I SHOULDN'T MOVE IF I WERE YOU UNTIL I HAD FINISHED COUNTING TO ONE HUNDRED! AU REVOIR!
A LITHE SPRING, AND THE STRANGE CREATURE MERGES WITH THE WANING DARKNESS!
WHILE INSIDE, THE MAN MAKES A HURRIED PHONE CALL..
HELLO... POLICE...? I'VE BEEN ROBBED..... ROBBED BY THAT WEIRD CREATURE, THE CAT!....YES! I SAID THE CAT!
AUTHENTICATED NEWS
NEW YORK CITY
WHO IS THE CAT ???
CAT NABS PARKER JEWELS
"CAT" ELUDES POLICE
MORNING SU
CAT WOMAN LOOTS SAFE
ONCE MORE NEWSPAPER EDITORS SHOUT ORDERS.... THE PRESSES TURN... THE CAT HAS STRUCK AGAIN!

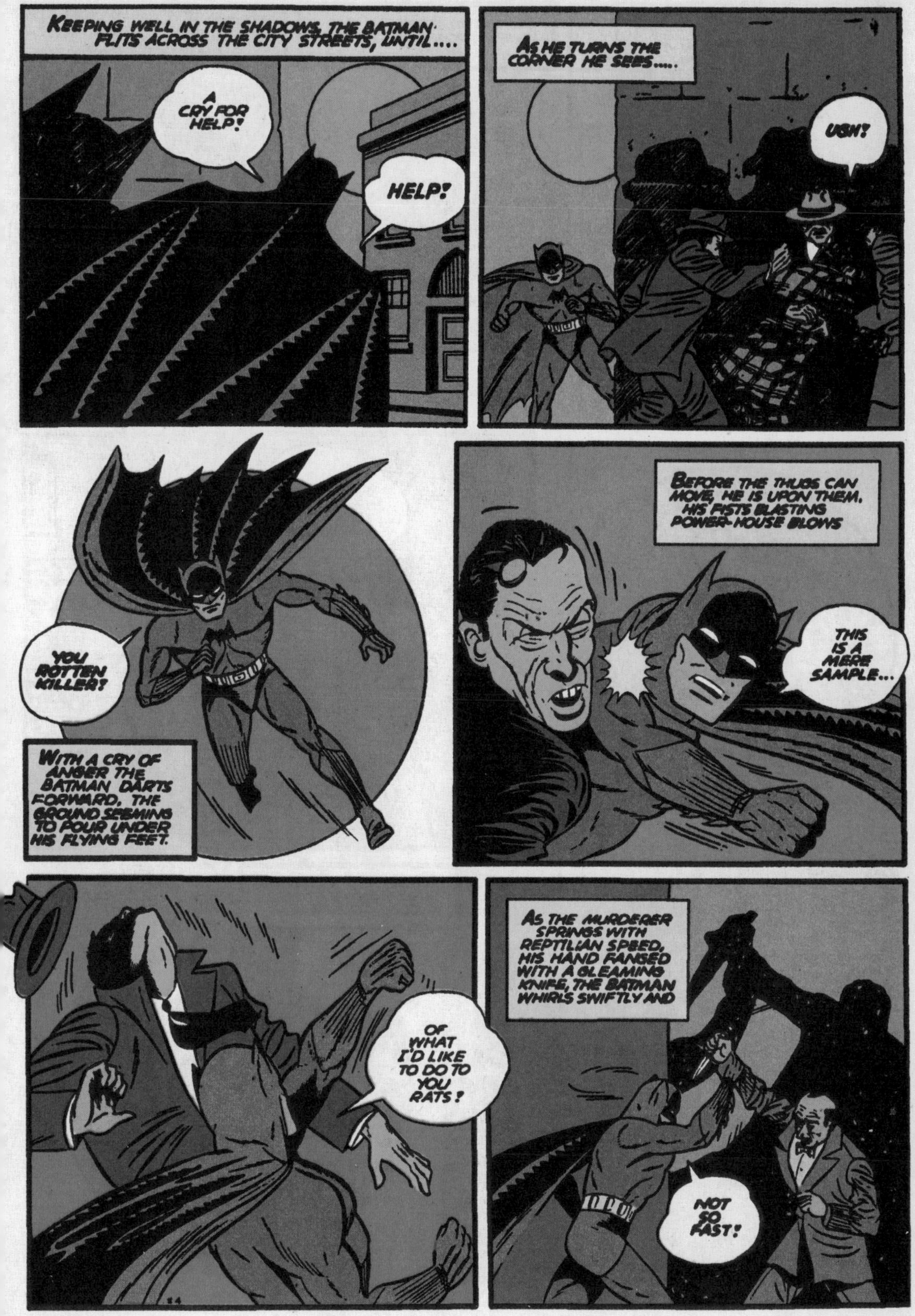
KEEPING WELL IN THE SHADOWS, THE BATMAN FLITS ACROSS THE CITY STREETS, UNTIL....
A CRY FOR HELP!
HELP!
AS HE TURNS THE CORNER HE SEES.....
UGH!
YOU ROTTEN KILLER!
WITH A CRY OF ANGER THE BATMAN DARTS FORWARD, THE GROUND SEEMING TO POUR UNDER HIS FLYING FEET.
BEFORE THE THUGS CAN MOVE, HE IS UPON THEM. HIS FISTS BLASTING POWER-HOUSE BLOWS
THIS IS A MERE SAMPLE...
OF WHAT I'D LIKE TO DO TO YOU RATS!
AS THE MURDERER SPRINGS WITH REPTILIAN SPEED, HIS HAND FANGED WITH A GLEAMING KNIFE, THE BATMAN WHIRLS SWIFTLY AND
NOT SO FAST!

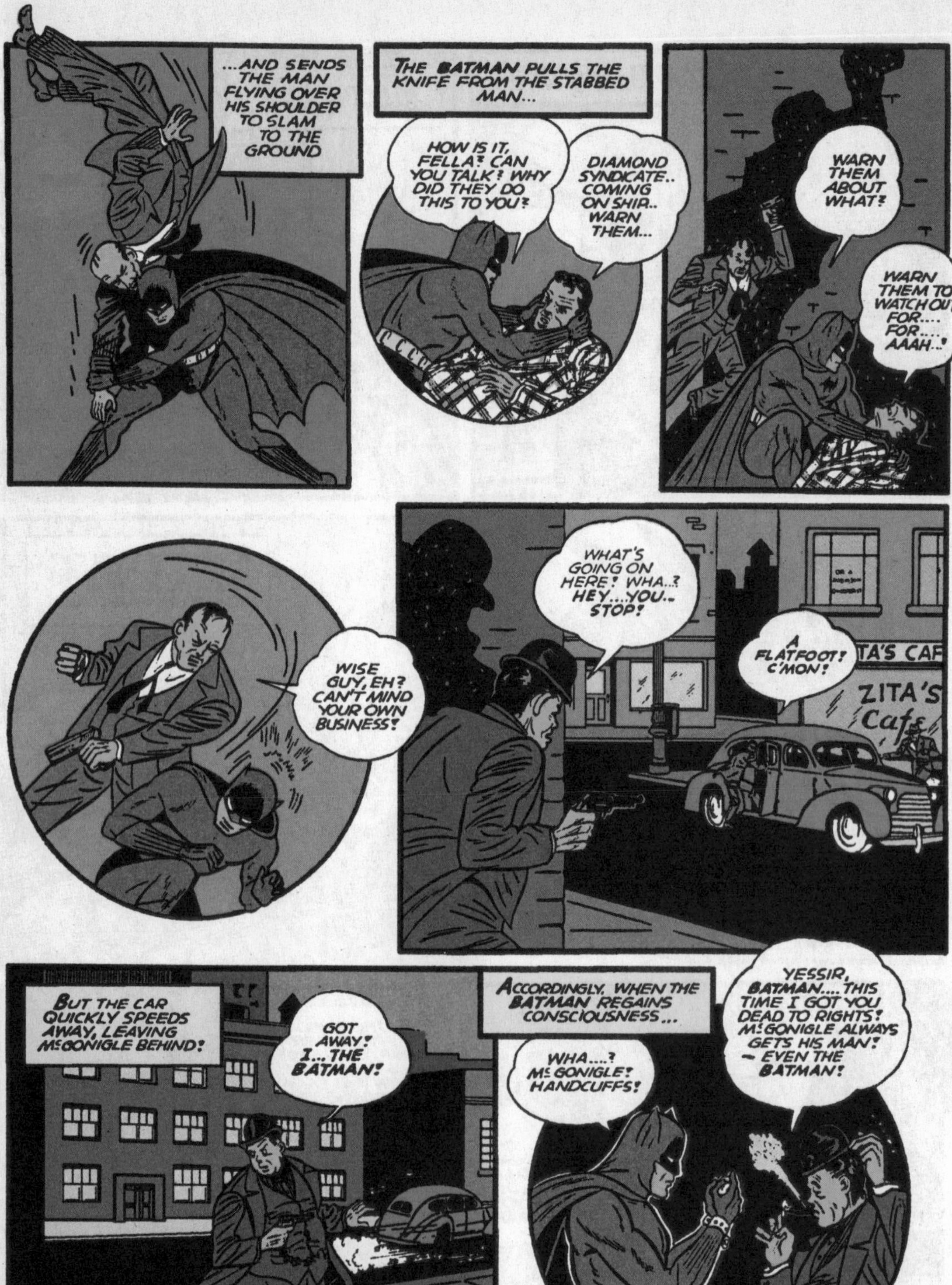
...AND SENDS THE MAN FLYING OVER HIS SHOULDER TO SLAM TO THE GROUND
THE BATMAN PULLS THE KNIFE FROM THE STABBED MAN...
HOW IS IT, FELLA? CAN YOU TALK? WHY DID THEY DO THIS TO YOU?
DIAMOND SYNDICATE.. COMING ON SHIP.. WARN THEM...
WARN THEM ABOUT WHAT?
WARN THEM TO WATCH OUT FOR.... FOR.... AAAH..!
WISE GUY, EH? CAN'T MIND YOUR OWN BUSINESS!
WHAT'S GOING ON HERE! WHA..? HEY...YOU.. STOP!
A FLATFOOT! C'MON!
ZITA'S Cafe
BUT THE CAR QUICKLY SPEEDS AWAY, LEAVING McGONIGLE BEHIND!
GOT AWAY! I...THE BATMAN!
ACCORDINGLY, WHEN THE BATMAN REGAINS CONSCIOUSNESS...
WHA....? McGONIGLE! HANDCUFFS!
YESSIR, BATMAN....THIS TIME I GOT YOU DEAD TO RIGHTS! McGONIGLE ALWAYS GETS HIS MAN! - EVEN THE BATMAN!

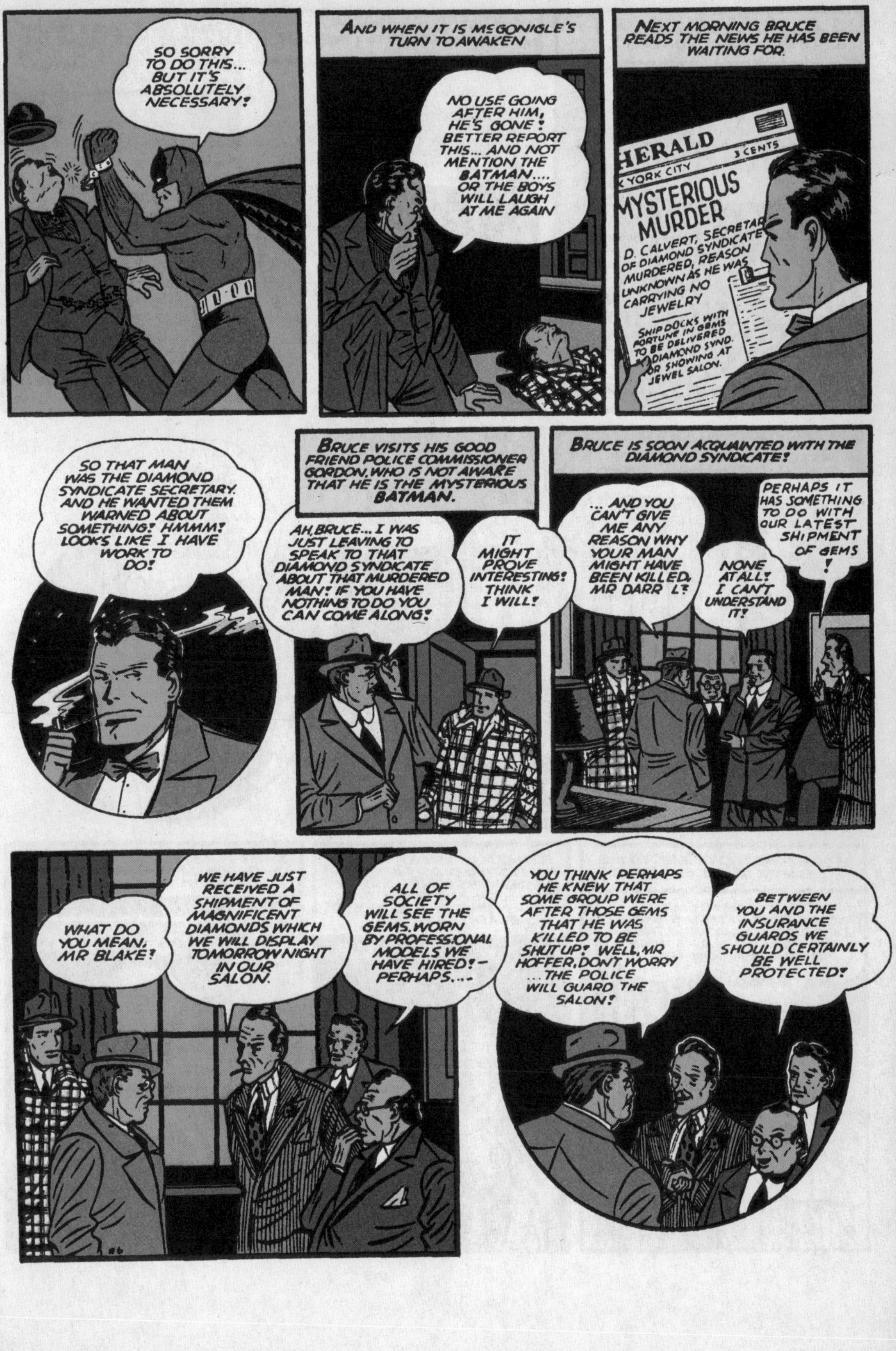
SO SORRY TO DO THIS... BUT IT'S ABSOLUTELY NECESSARY!
AND WHEN IT IS McGONIGLE'S TURN TO AWAKEN
NO USE GOING AFTER HIM, HE'S GONE! BETTER REPORT THIS... AND NOT MENTION THE BATMAN.... OR THE BOYS WILL LAUGH AT ME AGAIN
NEXT MORNING BRUCE READS THE NEWS HE HAS BEEN WAITING FOR.
HERALD
3 CENTS
YORK CITY
MYSTERIOUS MURDER
D. CALVERT, SECRETAR OF DIAMOND SYNDICATE MURDERED, REASON UNKNOWN AS HE WAS CARRYING NO JEWELRY
SHIP DOCKS WITH FORTUNE IN GEMS TO BE DELIVERED DIAMOND SYND. FOR SHOWING AT JEWEL SALON.
SO THAT MAN WAS THE DIAMOND SYNDICATE SECRETARY. AND HE WANTED THEM WARNED ABOUT SOMETHING! HMMM! LOOKS LIKE I HAVE WORK TO DO!
BRUCE VISITS HIS GOOD FRIEND POLICE COMMISSIONER GORDON, WHO IS NOT AWARE THAT HE IS THE MYSTERIOUS BATMAN.
AH, BRUCE... I WAS JUST LEAVING TO SPEAK TO THAT DIAMOND SYNDICATE ABOUT THAT MURDERED MAN! IF YOU HAVE NOTHING TO DO YOU CAN COME ALONG!
IT MIGHT PROVE INTERESTING! THINK I WILL!
BRUCE IS SOON ACQUAINTED WITH THE DIAMOND SYNDICATE!
... AND YOU CAN'T GIVE ME ANY REASON WHY YOUR MAN MIGHT HAVE BEEN KILLED, MR DARR L?
NONE AT ALL! I CAN'T UNDERSTAND IT!
PERHAPS IT HAS SOMETHING TO DO WITH OUR LATEST SHIPMENT OF GEMS!
WHAT DO YOU MEAN, MR BLAKE?
WE HAVE JUST RECEIVED A SHIPMENT OF MAGNIFICENT DIAMONDS WHICH WE WILL DISPLAY TOMORROW NIGHT IN OUR SALON.
ALL OF SOCIETY WILL SEE THE GEMS, WORN BY PROFESSIONAL MODELS WE HAVE HIRED! — PERHAPS....
YOU THINK PERHAPS HE KNEW THAT SOME GROUP WERE AFTER THOSE GEMS THAT HE WAS KILLED TO BE SHUT UP! WELL, MR HOFFER, DON'T WORRY ... THE POLICE WILL GUARD THE SALON!
BETWEEN YOU AND THE INSURANCE GUARDS WE SHOULD CERTAINLY BE WELL PROTECTED!

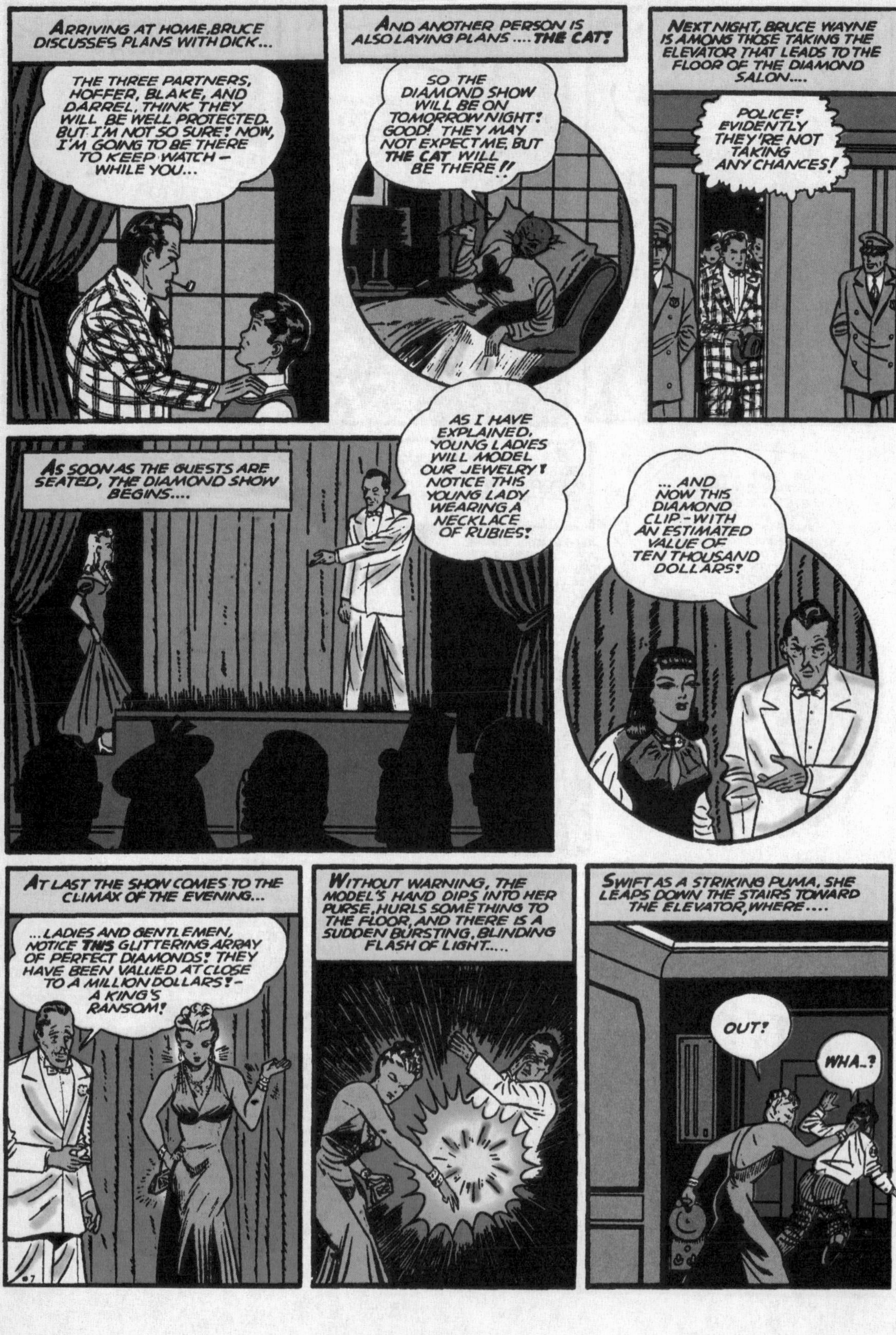
ARRIVING AT HOME, BRUCE DISCUSSES PLANS WITH DICK...
THE THREE PARTNERS, HOFFER, BLAKE, AND DARREL, THINK THEY WILL BE WELL PROTECTED. BUT I'M NOT SO SURE! NOW, I'M GOING TO BE THERE TO KEEP WATCH — WHILE YOU...
AND ANOTHER PERSON IS ALSO LAYING PLANS .... THE CAT!
SO THE DIAMOND SHOW WILL BE ON TOMORROW NIGHT! GOOD! THEY MAY NOT EXPECT ME, BUT THE CAT WILL BE THERE!!
NEXT NIGHT, BRUCE WAYNE IS AMONG THOSE TAKING THE ELEVATOR THAT LEADS TO THE FLOOR OF THE DIAMOND SALON....
POLICE! EVIDENTLY THEY'RE NOT TAKING ANY CHANCES!
AS SOON AS THE GUESTS ARE SEATED, THE DIAMOND SHOW BEGINS....
AS I HAVE EXPLAINED, YOUNG LADIES WILL MODEL OUR JEWELRY! NOTICE THIS YOUNG LADY WEARING A NECKLACE OF RUBIES!
... AND NOW THIS DIAMOND CLIP — WITH AN ESTIMATED VALUE OF TEN THOUSAND DOLLARS!
AT LAST THE SHOW COMES TO THE CLIMAX OF THE EVENING...
... LADIES AND GENTLEMEN, NOTICE THIS GLITTERING ARRAY OF PERFECT DIAMONDS! THEY HAVE BEEN VALUED AT CLOSE TO A MILLION DOLLARS! — A KING'S RANSOM!
WITHOUT WARNING, THE MODEL'S HAND DIPS INTO HER PURSE, HURLS SOMETHING TO THE FLOOR, AND THERE IS A SUDDEN BURSTING, BLINDING FLASH OF LIGHT.....
SWIFT AS A STRIKING PUMA, SHE LEAPS DOWN THE STAIRS TOWARD THE ELEVATOR, WHERE....
OUT!
WHA..?

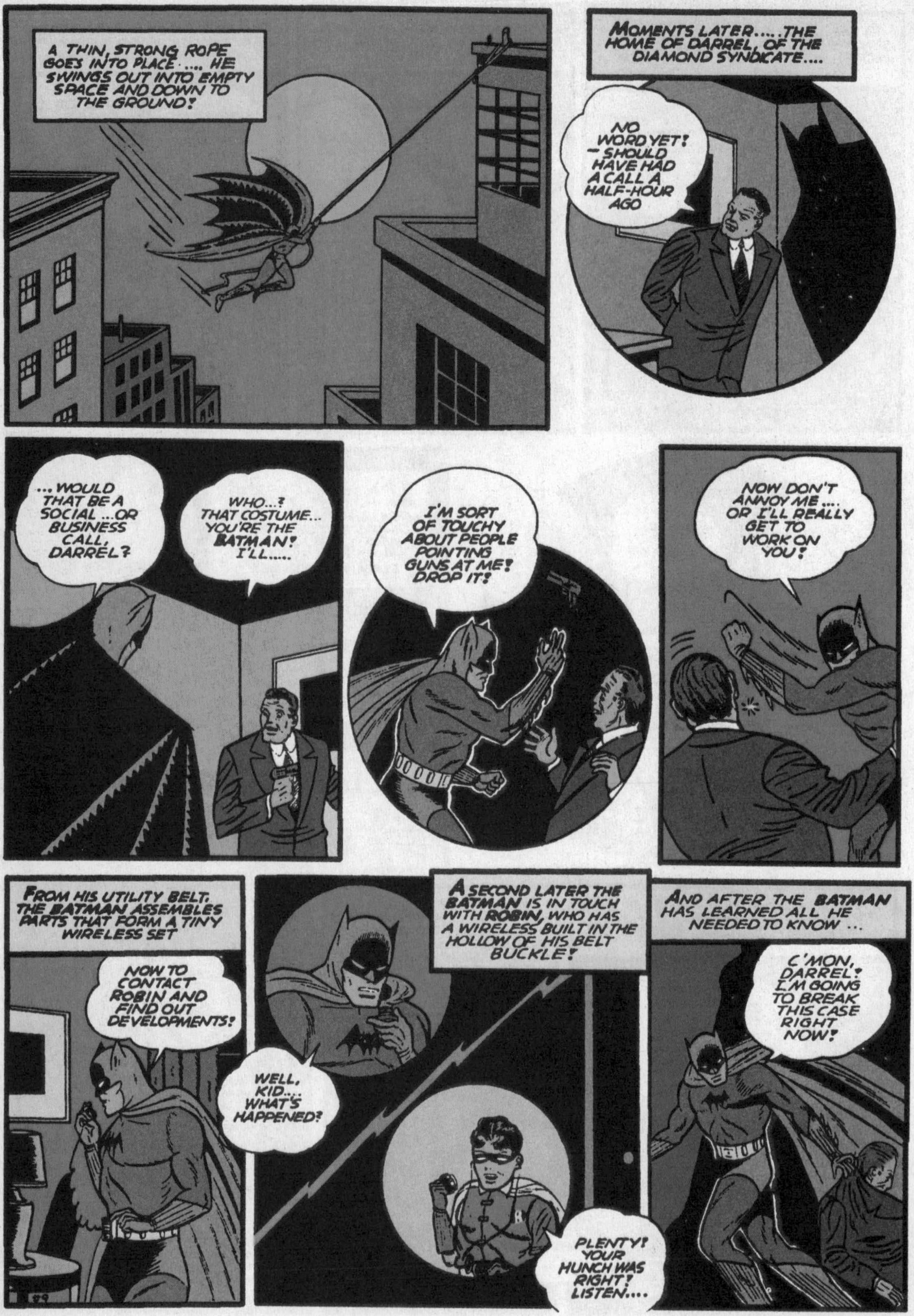
A THIN, STRONG ROPE GOES INTO PLACE .... HE SWINGS OUT INTO EMPTY SPACE AND DOWN TO THE GROUND!
MOMENTS LATER.....THE HOME OF DARREL, OF THE DIAMOND SYNDICATE....
NO WORD YET! —SHOULD HAVE HAD A CALL A HALF-HOUR AGO
...WOULD THAT BE A SOCIAL ...OR BUSINESS CALL, DARREL?
WHO...? THAT COSTUME... YOU'RE THE BATMAN! I'LL.....
I'M SORT OF TOUCHY ABOUT PEOPLE POINTING GUNS AT ME! DROP IT!
NOW DON'T ANNOY ME.... OR I'LL REALLY GET TO WORK ON YOU!
FROM HIS UTILITY BELT, THE BATMAN ASSEMBLES PARTS THAT FORM A TINY WIRELESS SET
NOW TO CONTACT ROBIN AND FIND OUT DEVELOPMENTS!
A SECOND LATER THE BATMAN IS IN TOUCH WITH ROBIN, WHO HAS A WIRELESS BUILT IN THE HOLLOW OF HIS BELT BUCKLE!
WELL, KID... WHAT'S HAPPENED?
PLENTY! YOUR HUNCH WAS RIGHT! LISTEN....
AND AFTER THE BATMAN HAS LEARNED ALL HE NEEDED TO KNOW ...
C'MON, DARREL! I'M GOING TO BREAK THIS CASE RIGHT NOW!

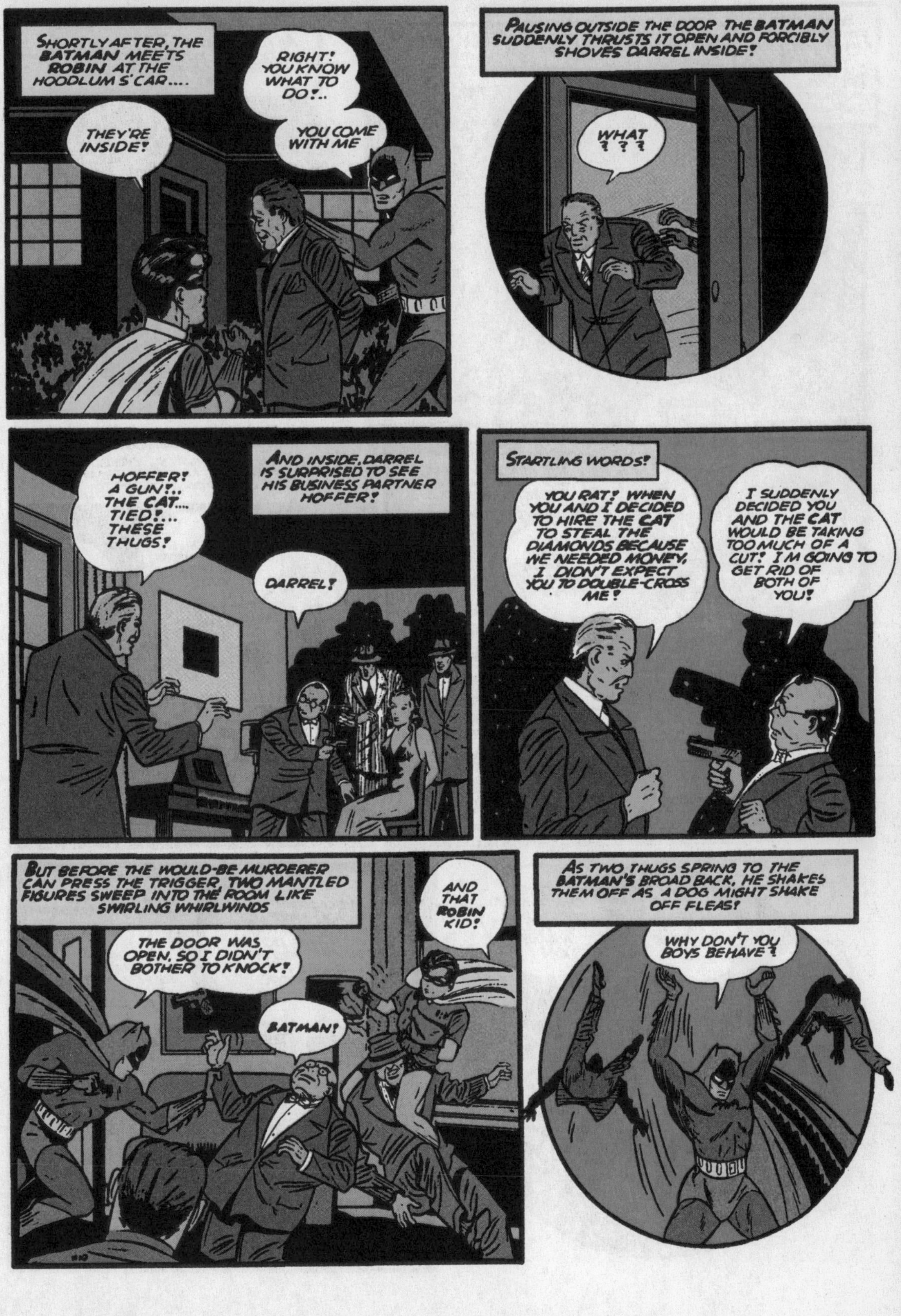
SHORTLY AFTER, THE BATMAN MEETS ROBIN AT THE HOODLUM'S CAR....
THEY'RE INSIDE!
RIGHT! YOU KNOW WHAT TO DO!..
YOU COME WITH ME
PAUSING OUTSIDE THE DOOR THE BATMAN SUDDENLY THRUSTS IT OPEN AND FORCIBLY SHOVES DARREL INSIDE!
WHAT ???
AND INSIDE, DARREL IS SURPRISED TO SEE HIS BUSINESS PARTNER HOFFER!
HOFFER! A GUN!.. THE CAT.... TIED!... THESE THUGS!
DARREL!
STARTLING WORDS!
YOU RAT! WHEN YOU AND I DECIDED TO HIRE THE CAT TO STEAL THE DIAMONDS BECAUSE WE NEEDED MONEY, I DIDN'T EXPECT YOU TO DOUBLE-CROSS ME!
I SUDDENLY DECIDED YOU AND THE CAT WOULD BE TAKING TOO MUCH OF A CUT! I'M GOING TO GET RID OF BOTH OF YOU!
BUT BEFORE THE WOULD-BE MURDERER CAN PRESS THE TRIGGER, TWO MANTLED FIGURES SWEEP INTO THE ROOM LIKE SWIRLING WHIRLWINDS
THE DOOR WAS OPEN, SO I DIDN'T BOTHER TO KNOCK!
AND THAT ROBIN KID!
BATMAN!
AS TWO THUGS SPRING TO THE BATMAN'S BROAD BACK, HE SHAKES THEM OFF AS A DOG MIGHT SHAKE OFF FLEAS!
WHY DON'T YOU BOYS BEHAVE?

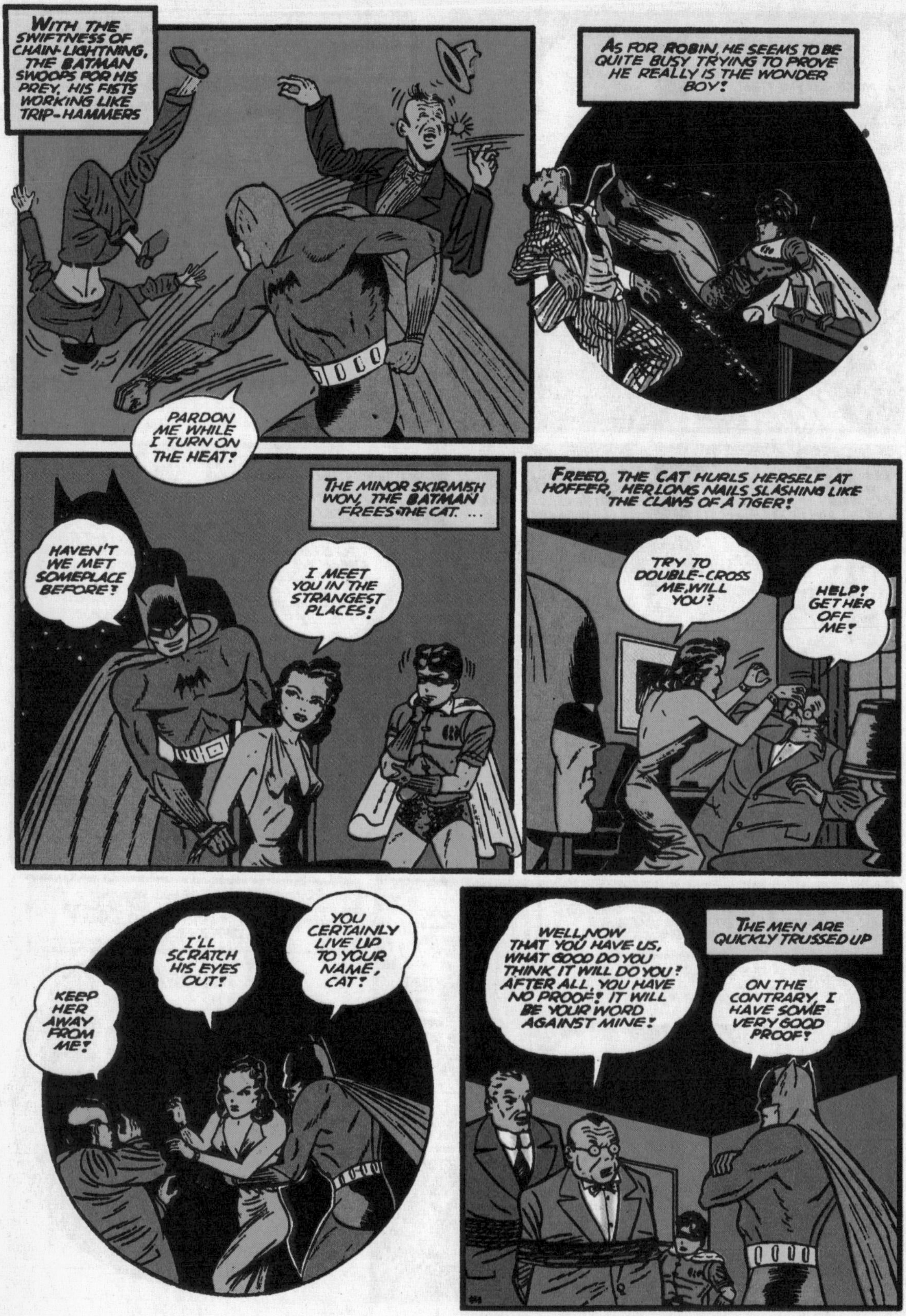
WITH THE SWIFTNESS OF CHAIN-LIGHTNING, THE BATMAN SWOOPS FOR HIS PREY, HIS FISTS WORKING LIKE TRIP-HAMMERS
PARDON ME WHILE I TURN ON THE HEAT!
AS FOR ROBIN, HE SEEMS TO BE QUITE BUSY TRYING TO PROVE HE REALLY IS THE WONDER BOY!
THE MINOR SKIRMISH WON, THE BATMAN FREES THE CAT. ...
HAVEN'T WE MET SOMEPLACE BEFORE?
I MEET YOU IN THE STRANGEST PLACES!
FREED, THE CAT HURLS HERSELF AT HOFFER, HER LONG NAILS SLASHING LIKE THE CLAWS OF A TIGER!
TRY TO DOUBLE-CROSS ME, WILL YOU?
HELP! GET HER OFF ME!
KEEP HER AWAY FROM ME!
I'LL SCRATCH HIS EYES OUT!
YOU CERTAINLY LIVE UP TO YOUR NAME, CAT!
THE MEN ARE QUICKLY TRUSSED UP
WELL, NOW THAT YOU HAVE US, WHAT GOOD DO YOU THINK IT WILL DO YOU? AFTER ALL, YOU HAVE NO PROOF! IT WILL BE YOUR WORD AGAINST MINE!
ON THE CONTRARY, I HAVE SOME VERY GOOD PROOF!

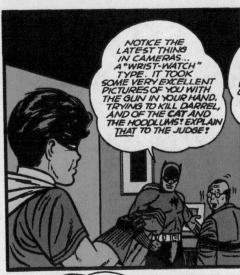

NOTICE THE LATEST THING IN CAMERAS... A "WRIST-WATCH" TYPE. IT TOOK SOME VERY EXCELLENT PICTURES OF YOU WITH THE GUN IN YOUR HAND, TRYING TO KILL DARREL, AND OF THE CAT AND THE HOODLUMS! EXPLAIN *THAT* TO THE JUDGE!

SO, UNKNOWN TO BLAKE, DARREL AND HOFFER HIRED YOU TO STEAL THE GEMS? THEY WERE INSURED, OF COURSE, SO THE, FIRM WOULDN'T SUFFER THE LOSS?

THAT'S RIGHT! DARREL AND HOFFER ARRANGED FOR ME TO BE HIRED AS A MODEL TO WEAR THE GEMS! BUT HOW DID YOU GET WISE TO ALL THIS?

I DID A LITTLE RESEARCH WORK AND FOUND OUT THAT HOFFER AND DARREL NEEDED MONEY TO COVER THEIR LOSSES ON THE STOCK-MARKET! I FIGURED SOMETHING WAS UP WHEN THAT CLERK WAS MURDERED!

YOUR MEN KILLED HIM... TO SHUT HIM UP — ISN'T THAT RIGHT, HOFFER!

MIGHT AS WELL ADMIT IT... HE OVERHEARD ME TALKING ON THE PHONE TO ONE OF THESE MEN. I SAW HE WAS SUSPICIOUS, SO...!

WELL, *CAT*... I'M SORRY... BUT I GUESS YOU'VE GOT TO GO ALONG TO THE POLICE TOO!

IT DOESN'T MATTER! YOU SAVED MY LIFE! I'D LIKE TO THANK YOU FOR THAT!

LIKE THIS!

SUDDENLY, WITH A SWIFT, SURPRISING MOVEMENT, THE *CAT* SHOVES THE *BATMAN* BACK.

..WHISKS OUT OF THE HOUSE AND SLAMS THE DOOR

The BATMAN SAYS:

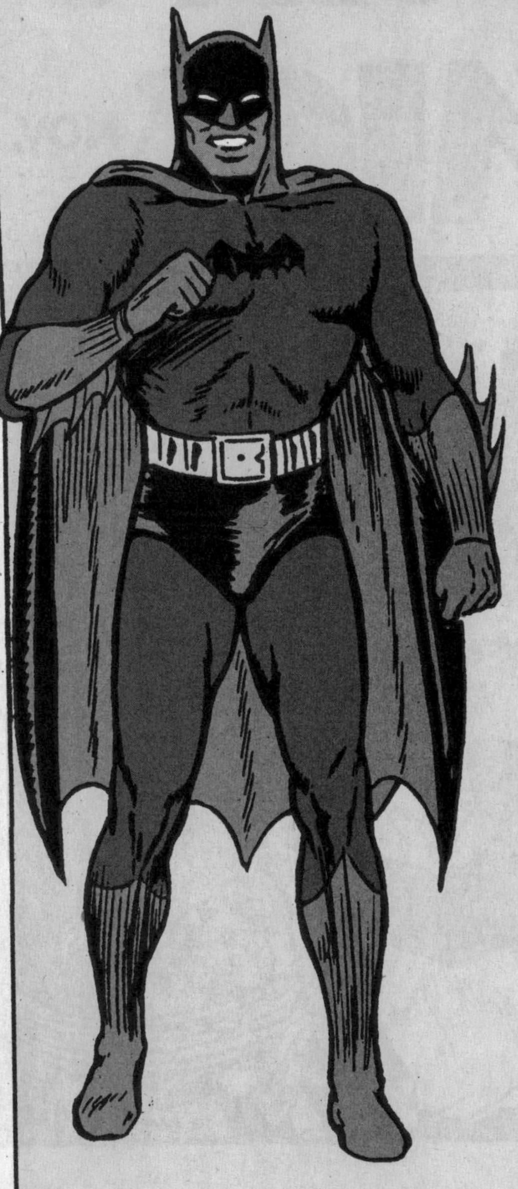

HELLO, Readers! Now that you've read all these new adventures of mine and Robin's, I'd like to talk right AT you for a minute or so.

I think Robin and I make it pretty clear that WE HATE CRIME AND CRIMINALS! There's nothing we like better than to crack down on the distasteful denizens of the underworld. Why? Because we're proud of being AMERICANS—and we know there's no place in this great country of ours for lawbreakers!

That phrase, "CRIME DOESN'T PAY," has been used over and over again to the point where I hesitate to repeat it. But remember this: IT'S JUST AS TRUE NOW AS IT EVER WAS—AND THAT'S PLENTY TRUE!

Sure, it may seem that lawbreakers DO get away with breaking the law. Some may get away with it longer than others. But in the end, every crook gets what's coming to him—and that means plenty of trouble with the law!

Robin and I hope that our adventures may help to "put over" that fact. We'd like to feel that our efforts may help every youngster to grow up into an honest, useful citizen.

It depends on YOU and YOU and YOU. You've got to govern your own lives so that they can be worthwhile, fruitful lives—not lives wasted in prison, or even thrown away altogether before the ready guns of the law-enforcement agents who duty it is to guard those of us who are honest from those of us who are not. And not only must you guide your OWN life in the proper channels—you must also strive to be a good influence on the lives of others.

If you do all this, if you are definitely on the side of Law and Order, then Robin and I salute you and are glad to number you among our friends!

....and what the BATMAN says goes DOUBLE for me!

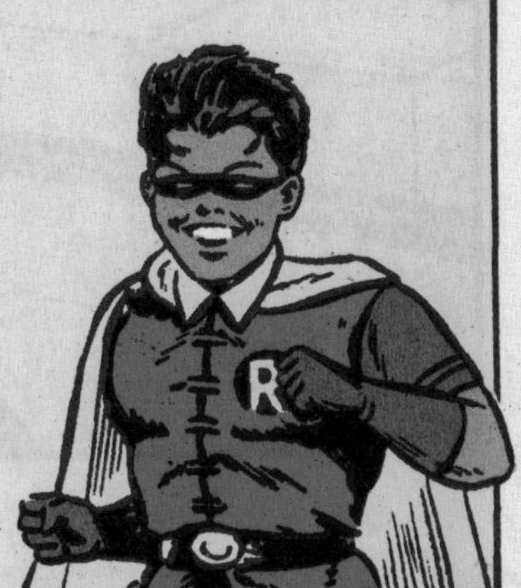
R

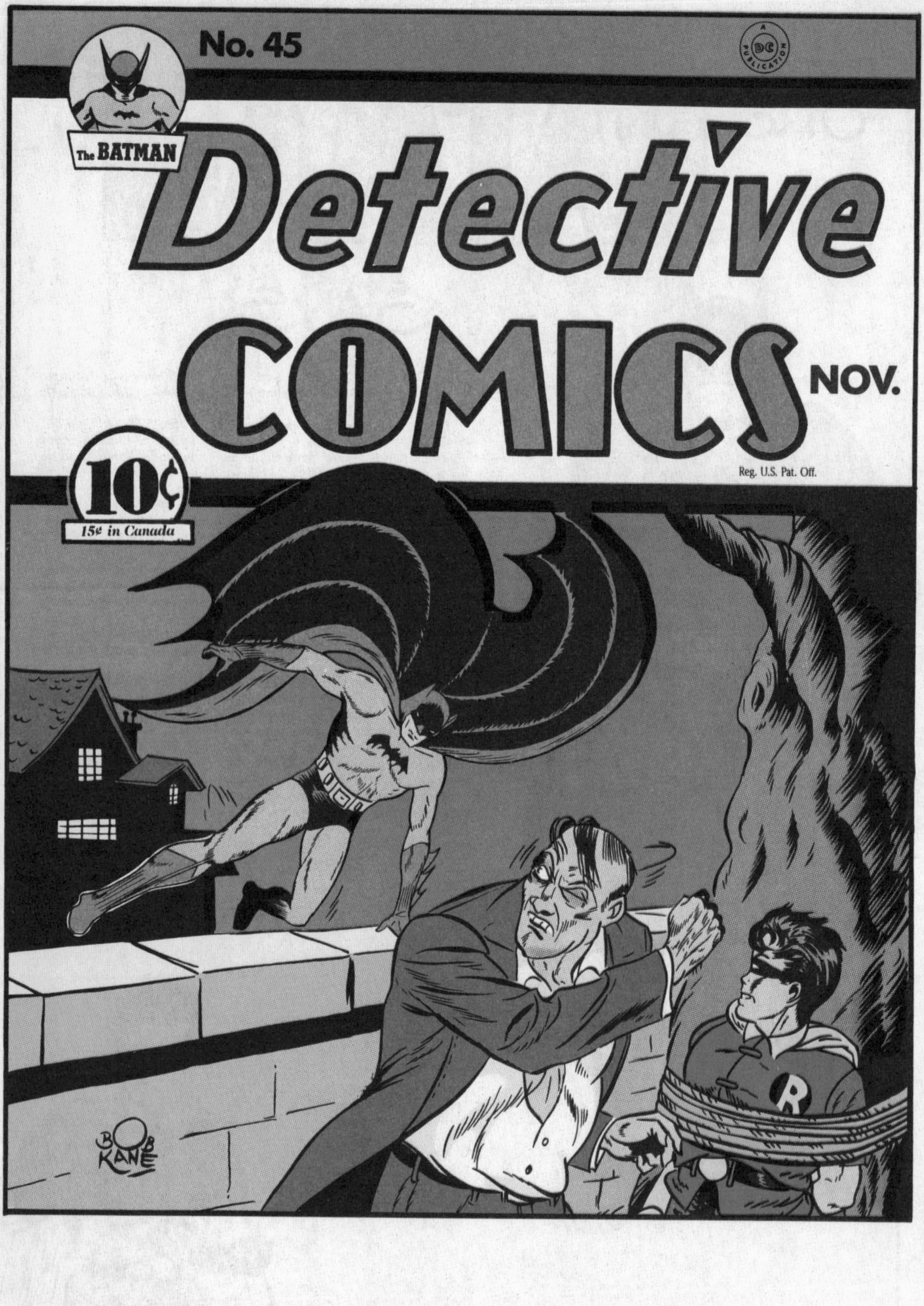
No. 45
A DC PUBLICATION
The BATMAN
Detective
COMICS
NOV.
Reg. U.S. Pat. Off.
10¢
15¢ in Canada
BOB KANE

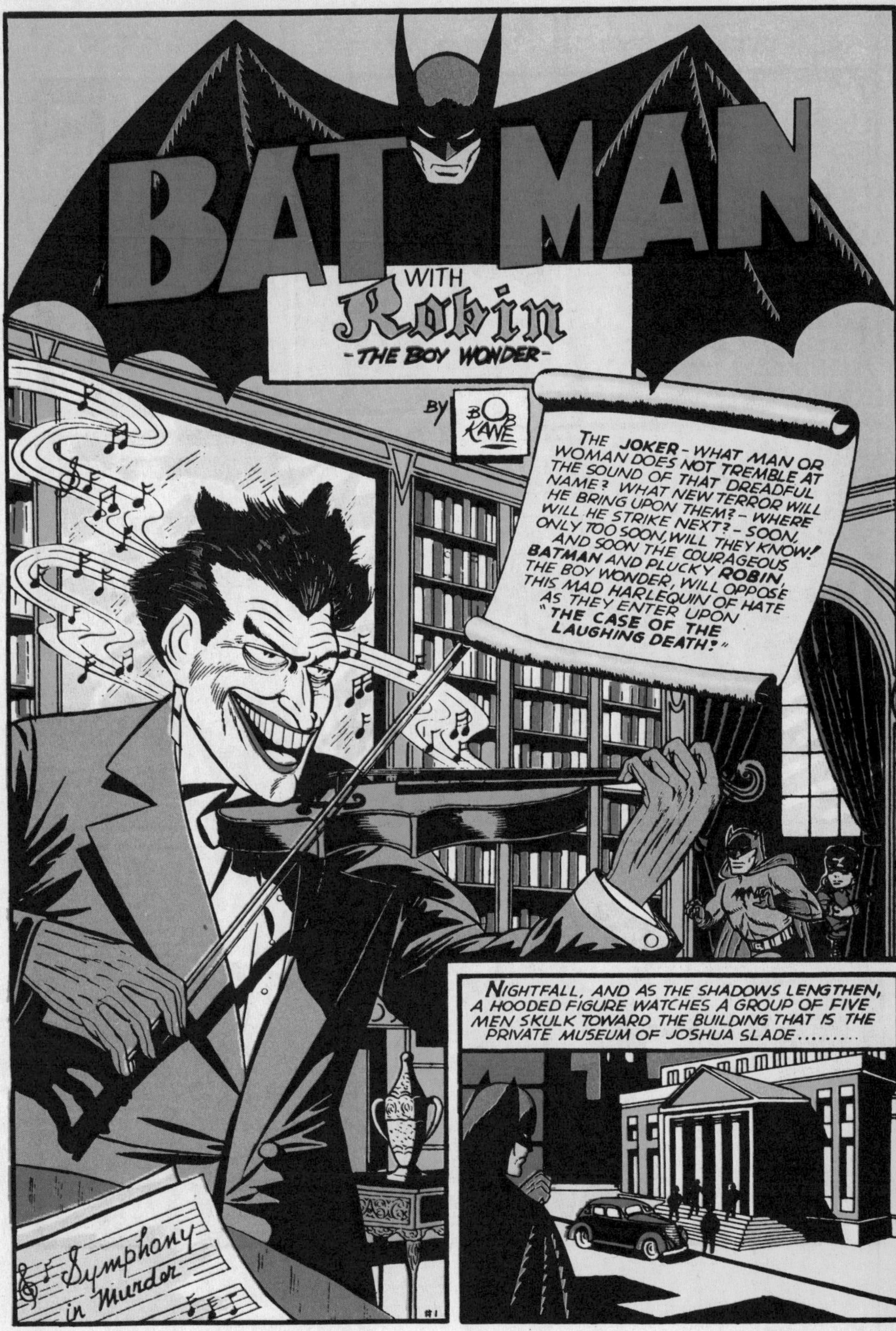
BATMAN
WITH Robin
-THE BOY WONDER-
BY BOB KANE
THE JOKER - WHAT MAN OR WOMAN DOES NOT TREMBLE AT THE SOUND OF THAT DREADFUL NAME? WHAT NEW TERROR WILL HE BRING UPON THEM? - WHERE WILL HE STRIKE NEXT? - SOON, ONLY TOO SOON, WILL THEY KNOW! AND SOON THE COURAGEOUS BATMAN AND PLUCKY ROBIN, THE BOY WONDER, WILL OPPOSE THIS MAD HARLEQUIN OF HATE AS THEY ENTER UPON "THE CASE OF THE LAUGHING DEATH!"
Symphony in Murder
#1
NIGHTFALL, AND AS THE SHADOWS LENGTHEN, A HOODED FIGURE WATCHES A GROUP OF FIVE MEN SKULK TOWARD THE BUILDING THAT IS THE PRIVATE MUSEUM OF JOSHUA SLADE.........

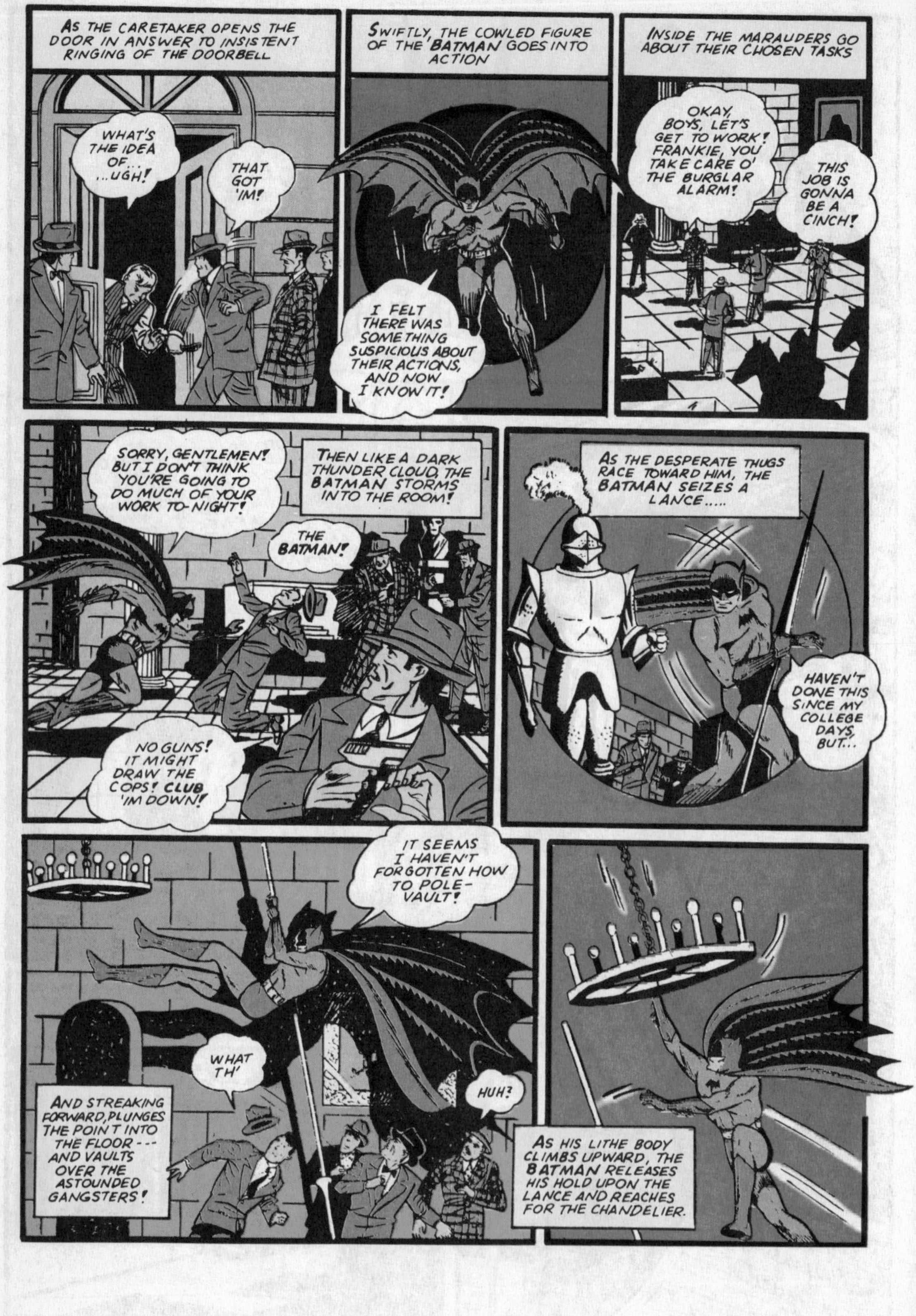

AS THE CARETAKER OPENS THE DOOR IN ANSWER TO INSISTENT RINGING OF THE DOORBELL
WHAT'S THE IDEA OF... ...UGH!
THAT GOT 'IM!
SWIFTLY, THE COWLED FIGURE OF THE BATMAN GOES INTO ACTION
I FELT THERE WAS SOMETHING SUSPICIOUS ABOUT THEIR ACTIONS, AND NOW I KNOW IT!
INSIDE THE MARAUDERS GO ABOUT THEIR CHOSEN TASKS
OKAY, BOYS, LET'S GET TO WORK! FRANKIE, YOU TAKE CARE O' THE BURGLAR ALARM!
THIS JOB IS GONNA BE A CINCH!
SORRY, GENTLEMEN! BUT I DON'T THINK YOU'RE GOING TO DO MUCH OF YOUR WORK TO-NIGHT!
THEN LIKE A DARK THUNDER CLOUD, THE BATMAN STORMS INTO THE ROOM!
THE BATMAN!
NO GUNS! IT MIGHT DRAW THE COPS! CLUB 'IM DOWN!
AS THE DESPERATE THUGS RACE TOWARD HIM, THE BATMAN SEIZES A LANCE.....
HAVEN'T DONE THIS SINCE MY COLLEGE DAYS, BUT...
IT SEEMS I HAVEN'T FORGOTTEN HOW TO POLE-VAULT!
WHAT TH'
HUH?
AND STREAKING FORWARD, PLUNGES THE POINT INTO THE FLOOR --- AND VAULTS OVER THE ASTOUNDED GANGSTERS!
AS HIS LITHE BODY CLIMBS UPWARD, THE BATMAN RELEASES HIS HOLD UPON THE LANCE AND REACHES FOR THE CHANDELIER.

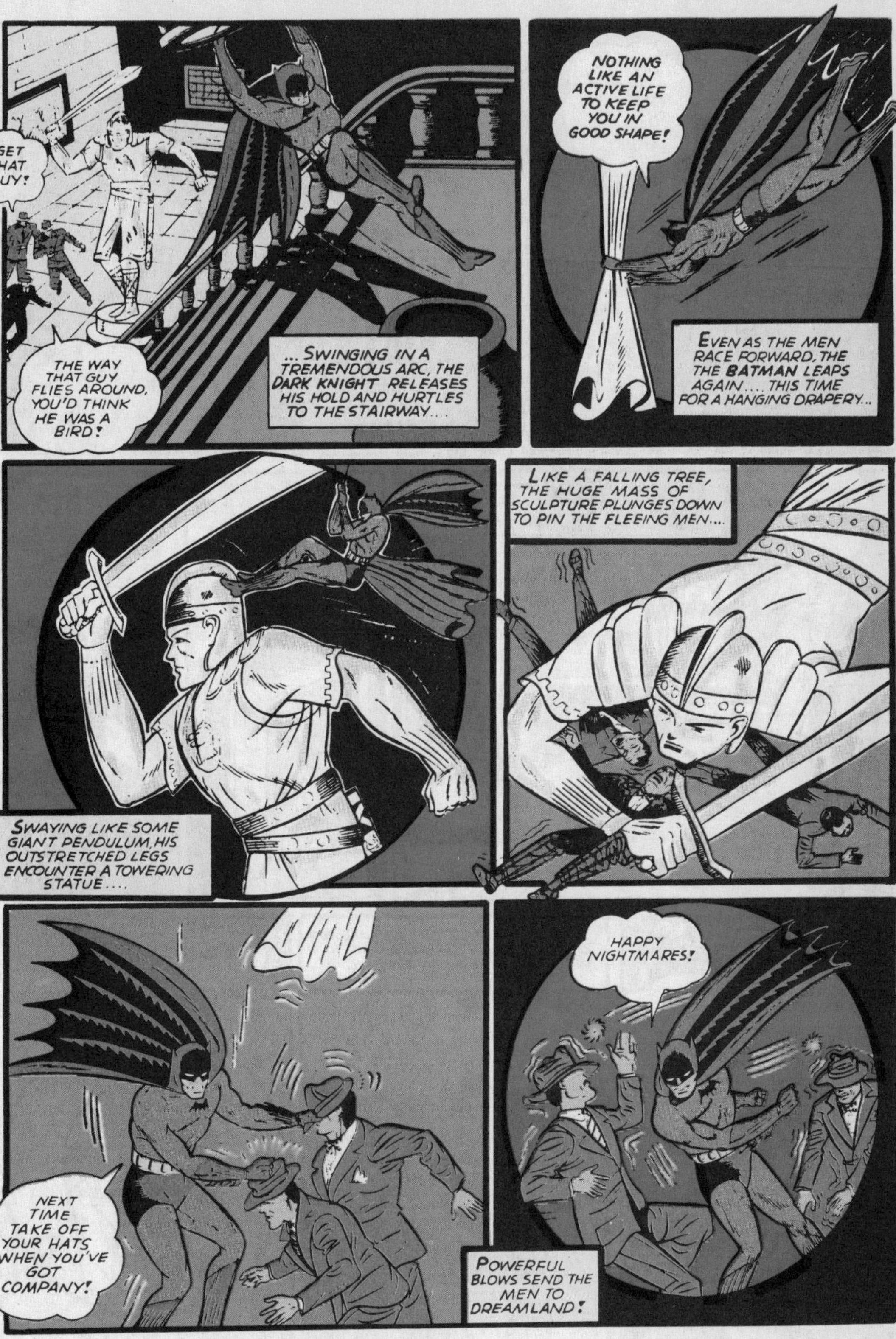
GET THAT GUY!
THE WAY THAT GUY FLIES AROUND, YOU'D THINK HE WAS A BIRD!
...SWINGING IN A TREMENDOUS ARC, THE DARK KNIGHT RELEASES HIS HOLD AND HURTLES TO THE STAIRWAY...
NOTHING LIKE AN ACTIVE LIFE TO KEEP YOU IN GOOD SHAPE!
EVEN AS THE MEN RACE FORWARD, THE THE BATMAN LEAPS AGAIN.... THIS TIME FOR A HANGING DRAPERY...
SWAYING LIKE SOME GIANT PENDULUM, HIS OUTSTRETCHED LEGS ENCOUNTER A TOWERING STATUE....
LIKE A FALLING TREE, THE HUGE MASS OF SCULPTURE PLUNGES DOWN TO PIN THE FLEEING MEN....
NEXT TIME TAKE OFF YOUR HATS WHEN YOU'VE GOT COMPANY!
HAPPY NIGHTMARES!
POWERFUL BLOWS SEND THE MEN TO DREAMLAND!

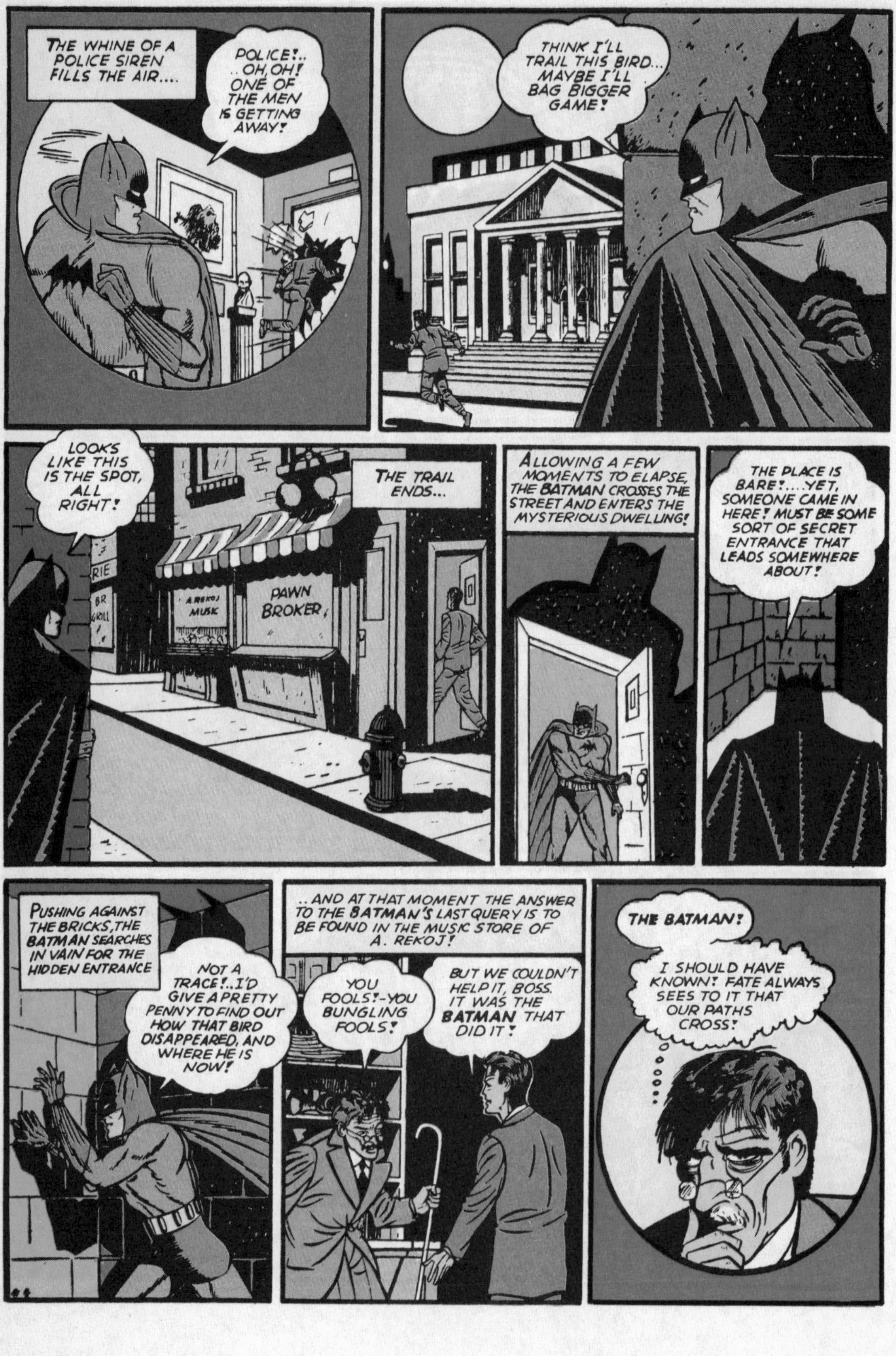
THE WHINE OF A POLICE SIREN FILLS THE AIR....
POLICE!.. ..OH,OH! ONE OF THE MEN IS GETTING AWAY!
THINK I'LL TRAIL THIS BIRD... MAYBE I'LL BAG BIGGER GAME!
LOOKS LIKE THIS IS THE SPOT, ALL RIGHT!
THE TRAIL ENDS...
A. REKOJ MUSIC
PAWN BROKER
ALLOWING A FEW MOMENTS TO ELAPSE, THE BATMAN CROSSES THE STREET AND ENTERS THE MYSTERIOUS DWELLING!
THE PLACE IS BARE!....YET, SOMEONE CAME IN HERE! MUST BE SOME SORT OF SECRET ENTRANCE THAT LEADS SOMEWHERE ABOUT!
PUSHING AGAINST THE BRICKS, THE BATMAN SEARCHES IN VAIN FOR THE HIDDEN ENTRANCE
NOT A TRACE!..I'D GIVE A PRETTY PENNY TO FIND OUT HOW THAT BIRD DISAPPEARED, AND WHERE HE IS NOW!
..AND AT THAT MOMENT THE ANSWER TO THE BATMAN'S LAST QUERY IS TO BE FOUND IN THE MUSIC STORE OF A. REKOJ!
YOU FOOLS!-YOU BUNGLING FOOLS!
BUT WE COULDN'T HELP IT, BOSS. IT WAS THE BATMAN THAT DID IT!
THE BATMAN!
I SHOULD HAVE KNOWN! FATE ALWAYS SEES TO IT THAT OUR PATHS CROSS!

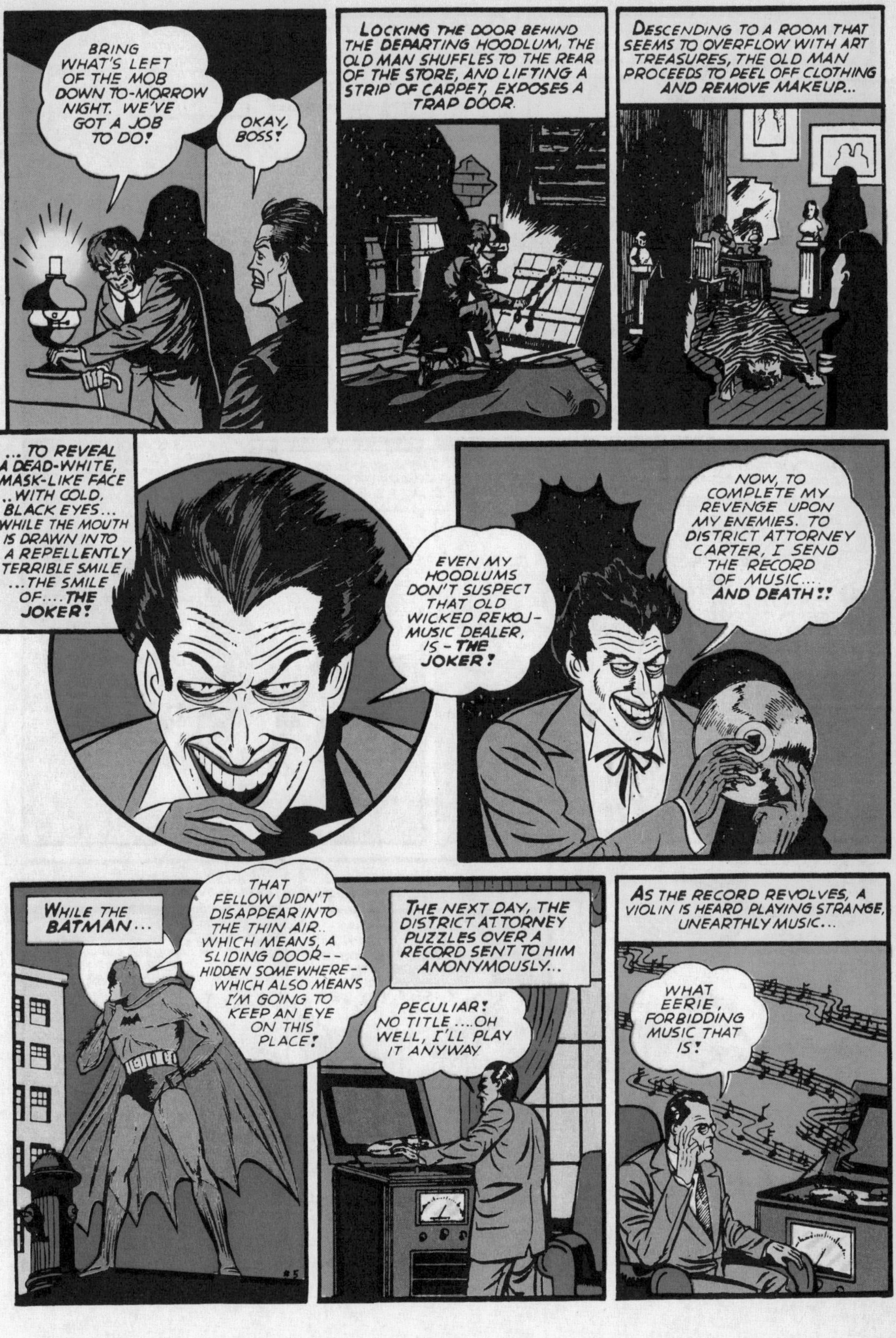
BRING WHAT'S LEFT OF THE MOB DOWN TO-MORROW NIGHT. WE'VE GOT A JOB TO DO!
OKAY, BOSS!
LOCKING THE DOOR BEHIND THE DEPARTING HOODLUM, THE OLD MAN SHUFFLES TO THE REAR OF THE STORE, AND LIFTING A STRIP OF CARPET, EXPOSES A TRAP DOOR.
DESCENDING TO A ROOM THAT SEEMS TO OVERFLOW WITH ART TREASURES, THE OLD MAN PROCEEDS TO PEEL OFF CLOTHING AND REMOVE MAKEUP...
...TO REVEAL A DEAD-WHITE, MASK-LIKE FACE ..WITH COLD, BLACK EYES... WHILE THE MOUTH IS DRAWN INTO A REPELLENTLY TERRIBLE SMILE ...THE SMILE OF....THE JOKER!
EVEN MY HOODLUMS DON'T SUSPECT THAT OLD WICKED REKOJ- MUSIC DEALER, IS - THE JOKER!
NOW, TO COMPLETE MY REVENGE UPON MY ENEMIES. TO DISTRICT ATTORNEY CARTER, I SEND THE RECORD OF MUSIC... AND DEATH!!
WHILE THE BATMAN...
THAT FELLOW DIDN'T DISAPPEAR INTO THE THIN AIR.. WHICH MEANS, A SLIDING DOOR-- HIDDEN SOMEWHERE-- WHICH ALSO MEANS I'M GOING TO KEEP AN EYE ON THIS PLACE!
THE NEXT DAY, THE DISTRICT ATTORNEY PUZZLES OVER A RECORD SENT TO HIM ANONYMOUSLY...
PECULIAR! NO TITLE ....OH WELL, I'LL PLAY IT ANYWAY
AS THE RECORD REVOLVES, A VIOLIN IS HEARD PLAYING STRANGE, UNEARTHLY MUSIC...
WHAT EERIE, FORBIDDING MUSIC THAT IS!

214

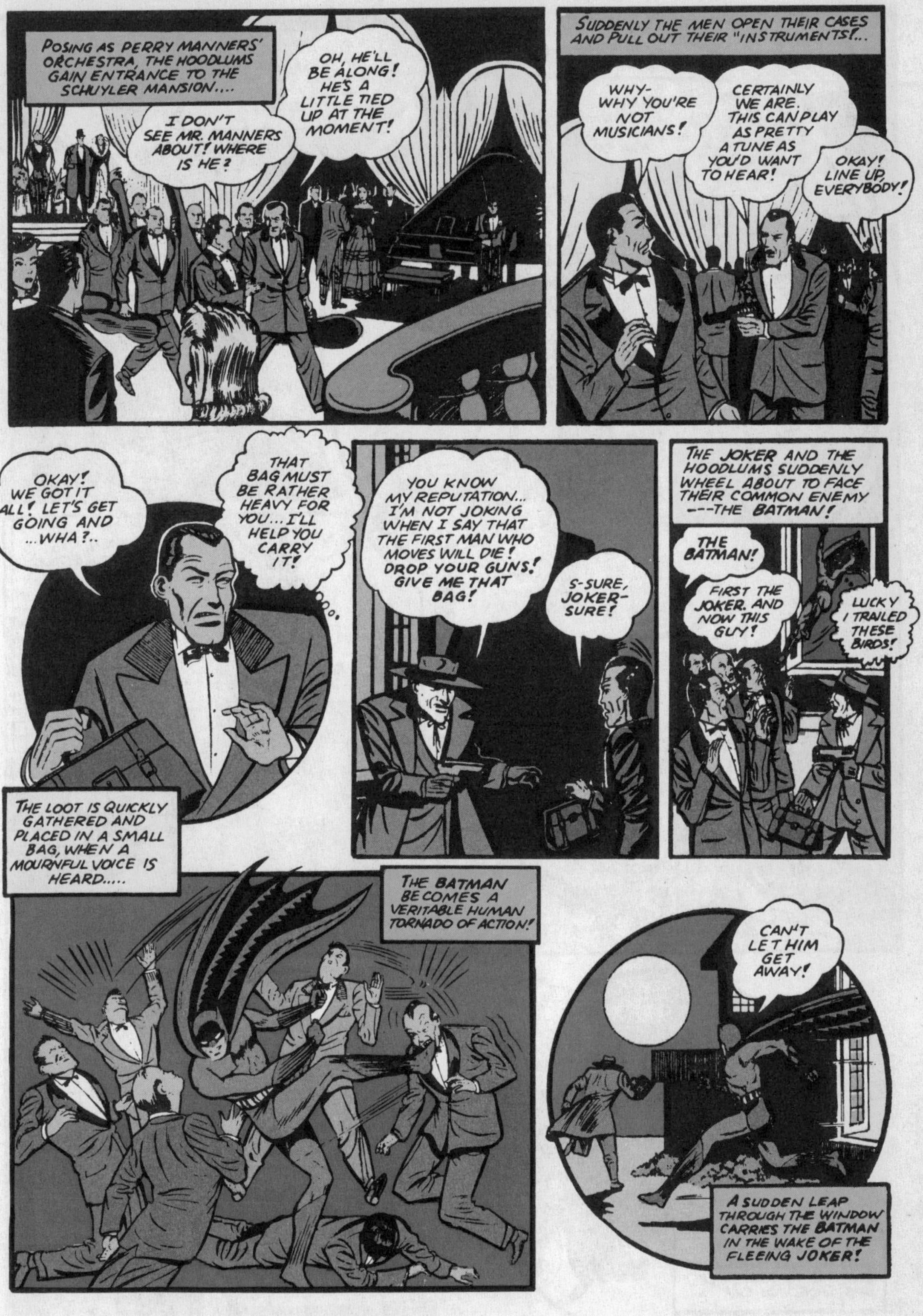
POSING AS PERRY MANNERS' ORCHESTRA, THE HOODLUMS GAIN ENTRANCE TO THE SCHUYLER MANSION....
I DON'T SEE MR. MANNERS ABOUT! WHERE IS HE?
OH, HE'LL BE ALONG! HE'S A LITTLE TIED UP AT THE MOMENT!
SUDDENLY THE MEN OPEN THEIR CASES AND PULL OUT THEIR "INSTRUMENTS!"...
WHY-WHY YOU'RE NOT MUSICIANS!
CERTAINLY WE ARE. THIS CAN PLAY AS PRETTY A TUNE AS YOU'D WANT TO HEAR!
OKAY! LINE UP, EVERYBODY!
THE LOOT IS QUICKLY GATHERED AND PLACED IN A SMALL BAG, WHEN A MOURNFUL VOICE IS HEARD.....
OKAY! WE GOT IT ALL! LET'S GET GOING AND ...WHA?..
THAT BAG MUST BE RATHER HEAVY FOR YOU... I'LL HELP YOU CARRY IT!
YOU KNOW MY REPUTATION... I'M NOT JOKING WHEN I SAY THAT THE FIRST MAN WHO MOVES WILL DIE! DROP YOUR GUNS! GIVE ME THAT BAG!
S-SURE, JOKER-SURE!
THE JOKER AND THE HOODLUMS SUDDENLY WHEEL ABOUT TO FACE THEIR COMMON ENEMY ---THE BATMAN!
THE BATMAN!
FIRST THE JOKER. AND NOW THIS GUY!
LUCKY I TRAILED THESE BIRDS!
THE BATMAN BECOMES A VERITABLE HUMAN TORNADO OF ACTION!
CAN'T LET HIM GET AWAY!
A SUDDEN LEAP THROUGH THE WINDOW CARRIES THE BATMAN IN THE WAKE OF THE FLEEING JOKER!

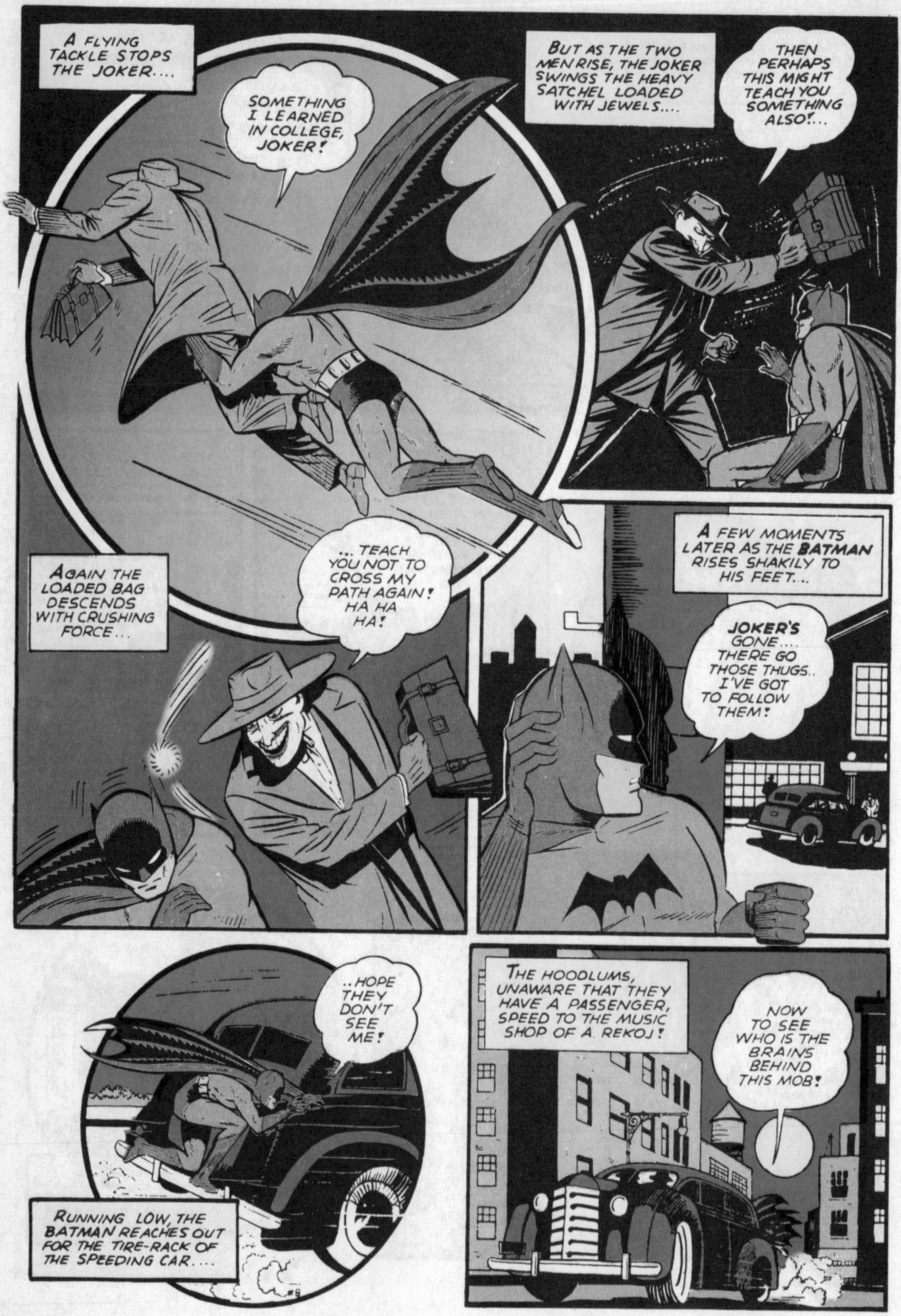
A FLYING TACKLE STOPS THE JOKER....
SOMETHING I LEARNED IN COLLEGE, JOKER!
BUT AS THE TWO MEN RISE, THE JOKER SWINGS THE HEAVY SATCHEL LOADED WITH JEWELS....
THEN PERHAPS THIS MIGHT TEACH YOU SOMETHING ALSO!...
AGAIN THE LOADED BAG DESCENDS WITH CRUSHING FORCE...
... TEACH YOU NOT TO CROSS MY PATH AGAIN! HA HA HA!
A FEW MOMENTS LATER AS THE BATMAN RISES SHAKILY TO HIS FEET...
JOKER'S GONE.... THERE GO THOSE THUGS.. I'VE GOT TO FOLLOW THEM!
..HOPE THEY DON'T SEE ME!
RUNNING LOW, THE BATMAN REACHES OUT FOR THE TIRE-RACK OF THE SPEEDING CAR....
THE HOODLUMS, UNAWARE THAT THEY HAVE A PASSENGER, SPEED TO THE MUSIC SHOP OF A. REKOJ!
NOW TO SEE WHO IS THE BRAINS BEHIND THIS MOB!

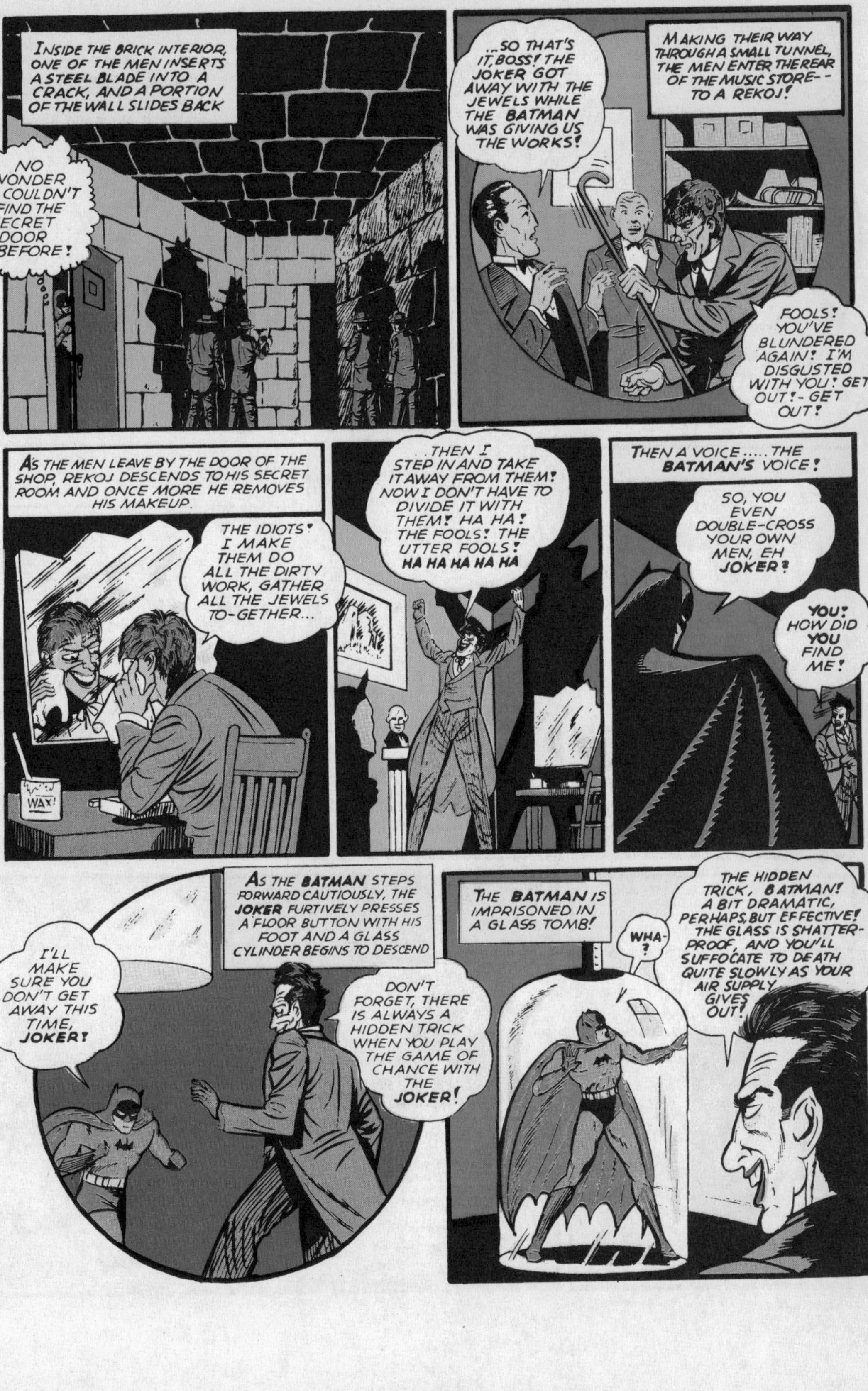
INSIDE THE BRICK INTERIOR, ONE OF THE MEN INSERTS A STEEL BLADE INTO A CRACK, AND A PORTION OF THE WALL SLIDES BACK
NO WONDER I COULDN'T FIND THE SECRET DOOR BEFORE!
MAKING THEIR WAY THROUGH A SMALL TUNNEL, THE MEN ENTER THE REAR OF THE MUSIC STORE-- TO A REKOJ!
..SO THAT'S IT, BOSS! THE JOKER GOT AWAY WITH THE JEWELS WHILE THE BATMAN WAS GIVING US THE WORKS!
FOOLS! YOU'VE BLUNDERED AGAIN! I'M DISGUSTED WITH YOU! GET OUT!- GET OUT!
AS THE MEN LEAVE BY THE DOOR OF THE SHOP, REKOJ DESCENDS TO HIS SECRET ROOM AND ONCE MORE HE REMOVES HIS MAKEUP.
THE IDIOTS! I MAKE THEM DO ALL THE DIRTY WORK, GATHER ALL THE JEWELS TO-GETHER...
WAX!
..THEN I STEP IN AND TAKE IT AWAY FROM THEM! NOW I DON'T HAVE TO DIVIDE IT WITH THEM! HA HA! THE FOOLS! THE UTTER FOOLS! HA HA HA HA HA
THEN A VOICE..... THE BATMAN'S VOICE!
SO, YOU EVEN DOUBLE-CROSS YOUR OWN MEN, EH JOKER?
YOU! HOW DID YOU FIND ME!
AS THE BATMAN STEPS FORWARD CAUTIOUSLY, THE JOKER FURTIVELY PRESSES A FLOOR BUTTON WITH HIS FOOT AND A GLASS CYLINDER BEGINS TO DESCEND
I'LL MAKE SURE YOU DON'T GET AWAY THIS TIME, JOKER!
DON'T FORGET, THERE IS ALWAYS A HIDDEN TRICK WHEN YOU PLAY THE GAME OF CHANCE WITH THE JOKER!
THE BATMAN IS IMPRISONED IN A GLASS TOMB!
WHA-?
THE HIDDEN TRICK, BATMAN! A BIT DRAMATIC, PERHAPS, BUT EFFECTIVE! THE GLASS IS SHATTER-PROOF, AND YOU'LL SUFFOCATE TO DEATH QUITE SLOWLY AS YOUR AIR SUPPLY GIVES OUT!

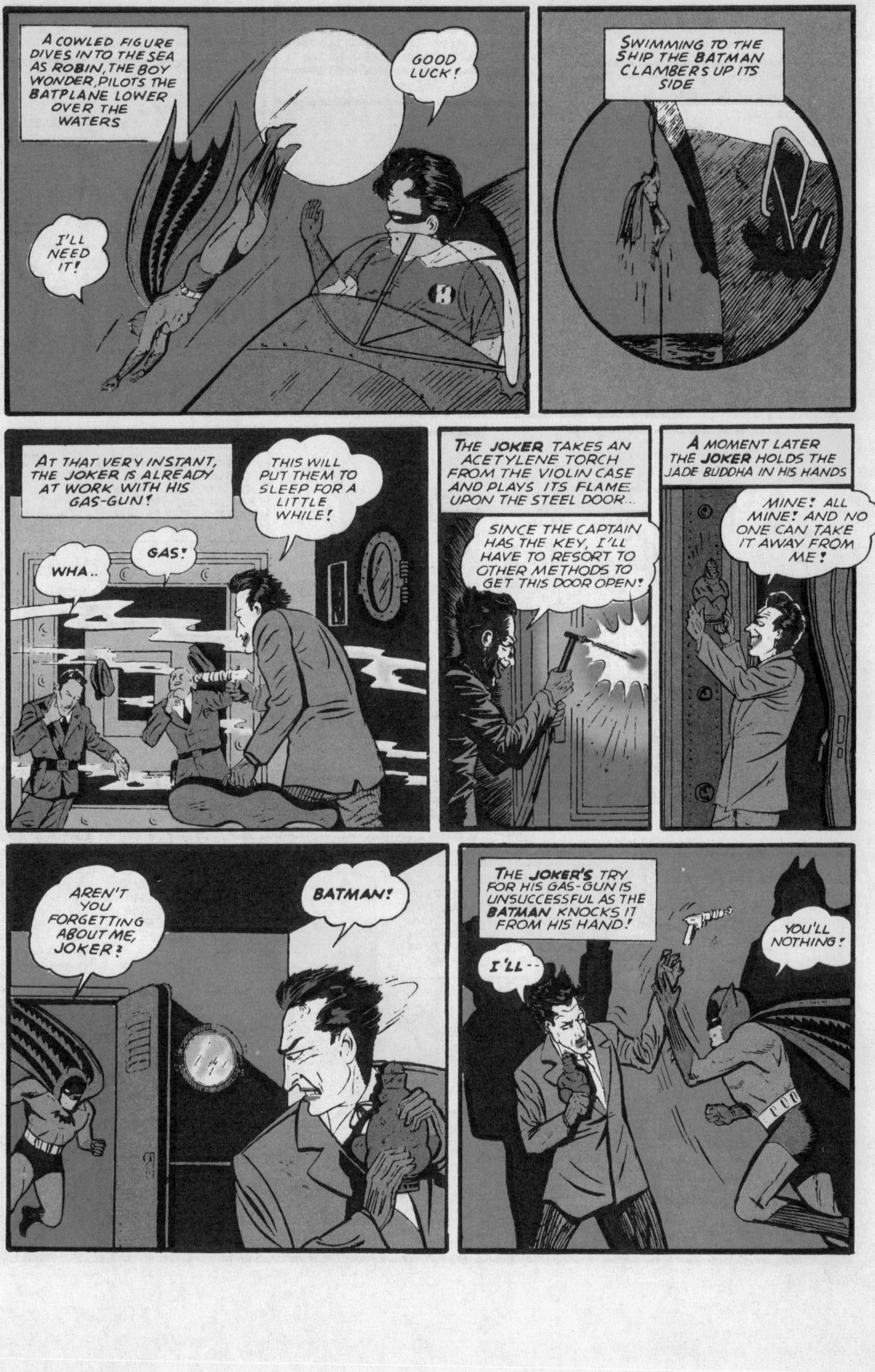
A COWLED FIGURE DIVES INTO THE SEA AS ROBIN, THE BOY WONDER, PILOTS THE BATPLANE LOWER OVER THE WATERS
GOOD LUCK!
I'LL NEED IT!
SWIMMING TO THE SHIP THE BATMAN CLAMBERS UP ITS SIDE
AT THAT VERY INSTANT, THE JOKER IS ALREADY AT WORK WITH HIS GAS-GUN!
THIS WILL PUT THEM TO SLEEP FOR A LITTLE WHILE!
WHA..
GAS!
THE JOKER TAKES AN ACETYLENE TORCH FROM THE VIOLIN CASE AND PLAYS ITS FLAME UPON THE STEEL DOOR...
SINCE THE CAPTAIN HAS THE KEY, I'LL HAVE TO RESORT TO OTHER METHODS TO GET THIS DOOR OPEN!
A MOMENT LATER THE JOKER HOLDS THE JADE BUDDHA IN HIS HANDS
MINE! ALL MINE! AND NO ONE CAN TAKE IT AWAY FROM ME!
AREN'T YOU FORGETTING ABOUT ME, JOKER?
BATMAN!
THE JOKER'S TRY FOR HIS GAS-GUN IS UNSUCCESSFUL AS THE BATMAN KNOCKS IT FROM HIS HAND!
I'LL--
YOU'LL NOTHING!

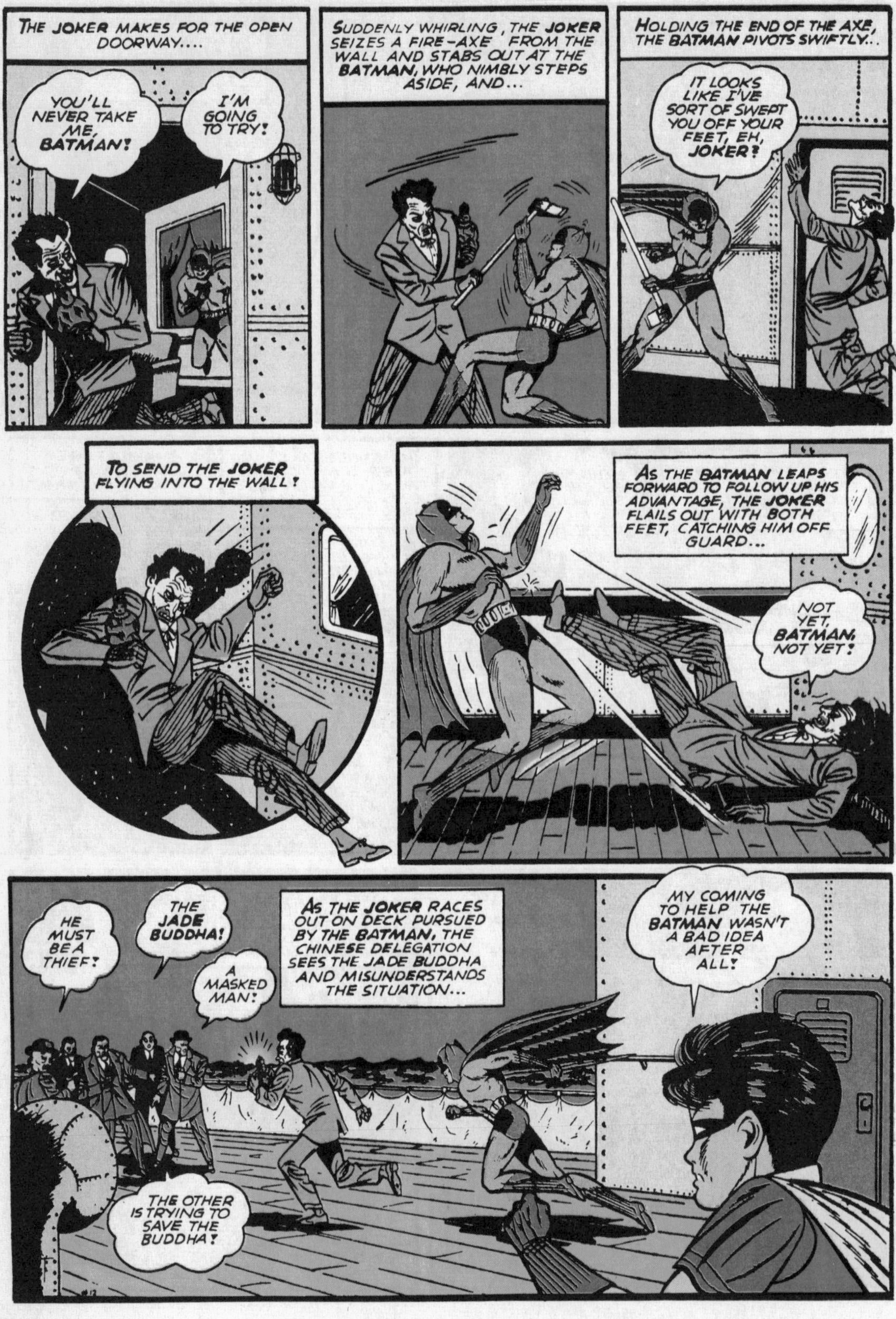

THE JOKER MAKES FOR THE OPEN DOORWAY....
YOU'LL NEVER TAKE ME, BATMAN!
I'M GOING TO TRY!
SUDDENLY WHIRLING, THE JOKER SEIZES A FIRE-AXE FROM THE WALL AND STABS OUT AT THE BATMAN, WHO NIMBLY STEPS ASIDE, AND...
HOLDING THE END OF THE AXE, THE BATMAN PIVOTS SWIFTLY...
IT LOOKS LIKE I'VE SORT OF SWEPT YOU OFF YOUR FEET, EH, JOKER?
TO SEND THE JOKER FLYING INTO THE WALL!
AS THE BATMAN LEAPS FORWARD TO FOLLOW UP HIS ADVANTAGE, THE JOKER FLAILS OUT WITH BOTH FEET, CATCHING HIM OFF GUARD...
NOT YET, BATMAN, NOT YET!
HE MUST BE A THIEF!
THE JADE BUDDHA!
A MASKED MAN!
AS THE JOKER RACES OUT ON DECK PURSUED BY THE BATMAN, THE CHINESE DELEGATION SEES THE JADE BUDDHA AND MISUNDERSTANDS THE SITUATION...
MY COMING TO HELP THE BATMAN WASN'T A BAD IDEA AFTER ALL!
THE OTHER IS TRYING TO SAVE THE BUDDHA!

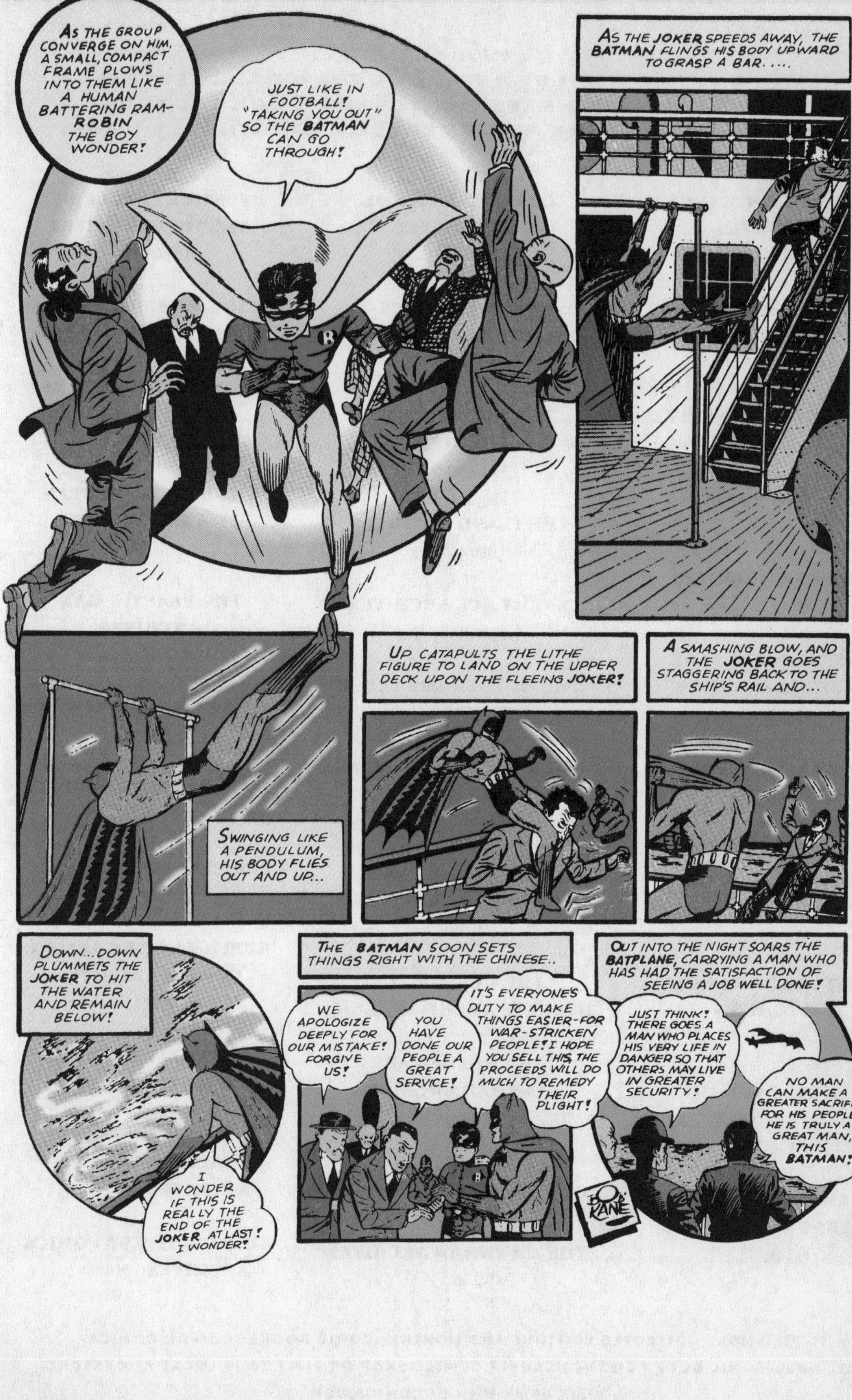

AS THE GROUP CONVERGE ON HIM, A SMALL, COMPACT FRAME PLOWS INTO THEM LIKE A HUMAN BATTERING RAM- ROBIN THE BOY WONDER!
JUST LIKE IN FOOTBALL! "TAKING YOU OUT" SO THE BATMAN CAN GO THROUGH!
AS THE JOKER SPEEDS AWAY, THE BATMAN FLINGS HIS BODY UPWARD TO GRASP A BAR.....
SWINGING LIKE A PENDULUM, HIS BODY FLIES OUT AND UP..
UP CATAPULTS THE LITHE FIGURE TO LAND ON THE UPPER DECK UPON THE FLEEING JOKER!
A SMASHING BLOW, AND THE JOKER GOES STAGGERING BACK TO THE SHIP'S RAIL AND...
DOWN...DOWN PLUMMETS THE JOKER TO HIT THE WATER AND REMAIN BELOW!
I WONDER IF THIS IS REALLY THE END OF THE JOKER AT LAST! I WONDER!
THE BATMAN SOON SETS THINGS RIGHT WITH THE CHINESE..
WE APOLOGIZE DEEPLY FOR OUR MISTAKE! FORGIVE US!
YOU HAVE DONE OUR PEOPLE A GREAT SERVICE!
IT'S EVERYONE'S DUTY TO MAKE THINGS EASIER-FOR WAR-STRICKEN PEOPLE! I HOPE YOU SELL THIS, THE PROCEEDS WILL DO MUCH TO REMEDY THEIR PLIGHT!
OUT INTO THE NIGHT SOARS THE BATPLANE, CARRYING A MAN WHO HAS HAD THE SATISFACTION OF SEEING A JOB WELL DONE!
JUST THINK! THERE GOES A MAN WHO PLACES HIS VERY LIFE IN DANGER SO THAT OTHERS MAY LIVE IN GREATER SECURITY!
NO MAN CAN MAKE A GREATER SACRIFICE FOR HIS PEOPLE! HE IS TRULY A GREAT MAN, THIS BATMAN!
BOB KANE

A SERIES OF DELUXE HARDCOVER COLLECTIONS RE-PRESENTING HISTORIC COMICS CHARACTERS AND THEIR STORIES AS THEY WERE ORIGINALLY SEEN.

THE ADAM STRANGE ARCHIVES
VOLUME 1

ALL STAR COMICS ARCHIVES
VOLUMES 0 - 11

THE AQUAMAN ARCHIVES
VOLUME 1

THE ATOM ARCHIVES
VOLUMES 1 - 2

BATMAN ARCHIVES
VOLUMES 1 - 6

BATMAN: THE DARK KNIGHT ARCHIVES
VOLUMES 1 - 4

BATMAN: THE DYNAMIC DUO ARCHIVES
VOLUMES 1 - 2

BATMAN: THE WORLD'S FINEST ARCHIVES
VOLUMES 1 - 2

THE BLACK CANARY ARCHIVES
VOLUME 1

THE BLACKHAWK ARCHIVES
VOLUME 1

THE CHALLENGERS OF THE UNKNOWN ARCHIVES
VOLUMES 1 – 2

COMIC CAVALCADE ARCHIVES
VOLUME 1

THE DC COMICS RARITIES ARCHIVES
VOLUME 1

THE DOOM PATROL ARCHIVES
VOLUMES 1 - 3

THE FLASH ARCHIVES
VOLUMES 1 - 4

ENEMY ACE ARCHIVES
VOLUMES 1 - 2

THE GOLDEN AGE FLASH ARCHIVES VOLUME 1

THE GOLDEN AGE GREEN LANTERN ARCHIVES
VOLUMES 1 - 2

THE GOLDEN AGE SANDMAN ARCHIVES
VOLUME 1

THE GOLDEN AGE SPECTRE ARCHIVES VOLUME 1

THE GOLDEN AGE STARMAN ARCHIVES
VOLUME 1

THE GREEN LANTERN ARCHIVES VOLUMES 1 - 5

THE HAWKMAN ARCHIVES
VOLUMES 1 - 2

JUSTICE LEAGUE OF AMERICA ARCHIVES
VOLUMES 1 - 9

LEGION OF SUPER-HEROES ARCHIVES VOLUMES 1 - 12

THE NEW TEEN TITANS ARCHIVES
VOLUMES 1 - 3

THE SILVER AGE TEEN TITANS ARCHIVES
VOLUME 1

THE PLASTIC MAN ARCHIVES
VOLUMES 1 - 8

THE SGT. ROCK ARCHIVES
VOLUMES 1 - 3

THE SHAZAM! ARCHIVES
VOLUMES 1 - 4

SUPERMAN ARCHIVES
VOLUMES 1 - 7

SUPERMAN: THE ACTION COMICS ARCHIVES
VOLUMES 1 - 4

SUPERMAN: THE WORLD'S FINEST ARCHIVES
VOLUME 1

WONDER WOMAN ARCHIVES VOLUMES 1 - 4

WORLD'S FINEST COMICS ARCHIVES VOLUMES 1 - 3

TO FIND MORE COLLECTED EDITIONS AND MONTHLY COMIC BOOKS FROM DC COMICS,
CALL 1-888-COMIC BOOK FOR THE NEAREST COMICS SHOP OR VISIT YOUR LOCAL BOOKSTORE.
VISIT US AT WWW.DCCOMICS.COM

READ MORE OF THE DARK KNIGHT DETECTIVE'S ADVENTURES IN THESE COLLECTIONS FROM DC COMICS:

BATMAN

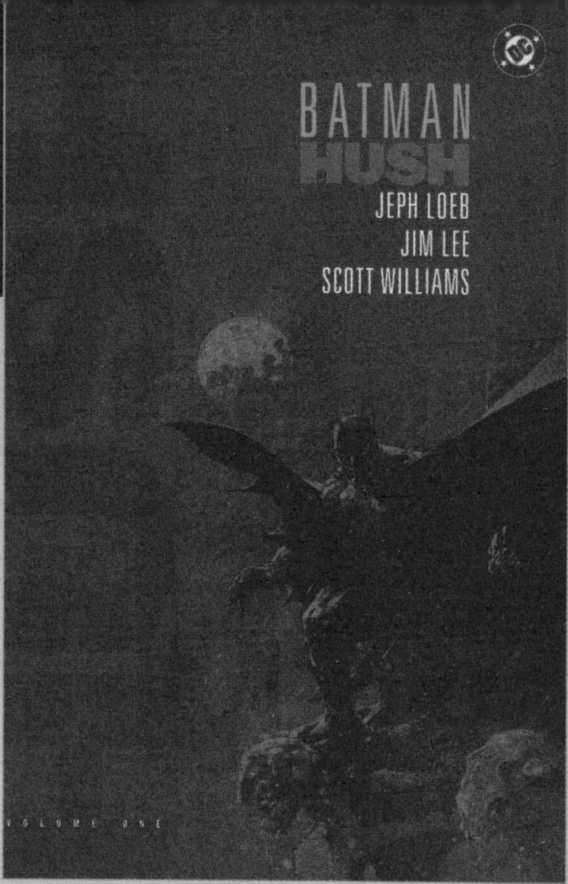
BATMAN
HUSH
JEPH LOEB
JIM LEE
SCOTT WILLIAMS
VOLUME ONE

BATMAN: HUSH VOLUME 1

Jeph Loeb, Jim Lee and **Scott Williams** tell an epic tale of friendship, trust and betrayal, in the first volume of a tale that spans a lifetime of the Dark Knight.

"THE ACTION IS EXCITING AND THE DETAIL IS METICULOUS."
— CRITIQUES ON INFINITE EARTHS

BATMAN: THE DARK KNIGHT RETURNS

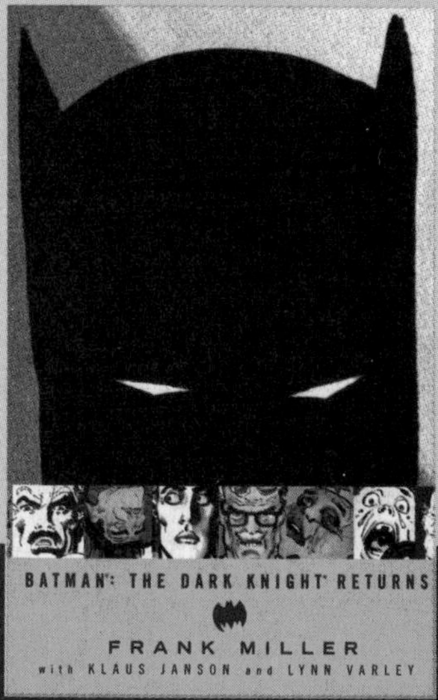
BATMAN: THE DARK KNIGHT RETURNS
FRANK MILLER
with KLAUS JANSON and LYNN VARLEY

FRANK MILLER
KLAUS JANSON
LYNN VARLEY

BATMAN: THE LONG HALLOWEEN

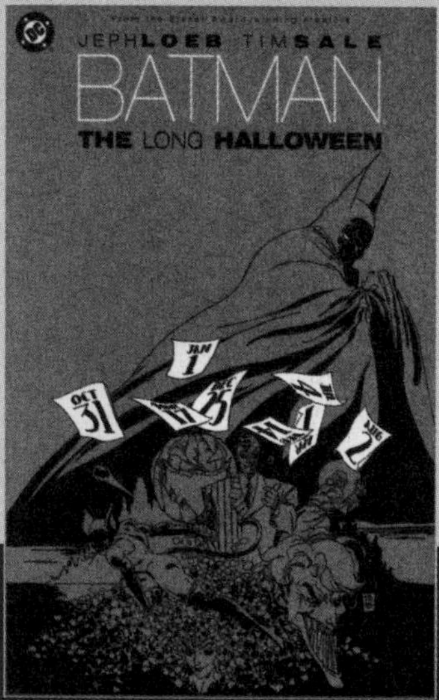
JEPH LOEB TIM SALE
BATMAN
THE LONG HALLOWEEN

JEPH LOEB
TIM SALE

BATMAN: YEAR ONE

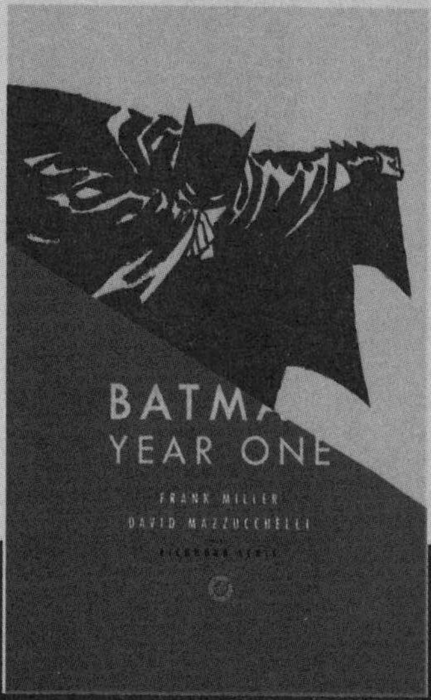
YEAR ONE
FRANK MILLER
DAVID MAZZUCCHELLI

FRANK MILLER
DAVID MAZZUCCHELLI